A Concise Survey of Western Civilization

Supremacies and Diversities throughout History

Fourth Edition

BRIAN A. PAVLAC

ROWMAN & LITTLEFIELD
Lanham • Boulder • New York • London

Acquisitions Editor: Ashley Dodge
Acquisitions Assistant: Haley White
Sales and Marketing Inquiries: textbooks@rowman.com

Credits and acknowledgments for material borrowed from other sources, and reproduced with permission, appear on the appropriate pages within the text.

Published by Rowman & Littlefield
An imprint of The Rowman & Littlefield Publishing Group, Inc.
4501 Forbes Boulevard, Suite 200, Lanham, Maryland 20706
www.rowman.com

86-90 Paul Street, London EC2A 4NE

British Library Cataloguing in Publication Information Available

Library of Congress Cataloging-in-Publication Data

Names: Pavlac, Brian Alexander, 1956– author.
Title: A concise survey of Western civilization : supremacies and diversities throughout history / Brian A. Pavlac.
Description: Fourth edition. | Lanham : Rowman & Littlefield, [2023] | "First Edition 2011." | Includes bibliographical references and index. | Contents: v. 1. Prehistory to 1500 — v. 2. 1500 to the present.
Identifiers: LCCN 2022046333 (print) | LCCN 2022046334 (ebook) | ISBN 9781538173350 (v. 1 ; paperback) | ISBN 9781538173374 (v. 2 ; paperback) | ISBN 9781538171103 (paperback) | ISBN 9781538173367 (v. 1 ; epub) | ISBN 9781538173381 (v. 2 ; epub) | ISBN 9781538171110 (epub)
Subjects: LCSH: Civilization, Western.
Classification: LCC CB245 .P38 2023 (print) | LCC CB245 (ebook) | DDC 909/.09821—dc23/eng/20221013
LC record available at https://lccn.loc.gov/2022046333
LC ebook record available at https://lccn.loc.gov/2022046334

♾️™ The paper used in this publication meets the minimum requirements of American National Standard for Information Sciences—Permanence of Paper for Printed Library Materials, ANSI/NISO Z39.48-1992.

Brief Contents

Contents

Diagrams, Figures, Maps, Primary Source Projects, Sources on Families, Tables, and Timelines

DIAGRAMS

FIGURES

MAPS

PRIMARY SOURCE PROJECTS

Sources on Families

Tables

Timelines

Acknowledgments

I was interested in history from a young age, as most kids are. Too often, as they grow older, kids lose their fascination with the past, partly because it becomes one more thing they have to learn rather than a path of self-understanding or even just "neat stuff." Wonderful teachers taught me history through the years, and, partly inspired by them, I foolishly went on to study history in college. Before I knew it, history became my intended profession. Since then I have been fortunate to make a living from history.

In teaching courses over the years, I found my own voice about what mattered. Instead of simply sharing my thoughts in lectures, I produced this book (and its companion website: **ConciseWesternCiv.com**). Former teachers, books I have read and documentaries I have viewed, historical sites I have visited, all have contributed to the knowledge poured into these pages. All photographs (figures) were taken by the author (except where credit is given in parentheses). Likewise, many students, too many to be named, have sharpened both words and focus through class discussion and comments on drafts. I owe thanks to the many readers whose suggestions have improved the text. For their help to me in getting this project as far as it has come, I have to thank a number of specific people. I appreciate my original editor, Susan McEachern, who gave the book her time and consideration, and even asked for this fourth edition. Now I also extend gratitude to my new editors, Katelyn Turner, Ashley Dodge, Jehanne Schweitzer, and Haley White. Various people have offered useful suggestions for all the editions: Nicole Mares, Cristofer Scarboro, Megan Lloyd, Mark Reinbrecht, and especially two readers, Ian Crowe and John Williams. Finally, most of all, my spouse, Elizabeth Lott, has sustained me through all the editions and permutations. Her skills in grammar, logic, and good sense have made this a far better book.

The final version is never final. Every new history source I read makes me want to adjust an adjective, nudge a nuance, or fix a fact. With every edition of this text, I find room for improvement. Should any inaccuracies or errors have crept in, please forgive the oversight and contact me with your proposed corrections.

How to Use This Book

Learning is difficult. If it were easy, everyone would be educated. In this age of multimedia, reading still remains one of the best ways to learn something. Of course, reading well is not always easy. You cannot read a nonfiction informative work such as this in the same way as you would a Harry Potter novel. Those novels, though, are full of information with strange new terms, from *muggles* to *Hogwarts*, that people learn easily and absorb into their knowledge. The same can be true of learning history, once it interests you.

The pictures on the covers of the various editions of this textbook illustrate people in the past writing something. Humans who lived before us have produced the sources that we use today to understand our heritage and ourselves. History is a product of people, by people, and for people. We create it, preserve it, and share it. The purpose of this text is to help you integrate the history of the Western past into your meaning of life.

I hope to make learning history as enjoyable as possible, even to those who are not in love with times gone by. As a survey, this book offers one person's opinion about what is good, bad, useful, and wasteful to know about our wider civilization. This book does cover the minimum historical information that educated adults should know—just compare it to other texts. Also, in the author's opinion, it offers a tightly focused narrative and interpretive structure, in a sometimes quirky style.

This text's distinctive approach uses overarching themes of conflict and creativity. The phrase *supremacies and diversities* describes the unifying threads through which this text has stitched together the historical record. Supremacies focus on the use of power to dominate societies, ranging from ideologies to warfare. Supremacy seeks stability, order, and amalgamation. Diversities encompass the creative impulses that concoct new ideas, as well as people's efforts to define themselves as different. Diversity produces change, opportunity, and individuality. A tension, of course, arises between the "supremacy" desire for conformity and the "diversity" idea of individuality. This interaction has clearly driven historical conflict and change. Other approaches might be equally valuable. Indeed, to be truly educated, you should be looking at a variety of views about the past. History is rarely simple. This version merely provides a foundation for learning more.

Fulfilling the survey function, this narrative examines political, economic, technological, social, and cultural trends, depending on the historical period. The book does not much emphasize the everyday-life aspects of people in the past. For more on this, and art and literature, see the website. Five main topical themes regularly inform how this text looks at change. These topics have significantly altered history and are still influential in the present. They are:

1. the question of truth. Historians play an essential role in verifying facts against misinformation, opinions, and myths that shape our understanding of what is important. What people at large think is true or not is often contested.

2. technological innovation and nature. Inventions of tools have enabled us to manipulate nature and build large, complex societies. Issues of environment and disease nonetheless still significantly impact human activity.

3. migration and conquest. Since the first humans outpaced their resources, people have been on the move to new places. Along the way, the species differentiated into various ethnicities. Once people occupied all useful land, their fights about who lives in various areas have changed history. Civilizations have defined themselves in trading with, fighting with, and trying to assimilate other cultures.

4. political and economic choices. This traditional focus of historical study illustrates how human decisions change about how to live together.

5. proposals about the meaning of life. Each individual while alive or a whole society as long as it exists determines what is to be done based on ideas. In concepts about class, ethnicity, and sexuality, humans especially express what is significant to them. Since religion has long had ascendancy over human belief, it requires some emphasis.

How could you best learn from this book? Read well. This time-tested advice applies to anything you might want to learn thoroughly for the rest of your life. Here are a few recommended steps:

1. Read the text in a space and at a time conducive to reading—not in the few minutes before class, not where others will interrupt, not with television or music blaring.

2. Prudently mark up, underline, highlight, and otherwise annotate your text as you study. Use the white space and margins for notes, questions, comments, and marks to remind yourself of some important point.

3. Critique the book as you read; enter into its conversation. You might comment in the margins or on blank pages on the following points:

connections between themes, ideas, or subjects;
ideas you agree with;
ideas you disagree with;
reactions provoked by the text;
material of particular interest to you; and
material you would like to know more about.

4. At the end of each section, jot down notes or write a brief comment about what you have just read. The review question at the end of each section and the space provided for a response encourage this learning skill.

5. Each chapter provides primary sources to help you think like a historian while determining your own perspective on the past and present. In the Primary Source Projects, you can compare and contrast the ideas from two different points of view (in a few cases within one source). Topics include the different roles of government, the power of religion, perceptions of good or bad leadership, the role of the individual, and social values. The Sources on Families present different views on the nature and experience of that basic social unit, further described in chapter 2. Such documents reveal issues about property, choice in forming a family, sexuality, social status, raising children, breaking spousal relationships, religious support, and alternatives to the "traditional" family. Answering the given questions for the sources in the space provided will help you understand and remember their content. The sources have usually been lightly edited from their cited printed versions for spelling, grammar, clarity, and length (with deletions marked by ellipses [. . .]).

More versions, questions, and information about these sources are available at the website http://www.concisewesternciv.com/sources.

The primary sources are just snippets. Longer texts can also provide essential perspectives or capture the spirit of their times. A list of suggested primary source readings (more of which are being put online all the time) is at http://www.concisewesternciv.com/sources/suggested.html.

6. A common question students have about history is "How important is it to know dates?" Understanding dates is essential. History is all about what happens before (which can affect causation), what events are happening at the same time (which adds to context), and what happens after (which may show results). The more dates connected with historical change you know, the better you will be at historical explanation. At least attempt to memorize the dates of the major periods (even if different approximate dates may be offered for the same large periods—historians do not always agree on exact beginnings and ends). The book presents dates in chapter subtitles, on most maps, throughout the text, and in the block timelines toward the end of the text. Use these block timelines to review and structure your knowledge according to theme or time period.

7. Another common question is "What details do I need to know?" The most important terms in the text appear in **boldface** and are listed in the block timelines. Additionally, terms representing significant ideas and ideologies are defined both in the text and again, for easy reference, in the glossary at the back of the book; these terms are set in ***boldface italics***.

8. To further help you learn dates, names, and terms, on the last page of each chapter is a "Make Your Own Timeline" feature. Use the terms in **boldface** and ***boldface italics*** from what you have just read and those in the block timelines toward the end of this text. See the sample timeline at the end of chapter 1 for an example of how you can make your own.

9. As is clear from the above, even more information is provided on the website: **ConciseWesternCiv.com**. The website offers more study guides, questions, outlines, summaries, maps in color, diagrams, tables, many of the figures (pictures), a history of art relevant to each chapter, and links to many more websites and primary sources. All of these materials can reinforce and expand on what you learn from the text.

10. Finally, connect what you learn here to the rest of your experience. The more you know, the more you can know. And according to the liberal arts creed, the more you know, the better will be your decisions about your life.

CHAPTER 1

History's Story

"Now" is over and done with. It can never take place again. Each moment retreats into the past, whether forgotten or remembered. In our personal lives, we treasure or bury memories on our own. Our larger society, however, has historians to preserve and make sense of our recollection as a community. Historians recapture the past by applying particular methods and skills that have been nurtured over the past few centuries. Although such processes are not without challenges, the work done by historians has created the subject of this book you are reading: **Western civilization**.

THERE'S METHOD

"How do we know anything?" is our starting point. As **humans**, some of our knowledge comes from instinct: we are born with it, beginning with our first cry and suckle. Yet instinct makes up a tiny portion of human knowledge. Most everything we know come from learning in one way or another. First, we learn through direct experience of the senses. These lessons of life can sometimes be painful (fire) other times pleasurable (chocolate). Second, other people teach us many important matters through example and setting rules. Reading this book because of a professor's requirement may be one such demand. Third, human beings can apply reason to figure things out.[1] This ability enables people to take what they know, then learn and rearrange it into some new understanding.

The discipline of *history* is one such form of reasoning. History is not just knowing something—names, dates, facts—about the past. The word *history* comes from the Greek word ιστορία for "inquiring," or asking questions. This questioning the past has been an important tool for humans gaining information about themselves and their communities.

---

1. This approach assumes we can correctly understand the world. When the title character in Shakespeare's play *Hamlet* pretends insanity in order to discover truth, another character rationally concludes that though "this be madness; yet there is method in it."

Quite often authorities, the people in charge, have used history to bind together groups of people so that they have shared identities. For peoples long ago, history has embodied a mythology that reflected their relationship to the gods. Or history chronicled the deeds of kings, justifying royal rulership. History also validated domination and conquest of one people over another. Most people are raised to believe that their own country or nation is more virtuous and righteous than those others beyond their borders. The history of Western civilization abounds with examples of these attitudes.

Then, about two hundred years ago, a number of scholars began to try to improve our understanding of the past. These historians began to organize as a profession based in the academic setting of universities (at which they did not allow women to study at that time). Historians imitated and adapted the scientific method (see chapter 10) for their own use, renaming it the **historical method** (see table 1.1). In the scientific method, scientists pose hypotheses as reasonable guesses about explanations for how nature works. They then observe and experiment to prove or disprove their hypotheses. In the historical method, historians propose hypotheses to describe and explain how history changes. The two main problems historians have focused on are **causation** (how something happened) and **significance** (what impact something had). History without explanations about how events came about or why they matter is merely trivia.

Unlike scientists, historians cannot conduct experiments or run historical events with different variables.[2] Historians cannot even obtain direct observational evidence of events before their own lifetimes—there are no time machines. Instead, historians have to pick through whatever evidence has survived. They call these data **sources**. At first, historians sought out sources among the written records that had been preserved over centuries in musty books and manuscripts. Eventually historians learned to study a wider variety of human-made objects, ranging from needles to skyscrapers.

Obviously, not all sources are of equal value. Those sources connected directly with past events are called **primary sources**. These are most important for historical investigation. Reading them, one encounters history in the raw.[3] When evaluating these primary sources, historians face two problems. For one, evidence for many events has not survived at all or remains only in fragments. Much of history is never recorded in the first place and dies with people's memories. Even for recorded sources, some are eaten by rats and rot, while others are obliterated in war or trashed on purpose (such as the records of the British Empire in Operation Legacy, where officials purged files to keep them out of the hands of their colonial successors). For another, some people have forged sources, in whole or in part, so that their version matters, even if false. Much of historical research involves questioning human character, deciding who is honest or deceitful, trustworthy

---

2. Alternative histories are an increasingly popular genre of fiction. Similar to science fiction's guesses about the future, alternative histories are based on "what-if" issues of the past: what would have happened differently if, for example, some leader had not been killed?

3. The "Primary Source Projects" and "Sources on Families" in this book offer opportunities to wrestle with such primary sources. For more explanation, see "How to Use This Book." More relevant primary sources can be found at http://www.concisewesternciv.com/sources/index.html.

Table 1.1.   The Historical Method

1. Find a problem.

2. Form a hypothesis (a reasonable or educated guess to the solution).

3. Conduct research into sources. Questions to ask of sources:

    A.   External: Is it genuine? Is it what it says it is? When and where was it made? How did it get from its original recording to the present? Who is the author? How was the author able to create the source? Are there any interpolations, emendations, or insertions by others?

    B.   Internal: What is its meaning? How is it significant? What is the source's ostensible or intended purpose? How accurate is the author (any competence, bias, or prejudice)? What is the source's content? How does it compare with other reliable sources? What do modern scholars say about the source?

4. Make the argument and conclusions, usually in written form.

5. Share the knowledge, usually through publication.

Note: The step-by-step process of the historical method rigorously questions sources in order to reconstruct the best version of the past. For an example of such a process, go to http://www .concisewesternciv.com/extras/methodxsmpl.html.

or undependable. Then, through careful examination and questioning, historians extract facts from sources and try to write the most reliable and accurate explanation of past events.

As the last and most important part of the historical method, professional historians have shared their information with one another. They produce **secondary sources**, usually books and articles.[4] At academic conferences and in more books and articles, historians learn from and judge one another's work. They debate and challenge one another's arguments and conclusions. Usually a consensus about the past emerges. Generally, agreed-on views begin to appear in **tertiary sources**, such as encyclopedias, handbooks, or this very textbook. Although tertiary sources are several steps removed, these sources offer convenient summaries and overviews but usually lack citations to sources.

Because the past is so vast, historians have always divided it up into smaller, more convenient chunks. Choosing what to examine begins historical work. Professional historians usually specialize, becoming experts in one small slice of the past. Since so many historians publish scholarship today, hardly anyone can ever read all that has been written about any single subject. New books and articles emerge each year, especially about popular topics such as the American Civil War or Hitler. The history of even one day covered in any detail would be long and confusing. A historian could not possibly cover every detail on even a small subject and remain interesting. Something is always left out.

---

4. A good secondary source has footnotes (at the bottom of the page) or endnotes (at the end of each chapter or the whole book or article) that cite the other primary, secondary, and tertiary sources. The footnotes in this text merely add some tangential commentary.

Therefore, historians prioritize to make the past manageable. They select certain events or places as more important than others. For example, in one person's life, a one-time decision, such as which college to attend, would probably be more essential to include in her biography than a description about what she chose to eat for breakfast on the day the decision was made. College choice deserves more attention, since that can change a life more than a routine meal. However, the description of breakfast choice might be valuable if, for example, years of eating too much bacon and eggs led to heart disease or a dose of poison killed a person. The quality of a unique, decisive historical moment is usually more interesting than a quantity of mundane events. Selection and generalization prevent us from becoming either overwhelmed or bored.

Historians therefore select only a few bits of the past, leaving out the vast majority of human activities. They then categorize or organize their selections into sensible stories and arguments. Historians once considered politics (how people organize themselves to make laws, choose leaders, go to war, collect taxes) as the only important human activities worthy of investigation. Within the past century, however, historians have broadened their interests to include a wider range of human pursuits. These days, many historians examine social manners: sex roles, food, fashion, and family.[5] Even a shift in breakfast habits from waffles and bacon cooked by Mom to a processed drive-through Egg McMuffin® can illustrate something about a **society**, a coherent group of people.

Historians categorize the past in three main ways. The first and most obvious division is **chronological**, using time as dividing points. The most natural division of time is the day, with its cycle of sunlight and darkness. Some particular days, like those on which battles are waged or a notable inspiration is put to paper, can change the course of history. A larger natural unit of time is the year, marked by seasons and the stars. Finally, the basic human experience stretches, for each of us, over a lifetime. Some lives are short and others seem long, but all end in death. Yet history marches on.

Aside from natural portions of time, historians divide up history into manageable segments. In the largest artificial division, historians split the past into two big eons: **prehistory** and history. Prehistory includes everything humans did up until the invention of writing, about five thousand years ago in the Middle East and East Asia. We can examine human activity before writing only through physical remains and artifacts, such as bones and shaped stones.

Technology (the study of people turning raw materials into tools), ideology (people's belief systems), and politics also define different eras. Many of the commonly used historical labels, terms such as *antiquity*, *medieval*, and *Renaissance*, were not drawn from the sources and lives of past people; instead, historians later coined those terms. The names for the Stone Age or the Iron Age are based on the use of those materials for making tools during those times. The term *Middle Ages* draws on the perceptions of politics and culture that fall between the ancient and modern epochs. The titles of the ages of Renaissance and Enlightenment derive

---

5. For interesting perspectives on marriage, children, and sex and gender, see the "Sources on Families" for each chapter after this one.

from artistic and intellectual achievements. Sometimes a country's ruling family provides a useful marker, such as England under its Queen Victoria. Given our preference for round numbers, a century fits into historical schemes, especially the more recent nineteenth or twentieth centuries. Historians apply such divisions to the past to show both what the people within a period shared in common and what they have to teach us. Acts of naming may simplify the complexities and contradictions of any given time interval, but we must treat beginning and end dates as tentative and flexible. Still, without choosing some limits it is difficult to frame a discussion.

While chronology applies time to divide up the past, **geographical** divisions, where events took place, are equally common. The largest unit for human activity is world or global history (with the minor exception of recent space exploration). By the twentieth century, people were clearly bound together through travel, communication, and trade. At the opposite end of size, the smallest unit could be a town, a college, or a person (biography). Most people have historically tended to view the world from their own vantage points, tending to focus on the history of the political states in which they live. American, European, Asian, or African historians have too rarely gazed across borders and boundaries to study their neighbors. Indeed, history became a profession in modern times because nations wanted origin stories for the modern nation-states.

The third method that historians use to slice up the past is a **topical** approach, separating the wide range of human activities into smaller groupings of human enterprise. For example, historians today often specialize in areas of intellectual, social, economic, constitutional, gender, literary, diplomatic, or military history. Topical approaches help us place comparable human experiences in context.

The timelines at the back of this book categorize historical activities into six different fields. First is *science* and **technology**: how we understand the universe and build tools to cope with it. Second is **economics**: how we create and manage the distribution of wealth. Third is **politics**: how people create systems to organize collective decisions. Fourth is **social structures**: the units and hierarchies (such as families and communities) within which people place themselves and the humble activities of daily life. Fifth is **culture**, especially those works and activities that people fashion in order to cope with, understand, or simply share their experiences of the world. Culture includes music, art (largely visual creations), literature (compositions of words read or performed), and recreation (acts ranging from sports to hobbies). Finally are both *philosophy* and *religion*: how people understand the purpose of life and the meaning of death, which usually involves belief in a supernatural reality beyond our senses. These six topics essentially embrace all human accomplishments.

This text uses the concept of **civilization** as an organizing principle. Historians see civilizations as large, coherent collections of peoples in a specific time and place that feature particular political, social, and cultural approaches, especially defined by cities. The notion remains slippery, however. Where any civilization began (or ended), whether in time, geographic boundary, or membership, depends on who defines it and by what criteria. And generalizations of what holds a society together often ignore contradictions and minority movements. Sometimes a civilization is dominated by one powerful people or idea (Chinese or Muslim civilizations), while Western civilization developed from the interaction of several cultures.

When historians formulated the subject of "Western" civilization about one hundred years ago, they intentionally took a broad view. After the United States had risen to become a world power, many American historians saw a shared past with other European nations that had also risen to global power from their location on the western edge of Eurasia. They argued that if Americans learned only US history without understanding how the United States fits into the larger culture of competing European powers, they would never really comprehend their own heritage.[6] The founders of classes on "the West" deliberately wove together American with European history, showing the common origins of so much that Americans, and Europeans, took for granted. Most designers of curricula considered Western civilization courses and texts essential until a few years ago. Then other historians argued to prefer world or global history courses, which try to cover all societies on planet Earth. An even newer trend is the "Big History," which covers both the natural history since the "big bang" origin of the universe as well as humanity's history.

The advantage of studying Western civilization is that it organizes a large portion of interrelated history relevant to today's problems in a world dominated by Western industrialized states and ideologies. The West is not necessarily better in creativity or virtue than many other civilizations that arose around the world, even if many past and even present historians have thought so (for more about studying Western Civ, see the epilogue). This text will often point out where the West borrowed knowledge and when its moral virtue fell short of its proclaimed ideals. People within this civilization also developed deeply contradictory ideas, many of which still clash with each other today. Undoubtedly, the West became more powerful, becoming the dominant culture of the contemporary world. To understand the West is to comprehend how many of the globe's institutions, practices, and ideologies came to function as they do, for good or ill.

The word **Western** obviously reveals a strong geographical component. While historians have not created a category for northern or southern civilizations, they used to apply the term **Eastern** (or **Oriental**, from the Latin for where the sun rises) to what they now prefer to call Asian civilizations (China and India, for example). Just as the name of the "Orient" comes from the place of the rising sun over the Eurasian landmass, the old-fashioned name for the West, the "Occident," derives from where the sun sets.

This book's narrative will show how a civilization that can be called "Western" began in the specific geographical area of **western Europe**, the northwestern extension of land from the vast landmass of Eurasia and Africa, bordered by the North Sea, the Mediterranean Sea, and the Atlantic. Its first inspirations lay in the so-called Middle East, the region including the river systems of the Tigris and

---

6. Be careful never to confuse "Western" history of culture rooted in European states with "Western" history of the expansion of the United States across the North American continent.

Euphrates and the Nile. The core of Western culture next developed around the Mediterranean Sea, until it shifted north into western Europe proper between fifteen hundred and a thousand years ago. About five hundred years ago, bearers of Western civilization began to conquer much of Eurasia and many overseas territories. The interactions of the West with other peoples around the world still decide the questions of where the West begins, endures, changes, or ends.

Just as geography defines the West, so does its chronology. Setting an exact starting date presents as many difficulties as setting its contemporary borders. One self-defining moment in Western tradition appears in its calendar, today accepted by many people around the world (as can be observed every December 31st). The Western chronology has traditionally divided history into two epochs, labeled with the initials **BC** and **AD**. These large periods mark the founding of Christianity by Jesus of Nazareth about two thousand years ago (see chapter 6). Most people can readily say BC means "before Christ," but fewer can explain that AD is the abbreviation for *anno Domini*, which means "in the year of the Lord" and refers again to Jesus of Nazareth. Many current history writers, apparently uncomfortable with the religious roots of our calendar, have switched to using the terms BCE and CE, meaning "before the common era" and "common era." These terms lack any historical content other than being placeholders for political correctness. No other event changed history around two thousand years ago to make any civilization more "common." This book's use of the terms BC and AD is not intended to privilege Christianity, but merely recognizes the actual origins of our dating system.

Rather than this simple duality centered on Christianity, historians more sensibly divide the Western past into three or four periods. Ancient history (which includes prehistory) usually ends around AD 500. The Middle Ages then follow, ending any time between 1300 and 1789, depending on the historian's point of view. Then early modern history might begin as early as 1400 or as late as 1660 and last until either the modern or contemporary periods take over in the past few centuries. The year 1914 seems useful as a starting point for contemporary history because of the first modern world war. To make the past still more manageable, this book divides it into fifteen parts, or chapters (including this introduction, and not counting an epilogue to both sum up and point forward). The above dates and eras, of course, make sense only in relation to the history of Europe. Other civilizations need other markers, although historians often try to impose Western categories on world history.

This survey assigns the beginning of Western civilization to between fifteen and eleven hundred years ago, as western Europe recovered from the disaster of the collapse of its part of the Roman Empire. Understanding how this civilization built on previous human experiences requires our reaching back beyond the fall of Rome to humanity's beginnings. Therefore, this particular book describes prehistory and the West's deep roots in the Middle East and Mediterranean regions. Some comparison between Western and other civilizations at different moments will also be pointed out. As descriptions approach the present, they will become more detailed, because recent events impact our lives more directly.

Chapter 2 lightly skims over several million years, while chapter 14 covers only a few decades.

Surveying much of Western history in fifteen chapters requires careful selection of the most resonant information. This narrative touches on the basic topics of politics, economics, technology, society, culture, and intellectual cultural trends, depending on the historical period. This story does not deal as much with the everyday-life aspects of people in the past, such as how families lived in their homes, or what they ate. Several topical themes regularly guide the flow: (1) the problem of how truth is asserted or contested, (2) interaction with nature through technological innovation, (3) the rise and fall of communities through migration and conquest, (4) disagreements about political and economic decision making, including conflicts about priorities in religion and government, and (5) proposals about the ultimate meaning of life. These topics have significantly affected the past and are still influential in the present.

This book, then, covers a lot of time, over a large part of the world, involving many human events. As a concise history, it necessarily leaves out a great deal. Historians are always making choices about what they want to study, what approach they take, and what stays in. As you learn more about history, you can choose for yourself what else to learn. For a beginning, this text should ground you in the basics of this civilization called the West.

Review: How do historians study and divide up the past?

Response:

WHAT IS TRUTH?

People make history. Every idea, institution, painting, document, movement, war, or invention originated with one or more human beings. If individuals have agency, they can take action, to believe in, fight for, kill for, and die for ideas. While natural forces such as floods, drought, and disease affect people and may influence the course of history, the survivors still must choose how to react to those disasters. No "force" works by itself to bring about historical events. Instead, people choose how they will fulfill their needs for sex, food, and material comforts (such as clothing, housing, and art) both with their intimate friends and family and for the larger societies with whom they bind themselves together as peoples.

People write history. One or more human beings decide to produce their version of something in the past worth recording for posterity. This text's version of history is shaped by the current broad culture of the modern West, the personal judgment of recent professional historians, and the author. Depending on their personal positions, people have always disagreed about the importance of particular issues of politics, economics, science, and even the meaning of words.[7] Cultural guardians have always argued over what information their contemporaries should know about the past. Disputes about how to honor or mourn the past with markers, statues, and memorials, as well as lesson plans, have been much in the news the past few years. How societies remember their past shapes their decisions about the future.

Degrees of *subjectivity* versus *objectivity* affect any accurate version of the past. Objectivity is seeing events and ideas in an impartial way, while subjectivity involves a view ranging from **bias** (inclination toward a particular point of view) through **prejudice** (dismissal of other points of view, usually out of ignorance) all the way to bigotry (stubborn intolerant hostility). Most people are somewhat biased based on how and where they were raised. The historian Herbert Butterfield notably referred to the "magnet in men's minds" where people best remember information that already aligns with their political and social inclinations. No one can entirely escape being somewhat subjective. Good historians strive toward objectivity, aware of their own inclinations.

These perspectives have always shaped or reflected the values of whole cultures who saw their past according to shared grand concepts, sometimes called paradigms. In our Western civilization, the ancient Greeks, Romans, and Germans believed in both the intervention of divine beings and a powerful role of unchangeable fate. The rise and fall of people, or nations, followed according to the will of the gods. The Jews saw themselves as being chosen by one all-powerful God who reserved for them a special place in history. The Christians of the Middle Ages supposed that they were caught in a battle of good versus evil. They condemned to hell their enemies, even if those enemies were fellow Christians. Intellectuals during the Enlightenment reasoned that history obeyed unalterable laws of nature. In reaction, Social Darwinists and nationalists in the nineteenth century embraced the jungle's competition of claw and fang and cheered on peoples warring against one another for supremacy. Story arcs explain causation and significance in terms of the rise or decline of societies, crises or stability, the primacy of foreign or domestic policy, sex or power, or any number of drives and choices. All of these versions of history's purpose made perfect sense to people at the time. Yet they can also obscure, simplify, and mislead (especially as they usually glorified their society's own achievements and diminished their flaws). Nor are we in our time exempt from the limitations of our own points of view, which may one day seem quaint or even wrongheaded.

Indeed, objectivity requires a great deal of educational effort in critical engagement with sources. Since history became an academic discipline, professional

---

7. For example, US president Bill Clinton (r. 1993–2001) notoriously responded to a question about knowledge of his extramarital affair: "It depends on what the meaning of 'is' is."

historians have striven to be impartial by applying the historical method. Historians found it self-evident that our empirical observation of the world through our senses, the scientific and historical methods, and reasoned debate of various viewpoints would arrive at indisputable truth. The trustworthiness of history depends on distinguishing whether something is **fact**, **opinion**, or **myth**. Facts are those pieces of historical information that all reasonable people agree upon. They are the data of history, extracted from the serious examination of sources. Once proved by historians, hard facts are the most reliable and least arguable information available. They come closest to anything we can call truth.

In the past few decades, historians have questioned whether true objectivity can be attained. First, the idea of *revisionism* involved younger historians critically reexamining sources and historical arguments in order to improve understanding. In correcting the works of their predecessors, they often try to promote better knowledge of oppressed people (such as the enslaved) and ignored subjects (such as women). Then the "linguistic turn" in philosophy and literature insisted that a source may be read one way superficially and officially, but when deconstructed it reveals hidden signs, meanings, and systems of discourses that explain both power and resistance to it. This *relativism* asserted that all knowledge was bonded with the culture in which it was produced (usually by elites).

These "postmodern" approaches seemed to question whether anything could be known for certain about history. Even more, modern neuroscience seems to indicate that an individual human brain cannot tell the difference between real and false memories. As these ideas filtered into the popular culture, those with political agendas have created their own historical discourse. Revisionism now can mean attacking accepted historical events, such as denying the Holocaust or the moon landing or claiming that Elvis or John Kennedy Jr. is alive or that earth has been visited by space aliens.[8] Conspiracy theories are spread and fed by social media through the internet, which has given rise to not insignificant segments of society insisting on falsehoods without good supporting evidence. Most recently, even partisan government spokespeople deny obvious lies and errors with claims of "fake news," "alternative facts," and "Big Lies."[9]

Yet even those facts which most people agree upon as true mean little by themselves. Only when they have been selected and interpreted do they explain historical causation and significance. Even facts become what people make them into. People may blow them out of proportion or neglect them into nonexistence. To use a metaphor, facts are the bricks of historical work. Hard and rough, they can be used to frame a hearth or build a wall, but they can also be tossed aside

8. To be clear, there exists substantial and conclusive evidence that (1) Nazis during World War II carried out the systematic murder of millions of Jews and others, and (2) American astronauts personally explored the lunar surface between 1969 and 1972. There exists no valid evidence that (1) Elvis Presley did not die partly from an overdose in 1977 or (2) John F. Kennedy Jr. did not die in a plane crash in 1999. There exists no good evidence that extraterrestrials have buzzed the skies in flying saucers, landed on earth in their chariots of the gods, or are kept in Area 51.

9. For links to good websites that help separate fact from fiction on current events, see http://www.concisewesternciv.com/links/ferret.html.

Figure 1.1. What appears to be a random pile of stones in the foreground is clearly organized in the background as a cairn or burial place. Four thousand years ago at Clava, now in Scotland, people stacked the foundations of these tombs and set up the standing stones in the background for a few of their dead. The doorway is oriented to face the rising sun on the first day of winter. What beliefs they associated with death, we do not know.

or thrown through a window. They may have been part of some ancient ruin, but because of gaps in historical preservation, many details will be missing. A historian digging into that ancient ruin has incomplete information, since bricks have been lost, destroyed, or perhaps never even made in the first place. Someone may have reconstructed part of the ruin with modern materials. In contrast, a historian reviewing recent history may have too much information, piles upon piles of construction materials. Either way, we cannot really see behind the façade of the source (see figure 1.1). We try to read the minds of people in the past, attempt to see through their eyes, but perfect clarity is impossible.

Historians construct arguments choosing from whatever facts are available. Conclusions in lectures, articles, and books (and now other media) explain what happened in history. Such judgments argue the significance of the details and show how they mattered to people in the past or to us now. Debates among historians with differing viewpoints improve the accuracy of their answers. To extend the above metaphor, a historian may say that one set of bricks belongs to a palace, yet another historian, looking at the same bricks, might say they come from a fortress. Whether either or neither is correct is the ongoing labor of historians.

Without conclusive evidence (blueprints, foundations, illustrations, eyewitness accounts), disputes may remain tangled. Usually the weight of scholarly opinion will lean one way or another. Sometimes new insights might lead to an alternative suggestion, such as a compromise—a palace-fortress. Good historians are ready to change their opinions, given solid evidence and cogent argument. This author might conceivably rewrite and improve every sentence of this book to respond to new information in the future. Every new source provides new nuance. This changeableness is not inconsistency, dodging, or flip-flopping, but rather a result of sound judgment. Historians build on each other's work.

A concise survey such as this book depends on the writings of many historians. This author, though, provides his own viewpoint on the grand sweep of time. This book's themes of supremacies and diversities help to explain our complex past. Supremacies focus on how the use of power dominates societies. Those who want *supremacy* usually seek stability, order, and consolidation. They also often desire to expand their power over others by using anything from warfare to ideologies. People react to such power either by accommodating and transforming themselves in compliance or by resisting in public or covert ways. Power may flow from the top down, from rulers to subjects, or from the bottom up, from the masses to the leaders. *Diversity*, on the other hand, reflects the creative impulse that produces new ideas, as well as people's efforts to define themselves as different. Those who promote diversity create change, opportunity, and individuality.

These two trends do not necessarily oppose each other. They are not a version of dialectical materialism (see chapter 11). The opposite of supremacy is inferiority; the contrast of diversity is conformity. People who want supreme power usually demand **universalism**, applying the same beliefs and practices to everyone. They would promote **acculturation**, where one ethnic group conforms its culture to another. Likewise, people's frequent tendency toward diversity often encourages *particularism*, requiring that various ideas and activities differ according to location. In addition, the mixture of cultures may result in *syncretism*, where elements of one join or blend with another. A tension thus may arise between the supremacy desire for similarity and the diversity push for variety, or the two may align together. One or the other, or both, intermingle in different ages and societies. Whether applied to politics, culture, or society, supremacies and diversities offer a structure in which to illustrate historical conflict and change. They are not the only way to understand history, just this author's attempt to help make sense of facts and opinions about the past.

Explanations based on these facts and opinions can sometimes mutate into myths, which then complicate a historian's task. Myths are stories that give meaning to a society's existence. Because myths obscure the facts they draw on, they complicate understanding the past. People embrace myths as true because they make sense of a confusing world. Passed on from generation to generation, myths stubbornly exist beyond rational proof (see figure 1.2). These stories justify both the worst and the best behavior of individuals, societies, and states. The myths inherent in religion and the so-called lessons of history are problematic because they shape the meaning of life. Even religion, however, may not always offer clarity. For an example with real specifics (see chapter 6 for more context), in

Figure 1.2.   This round stone disk is now called the Bocca della Verità (Mouth of Truth). Historians suggest that it was a sculpture representing Oceanus, ancient god of the seas, made during the Roman Empire, and served as a drain cover. In the Middle Ages someone brought it to a church in Rome, where it now serves as a tourist attraction (cinematically seen in the movie *Roman Holiday*). If one lies while putting one's hand in the mouth, the hand gets bitten off. How can that be true?

the Gospel of John, chapter 18, verse 38, translated from the Greek, the Roman procurator Pontius Pilate asks Jesus, "What is truth?" and does not get an answer.

In striving for objectivity, most modern historians try not to favor one religion or belief system as being more true than any other. Indeed, the rational and empirical historical method cannot assert any religion's validity or falsity. Religions draw on the **supernatural**, which is beyond the limits of nature, to which historians are confined. Historians cannot prove any religion true in all its supernatural aspects. The historian instead examines what the followers of any religion believed and, based on those beliefs, how they affected history.

People also want to believe good things about their own society. Thus, myths are often disguised as comforting lessons learned from history. In particular, historical figures are often mythologized into heroes. Our own society promotes potent myths about figures such as Christopher Columbus, George Washington, and Robert E. Lee that resist change in the face of reality. Most of Columbus's contemporaries knew the world was a globe; good evidence is lacking that Washington chopped down a cherry tree and confessed it to his father. These men might be notable, but their significance should not be based on stories that mislead. Even more tricky, from opposing points of view the heroes are actually villains. In the judgment of many Native Americans, Columbus began genocide. Some British consider Washington a traitor, and some Americans believe Lee committed treason. Accurate portrayals of such figures require subtlety. Yet cracking open myths and examining their core is essential to learning from history.

The best history makes us self-critical, not self-congratulatory. Too often, someone's victory and satisfaction is someone else's defeat and suffering. Everyone joins in to take collective credit for victories, but resulting atrocities are blamed on isolated others. The American philosopher George Santayana wrote in 1905, "Those who cannot remember the past are condemned to repeat it." Since then, many have tried to learn from history but have nonetheless committed the same mistakes as their predecessors.[10] What historians can do, instead, is to help us think more critically about how humans stumble into particular moments of crisis. Learning history may be dangerous, especially when opinions sprout into myths.

This text will regularly offer "basic principles," clear statements of obvious common historical behavior. They are not so much "lessons" of history as contradictions of common myths and suppositions (although there are always exceptions). They should challenge you to test them against historical experience. The first basic principle is:

> **There is no such thing as the "good ol' days," except in a limited way for a few people.**

People like to believe that there was once a golden age to which we should aspire to return. But only a small number of people led lives of comfort and calm during some so-called good ol' days. Whether in first-century Rome or eighteenth- and nineteenth-century Virginia, social elites proclaimed myths of their own supremacy to justify their status and power. If they lost those privileges, then they could ostensibly claim that their way of life had once been better. Both Rome and Virginia, of course, benefited from enslaved people who did not enjoy the same luxuries as their masters. That good life of the few has often required the exploitation of a much larger number of other people. And the interesting parts in history often portray the trials and tribulations that humans inflicted on other humans.

The challenge for this book is making sense of the Western past for someone unfamiliar with its history, through the words of one particular author and the few translated voices of people from the past. As should be clear from the above discussion, no single view can be true for everyone, everywhere, forever. This historical account will regularly note the disputes and unknowns of what historians know. Like a reviewer of a book or film, this text both describes what happens and offers some value judgments. It often criticizes the flaws, failures, and contradictions inherent in the West. As the story unfolds, it points out the diverse options created during centuries of new ideas and practices by the many

---

10. The German Philosopher G. W. F. Hegel in 1824 suggested that history teaches that no one has ever learned from history and used its lessons. He kept trying to teach it anyhow.

peoples that make up Western civilization. Further reading and learning in history should reveal where this version is more or less objective, and what it has omitted or overinterpreted. In a comparatively few pages, you are offered a starting point to understand the essential people, events, and ideas of a culture that dominates the world today.

Unfortunately for us all, few people really learn from history; most people use history only to confirm what they already believe. Historians offer the hope that we can learn from history to improve ourselves. They write some things with certainty, much with confidence, and some with caution. The ultimate challenge for each of us is to form an opinion about history. Ask yourself: What can I learn that gives life more meaning? How can I make better decisions today based on the successes and failures of our ancestors? What knowledge of our heritage should I pass on to our descendants? This book offers some perspectives to help you answer those questions.

Review: How can we evaluate history?

Response:

PRIMARY SOURCE PROJECT 1: THUCYDIDES VERSUS VON RANKE ABOUT THE AIM OF HISTORY

Modern historians often credit the ancient Greek writer Thucydides with the first work of critical historical writing. His work called The Peloponnesian War *describes a conflict fought during his lifetime. Thucydides thought it the most significant of all wars up until then. In this passage, he describes his approach to writing the book. More than two thousand years later, the young Leopold von Ranke produced his work on other wars, fought four hundred years before his own lifetime. He began* his History of Roman and German Peoples from 1494 to 1535 *with a preface that called for a new, more methodological and neutral kind of historical writing. Both texts offer some insight into the historical method.*

Source 1: *The Peloponnesian War* by Thucydides (ca. 400 BC)

Having now given the result of my inquiries into early times, I grant that there will be a difficulty in believing every particular detail. The way that most men deal with traditions, even traditions of their own country, is to receive them all alike as they are delivered, without applying any critical test whatever. . . .

So little pains do the vulgar take in the investigation of truth, accepting readily the first story that comes to hand. On the whole, however, the conclusions I have drawn from the proofs quoted may, I believe, safely be relied on. Assuredly they will not be disturbed either by the lays of a poet displaying the exaggeration of his craft, or by the compositions of the chroniclers that are attractive at truth's expense; the subjects they treat of being out of the reach of evidence, and time having robbed most of them of historical value by enthroning them in the region of legend. Turning from these, we can rest satisfied with having proceeded upon the clearest data, and having arrived at conclusions as exact as can be expected in matters of such antiquity. . . .

With reference to the speeches in this history, some were delivered before the war began, others while it was going on; some I heard myself, others I got from various quarters; it was in all cases difficult to carry them word for word in one's memory, so my habit has been to make the speakers say what was in my opinion demanded of them by the various occasions, of course adhering as closely as possible to the general sense of what they really said. And with reference to the narrative of events, far from permitting myself to derive it from the first source that came to hand, I did not even trust my own impressions, but it rests partly on what I saw myself, partly on what others saw for me, the accuracy of the report being always tried by the most severe and detailed tests possible. My conclusions have cost me some labor from the want of coincidence between accounts of the same occurrences by different eye-witnesses, arising sometimes from imperfect memory, sometimes from undue partiality for one side or the other. The absence of romance in my history will, I fear, detract somewhat from its interest; but if it be judged useful by those inquirers who desire an exact knowledge of the past as an aid to the interpretation of the future, which in the course of human things must resemble if it does not reflect it, I shall be content. In fine, I have written my work, not as an essay which is to win the applause of the moment, but as a possession for all time.

Source 2: *History of Roman and German Peoples from 1494 to 1535* by von Ranke (1824)

Some have claimed for history the aim to judge the past, to instruct us today for the benefit of future years. The present attempt does not dare to reach such high aims: it will merely state, how it actually was [*wie es eigentlich gewesen*].

Yet how could this be newly researched? The foundation of this present text, the origin of its material are memoirs, diaries, letters, diplomatic reports and original testimonies of eyewitnesses; other writings are used only when they are directly derived from those sources, or when they appear to be equivalent to them through some original knowledge. Every page cites the relevant works; the manner of research and the critical results will be presented in a second volume, that will be published with the present one on the same day. . . .

Intention and material give rise to the form. One cannot expect from a history the free expression, which at least, in theory, one seeks in a poetical work. And I do not know whether in fairness one could believe the like is found in the works of Greek or Roman masters. The strict description of the facts, as limited and uncomfortable as they may be, is without doubt the highest law. A second, for myself, was the development of unity and the sequence of events. It might have been expected, that I begin with a general description of the political relationships in Europe. Such an approach might not have confused the perspective, but it certainly would have diverted the focus. Instead, I have prioritized, every people, every power, every particular, as they were, only then to describe them thoroughly only when they enter upon the stage as significantly active or notable. It does not worry me—for how could their existence have forever remained untouched?—that already ahead of time, here and there, they must be mentioned. In this manner at least, the course that they held in general, the path that they followed, the thoughts that moved them, could all the better be delineated.

Finally, what can one say about such treatment in detail, as an essential part of historical works? Will it not appear often hard, fragmented, bland, and tiresome? There exists for this problem noble models, both old—and not to be forgotten—also new; yet I have not attempted to imitate them: their world was another one. There exists an exalted ideal to strive toward: that is the event itself in its human dimension, its unity, its fullness. I know how far I have remained from that. What else is to say? One makes the effort, one strives, in the end one has not reached the goal. If only nobody would be impatient with that! The main thing is always that we are dealing with humanity as it is, explainable or inexplicable: the life of the individual, the kinfolk, the people, now and then with the hand of God over them.

Questions:

- *What kind of sources does each historian draw on and what is the difficulty with them?*
- *Against what kind of history does each historian write and toward what goal(s) does each historian aspire for his own work?*
- *How do these authors' comments illustrate the value of studying history?*

Responses:

Make your own timeline! Here is an example of information you could add to the blank timelines at the end of each chapter. Just write down terms, names, dates, whatever you think important, in chronological order. Do not worry about spacing or neatness—just get it down.

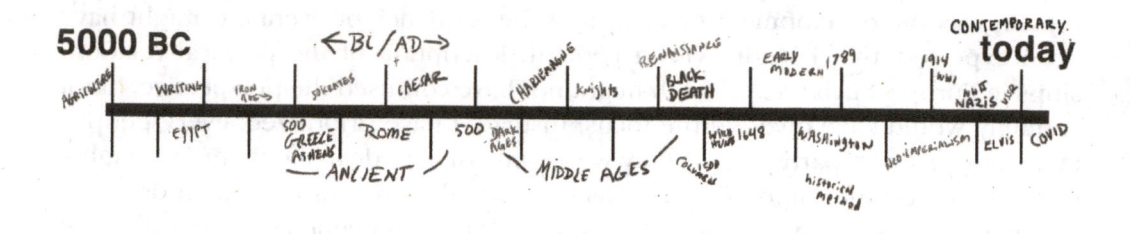

For more on these sources, go to http://www.concisewesternciv.com/sources/psc1a.html. For a comparison by Voltaire and Macaulay on historical point of view, go to http://www.concisewesternciv.com/sources/psc1.html.

CHAPTER

Wanderers and Settlers

The Ancient Middle East to 400 BC

Every human society tells stories that explain the dawn of the universe, the world, and human beings (see timeline A). In our society, the beginnings of human history have become controversial. Some people today agree with ancient peoples who calculated that the age of the world was only a few thousand years. Most people agree with current scientific and historical methods that the origins of both the earth and humanity stretch much further back into time. The scientific-historical viewpoint of this textbook presumes that the first human beings wandered out of our ancestral home in Africa many tens of thousands of years ago. Several thousand years ago, some humans settled on the civilized way of life. From those beginnings, the ancient civilizations in Egypt and Mesopotamia produced knowledge used by the early Europeans.

THE APES' COUSINS

What we know about our oldest ancestors comes from the archaeological record of their physical remains, in their bones and creations, as well as comparisons to primates and hunter-gatherer groups that have survived until today (whose contact with or avoidance of civilization may have altered their behavior). Thus our knowledge is fragmentary and tentative, subject to revision with new discoveries and studies. The first humanlike creatures, called **hominins**, appeared on the earth millions of years ago. One of our earliest direct ancestors, *Australopithecus* (southern ape), lived about four million years before us. These hominins shared much of their genetic structure and basic anatomy with their closest great ape relatives, hominids, whose descendants would eventually evolve into modern primates of orangutans, bonobos, chimpanzees, and gorillas. Various differences gave hominins and their descendants advantages in the life-and-death struggles in a dangerous world of predators. From about three to one million years ago, the separate species of early humans had evolved (such as *Homo erectus*, then *Homo habilis* and *Homo rhodesiensis* or *heidelbergensis*).

First, physical differences made up for their inferiority of sight and smell, strength, and speed. The erect stance on two legs distinguished hominins from most other creatures. The hominins came down from the trees of the jungle and began to walk on two legs across the African savanna. Because they could see and travel farther than other apes, they gained access to wider varieties of food. An opposable thumb allowed hominins to make a fist and grasp **tools**.

Second, this ability to manipulate material objects into complex tools gave hominins another advantage. Although an ape might be able to make a primitive tool from a rock or a stick, hominin hands began to craft much more efficient and useful devices. **Weapons** made up for their lack of claw, fang, and muscle. Knives, needles, hooks, and hatchets fashioned from stone and bone were the evidence left behind by the first humans. Using these, our ancestors fashioned protective **clothing** and carrying bags that made them still more mobile. Hundreds of thousands of years ago, they learned to control fire, which both provided warmth and made more varieties of food edible by cooking. Instead of being food for saber-toothed cats, early humans ate what saber-tooths ate, even if they had to steal carrion from big cats rather than kill their food themselves. Tools became one of the great driving forces of human history. Indeed, historians call this long period of human evolution, from over two million to ten thousand years ago, the **Paleolithic Age** (from the Greek for "Old Stone Age"), named after the stone tools used then.

Third, a larger and more complex brain enabled more advanced thought and speech. Gorillas and chimpanzees can be taught some simple ways to form basic words and phrases. As far as science can detect, though, they lack anything approaching our sophistication of narrative language. Communication through human words and sentences allowed more extensive exchange of ideas than did the squeaks, yelps, and buzzes of other animals. This complexity allowed people to better survive through words, games, and role-playing. Humans with their more flexible and adaptive brains have relied less on instinct and more on learning. Instinctually, someone threatened will react with fighting, fleeing, or freezing still. Skilled humans can make choices among those reactions.

Perhaps the most important idea conveyed by speech and human experience is that we die. On their own, children, teenagers, and even often adults have a sense of invulnerability and immortality. Yet stories and experience teach that death is certain. Our consciousness of our own mortality leads to another basic principle:

> **Humans know they are going to die; therefore, most people form supernatural beliefs about what their purpose is in this life and what happens after death.**

Religion, the structure we give to a set of supernatural beliefs, may have been the first human invention. Religion answers that most basic of human questions: "What is the meaning of life?" This very question recognizes that for each of us, life ends in death, at least in the natural world. Yet nearly all religions suppose that a "super"-natural world also exists beyond or above our senses. Most humans rely on beliefs about a supernatural realm to help them cope with everyday troubles in the struggle for survival. Our first ancestors probably practiced some form of *animism*: the belief that nature is alive with spirits and ghosts who can affect our world and us.

Religion's development depended on another difference between the apes and humans, namely our ability for complex verbal and pictorial communication. In human culture, the ideas of religion were conveyed in stories and images. Religious information through symbols was probably the first form of art, in **paintings** and small **sculptures**.[1] Cave paintings and artifacts portrayed what people were interested in, primarily beasts being hunted, sexualized figures of men and women, and strange beings mixing the animal and the human.

Fourth, hominins moved in social **communities**, since there was strength in numbers. Even the behavior of our ape cousins shows the usefulness of groups for individual survival. Like baboons and gorillas, early peoples seem to have formed packs, often called bands or tribes, ranging from probably twenty to a hundred individuals. Leadership to solve disputes was divided between chiefs who connected with people and shamans who communicated with the supernatural spirits. Observations of bonobos and chimpanzees interestingly reveal two different attitudes toward social structure. Chimpanzees usually live in relative peace with one another under a dominant male who keeps order, but sometimes they break out in murderous violent slaughter. In contrast, bonobos remain peaceful under the guidance of females, with social tensions soothed by all kinds of sexual activity.

As for humans, tribes developed more complex social hierarchies involving bonds among individuals, young and old, each mutually dependent and involved with the other in order to remain alive. The increasing numbers of distinct groups reveal a common human attitude of dividing into opposing factions. This **tribalism** was the tendency to band together by defining members as different from "other" people. Such tribalism could both unite one tribe against others and divide a community against itself. Another point of both unity and division was the **family** as a vital social unit. The smallest grouping modern sociologists call a family was a parent and child (whether born of sexual reproduction or adopted). Larger collections included parents united through marriage, grandparents, aunts and uncles, cousins, friends, helpers, hangers-on, or anyone defined by its members as belonging. One family could not exist by itself for long, given questions of safety and prohibitions against inbreeding. Maybe a half dozen to a few dozen families made up the typical human community for many of the millennia during which our ancestors evolved.

Within these families and communities, the interrelationship of men and women and their children varies widely within our historical heritage. Since women bear the children, they have throughout history devoted much of their

---

1. A brief history of art to accompany this text, with links and illustrations, can be found at http://www.concisewesternciv.com/arth/index.html.

time and energy to raising the young. Men found it easier to get away from their children, whether on the hunt or (later) in the public square. Yet some men could not hunt well enough to bring home much meat, and some women can be terrible or murderous mothers. A basic principle expresses a more realistic perspective on family relationships:

> **The only people who can bear children are those with the necessary reproductive organs; everything else about people's social roles is up for discussion.**

There are very few ways in which everyone agrees that people are either essentially the same or different from one another. Otherwise, societies construct opinions about morality, customs, and expectations, which they then use to force people into categories or compartments. Certainly, biological differences between men and women exist, but how significant are they, especially when technology can be an equalizer? Some people argue that because men on average are bigger, stronger, and more aggressive than women, they should naturally have the superior social role. Yet we know that the biggest man can be the gentlest father, while the smallest mother with a weapon can kill the largest man.

Recorded history is dominated by men. One reason is that historical and scientific studies show that males are statistically more aggressive and possess more upper-body strength than females, especially because of the hormone testosterone. This quality has both a positive and a negative side for human society. Too much violence and the community is destroyed from within; too little ferocity and it can be destroyed by outsiders. Hence, male aggressiveness is useful when warriors are trained to kill for their community but harmful when men murder their family, friends, or neighbors. Much of our history has been a harsh tale of channeling aggression.

The other side of history is peaceful management of the inevitable squabbles within and quarrels among these communities. Our ancestors' first political arrangements organized where to camp, when to move, how to punish, and even how to protect the young and raise them with all the knowledge necessary for survival. Hominins developed increasingly complicated rules of behavior of command and obedience, without which communities would fall apart in anger and jealousy. The first political organization meant the choosing of leaders who could interact well with the rest of the group and resolve conflicts. Sought-after qualities were usually wisdom, charisma, and the ability to persuade or intimidate. While women rarely gained leadership, as wives and lovers they could influence their spouses and mates. Possession of better weapons technology also made a difference, allowing those organized with better weapons to dominate those less well prepared.

Hominins formed a primitive economic system of **hunting and gathering** that wrung the necessities of life from nature. Hunter-gatherers followed the game and the ripening plants as nomads. Everyone in the community participated in foraging for food and raw materials and in consuming them. Tribes traded and exchanged with other tribes for food, tools, and breeding partners. In these early tribal communities, everyone knew one another.

These tribes then interacted with others for the purposes of sharing goods, people, and worship. Many different tribes may have come together in large gatherings of thousands during seasons of plenty, living briefly in more complex social hierarchies. Ancient burials have been found with bodies surrounded by enormous wealth and possessions untypical of nomads. Many peoples without settled cities organized massive effort to build megaliths (large standing stones, often in circles, such as Stonehenge) and more permanent homes (notably Göbekli Tepe, a Neolithic archaeological site in modern-day Türkiye). Then they would go their separate ways, as nomads only able to own what they could carry. Meanwhile, isolated humans found it much more difficult to survive. Without family and friends, their death, of course, ended their history. Social bonds among people were essential for culture to grow and for knowledge to be passed to the next generation, to better the chances of survival.

Superficial differences in appearance and behavior soon emerged in the tribes that multiplied and spread to different regions. Dissimilarities increased about sixty thousand years ago when some members of *Homo sapiens* ventured out of Africa to spread over much of Eurasia, and then the Americas.[2] Scholars describe these variations as ***ethnicity***. Humans used the idea of ethnicity to create, unify, or separate themselves into communities we often categorize as "peoples." Over time, groups of people who intermarried had inherited certain physical attributes (skin color, eye shape, hair, height, etc.) that set them visually apart from others. While scientific studies have shown no significant genetic impact caused by these attributes, peoples have often found such noticeable distinctions essential in deciding who did or did not belong. More important in determining ethnicity has been learned culture (tradition, fashion, cuisine, manners, religion, etc.). The most powerful signifier of ethnic difference is probably how a people talked among themselves, whether just with a different accent or dialect having some minor vocabulary variation, or with full-fledged new languages. Ethnic use of speech includes those who belong and excludes outsiders. Today various ethnic groups speak around seven thousand different languages, and many hundreds have already gone extinct.

When this text refers to "a people," such as the Greeks, the Vikings, or the English, it recognizes a society of those who formed a certain ethnicity, meaning cultural and social (as well as, perhaps, political) coherence from their own point of view at some time in the past or from the vantage point of the present. This text does not use "race" as a useful concept. Race is a fictional idea. It has no scientific

---

2. These humans sometimes encountered other close human relatives, such as Neanderthals or Denisovans. Neanderthals were named after the German valley where modern archaeologists found the first skull attributed to the species; Denisovans were named after a cave in Siberia where archaeologists found a finger bone. Those hominins went extinct, while *Homo sapiens* continued to thrive. Traces of contacts between them survive in the DNA of many modern people.

empirical reality.[3] **Racism**, however, is very real. Racists impose imaginary biologically inherited "differences" on people of various so-called "races." Alleged racial characteristics are either literally superficial or dependent on personality dualisms (sneakiness/boldness, smartness/stupidity, hardworking/lazy), which are often used to discriminate against ethnic groups. Many societies have incorporated racism into their belief systems, and sometimes those attitudes changed history. Nonetheless, all humans have substantially the same DNA, inherited from the same ancestors, first born in the original human homeland of Africa over two hundred thousand years ago. Yet during the course of history, diverse ethnic communities formed, reformed, fell apart, vanished, or flourished. Sometimes differing societies settling near one another provoked hostility and conflict; other times closeness fostered friendship and cooperation. Many ethnic groups define others as inferior or superior to others, focusing on socially constructed differences rather than common humanity. Worst of all, groups of humans have often dehumanized other people in order to rationalize killing them. Whatever nominal ethnic divisions, however, all human beings are of the species *Homo sapiens sapiens* (thinking, thinking human).

In sum, the anatomy of human ancestors, their tools and weapons, their creative minds, and their social, political, and economic cooperation gave them advantages over most other animals. These attributes allowed humans to survive four great ice ages that began about 130,000 years ago and lasted, off and on, for tens of thousands of years. The global climate change was catastrophic for many species of plant and animal life. Vast ice sheets covered much of the landmasses. Growing seasons shortened. Those living things that could not cope became extinct. Scientists have not yet established what began or ended those ice ages in the past, and we ourselves might just be living in a brief geologic pause between one ice age and another.

In the midst of those ice ages, humans adapted themselves to every climate on the entire planet, from the sweltering jungle to the frigid Arctic. Successful humans reproduced more humans and often outstripped the natural resources in a particular range. So they went looking for better lands. Aside from descendants of the original humans in Africa who remained where they had evolved, everyone else is an immigrant. Humans entered Asia about sixty thousand years ago, getting all the way to Australia about forty thousand years ago, and some tens of thousands of years after that they sailed to islands in the Pacific Ocean. From the Bering Strait in northern Asia, perhaps on a land bridge created by lower sea levels or on boats hugging the coastline, humans crossed into the Americas about fourteen thousand years ago (see map 2.1).[4] And everywhere since, new human inhabitants moved in where others already lived. People traveled and encountered others. Would they exchange ideas and goods or would they fight and kill? Could they live with their differences or force conformity? Modern humans (once called "Cro-Magnons") immigrated to Europe about forty-five thousand years ago. About

---

3. For more on issues of race and racism, go to http://www.concisewesternciv.com/sources/psrace.html.

4. For help understanding maps, go to http://www.concisewesternciv.com/extras/maps help1.html.

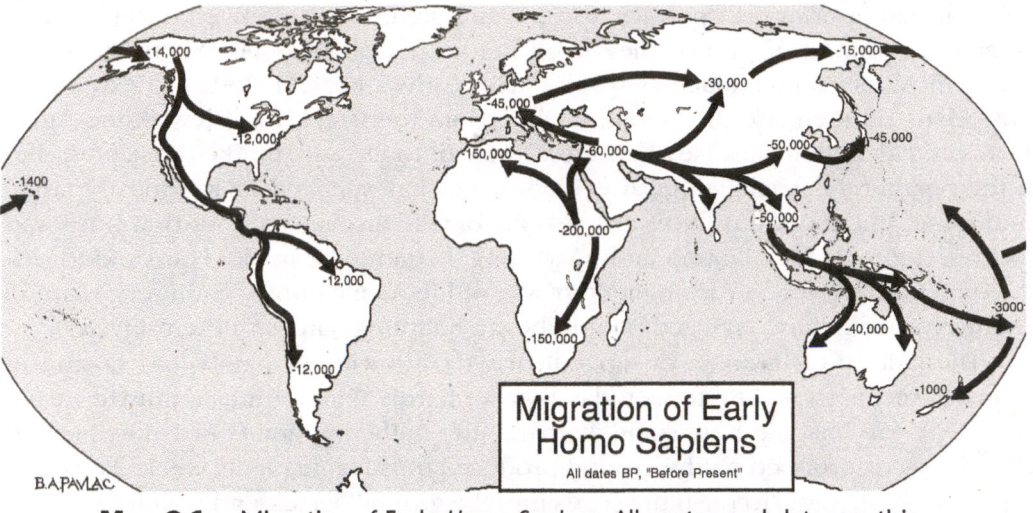

Map 2.1.   Migration of Early *Homo Sapiens*. All routes and dates on this map are based on current educated estimates and may change with new evidence. Temperatures were colder and sea levels were lower during many of these dates, increasing the size of most landmasses and coverage by ice and glaciers. How would that and other geographic factors have affected migration?

ten thousand years ago, the climate warmed again, the summers lengthened, and the glaciers retreated. Much of the planet then basked for millennia under a temperate climate. Homo sapiens soon took advantage of such agreeable weather.

Review: *What important cultural survival techniques did our hunter-gatherer ancestors use in the Old Stone Age?*

· ***Response:***

BOUND TO THE SOIL

The end of the last ice age allowed what could be considered the most fundamental and radical change in human history, the so-called **Neolithic Agricultural Revolution**. For historians, the term *revolution* often represents a major transformation of human politics, society, and culture. People lived different lives after revolutions from those they lived before. By about 8000 BC, hunters had killed most megafauna (such as woolly mammoths and giant sloths) to extinction. Historians differentiate the Neolithic Age (from the Greek for "New Stone Age") from the Paleolithic because of the new kinds of tools used, unlike those of earlier hunter-gatherers. Archaeological evidence that has survived is still mostly stone and bone, but about ten thousand years ago, evidence also shows that hoes and sickles, the tools for planting and harvesting, began to be made. Humankind discovered farming, forever changing our way of life. While hunter-gatherers adapted themselves to nature, civilized people began adapting nature to themselves.

The culture of farming, or **agriculture**, the growing of plants and raising of animals, seems so natural to us today that we hardly think of it as a human invention. One can imagine how some woman, after gathering grains or fruits, noticed that the seeds dropped on the ground produced those same plants weeks later. The logical next step was to push the seeds into the ground herself and wait for them to grow. Then she did not have to go wandering around to gather food. Once people could grow and store enough edibles to live on year-round, they could simply stay put. So rather than living in moveable tents or temporary huts, people built sturdy **houses** from logs, mud, or baked clay bricks. And homes offered better shelter against the bad weather. As they settled into their houses, these new farmers used their growing knowledge of husbandry, or planned breeding, to get better crops and animals. Hunter-gatherers had already begun the **domestication** of animals with dogs during the ice ages. Hunters bred the dangerous instincts out of wolves and fostered canine affection for humans and usefulness as hunting companions. Today, selective breeding of dogs has produced working dogs and pets ranging from Great Danes to Chihuahuas. The new farmers surely reasoned that if dogs could be tamed, why not try it with the beasts that they hunted? Some animals could not be domesticated. Yet aurochs became cattle, boars became pigs, and jungle fowl became chickens. With taming of both plants and animals, humans bound themselves to plots of land to raise their food. This switch to farming moved very slowly at first, taking thousands of years for the new way of life to spread across the world. Others kept a mobile existence of low-impact agriculture as animal herders (pastoralists). And some people refused to join in, remaining hunter-gatherers.

Agriculture's vast change for the history of the world can hardly be exaggerated. The surface of the earth began to yield to human power. Before agriculture, everyone had been at the mercy of the environment, depending on nature to provide sustenance. Climatic change with ice ages had prevented agriculture and made hunting and gathering difficult in many places. Since the last ice age ten thousand years ago, nature could still frighten with earthquakes, threaten with heat waves and drought, beat down with thunderstorms and hurricanes and floods, and endanger with fires across prairies and forests. Humans plowed through these difficulties to reshape nature herself. They cleared farmland by removing forests with axes or burning and slashing. They irrigated crops by damming and digging trenches to change the shape and course of streams and lakes. They chased away or killed any and all wildlife that might harm their domesticated crops and animals. From all this hard work and innovation, people produced more food, allowing families to grow as fast as hungry infant mouths could be filled, reproducing much faster than hunter-gatherers had. Farmers soon grew enough extra provisions so that a few people no longer had to work in agricultural production.

This transition to farming varied widely as to when or where or whether people made it happen. Archaeological evidence shows a wide range of creative adaptations as people better controlled their surroundings. Some peoples tried agriculture and returned to hunting and gathering. Others practiced agriculture seasonally and turned to old ways in winter or times of drought or flood. These mixed hunter-gatherer and settled cultures increasingly either failed or gave way to civilizations where agriculture ruled year-round.

Farming opened up a whole range of new occupations beyond tilling the soil and tending animals. **Division of labor** made urban life more efficient. While all hunter-gatherers hunted and gathered, civilized people might focus on work for which they were most suited or that they found most enjoyable. Some people could devote their energy to making garments. Weavers wove the fibers of flax and hemp on a loom to produce cloth. Tailors cut cloth into unusual styles and colored it with dyes in patterns never seen on plant or animal. Some fashions promoted comfort and protection from weather; others emphasized social roles at the expense of comfortable fit. Cooks soaked, fermented, mixed, roasted, baked, and boiled increasing varieties of plant and animal stuffs into cuisine. Potters baked clay pots that better preserved food, free from spoilage and vermin. Cartwrights built wagons to transport large loads over long distances. Masons stacked bricks and stone into durable buildings, beginning the art of **architecture**.

Especially where land could be put to use for growing crops or raising animals, economic success led to growing communities where larger numbers of families could reside within a limited geographic space. Small **villages** might contain a few families or numbers up to two hundred people. Villages might grow into **towns**, which might hold a few thousand people. Then great **cities** bloomed, ranging from many thousands to today's huge urban areas of millions of people. This complex life of interconnected cities with supporting farmland gives us **civilization**. Urban living provided a rich, creative, evolving dynamic that expanded and intensified human domination of the planet, changing the environment to suit human buildings and farmlands. Forests fell, rivers shifted, hills altered, grasslands converted to pasture or farmland. People invented the idea of weeds—plants that grew where humans did not want them.

Early civilizations often showed several common structures. The first civilized political organization, the **city-state**, was literally the smallest viable unit of civilization. It included the city itself (made up of homes, businesses, and public buildings) and the surrounding countryside of farmland from which the people of the city fed and supplied themselves. These larger numbers of people confined in a small area often created new kinds of leaders to organize the increasingly complex human activities.

The first important leaders perhaps made use of religion as a key source of convincing others to obey. Agriculture and its new concepts of property

Table 2.1. Comparisons of Gods and Goddesses of Ancient Polytheisms

Attribute	Mesopotamian	Egyptian	Greek	Roman	Norse
Ruler of gods	Enlil, Marduk, Asshur	Ra	Zeus	Jupiter	Odin
Sky/storm	Anu	Nut, Horus	Zeus	Jupiter	Thor
Earth	Ninhursag	Geb	Gaia	Terra/Tellus	Erda
Water/sea	Apsu, Enki	Tefnut	Poseidon	Neptune	Aegir
Sun	Shamash	Ra	Apollo	Apollo	Sunna
Moon	Sin	Thoth	Artemis	Diana	Moon
Wisdom	Ea, Nabu	Thoth	Athena	Minerva	Odin
War	Ninurta/Ishtar	Nit, Menhit	Ares	Mars	Tyr
Magic	Enki	Isis	Hermes	Mercury	Odin
Crop fertility	Dumuzi	Ernutet	Demeter	Ceres	Freyr
Alcoholic drink	Ninkasi, Geshtinanna	Osiris	Dionysius	Bacchus	Byggvir
Technology			Hephaestus	Vulcan	
Trickster		Set	Hermes	Mercury	Loki
Love	Ishtar	Hathor	Aphrodite	Venus	Freya
Fire/hearth	Gibil	Bes	Hestia	Vesta	Frigga
Marriage	Innana	Hathor	Hera	Hymen, Juno	Frigga
Death	Ereshkigal	Osiris	Hades	Pluto	Hel

Note: The deities of ancient religions performed similar functions for agricultural peoples in early civilizations.

encouraged new, more complex religions. Most were a form of **polytheism**, the belief in many gods and goddesses, divine beings connected to the new practices of farming (see table 2.1). These new storm gods and earth goddesses tended to have more individual personalities and defined attributes than the vague spirits of animism. **Priests** (and, less often, priestesses) conducted elaborate rituals and prayers intended to appease the gods. People often shared in communal meals to celebrate the goodness of what the gods had provided in nature. Ironically, priests and priestesses who managed the temples as centers of worship actually drew much of their alleged power not from their communication with supernatural beings but from their practical, more systematic knowledge of nature.

This brings up one of the most important basic principles:

Knowledge is power.

As these ancient religious leaders studied the natural world, looking for evidence of the gods, they found data about seasons, climate, and soil conditions. Priests observed the heavens and calculated the **calendar**; they measured, added, and divided to plan and build their temples and irrigation canals; they quantified trade and agricultural production; they told stories, often describing the relations of humans to gods; they invented **writing** to keep track of it all. Thus, the fields of astronomy, mathematics, and literature became basic to the civilized way of life.

The priests passed on their knowledge in **schools**, one of the essential institutions of civilization. Instead of having education provided by parents and community leaders, as in hunter-gatherer societies, children from separate families more efficiently learned from professional teachers. Usually, though, privileged elites allowed only boys from prosperous families access to a formal education, excluding girls and the poor.

Priests had to share leadership of society with **kings**, who became the dominant political figures. **Monarchy**, the rule of kings, was the most frequent form of government throughout civilized history until the last century. The first kings probably came to power either by election or usurpation. People chose a king or he claimed authority for himself, probably in the name of the gods, and people went along with it. The essential political questions then became (first) how many decisions affecting other people's lives could the king make and (second) who might influence or share in making those decisions. Some kings possessed only minimal power to command obedience, enjoying tightly limited roles as figureheads or mere symbols of authority. Members of the royal family, favorites, and court officials or the upper classes might actually run the kingdom behind the scenes. Kings typically strove to rule according to **autocracy** or **absolutism**, the practice that one person should dominate as much as possible in authority and decision making.[5] The acceptance of absolute monarchy allowed a ruler to exercise as much power as human limitations allowed. Attempts by rulers to establish autocracies, as well as resistance to such efforts, have driven many political changes in history.

Whether weak or strong, kings held three essential roles. First, they represented the unity of the people. Each was symbolically the father of his country, the head of the most important family of families. The importance of family often eased the creation of a **dynasty**, where political power passed from parent to child. Dynasts often justified their monopoly on power by claiming connections to the gods. The gods were their relatives or specially chose them to be rulers. Even today, powerful political leaders endowed with charisma are often seen as superior to normal citizens. People worshipped these "Oriental despots" almost as elaborately as the gods they represented. Despite such divine connections, however, accident, disease, and infertility might end dynasties. Lack of a proper successor sparked political violence, often civil war, about who should rule next.

A king's second role was to preserve peace among his own people. In this role, a king usually acted as supreme judge (which was also a divine attribute). People petitioned the ruler for the righting of wrongs. To settle the increasing number of cases brought about by the rising populations of cities, kings began to establish **laws**. The most famous early law code was that which King Hammurabi of Babylon commanded to be carved onto a black stone pillar around 1700 BC. A picture above the **Law Code of Hammurabi** shows a god himself handing the laws to the king. Here the king was not going through the priests but interacted

---

5. Historians and political theorists most often apply the term *absolutism* to European monarchs of the seventeenth and eighteenth centuries AD. While queens and kings during those years clearly argued for unlimited authority, the concept has relevance for all ages.

directly with the gods, becoming the lawgiver within the cosmic order. Many early peoples believed that keeping the law pleased the gods.

The laws, of course, laid out right and wrong in practical ways, dealing with social conflict. Culture is encoded in a society's laws, which reflect what matters and what does not. One of the most essential rights in societies throughout recorded history has been protecting **property**, whether land for farming or other possessions accumulated by civilized people. Hunter-gatherers could possess only as much property as they could carry. Civilized people could claim as much property as they could defend or get others to defend for them.

At the foundation of all private property is the government's protection of the right to own possessions. Such a social contract began when our ancestors turned from hunter-gatherers into agriculturalists. Laws guaranteed that land could not be easily taken away from owners and ensured that after the owner's death it went to the correct heirs. Laws defined which property belonged to whom and prescribed punishments for those who damaged, destroyed, or tried to take it. Courts, police forces, and armies, all paid through taxes, enforced those laws. Without the social contracts maintained by governments, each one of us as individuals would be responsible for protecting and defending our private property against any ruthless person's force to take it.

Another universal legal issue for rulers has been regulating violence among people. While hunter-gatherers often punished crimes with isolating or exiling offenders, civilized regimes punished by confiscating wealth or inflicting physical pain. A fundamental question for all societies has been to categorize the killing of one human by another. Was it the defense of the nation by a soldier or of his family by a parent? Was it capital punishment inflicted by the state for justice? Was it a vicious crime by a murderer? Was it manslaughter by accident? Or did it matter at all? Many ancient laws, like Hammurabi's, punished a wide variety of crimes with death. Laws also began to regulate drunkenness, after ancient farmers discovered how to manage the fermentation processes for turning grapes into wine and grains into beer. For example, a wine seller not reporting rowdy customers to the authorities might be executed for that oversight. Many other punishments involved mutilation. In Hammurabi's Code, for example, a son who hit his father deserved having his hand cut off. Fines and banishment also were common, but not prison, because of the high cost of keeping a person confined.

The third role of a king was as a war leader against foreign foes. Brute force and the ability to kill is an obvious form of power. Yet no king could fight on his own, except in legend, such as the superhuman hero Gilgamesh of Sumerian literature (see below). A king needed warriors. One of the basic questions through history is, "Whom do the soldiers obey?" Whoever can successfully order others to kill has real power.

The king's command over life and death in peace and war gave him supreme authority within a society. The earliest kings ruled over city-states, the smallest and most cohesive political units. Yet city-states were vulnerable owing to their small size. Their wealth and resources tempted other kings, who soon desired to dominate their neighbors. If a king gained power over similar people of a similar ethnicity in a number of cities, he would rule a **kingdom**. If a king conquered foreign neighbors, he would rule those combined kingdoms as an **emperor** over an **empire**. Thus arose the practice of *imperialism*, one people who might differ in ethnicity, religion, language, history, or any number of other ways governing other peoples. Empires became the largest political structures of all, even if they were inherently unstable because of the diversity of the emperor's subjects. Many successful empire builders tried to unite their imperial subjects through accultura-tion. When voluntary cooperation failed, forced obedience often followed.

At first, civilized agriculturalists and their uncivilized neighbors lived side by side. The world seemed big enough for everyone. By about 3000 BC, however, most good farmland was already claimed by one empire, kingdom, city-state, or another. The economic and political expansion of people living in civilizations, nevertheless, progressively destroyed nonagricultural societies. The civilized peo-ple justified their superiority over the uncivilized by calling them *barbarian* (a word suggesting that they merely babbled "ba ba ba" instead of speaking coher-ently). City dwellers set up a dichotomy of themselves as generous, refined citi-zens (what the word *civilized* also means to many people) and of those who had no settled dwellings as selfish, ignorant savages. Of course, virtue does not live only in cities and wickedness among the nomads. Regardless, powerful, organized agricultural societies relentlessly grabbed whatever good land could be found for farming, mining, or building. Pastoral herders of animals and hunter-gatherers only survived because they lived on land poorly suited for agriculture (being too dry, too wet, too hilly, too hot, too cold, or with too little fertile soil). This trend continues even today, where modern encroaching civilizations seem to require the last few "barbarians" either to convert to civilization or die out.

Historians still argue about which civilization was the first. Evidence is too fragmentary to fully determine which people get boasting rights for being number one. In general, between seven and six thousand years ago, the first civilizations sprouted up along great river systems that provided enough water for agriculture. In South Asia the Indus River nurtured Indian civilization, in East Asia the Hwang Ho (Yellow River) gave rise to Chinese civilization, and the valleys of the Nile and those of the Tigris and Euphrates fertilized Middle Eastern civilizations. These three regions first cultivated the shared new way of life of cities (the social, political, and economic roles of priests, schoolteachers, kings, private property, and laws).

Review: *What did agriculture cultivate as the key components of civilization?*

Response:

THE PRICE OF CIVILIZATION

Although the vast wealth of civilization produced numerous comforts, life in cities clearly had some serious drawbacks. Humans had evolved over millions of years to be nomadic hunters and gatherers. Then, in a few centuries, people found themselves transplanted into a completely unfamiliar way of life. We continue to suffer complications from choosing urban lifestyles; unless we recognize these problems, we cannot solve them.

For instance, serious health issues arose with life in cities. Famine could easily strike, since despite the best planning, a drought or flood could destroy all the food available in a particular region. The limited abilities of transportation often meant that little food could be imported. In contrast, hunter-gatherers faced with natural disaster could move on to other hunting grounds. Agricultural people instead felt compelled to stay for two main reasons. First, they believed that one day the land would be productive again, and so they remained to prevent anyone else from taking it over. Second, most other nearby land suitable for farming was already taken. Good farmland is a precious and limited commodity. Farming peoples stuck out the hard times and, consequently, many died where they had planted.

Surprisingly, another health problem was poor nutrition. The hunter-gatherers had evolved to eat a balanced diet out of what nature provides. In contrast, civilized people chose what they wanted to eat rather than what nature offered to them. They often wanted to go heavier on the meats, avoided certain roots and vegetables, and devoured sweets. Our "sweet tooth" derives from our body's requirements for carbohydrates and fats. For hunter-gatherers, concentrated sugars were limited and rare in the wild. Agricultural people, however, could produce and consume sugars in large qualities, unaware of how obesity put health at risk and sugar rotted teeth.

Contagious diseases also threatened civilized society. Hunter-gatherers lived in small groups that wandered regularly. Their contact with other groups of people was brief. In contrast, cities opened themselves up for illness, encouraging close and regular contact with travelers and traders from other communities. Widespread outbreaks of disease, called **plagues**, regularly devastated urban populations. Harmful germs flourished as civilized people lived in large groups that dumped their waste all around themselves and possessed animals that carried diseases. Epidemics affected smaller populations, while pandemics could spread over vast distances, even around the world. We know now that the causes of many sicknesses (as explained in chapter 11) are microscopic bacteria and viruses, which live all around and on us. Some historical epidemics spread by water (dysentery, cholera, typhoid), some by human contact (measles, smallpox), some through insects (fleas and lice for typhus and bubonic plague, mosquitoes for malaria, and ticks for Lyme disease), and some through the air (influenza, pneumonia). Until roughly a century and a half ago, few people cared much about cleanliness, which helps prevent some contagion. Ignorant of the real causes of disease, civilized people could often do little more than suffer through them and complain to their gods.

Another negative consequence of civilization, for half the human species at least, was an increase in **sexism**. Sexism is the belief that one sex (usually the male) is better than the other (usually the female). From birth, we usually separate humans into these two groups, male and female, with that common first question, "Is it a boy or a girl?" Sometimes physical or genetic irregularities complicate the answer to that question.[6] Regardless of the biology of chromosomes and anatomy, all societies set expectations about gender behaviors. They use both custom and law to shape how individuals should perform gender attitudes of masculinity or femininity, as well as romantic feelings and physical desire. Studies by modern social scientists and historians suggest that differences of sexual attraction and gender identity are much more complicated than commonly believed.

In hunter-gatherer families and tribes, sex roles seem to have been much more undifferentiated and fluid than in civilized societies. In a community on the move, where everyone bore his or her own share, men and women were more equal in status. Also, in such small communities, everyone knew one another. Some matriarchies, or societies where women set the tone and had public positions of influence, seem to have existed among hunter-gatherers and a very few early civilizations.

In civilization, however, sexism began to grant more advantages to males. The acquisition of property changed everything. Ownership of farmland led to yet another, and simple, basic principle:

> **Land is wealth; wealth is power.**

Of course, land is not the only means to wealth—later, commerce, industry, and finance would provide much more efficient ways to become wealthy. Nor is wealth the only route to power—charisma, military force, ruthless violence, and other methods can all be useful in seizing dominion. When agriculture has dominated the economy, though, land has meant power.

Once civilized through owning land, men effectively excluded women from power by their near-exclusive control of property within the family or even within society at large. Such a system is often called patriarchy. The preference for male, paternal authority often meant that power went from father to son, whether in a household or a kingdom. This control by men had nothing to do with our Western, traditional idea that the men are out sweating in the fields while the women are keeping house. Indeed, in many farming societies women work in the fields as much as or more than men, especially during planting and harvest. The first governments and their laws intervened with family structures and have ever since. Formal laws regulated property transferred through inheritances, or as gifts at the time of betrothal or marriage; laws turned those

---

6. People who say humans are born either biologically male or female are ignorant of conditions that modern physicians label as intersex or disorders of sexual development, once named hermaphroditism (after a figure in Greek mythology).

agreements into legal contracts; laws monitored sexual fidelity (usually allowing husbands more leeway than wives). How spouses treated one another, and how parents raised their children, even with the power of life and death, were matters of community, not just private, concern.

Another reason for women's exclusion from public roles may be that once people settled down, women had more young children to care for (since only women bear children). With increased food production, more children could be fed. Since women did not have to worry about long treks as nomads, they could more easily endure pregnancies, while looking after other young children at the same time. In turn, more children provided cheap labor for farmwork. Women undoubtedly worked behind the scenes, in the kitchens and bedrooms, at mealtimes and in the fields, influencing the decisions of fathers and brothers, husbands and sons. Nevertheless, men largely monopolized the formal and accepted social roles of status and power that developed in civilization. Women did, if rarely, achieve political power and economic wealth throughout history, but even then their success was usually in defiance of custom and tradition. Women's domestic work freed the men from chores so that they could take the lead in public life. Given women's typical exclusion from real power, cultures instead praised them in their roles as mothers. While they may have crucially formed the character of their children (leading to the later cliché, "The hand that rocks the cradle rules the world"), women's limited opportunities wasted much human potential.

It remains difficult to illuminate gender roles within families, since comparatively few sources survive (although examples for some that do are the Sources on Families in this and each following chapter). Therefore, women's roles in driving decisive changes in history were once rarely examined. Only in the twentieth century did numbers of Western women gain rights comparable with or the same as those that men have long had (see chapter 14). Until then, the dominance of men over subservient women became traditional in civilizations.

In most societies, other social divisions initiated by civilization have gone unquestioned. **Social classes**, groups of people defined around intersecting cultural and economic status, are commonplace in urban situations. These developed out of a division of labor or specialization in economic production. As mentioned already, weavers, tailors, potters, cartwrights, smiths, bakers, and masons carried out their crafts with greater efficiency than if each individual personally wove and sewed cloth, fired clay pots, built carts, forged tools, baked bread, and laid bricks. Instead of treating all kinds of labor as equal, some people earned a greater portion of wealth from their work than others did from theirs. Urban cultures usually separated people into at least three groups, traditionally reflecting a hierarchy of political power, wealth, and social influence. First, the **upper class** lorded their status over the other classes. A tiny minority of people took charge, controlling access to knowledge, possessing most of the land, and taking the best goods that society had to offer. They became **royalty** at the top, followed by **aristocrats**, with the **nobles** just below, who declared themselves destined to pass on inherited dominance from generation to generation. These elites organized society. Second, a tiny **middle class** formed around **artisans** (who made pots, shoes, and furniture) and **merchants** (who bought and sold goods). Third, the vast majority of others, the **lower class** or commoners, did the heavy labor of building and farmwork. Through most of civilized history they were simple farmers called **peasants**. They worked the land and produced the food so that the aristocrats and artisans did not have to. The hard work of peasants raising food from the land was at first, and often still is, the foundation of civilization. Although they created much wealth, peasants often saw few of its benefits. Ranked even below them, however, were the jobless poor, who hardly even counted as a class. Poverty did not exist among hunter-gatherers, since all members shared in the group's resources, while those who did not belong died in the wilderness. In cities, though, people who had lost most social connections and the ability to work could still survive on the margins and with the scraps of urban wealth. Some took up what has been called "the oldest profession," namely prostitution, where people earned wealth through sex work.

Throughout most of civilized history, the majority of people remained in the class they were born into. Response to pressure for change sometimes led to adding new classes or subdividing old ones, with each new group placed in the established pecking order. Usually, though, one's parents determined one's status. Born to upper-class parents, one could easily stay upper class. Born to poor parents, one could hardly ever rise in status. So a few families sat at the top of society and decreed economic, political, and religious decisions. The large numbers of people without power usually obeyed these decisions and reinforced the authority of the elites in the marketplace, on the battlefield, and within sacred spaces. The masses had little choice.[7]

Class conflict, or attempts by the masses to achieve power alongside the elites, did drive some historical change. Now and then the thought crossed common people's minds, "Why should we suffer just because we were born to lowborn parents?" Resentful of their imposed inferiority, the lower classes every so often rebelled against their superiors. Mostly they failed.

Two aspects of civilization explain how a few aristocratic families exercised supremacy over the multitude of peasants for so long. One was the aristocratic role in warfare at the beginning of civilization. In hunter-gatherer groups, most adult males fought. Hunting even provided the weapons and training in tactics similar to battle, with its organization of killing. Farming techniques, however, did not resemble warfare. Civilized warfare thus became the work of specialists: warriors were freed from the daily grind of farming so that they could dedicate themselves to training for combat with weapons designed to kill people. The king as war leader shared with a few associated warriors some of his aura of power.

Another change to explain the rise of the aristocracy was stability. In a hunter-gatherer group, the nomadic wandering imposed equality. People could possess only as much property as they could carry. Most everyone, from chief to child,

---

7. Some societies instituted castes to rank people into groups with different power and benefits. Unlike the status class, which might change according to one's economic situation, caste remained permanent from birth. India in South Asia is best known for having such a system, although some historians suggest the USA's social divisions often work like castes.

did the same kind of work: hunting and gathering. In civilization, however, any one person had as much property as could be accumulated, stored, and defended, by oneself or with the support of others. Leadership soon became held by the few, while followers were many. Through most of civilized history, in most places, a few powerful families have run large human communities.

The elites kept their superiority through law and custom. Clothing, in particular, often denotes social status. With civilization, higher-status people imposed sumptuary laws about fashion, making it obvious to any passersby on the street to which class one belonged. Where one lived, in how elaborate a residence, also reflected status. The earliest laws of Hammurabi recognized distinctive classes of people, divided at least into nobles and commoners (as did most laws until the eighteenth century AD). Even crime and punishment usually depended on one's social status. If an aristocrat stole something, he paid compensation thirtyfold; a commoner paid only tenfold. Those who lacked money, however, paid with their life.

With these divisions of labor and class arrived the first **taxes**. Governments can tax anything at any rate they can get away with. Two and a half centuries ago, Benjamin Franklin famously quipped that death and taxes were the only sure things in life. More accurate is the following basic principle:

> **The only certainty in civilization is death and taxes. The essential questions are these: Who pays, and how much?**

Not everyone pays taxes. In some civilizations, the privileged are tax exempt. Uncivilized barbarians do not pay taxes either: in their small, self-sufficient groups, hunter-gatherer peoples do not divide up their labor and leadership. Yet civilized society cannot exist without the taxes that pay for the rule keepers, warriors, and infrastructure that have kept human interchanges functioning smoothly. Most of the time, the poorer classes, hardworking peasants, have paid for the privileges of the richer classes, landowning aristocrats.

The lowest of all people in a society were those enslaved. **Slavery** denied any position in class or caste to certain humans who became property, their bodies and labor owned by someone else. Some persons were sold into slavery to pay off debt (for example, fathers could sell their daughters for such purposes). Others were condemned to servitude as punishment for crime. Many people defeated in conquest endured bondage in captivity rather than suffer death. The harshness of the slave system—how well the enslaved peoples were cared for or how hard they were worked—varied according to the customs of a civilization and the behavior of individual masters.

Despite being inhumane, slavery has been a component of almost every civilization until modern times. Hunter-gatherers, in contrast, found it difficult to enslave people. If a hunter-gatherer was enslaved but managed to escape, she knew how to live off the land until she managed to find some friendly people of her own. In contrast, a civilized person who escaped enslavement did not know how to survive in the woods, which plants to eat, or how to make shelter. Thus, the civilized form of slavery more easily trapped people in its system.

Slave economies were supported by a final negative consequence of the rise of civilization: the perfection of **war**. Some romantics have suggested that human conflict did not exist among hunter-gatherers, who reputedly lived in some idyllic paradise. It seems, however, that humans have always organized to fight with one another, whether over pride, power, or possessions. When hunter-gatherers came under attack, though, they often could run away—they knew how to live in the wild and thus could give up a hunting ground rather than be exterminated. Further, the world was less crowded when most people were nomads. Hunter-gatherers also possessed comparatively few valuable goods to plunder.

Agriculture and cities added a more lethal intensity to human conflict. Once people settled down as farmers, the available space became much more restricted: good farmland was limited to well-watered plains. Farmers would not leave their land when threatened by invaders any more than when threatened by flood or famine. Thus, people stayed and fought with more determination and more destruction. The wealth of cities provided more temptation for invaders to take quickly and easily what others had wrung from the soil by long, hard labor. Agriculture also enabled the recruiting and supplying of larger and more complex armies, which in turn could more readily devastate a region.

Although commonly directed toward deadly division, war also promoted forms of cooperation. First, since equipping and training warriors became increasingly expensive, those who were not warriors often had to pay for those who were. The "noncombatants," mostly old men, all women and children, and those dedicated to religions, provided weapons, equipment, food, and emotional and ideological support. In some cultures warriors affirmed an ethos of the protection of noncombatants, the companionship of fighters, and the trust of allies. Second, any army must have a cooperative system of obedience and command in order to coordinate individual soldiers into a killing unit. Third, the nature of battle encouraged people to limit participants to two opposing sides. Any more than two participants in a battle too easily exposed the flanks or rear of an army, a sure way to defeat it. This battlefield reality led to alliances. Thus, kings and emperors started a pattern that has endured throughout the history of civilization: conquest and subjugation. Many people have died as a result. Ironically, however, until recently more soldiers actually died from infectious disease than from wounds inflicted in battle.

History may sometimes appear to be a record of wars and battles. Yet no history can ignore these events, for they often determined the rise or fall of kingdoms and empires. Most successful peoples in history defended their supremacy through warfare. Many failed peoples dissolved by losing wars. A war won or lost, though, is usually not the only reason for a civilization's expansion or disappearance. Wars have melded or destroyed groups of peoples who become part of one civilization or another. Because most rulers encourage uniformity, it could be hard to preserve an ethnic identity. Once conquered, peoples have assimilated, or merged, into the ethnicity of their masters. Sometimes, if the conquered peoples were numerous enough, they have blended with the conquerors, both creating a new identity. Or conquerors have even been absorbed into the conquered. On occasion, conquered peoples have broken free again, either through their own power or through allies. Civilization and war have been close companions throughout history.

Review: *What often-ignored problems did civilization create?*

Response:

SOURCES ON FAMILIES:
LAW CODE OF HAMMURABI (CA. 1750 BC)

Hammurabi's Law Code shows how family has been a focus of government since the beginning of civilization. A number of his laws relate to family issues such as marital fidelity, male authority, women's roles, rights of children, and procreation. While the Babylonian concepts of marriage and family differed in significant ways from our own, we share with them the desire to regulate personal behavior.

110. If a consecrated woman, who is not living in the convent, has opened a wine shop or has entered a wine shop for drink, one shall burn that woman.

117. If a man has seized another for debt, and the debtor has given his wife, his son, his daughter for the money, or has handed them over to work off the debt, for three years they shall work in the house of their buyer or exploiter, who in the fourth year shall give them their liberty.

129. If the wife of a man has been caught in lying with another male, one shall bind them and throw them into the waters. If the owner of the wife would save her or if the king would save his servants (he may).

130. If a man has forced another man's betrothed who has not known men and is dwelling in the house of her father, and he has lain in her bosom and one has caught him, that man shall be killed, while the woman herself shall go free.

131. If a husband has accused his wife, and she has not been caught in lying with another male, she shall swear by the gods and shall return to her house.

134. If a man has been taken captive, and his house is not being maintained, and his wife has entered into the house of another, that woman shall not be blamed.

138. If a man has put away his bride who has not borne him children, he shall give her money as much as her dowry, and shall pay her the marriage portion which she brought from her father's house, and shall put her aside.

142. If a woman hates her husband and has said "Thou shalt not possess me," one shall enquire into her past about what her faults are. And if she has been economical, and has no vice, and her husband has gone out and greatly belittled her, that woman has no blame; she shall take her marriage portion and go off to her father's house.

143. If she has not been economical, has been a goer about, has wasted her house, and has belittled her husband, one shall throw that woman into the waters.

148. If a man has married a wife and a sickness has seized her, and then he has set his face toward marrying a second wife, he may marry her but his wife whom the sickness has seized he shall not put her away; in the home she shall dwell, and as long as she lives he shall sustain her.

152. If from the time that a woman has entered into the house of the man and a debt has come upon them, both together they shall repay the merchant.

162. If a man has married a wife and she has borne him children, and that woman has gone to her fate, her father shall have no claim on her marriage portion; her marriage portion is her children's.

165. If a man has apportioned to his son, the first in his eyes, field, garden, and house, has written him a sealed deed, after the father has gone to his fate, when the brothers divide, he shall take the present his father gave him, and over and above that he shall share equally in the goods of the father's house.

194. If a man has given his son to a wet nurse, and that son has died in the hand of the wet nurse, then the wet nurse without consent of his father and his mother has procured another child, one shall put her to account. And because without consent of his father and his mother she has procured another child, one shall cut off her breasts.

195. If a man has struck his father, one shall cut off his hands.

209. If a man has struck a gentleman's daughter and caused her to drop what is in her womb, he shall pay ten shekels of silver for what was in her womb.

210. If that woman has died, one shall put to death his daughter.

211. If the daughter of a poor man through his blows he has caused to drop that which is in her womb, he shall pay five shekels of silver.

212. If that woman has died, he shall pay half a mina of silver.

213. If he has struck a gentleman's maidservant and caused her to drop that which is in her womb, he shall pay two shekels of silver.

214. If that maidservant has died, he shall pay one-third of a mina of silver.

Questions:

- *What role does wealth and property play in civilization?*
- *What opportunities for agency do women have?*
- *How does social status intersect with sex roles?*

Responses:

For more on this source, go to http://www.concisewesternciv.com/sources/sof2 .html.

THE RISE AND FALL OF PRACTICALLY ALL MIDDLE EASTERN EMPIRES

Peoples in the Middle East laid the foundations for the later rise of peoples in the West (see map 2.2). Americans coined the name *Middle East* about a hundred years ago as they were defining this region as different from both the Far East of India and China and their own former "Wild West." Europeans often call it the Near East; some geographers prefer labeling the regions North Africa and Southwest Asia. Whatever the name, the Middle East today includes countries stretching from northeast Africa through the Arabian Peninsula; northward through the Levant (the eastern coast of the Mediterranean), Asia Minor, and Mesopotamia; and eastward to Iran. Today, Islam substantially defines the culture (see chapter 6). But long before Islam, the Middle East was home to rich, powerful, and influential civilizations.

Today we often think of the Middle East as dominated by desert. Indeed, thousands of years of human overpopulation, soil exhaustion, deforestation, and water overuse, as well as climatic change, have left much of the area arid. In ancient times, however, ten thousand years ago, the core of the region deserved the name Fertile Crescent. An arc of agriculturally productive land from the Nile River valley up through Palestine and down across the Tigris and Euphrates to the Persian Gulf soon fed peoples far more advanced than their neighbors in Europe, Africa, and Asia.

Helping these new agricultural civilizations succeed was their discovery of how to make **metal** tools. Humans had been using wood, bone, and stone for millions of years. Embedded in many stones were ores that, when heated or smelted,

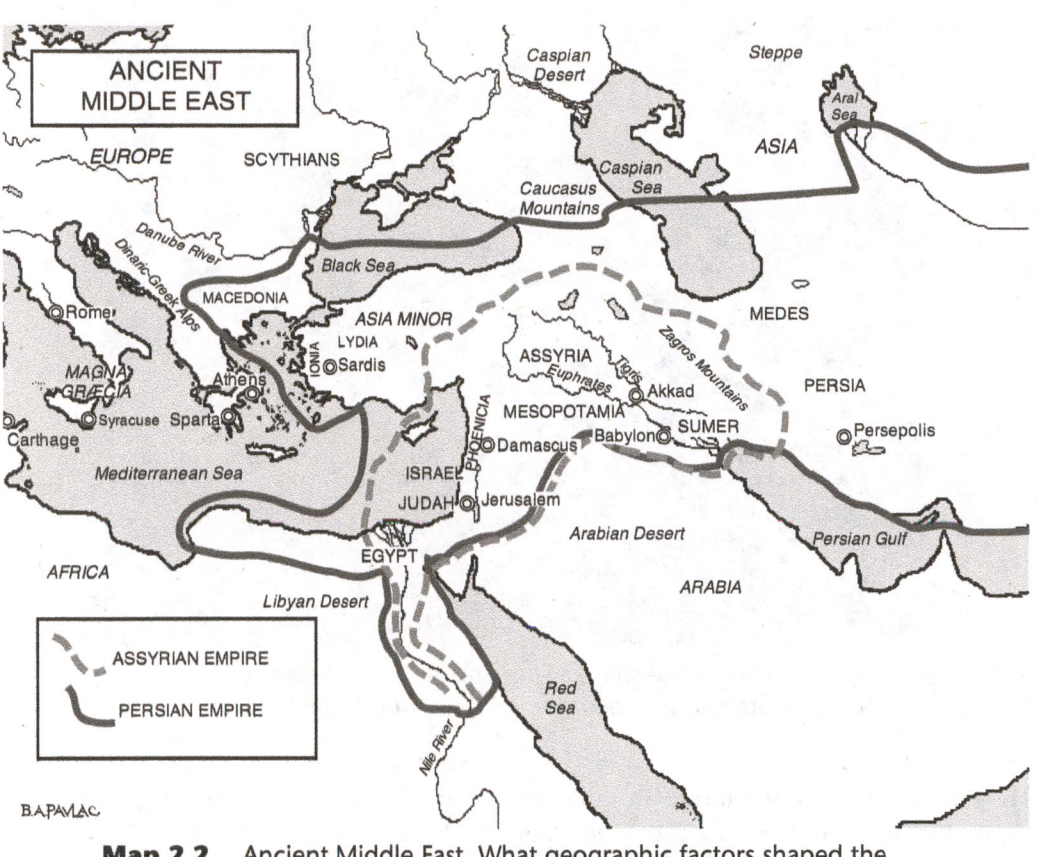

Map 2.2.   Ancient Middle East. What geographic factors shaped the Middle Eastern empires?

could be purified into an elemental metal, such as copper or tin. Thus, the Neolithic or New Stone Age of technology began to end around 4000 BC as humans began to mine copper for tools. They soon learned how to make an even better alloy, blending copper and tin into bronze. Technology of the **Bronze Age** prevailed from about 3000 to 800 BC. Based on these technologies, two civilizations arose in the Middle East, in **Mesopotamia** and **Egypt**. Each was relatively isolated from the other at first, but both were soon joined in commerce and conquest.

Mesopotamian civilization began around 3500 BC, when the Sumerians migrated from South Asia into the land of the two rivers of the Tigris and Euphrates (mostly in modern-day Iraq). The Sumerians were the first of many Mesopotamian peoples who shared a similar culture. They founded the earliest significant political units in the form of city-states. As their most important public buildings they built ziggurats: huge step pyramids of baked brick that served as temples for worship of the gods and storehouses for grain. Priests and priestesses celebrated **fertility rituals**. In doing so, they imitated the imagined sexual couplings of the gods, believing that such activity sustained the annual cycle of seasons (in other words, sex made the world go round). By studying and learning about the skies, the priests divided the stars into the twelve constellations of the zodiac (creating twelve months) and set twenty-four hours to the day and seven days to the week.

Figure 2.1.   The wedge-shaped lines of cuneiform, the writing of ancient Mesopotamia, scrawled over the sculpture of an Assyrian.

They wrote such knowledge in cuneiform, block symbols formed by a wedge-shaped stylus pressed into clay (see figure 2.1).

On such tablets they composed **epic poetry**, the most enduring form of literature, popular for thousands of years. Epics are long poems (using verse, rhythm, and sometimes alliteration or rhyme) composed to tell stories of heroes and gods. The oldest surviving epic poem told the story of the king **Gilgamesh**; it was written six hundred years after his reign and portrays the human ruler as two-thirds divine. The poem recounts how after the death of his friend, Enkidu, with whom he had shared many adventures and hardships, the sorrowful Gilgamesh sought the meaning of life. The hero learned that although the gods failed at wiping out all humankind by a great flood, they still doomed men to death by wild animals, famine, and plague. Such a gloomy view of existence seemed common in Mesopotamia, despite the riches of the civilization.

The second great Middle Eastern civilization, Egypt, arose in the Nile River valley of northeastern Africa. Powerful kings called pharaohs united Egypt by around 3100 BC. These men (and a few women, such as the now-famous Hatshepsut) not only held the power of kings but were also believed to have been actual gods incarnate on earth.[8] They often intensified their bloodline connection to the gods

---

8. History forgot about Hatshepsut (r. ca. 1479–1458 BC) for millennia because her son and heir tried to erase every single mention of her after he came to power. Historians rediscovered her impressive and peaceful reign only about a hundred years ago. To reinforce her status as ruler, she often wore the same artificial long, thin beards that male pharaohs wore. Perhaps to compensate for his "mommy issues," her son started a number of wars.

by marrying their royal siblings. As divine beings, pharaohs were exempt from the usual social prohibition against incest. The pharaohs, their officials, and priests wielded power through their abilities to calculate and to write (in pictographs called hieroglyphics) (see figures 2.2 and 2.3). With these skills, they controlled agriculture: they accurately predicted the regular annual rise and fall of the Nile floods that nourished the fields. The Egyptian kingdom offered comparative stability and prosperity.

Hence, Egyptians seemed more optimistic about the afterlife than their Mesopotamian neighbors. The Egyptians hoped that, after death, their souls would be judged worthy by the gods, and thus they could spend a luxurious afterlife full of pleasure. According to *The Book of the Dead*, the deceased appeared before the god Osiris, who had each one's spirit weighed on scales against a feather. The dead person recited a long list of sins not committed and good deeds done. Based on the truth of the declaration and the weight, souls lighter than a feather departed to heaven; souls heavier suffered from the Devouress; those equally balanced served the gods in the afterlife (see figure 2.2).

Their belief in some sort of bodily resurrection after death led the ancient Egyptians to mummify their loved ones' dead bodies. So many hundreds of thousands of mummified people (and cats) survived to the nineteenth century that they were ground up for fertilizer or medicine (although Mark Twain joked that mummies were also used to stoke fires for locomotives). For the ancient Egyptians, the most wealth and effort was spent on the bodies of the pharaohs. Several pharaohs commanded tens of thousands of people over decades to build giant pyramids as funereal monuments to house their own mummies and treasure. Sadly for them (and for our ability to appreciate the past), most tombs were looted over the centuries, even when they were buried in the isolated Valley of the Kings. At the height of the Egyptian civilization, though, the regular pattern of life and death, the flood and fall of the Nile, and the rising and setting of the sun offered Egyptians a comforting cycle of expectation in this world while they also hoped for a better life in the next.

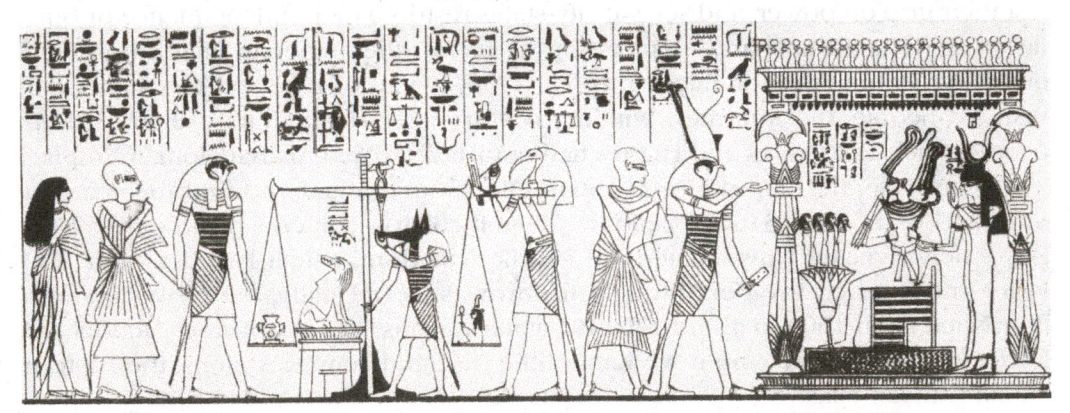

Figure 2.2. This drawing of an ancient Egyptian scene portrays the weighing of a dead person's soul, awaiting the judgment of the gods according to *The Book of the Dead*. (NYPL Digital Collection)

One brief exception in Egypt's cyclical history was the Amarna period, created by the rule of Pharaoh Ahkenaton (r. ca. 1352–1335 BC). He came to power with the traditional name Amenhotep IV but was inspired to transform Egyptian religion and, thus, his status as pharaoh. Instead of the many gods of traditional Egyptian polytheism, he encouraged worship of one god, Aton, the sun, with whom Ahkenaton had a special, divine connection (of course). Some historians think this focus on Aton established the first *monotheism*, or belief in only one god. Ahkenaton's ideas, though, did not long outlive him. Whether the priests saw him as a creative individualistic innovator or an ugly slothful fanatic, they and most Egyptians soon went back to worshipping according to the traditional patterns. Later pharaohs erased Ahkenaton's very name from their dynastic records. A brief artistic revolution, though, created lively and fascinating art of the Amarna period that differed from the static, unchanging forms of most Egyptian painting and sculpture. This art has come down to us in the treasures from the rare unplundered tomb of his successor, the boy pharaoh Tutankhamen (r. ca. 1335–1325 BC), or King Tut. Archaeologists discovered Tut's tomb in AD 1922. Stories of a mummy's curse that afflicted the tomb's excavators exaggerate the mundane circumstances surrounding the deaths of a few of those treasure hunters.

The curse of warfare, though, nearly killed off these early Middle Eastern civilizations in Mesopotamia and Egypt. Mesopotamia was particularly vulnerable to attack. Again and again, warriors from the surrounding hills stormed into the fertile valleys to plunder and conquer. Similarly, neighboring kings fought to dominate one another. Mesopotamia, never united for long, offered a dismal and depressing chronicle of slaughter.

After 2500 BC, various peoples, called Semites by modern scholars, entered Mesopotamia from the Arabian Peninsula. Their name is based upon the similar languages they spoke, supposedly linked to a biblical character, Shem, son of Noah. Semitic languages included Aramaic, Hebrew, and Arabic. Soon, the Semitic speakers began to dominate the region's politics even as they adopted Sumerian culture. By 2300 BC, Sargon of Akkad had formed one of the first great empires by conquering Sumer and many of his Mesopotamian neighbors. His descendants lost their grip on power, and several city-states restored their independence or built new, fragile kingdoms and empires. In the chaos, the Sumerian civilization died out. King Hammurabi of Babylon (r. ca. 1790–1750 BC) replaced the Sumerians with his people, the Amorites. Within a century after Hammurabi's reign, various peoples such as Kassites and Hittites had in turn destroyed his Babylonian Empire.

Meanwhile, the impressive Egyptian Old Kingdom had endured for nearly a thousand years, from 3100 to 2200 BC. Then it collapsed in civil disorder. By 2050 BC, a new dynasty consolidated the Middle Kingdom, which lasted a mere 250 years until foreign invaders brought it down as well. Finally, the New Kingdom flourished from 1600 to about 1200 BC when various "Sea Peoples" or "Raiders of Land and Sea," about whom we know little, ravaged countries along the eastern Mediterranean coast.

During this time, another people, the **Phoenicians**, built a different kind of empire, based on trade. Beginning around 1500 BC this Semitic people occupied the Levantine or eastern coast of the Mediterranean Sea that runs from Asia Minor to Egypt. Unlike the imperialism of Mesopotamians and Egyptians, who marched to conquer their neighbors, the Phoenicians sailed across the Mediterranean to begin their *colonialism*. This form of rule meant a people established settlements called colonies in foreign territory at a distance, usually across the sea from their homeland. Through this piecemeal migration, the Phoenicians gained footholds in new lands and prospered through trade in dyed cloth, dogs, and wine. Soon Phoenician cities dotted the Mediterranean coast and all the way beyond Gibraltar to the Atlantic shores of the Iberian Peninsula and North Africa. Some Phoenicians sailed as far north as Great Britain, south around the coast of Africa, and perhaps even west to the Americas.

The Phoenicians' invention of the first **alphabet** gained them efficiency in communication of knowledge. All previous and contemporary civilizations, Sumer with its cuneiform and Egypt with its hieroglyphics (or, for that matter, China and India), used written systems composed of thousands of individual symbols, many of which represented only one word. Instead, the Phoenicians chose about two dozen symbols to represent sounds. With these few symbols to signify consonants and vowels, they could spell out phonetically (from *Phoenicians*!) any word that could be pronounced.[9] Most neighboring cultures, including the Hebrews, the Hellenes, and even the Egyptians, adapted the Phoenician alphabet idea to their own languages. Indeed, soon people forgot how to read cuneiform or hieroglyphics, and much of the rich culture of Middle Eastern civilizations remained unknown until Western scholars relearned those writing systems in the nineteenth century (using, for example, the famous Rosetta Stone to translate ancient Egyptian) (see figure 2.3).

The Phoenicians with their colonies managed to survive massive invasions by the mysterious "Sea Peoples" that overwhelmed much of the Middle East beginning around 1200 BC. Two technological innovations about this time made war even more destructive. First, around 1500 BC, the Hittites of Asia Minor figured out how to smelt iron ore and forge iron tools. Iron, except for the problem of rust, was stronger and could hold an edge far better than bronze. Iron swords, spear points, and arrowheads became more lethally efficient. Heavy iron helmets, breastplates, and shields likewise offered better protection, although only to those who could afford them or bear their heavy weight. As other peoples adopted this metal as their key material, the **Iron Age** (1200 BC–AD 1870) began and endured until just over a century ago. Second, the Hittites domesticated horses from the steppes of Asia, either as military transportation for individual riders or harnessed to chariots. Both of these new warfare techniques enabled ambitious kings more easily to dominate others and build empires. While these invaders by land and sea soon vanished from the historical record, their destruction of dominant powers left room for others to develop.

The **Assyrian Empire** (ca. 750–600 BC) was the first new state to make a mark in the region. Historians call it the first "universal empire," a historical term

---

9. English is not a very phonetic language. For example, the phrase "write the right way" could be misspelled as "wright the rite weigh." Languages such as Latin and Greek or German, on the other hand, are spelled pretty much the way they sound when pronounced.

Figure 2.3.   This picture of a replica of the Rosetta Stone shows three kinds of writing: Egyptian hieroglyphics, Egyptian common writing (Demotic), and Greek (at the bottom). In 1799, a soldier in Napoleon's army found the Rosetta Stone at the place it is named after. Historians used the stone to finally unlock the lost reading of hieroglyphics, enabling them to study Egyptian history more thoroughly.

that sounds as if it includes the entire earth, but actually only refers to the political unification of most of the peoples of the early Middle East. It stretched from the Persian Gulf to the Nile, uniting both Egypt and Mesopotamia. The Assyrians, with their swift cavalry, iron swords, and utter ruthlessness, were among the early wholehearted believers in *militarism*: the idea that virtues such as discipline, obedience, courage, and willingness to kill for the state are the highest values a civilized society can hold. Assyrians loved the hunt and warfare. Their brutality, however, inspired little affection among the dozens of peoples they conquered. If any people dared to resist conquest, the Assyrians punished the defeated populations either by burning alive many men, women, and children or by beheading them and flaying off their skins to drape over city walls; they mutilated many survivors by hacking off hands, arms, noses, ears, or genitals. Most of those who surrendered they enslaved. These practices swiftly destroyed many ethnic groups.

Some survivors, though, organized against their Assyrian conquerors. The Assyrian Empire lasted only about 150 years. Two allied peoples destroyed the Assyrians in 600 BC: the Chaldeans (or Neo-Babylonians, since they had occupied Babylon) and the Medes from the hills north of Persia (as it was called by the Greeks, although the Medes named their own country Iran, as it is called today). The Neo-Babylonian–Median alliance completely wiped out the Assyrians, as they themselves had done to so many others. Of the Assyrian civilization only the ruins of their grand monuments to hunting and war survived.

After ridding themselves of the Assyrians, the Neo-Babylonians and Medes lived in an uneasy competition for supremacy over weaker societies. During one of the wars, there occurred the first scientifically verifiable date in history: 28 May 585 BC—when a battle between the Medes and the Lydians in Asia Minor was broken off because of a solar eclipse (whose exact date modern astronomers can confirm).

Following a few decades of intermittent warfare, both Neo-Babylonians and Medes were surprised by the sudden rise of Cyrus "the Great" of Persia (r. 559–530 BC). In 550 BC, Cyrus defeated the Medes and eleven years later took Babylon. Cyrus established the **Persian Empire** (550–330 BC), the second, even larger universal empire, comprising Egypt, the Fertile Crescent, the Medes' lands, and his own Persia. As the *shahanshah*, the "king of kings," Cyrus ruled over all, venerated like a god on earth. Yet his rule was benevolent compared with that of the Assyrians. He set up satraps (provincial governors) as his eyes and ears throughout the empire. With broad authority, they kept his various subjects in order. The native Persian religion of **Zoroastrianism**, founded by a prophet named Zarathustra, spread through the empire. Its belief system is called **dualism**, recognizing two powerful divine forces at war with each other in the universe: the good of spirit and ideas against the evil of matter and flesh. Humanity had to choose between the two. While Cyrus and his dynasty favored their own dualistic faith, they did not force conversions. Instead, Cyrus allowed many of his subject peoples to keep their unique customs and religions. The Persians even encouraged the foreign (to them) Semitic language of Aramaic as a common means for most people to communicate with one another, rather than their own Farsi.[10] Most of the diverse peoples found the Persian shah's rule beneficial (see Primary Source Project 2).

The Persians encouraged trade, helped by the invention of **money** in their recently conquered province of Lydia in Asia Minor. Money appeared surprisingly

---

10. The Assyrians had first replaced Sargon's Akkadian with Aramaic as a *lingua franca*, or a common language used by widespread peoples to communicate. Aramaic became so accepted that even Jews such as Jesus of Nazareth spoke it rather than Hebrew. A few people in modern-day Lebanon, Syria, and Iraq still speak it, although it is now in danger of going extinct.

late as a means of economic exchange, or at least it might seem so to us who take it for granted. For thousands of years of civilization, though, no one could trust it. Before money, people bartered for goods and services, trading their labor or goods such as pots, cows, or women. Using money meant that specially made lumps of precious metals (usually copper, silver, or gold) could be used instead, creating a more stable and consistent pricing system. One problem, though, with any precious metal was determining its purity. Money will circulate only when people trust its value. Copper, silver, and gold could be easily degraded with baser metals such as tin or nickel into alloys and thus be worth less than the expected value. Gold could be tested somewhat because of its softness—and thus the custom arose of people biting gold coins to see whether they dented. Silver was a much more common and useful metal for making money, especially after the Lydians figured out how to use a touchstone (a rock on which metals left a specific color streak) to prove the purity of silver coins. The power of government also contributed to the use of money. Rulers put their own faces on the coins and ensured their value by setting purity standards and punishing forgers who debased coins. Hence, out of the Persian Empire came the long-standing practice that the government is responsible for money and is therefore always intimately involved in the economy.

The Persians were great and powerful, yet even their empire survived little more than two centuries before another people conquered it. Nevertheless, the Persian Empire represented the summit of ancient Middle Eastern civilizations. The diverse peoples of the Fertile Crescent and Nile River basin had developed much of agriculture and architecture, metallurgy and mathematics, literature and law. Their influence on Western civilization was to set an example of these basic practices for other peoples who lived on the fringes of the great empires.

While Bronze Age Egypt and Sumer first reached their high points, various peoples lived without the benefits of civilization in what we now call Europe. The European peninsula in the far western corner of Eurasia was off the beaten track of the major civilizations of India, China, and the Middle East. About seven thousand years ago, agriculturalists began to push into Europe from the Middle East along the Mediterranean coast or up the Danube River, and across the Urals from the steppes of northern Siberia. Early European farmers who put down roots found an area well suited for human habitation. Flooding was less devastating than along the great rivers of Africa, the Middle East, or Asia, since the major waterways were not nearly so vast. Europe suffered few earthquakes. The temperate climate prevented many insects that bore lethal tropical diseases. The hills contained rich deposits of mineral ores. As immigrants cleared dense forests to create farmland, the plentiful wood provided excellent building material and fuel. Their domesticated animals and plants easily adapted to the new environment.

Waves of European immigrants thrust their way in over many centuries. Whether by absorbing or killing, they eliminated the hunter-gatherers, except those shoved to the fringes in the far north, such as the Sami of Lapland. While archaeology has illuminated little about the first farmers, recent scientific studies in genetics have opened up new vistas. The earliest excavated agricultural

Figure 2.4.   The mysterious, massive blocks of Stonehenge rise from a meadow in the south of England. The monument is clearly connected to astronomy, with various stones aligned with heavenly bodies. Beyond that, the reasons why people built it remain a mystery.

settlement in Europe, Lepenski Vir on the Danube River, dates back to 6500 BC. A tiny portion of the DNA of these people still lives on in some modern-day Serbians. The oldest Europeans surviving today as an ethnic group (because of their unique language) are probably the Basques. Their settlements in modern southwest France and north-central Spain were protected by the Pyrenees Mountains, sheltering them from later acculturation. The 1991 discovery in the Alps of a mummy, since nicknamed Ötzi, provided a few new insights into the hunter-gatherers of five thousand years ago.[11] The huge ring of standing stones at Stonehenge in present-day England is impressive in size and its ability to synchronize with astronomical events (see figure 2.4). But the stone circles tell us little of the people who began it around 3500 BC or added to it over many centuries.

About four thousand years ago, peoples from the Yamna or Kurgan culture in the northern Caucasus Mountains, southern modern Ukraine, and western modern Kazakhstan migrated westward into Europe and to the southeast into Asia. Scholars call them Indo-European peoples because of their related languages spoken now across Eurasia. Most modern European languages grew out

---

11. One of the lessons taught by Ötzi and other mummies is the legacy of human violence. Several years after his discovery, scientists discovered that he had been shot and killed by an arrow in the back. Bog bodies, such as the twenty-four-hundred-year-old Tollund man from Denmark, seem to have been executed by strangling and then tossed into a swamp, which preserved them.

of those spoken by these new immigrants. Military victories with their horses and chariots allowed them to conquer and replace in Europe most of those peoples who were not Indo-Europeans. Kings ruled the subgroups of these peoples, priests communicated with their gods and maintained their mythologies, the common people labored as pastoralists and farmers, and society was organized along patriarchal lines.

Despite their overwhelming success, these new Europeans maintained contact with the civilized peoples of the Middle East, Asia, and Africa. They readily borrowed or stole political practices, economic systems, social customs, art and literature, and religion. Drawing on the wisdom of ancient Mesopotamia and Egypt, two Indo-European peoples of the Greeks and Romans who had settled on the southern edge of Europe along the Mediterranean Sea would build their own civilizations. First, however, the obscure Middle Eastern Jews, who barely survived the rise and fall of empires, became essential to the West.

Review: *What did various ancient Middle Eastern civilizations offer to the early peoples of the West?*

Response:

PRIMARY SOURCE PROJECT 2:
XENOPHON VERSUS HERODOTUS ABOUT REPUTATION

Two Greek historians offer perspectives on the death of Cyrus "the Great" of Persia. Xenophon in his Cyropaedia *tells of Cyrus speaking from his deathbed to his two heirs, Cambyses (who inherits most of the realm) and Tanaoxares. The shah gives them counsel about good rule based on kindness toward all and support for one another. After his death, the brothers did not follow his advice. Herodotus in his* History *presents Cyrus as more of a villain, dishonest and dishonorable. He suffers a brutal death at the hands of the Massagetai, whose kingdom lay between the Black and Caspian Seas. Where does the truth lie?*

Source 1: *The Death of Cyrus* by Xenophon (ca. 380 BC)

My sons, and friends of mine, the end of my life is at hand. And as the years passed, I seemed to find my powers grow with them, so that I never felt my old age weaker than my youth, nor can I think of anything I attempted or desired wherein I failed. Moreover, I have seen my friends made happy by my means, and my enemies crushed beneath my hand. This my fatherland, which was once of no account in Asia, I leave at the height of power, and of all that I won I think I have lost nothing. . . .

These are the principles that I leave with you, sanctioned by time, ingrained in our customs, embodied in our laws. Cambyses, you know of yourself, without words from me, that your kingdom is not guarded by this golden scepter, but by faithful friends; their loyalty is your true staff, a scepter which shall not fail. But never think that loyal hearts grow up by nature as the grass grows in the field; if that were so, the same men would be loyal to all alike, even as all natural objects are the same to all mankind. No, every leader must win his own followers for himself, and the way to win them is not by violence but by loving-kindness.

Let no one, Tanaoxares, be more eager than yourself to obey your brother and support him: to no one can his triumph or his danger come so near. Ask yourself from whom you could win a richer reward for any kindness? Who could give you stouter help in return for your own support? And where is coldness so ugly as between brothers? Or where is reverence so beautiful? And remember, Cambyses, only the brother who holds pre-eminence in a brother's heart can be safe from the jealousy of the world. . . .

And after the gods, I would have you reverence the whole race of man, as it renews itself for ever; for the gods have not hidden you in the darkness, but your deeds will be manifest in the eyes of all mankind. And if they be righteous deeds and pure from iniquity, they will blazon forth your power. But if you meditate evil against each other, you will forfeit the confidence of every man. For no man can trust you, even though he should desire it, if he sees you wrong him whom above all you are bound to love.

Therefore, if my words are strong enough to teach you your duty to one another, it is well. But, if not, let history teach you, and there is no better teacher. For the most part, parents have shown kindness to their children and brothers to their brothers, but it has been otherwise with some. Look, then, and see which conduct has brought success, choose to follow that, and your choice will be wise. . . .

Remember my last saying: show kindness to your friends, and then shall you have it in your power to chastise your enemies. Good-bye, my dear sons, bid your mother good-bye for me. And all my friends, who are here or far away, good-bye.

Source 2: *Death of Cyrus* by Herodotus (ca. 420 BC)

At this time the Massagetai were ruled by a queen, named Tomyris. To her Cyrus sent ambassadors, with instructions to court her on his part, pretending that he wished to take her to wife. Tomyris, however, aware that it was her kingdom, and not herself, that he courted, forbade the men to approach. Cyrus, therefore, finding that he did not advance his designs by this deceit, marched . . . openly displaying his hostile intentions. . . .

Tomyris sent a herald to him, who said, "King of the Medes, cease to press this enterprise. . . . Be content to rule in peace your own kingdom, and bear to see us reign over the countries that are ours to govern. . . ."

But Croesus the Lydian [said] . . . "[W]ere it not disgrace intolerable for Cyrus the son of Cambyses to retire before and yield ground to a woman? My counsel, therefore, is that we . . . get the better of them by stratagem. I am told they are unacquainted with the good things on which the Persians live, and have never tasted the great delights of life. Let us then prepare a feast for them in our camp; let sheep be slaughtered without stint, and the wine cups be filled full of noble liquor, and let all manner of dishes be prepared. Unless I very much mistake, when they see the good fare set out, they will forget all else and fall to. Then it will remain for us to do our parts manfully." . . .

Cyrus, having advanced a day's march from the river, did as Croesus had advised him. Soon afterwards, a detachment of the Massagetai, one-third of their entire army, led by Spargapises, son of the queen Tomyris, seeing the banquet prepared, they sat down and began to feast. When they had eaten and drunk their fill, and were now sunk in sleep, the Persians under Cyrus arrived, slaughtered a great multitude, and made even a larger number prisoners. Among these last was Spargapises himself.

When Tomyris heard what had befallen her son and her army, she sent a herald to Cyrus, who thus addressed the conqueror: "You bloodthirsty Cyrus, pride not yourself on this poor success; . . . it was this poison by which you ensnared my child, and so overcame him, not in fair open fight. Restore my son to me and get you from the land unharmed. Refuse, and I swear by the sun, the sovereign lord of the Massagetai, bloodthirsty as you are, I will give you your fill of blood."

To the words of this message Cyrus paid no manner of regard. As for Spargapises, . . . he killed himself.

Tomyris, when she found that Cyrus paid no heed to her advice, collected all the forces of her kingdom, and gave him battle. The greater part of the army of the Persians was destroyed and Cyrus himself fell, after reigning nine and twenty years. Search was made among the slain by order of the queen for the body of Cyrus. And when it was found she took a skin, and, filling it full of human blood, she dipped the head of Cyrus in the gore, saying, as she thus insulted the corpse: "I live and have conquered you in battle, and yet by you am I ruined, for you took my son with guile. But thus I make good my threat, and give you your fill of blood."

Of the many different accounts which are given of the death of Cyrus, this which I have followed appears to me most worthy of credit.

Questions:

- *How do the two sources differ in their method of conveying information?*
- *What specific words or deeds show how Cyrus respected law and justice, or not?*
- *What do the authors seek to have readers understand about Cyrus's legacy?*

Responses:

Make your own timeline.

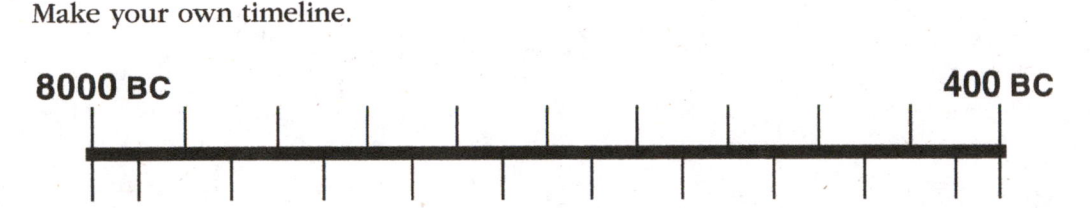

8000 BC   400 BC

For more on these sources, go to http://www.concisewesternciv.com/sources /psc2.html.

CHAPTER 3

The Chosen People

Hebrews and Jews, 2000 BC to AD 135

At first, the history of the ancient **Hebrews** might seem insignificant compared with the peoples of ancient North Africa, Mesopotamia, Persia, and Asia Minor who developed essential practices of civilization upon which the West would build. The Hebrews lived in a tiny territory near the Dead Sea, along the Levantine coast of the Eastern Mediterranean. Their petty kingdoms barely budged the course of history, while numerous vast empires rose and fell around and over them. Amazingly, they survived these cataclysms. They came to be called **Jews** during their domination by the Persian Empire. Then and after, many Jews moved into cities of the Middle East and Europe, where they participated in ancient and modern civilization. They and their religion of *Judaism*, which asserted that they were the special people of a single omnipotent God, became a key component of the West.

BETWEEN AND UNDER EMPIRES

A century ago, modern professional historians enthusiastically accepted the Hebrews' version of their past as presented in their own sacred scriptures, since those accounts reinforced the historians' own cultural view of their significant religious legacy. More recently, however, archaeologists and historians have qualified much of what the ancient Hebrews wrote about their foundations and origins. Because this history is intimately interwoven with the Hebrew faith of Judaism, determining the truth has been all the more complicated. As so often happens, myths overshadow the verifiable facts.

Over the course of many centuries Jews collected their most important sacred scriptures into a collection called the Tanakh, an acronym for its contents: the Torah (the first five books), the proclamations of prophets, and other writings such as poetry, proverbs, and (most relevant to this study) history. Later, Christians included Hebrew scriptures as the **Old Testament** of their **Bible**. According to the

Hebraic Bible stories, God's influence on humanity started with the beginning of all history, with a story about creation.[1] In the beginning, God created the heavens and the earth. Since this Hebrew God would also later be revered by most of Western civilization, His name in English is conventionally spelled with a capital *G* to distinguish "Him" from all other (false) gods. The Hebrews believed that God created two human beings, a man and a woman (although there are two versions of the story offering two contradictory accounts of their formation). They believed that all the rest of humanity descended from these first two people, Adam and Hawwah (Eve in English).

This creation myth not only narrated how God created the universe but also described how things went wrong for humans because of bad choices. The Archangel Michael threw Adam and Hawwah out of paradise as punishment for eating the fruit of the tree of knowledge of good and evil. As generation begot generation, sins multiplied. At one point, God became fed up with humanity and killed almost everyone with a great flood. Only Noah and his family survived in a large ship, the ark, which also harbored pairs of all living creatures.

Many cultures have similar myths of original couples falling from perfection and of devastating floods covering the earth. No valid scientific or historical evidence exists to prove such creation or flood myths. No physical location for paradise has been found; its existence is improbable in this world. A ship built according to the biblical design could not possibly hold all species of animals and sustenance for them. The writers of sacred texts aimed to convey something about the relationship between humans and God. Although these origin myths cannot be literally true, they have long been believed to be the start of history.

In addition to Noah, archaeologists and historians have difficulty connecting many other biblical people and timelines with evidence from their digs and from the few surviving written records. They have found many places and names of peoples and empires in the sources, but few specifics when it comes to the early Hebrews. The first founding figure of Judaism, the biblical Noah's descendant Abram (later Abraham), followed his God's call to leave Mesopotamia. Abram and his people allegedly settled in the land of the Canaanites (or the Phoenicians!), where a diverse number of other peoples, such as Hivites, Perizzites, Girgashites, and Jebusites, also lived. The early Hebrews prospered as pastoral herders of livestock. The biblical Abraham's grandson, Jacob (also called Israel), gave this latter name to a territory divided among his ten sons and two grandsons whose names in turn identified the twelve "tribes" who lived there. Then, the Bible story relates that during a time of famine, the Hebrews fell under Egyptian domination and moved to the kingdom of the pharaohs.

The Egyptian sojourn became central to Hebrew nation forming, even though modern historians have yet to find any Egyptian source material to date (or even

---

1. Most Jewish authorities calculate their calendar from the year AM 1 (from the Latin *anno mundi*—in the year [since the beginning] of the world), equivalent to 3761 BC. The Jewish calendar is lunar based (thus changing the number of days in the year), and so the New Year holiday moves, usually taking place in the Gregorian month of September. Thus, most of the year AD 2023 is AM 5783.

mention) their stay.[2] The defining moment of Hebrew history had a leader named Moses lead his people out of Egypt in an event called the Exodus (celebrated ever since in the religious festival of the Passover). According to their scriptures, the Hebrews afterward wandered in the wilderness for forty years (probably a mythologized number). Along the way many died, some from divine punishments (especially plagues). Then the Hebrews invaded the land of the Canaanites (although the region was actually ruled by Egypt) and quickly won it by conquest and slaughter. The story about their leader Joshua blowing horns to bring down the walls of the ancient city of Jericho is popular in children's Bible stories (but is unproven by archaeology). Usually, children do not hear that the Hebrews then completely destroyed the city and put to the sword all the men and women, whether young or old, sparing only the family of Rahab the harlot, who had helped Joshua's spies. All that archaeologists can confirm about this Exodus is that identifiable Hebrews lived among the Canaanites by about 1200 BC. About the same time, beginning in 1150 BC, a raiding "Sea Peoples," the Philistines, seized part of the Levantine coast. The Philistines' superior iron weapons assured their successful migration and conquest. They also gave their name to the region: **Palestine**.

Meanwhile, the Hebrews held a precarious place in a dangerous land, living among foreigners whom their scriptures instructed them to treat well. Their political organization remained fragile, with a loose confederation led by figures called judges (such as Gideon, Samson, and even a woman, Deborah). The judges' leadership derived both from their military ability and apparent divine sanction. Still, many Hebrews began to insist on having a king, just as their neighboring peoples had. The failures of the first king, Saul, prompted a rebellion by David, son of the shepherd Jesse. Even after Saul's death in battle against the Philistines, the new King David needed to fight for the loyalty of all Hebrews. He eventually succeeded and established a dynasty, passing the crown to his son Solomon. Under Solomon, the Hebrew kingdom reached its peak during a weak period for neighboring Egypt and Mesopotamia. The Bible describes these Hebrew kings as important and wealthy, yet historical evidence so far suggests that they were insignificant and poor compared to the rulers of nearby states.

The fragile unity achieved by these early Hebrew kings broke down after Solomon's death, shortly after 1000 BC. The Northern Kingdom, including ten of the tribes, kept the name of their forefather **Israel**. The Southern Kingdom of the other two tribes became **Judaea** (or **Judah**), named after one of Israel/ Jacob's sons. The uneasy rivalry of these kingdoms made them an even more tempting target for neighboring empires. The militaristic Assyrians attacked in 722 BC. Within two years they had annihilated the Northern Kingdom: its people disappeared, either killed or enslaved and assimilated, becoming known as the "lost ten tribes of Israel." The people known as Samaritans repopulated the northern lands. The Samaritans adopted a version of the Hebrews' faith, but their worship at shrines on mountaintops offended the temple priests of Jerusalem.

---

2. In any case, they did not help build the pyramids, which had been finished centuries earlier.

The Southern Kingdom narrowly escaped Assyrian conquest in 701 BC (see the Primary Source Project). Nevertheless, Judaea's time was limited. In 598/597 BC, the Neo-Babylonians, who had recently destroyed the Assyrians, picked up where the latter had left off. The Babylonian Empire conquered the Southern Kingdom and dragged off many thousands to Mesopotamia to be enslaved.

The years between 598 and 538 BC became known as the **Babylonian Captivity**, another important turning point for the Hebrew people. Instead of disappearing into the large category of lost peoples of history, however, the Hebrews endured. They kept their religion; they held their social integrity; they survived despite oppression. After only a few generations of suffering, a rescuer appeared in the person of Cyrus "the Great" (r. 559–530 BC), the same who destroyed Babylon and founded the new Persian Empire. The magnanimous Cyrus took pity on the Jews and allowed them to return to Judaea once again. Many did return, and they rebuilt their temple in Jerusalem, resuming life under the benevolent protection of the shahs of Persia. The Hebrews' history to that point was indeed remarkable in that they had managed to survive as a people. Many cultures and nations had already become extinct over the millennia, including the Sumerians, Hyksos, Hittites, most "Sea Peoples," Assyrians, and many Canaanites. All these peoples had been far more powerful than the Hebrews. Yet the Hebrews persevered despite their stories of multiple migrations: into Palestine, out of Palestine, into Palestine, out, again and again. Nevertheless, this achievement of surviving between and under the power of various empires would not have rated the Hebrews much of a mention in ancient history were it not for their religion.

Review: *How did the history of the Hebrews/Jews contrast with that of other ancient peoples?*

Response:

PRIMARY SOURCE PROJECT 3: SENNACHERIB'S ANNALIST VERSUS CHRONICLES' WRITER ABOUT DIVINE FAVOR

Although the Assyrians overran the Kingdom of Israel, they did not conquer the Kingdom of Judaea with its capital of Jerusalem. These two sources offer two different versions about why. On a prism-shaped clay object, an unknown writer provided the Assyrian point of view. The Assyrian ruler Sennacherib's actions against the Hebrew king Hezekiah are recorded here, as well as details of his other successful conquests. In contrast, the Book of Chronicles *from the Hebrew sacred scriptures (or Christian Old Testament of the Bible) offers another explanation for Judaea's survival.*

Source 1: *Sennacherib Prism Inscription* by Anonymous (written ca. AD 121)

In my Third Campaign to the land of Syria I went. Luliah, King of Sidon (for the fearful splendor of my Majesty had overwhelmed him), to a distant spot in the midst of the sea fled. His land I entered. [Many provinces], his cities and castles, walled and fenced, and his finest towns (for the flash of the weapons of Ashur my Lord had overcome them) made submission at my feet. Tubal, upon the throne over them I seated. A fixed tribute to my Majesty, paid yearly without fail, I imposed upon him. . . .

The chief priests, noblemen, and people of Ekron whom Pariah their King (holding the faith and worship of Assyria) had placed in chains of iron, and unto Hezekiah king of Judah had delivered him and had acted towards the deity with hostility: these men were now terrified in their hearts. The Kings of Egypt and the soldiers, archers, chariots, and horses of Ethiopia, forces innumerable, gathered together and came to their assistance. In the plains of Altaku in front of me they placed their battle array: they discharged their arrows: with the weapons of Ashur my Lord, with them I fought, and I defeated them. . . .

Then I drew nigh the city of Ekron. The chief priests and noblemen who had committed these crimes, I put to death; on stakes all round the city I hung their bodies: the people of the city who had committed sins and crimes to slavery I gave. The rest of them who had not been guilty of faults and crimes, and who sinful things against the deity had not done, to spare them I gave command. Pariah their King from the midst of Jerusalem I brought out, and on a throne of royalty over them I seated. Tribute payable to my Majesty I fixed upon him.

And Hezekiah, king of Judah, who had not bowed down at my feet, 46 of his strong cities, forts, and the smaller towns in their neighborhood beyond number, with warlike engines I attacked and captured. 200,150 people small and great, male and female, horses, mares, asses, camels, oxen, and sheep beyond number, for the midst of them I carried off and distributed as spoil. He himself, like a bird in a cage, inside Jerusalem his royal city, I shut him up: siege-towers against him I constructed, (for he had given command to renew the bulwarks of the great gate of his city). His cities which I plundered, from his kingdom I cut off. I diminished his kingdom. Beyond the former scale of their yearly gifts their tribute and gifts to my Majesty I augmented and imposed upon them. He himself Hezekiah the fearful splendor of my Majesty had overwhelmed him. The workmen, soldiers, and builders whom for the fortification of Jerusalem his royal city he had collected within it, now carried tribute and with 30 talents of gold, 800 talents of silver; woven cloth, scarlet, embroidered; precious stones of large size, couches of ivory, moveable thrones of ivory, skins of buffaloes, teeth of buffaloes, dan wood, ku wood, a great treasure of every kind, and his daughters, and the male and female inmates of his palace, male slaves and female slaves, unto Nineveh my royal city after me he sent; to pay tribute and do homage he sent his envoy.

Source 2: 2 Chronicles 32:1–30 (written ca. 350 BC)

After these things, and the establishment thereof, Sennacherib king of Assyria came, and entered into Judah, and encamped against the fenced cities, and thought to win them for himself. And when Hezekiah saw that Sennacherib was come, and that he was purposed to fight against Jerusalem, he took counsel with his princes and his mighty men to stop the waters of the fountains which were without the city: and they did help him.

So there was gathered much people together, who stopped all the fountains, and the brook that ran through the midst of the land, saying, Why should the kings of Assyria come, and find much water?

Also he strengthened himself, and built up all the wall that was broken, and raised it up to the towers, and another wall without, and repaired Millo in the city of David, and made darts and shields in abundance. And he set captains of war over the people, and gathered them together to him in the street of the gate of the city, and spake comfortably to them, saying,

"Be strong and courageous, be not afraid nor dismayed for the king of Assyria, nor for all the multitude that is with him: for there be more with us than with him. With him is an arm of flesh; but with us is the Lord our God to help us, and to fight our battles." And the people rested themselves upon the words of Hezekiah king of Judah.

After this did Sennacherib king of Assyria send his servants to Jerusalem, (but he himself laid siege against Lachish, and all his power with him,) unto Hezekiah king of Judah, and unto all Judah that were at Jerusalem, saying,

"Thus saith Sennacherib king of Assyria, Whereon do ye trust, that ye abide in the siege in Jerusalem? Doth not Hezekiah persuade you to give over your-selves to die by famine and by thirst, saying, 'The Lord our God shall deliver us out of the hand of the king of Assyria?' Hath not the same Hezekiah taken away his high places and his altars, and commanded Judah and Jerusalem, saying, 'Ye shall worship before one altar, and burn incense upon it.' Know ye not what I and my fathers have done unto all the people of other lands? Were the gods of the nations of those lands any ways able to deliver their lands out of mine hand? Who was there among all the gods of those nations that my fathers utterly destroyed, that could deliver his people out of mine hand, that your God should be able to deliver you out of mine hand? Now therefore let not Hezekiah deceive you, nor persuade you on this manner, neither yet believe him: for no god of any nation or kingdom was able to deliver his people out of mine hand, and out of the hand of my fathers: how much less shall your God deliver you out of mine hand?"

And his servants spake yet more against the Lord God, and against his servant Hezekiah.

He wrote also letters to rail on the Lord God of Israel, and to speak against him, saying, "As the gods of the nations of other lands have not delivered their people out of mine hand, so shall not the God of Hezekiah deliver his people out of mine hand."

Then they cried with a loud voice in the Jews' speech unto the people of Jerusalem that were on the wall, to affright them, and to trouble them; that they might take the city. And they spake against the God of Jerusalem, as against the gods of the people of the earth, which were the work of the hands of man.

And for this cause Hezekiah the king, and the prophet Isaiah the son of Amoz, prayed and cried to heaven. And the Lord sent an angel, which cut off all the mighty men of valor, and the leaders and captains in the camp of the king of Assyria. So he returned with shame of face to his own land. And when he was come into the house of his god, they that came forth of his own bowels slew him there with the sword.

Thus the Lord saved Hezekiah and the inhabitants of Jerusalem from the hand of Sennacherib the king of Assyria, and from the hand of all other, and guided them on every side.

And many brought gifts unto the Lord to Jerusalem, and presents to Hezekiah king of Judah: so that he was magnified in the sight of all nations from thenceforth. . . .

And Hezekiah had exceeding much riches and honor: and he made himself treasuries for silver, and for gold, and for precious stones, and for spices, and for shields, and for all manner of pleasant jewels; storehouses also for the increase of corn, and wine, and oil; and stalls for all manner of beasts, and cotes for flocks. Moreover he provided him cities, and possessions of flocks and herds in abundance: for God had given him substance very much. And Hezekiah prospered in all his works.

Questions:

- *What qualities does each source give its ruler and his rival?*
- *What specific actions prevent Judah from being conquered, according to each source?*
- *What roles do supernatural beings play in each source?*

Responses:

For more on these sources, go to http://www.concisewesternciv.com/sources/psc3a.html.

BOUND BY LAW

During the course of their mythic history, the Hebrews continued claiming that they could see the hand of God regularly revealed. History permeated their religion of Judaism and vice versa. Other Middle Eastern religions emphasized the cyclical nature of creation and destruction, where nothing really changed. The rulers ruled, the people worked, year after year, century after century, millennium after millennium. In contrast, the Hebrews saw a direction to their experiences. From the Hebrews' point of view, the whole purpose of history was to illuminate their relationship with their God, who, for unknown reasons, had selected the people of Israel as His special favorites. The Hebrew people sinned and failed as much as any other group of people. Nonetheless, they claimed that a special relationship grew out of their obedience to God.

The Babylonian Captivity catalyzed a number of revisions to the religion of Judaism. While in Mesopotamia they developed a strict monotheism, devotion to one divine being, transcendent, beyond nature, not of this world. All the other polytheistic gods and their fertility cults were false. The core of Judaism was the **covenant** that their God had concluded with the Hebrews alone. Covenants were political treaties and contracts between greater and lesser peoples. God's contract was laid out not only in the famous **Ten Commandments** (see table 3.1) but also in more than six hundred other laws and regulations for everything from murder and debt to food and sex. The Hebrews believed that if they kept these laws, God would make of the Hebrews a great nation, multiplying them, giving them a promised land of milk and honey, and cursing their enemies.

The exact nature of this promised land of milk and honey was a matter of dispute. Some Hebrews held that it was the land of Canaan/Palestine/Israel/Judaea—a land physically in this world. Others believed that it was a metaphysical land in the next world, where Jews lived on after death. Either way, Judaism emphasized living a moral life for God in this world, not the afterlife. The Jewish emphasis on morality later influenced its successor faiths of Christianity and Islam.

Besides monotheism, another remarkable feature of Judaism was its organization. God made the covenant with the people without the intervening mediation of kings or priests. A hereditary caste of priests did maintain the single temple in Jerusalem, but the most important religious figures were the **prophets**, who tried to share with the people their direct communication with God. During their lifetimes, prophets often suffered rejection, frequently ignored and punished. Yet the moral voices of the prophets like Samuel, Ezekiel, Jeremiah, and Isaiah have resonated through the scriptures.[3]

The Hebrews were likewise unusual in the less-than-divine nature of their kings. The early history of the Hebrews included no kings; the judges who conquered Canaan were not kings. And what happened (according to their scriptures) once God granted the Hebrews a king? Saul, their first king and allegedly chosen by God, suffered civil war and committed suicide after defeat by the Philistines.

---

3. For contrasting prophecies about violence and end times, go to http://www.concisewesternciv.com/sources/psc3.html.

Table 3.1. Which Ten Commandments?

Jewish	Orthodox	Most Protestant	Roman Catholic	Exodus 20: 2–17
1				2 I am the LORD thy God, which have brought thee out of the land of Egypt, out of the house of bondage.
		1		3 Thou shalt have no other gods before me.
2			1	4 Thou shalt not make unto thee any graven image, or any likeness of any thing that is in heaven above, or that is in the earth beneath, or that is in the water under the earth: 5 Thou shalt not bow down thyself to them, nor serve them: for I the LORD thy God am a jealous God, visiting the iniquity of the fathers upon the children unto the third and fourth generation of them that hate me; 6 And shewing mercy unto thousands of them that love me, and keep my commandments.
3			2	7 Thou shalt not take the name of the LORD thy God in vain; for the LORD will not hold him guiltless that taketh his name in vain.
4			3	8 Remember the sabbath day, to keep it holy. 9 Six days shalt thou labour, and do all thy work: 10 But the seventh day is the sabbath of the LORD thy God: in it thou shalt not do any work, thou, nor thy son, nor thy daughter, thy servant, nor thy maidservant, nor thy cattle, nor thy stranger that is within thy gates: 11 For in six days the LORD made heaven and earth, the sea, and all that in them is, and rested the seventh day: wherefore the LORD blessed the sabbath day, and hallowed it.
5			4	12 Honour thy father and thy mother: that thy days may be long upon the land which the LORD thy God giveth thee.
6			5	13 Thou shalt not kill.
7			6	14 Thou shalt not commit adultery.
8			7	15 Thou shalt not steal.
9			8	16 Thou shalt not bear false witness against thy neighbour.
10			9	17 Thou shalt not covet thy neighbour's house, thou shalt not covet thy neighbour's wife,
			10	nor his manservant, nor his maidservant, nor his ox, nor his ass, nor any thing that is thy neighbour's.

Note: While people often refer to the Ten Commandments as the foundational laws of our culture, the exact rules are difficult to pin down. Two slightly different versions exist, one, as here, and the other, as in Deuteronomy 5:6–21. Translation challenges lead to different word choices ("kill" or "murder") or archaic phrasing, such as in this, the King James Version. In the original Hebrew, there was no numbering—verse numbers appeared only as late as the twelfth century AD. Jews, Orthodox, Roman Catholics, and Protestants numbered the commandments in different ways, so where some commandments ended and others began was open to interpretation.

The next two, David and Solomon, did much good and lived into old age, but they also sinned mightily. The kingdom broke into two parts, and both were conquered. What use were kings for the chosen people of God? They did just as much harm as good. Judaism absorbed the lesson that political states were not essential for faith. God made a covenant with the people of Israel, not the kings of Israel.

Thus originated the Western principle of the separation of church and state. This ideal certainly did not mean that the populace lacked religion. On the contrary, the Hebrew people were religious (or not) independent of the status of their government. The emphasis on God's rule did incline them toward **theocracy**, the idea that religion ruled a society through its officials and ministers. Such tendencies, though, never lasted for long. While Hebrew priests played an essential role in ritual and the maintenance of religious laws, the Hebrews insisted on having secular rulers.

This practice differed from Mesopotamian kings who claimed divine powers or Egyptian pharaohs who asserted themselves as gods incarnate. When those states fell, so did their religions. No one today reveres Ishtar or Osiris. For most of history, however, the Hebrews, the Jews, have done without any state at all. They and their religion nevertheless survived. Their God did not care about what constitution a kingdom has, they believed, but how faithful His people were.

The failure of the postexilic Jews to have a powerful kingdom like other peoples did not doom them. At first they prospered under the tolerant Persian Empire. When the Persian Empire fell in 330 BC to Alexander (see the next chapter), Greek kings based in Egypt or Syria ruled the Jews for several centuries, often allowing them substantial autonomy.

That conquest by the Greeks began the last great turning point of Jewish history: the **Diaspora** (dispersion or scattering). Some Jews were dragged out of Palestine to be forced into soldiery or slavery. Others, encouraged by cosmopolitan freedom under other Greek rulers, left their chosen home for distant lands to live among other peoples. Within an international cultural and political system dominated by Greeks, many Jews found it easy to emigrate from Palestine and settle in enclaves in distant cosmopolitan cities throughout the Mediterranean and Middle East, even as far as India.

Jews who remained in Judaea found one more brief moment to claim their own worldly kingdom. In 165 BC, a Hellenistic king desecrated the temple in Jerusalem in honor of his own Greek gods. In reaction, the Maccabee (or Hammer) family led a revolt, winning about a century of independence again for the Jews. The victors proclaimed a brief theocracy, unifying the kingship under the office of high priest. Then, in the first century BC, Roman armies marched into the Middle East (see chapter 5). By 63 BC, the Romans had easily conquered the weak Jewish kingdom, although keeping order among the Jews proved much more difficult. A Jewish civil war became a rebellion against the empire, which led the Romans to destroy the temple in Jerusalem in AD 70 (see figure 3.1) and intensify the Diaspora by forcefully ejecting many Jews from Palestine after AD 135. From that time until the twentieth century, most Jews lived outside of their ancient homeland and

Figure 3.1.   The Romans take plunder from the Jerusalem temple (most notably the menorah) and commemorate their success in crushing the Jewish rebellion, on the Arch of Titus in the forum in Rome.

had no political autonomy of their own. They lived in small enclaves in the cities of the kingdoms and empires of other peoples.

The Jews lost their kings, their temple and its priests, and their agricultural base as they moved into foreign cities. Out of necessity, the Jews no longer were peasant farmers and instead became urban traders and merchants. Teachers trained in their scriptures, called **rabbis**, led both worship in synagogues and entire Jewish communities. Their written commentaries collected into the Talmud (a compendium of the Torah with scholarly elucidation) helped to maintain some religious unity. Due to the Diaspora and lack of central authority, Jews often differed in their interpretation of scripture and manner of living. Jews may have been monotheists, but they were not monolithic. Nevertheless, enough tolerance in the Hellenistic and Roman cosmopolitan cities allowed the fragmented Jews to keep practicing their religion across the Mediterranean world.

Toleration went only so far, however. Most states have justified their existence through a divine connection; thus a different faith implied a lack of allegiance to the state religion. Jews remained a perpetual irritant for authorities who preferred conformity, because the Jews were implacably capable of maintaining their distinct religion. As the Jews came under Roman rule, their refusal to make religious sacrifices to the Roman gods, especially the emperor, might have led to persecution. Fortunately, the Romans concluded, in their usual tolerant manner toward religion, that Judaism predated their own rituals. Abraham, Moses, and David had lived centuries before the founding of Rome. So the Romans exempted the Jews from worship of the gods, by special license.

Despite this sympathy for differences, Jewish cultural identity has continually provoked hostility from their neighbors. Our modern word for this hatred toward Jews is *antisemitism*.[4] Through the centuries, the results of that hatred have ranged from mere dislike for Jews as "different," to discrimination in jobs and housing, to violent persecution, and even to extermination. Had the Jews assimilated, given up any unique clothing, religious practices, and ways of speech or life, then antisemitism might have disappeared. But then Jews would have ceased to be Jews. Since many Jews have remained faithful to their concept of how to obey God, they have often faced difficulties with majorities who wanted them to conform or convert.

The Jews survived as a small but significant minority in the ancient world of the Middle East, Europe, and even deeper into South and East Asia. But compared with the rise of the other ancient empires, the political history of the Hebrew kingdoms mattered little. Nonetheless, the Jewish people have endured without a homeland as few peoples in world history have done. Also, out of their religion arose other beliefs that would reshape the West and the world. As residents in the cities of Europe, they would contribute from their culture to the growth of Western—or what some call Judeo-Christian—civilization. Before those moments, however, two other Mediterranean peoples added their own groundwork to Western civilization.

Review: *How did the Jews maintain their cultural identity?*

Response:

---

4. The word *antisemitism* is highly contested. It was coined during the growth of racist ideology in the nineteenth century (see chapter 12). Some say the term obscures the difference between Jews and other Semitic peoples, while classifying them as ethnically "semitic" ignores hostility toward Judaism as a religion. Scholars also question whether it is appropriate to apply the concept of antisemitism to the ancient world, or even medieval or early modern European history. While the label can be spelled using a hyphen and a capital first *S*, the all-lowercase version seems now preferred.

SOURCES ON FAMILIES: DEUTERONOMY (CA. 625 BC)

The book of Deuteronomy (or Second Law) in the Torah (or Christian Old Testament in the Bible) presents directions for ritual practices along with rules for behavior. These rules for the Hebrews resembled those of other Middle Eastern civilizations, such as presented in Hammurabi's Law Code. These particular selections from chapters 20–25 mostly focus on the relations of men and women, both within a marriage and without, in violence and in peace. Today's Jews and Christians have to choose how many of these laws to follow or ignore.

When thou goest forth to war against thine enemies, and the Lord thy God hath delivered them into thine hands, and thou hast taken them captive, And seest among the captives a beautiful woman, and hast a desire unto her, that thou wouldest have her to thy wife;

Then thou shalt bring her home to thine house, and she shall shave her head, and pare her nails; And she shall put the raiment of her captivity from off her, and shall remain in thine house, and bewail her father and her mother a full month: and after that thou shalt go in unto her, and be her husband, and she shall be thy wife. And it shall be, if thou have no delight in her, then thou shalt let her go whither she will; but thou shalt not sell her at all for money, thou shalt not make merchandise of her, because thou hast humbled her.

If a man have two wives, one beloved, and another hated, and they have born him children, both the beloved and the hated; and if the firstborn son be hers that was hated: Then it shall be, when he maketh his sons to inherit that which he hath, that he may not make the son of the beloved firstborn before the son of the hated, which is indeed the firstborn: But he shall acknowledge the son of the hated for the firstborn, by giving him a double portion of all that he hath: for he is the beginning of his strength; the right of the firstborn is his.

If a man have a stubborn and rebellious son, which will not obey the voice of his father, or the voice of his mother, and that, when they have chastened him, will not hearken unto them: Then shall his father and his mother lay hold on him, and bring him out unto the elders of his city, and unto the gate of his place; And they shall say unto the elders of his city, This our son is stubborn and rebellious, he will not obey our voice; he is a glutton, and a drunkard. And all the men of his city shall stone him with stones, that he die: so shalt thou put evil away from among you; and all Israel shall hear, and fear.

The woman shall not wear that which pertaineth unto a man, neither shall a man put on a woman's garment: for all that do so are abomination unto the Lord thy God.

If a man be found lying with a woman married to an husband, then they shall both of them die, both the man that lay with the woman, and the woman: so shalt thou put away evil from Israel.

If a damsel that is a virgin be betrothed unto an husband, and a man find her in the city, and lie with her; Then ye shall bring them both out unto the gate of that city, and ye shall stone them with stones that they die; the damsel, because she cried not, being in the city; and the man, because he hath humbled his neighbor's wife: so thou shalt put away evil from among you.

But if a man find a betrothed damsel in the field, and the man force her, and lie with her: then the man only that lay with her shall die. But unto the damsel thou shalt do nothing; there is in the damsel no sin worthy of death: for as when a man riseth against his neighbor, and slayeth him, even so is this matter: For he found her in the field, and the betrothed damsel cried, and there was none to save her.

If a man find a damsel that is a virgin, which is not betrothed, and lay hold on her, and lie with her, and they be found; Then the man that lay with her shall give unto the damsel's father fifty shekels of silver, and she shall be his wife; because he hath humbled her, he may not put her away all his days.

He that is wounded in the stones, or hath his privy member cut off, shall not enter into the congregation of the Lord.

A bastard shall not enter into the congregation of the Lord; even to his tenth generation shall he not enter into the congregation of the Lord.

When a man hath taken a wife, and married her, and it come to pass that she find no favor in his eyes, because he hath found some uncleanness in her: then let him write her a bill of divorcement, and give it in her hand, and send her out of his house. And when she is departed out of his house, she may go and be another man's wife. . . . Her former husband, which sent her away, may not take her again to be his wife, after that she is defiled; for that is abomination before the Lord: and thou shalt not cause the land to sin, which the Lord thy God giveth thee for an inheritance.

When a man hath taken a new wife, he shall not go out to war, neither shall he be charged with any business: but he shall be free at home one year, and shall cheer up his wife which he hath taken.

When men strive together one with another, and the wife of the one draweth near for to deliver her husband out of the hand of him that smiteth him, and putteth forth her hand, and taketh him by the secrets: Then thou shalt cut off her hand, thine eye shall not pity her.

Questions:

- *What euphemisms does the source use (such as for love, desire, sexual intercourse, genitals)?*
- *What opportunities for agency do women have?*
- *What role does "the Lord thy God" play in maintaining these laws?*

Responses:

Make your own timeline.

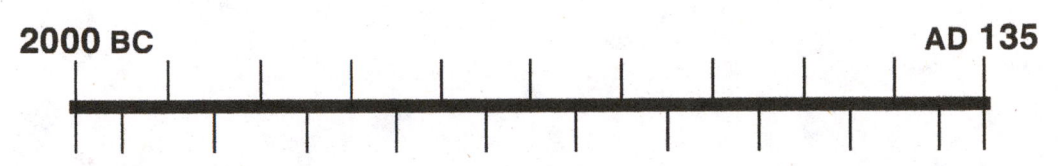

For more on this source, go to http://www.concisewesternciv.com/sources/sof3
.html.

CHAPTER 4

Trial of the Hellenes

The Ancient Greeks, 1200 BC to AD 146

While the ancient Hebrew kingdoms were oppressed on all sides by conquerors, far away from the dangerous Middle East another people, the **Greeks**, were able to prosper, at least at first. For shortly after the Persian Empire restored the Jews to Palestine, a new *shahanshah* turned his wrath on the Greeks. Persia might have utterly destroyed the Greeks like the "lost tribes" of Israel or beaten them into political impotence like the last Kingdom of Judaea. Instead, for a brief moment in history, the Greeks triumphed to dominate the Eastern Mediterranean and much of the Middle East. While a tragic flaw in their success eventually drove the Greeks into political irrelevance, their cultural achievements made them the second founding people of Western civilization.

TO THE SEA

The Greeks called themselves Hellenes, the descendants of a legendary founder named Hellas. They first came together as a people sometime at the dawn of the Iron Age around 1200 BC, when so many other civilizations suffered attacks from the "Sea Peoples." At that time two small civilizations collapsed: the Mycenaeans (who had lived at the southern tip of the Balkan Peninsula) and the Minoans (who had ruled from the nearby island of Crete). Their culture survived only through myths and stories of the Trojan War (for the former) and the Minotaur of the labyrinth (for the latter). From about 1200 to 800 BC, the first Hellenes invaded and took over the southern Balkans, displacing, intermarrying, and blending with the surviving indigenous people to become the Greeks.

These were the Greek "Dark Ages," so called because we know so little about what happened then, since records are sparse. Although the Greeks remained loosely connected through their language and culture, geography inclined them toward political fractiousness. They themselves distinguished three main ethnicities: Dorians, Ionians, and Aeolians. Greece's sparse landscape seemed inadequate for agriculture compared with the vast fertile plains of the Nile and Mesopotamian river valleys. The southern end of the Balkan Peninsula and the neighboring islands in the Aegean Sea were mountainous and rugged, with only a few regions suitable for grain farming. Grapevines and olive trees, though, grew well there and provided useful produce of wine and oil for export. Also, numerous inlets and bays where the mountains slouched into the sea provided excellent harbors. Therefore, the Greeks became seafarers, prospering less by farming and more by commerce, buying and selling, as they exchanged what they had for what they needed. And if a little piracy was necessary now and then, they did not mind that either.

The Greeks were so successful that by 800 BC the southern Balkan Peninsula and the Aegean islands had become too crowded. In the Greek homeland, the Greeks did away with their kings. Instead, they divided into separate, independent city-states, each one called a **polis** (in the singular; poleis in the plural). Throughout the rest of the Mediterranean, though, good farmland lay available for those who could take it. So the Greeks seized upon the form of imperialism called colonialism, just as the Phoenicians had done before them. In forming colonies, a crowded city-state would encourage groups of families, as many as two hundred men and their dependents, to emigrate. The Hellenes sailed across seas rather than crossing plains or rivers or mountains to conquer neighboring lands. There, on some other island or distant shore with a good harbor and a hill to build a fort, the emigrants would found a new city-state. Many indigenous peoples were killed, assimilated, enslaved, or driven away to live in the areas not held as Greek territories. The new colonies, however, remained only loosely connected to their founding state. They too became free poleis, responsible to no higher political authority even if they shared in the Greek way of life of the homeland. Each Greek held allegiance to his own polis before and above any allegiance to the Hellenes as a whole.

Most of these independent new colonies succeeded. First, the Greeks occupied all the islands of the Aegean Sea, where they still live today. More Greek populations migrated to western Asia Minor (called Ionia, now the western edge of modern Turkey), along the shores of the Black Sea, and all around the Mediterranean, often near Phoenician colonies. Greek settlements survived for many centuries, although people of Greek ethnicity no longer live in those places today (see chapter 14). By 500 BC, more Greeks were actually living in the region of southern Italy and Sicily called Magna Græcia (or Greater Greece) than in the original Greek homeland. The colonies promoted trade networks and encouraged innovation and invention as the Greeks built new homes and thrived in strange lands.

The Greeks, in fact, succeeded beyond anyone's imagining, except perhaps their own. The Hellenes had a remarkable confidence in their own superiority. They called all non-Greeks "barbarians," a word derived from nonsense syllables which the Greeks heard foreigners speak, namely babbled nonsense. For the Greeks the word included more than the hunter-gatherers usually called that name by civilized societies, since the Greeks also labeled as barbarians peoples like the Egyptians and Babylonians, who had brought forth great civilizations centuries before the Greeks existed and were still wealthy. Such distinctions were of no importance to the Greeks. They felt themselves to be the only truly civilized people.

Some Greek attitudes seemed rather strange to their neighbors at the time. For one, romantic and sexual relationships between men were more common and accepted in ancient Greece than elsewhere. With limited evidence from pottery, philosophical writings, poetry, and some court cases, historians do not fully understand these relationships. On the one hand, it seems that often a male prepubescent was initiated into adulthood through a liaison with an older man. These relationships were not like modern homosexuality and might not necessarily have had a physical sexual dimension—Plato wanted them to follow his ideal of sexless "Platonic love." Warriors of the Sacred Band of Thebes or the Spartans seem to have had strong same-sex customs. On the other hand, some Greeks (even Plato in one dialogue) condemn same-sex relationships. Idealization of male beauty is reflected in the practice of Greek men exercising in gymnasia or competing in sports in the nude. The athletes in the famous **Olympic Games** ran, hurled, boxed, and wrestled in the nude, watched by male spectators (although some young virgin girls were allowed to attend, possibly to check out prospective husband material). Not only women, but also non-Greek men were excluded from competing in the Olympics. The Hellenes played out our modern Olympic ideal of bringing together all nations of the world in sports on a more restricted scale. Although famous through the ancient world, the Olympic Games expressed *pan-hellenism*, the idea that Greeks were a special community. They used the competitions to bind together the different poleis (who were forbidden to make war while the games were in session). "Barbarians," meaning anyone who was not Greek, were not welcome on the playing field.

Their political particularism further intensified into the idea of personhood called *individualism*. The heroic individual mattered more than the family, more than the city or its people. Homer's *Iliad*, a great epic poem, shows how Achilles and his many virtues, called *arête*, were hard to balance against the needs of the larger community. As the hero sulked in his tent, the Greeks were stalemated in their war against the Trojans. Many died because of the pride of Achilles, including his best friend, Patroclus. Should readers admire Achilles or admonish him? In any case, Achilles earned praise for being the best warrior. In everything, from war to theater, the Greeks competed with one another. How the Greeks would deal with this feeling of superiority, exclusiveness, and individuality became their greatest trial.

Review: *How did the Greeks begin as a people and expand through the Mediterranean?*

Response:

THE POLITICAL ANIMAL

As the Greeks built their civilization, they entered a remarkable period of political experimentation. The word *polis* gives us our word *politics*. The Mesopotamian kings and emperors, Egyptian pharaohs, and Persian shahs lacked politics in our modern, Western sense. Their royal and imperial commands were to go unquestioned, endorsed by divine mandate. Only a few select elites, the aristocrats, had any part in the decision-making process that affected tens of thousands of subjects. In contrast, some Greeks exercised **democracy** as a form of government. The Hellenic practice of politics broadened the decision making to include many people, which is what *democracy* literally means: rule by the people. More people participated in deciding who paid taxes and how much, or whether to preserve peace or make war against others. Achieving democracy required a long struggle against the elites who wielded power.

The first step toward power for the people had already taken place during the "Dark Ages." The Greeks rejected monarchy, the most common political institution of the ancient world. Instead of allowing their kings to become gods like most other ancient peoples, the Greeks dispensed with most of them. The Greeks did not, of course, cast off the gods. They still believed their societies depended upon the favor of deities. At the heart of every city was an acropolis, "the high citadel," in which the people built their temples, held their most important religious ceremonies, and hoarded their treasures. Yet the Greeks got rid of kings and a priestly caste as mediators with the divine. Instead, members of the community shared and alternated in the role of priests and officiators in religious ceremonies.

The next step, of breaking the power of the wealthy and well-born families, was much more difficult. **Aristocracy**, rule of the "better born," replaced monarchy at first. Recall that a few well-connected families usually ran things. Such happened also in ancient poleis. The aristocrats supported their power through their wealth in land, control of commerce, and monopoly of leadership in war. The expensive bronze armor and weaponry of the aristocratic warrior, such as Achilles had wielded in myth, made the aristocrats dominant on the battlefield, which in turn secured their monopoly in political counsels.

In the seventh century BC, politics changed when new military technology and tactics created new kinds of warriors. The rough terrain of the southern Balkans was unsuitable for cavalry, and so foot soldiers became the most important fighters. Then the growing use of iron allowed for new weapons, as it had for the Assyrians. A new type of Greek warrior, the **hoplite**, was lightly protected by a helmet and a large round shield while armed with a long spear and a short sword.

The key to the hoplite's success on the battlefield was fighting in coordination with other hoplites in a **phalanx**. Each phalanx consisted of about four hundred men standing in lines eight ranks deep; each man defended himself with his helmet and large shield that covered both part of himself and his fellow soldier. To attack, the hoplites wielded nine-foot-long spears as they ran forward together to smash the enemy. The battle often turned into a shoving match, each side pushing until the other started to give way from exhaustion, fear, or the loss of combatants to wounds. If spears became unwieldy or broke in close combat, then soldiers swung their short swords through the gaps in the shield wall of their enemy.

At the same time, the Greeks perfected a new warship for the all-important battles at sea: the trireme. While triremes did have sails, rowers called *thetes* provided the essential means of propulsion. A large ram on the prow could crash into an enemy ship, aiming to sink it. If that was unsuccessful, armed *thetes* would leave their rowing banks and board the enemy ship, fighting hand to hand to seize it. Navies organized ships to fight in groups, like a phalanx at sea.

Repeatedly in history, innovations in military methods have forced changes in political structures. These two innovations by the Greeks, hoplite and trireme, broke the dominance of the aristocracy in combat and lost them their political monopoly. In ancient Greece, a simple peasant could afford the few weapons of a hoplite and then spend several weeks training to march in formation and kill. Anyone with a strong back and limbs could be a *thete*. Once the peasants and merchants realized that they were putting their lives on the line for their "country," they demanded a share of the power and wealth controlled by the aristocrats. Many peasants called for **land reform**, taking away some land from those who had inherited a great deal and giving it to those who had little. Peasants have called for this redistribution regularly throughout the history of Western civilization. Getting the great landowners to surrender power, however, has been more of a challenge.

The struggle for dominance in Greek city-states reflected the eternal interconnection between politics and violence. Ideally, politics should mean that people peacefully make a decision after civil discussion. All too often, however, discourse among the people of the poleis failed and violence followed. Violence then could escalate from riots to rebellion. The Greek aristocrats resisted any land reform, correctly perceiving it as not in their own best interest. They believed themselves to personify warriors of privilege, whose dominance had been granted by the gods. The Greek peasants, equally determined to gain their version of justice, fought for it. Thus, rebellion and strife have been political tools just as often as laws and votes. When all political discourse had broken down into rioting, the Greeks called it anarchy (from their word for a society without archons, the appointed administrators).

A few aristocrats who sympathized with the plight of the peasants assisted the commoners in the seventh and sixth centuries BC. These leaders seized power for themselves from their fellows and won the favor of the masses by pushing through reforms. These popular rulers have been given the name of **tyrants**. To accuse someone of *tyranny* nowadays implies ruthless rule for one's own gain, and indeed that did happen in Greece. More often, though, the Greek tyrants ruled with harshness in order to break the power of their fellow aristocrats and grant land and rights to the peasants. Greek tyrants were rarely able to establish a dynasty and pass power to their descendants. Instead, the commoners who had helped the tyrants subsequently overthrew them, believing, correctly, that they no longer needed the tyrants once the power of the aristocrats was broken. The mechanisms of political power had shifted.

After much bloodshed and suffering, most Greeks settled on some form of democracy by 500 BC. How democratic any city-state became depended on how many of its residents held the political rights of **citizenship**. Citizens exercised defined rights and responsibilities in making group decisions and supporting the safety of their polis. The ancient Athenians regarded a citizen who neglected public service as literally an "idiot." The majority of residents of a polis, though, could not be citizens. First of the excluded were resident "foreigners," anyone not descended from the founders of the particular polis, whether ethnic Greek or not. Second, adult women had no legitimate political role (as would continue to be true in the West until the twentieth century), even if they technically held citizenship. Third, children of citizens were left out, as they are today. Fourth, the large numbers of enslaved persons held very few legal rights at all. Fifth, not possessing enough property prevented many of the poor from political participation. In sum, Greeks usually limited participation in democracy to adult male citizens who held a defined amount of wealth, which varied from city to city. Overall, the percentage of people actually engaged in democracy ranged from 30 percent down to only 3 percent of any city-state's population. Nevertheless, this percentage was a substantial improvement on the less than 1 percent of people involved in early Greek states or most Middle Eastern civilizations of the time. The number also compares well with modern democracies, where sometimes only one-third of the population votes in elections. The Greek philosopher Aristotle may have called man "a political animal," but even he did not expect all people to participate.

These restrictions on voting in Greek poleis created the first tension within democracy, which leads to another basic principle:

Democracy is difficult.

Throughout the history of democracy, people not only argued but also killed one another over political principle. Most people cannot easily give up power. Many people cannot peacefully accept that others with whom they disagree should have power over them. Others cannot resist the temptation to enrich themselves through political office rather than work to improve the community as a whole. Despite these sad realities, sometimes people have accepted the rules of democracy and created real and just democratic governments. A truly functional democracy requires the rule of law and at least two different ideological positions that can both legitimately disagree and yet compromise with the other. Rules require that political process, not violent power, should guide decisions within a polity.

The Hellenes developed two basic political directions that are still with us today. Now as then, the word *democracy* had a double meaning.[1] First, it stands today for the general political principle of the direct rule by the people, under

---

1. The two dominant American political parties since the 1850s have been the Democrats and Republicans. Both have usually supported the ideology of democracy and republicanism (as explained in the next chapter), even when they disagree with each other on what should be done.

laws, and through argument and compromise. Second, it indicated the particular polities formed by factions of citizens in Greek poleis that included the free adult males of the lower classes. Likewise the term *oligarchy* today means any government managed by a small number of privileged people, while in ancient Greece factions of oligarchies formed regimes limited to aristocratic and newly wealthy adult males. In their contrasting ideologies, oligarchs leaned toward the past tradition (often mythologized), while democrats inclined toward the unknown future (always idealized). While oligarch and democrat factions challenged one another for political supremacy in most city-states, two poleis exemplified each political ideal: **Sparta** and **Athens**. Both city-states included more people in political decision making in a general way than the monarchies of the ancient world. Both also adopted different political structures.

The oligarchic Spartans called themselves Laconians, which has given us the expression "speaking laconically"—using few words to convey great meaning. Their city-state was unique among the Greeks because it founded almost no overseas colonies. Instead, the Spartans conquered their neighboring Greeks in the Peloponnesus, the hand-shaped peninsula at the southern tip of the Balkans. Most of those conquered Greeks became helots, Spartan subjects who held no political rights and had to surrender half of their agricultural produce annually. The free citizens of Sparta who ruled over all made up only a small subset, perhaps 3 percent of the total population. Since the unfree helots retained their Greek inclination for fierce independence, the Spartan citizens always feared revolt.

To prevent a successful slave rebellion, the Spartans therefore organized their entire state around militarism and *egalitarianism*, claiming that these values were an ancient tradition. Egalitarian values meant that all citizens were considered rigorously equal. For example, the government divided up the agricultural plantations into relatively equal portions, one for each family. Money was made of large iron weights, which were too difficult to store, spend, or steal. Trade and artisanship in luxury goods was discouraged, since it would have increased the display of wealth. The common good (for the elite minority) was seen as better than the individual good.

More famous has been the Spartan commitment to militarism. The first priority of all male citizens was military service. Male children were taken away from their parents at the age of seven, and from then on they were raised in military barracks to train for the army. As part of their training, they were supposed to sneak and steal food from the local population. If an adult caught a boy stealing, he could beat the young one, sometimes so harshly that the boy died. At eighteen, a man who survived was allowed to marry. Even then, a married man ate meals in the warriors' mess until he was sixty. Even on the wedding night, the husband had to return to the barracks after consummation of the marriage. Women were esteemed if they produced male children. Spartan parents often exposed female babies to the elements to die because, as was common in the ancient world, they valued girls less than boys. Likewise, the Spartans tossed into a chasm any male infant whom a group of elders deemed unlikely to mature into a proper warrior. The public interest in strong children overrode any parental rights or affections.

Sparta's oligarchic government nevertheless functioned democratically, at least for those few considered full-fledged citizens. No one person could be all powerful. At age thirty, men became citizens with full political rights. Two traditional kings ruled Sparta as a pair, but they were really figureheads—real power rested with appointed magistrates and a council of elders (about thirty of the leading citizens over age sixty). Generations of Spartans tried to maintain this system with as little change as possible because for them it embodied the virtues of the past and their founding father, Lykurgus. When a political crisis arose, those who promoted a policy always tried to claim, "It's what Lykurgus would have wanted!"

The democratic Athenians contrasted with the Spartans in many ways. Our concept of the civilization of ancient Greece is usually their direct democracy and classical culture. The Athenians emphasized individualism rather than Sparta's egalitarianism and militarism. Athenian society encouraged its citizens to excel in politics, business, art, literature, and philosophy, according to each person's talents. Athens's location on a broad fertile plain with easy access to the sea allowed its inhabitants a prosperous economy and a large population. From early on, however, Athens needed to resolve differences among three competing constituencies: those of the city, those of the plain, and those of the hills. Each had different priorities and loyalties.

These divisions hindered the formation of a more democratic form of government until a series of tyrants began reforming the system. Draco, one of the first tyrants, became infamous for his set of laws issued in 621 BC. Many of the laws mandated the death penalty, even for minor crimes. Consequently, his name has become a byword for excessive harshness: *draconian*. A few years after 600 BC, the tyrant Solon solved so many problems that his name became a byword for someone with political wisdom. To stop unrest, Solon divided the people into classes based on property, canceled farmers' debts outright, and expanded citizenship to the poor. Finally, by about 500 BC, Cleisthenes left Athens with a substantially inclusive and stable democratic structure.

Cleisthenes's balanced constitutional system served Athens for most of the fifth century BC. First, Cleisthenes brought all citizens together into a political body called the Assembly. As the highest legislative body, it included all male citizens over eighteen, about 10 percent of the population. Anyone was allowed to speak and vote, and a simple majority decided most issues. The Assembly declared war, made peace, spent tax money, chose magistrates, and judged capital crimes. Thus, every citizen was involved in making the most important state decisions. How was the citizen to make up his mind how to vote in the Assembly? Politicians became orators, speechmakers striving to sway the crowd. If a politician became too powerful, the citizens could impose **ostracism**. Each citizen "voted" by writing a politician's name on a piece of broken pottery (*ostracon*), and the winner was sent into exile. To prevent getting ostracized and hold on to power, politicians built up factions, groups of followers on whom they could rely. In Athens, as in most city-states, one faction preferred democracy, the other oligarchy.

The Assembly met only periodically. Select citizens carried out the day-to-day administration of the city. Interestingly, the Athenians filled most administrative positions and juries by lot: a randomizing machine selected names of citizens. They reserved actual voting within each tribe (*ethnos*, the word from which we get our *ethnicity*) for elections of generals (*strategoi*, the word from which we get our *strategy*). One advantage was that election ensured the generals had the support of their troops. The troops could hardly disobey someone they themselves had elected. A disadvantage was that soldiers did not always elect the best strategists or tacticians. Popular charisma is not always the best quality in battle. From the point of view of the city's leaders, though, dividing power among ten commanders prevented any one general from possessing too much military power.

Cleisthenes's second innovation aimed to end old feuds between people living in the three different geographic regions. The merchants of the city, the farmers of the plain, and the shepherds of the hills felt they had little in common with one another. Cleisthenes broke up loyalties by imposing new ties that were not based on location, blood, occupation, or social status. He divided each of the three regions (city, plain, and hills) into ten districts. One district from each of the three regions was then combined into a new "tribe," artificially forcing the divergent people of city, plain, and hills to work and fight together. These ten amalgamated tribes determined both a citizen's role in the rotating administration and their own units in military service. Finally, the ten tribes sent fifty representatives each to the Council of Five Hundred. This important body prepared bills for the Assembly, supervised the administration and magistrates, and negotiated with foreign powers.

The Athenian democratic idea, as we shall see in later chapters, would survive to inspire change, even violent revolutionary change, up to the present day. Nevertheless, throughout most of Western history, cultural conservatives have attacked democracy and democratic tendencies. Indeed, most Hellenes themselves admired oligarchic Spartans more than the democratic Athenians. It seemed less messy to have a more authoritarian system of government. The chaotic debate and passions of the Athenian crowd seemed undignified compared with the stoic calm of Spartan deliberation. Either way, as both city-states entered confidently into Greece's **Classical Age** (ca. 500–338 BC), this whole argument was nearly lost to history. Just as these early experiments in self-government had begun, the most powerful empire of the age nearly wiped them out.

Review: *How did the ancient Greeks practice divergent democratic politics?*

Response:

METAMORPHOSIS

The Greeks almost vanished as a people because the *shahanshah* of the vast and powerful Persian Empire decided to crush them. Instead, the Greeks metamorphosed (their word for transformed) into a political power to be reckoned with. The first stage of this transformation was their defeat of the Persian invasions. After that, however, they nearly defeated themselves in civil war. They regrouped under new leadership to invade and conquer the Persian Empire itself, only, in the end, to become a conquered people themselves.

As seen in chapter 2, by 500 BC Persia's empire had extended westward into most of Asia Minor, where many Greeks lived. Although the absolutism of the shah satisfied most of his diverse subjects, the independent-minded Greeks chafed under the imperialist Persian yoke. The Greeks put the conflict in simple terms: freedom versus servitude. In 499 BC, many Greeks in Ionia rebelled against their Persian imperial masters and burned the city of Sardis, a provincial capital. The Persians simply saw arson and violent rebellion. In retaliation, Persian troops burned the Greek cities in Ionia and enslaved their residents. Then Emperor Darius found out that the rebels had received help from across the Aegean, from the Athenians and a few of their fellow Greeks. In the opinion of the king of kings, these supporters of rebels should be smashed. So Darius invaded Greece. Thus began the **Persian Wars** (494–449 BC).

In 490 BC, the Persian forces landed about twenty-four miles east of Athens, near the village of Marathon. The story of a messenger who ran to the Spartans for aid soon grew into the myth of the heroic marathon runner who delivered his message with his dying breath. The distance from Athens to Marathon has given us the modern Olympic race, although the Greeks themselves never ran such a long distance in sport. Surprisingly, the Athenians did not actually need help from the militaristic Spartans. The Athenians and a few allied forces of hoplites managed to push the Persians back from the beaches into the sea, even though the enemy landing force was twice their number.

Ten years later, Darius's successor, Xerxes, decided to avenge his father's defeat, especially after the Greeks encouraged a revolt by Egyptians against Persian imperial rule. Xerxes amassed the largest army that had ever been assembled in the region, reportedly several hundred thousand troops from all corners of the diverse empire (including Greeks who had submitted to his authority). To avoid the dangers of a sea-to-land invasion, he built a bridge across the narrow straits of the Dardanelles that separated Europe from Asia. As the Persian army marched into Greece, most Greeks surrendered and begged for mercy.

A few city-states, led by Athens and Sparta, resolved to fight. Athens had built a major fleet of triremes, financed by a recently discovered silver mine. Sparta, not surprisingly, already had the best hoplites. But a majority of Spartans refused to commit themselves to a common defense of Hellas. So out of a possible Spartan army of eight thousand, only a small force of three hundred Spartans advanced to hold off the advancing Persian army in the narrow pass at Thermopylae (or Hot Gates). Several hundred hoplites from other city-states, such as Thebes and Thespia, joined them. Mountains protected the Spartans' left flank, and the Athenian and allied navy supported their right. After three days of heroic resistance, some traitorous Greeks led Persian forces along a mountain path around and behind the Spartan line. The Persian army surrounded and slaughtered the Spartans. The Greek naval forces, which had also fought well against the Persians, withdrew.

With the road now clear of opposing armies, all of Greece lay open to annihilation. The Persian army marched into Athens only to find it abandoned. Xerxes set fire to the city and waited for his fleet to bring essential support to his troops. Then, as the Persian fleet entered the straits of Salamis, the Athenian and allied Greek navy sprang a surprise attack. In the narrow strait, the Persian captains panicked. One Persian captain, Queen Artemisia of Halicarnassus, even attacked her Persian allies in order to retreat. Xerxes had to withdraw. He invaded again the following year, but the phalanxes of the main Spartan army and of many allied Greeks defeated his army at Plataea. Against all odds, the puny Greeks had beaten the greatest empire in their world.

The Greeks characterized their victory as liberty and civilized virtue triumphing over oppression and barbarian vice. We might, however, be skeptical about such labels. On their own side, Greek prosperity made the most of slavery (or, in Sparta, exploiting helots). And on the other side, the Persians had maintained a relatively tolerant empire. They had allowed the Jews to resettle Palestine. They had created general prosperity and stable rule with which many of their subjects were satisfied. If the Persians had won, some sort of Western civilization still might have developed. Perhaps the Persians might have gone on to conquer the rest of Europe. Or maybe the Romans or Phoenicians might have stopped and reversed the Persian advance. In any case, the Greek triumph did not guarantee success for their versions of liberty and virtue. They would betray those values themselves.

Nevertheless, momentarily buoyed by victory, the Athenians entered their brief Golden Age, which lasted only fifty years, from 480 to 430: less than one lifetime. To commemorate their success, some Greeks invented a new literary genre: history. Two famous books frame that age: one describes the war that enabled the Golden Age, the other the war that ended it. Both are early examples of historical writing since they relate how human choices rather than divine intervention drove events. First, Herodotus of Halicarnassus wrote his *History*, a retelling of the Persian Wars. Herodotus developed the theme of Europeans versus Asians, the Hellenes against the barbarians, but carefully evaluated and balanced his sources. For this achievement he is considered the father of historical writing. Second, Thucydides wrote of the civil war fought by Greeks against Greeks, now known as *The Peloponnesian War*. Thucydides was an even better historian than Herodotus, insightfully examining events and evenhandedly assigning fault or merit to the historical players. He also reimagined dialogues and speeches made by leading and representative participants. Such dramatic invention is not like the methodological writing of modern historians, but it makes for great reading.

To some extent, the **Peloponnesian Wars** (460–404 BC) inevitably followed from Greek particularism. After having survived the Persian threat, each polis pursued its own aims, usually without regard for the greater good of all Greeks. At the heart of these differences was the contradiction between the ideologies of Athens and Sparta. Democratic Athens looked outward and reveled in culture. Oligarchic Sparta gazed inward and worked at discipline. Could two such different cultures coexist as part of the same civilization? At first, the necessity of the Persian threat demanded it. Even after the defeat of the Persians at the Battles of Salamis and Plataea, many Greek poleis remained together in an alliance dedicated to the final defeat of Persia and the liberation of the Ionian Greeks. This **Delian League** had its original headquarters and treasury on the Aegean island of Delos. All too soon, however, the Athenians manipulated the Delian League to support their empire building. In most of the key battles, the Athenians bore the brunt of the fighting because they had the largest war fleet. For them, this sacrifice fully justified their new supremacy among the Greeks. Athenian culture was enormously expensive and cost far more than what the city-state of Athens produced. Eventually, the Athenians extracted tribute from the other member poleis to pay for the navy and troops. The other states submitted to Athens because they, like most people, were willing to let others fight for them.

Soon Athens was a mere city-state no longer—it had become an empire uniting many Greeks. In 455 BC, the Athenians ceased all pretense about their own imperial ambitions and moved the league's treasury from Delos to Athens. Even after Persia officially made peace with the Greeks in 449 BC, the Athenians maintained their dominion. When member poleis tried to withdraw from the Delian League, Athens seized control of their cities. If nonmember poleis threatened Athenian power and prosperity in any way, Athens attacked them (see Primary Source Project 4). Thus, Athens began to achieve political unity for the Greeks through oppression. In their own eyes, they were deservedly the leaders of the Hellenes. Not for the first time would a people practice democracy at home yet imperialism abroad.

The leader of Athens toward the end of this Golden Age was Perikles (b. ca. 490–d. 429 BC). Perikles rose to power as the head of the democratic faction, based on a reputation for honesty and skill in public speaking. He proudly rebuilt the city after the Persian devastation with glorious marble temples paid for with the profits of empire. Perikles also wanted to use imperial wealth to subsidize the lower classes of Athens. For example, he arranged to pay jurors, thus enabling simple laborers to take time off from their jobs to hear cases. The oligarchic faction of well-born gentlemen opposed policies that favored their social inferiors, even including the building of the Long Walls to protect the city and its port. The expensive project may have protected the homes of vulgar commoners, but it left exposed the oligarchs' fields outside the walls. Since they could not attack Perikles directly, the oligarchs tried to discredit him by bringing corruption charges against those close to him, such as his mistress Aspasia (a former *hetaira*, or high-class prostitute/courtesan) or Phidias, whose sculptures decorated the Parthenon.

Outside Athens, other Greeks opposed Athenian supremacy. Sparta formed a rival Peloponnesian League, which believed that Athenian expansionist policies threatened liberty as much as the Persians had. Initial fighting between the allies of Athens and Sparta began in 460. Neither side, however, could achieve victory because the Spartans were putting down revolts by helots and the Athenians were still fighting the Persians. A thirty-year truce in 445 BC lasted only half that long. In 431, when some of the subsidiary allied states began fighting one another, both Athens and Sparta thought the situation serious enough to declare war.

These Peloponnesian Wars were the greatest tragedy for Greece. At first, neither side could effectively fight the other. The Athenians ruled the waves with their navy, but they could not land enough infantry to defeat Sparta. The Spartans dominated land with their infantry, but they could not breach the high, long walls enveloping Athens. And the defensive strategy of the Athenians backfired when a plague struck the crowded, besieged city in 430 BC. The death toll of disease gravely weakened Athenian ability to strike at Sparta. Even worse, the plague killed Perikles. No politician who followed shared his qualities of statesmanship.

As the war dragged on, both Athens and Sparta attacked neutral states, thereby forcing all Hellenes to choose sides. Each side basically told other Greeks, "You can have liberty, but only on our terms." In a famous example, the polis of Mytiline tried to secede from the Delian League after Athens had been weakened by the plague. In 427 BC, the once-again strong Athenians decided to punish the Mytilines by killing every male and selling the women and children into slavery. They had second thoughts, however, and killed only a thousand of Mytiline's men. The Athenian attack on the neutral island city-state of Melos in 416 BC resulted in more horrors (see the Primary Source Project). Such political slaughters by winners on both sides piled up more casualties from battle and disease. Class conflict also increased as Sparta supported oligarchic factions in various poleis and Athens encouraged democratic factions. Rather than solving their disagreements through political dialogue and voting, extremists took to violence, assault, rape, arson, and murder. Ferocity ravaged Greek political structures from both without and within.

The Athenians' worst mistake was a poorly planned and unnecessary attack on Greek city-states in Sicily, part of Magna Græcia, and the key to control of the central Mediterranean. Led by the young politician Alkibiades, a majority in the Assembly strategized how to outflank the Spartans. They seized a convenient excuse: helping an allied polis that had complained of oppression by the great city-state Syracuse. The Syracusans were related to the Spartans but had managed to remain neutral. In 415 BC, the Athenians landed and found a well-prepared enemy and few allies. Instead of withdrawing or gaining a quick victory by assault, they got bogged down in a siege that lasted two years. The Syracusans defeated the exhausted Athenians, killing thousands of their best warriors and enslaving thousands more who slowly died digging in quarries. Athens lacked the resources to recover from this defeat. Sparta itself finally counterattacked with its own new navy, built with the help of its old enemy and new ally, Persia. The Spartans then besieged Athens by both sea and land, forcing the city to surrender in 404 BC.

Sadly, neither peace nor prosperity followed. Persia stoked the mutual suspicions of the Greeks against one another. Sparta began to act as imperialistically as Athens had. The city-states of Thebes and Corinth attacked their former ally

Sparta. Then the Greek helot-slaves of Sparta successfully revolted. Without slave labor, the once-mighty Sparta declined into an obscure village of no account. Meanwhile, Corinth and Thebes were each too weak to make other poleis submit. Everywhere, **demagogues** (partisan public speakers) inflamed emotions and manipulated public opinion toward short-term thinking and *factionalism*, where opposing groups refuse to cooperate with one another. Class warfare led to riots and rebellions. Thus, the Greek polis failed politically. Democracy had proven too difficult.

A political solution to this chaos came from the north: old-fashioned kingship. The Kingdom of **Macedon** lay along the mountainous northern reaches of Greek civilization. The southerners had always disregarded the rustic Macedonians as insufficiently civilized compared to true Greeks. The Macedonians did not live in cities, they spoke with strange accents, and they had been weak politically. That changed with King **Philip II** (r. 359–336 BC). As a youth, he had been held hostage in the polis of Thebes. While classical Greek culture impressed him, the politics of the polis did not. He returned to Macedon, reformed the administration of his kingdom, and strengthened his army along Greek lines. He also added cavalry to defend the sides and rear of a more flexible Macedonian phalanx and improved siege machinery to take city walls. Armed with these advantages, Philip began his conquest of Greece, capturing city-state after city-state. At the Battle of Chaeronea in 338 BC, Philip's army crushed the last Greek resistance to his rule on the mainland. He was now *hegemon*, captain-general-ruler of the Greek world (from which we get the word *hegemony* for political supremacy). The **Hellenistic Age** (338–146 BC) supplanted the Classical Age of Greece (see map 4.1).

Philip was assassinated at the height of power.[2] The new twenty-year-old King **Alexander** III (r. 336–323 BC) soon gained the title "the Great" for his conquest of much of the known world. Alexander carried out his father's proposal to attack the age-old enemy, Persia. His Macedonian and Greek armies routed the Persian forces in Asia Minor, liberated Egypt from Persian imperial power to put it under his own, and then swept through Mesopotamia to take Iran itself. So awed were people, and he himself, by his success that *deification* began, the belief that a person became a god. Alexander did not discourage the trend and may have believed in his divinity himself.

Whether Alexander "the Great" was god, emperor, general, or fool, his soldiers followed him farther eastward into the foothills of Afghanistan and into the Indus River valley. Only the fierce resistance by the vast populations of the Indian subcontinent finally allowed his soldiers to convince the not quite thirty-three-year-old Alexander to turn home toward Greece. On the way back, after a night of heavy drinking, Alexander fell into a fever. A few days later, whether from too much alcohol, infection, or poison, the conqueror lay dead.

---

2. It might be argued that he was murdered rather than assassinated for political reasons. His killer, Pausanias, had been a lover of Philip but had been gang-raped by Philip's allies, a crime about which the king did nothing. Some conspiracy theorists then and today suggest also that Philip's wife Olympia and his son Alexander were participants in the conspiracy since Philip's new wife and son threatened their positions. The official excuse given to the public cited Persian and foreign intervention.

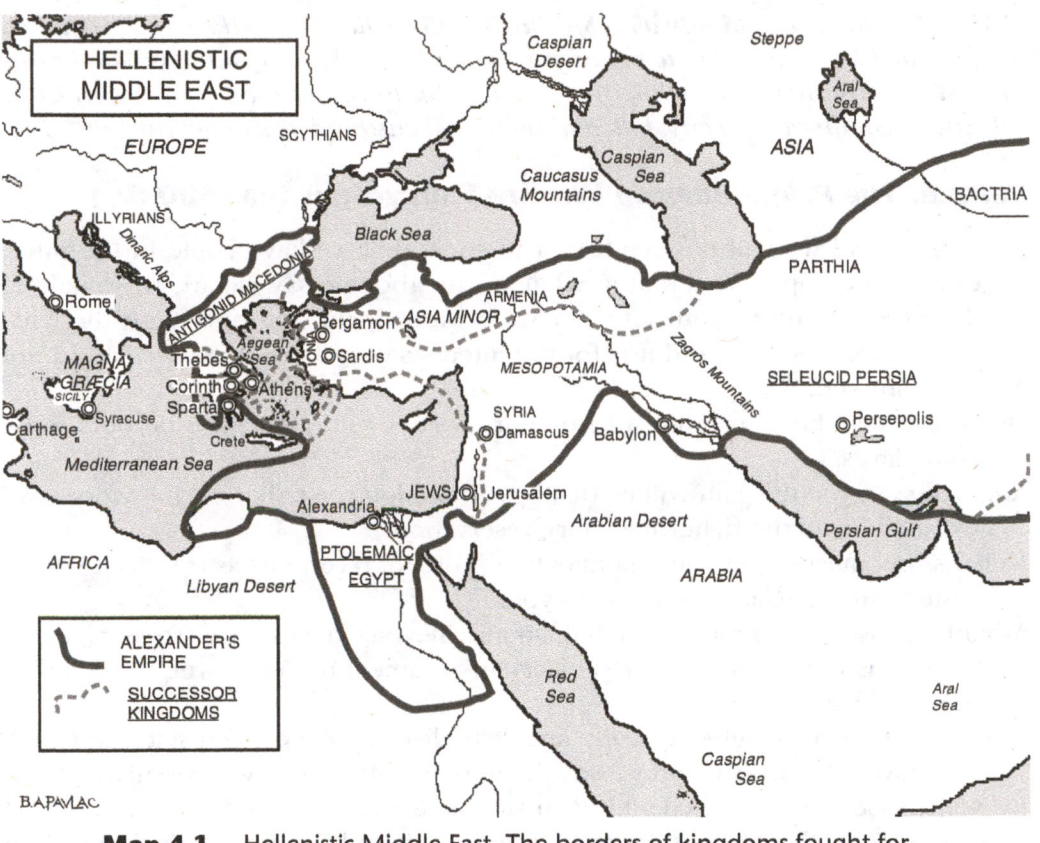

Map 4.1. Hellenistic Middle East. The borders of kingdoms fought for by the successors of Alexander were constantly in flux, as battles were lost and rulers were killed. Why did Alexander expand his empire only in certain directions?

Review: *How did the Greeks enter a brief Golden Age, and how did it collapse?*

Response:

PRIMARY SOURCE PROJECT 4:
ATHENIANS VERSUS MELIANS ABOUT THE RULES OF WAR

The Peloponnesian War between Sparta and Athens opposed the idea of liberty against the idea of power. In 416 BC, Athenian forces attacked the neutral city-state of Melos, afraid it would ally with Sparta. The historian Thucydides reconstructed the so-called Melian Dialogue between representatives of each side: the Athenians suggest the city surrender while the Melians ask to be left alone. In the end, the Athenians conquered the city, killed its men, and enslaved its women and children.

Source: *The Peloponnesian War* by Thucydides (ca. 400 BC)

Athenians: And we will now endeavor to show that we have come in the interests of our empire, and that in what we are about to say we are only seeking the preservation of your city. For we want to make you ours with the least trouble to ourselves, and it is for the interests of us both that you should not be destroyed.

Melians: It may be your interest to be our masters, but how can it be ours to be your slaves?

Athenians: To you the gain will be that by submission you will avert the worst; and we shall be all the richer for your preservation.

Melians: But must we be your enemies? Will you not receive us as friends if we are neutral and remain at peace with you?

Athenians: No, your enmity is not half so mischievous to us as your friendship; for the one is in the eyes of our subjects an argument of our power, the other of our weakness.

Melians: But are your subjects really unable to distinguish between states in which you have no concern, and those which are chiefly your own colonies, and in some cases have revolted and been subdued by you?

Athenians: Why, they do not doubt that both of them have a good deal to say for themselves on the score of justice, but they think states like yours are left free because they are able to defend themselves, and that we do not attack them because we dare not. So that your subjection will give us an increase of security, as well as an extension of empire. For we are masters of the sea, and you who are islanders, and insignificant islanders too, must not be allowed to escape us. . . .

Melians: Surely then, if you and your subjects will brave all this risk, you to preserve your empire and [rebellious city-states] to be quit of it, how base and cowardly would it be in us, who retain our freedom, not to do and suffer anything rather than be your slaves?

Athenians: Not so, if you calmly reflect: for you are not fighting against equals to whom you cannot yield without disgrace, but you are deciding whether or not you shall resist an overwhelming force. The question is not one of honor but of prudence.

Melians: But we know that the fortune of war is sometimes impartial, and not always on the side of numbers. If we yield now, all is over; but if we fight, there is yet a hope that we may stand upright.

Athenians: Hope is a good comforter in the hour of danger, and when men have something else to depend upon, although hurtful, she is not ruinous. . . .

Melians: We know only too well how hard the struggle must be against your power, and against fortune, if she does not mean to be impartial. Nevertheless we do not despair of fortune; for we hope to stand as high as you in the favor of heaven, because we are righteous, and you against whom we contend are unrighteous. . . .

Athenians: As for the Gods, we expect to have quite as much of their favor as you: for we are not doing or claiming anything which goes beyond common opinion about divine or men's desires about human things. For of the Gods we believe, and of men we know, that by a law of their nature wherever they can rule they will. This law was not made by us, and we are not the first who have acted upon it; we did but inherit it, and shall bequeath it to all time, and, we know that you and all mankind, if you were as strong as we are, would do as we do. . . .

[Y]ou are showing a great want of sense. For surely you cannot dream of flying to that false sense of honor which has been the ruin of so many when danger and dishonor were staring them in the face. Many men with their eyes still open to the consequences have found the word "honor" too much for them, and have suffered a mere name to lure them on, until it has drawn down upon them real and irretrievable calamities; through their own folly they have incurred a worse dishonor than fortune would have inflicted upon them. If you are wise you will not run this risk.

You ought to see that there can be no disgrace in yielding to a great city which invites you to become her ally on reasonable terms, keeping your own land, and merely paying tribute; and that you will certainly gain no honor if, having to choose between two alternatives, safety and war, you obstinately prefer the worse. To maintain our rights against equals, to be politic with superiors, and to be moderate towards inferiors is the path of safety. Reflect once more when we have withdrawn, and say to yourselves over and over again that you are deliberating about your one and only country, which may be saved or may be destroyed by a single decision.

The Athenians left the conference; the Melians, after consulting among themselves, resolved to persevere in their refusal, and made answer as follows:

"Men of Athens, our resolution is unchanged. We will not in a moment surrender that liberty which our city, founded seven hundred years ago, still enjoys. We will trust to the good fortune which, by the favor of the Gods, has hitherto preserved us, and for human help to the Spartans, and endeavor to save ourselves. We are ready, however, to be your friends, and the enemies neither of you nor of the Spartans, and we ask you to leave our country when you have made such a peace as may appear to be in the interest of both parties."

Questions:

- *What choices are open to each side of the dialogue?*
- *How does each side define its ultimate goal?*
- *What are the principles or beliefs that are common to both sides, even if interpreted differently?*

Responses:

For more on this source, go to http://www.concisewesternciv.com/sources/psc4 .html.

THE CULTURAL CONQUEST

Opinions about the rise of Macedonian power stir controversy. Critics of Philip and Alexander condemn their use of conquest, destruction of democracy, and overemphasis on the cult of personality. Supporters praise their heroism, reform of government, and unification of Greeks among themselves and with other peoples. Alexander even encouraged his Greek soldiers to marry Persian women. Regardless, Philip and Alexander's brief reigns changed history for the Greeks and all their neighbors. The Hellenistic Age saw Greek power reach diverse peoples across the ancient world. The great cultures of Egypt, Mesopotamia, and Persia briefly collapsed before the armies of Alexander.

Although the political unity of Alexander's empire died with him, the Greeks stayed on as regional rulers. They founded new poleis and colonies of Greeks throughout their kingdoms. Greek became the *lingua franca* or common language, and Greek practices dominated economics, society, and the arts. The conquered peoples adapted to Greek civilization in a process called *hellenization*. Eventually, being Greek became a cultural attitude, not solely a biological descent from a forefather Hellas.

Political democracy, though, was not part of this expansion, since classic Greek democracy lay in ruins. Ending the give-and-take of political debate, Alexander imposed absolutism, like other Middle Eastern semidivine potentates or "Oriental despots." Alexander's successors were generals who seized power and set up their own royal dynasties. As Hellenistic kings, they likewise employed deification with elaborate rituals emphasizing their association with the gods. In the constant tension between independent local control and centralized authority, the city-state vanished under the Hellenistic monarchs.

Alexander's fragile empire fell apart into three great power blocs. One general took Macedon and from there tried to impose Macedonian rule on the Greeks of the south. Another, Ptolemy, seized Egypt, whose rich farmlands and ancient heritage provided the most secure and long-lasting power base. A third, Seleucus, controlled the riches of Asia Minor and ancient Persia. The Macedonian, Ptolemaic, and Seleucid dynasties dominated the Western Mediterranean and Middle East for about two hundred years, until replaced yet again by other rulers (as told in chapter 5).

While the Hellenistic kingdoms failed to establish enduring political unity, they fostered a cultural success that endured for many more centuries. The Greeks lost political choices, but they gained a role in history that would have amazed even the most optimistic Athenian of the Golden Age. Greek culture became the standard for much of the ancient world, as well as a foundation of Western civilization.

Most of that culture reflected Athens and its Golden Age of fifty years after the Persian destruction of 480 BC. The Athenians under Perikles had rebuilt their ruined city in shining marble. The crowning achievement was the temple atop the acropolis, the Parthenon, dedicated to the city's namesake, Athena, the goddess of wisdom (see figure 4.1). It pleases the eye, perfectly proportioned and harmonious, while its design contains nary a perfectly straight line in the Euclidian sense. The Athenians decorated the Parthenon with the most anatomically correct sculptures done by anyone in the West up to that point (although they usually painted the figures in garish colors that would strike us as strange and would horrify later art critics who had learned to admire the shimmering pallid blank white of marble).[3] **Realism** and **naturalism**, mixed with a poised serenity, characterized the art of the Classical Age.

Figure 4.1.   The remains of the temple of the Olympian Zeus, with the Parthenon on the Acropolis of Athens looming beyond.

---

3. The Parthenon survived largely intact for almost two thousand years. In AD 1687, during a war between Venice and the Ottoman Empire, the Turks stored ammunition in the temple, and a direct hit blew off the roof. In the early 1800s, the British Lord Elgin took to England many of Phidias's sculptures, which had been neglected by Turkish officials. The Greeks and the British continue to argue about returning the originals.

The effort spent on the temple of the Parthenon demonstrated again how religion was the heart of Greek society. The Greek myths and legends showed that the **Olympian gods** were uninspiring from a moral or spiritual sense. The gods exemplified *anthropomorphism*; they not only looked like humans but also behaved like them, usually at their worst. For example, the ruler of the gods, Zeus, reigned as a petty tyrant with his thunderbolts. He was notorious for his many affairs with goddesses, mortal women, and even the occasional boy. Likewise, the beauty of Aphrodite, the goddess of love, usually ruined men's lives. The gods' quarrels with one another spilled over into human affairs, and they quickly avenged insults to their divinity. Their divine interference is best recounted in Homer's epic poems, *The Iliad* and *The Odyssey*. The latter tells of a Greek king trying to return home after the Trojan War. Because he offends the gods while trying to survive, they throw many obstacles in his way: sirens, cyclopes, sorceresses, and even suitors for his faithful wife, Penelope. The legendary Trojan War itself had started because three goddesses fought over who was the most beautiful. Despite, or perhaps because of, this divinely trashy behavior, the Greek myths conveyed a rich and deeply textured heritage. How the human spirit rose above fate and the cruelty of the gods inspires us even today.

The Greeks revered their gods and ancestors by forming restrictive cults that kept those who did not belong out of each polis. Indeed, they dedicated each city to a deity, whom they also believed to have sired or borne semidivine heroic founders. **Civic cults** structured the worship of the city's gods in particular and of all gods (out of concern not to neglect any divine power). The polis organized religious ceremonies as a political responsibility. As mentioned before, the Greeks had no priestly caste or class. Instead, every citizen accepted an obligation to ensure that the civic rites of appeasing and worshipping the gods were performed properly. Consulting the gods through **oracles** provided guidance for everyday activities and major political decisions. The city fathers brought the cultic practices into their own homes by tending sacred fires (of which the Olympic torch is an offshoot) and sharing sacred meals.

Some Classical Greeks soon turned away from the austere formality of civic cults and the lack of spirituality found in the Greek pantheon. They instead embraced **mystery cults**, which were centered on rituals of fertility, death, and resurrection. We know little about the worship that focused on deities such as Demeter (fertility) or Dionysius (wine), since their followers kept most of their activities secret. The cults seemed to promise a conquest of death. Although the cults were popular for private worship, every citizen still upheld the civic rituals in public. All governing was performed in a religious context.

Even the religious cults, however, offered little in the way of a guide for the moral or ethical decisions that always have been at the heart of politics. For answers, the Greeks took one important step beyond religion with their invention of philosophy, named from the Greek for "love of wisdom." At about the same time, important philosophical progress appeared in both South Asia (Siddhartha Gautama or the Buddha) and East Asia (K'ung Fu-tzu or Confucius), but these ideas did not reach Europeans until many centuries later. In the sixth century BC in Ionia, some Greeks began to wonder about the nature of the universe. Compared with modern scientific investigation (explained in chapter 10), the Greek theories about how the universe was based on air or water seem rather silly. But they represented progress. Instead of relying on myth for explanation, philosophers began to apply reason. *Rationalism*, the concept that the human mind can comprehend the natural world, became a key component of Western civilization.

Since Greek philosophers could not provide definitive answers to the meaning of life, diverse views flourished. By the fifth century, the so-called Sophists (wise men) had started to create ideas about moral behavior that are still with us today. They were itinerant teachers who, for a fee, educated Greeks about the ways of the world. Several distinct schools of thought competed for attention. *Skepticism* doubted knowing anything for certain. *Hedonism* pursued pleasure as the highest good. *Cynicism* rejected all possessions and social restraints. The most famous cynic, Diogenes, supposedly lived in a barrel. When the great king Alexander visited this wise man, the philosopher allegedly told the monarch to step aside because he was blocking the sunlight. Many Sophists seemed to offer methods for becoming wealthy without worrying about moral scruples. Against them, a trinity of Greek philosophers offered lasting alternative suggestions for human action.

First, **Socrates** (b. 469–d. 399 BC) argued against the materialism of the Sophists. As he strolled through the streets and plazas of Athens, Socrates constantly asked questions of his fellow citizens. Moreover, his questioning challenged his fellow men to ponder true values. Such is the Socratic method. Socrates claimed to hold no set of doctrines he wanted to teach; he only desired to seek the truth. Indeed, he said that he knew little at all. When the Delphic Oracle had answered someone's query as to who was the wisest man in Greece with the answer "Socrates," the philosopher was at first puzzled. Then he realized that his self-description ("the only thing I know is that I know nothing") explained the oracle. He concluded that genuine wisdom was self-knowledge. Therefore, Socrates advocated that every person should, according to the Delphic Oracle's motto, "know thyself."

Amid the conflict of the Peloponnesian Wars, the trial of the philosopher Socrates highlights the Greeks' failure to live up to their high ideals. In 399 BC, as the Athenians tried to recover from their defeat by Sparta, a new democratic leadership charged the oligarchic Socrates with two crimes: blasphemy and corruption of the young. One day, a jury of five hundred citizens who had been chosen by lot heard the arguments, where plaintiffs and defendants represented themselves. Socrates defended himself of the first charge by openly mocking the nonsense of Greek mythology. How could someone believe in, let alone blaspheme, gods who did so many silly and cruel things to humans? He defended himself against the second charge by saying he only encouraged young people to think critically about their elders and society. Socrates gladly saw himself as an annoyance, a gadfly, provoking and reproaching the leaders of Athens. The jury found him guilty.[4] Consequently, when he wryly suggested his own punishment be a state pension, they sentenced him to death. Obedient to the laws of his city, Socrates committed

---

4. For more of his "Apology," go to http://www.concisewesternciv.com/sources/socrates1.html.

suicide by drinking hemlock, a slow-acting paralytic poison. This political trial illuminated how democracy failed to adapt to changing circumstances.

Second, Socrates's pupil **Plato** (b. 427–d. 347 BC) explored new philosophical directions. Since Plato wrote his philosophy in the form of dialogues conducted by his master Socrates, it is sometimes difficult to decide where Socrates's views end and Plato's begin. Still, Plato offered the doctrine of ideas, or *idealism*, as an answer for the nature of truth. In his famous allegory of the cave, Plato suggested that our reality is like people chained in a cave who can see only strange shadows and hear only odd noises. But if a person were to break free and climb out of the cave, though blinded by sunlight, he would confront the genuine reality. Actual forms in our world only poorly imitate real universal ideas. How could the person who sees truth then describe it to those still inside the cave, who do not share such an experience? Plato argued that the philosophers described ultimate reality.

Third, Plato's student **Aristotle** (b. 384–d. 322 BC) turned away from the more abstract metaphysics of his teacher to refocus on the natural world and people's place in it. Thus, he studied nature and wrote books on subjects from zoology to meteorology that would define scientific views for centuries (even if many were ill informed by our modern standards). Aristotle's rules of logic covered politics, literature, and ethics. He used *syllogisms*, called *dialectic logic*, where two pieces of known information are compared in order to reach a new knowledge. It was the most powerful intellectual tool of its day and indeed for long after. Finally, Aristotle promoted the "golden mean" of living a life of moderation.

Altogether, Socrates, Plato, Aristotle, and many other Greek philosophers helped to establish an idea called *humanism*. As this book will use it, *humanism* means that the world is understood as existing for humans. A phrase by the philosopher Protagoras, that "man is the measure of things," embodies the approach.[5] According to humanism, our experiences, perceptions, and practices are important and useful in dealing with life here and now. This belief has repeatedly offered an alternative to religious ideas emphasizing life after death. Greek philosophers who studied nature gained enduring knowledge in astronomy, mechanics, and medicine. On the last field, Hippocrates around 400 BC helped to establish the study of medicine by asserting that the gods were not involved in causing disease. On the positive side, he studied anatomy, sought natural causes for disease, and proposed gentle therapies of treatment. On the negative side, he thought that the relationship of four "humors" or qualities of bodily fluids he named blood, phlegm, yellow bile, and black bile affected health. These humors revealed themselves in patients' personalities and sex differences (men being superior with warm and dry balances, while women were inferior because they were cold and wet). This theory of humorism misleadingly dominated medical knowledge for many centuries. There is no good scientific evidence that humors exist or affect health.

One of the great humanistic triumphs of Greek culture was its literature. Many educated people knew the epic poems of *The Iliad* and *The Odyssey* by heart. Lyric

---

5. And the Greeks (especially Aristotle) usually meant specifically "men," since, following the assertions of Aristotle, they considered women to be an inferior version of the idealized male person.

poetry also was quite popular. Then, as today, that meant shorter, personal poems about feelings. In Greece, all poetry was literally said, or sung, while someone played the lyre, a stringed instrument, or a flute. Many Greeks declared Sappho as one of the greatest lyric poets. Today, more people now know her name as standing for female same-sex love, ***sapphism***; the alternate term ***lesbianism*** also is connected to Sappho, namely from the island where she had her school, Lesbos. As far as literary historians can tell, though, Sappho loved both men and women. Christians offended by her sensuality later destroyed much of her poetry, so only a few fragments have come down to us.

When the Greeks combined literature and performance, they invented **theater** (see figure 4.2). Like politics, theater had a religious context in Greek culture. Recitation of ritual stories of the gods turned into festivals, where actors dramatized the poetry with voice, movement, music, and even special effects. The most famous of the last is the *deus ex machina* (Latin for "god from the machine"), where a tangled plot could be instantly resolved by divine intervention, an actor playing a god lowered onto the stage from above. The most popular and important plays were tragedies, where the protagonist of the story fails, often due to pride (in Greek, *hybris*). The most famous tragedy is *Oedipus Tyrannos* (*Clubfoot the Tyrant*, usually translated as *Oedipus Rex*). By trying to do what is right, the title character causes suffering. Oedipus discovers that he had unknowingly killed his own father and had married his mother. She hangs herself; he blinds himself and goes into exile. No happy ending there.

Figure 4.2.   The curved rows of a theater are carved into the hillside of Ephesus, today a ruin in Türkiye. In the first century AD, a crowd gathered in the theater to accuse Paul of Tarsus and his Christian companions of blasphemy against the goddess Artemis.

Festival performances of several tragedies would be balanced by a comedy. Some Greek comedies were merely bawdy farces, but others rose to transcendent political satire. For example, *Lysistrata* by Aristophanes, first performed during the Peloponnesian Wars, struck a blow at both male aggression and ego. The heroine of the title successfully organizes the women of two warring poleis to go on a sexual strike until their men stop fighting.

It often happens that enduring culture is produced during brutal war. As rival Greek kings too often fought over their shares of Alexander's empire, the ruling Greek elites fostered a new phase of creativity called Hellenistic civilization (338–146 BC). While critics often characterize Hellenistic culture as less glorious than Athens's Golden Age, elites spread that age's classic works while also fostering their own new products. Cities became cosmopolitan, growing vibrant with peoples from many diverse ethnic groups. Alexander founded several urban centers and named them after himself, such as the most successful Hellenistic city, Alexandria, located at the mouth of the Nile. Streets laid out on grids connected places of education and entertainment: schools, theaters, stadiums, and libraries. Commerce in the Eurasian-African trade networks supported luxuries. Sculpture conveyed more emotion and character than the cool calm statues carved and cast during the Classical Age.

The two most popular philosophies to come out of the Hellenistic period reflected pessimism about the future, however. **Epicureanism** sought to find the best way of life to avoid pain in a cruel world. Epicureans taught that the good life lay in withdrawal into a pleasant garden to discuss the meaning of life with friends. In contrast, **stoicism** called for action. Stoics accepted the world's cruelty but called on everyone to dutifully reduce conflict and promote the brotherhood of mankind (women not included, as usual). This duty should be pursued even if one failed, which was likely.

The Greeks ultimately failed in their politics because of fighting among themselves, not because of external enemies. They changed history because a few of their city-states managed to defeat the great empire of Persia. Although their civil war led to them being conquered by Macedonians, their combined forces won mastery over masses of Asians and North Africans. The Greeks, however, were too few and too divided to permanently dominate these peoples. Although they contributed many high ideals, they betrayed them just as often. The Greek heritage of art, literature, and philosophy enriched the peoples of the ancient world, as it continues to do for many in the world today. Nevertheless, democracy fell to imperialism, imperial unity fell to particularism, and the intellectual honesty of Socrates fell to fear. The Greeks' cultural arrogance condemned them for a time to become marginalized instead of being the ongoing shapers of history. The next founders of Western civilization, the Romans, would soon conquer most of what Alexander had and add yet more to the foundations of the West.

Review: *What Greek culture expanded through the ancient West?*

Response:

SOURCES ON FAMILIES: PLATO, *THE REPUBLIC* (380 BC)

In The Republic, *the philosopher Plato relates a conversation proposing an ideal kind of society. Plato suggests that the utopian polis should be ruled by philosopher-kings who are aided by an elite group of "guardians." In this selection from Book V, Plato radically proposes that the guardians should have a unique kind of family, removing them from personal loyalties in order to concentrate on the good of the polis.*

Glaucon: What sort of community of women and children is this which is to prevail among our guardians? And how shall we manage the period between birth and education, which seems to require the greatest care? Tell us how these things will be. . . .

Socrates: For men born and educated like our citizens, the only way, in my opinion, of arriving at a right conclusion about the possession and use of women and children is to follow the path on which we originally started, when we said that the men were to be the guardians and watchdogs of the herd. Let us further suppose the birth and education of our women to be subject to similar or nearly similar regulations; then we shall see whether the result accords with our design.

Glaucon: What do you mean?

Socrates: What I mean may be put into the form of a question, I said: Are dogs divided into hes and shes, or do they both share equally in hunting and in keeping watch and in the other duties of dogs? Or do we entrust to the males the entire and exclusive care of the flocks, while we leave the females at home, under the idea that the bearing and suckling their puppies is labor enough for them?

Glaucon: No, they share alike; the only difference between them is that the males are stronger and the females weaker.

Socrates: But can you use different animals for the same purpose, unless they are bred and fed in the same way?

Glaucon: You cannot.

Socrates: Then, if women are to have the same duties as men, they must have the same nurture and education?

Glaucon: Yes.

Socrates: . . . Then women must be taught music and gymnastic and also the art of war, which they must practice like the men?

Glaucon: That is the inference, I suppose.

Socrates: I should rather expect that several of our proposals, if they are carried out, being unusual, may appear ridiculous.

Glaucon: No doubt of it.

Socrates: Yes, and the most ridiculous thing of all will be the sight of women naked in the arena, exercising with the men, especially when they are no longer young; they certainly will not be a vision of beauty, any more than the enthusiastic old men who in spite of wrinkles and ugliness continue to frequent the gymnasia. . . .

[The male and female guardians] must live in common houses and meet at common meals. None of them will have anything specially his or her own; they will be together, and will be brought up together, and will associate at gymnastic exercises. And so they will be drawn by a necessity of their natures to have intercourse with each other—necessity is not too strong a word, I think? And can there be anything better for the interests of the State than that the men and women of a State should be as good as possible? Then let the wives of our guardians strip, for their virtue will be their robe, and let them share in the toils of war and the defense of their country; only in the distribution of labors the lighter are to be assigned to the women, who are the weaker natures, but in other respects their duties are to be the same. And as for the man who laughs at naked women exercising their bodies from the best of motives, in his laughter he is . . . ignorant of what he is laughing at. . . .

. . . The proper officers will take the offspring of the good parents to the pen or fold, and there they will deposit them with certain nurses who dwell in a separate quarter; but the offspring of the inferior, or of the better when they chance to be deformed, will be put away in some mysterious, unknown place, as they should be.

Glaucon: Yes, that must be done if the breed of the guardians is to be kept pure.

Socrates: They will provide for their nurture, and will bring the mothers to the fold when they are full of milk, taking the greatest possible care that no mother recognizes her own child; and other wet-nurses may be engaged if more are required. Care will also be taken that the process of suckling shall not be protracted too long; and the mothers will have no getting up at night or other trouble, but will hand over all this sort of thing to the nurses and attendants.

Both the community of property and the community of families, as I am saying, tend to make them more truly guardians; they will not tear the city in pieces by differing about "mine" and "not mine"; each man dragging any acquisition which he has made into a separate house of his own, where he has a separate wife and children and private pleasures and pains; but all will be affected as far as may be by the same pleasures and pains because they are all of one opinion about what is near and dear to them, and therefore they all tend towards a common end.

Questions:

- *What does Plato see as the differences between men and women?*
- *How are Plato's proposals different from Athenian or modern concepts of family?*
- *How much do Plato's proposals resemble Spartan society?*

Responses:

Make your own timeline.

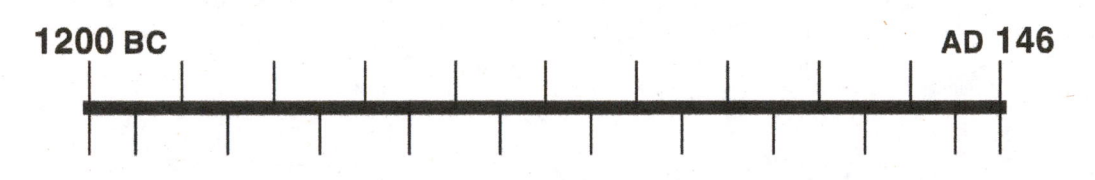

1200 BC   **AD 146**

For more on this source, go to http://www.concisewesternciv.com/sources/sof4 .html.

CHAPTER 5

Imperium Romanum

The Romans, 753 BC to AD 300

While the Greeks quarreled themselves into fragmentation, another people, the Romans, were proving much more adept at power politics. The Romans forged the most important and enduring empire of the ancient world. This achievement is all the more impressive since Rome started out as just one small city-state. Roman success can perhaps be attributed to the Romans' tendency to be even more vicious and cruel than the Greeks, who, as seen in the preceding chapter, could be fairly nasty themselves. Roman brutality could nevertheless also give way to tolerance and inclusivity. Their empire rose through military fortitude, cultural diversity, and political innovation (see map 5.1). The glory of the *Imperium Romanum*, the **Roman Empire**, still appeals to the historical imagination.

WORLD CONQUEST IN SELF-DEFENSE

At first, the city-state of **Rome** was small and surrounded by enemies, many of whom spoke similar "Italic" languages. According to Rome's own mythological history, refugees from the destroyed city of Troy in Asia Minor had fled westward and eventually immigrated to the province of Latium, which was halfway down the western coast of the Italian Peninsula. It was there, according to the story, that a she-wolf raised twin brothers, Romulus and Remus. As adults, they argued about the founding of a new city. In one version, in the year 753 BC, Romulus killed his brother Remus and named the new city after himself. Thus Rome was founded on fratricide. The Romans were proud of their violent inheritance; they themselves later became some of the best practitioners of state-sponsored violence in the history of the world.

Whatever truth may lie in the myth of Romulus, Rome's actual founders took advantage of a good location. The Tiber River provided easy navigation to the sea, yet the city was far enough inland to avoid regular raids by pirates. The city also lay along north–south land routes through central Italy. Hence, the founders

Map 5.1. Roman Europe. What geographic factors limited the empire's expansion?

had ready contact with nearby stronger societies and began to borrow from them liberally. The early Romans cobbled together a hodgepodge culture. They learned much from the Greeks who lived in the cities of Magna Græcia in southern Italy and Sicily. From them the Romans borrowed the Greek Olympian gods and goddesses, usually giving the deities new names better suited to the Romans' language of **Latin**. Another important influence were the neighbors to the north, the Etruscans (who have lent their name to Tuscany). For much of Rome's early history, the city itself was so weak that Etruscan kings ruled the Romans.

Roman myth supplied another violent story about winning freedom from the Etruscans. According to legendary history, Sextus, the son of an Etruscan king, lusted after Lucretia, the virtuous wife of a Roman aristocrat. When the husband was away from home one day, Sextus demanded that Lucretia have sex with him. If she did not, he promised to kill both her and a male servant. He promised he would then put them in bed together and report that he had found and rightfully killed them for shameful adultery and violation of class distinctions. So Lucretia gave in to Sextus. When her husband and his companions returned home, Lucretia confessed what had happened and then stabbed herself to death to remove her shame. The outraged Romans organized a rebellion and threw the Etruscans out of their city. Thus, rape and suicide inspired Roman political freedom.

This charming myth passed down through the generations probably has as little fact behind it as the legend of Romulus and Remus. For the Romans, though, this story proudly showed once again how violence and honor were woven into their history. Moreover, historical and archaeological evidence indicates that around 500 BC the Romans did indeed win freedom from Etruscan domination.

What the Romans then did with their new freedom was something remarkable: they chose a democratic form of government. Technically, the Romans founded a **republic**, where citizens elected other citizens to represent them. So, like the Greeks, they had no kings. Unlike the Greeks, they did not require all citizens to hold public office. The most important government institution was the **Senate**, a council of elders who protected the unwritten constitution and were involved in all major decisions. Initially, the Senate had three hundred members who served for life and were supposed to embody the collective wisdom of the republic. To lead their city-state, the Romans elected two consuls as administrators. These two ran the city government, commanded the army, spent the money, and exercised judicial power. The two consuls held office at the same time, and each had veto power over the other. The consuls served only a year, with only two terms permitted for any individual in a lifetime. Many other magistrate positions (praetors, quaestors, censors, lictors) were similarly limited.

Thus, the Senate and People of Rome (using the initials SPQR) began an elaborate system of **checks and balances**. In such a constitutional structure, offices and representative bodies were arranged with specific limits and overlapping jurisdictions. Thus no single individual, family, faction, class, officeholder, or institution could gain too much influence. For times of war or other emergency, however, the Senate could appoint a dictator for a six-month term. Such dictators had broad powers of military command unrestricted by another consul second-guessing decisions during the crisis. Then when the danger had passed, dictators retired to private life, like the famous Cincinnatus.

Officially, all male citizens voted and could hold official government offices. In actuality, though, a handful of families made the major decisions behind the scenes. Roman society was divided into two main groups: the aristocrats (a few dozen families called **patricians**) and the free-born peasants (called **plebeians**). In the early centuries of the Roman Republic, patricians controlled all the political positions. Indeed, someone could hardly hold office without living off of patrician wealth since government service was unpaid.

Suddenly, Rome's near destruction by the **Celts** (or **Gauls**) galvanized the Romans to improve their military. From the sixth through the fourth centuries BC, the Celts had been migrating through and settling down across Europe. One branch of the Celts conquered much of the northern Italian Peninsula at the end of the fourth century BC. In 390 BC, they attacked Rome itself. Celtic warriors occupied and destroyed much of the city, pushing the Romans back into a fortress on the Capitoline Hill. The legend goes that a sneak attack by Celts disturbed geese whose honking warned the Romans in time. The Romans then regrouped and drove off the Celts. Because of this narrow escape from defeat, the Romans decided to militarize their nation so that it would never be conquered. For about eight hundred years they succeeded in this goal—a good run for any empire.

The key military innovation that enabled this success was the Roman **legion**. The Romans improved upon the Greek and then Macedonian phalanx, which they must have encountered in Magna Græcia. On the battlefield the legion used smaller, more maneuverable groups of men who marched in formation and blocked enemy infantry with a shield wall, threw their "missiles" (spears, darts, rocks) to break up opposing ranks, and finally stabbed in close combat with their short swords. Meanwhile, the cavalry would attack the enemy on the flanks. The need for mounted troops gave rise to a new equestrian class, named after its members' ability to afford horses. Legions could successfully assault walled cities supported by improved siege weapons. The Romans surpassed the Greeks as the best warriors of antiquity.

While the city-state used aggression against its neighbors, Roman citizens sought more representative government where disagreements could be worked out peacefully. As in Greece, the new warfare left the aristocratic patricians less essential. Since plebeian farmers and craftsmen supplied most of the troops for the burgeoning empire, they wanted a larger say in government. Unlike the Greeks who went through the phase of violent tyranny against aristocrats, Roman plebeians threatened to strike rather than fight. The aristocratic patricians, numerically incapable of defending Rome on their own, began to make concessions. Patricians created the political office of the **tribunes**, who protected the plebeian citizens from aristocratic magistrates who unjustly intimidated them. Tribunician authority was one of the broadest and most powerful in the state. Patricians soon allowed the plebeians a major political body of their own: the Assembly of Tribes. By 287 BC, the assembly gained the power to make binding laws, declare war and peace, and elect judges. Patricians finally allowed wealthy plebeians to become magistrates as well. Thus, more checks and balances perfected the ideal republican government of the SPQR (see diagram 5.1).

Although the Romans developed republican government at home, they had to decide how to adapt politics to their conquered peoples in what was becoming an empire. By 250 BC, the Roman legions had subdued most of Italy, including "foreigners" such as the Samnites, who were actually more native to the peninsula than the Romans were. The secret to Roman success was not pure military force but a good dose of inclusiveness, which had been so foreign to the Greeks. Resistance to Rome might mean annihilation. They wiped out the Etruscan civilization, which had helped to civilize them, leaving only charming tombs and indecipherable records. Italic neighbors such as fellow Latins, Sabines, Aurunci, Hernici, Volsci, and Samnites all fell under the Roman yoke. Yet the Romans offered a *romanization* policy to many of the survivors in their new conquests. The vanquished were allowed to become more like Romans instead of beaten people. Subjected people had the option of keeping local government and even traditional gods and religion. All they had to do was accept Roman control of foreign affairs,

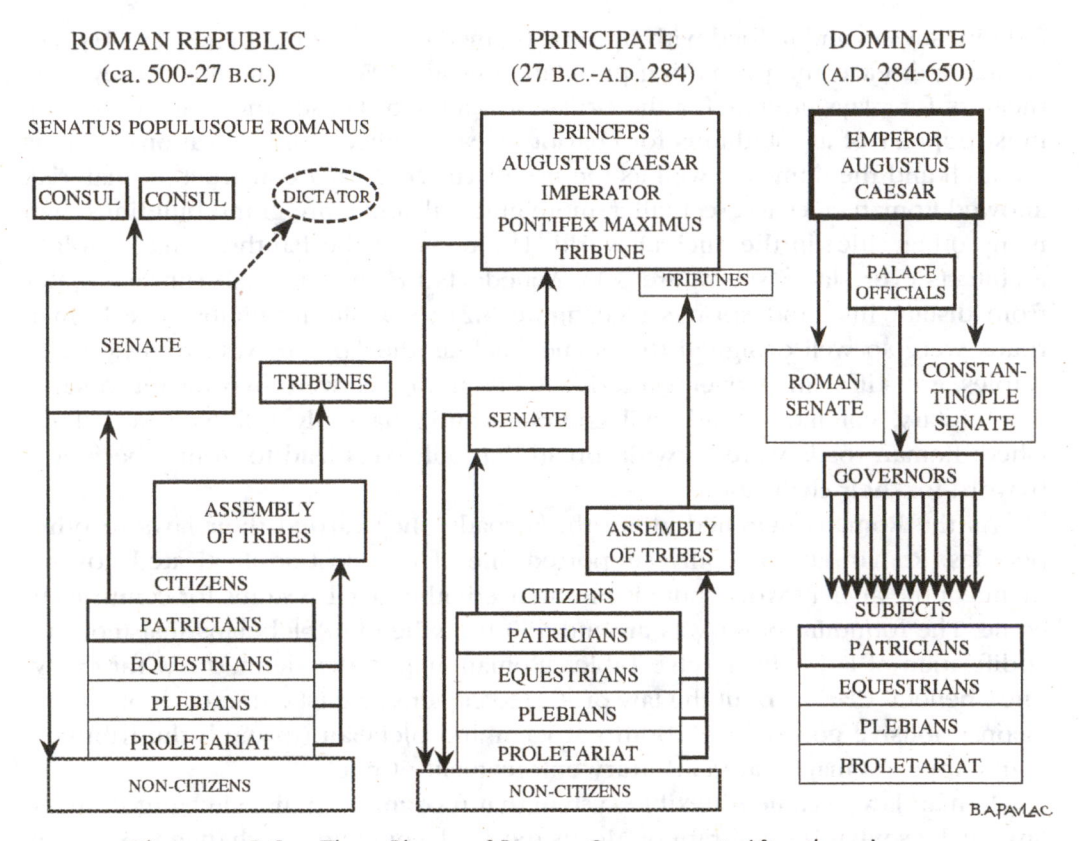

ROMAN REPUBLIC
(ca. 500-27 B.C.)

PRINCIPATE
(27 B.C.-A.D. 284)

DOMINATE
(A.D. 284-650)

SENATUS POPULUSQUE ROMANUS

CONSUL CONSUL DICTATOR

SENATE

TRIBUNES

ASSEMBLY
OF TRIBES

CITIZENS

PATRICIANS

EQUESTRIANS

PLEBIANS

PROLETARIAT

NON-CITIZENS

PRINCEPS
AUGUSTUS CAESAR
IMPERATOR
PONTIFEX MAXIMUS
TRIBUNE

TRIBUNES

SENATE

ASSEMBLY
OF TRIBES

CITIZENS

PATRICIANS

EQUESTRIANS

PLEBIANS

PROLETARIAT

NON-CITIZENS

EMPEROR
AUGUSTUS
CAESAR

PALACE
OFFICIALS

ROMAN
SENATE

CONSTAN-
TINOPLE
SENATE

GOVERNORS

SUBJECTS

PATRICIANS

EQUESTRIANS

PLEBIANS

PROLETARIAT

B.A.PAVLAC.

Diagram 5.1.   Three Phases of Roman Government. After throwing
out the Etruscan kings, the Romans established the Roman Republic.
Representatives of the people worked through various governing
institutions, calling on a dictator only in case of emergency. Later, under
the Principate, the emperor's power worked through lingering republican
institutions. With the Dominate, the overwhelming power of the emperor
reduced participatory citizens to obedient subjects.

contribute taxes, and provide military service. While originally only Roman citizens
could vote and hold important offices, their subject peoples slowly gained these
privileges as well, especially as they intermarried with Roman families. Slowly,
naturally, Roman culture took over as all of the peoples throughout the Italian
Peninsula were romanized, gave up their own languages, and adopted Latin. From
these small beginnings, Romans would come to rule most of western Europe.

The city of Rome's urbanity became imitated throughout what was essentially
an empire (in fact, if not yet in name). The center of Roman society were the
cities, even though most people lived and worked in the countryside as farmers.
Where cities existed, the Romans transformed them; where cities did not exist,
the Romans built them. Most of these cities were small, with only a few thousand
inhabitants each. The heart of each city was the **forum**, a market surrounded by
government buildings and temples. The public bathhouse was the most essential
institution of civilized life—the Romans were clean people. Their public latrines

fed into sewers and helped with hygiene (named from the Roman goddess Hygia), reducing disease and promoting population growth. For entertainment they built theaters for plays, arenas for the brutal slaughter of beasts and gladiators, and, most popular of all, stadiums for chariot races. Architectural innovations such as the arch and the dome, as well as the use of **concrete** as a construction material, allowed Roman cities to erect taller, more graceful, and more grand buildings than many other cities in the ancient world. The dome of the Pantheon has inspired architects ever since (see figure 5.1). Aqueducts brought in fresh running water from distant hills and springs (see figure 5.2) to public fountains. The Roman roads were so well designed that some, such as the Appian Way from Rome to Naples, are still being driven on today. While the roads were first meant to serve the military, commerce and civil communication naturally followed and flourished. Roman roads were so widespread that "all roads lead to Rome" became a byword for their civilization.

As the Romans marched along these roads, they carried their laws to other peoples. Roman law not only supported one of the most sophisticated governments of the ancient world but also influenced other legal systems for centuries to come. The founding point was around 450 BC, when the plebeians insisted on a codification of laws, the Twelve Tables. Roman magistrates defined law for everyone's benefit. Clarity about the law protected citizens against either each other and against abusive government. Both patrician and plebeian (through the tribunes) could appeal a magistrate's arbitrary enforcement of rules.

Roman law became a flexible system that recognized political change. Divine law, such as what Hammurabi or Moses received, could not be changed except by the gods. But the Romans began to invent the *theory of natural law*. This idea accepted that deities designed nature and humans to act in a certain way, but it proposed that human understanding of nature could change as people learned more. Through practice and experience, humans could create laws that were in better harmony with the natural order, consequently shaping a more just society. The Romans thought that if a law did not work, then a new one should be fashioned. Legal decisions and judgments were supposed to be founded on facts and rational argumentation, not divine intervention. As such, Roman law became the basis for many European legal systems today.

The Romans also established that all citizens should be treated equally by the law. Expanding rights of citizenship broke down the barriers between upper and lower classes, ethnic Romans, and others. Citizenship granted important status and political participation (although, of course, while women might be citizens and had some rights over property, the political system shut them out). To manage this growing and complicated system, the Romans also invented professional helpers in the law: lawyers. Roman lawyers had as bad a reputation in their own time as many lawyers have today. They were seen as greedy, loud, and annoying. Regardless, lawyers were essential to the smooth functioning of civil society. The Roman legal and political systems allowed people to have more of a voice and choice in politics than in most other societies in the ancient world. This republican government designed for a city-state, however, found itself unable to resolve increasing tensions within Rome's expanding rule.

Figure 5.1. Light shining through the oculus of the dome of the Pantheon in Rome. Into this temple the Romans welcomed all the gods worshipped by people in the empire.

Figure 5.2. Roman civilization relied on clean, fresh water, here brought by a tall aqueduct into Segovia, now in modern Spain.

Review: How did Rome grow from a small city-state to a vast multicultural empire?

Response:

THE PRICE OF POWER

Despite admirable legal innovation, civil society in Rome nearly collapsed in the third century BC because of the Roman addiction to world domination. The next hill always hid some possible danger to Rome, and such potential threat constantly justified another military expedition. Soon the Romans decided not to stop at the water's edge of the Italian Peninsula and set their eyes on Sicily. This target, however, led to a life-or-death crisis for Rome.

Previously, the Phoenicians had been competitors with the Greeks in forming colonies across the Mediterranean. Their major city of **Carthage** (which meant "New City"), located on the north coast of Africa across the sea from Sicily, controlled the central Mediterranean sea routes. Greek cities in Sicily complained of Phoenician oppression. The Romans intervened, using the excuse of defending liberty. Thus began the **Punic Wars** (named after the Latin word for the Phoenicians), which were fought in three phases over several generations from 264 to 146 BC.

The most memorable stage of the Punic Wars was the invasion of Italy by the Carthaginian general **Hannibal**. In 218 BC, he marched his armies (including war elephants) from Carthaginian territories in the Iberian Peninsula (Hispania) over the Pyrenees and Alps to enter Italy from the north. This brilliant feat of military command and logistics astonished the Romans. Unfortunately for Carthage, Hannibal failed to seize his most important objective, Rome itself. He did rampage up and down the peninsula, causing great fear and considerable damage, but he was unable to inflict a fatal defeat on Rome. This delay in capturing Rome gave the Romans the chance to learn from Hannibal's strategy and tactics. The Romans also proved their organizational abilities by recovering from defeats in particular battles and raising new troops in a country under constant threat. They then counterattacked by invading Africa in 203. Hannibal returned to defend his own capital city of Carthage at the Battle of Zama. The Romans defeated the fearsome Phoenician elephants by frightening them with trumpets or by letting them pass harmlessly through their lines without opposition. The legions surrounded the rest of the Carthaginian army and forced Hannibal to surrender. Rome wielded undisputed mastery over the Western Mediterranean.

The Phoenicians, severely weakened by this defeat, offered no further threat to Roman expansion. Within only a few years, though, demagogues in Rome began to chant the slogan "Carthago delenda est" (Carthage must be destroyed). The Romans finally carried out that final devastation in 146 BC, tearing down the city and sowing the fields with salt to inhibit any crops from growing again. All around the Mediterranean the Romans erased Phoenician civilization, its literature, and its culture from history.

In contrast, as the Romans conquered the Greeks, they embraced Hellenistic civilization. Also in 146 BC, the same year they demolished Carthage, the Romans destroyed Corinth, the last independent Greek city-state in the Balkans. Ever since the collapse of Alexander's empire, the Greeks had been fighting among one another. The Macedonian kingdom had tried to dominate the Greeks in the southern tip of the Balkan Peninsula, but supremacy remained elusive. One faction of Greeks sought help against the Macedonians by inviting the Romans in, first as mediators, then as protectors. Soon the Romans stayed as rulers. Any Greeks who resisted were conquered and enslaved, of course, but the Romans used many of them to spread Greek culture rather than for manual labor. And many Greeks accepted the Romans, who brought order and peace. With the fall of Corinth, Romans were well on their way to claiming the entire Mediterranean as *Mare Nostrum* (Our Sea). They pushed farther into Africa to absorb Egyptians, Nubians, and Ethiopians; into the Middle East to take on more Greeks, Jews, Syrians, and other Mesopotamians; and then north to the Celts. Many diverse peoples were unified by Roman armies.

The Romans did not notice at first that their victories came at great cost, as imperialism so often does. How could the political institutions designed for a city-state manage a vast multiethnic empire? The weak spots in Rome's society worsened. One great flaw was the classic economic recipe for social disaster: the cliché that "the rich get richer while the poor get poorer." The vast and productive new provinces fell under the exploitation of the aristocrats of Rome. As these patricians profited from the distant lands, discontent spread abroad while envy arose at home. One of the great new sources of wealth was the enslavement of the defeated peoples, who were forced to work on large plantations (called *latifundia*). The plantation owners began to grow cash crops such as olives and wine, which outsold the produce of simple farmers. Before the Punic Wars, the farmer-plebeians had been the backbone of Roman society and the army. Afterward, rich slave owners prospered from slave labor while free peasants lost their farms. These unemployed masses, forming the new social underclass of the **proletariat**, migrated to the cities, especially to Rome itself.

This mass urban migration shredded the social fabric of urban life. To keep the poor occupied, the patricians created an expensive welfare system known as "bread and circuses." They handed out grain (the bread) and provided entertainments (the circuses—meaning chariot races on which people gambled). Many other Romans increasingly complained that traditional values were vanishing.

Some Romans blamed imported "Greek customs," such as fashion, legal and political procedures, sexual practices, and alleged hedonism. Meanwhile the Roman noble equestrian class had become well-off from the burgeoning trans-Mediterranean trade. They resented the aristocratic patricians who excluded equestrians from the true mechanisms of power and treated them like plebeians.

By the late second century BC, these social tensions sparked civil wars that lasted for the next hundred years. The patricians divided into two factions. Those called *optimates* united to preserve oligarchy with as few social or economic reforms as possible. Those called *populares* advocated democracy, a broader political base, and land reform. Two patrician brothers in the *populares* party, **Tiberius** and **Gaius Gracchus**, tried to help the plebeians, as the tyrants had once done for the commoners in Greece. In doing so, the Gracchi brothers used extralegal violence to their advantage. In turn, the rival *optimates* led mobs to kill them both in 133 BC. Their deaths meant that the previous system of democratic politics, where checks and balances peacefully mitigated class differences, degenerated into fights over tyranny.

Violence soon became routine politics. A new permanent army only fueled the bloodshed. Rome had risen to regional supremacy based on the idea of citizen-soldiers, peasants who would serve for set terms during an emergency. Imperial defense and the danger of slave revolts required a standing army of recruits who served throughout their working lives. Many legionaries no longer came from Italian plebeians but from the newly conquered peoples who had not been fully converted to republican-style politics. This professionalization led to soldiers becoming more loyal to their commanders than to the idea of Rome.

Soon, generals such as Marius and Sulla began to fight one another over the wealth and power of the empire, while soldiers and citizens paid with their lives. They revived the position of dictator, which had faded after the Punic Wars. Dictators now stayed in power for the long term instead of only during a crisis. They escalated **proscription** to remove their political enemies. When a politician's name was posted on the *rostrum*, the speaking platform of the tribunes in the main forum, he was declared an outlaw. Anyone could kill him without penalty—a fate rather more harsh than the Athenian ostracism and exile. The ability to intimidate and kill mattered more than the talent to persuade. The Roman Republic staggered from bloody crisis to crisis.

Review: *How did Rome's conquests end in a long civil war?*

Response:

THE ABSOLUTIST SOLUTION

Only the collapse of the democratic-republican government and the establishment of absolutism resolved Rome's political and social crises. One politician and general, **Julius Caesar** (b. 100–d. 44 BC), almost succeeded in restoring order. Caesar rose to prominence and popularity as a leader of the *populares* faction. In 62 BC he formed the First Triumvirate, a three-man coalition with two other powerful Romans, Pompey and Crassus. They briefly restored peace to the political system.

Caesar's ambition was to surpass his two partners, who had also gained renown as generals. Pompey already had a solid reputation, having conquered Hellenistic kingdoms in Asia Minor and the province of Judaea, thus bringing the homeland of the Jews into the growing Roman Empire. Crassus achieved fame by crushing a dangerous slave revolt. In 73–71 BC, Spartacus, a free man who had fought in Rome's army only to be enslaved to fight as a gladiator, raised an army of gladiators and other people freed from slavery. Crassus upheld the Roman social order and defeated the slave army. To warn against further rebellion, he crucified more than six thousand captured rebels along the Appian Way. Caesar, in turn, sought to outdo his two colleagues by conquering the Celts in central and northern Gaul.

After their near conquest of Rome in 390 BC, the Gauls had done little to harm the Romans. Since they had no written culture, we know very little about the Celts, except what was written by their enemies (such as the Romans) and as exposed by archaeology. They had beautiful arts and crafts, growing cities, and even wore pants (while Roman men still wore skirts—in the form of tunics and togas). The Romans especially hated the Celtic Druidic religion and exterminated it wherever they could. As so often in religious conflicts, the victors accused their foes of rampant human sacrifices. Celtic merchants, however, readily traded with the Græco-Romans around the Mediterranean, supplying agricultural products and prisoners captured in wars between tribes to be enslaved. Several tribes had even agreed to defense treaties with Rome. When the Helvetii (ancestors of the modern Swiss) tried to move through a territory of a tribe allied with Rome, those Gauls asked for Roman help.

Caesar seized the opportunity to enhance his reputation by expanding Roman dominion (see map 5.1). For eight years, from 59 to 50 BC, Caesar exploited the fighting among different Celtic tribes to conquer Gaul (and even briefly to invade Britain). Nevertheless, many generations were needed to assimilate the Celts into becoming Romans. A few Celtic communities managed to escape the domination of Rome. Survivors with their own language and cultures lived on in Brittany on the Continent and in Devon, Cornwall, and Wales on the island of Great Britain. And Roman power never reached at all into what would become Scotland and Ireland. These small numbers of Celts would contribute a good share to Western civilization in the future.

Meanwhile, Caesar wrote a book about his "successful" conquest, *The Gallic War*, to make sure people recognized his good leadership (and the deserved defeat of the Celts). With his fame established, Caesar turned to his real aim: leadership in Rome. He declared his intentions of becoming sole dictator by leading his army from Gaul into Italy in 49 BC. His crossing of the river Rubicon (now a metaphor for an irrevocable decision) set him at war with his former allies and with the Roman constitution itself. Inevitably, might made right. By 46 BC Caesar had defeated his rivals and become dictator. He built on his success by making an alliance with Egypt, the breadbasket of the Mediterranean. Its queen, Cleopatra VII (r. 51–30 BC), who had been quarreling with her brother over sharing power, became Caesar's lover and ally.

Like the better Greek tyrants, Julius Caesar did not rule solely to satisfy his own lust for power; he also addressed real issues. He carried out land reform, especially by rewarding his army veterans with confiscated property. He extended Roman citizenship to conquered Celtic and Phoenician peoples in Gaul and Hispania (the Iberian Peninsula), improved the administration, lowered taxes, and built public works such as aqueducts, baths, and temples. Caesar's **Julian calendar** reform gave us the basic system that we use now.[1]

Caesar's enemies both envied his success and feared that he might make himself king. The Romans had disliked kingship ever since they had rebelled against Etruscan kings at the beginning of their republic. For some, a monarchy defiled Roman identity, so a handful of senators plotted to assassinate Caesar. In 44 BC, during the ides (the middle of a month) of March, as Caesar entered the Senate's meeting place, they stabbed him twenty-three times.

Yet this political murder still did not resolve the constitutional difficulty of governing Rome. Immediately, civil war broke out over Caesar's legacy, about who could inherit his mantle. Rather than being hailed as heroes who liberated Rome from tyranny, Caesar's assassins became outlaws, quickly discredited and killed. Caesar's lieutenant, Marc Antony, first claimed succession.[2] But Marc Antony had fatefully taken up with Caesar's paramour Cleopatra. Many Romans disapproved of the queen of Egypt, who was too Greek and too female. To prevent civil war, Antony briefly formed the Second Triumvirate with the wealthy patrician Lepidus and with **Octavian**, Caesar's eighteen-year-old grandnephew and posthumously adopted heir. The arrangement did not last long. In the course of several years of warfare, Octavian grew into leadership until he had utterly destroyed all rivals, including Antony and Cleopatra. With this takeover, the last surviving Hellenistic kingdom formed by Alexander's generals ended its independent existence. By 27 BC, Octavian ruled over an empire that came to symbolize Roman greatness. With the civil wars largely ended, the empire entered the period called the Pax Romana—a period of relative peace and prosperity upheld by Roman power.

---

1. The twelve months that we use now were set then, with February shortchanged because of a periodic leap day, which better accounted for the fraction of a day longer than 365 days in an astronomical year. The Romans had not fully settled on a clear beginning of each new year, however. September through December were originally their seventh through tenth months, as their Latin translations indicate. And the Romans honored Julius by renaming the "fifth month" July. When they honored Caesar's nephew with August, poor February lost another day. For more on Caesar's accomplishments, go to http://www.concisewesternciv.com/sources/caesar1.html.

2. Marc Antony and his claim are linked forever with the ironic speech that Shakespeare put in his mouth: "Friends, Romans, countrymen, lend me your ears. I come to bury Caesar, not to praise him."

Octavian replaced the Roman Republic's form of democracy with his own version of autocracy, which historians call the **Principate** (27 BC–AD 284) (see diagram 5.1). The new master of Rome was smart enough not to repeat his late uncle's mistakes. He vigorously professed modesty and a reluctance to assume power. Octavian claimed to restore the order and stability of the old republic and refused the title of king. Instead, he merely accepted the rank of "first citizen" or *princeps* (from which we derive our word *prince*, a powerful ruler, not only the son of a king). The republic's name lived on, since officially the Senate and People of Rome (SPQR) retained their traditional government roles.

Despite his humble platitudes, Octavian actually concentrated all power in his own hands. His actions reveal another basic principle:

> **Sometimes politicians do the exact opposite of what they say they are doing.**

He continued to collect titles and offices, such as consul, tribune, and even *pontifex maximus*, the head priest. To make sure he was not assassinated, he assembled a special group of soldiers to protect his person, the **Praetorian Guard**. The key to Octavian's power was the office of *imperator*, or commander of the armed forces (and from which we derive the word *emperor*). For the common people, Octavian continued the reforming trends begun by Julius Caesar and set standards of behavior and efficiency for the imperial **bureaucracy** (which means administration by officials storing documents and records in bureaus, cupboards with drawers). Even the census called by him was to promote efficient and fair taxation.

Senators authorized the changes that violated the old constitution. Octavian granted to many of them a large share of the empire's wealth, although retaining for himself a larger share of the rule and profits of the overseas provinces. The senators called Octavian the father of the country and granted him the title **Augustus** (r. 31 BC–AD 14), or "honored one," by which he is often known today. Indeed, both his family name of Caesar and his honorific Augustus became synonyms for the word "emperor." Even more, he proclaimed the spirit of his "father" Julius Caesar to be elevated to godhood. As his heir, of course, Augustus shared in some of that divinity. Therefore, Augustus began the process of deification in Rome; the emperors became gods, as important for worship as the old mythological civic gods had been. The Romans thus imitated the "Oriental despots" of Persia, as Alexander also had, harnessing godhood for political stability. And so Augustus became the first Roman emperor; the Republic was a memory.

Augustus's system functioned well, but it possessed one great weakness: it was based on lies. Rome, of course, had been an empire for centuries, based on its widespread rule of many different peoples. The republican labels survived, but the Principate concentrated government in Augustus's hands (see diagram 5.1). Officially, Augustus pretended not to be as powerful as a king or emperor, but everyone knew he was. Since there was officially and legally no emperor, the

Romans lacked a formal process for succession. As a consequence, the emperor's death raised questions of legitimacy.

Members of Augustus's family, called the Julio-Claudian dynasty, used the lack of clarity to assume rule of the empire after his death. Roman historians tell lurid tales of their imperial excesses. Augustus's first heir, Tiberius, almost lost control as he brooded in his sex den on the resort island of Capri while his lieutenant Sejanus gathered power. Just in time, Tiberius had Sejanus, his wife, and their young children bloodily executed. The next emperor, Caligula, was probably insane, believing that he had indeed become a god. Caligula named his horse to be a senator, raped senators' wives, and married his own sister before being murdered by his own Praetorian Guard. Caligula's older uncle Claudius survived to become emperor because until Caligula's death, everyone thought Claudius was a fool. Although Claudius ruled reasonably well, his third wife, Messalina, was a sex maniac, while his fourth, Agrippina, probably poisoned him. Nero, Agrippina's son from a previous marriage, followed as emperor and soon had his helpful mother assassinated. He proclaimed himself the world's greatest actor and forced rich and poor to sit through his awful performances of singing and strumming a lyre.[3] He flamboyantly staged public orgies and capriciously executed many of his generals. After revolts in the provinces, the fed-up Senate ordered him to be stripped naked and flogged to death. Instead, his servant helped him commit suicide with a knife in the throat. Just before he died, he lamented, "Thus perishes a great artist."

Since Nero's death meant that all male heirs in Augustus's dynasty had died, the Romans fought a brief civil war in AD 69, the "year of four emperors." The winner was the new dynasty of the Flavians, who started out well with Vespasian and his elder son Titus. Each ruled briefly, with sense and moderation. Then the younger son Domitian followed. He became so increasingly paranoid and violent that his servants murdered him in AD 96. That Rome did not collapse into anarchy under so many cruel and capricious rulers was a testament to its own vitality and the success of the reforms made by Julius and Augustus Caesar.

The leaders who followed Domitian from AD 96 to 180 have become known as the "Five Good Emperors." They secured Rome's everlasting glory. The great eighteenth-century historian of Rome, Edward Gibbon, credited the greatness of Rome to the wise and virtuous reigns of Nerva, Trajan, Hadrian, Antoninus Pius, and Marcus Aurelius. Under Trajan, Rome's supremacy reached its greatest extension. He conquered and plundered one final major province for Rome, exterminating the people of Dacia north of the Danube River by the Black Sea (see figure 5.3). The Romans who replaced the Dacians laid the foundation of the modern Romanian language.

While Gibbon certainly exaggerated, this golden age of Rome has always been attractive to readers of history. Rome flourished by providing a structure for political peace while allowing substantial cultural freedom. The empire of this period stood for universalism—"all is Rome"—but the emperors did not crush

---

3. He is infamous for "fiddling" while a good part of the city of Rome burned, although he was probably innocent of that bad behavior. He certainly did not play a fiddle, since it had not yet been invented.

Figure 5.3. Trajan's Column presents the victorious Romans holding up heads of the Dacians for their emperor. The province was Rome's last significant conquest.

particularism. People worshipped diverse gods and deities, wore their own ethnic fashions, and ate their exotic cuisine. Their trade network extended to India and China where they bought textiles, spices, and precious stones. The Roman urban culture, fostered by planting colonies of retired Latin soldiers, helped diverse peoples become romanized to various degrees. Previous cultures gradually and peacefully faded as everyone adopted Roman social ways and the responsibilities and benefits of citizenship. While some local ways of life dwindled away altogether, other regional and ethnic diversity remained. The Romans advocated Latin as a language, yet every educated Roman also spoke Greek. Many Greeks, who predominated in the eastern regions of the empire, barely bothered to learn Latin. The protections of Roman law increasingly covered non-Latin speakers as citizens, until virtually everyone born free within the borders of the empire could claim the privilege of Roman citizenship (although it counted more for men than women). Even many enslaved persons had opportunities to win their freedom. Ironically, citizenship no longer meant participation in the most important decisions of government. Those were left to the emperor.

Just outside the empire's borders, though, lived many peoples who did not share in its riches and resented Rome. The Romans had tried to conquer the world in self-defense, but they had not succeeded. Their ability to organize resources and raise armies hit a metaphorical wall. Two of the empire's borders seemed secure. In the far north, much of Great Britain had been brought under the Roman yoke in the first century AD despite sometimes fierce British opposition, such as the rebellion led by Queen Boudica (see Primary Source Project 5). The ferocious Celts called Picts in the island's north did halt Roman advancement. Deciding against expansion into the highlands, Emperor Hadrian built a wall across the island to separate and defend the Roman province from the wild northerners. The Celts on the island of Hibernia (Ireland) were not even considered worth conquering. After all, the free Picts and Irish hardly threatened the empire's interests. Likewise, on the border in the south, the Sahara Desert provided a natural barrier to the rest of Africa. Most of Rome's other borders, however, remained dangerously vulnerable. Slow communications by foot, horseback, or ship meant that responses to emergencies took much too long. The first major threat to the empire's border loomed northward, in the heartland of Europe. There the **Germans** or **Goths** dwelt in dark forests and resisted seizure by Rome. Many Romans categorized the Germans as barbarians, since they did not live in cities. Instead, they remained in loose and quarreling pastoral and agricultural tribes along Rome's central European borders. They sometimes traded and other times raided to gain Rome's luxury goods. In his book *Germania*, the Roman historian Tacitus actually admired the Germans, contrasting their egalitarian lives, enjoying hunting and warfare, with the decadence in Rome (see Primary Source Project 5 and Sources on Families in chapter 7).

During the age of Augustus, a German leader called Arminius (in Latin; Hermann in German) briefly frustrated Roman ambitions. Hermann learned Roman ways from his life as an imperial soldier who rose through the ranks. Back in his homeland, Hermann led his people to ambush and slaughter three Roman legions in the Teutoburg Forest in Germany in AD 9. This defeat seemed so decisive that Augustus and the later Romans refrained from further expansion in that direction. Instead, the Romans built a line of defensive fortifications, the *limes*, along the Rhine and Danube Rivers, trying to defend against repeated raids by bands of unconquered Germans. Emperor Marcus Aurelius led some successful campaigns against the Germans, but the Antonine Plague (AD 165–180), which killed a tenth of the Roman population, limited what he could achieve.

To the east of Mesopotamia, the long-civilized Persians presented the second threat to Rome. In 247 BC, the Parthians, horse-riding archers migrating westward from the Asian steppes, seized most of the Persian Empire from the Seleucid Hellenistic dynasts. By 139 BC they had fully defeated the last Seleucid, leaving him only a rump state around Antioch, itself seized by the Roman general Pompey in 63 BC. Now Rome inherited the Greeks' traditional enemy of the Persians, both desiring the rich Mesopotamian heartland of Middle Eastern civilization. After overcoming stiff Parthian opposition, the Romans occupied much of Mesopotamia by the end of the second century AD. Yet despite many attacks, the Romans failed to conquer Persia, unlike Alexander the Great.

Thus Rome could no longer expand, limited by the Germans in central Europe and the Parthian/Persian Empire in the Middle East. Failure either to defeat or to befriend the Germans and Persians sealed the Romans' doom. Only internal rivalries among both the German tribes and the Parthian elites postponed for a few decades their catastrophic confrontations with Rome.

As the second century AD drew to a close, preservation of the Roman Empire became more urgent than its expansion. First foreign threats and then internal weaknesses brought on crises that threatened to tear the Roman Empire apart, as had almost happened in the civil wars of the first century BC. The office of emperor finally failed to maintain the efficient functioning of the bureaucracy. The Five Good Emperors also did not solve the problem of finding successors. The first four of those five emperors, who had no sons, did implement a policy of "adoption and designation," which showed promise. Each reigning emperor sought out a younger, good, qualified successor and then adopted that person as his heir. This imitation dynasty borrowed the stability of family rule to ensure talented leadership. Tragically, in AD 180, Marcus Aurelius's son, Commodus, inherited the empire from his father. This end to the successful policy of adoption and designation was bad enough, but Commodus's insanity (combining paranoia with the belief that he was Hercules incarnate) was catastrophic. Conspirators had his wrestling partner strangle him, launching a series of briberies, murders, and civil war over who would take the imperial office. Without the plunder from new conquests, defending the borders depleted the treasury. Waves of plague also repeatedly ravaged the empire. The resulting population and tax losses reduced the ability of Rome to recruit and pay for soldiers.

Then, in the late second century, both the Germans and the Persians attacked. Clumsy Roman interventions in Mesopotamia allowed the Persian Sassanian dynasty to replace the weakened Parthian rulers of the Persian Empire and revive its power. The Sassanian-led Persians aggressively pushed the Romans back toward the Mediterranean. Meanwhile, in central Europe, the Germans invaded across the *limes*.

This time when Rome required capable leadership, it had none. Constant violence crippled imperial authority. Just as during the collapsing republic of the second century BC, "barracks emperors" were too busy fighting one another to rule Rome well. Unfortunately for political stability, generals have rarely been successful as politicians. Between 197 and 235, several women named Julia, who were wives and mothers of emperors, were able to bring some stability, but they died in rebellions that overthrew their husbands and sons. Indeed, in the rough century between AD 180 and 284, out of thirty-six emperors, fifteen served less than a year each. Such brief reigns weakened government, as did the manner of their deaths. Only two or three died naturally and peacefully in their beds; the Praetorian Guards, other bodyguards, or their own troops killed most of the others. The "barbarian" Germans actually killed in battle one "civilized" emperor, Decius, and then his son and heir. The Persians captured and enslaved another, Valerian, who became a human footstool for Shah Shapur I. Such humiliations deeply shocked the proud Romans. Even worse, rampaging Germans sacked Roman cities. Emperors tried to cover expenses by minting too many coins, which fed inflation. Around AD 250 and again around 270, plagues killed hundreds of thousands of Romans. Trade suffered, urban life cracked, and citizens turned to local leaders for organization and defense. Many towns hurriedly built walls, believing the far-off emperor could not help. The Roman Empire almost fell apart in the third century AD.

Then, in AD 284, one more general, **Diocletian** (r. 284–305), seized the imperial throne. As the son of a freedman (a bondsman who had been manumitted or emancipated), he had worked his way up through the army ranks and through the rivals for the empire until he stood alone at the top. Fortunately for Rome, Diocletian proved to be a man of rare talent and vision. He created Rome's third system of government, an autocracy that historians call the **Dominate** (284–ca. 650) because it finally recognized the emperor's domination (see diagram 5.1). Diocletian kept only traces of the republican system of citizen rule. Instead, based on the style of "Oriental despots," he wanted his subjects to exalt him as mysterious and semidivine. He reinforced deification and emperor worship. More importantly, he implemented practical solutions for the challenges of good government. He appointed governors to run his administration across double the former number of provinces, and he made them more professional and well paid. He also planted secret informers to report on government abuses. At the same time, the military abandoned the now-outdated legion system. The emperor created a large field army under his direct command. Its heavy cavalry could strike more quickly where needed. Diocletian also strengthened border defenses with more forts.

All these government expenses, especially armies and war, required a great deal of money, so Diocletian raised taxes. To collect sufficient taxes, he needed a good economy. Since inflation seems to ruin good economies, he instituted government controls on wages and prices. Indeed, Diocletian went so far as to make professions hereditary. If a man's father was a soldier, the son soldiered; if the father was a baker, then the son baked. Such restraints were not so burdensome, since before modern times most children followed in their parents' professions. Still, these limitations on economic freedom sparked complaints and did not work as well as hoped, but neither did the economy collapse. By expanding the emperor's absolutism and reducing people's rights, Diocletian lengthened the life of the Roman Empire for centuries. Diocletian's policies show that sometimes the solution is more government, not less.

Diocletian's creative solution to the ongoing problem of regulating the imperial succession also brought mixed results. First, Diocletian recognized that the empire was too difficult for one man to govern, so he divided the empire in half on a north–south line along the western edge of the Balkans. Second, he aimed to revive a form of the adoption and designation policy used by the "Good" emperors in the second century AD. Diocletian ordained four joint rulers called a tetrarchy. For the two halves of the empire, he designated himself and a co-emperor as leaders, each called "Augustus." Each Augustus then designated an assistant, called "Caesar." When the Augustus retired or died, the Caesar would succeed him as Augustus and then designate a new assistant as Caesar. Such a complicated system could not last. Diocletian's successors altered his model of succession, although they largely preserved and expanded his other governmental reforms, including the partitioned empire.

In the year 300, Rome still reigned as one of the great empires of the ancient world. From the Roman Republic through the Principate, Rome's greatness once more seemed secure under the Dominate. Having risen from an obscure city-state, Rome had survived internal political conflict, invasions by external enemies, and success itself. The Romans of course thanked their gods for these triumphs. The new god-emperor Diocletian, however, particularly hated one religious sect, the Christians. These "criminals" refused to recognize his divinity or that of any of the gods of Greece and Rome. Diocletian stepped up persecuting Christians but could not wipe them out. Nevertheless, these survivors of Diocletian's religious intolerance would, surprisingly, be running the empire within only a few years.

Review: *How did key rulers establish order within the Roman Empire?*

Response:

PRIMARY SOURCE PROJECT 5: GALGACUS VERSUS AGRICOLA ABOUT MOTIVATIONS FOR BATTLE

The Roman historian Tacitus reconstructs two speeches offering opposing views of Roman conquest just before the Battle of Mons Graupius (AD 83 or 84) in the north of the island of Great Britain. First, Galgacus, the chief of the Caledonians or Picts, gives his troops reasons to fight. Second, Tacitus's hero, the Roman commander Agricola, encourages his legions. At the end of the day, the Romans won a decisive victory, briefly securing most of the island of Great Britain for the empire.

Source: *The Life of Agricola* by Tacitus (ca. AD 100)

Galgacus

Every time that I look at the reasons we have for fighting, and the fact that we have no choice but to fight, my heart beats high at the thought that this morn, which sees your united hosts assembled, is the dawn of liberty for all Britain. . . .

During the struggles waged in the past by the Britons against the Romans, struggles sometimes lost and sometimes won, we were always in the background as a last hope and resource. No other tribe stands behind us; naught is yonder but the rocks and waves, and the Romans more cruel yet. The plunderers of the world, they have laid waste the land till there is no more left, and now they scour the sea.

If a people are rich they are worth robbing, if poor they are worth enslaving; and not the East and not the West can content their greedy maw. They are the only men in all the world whose lust of conquest makes them find in wealth and in poverty equally tempting baits. To robbery, murder, and outrage they give the lying name of government, and where they make a desert they call it peace.

. . . Cast away, then, all hope of finding mercy, and summon up your courage like men who fight for dear life as well as for love of honor. . . . Do you really imagine that the courage of the Romans in war is equal to their licentiousness in peace? It is our quarrels and our discords that give them their fame, for they turn the faults of their enemies to the glory of their own army, that mongrel army of a mixed multitude of peoples which is only kept together by prosperity, and must assuredly dissolve under defeat. Or can you believe that the Gaul, the German, and the Briton—yes, shame that I must say it! of Britons not a few—are following the standards of Rome from loyalty and love? . . . Fear and dread are the bonds that bind them, bonds all too weak in the place of love.

Break their bonds, and, as their fears vanish, hatred will spring to life. On our side is everything that can spur men on to victory. The Romans have no wives to fire their hearts, no kinsfolk to brand them as cowards if they fly. Most of them are men without a country, or if they have one it is some other than Rome. Few in number, bewildered and lost, they turn their eyes to sky, and sea, and forest, and all alike are strange to them. Verily they are as men fettered and taken in the snare, and thus the gods have delivered them into our hands.

. . . Here before you stand their general and their army; behind them come the tribute, the penal labor in the mines, and all the anguish of slavery, which you must endure forever and ever; or else strike home upon this field today. Remember your fathers, remember your children, and let your last thoughts be of them ere you rush upon the foe.

Agricola

It is now eight years, comrades, that I have shared in your conquests in Britain; conquests due to your loyalty and your devotion, inspired by the valor and the majesty of imperial Rome. Side by side in many a march and many a fight, whether the call was for courage against the foe, or for patient effort to overcome the obstacles offered by nature herself, we have been well content with each other, you and I. We have pushed our way far beyond any point that other generals and other armies have ever reached, and are masters of this extremity of the land, thanks not to our prestige or our reputation, but to our camps and our good swords. You have been the explorers of Britain, you have been its conquerors as well.

. . . In our triumphant advance we have traveled a long, long road, we have threaded forests, and we have forded estuaries, all of which are so many additions to our glory. If we flee now, all these things do but multiply our perils. We have no knowledge of the country, such as our enemies have; we have no means of getting supplies like them; what we have are our swords and our strong arms, and having them we have all things. . . . Death on the field of honor is better than a life of shame; but in our position life and honor go hand in hand, while to fall at the point where the natural world itself comes to an end would be to find a glorious tomb.

. . . As it is, I say count over your own victories and ask your own eyes. Thus, the stoutest-hearted of the Britons have long since bitten the dust; the remainder are but a pack of panic-stricken poltroons.

The reason that at last you find them here in front of you is not that they have turned to bay, but that they are caught in a trap. Their desperate case and their paralyzing fears have nailed them to the spot where they stand, and on that spot you shall show the world the spectacle of a brilliant and memorable victory.

Here make an end to these campaigns. Let fifty years of conquest have their crowning day. Prove to Rome that her army never falters with its work, nor leaves behind it the seeds of fresh rebellions.

Questions:

- *How does each speaker criticize his opponents?*
- *What virtues does each speaker claim for his own side?*
- *What will be the final result of the battle, according to each speaker?*

Responses:

For more on this source, go to http://www.concisewesternciv.com/sources/psc5 .html.

THE ROADS TO KNOWLEDGE

If Rome's greatness had been based only on its ability to conquer, it would have faded as quickly as had the Assyrian Empire. The Romans, though, believed they were civilizers. Their efforts at romanization succeeded in making diverse peoples loyal to the empire. Likewise, they absorbed much from those they ruled over, laying a foundation of classical antique culture that has inspired people through the Middle Ages, into the Renaissance of the fifteenth century, through the Enlightenment, and even into the twenty-first century.

Three hundred years ago, digging Italians struck upon treasure troves of lost history, the buried Roman cities of Herculaneum and Pompeii. In AD 79 the sudden eruption of the nearby volcano Vesuvius entombed both cities. As the earth shook and a dark mushroom cloud filled the sky, many people started to flee toward the sea; others took refuge where they could. Poisonous overheated gas killed many people (see figure 5.4). Hot mud drowned Herculaneum, while fiery ash, cinder, and stone smothered Pompeii. Archaeologists have restored a semblance of the bodies of the dead with gray, rough castings. Their silence still speaks to us of human mortality. Nevertheless, much of the cities themselves and their evidence of the everyday life of the Romans survived. Their art of frescoes, mosaics, and sculptures depicting gods, heroes, and friends; their taverns, villas, and brothels; their gardens, stadiums, and baths; and their utensils, furniture, and jewelry and even graffiti all offer invaluable artifacts to help us appreciate the civilized, urban culture fostered by the Roman Empire at its height.

Figure 5.4. The casts of Romans who died in the eruption of the volcano Vesuvius near Pompeii show their huddled attempt to survive. The molds were made by injecting plaster before excavating into where the bodies had decomposed under volcanic ash.

One of the most important cultural attitudes of the Romans was their appreciation of Hellenistic civilization. From their earliest history, the Romans accepted Greek influences, beginning with the stories of the Olympian gods. Roman polytheism simply renamed and rewrote the Greek gods and their myths (see table 2.1). Ovid's *Metamorphoses* retold many of the amusing, tragic, and bawdy stories about gods and people changing forms. From the Eastern Mediterranean the Romans also imported various mystery cults, as long as their followers did not disturb the peace. **Mithraism** was particularly popular among the soldiers of the legions. This religion believed that the son of the sun god born from a rock on 25 December grew up to slaughter a magical bull to provide fertility for the world, died, was reborn, and served as a mediator between heaven and earth. Mithras's followers (men only) were baptized in blood, celebrated with a common meal of bread and wine, and believed they would attain eternal life. These elements of belief may sound familiar to the followers of Christianity.

The Romans also loved Greek art. Most of the white marble statues of Hercules or Venus we have today are copies made for eager Roman collectors from Greek originals of brightly painted Herakles or Aphrodite. Roman architecture used the Greek styles or orders of columns: Doric, Ionic, and Corinthian (the last especially favored by Roman architects). In their own right, Roman artists developed a particular talent for portraiture. Paintings and busts not only capture unique features but the underlying feelings of their subjects. The Romans pushed much of their artistic effort into propaganda. The impressive temples of the forums, lofty triumphal arches, and noble statues of emperors reminded people in the cities of their rulers.

Not only art, but also Greek literature flourished under Roman rule. As mentioned earlier, every educated Roman learned Greek and often spoke it in everyday life. Most of the populations in the Eastern Mediterranean who spoke Greek as a *lingua franca* before Roman rule continued to do so. The Romans read Herodotus about the Persian Wars and Thucydides about the Peloponnesian Wars. Newer Greek writers found patrons in Rome to support them as they wrote their poetry, history, and science. Plutarch's popular collection of biographies, *Parallel Lives*, compared Greek and Roman heroes and villains. Ptolemy's views on astronomy and Galen's on medicine, translated into Latin, would have a long-lasting influence on the West for more than a thousand years after they wrote. Ptolemy reasoned that the earth was the center of the universe; Galen further developed Hippocrates's theory of humorism and encouraged bloodletting as a useful medical treatment. Much of the "science" they taught has been proven wrong.

The Romans also produced their own literature in Latin. They especially differed from the Greeks in their plays for the theater. Rather than the tragedies preferred by the Greeks, where the violence usually happened offstage, Romans most enjoyed bawdy comedies or violent melodramas, where murder and mayhem were reenacted onstage. Actual killing, of course, happened in the amphitheaters, such as the Colosseum. In rhetoric, or the art of communication, the greatest orator or speechmaker was Cicero, who during the fall of the republic opposed Caesar and was killed by Antony's proscription. His writings provide us with models of rhetorical discourse on the duties of citizens. In the next generation, Vergil's epic poem *The Aeneid*, about the founding of Rome by refugees from the Trojan War, celebrated the virtues of Augustus's Principate. Later historians, such as Suetonius and Tacitus, however, insightfully analyzed both the virtues and the vices of emperors.

The Romans appreciated Greek philosophy, although their favorites were Epicureanism and stoicism. Romans particularly found in stoicism a reflection of their traditional values of following rules, performing one's duty, and doing hard work. The stoic philosopher Seneca's failure to satisfy the emperor Nero led to his dutiful suicide. Emperor Marcus Aurelius himself penned a collection of stoic sayings called the ***Meditations***.

Late in the empire's history, some scholars organized the Roman educational curriculum, which in Latin means a "running path" to follow toward knowledge. They chose seven subjects, called the **seven liberal arts**, which they split into two parts. The first part was the "three roads," or *trivium* (from which we unfairly derive the word *trivial*). These included grammar, rhetoric, and logic. Second was the "four roads," or *quadrivium*, of arithmetic, geometry, music, and astronomy. All seven of these subjects taught the skills (arts) that would enable people to be free (the "liberal" in liberal arts equated to liberty). Later generations in the West would draw on this heritage of Rome to emphasize freedom from the slavery of ignorance.

Actual freedom in Rome, despite the rhetoric, could be quite limited. The economy relied on millions of enslaved persons drawn from diverse peoples both within and without the empire's borders. Female citizens did not enjoy the same status as their male counterparts. Many nations were forced into the empire by conquest, not by choice. The Romans purposefully destroyed the cultures of the Etruscans, Phoenicians, Celts, Dacians, and others; ignored the Germans as barbarians; and opposed the Persians as traditional enemies of Europe. At the height of its creative power, though, the mixed pagan culture of Greece and Rome gained a new, unexpected enemy in Christianity. This religion would claim to offer classical antiquity a new kind of freedom.

Review: *How did the Romans bring together the cultural heritage of classical antiquity?*

Response:

SOURCES ON FAMILIES:
SUETONIUS, *THE TWELVE CAESARS*, AUGUSTUS

Proper marriages and family were an important part of Roman cultural values. The first Roman emperor Augustus does not represent a typical Roman because of his high status and power, but his biographer, the historian Suetonius, appropriately covers issues of marriage and family. In the first section (XXXIV), Suetonius tells how Augustus tried to improve marriage through government regulation. In the second section (LXII–LXV), the story of Augustus's own family problems illustrates how actual lives failed to live up to ideals.

XXXIV. He revised existing laws and enacted some new ones, for example, on extravagance, on adultery and chastity, on bribery, and on the encouragement of marriage among the various classes of citizens. Having made somewhat more stringent changes in the last of these than in the others, he was unable to carry it out because of an open revolt against its provisions, until he had abolished or mitigated a part of the penalties, besides increasing the rewards and allowing a three years' exemption from the obligation to marry after the death of a husband or wife. When the equestrians even then persistently called for its repeal at a public show, he sent for the children of Germanicus [possibly Nero and Caligula] and exhibited them, some in his own lap and some in their father's, intimating by his gestures and expression that they should not refuse to follow that young man's example. And on finding that the spirit of the law was being evaded by betrothal with immature girls and by frequent changes of wives, he shortened the duration of betrothals and set a limit on divorce.

LXII. In his youth he was betrothed to the daughter of Publius Servilius Isauricus, but when he became reconciled with Antonius after their first quarrel, and their troops begged that the rivals be further united by some tie of kinship, he took to wife Antonius's stepdaughter Claudia, daughter of Fulvia . . . although she was barely of marriageable age; but because of a falling out with his mother-in-law Fulvia, he divorced her before they had begun to live together. Shortly after that he married Scribonia, who had been wedded before to two ex-consuls, and was a mother by one of them. He divorced her also, "unable to put up with her shrewish disposition," as he himself writes, and at once took Livia Drusilla from her husband Tiberius Nero, although she was with child at the time; and he loved and esteemed her to the end without a rival.

LXIII. By Scribonia he had a daughter Julia, by Livia no children at all, although he earnestly desired issue. One baby was conceived, but was prematurely born. . . . Augustus, after considering various alliances for a long time, even in the equestrian order, finally chose his stepson Tiberius, obliging him to divorce his wife, who was with child and by whom he was already a father. . . .

LXIV. In bringing up his daughter and his granddaughters he even had them taught spinning and weaving, and he forbade them to say or do anything except openly and such as might be recorded in the household diary [a record of the imperial household, which apparently dated from the time of Augustus]. He was most strict in keeping them from meeting strangers. He taught his grandsons [Gaius and Lucius] reading, swimming, and the other elements of education, for the most part himself, taking special pains to train them to imitate his own handwriting; and he never dined in their company unless they sat beside him on the lowest couch, or made a journey unless they preceded his carriage or rode close by it on either side.

LXV. But at the height of his happiness and his confidence in his family and its training, Fortune proved fickle. He found the two Julias, his daughter and granddaughter, guilty of every form of vice, and banished them. He lost Gaius and Lucius within the span of eighteen months. He then publicly adopted his third grand-son Agrippa and at the same time his stepson Tiberius by a bill passed in the assembly of the curiae; but he soon disowned Agrippa because of his low tastes and violent temper. . . . He bore the death of his kin with far more resignation than their misconduct . . . and for very shame would meet no one for a long time, and even thought of putting [the elder Julia] to death. At all events, when one of her confidantes, a freedwoman called Phoebe, hanged herself at about that same time, he said: "I would rather have been Phoebe's father." After Julia was banished, he denied her the use of wine and every form of luxury, and would not allow any man, bond or free, to come near her without his permission, and then not without being informed of his stature, complexion, and even of any marks or scars upon his body. . . . But he could not by any means be prevailed on to recall her altogether, and when the Roman people several times interceded for her and urgently pressed their suit, he in open assembly called upon the gods to curse them with like daughters and like wives. He would not allow the child born to his granddaughter Julia after her sentence to be recognized or reared. [A]t every mention of [Agrippa] and of the Julias he would sigh deeply and even cry out: "Would that I ne'er had wedded and would I had died without offspring" [a quote from *The Iliad* III.40]; and he never alluded to them except as his three boils and his three ulcers.

Questions:

- *What policies does Augustus institute to promote families and children?*
- *How does Augustus's own family history compare to his official policies?*
- *What do Augustus's problems with his own family indicate about how families can be challenging?*

Responses:

Make your own timeline.

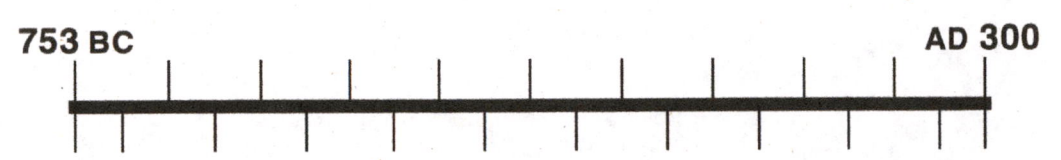

753 BC   **AD 300**

For more on this source, go to http://www.concisewesternciv.com/sources/sof5 .html.

CHAPTER 6

The Revolutionary Rabbi

Christianity, the Roman Empire, and Islam, 4 BC to AD 1453

While Augustus was sorting out his new imperial government, in one small part of his empire called Palestine many Jews resented Roman rule. A handful of them soon began an obscure cult that later grew into the major religion called *Christianity*. From its insignificant beginnings among a few believers in Judaea, this new faith triumphed over the whole Roman Empire, becoming an essential part of Western civilization.

THE SON OF MAN

Christianity started with Yeshua (or Joshua, meaning "Yahweh is salvation") ben Joseph of Nazareth. He has since become better known by the Latinized version of his name: **Jesus Christ**. The Yeshua of history became the Jesus of religion. Later myths settled the date of his birth on 25 December, the year 1 "of the Year of the Lord" (AD, or in Latin, *anno Domini*). According to the best modern historians, Jesus was actually born in the springtime in one of the years between 7 and 4 BC.[1] As mentioned in the first chapter, medieval historians considered the appearance of Jesus in this world important enough to create the major dividing point in the calculation of the history of the universe, between BC ("Before Christ") and AD.

Historically, Yeshua lived and died a Jew. The **Gospels** ("Good News") are the only surviving descriptions of his life, written years later. The nominal authors of these stories, Matthew, Mark, Luke, and John, were probably not those named in the Gospels themselves as Yeshua's disciples. His followers (and, later, the leaders of Jewish communities) called him by the title "rabbi," which meant "teacher" or "master." His ministry, which lasted just a few years, consisted of preaching to large crowds, teaching to a smaller group of disciples, and sending out apostles to convert and heal others in Yeshua's name. These Gospels did not always clearly

---

1. Roughly five hundred years after Christ's birth, the medieval monk Dennis Exiguus ("the Short" or "the Humble") miscalculated his proposed year Anno Domini 1 for Jesus's birth, at least according to modern scholars.

reveal Yeshua's teachings, complicating all interpretations about him ever since. Yeshua often used challenging parables to illustrate his teachings and did not propose a systematic set of principles. Therefore, much of what we know about Jesus Christ has to be taken on faith, not facts.

Still, some general trends are observable. Yeshua criticized the Jewish religious establishment of his day and other diverse Jewish groups such as Pharisees, Sadducees, Zealots, and Essenes. He taught that people were to repent of their faults or sins to prepare properly for the Kingdom of God. Our life in this world determined our place in the next world, after death. The life after death, the Kingdom of God, was far more important than treasures accumulated in this worldly existence. People were to love God and their neighbor (including their enemies and foreigners). Yeshua constantly emphasized moral action and repentance of sin over strictly following the letter of the Jewish religious laws. He criticized the rich, wanted to help the poor, and preached pacifism and forgiveness. According to the Gospels, he worked miracles (especially healing the sick and exorcising demons) to confirm and reinforce his mission.

During his three years of ministry, Yeshua generally avoided trouble with the Roman Empire ("Give to the emperors the things that are the emperors', and to God the things that are God's," Mark 12:17). About the year AD 27, certain Jewish leaders who feared that Yeshua wanted to overthrow their system put pressure on the local Roman imperial governor, Pontius Pilate. He convicted Jesus of treason on an alleged claim to be the king of the Jews. Instead of resisting, Yeshua surrendered himself to death and ended up more powerful than ever. Pilate had Yeshua executed in the same way as the Romans did many other condemned criminals: crucifixion. The victims of crucifixion were nailed alive to a large cross and hung on it until dehydration, hunger, exhaustion, or suffocation finally killed them in a painful ordeal that was designed to last for days.

After Yeshua's execution by the Romans, his followers claimed that Jesus "the Christ" was resurrected in a new body—that he physically became alive again and walked the earth until he ascended into heaven. Belief in resurrections was not unusual in those times (indeed, Yeshua is recorded as himself raising several people from the dead). Regardless of any debate about the truth of the resurrection, belief in it encouraged his followers. They multiplied from a small, persecuted group of Jews to a force that changed the course of Roman history.

"Who exactly was Jesus?" was the first question faced by his followers after Jesus's departure from this world. During his lifetime, he referred to himself most often as the "Son of Man," but that term's meaning is unclear. A few times he is recorded as using the name "Anointed One" ("**Messiah**" in Hebrew or "Christ" from the Greek). The concept of the Messiah was a recurring theme in Jewish thought at the time. Many Jews in the first century were awaiting a savior who would rescue them from the troubles of this world. Jewish believers disagreed upon the exact manner of salvation, but they most often imagined a warrior-king. While Jesus certainly did not fit that view, Christians soon considered him to be much more than the Messiah. According to two of the Gospels, Jesus had a human as a mother and God as a father—but what does that actually mean? What is Jesus's connection to God and vice versa? These questions challenged the first Christians and still confuse many Christians today.

His followers' explanation about who Jesus was took four centuries to work itself out. They had to decide what was **orthodoxy**, the genuine position supported by most of tradition, and what was **heresy**, a belief close to, but rejected by, the religious authorities. A large group eventually identified as heretics held to **Gnosticism**. Gnostics believed in secret knowledge that emphasized dualism, considering Jesus's human aspects as bad but his divine as good. Christian leaders eventually concluded that Jesus was not merely the Christ, or the Son of God; Jesus was God, incarnate, in the flesh, divine and human at the same time. Christians asserted that the Trinity of God the Father, God the Son, and God the Holy Spirit has ordained a universe where people live and die. After death, humans could end up in either one of two places: righteous Christians who believed in Jesus's resurrection and behaved morally would be saved to spend eternity in blissful unity with God in heaven; sinners would be forever damned to hell, surmised as a place of horrible suffering.

In coming to these conclusions about Jesus, the Christians worked their way through available sources. It took until the fourth century for orthodox Christians to agree that their Bible (which means "book") would include, and only include, the Hebrew scriptures as an Old Testament and a **New Testament** of the four Gospels, the Acts of the Apostles, twenty-one letters (epistles), and an apocalyptic text (about the future end of this world). Some writers who brilliantly expounded on the faith during the first few centuries of Christianity came to be called Church Fathers. They often took the role of apologists, which meant defending Christian viewpoints against those of Judaism, ancient philosophies, and mystery cults. Other writings, such as the Gospels of Thomas or of Mary Magdalene, were excluded, banned, and destroyed as heretical misinformation.

Another early action of the Christians was to assemble themselves into an institution called the "Church" (capitalized to distinguish between the body of believers and a specific building). While all baptized Christians could be considered members of the Church, selected people became the organization's leaders and administrators. Many Christians accepted the idea of **apostolic succession**, the belief that those whom Jesus had charged with his mission could pass on that authority to others, one to the next, and they, in turn, to still others (see figure 6.1). Thus began a distinction between the laity (normal Christians) and the **secular clergy** (Church officials). Overseers (later evolving into **bishops**) began to manage elders (priests) and servers (deacons). Soon each bishop had a special church called a cathedral (from the Latin for the "bishop's chair") from which he administered a territory called a diocese (or a see, or a bishopric). Church **councils**, starting with the first major one described in the Acts of the Apostles, brought the Christian leaders together to debate and resolve important controversies (guided, they believed, by the Holy Spirit).

Through these discussions and interpretations of the scriptures, the Church leaders established several methods to help people in their earthly pilgrimage toward heaven. The Church taught that grace (God's gift of salvation) could be

Figure 6.1.   A graffito in Rome of an early priest shows him standing behind an altar, his arms raised in prayer (and perhaps the presence of the Holy Spirit in the form of a bird).

obtained through the beliefs, sacraments, and ceremonies of Christian worship. Centuries later, the "Western Church" eventually settled on seven sacraments or holy acts important on the earthly path. First, ***baptism***, performed on all infants, initiated involvement in church life. In the sacrament of reconciliation, one was supposed to confess one's sins and be absolved before the most important regular sacrament, the **Eucharist**, also called Communion or the mass. Like many religious services in a variety of cultures, the mass involved a performance with processions, prayers, readings, songs, and a sermon, which culminated in a sacred meal. For most people it became the custom to attend mass on Sunday morning, which the Christians turned into their Lord's Day, replacing as their day of worship the Jewish Sabbath (sundown Friday to sundown Saturday). Young people underwent confirmation, recommitting themselves to vows made in their name as babies. As an adult, one might be married or be ordained into holy orders of priests or monastics. Last, extreme unction (or last rites), a final blessing at the time of death, carried one into the afterlife (although nowadays it has become more commonly an anointing of the sick).

The sacraments became so important that the Church could threaten anyone who strayed from the proper orthodox path with ***excommunication***. That punishment excluded a sinner from the sacraments until he or she asked for forgiveness. The average person rarely worried about excommunication, though. The beliefs and rituals of Christianity did relieve some of the daily grind of life and the fear of death. The Christian calendar of the seven-day week, ending with a day of worship and rest, combined with various holidays (holy days) such as Easter (the day of Christ's resurrection) or Pentecost (fifty days later, when the Holy Spirit entered Christ's followers), increasingly shaped the living patterns of Christian society for the next few centuries.

In these early formative centuries, Christianity did not appear fully organized and obvious. The Christian Church rose from discussions and controversy among believers. The early Christians disagreed with one another over what Jesus actually taught, either about morality and behavior or about authority and obedience. Some of these distinctions also derived from the languages believers used to interpret scripture. The Old Testament was written in Hebrew and the New Testament in Greek, with little bits of Aramaic in each part. As Christians translated and argued in Latin, Coptic, Syriac, Armenian, and other languages, misunderstandings multiplied. These same problems confront Christians today, who have splintered into many different denominations. The solution to these questions was even more difficult in antiquity because the early Christians lived within a culture that was hostile to them.

Review: *How did the new religion of Christianity begin and define itself?*

Response:

SOURCES ON FAMILIES:
PAUL, FIRST EPISTLE TO TIMOTHY (AD 65–150)

Early Christians called for family values that were different from those of contemporary pagans. The First Epistle to Timothy touches on issues of morality and marriage, especially for the new leaders of bishops and deacons. Although attributed to Paul of Tarsus, many scholars argue that the I Timothy letter was written by a follower using his name, decades after the apostle's death. Either way, many modern Christians use these verses to assign roles and determine policies for both men and women.

. . . But we know that the law is good, if a man use it lawfully;

Knowing this, that the law is not made for a righteous man, but for the lawless and disobedient, for the ungodly and for sinners, for unholy and profane, parricides and matricides, for manslayers, for whoremongers, for them that defile themselves with mankind [*arsenokoitai*],[2] for kidnappers, for liars, for perjured persons, and if there be any other thing that is contrary to sound doctrine; according to the glorious gospel of the blessed God, which was committed to my trust. . . .

I want, therefore, that men pray everywhere, lifting up holy hands, without wrath and doubting.

In like manner also, that women adorn themselves in modest apparel, with shamefacedness and sobriety; not with braided hair, or gold, or pearls, or costly array; but (which becomes women professing godliness) with good works.

Let the woman learn in silence with all subjection. But I suffer not a woman to teach, nor to usurp authority over the man, but to be in silence. For Adam was first formed, then Eve. And Adam was not deceived, but the woman being deceived was in the transgression. Notwithstanding she shall be saved in childbearing, if they continue in faith and charity and holiness with sobriety.

This is a true saying, if a man desire the office of a bishop, he desires a good work. A bishop then must be blameless, the husband of one wife, vigilant, sober, of good behavior, given to hospitality, apt to teach; not given to wine, no striker, not greedy; but patient, not a brawler, not covetous; one that rules well his own house, having his children in subjection with all gravity. (For if a man know not how to rule his own house, how shall he take care of the church of God?) Not a novice, lest being lifted up with pride he fall into the condemnation of the devil. . . .

Likewise must the deacons be grave, not double-tongued, not given to much wine, not greedy; holding the mystery of the faith in a pure conscience. And let these also first be proved; then let them use the office of a deacon, being found blameless. Even so must their wives be grave, not slanderers, sober, faithful in all things. Let the deacons be the husbands of one wife, ruling their children and their own houses well. . . .

Now the Spirit speaks expressly, that in the latter times some shall depart from the faith, giving heed to seducing spirits, and doctrines of devils; speaking lies in hypocrisy; having their conscience seared with a hot iron; forbidding to marry, and commanding to abstain from meats, which God hath created to be received with thanksgiving of them which believe and know the truth. For every creature of God is good, and nothing to be refused, if it be received with thanksgiving: For it is sanctified by the word of God and prayer. . . .

Rebuke not an elder, but treat him as a father; and the younger men as brethren. The elder women as mothers; the younger as sisters, with all purity.

Honor widows that are widows indeed. But if any widow have children or nephews, let them learn first to show piety at home, and to support their parents: for that is good and acceptable before God. Now she that is a widow indeed, and desolate, trusts in God and continues in supplications and prayers night and day. But she that lives in pleasure is dead while she lives. . . .

But if any provide not for his own, and specially for those of his own house, he has denied the faith, and is worse than an unbeliever. Let not a widow be taken into the membership under sixty years old, having been the wife of only

---

2. About the difficulty in translating the word *arsenokoitai*, see http://www.concisewest ernciv.com/sources/sof6.html.

one man, well reported of for good works; if she have brought up children, if she have lodged strangers, if she have washed the saints' feet, if she have relieved the afflicted, if she have diligently followed every good work.

But the younger widows refuse: for when they have begun to wax wanton against Christ, they will marry, earning damnation, because they have cast off their first faith. And at the same time they learn to be idle, wandering about from house to house; and not only idle, but tattlers also and busybodies, speaking things which they ought not.

I intend, therefore, that the younger women marry, bear children, guide the house, give no occasion for opponents to speak reproachfully. For some are already turned aside toward Satan.

If any man or woman who is a believer has widowed relatives, let them care for them, and let not the church be obligated, so that it can care for those who are really widows. . . .

Questions:

- *What specific restrictions are suggested for women as opposed to men?*
- *What standards in marriage are outlined for bishops and deacons?*
- *Why should the early Church have been so concerned about who was a deserving widow?*

Responses:

For more on this source, go to http://www.concisewesternciv.com/sources/sof6.html.

THE CULTURAL WAR

Not surprisingly, the Jews were the first to attack the Christians, who had all originally been Jewish. From Judaism the Christians had adapted the key belief system regarding Jesus as Messiah and God. For the Jews, however, Christianity was heresy. Many hostile Jews had Christians arrested or stoned to death. Foremost among the persecutors was Saul of Tarsus. Then, on the road from Jerusalem to Damascus one day, Saul claimed to have had a vision of Jesus and converted to Christianity. He changed his name to **Paul of Tarsus** and became one of the leading apostles.

Encouraged by Paul's missionary work among the Gentiles (non-Jews) of Asia Minor and Greece, Christians took a decisive step away from Judaism when they opened up Christianity as a universal religion. While theoretically anyone could convert to Judaism, Jews tended to emphasize ethnic inheritance. In contrast, Christians abandoned obligations to many of the Jewish dietary rules and other restrictive laws to make their faith more hospitable to Gentiles. Unlike the Jews, Christians regularly used syncretism, adapting foreign customs to Christian practices, such as replacing pagan holidays with Christian ones. For example, Church authorities chose 25 December as the date for Christmas because it could replace popular pagan festivals of the winter solstice. Indeed, almost anyone could easily become a Christian, even among socially disadvantaged groups such as women, the poor, outcasts, and bond servants. Women even took on leadership roles as patrons, deacons, and apostles in the early Church. The Christian message of love and the example of charity attracted many who found little interest in kindness and caring within the practices of other ancient religions and philosophies.

Christianity quickly spread outward from Palestine, whether to Jewish communities of the Diaspora or directly into the hellenized and Roman towns and cities of antiquity. At first, Christianity was an urban religion, as opposed to ancient polytheism, which became known as either *paganism* (after the word for farmers) or *heathenism* (after those who live on uncultivated land). As a belief system, Christianity offered something different from other civic religions, mystery cults, and schools of philosophy, which were all sanctioned and supported by the state. The official myth-based religions were too empty of fervor, the mystery cults were too exclusive and secretive, and philosophy was too intellectually challenging. In comparison, Christianity offered a relatively simple and open religion of passion, available to all, Greek or Roman, rich or poor, male or female, enslaved or free.

The Roman Empire, however, did not make life easy for Christians. By the first century AD, the Romans had unified their vast and diverse empire through a state religion based on sacrifices to the gods of Rome, including their deified emperors. We do not know how sincerely they believed in the reality of these gods. And they were relatively tolerant of people holding any number of philosophical or religious beliefs. Nevertheless, the Romans insisted that only diligent sacrifices prevented the gods from punishing the state with destruction. The government labeled as a traitor anyone who refused to support the state through ritual civic sacrifice. Thus, all citizens and subjects were obligated to acknowledge the Græco-Roman gods through a simple act, usually burning incense or sacrificing a bird on an altar. Christians, however, refused to perform even such superficial rites (see the Primary Source Project).

In the view of the imperial authorities, that refusal made Christianity a crime. As explained in chapter 3, the Jews, who regarded such actions as idolatry, were exempted from performing this sacrifice since their beliefs predated Rome's founding. In contrast, the Romans considered that since Christianity had been founded within living memory, it deserved no special exemption. Some emperors and magistrates therefore persecuted the Christians by arresting and punishing them in various creative ways. Christians were sold for use as enslaved miners, forced to become temple prostitutes, beheaded, or even ripped apart at gladiatorial games by wild animals. Christians who suffered death for the sake of faith were believed to become **martyrs** and immediately enter heaven.[3]

Fortunately for the Christians, these persecutions failed to destroy the faith, because the Roman emperors could neither apply enough pressure nor maintain the scope of hunting down Christians for very long. The Christians were able to outlast the attention span and strength of the most powerful rulers in the ancient world. Also, the noble death of so many Christians inspired many Romans to consider Christianity more seriously. Still, by AD 300, Christians had not convinced a large number of Romans to convert. Christians probably made up only 10 percent of the empire's population then.

In the fourth century AD, Emperor **Constantine** (r. 306–337) suddenly decriminalized Christians. His father had become an Augustus in Diocletian's system of imperial succession (see figure 6.2). But the system of four emperors did not work.

Figure 6.2.   Statues of four Roman emperors, two *augusti* and two *caesares*, cling to one another as they try to hold the empire together.

---

3. In case you wondered, no one can choose martyrdom; it has to be forced on a person. Thus Christians were not allowed to simply walk up to Romans and announce their faith, hoping to be executed and thus become martyrs.

Figure 6.3.   The colossal face of Emperor Constantine stares into the future.

The co-rulers just made war on each other, fighting to come out on top. Constantine's troops proclaimed him an imperial successor upon his father's death in AD 306 (see figure 6.3). Over the next few years, Constantine successfully defeated all other claimants, seizing the imperial supremacy for himself.

As the sole Roman emperor, Constantine continued the strong imperial government revitalized by Diocletian, adding three improvements of his own. First, he solved the question of succession by creating an old-fashioned dynasty. A son (or sons in the divided empire) would inherit from the father. While this system had the usual flaw of dynasties (both that heirs might not be competent and that sons and cousins might still fight over the throne), bloodlines limited the claimants to within the imperial family rather than allowing legions to proclaim ambitious generals. Second, Constantine built a new capital for the eastern half of the administratively divided empire. He chose the location of the Greek city of Byzantion, situated on the Bosphorus, the entrance from the Aegean to the Black Sea. Strategically, it was an excellent choice: close to key trade routes, in the heart of the vital Greek population, and easily defensible. He modestly named the new capital after himself, **Constantinople**.

Constantine's third improvement reversed Diocletian's religious policy of exterminating all Christians. Instead, Constantine decided to help them. As the story went, Constantine was fighting against a rival who was a great persecutor of Christians. Constantine had a vision and a dream of the Christian symbol of the *labarum* (similar to the letter *P* with a crossbar) in the sun (which held a special connection to his family as a patron deity). He won victory over the imperial rival under this sign in a battle at the Milvian Bridge, just to the north of Rome. Although Constantine himself probably remained a pagan until his death, the victorious emperor ordered all of the empire to tolerate Christians by issuing the **Edict of Milan** in 313. This law reinforced a previous Edict of Toleration of two years earlier. In this edict, the Christians were exempted from making sacrifices to the emperors. After 313, Christians in the Roman Empire were no longer criminals because of their faith.

Beyond simply tolerating the Christians, Constantine showered his imperial largesse upon them. He favored them with land and buildings. The design of the new public Christian churches was based on imperial meeting halls called basilicas. Constantine bestowed special privileges on Christians, such as rights of self-government and exemptions from imperial services. He probably thought Christianity, which had proved so resistant to persecution, could help the empire through its prayers and zeal. Overnight, Christianity had moved from being the illegal counterculture to representing the establishment.

Saints served as new role models for Christian society, since without persecution, martyrs became a rarity. Originally, a saint referred to any faithful Christian. Over time, the term *saint* became restricted to those who both lived the virtuous life in this world and proved their divine connection by working miracles after their death. Saints' lives became meaningful not only in stories but also in their physical remains. The faithful believed that parts of saints' bodies or objects associated with them channeled divine power to work miracles long after the saint's death. The relics of specific saints preserved in and around altars often gave churches their names. For example, the grill on which Saint Lawrence was roasted and the headless body of Saint Agnes reside at their respective churches located outside the walls of ancient Rome. New churches began to be built openly in great numbers to hold all the recent converts.

In one of those amazing ironies of history, just when they reached social acceptance, Christians began to attack one another. Uncertainty raised by Gnostics about the combined humanity and divinity of Jesus burst out into the open. These conflicts threatened Constantine's aim for Christianity to provide stability, so he called the **Council of Nicaea** in 325 to help the Church settle the matter. The majority of church leaders decided on the formula that Jesus was simultaneously fully God and fully human, embedding this idea and other basic beliefs into the Nicene Creed, which is still professed in many Christian churches today. That creed became catholic orthodoxy (the universally held, genuine beliefs). The large majority believed along catholic (universal) orthodox (genuine) lines. Orthodox catholics labeled those who disagreed with them as heretics, no longer Christian.

Another large group of heretics, the Arians, remained unconvinced about Jesus's complete combination of divinity and humanity.[4] They continued to spread their version of the faith and tried to convince the majority to change its mind. Over the next few decades, they even convinced emperors to switch sides. They also succeeded in converting many Germans along and beyond the borders of the Roman Empire to their version of the Christian faith. For a long time, heretical *Arianism* looked as if it would become the orthodox faith. The Christian leadership, however, remained convinced that the Holy Spirit worked through them. They converted, persecuted, exiled, or even executed the heretics. By the sixth century, only a few Arian Christians survived in the empire, although many, called Nestorians, spread their version of Christ throughout Asia.

With their new political power, many Christians turned toward antisemitism or hating Jews. Under Roman rule, the Jews had legally maintained their distinct religion and avoided completely assimilating. And Judaism was the undoubted foundation for Christianity, as recognized by the inclusion of Hebrew scripture as the Old Testament of the Bible. Nominal excuses for inflamed hostility ranged from blaming Jews for killing Christ, through disliking Jewish refusal to recognize their truth of Jesus as the Messiah, to resenting Jewish religious obligations that the Christians had rejected. Other untrue reasons included blaming the Jews for plague or for committing ritual murders. Whatever the excuses, increasingly over the centuries Christians passed laws restricting Jewish civil rights. Christians limited Jews to certain occupations, had them confined in ghettoes, forced them to convert or emigrate, or simply killed them. Even if many Christians respected the Jews, even recognizing them as God's chosen people, intolerance and discrimination remained the dominant policy for many centuries.

Besides deciding on orthodox beliefs and how to relate to the Jews, early Christians needed to resolve their attitude toward Græco-Roman culture, which dominated the Roman Empire during the centuries after Christ. With the famous question, "What has Athens to do with Jerusalem?" some Christians attacked and wanted to reject the classical heritage. Indeed, Christianity threatened to wipe out much of Græco-Roman civilization, even through violence. Many Christians thought that pagans like Socrates, Plato, or Aristotle had little of value to say to the followers of Jesus Christ. What could the histories of Herodotus or Thucydides possibly teach those who followed the greater history of the Hebrew people, the apostles, and the saints?

---

4. Arians take their name from one of their important theologians, Arius. They are not to be confused with "Aryans." That term is a racist-tinged and outdated concept describing European ancestors who originated in India (see chapter 13).

When Christianity became the sole legal religion of the Roman Empire in 380, the government banned paganism and many of its works. Christians toppled temples and shrines, chopped down sacred groves, shredded and burned classical literature, shut philosophical schools that had been started by Plato and Aristotle, silenced oracles, halted gladiatorial contests, and abolished the Olympic Games. A Christian mob murdered the mathematician and polytheist philosopher Hypatia by cutting her down with shards of pottery in the middle of a public street. The murderers and instigators of her death (who may have included the bishop) went unpunished.

Eventually, however, the Christian Church embraced much from classical antiquity. This attitude was an important milestone in the West's cultural development, perhaps the most important. If narrow-minded zealots had won this culture war, Church leaders might have only gazed inward at the Gospels and focused on the Kingdom of Heaven alone. Such *anti-intellectualism*, or rejecting human rationalism and empiricism by educated people, would have stagnated civilization. To this day, some Christians still condemn knowledge that does not fit in with their view of what is godly. Instead, a majority of Christian scholars usually embraced *intellectualism*, requiring advanced education for its leaders. Christianity partly succeeded because it compromised with the secular world and opened itself up to the voices of polytheist others. In doing so, Christianity adapted and prospered in unexpected ways over the centuries and eventually spread around the world. Before that could happen, however, barbarians almost wiped out this newly Christian civilization.

Review: How did conflicts among the Jews, Christians, and pagans lead to the Romans creating a new cultural landscape?

Response:

PRIMARY SOURCE PROJECT 6: PAUL VERSUS PLINY AND TRAJAN ABOUT THE VALUE OF CHRISTIANITY

Christianity offered new ways of believing in and experiencing the supernatural divine. The first source witnesses the apostle Paul of Tarsus preaching at the Areopagus (Mars' Hill), where the Athenians held their trials. The second source is an

*exchange of letters between Pliny the Younger (Gaius Plinius Caecilius Secundus)
and the Roman emperor Trajan. As governor of Bithynia-Pontus (in northern Asia
Minor, along the Black Sea), Pliny often sought the advice of his superior. This particular exchange provides some of the earliest evidence of Roman attitudes about
the new Christian faith.*

Source 1: Sermon at the Areopagus from the Acts of the Apostles (ca. AD 90)

Now while Paul waited for them at Athens, his spirit was stirred in him, when
he saw the city wholly given to idolatry. Therefore, he disputed in the synagogue
with the Jews, and with the devout persons, and in the market daily with them
that were there. Then certain philosophers of the Epicureans, and of the Stoics,
encountered him. And some said, "What will this babbler say?" Others said, "He
seems to be a setter forth of strange gods," because he preached to them Jesus
and the resurrection.

And they took him, and brought him to the Areopagus, saying, "May we know
what is this new doctrine of which you speak? For you bring certain strange things
to our ears: we would know therefore what these things mean." (For all the Athenians and foreigners which were there spent their time in nothing else, but telling
or hearing about new things.)

Then Paul stood in the midst of Mars' Hill, and said, "You men of Athens, I
perceive that in all things you are too superstitious. For as I walked around and
beheld your devotions, I found an altar with this inscription: 'TO THE UNKNOWN GOD.'
Whom you ignorantly worship there, Him I declare unto you. God that made the
world and all things therein, seeing that He is Lord of heaven and earth, He dwells
not in temples made with hands. Neither is He worshipped with men's hands, as
though he needed anything, seeing as He gives to all life and breath and all things.
And He has made from one ancestor all nations of men to dwell on the face of
the earth, and has determined the times of their lives, and the bounds of their
habitation. Thus they should seek the Lord, so that perhaps they might seek after
Him, and find Him, though He is not far from every one of us: 'For in Him we live,
and move, and have our being'; as certain also of your own poets have said, 'For
we are also His offspring.'

"Forasmuch as we are the offspring of God, we ought not to think that the
Godhead is like gold, or silver, or stone, graven by art and man's device. And God
winked at such times of ignorance; but now commands all men everywhere to
repent: Because He has appointed a day, in the which He will judge the world in
righteousness by that man whom He had ordained; whereof He has given assurance to all men, in that He has raised him from the dead."

And when they heard of the resurrection of the dead, some mocked: and others said, "We will hear you again on this matter." So, Paul departed from among
them. Yet certain men clung to him, and believed, including Dionysius the Are-
opagite, a woman named Damaris, and others with them.

Source 2: Letters by Pliny the Younger and Trajan (ca. AD 112)

Pliny the Younger to Emperor Trajan

It is my custom, lord, to refer to you all things concerning which I am in doubt. For who can better guide my indecision or enlighten my ignorance?

I have never taken part in the trials of Christians: hence I do not know for what crime or to what extent it is customary to punish or investigate. Meanwhile I have followed this procedure in the case of those who have been brought before me as Christians. I asked them whether they were Christians a second and a third time with threats of punishment; I questioned those who confessed; I ordered those who were obstinate to be executed. For I did not doubt that, whatever it was that they confessed, their stubbornness and inflexible obstinacy ought certainly to be punished. There were others of similar madness, who because they were Roman citizens, I have noted for sending to Rome.

Soon, . . . more cases arose. Those who denied that they were or had been Christians, ought, I thought, to be dismissed since they repeated after me a prayer to the gods and made supplication with incense and wine to your image and since besides they cursed Christ, not one of which things, they say, those who are really Christians can be compelled to do. . . .

[Christians] continued to maintain that . . . on a fixed day, they used to come together before daylight and sing by turns a hymn to Christ as a god; and that they bound themselves by oath, not for some crime, but that they would not commit robbery, theft, or adultery, that they would not betray a trust or refuse to repay a debt when called upon. After this it was their custom to disperse and to come together again to partake of food, of an ordinary and harmless kind; however, even this they ceased to do after the publication of my edict, in which according to your command, I had forbidden secret associations. Hence, I believed it necessary to examine two female slaves, who were called ministers, in order to find out what was true, and to do it by torture. I found nothing but a vicious, extravagant superstition.

Consequently I postponed the examination and make haste to consult you. . . . For many of all ages, of every rank, and even of both sexes are and will be called into danger. The infection of superstition has not only spread to the cities, but even to the villages and country districts. It seems possible to stop it and bring about a reform. It is clear that the temples, which had been almost deserted, have begun to be frequented again, that the sacred rites, which had been neglected for a long time, have begun to be restored, and that sacrificial animals, for which until now there was scarcely a purchaser, are being sold. From this, one may readily imagine that a great many people can be reclaimed if penitence is permitted.

Trajan's Reply

You have followed the correct procedure, my Secundus, in conducting the cases of those who were accused before you as Christians, for no general rule can be laid down as a set form. They ought not to be sought out; if they are brought before you and convicted, they ought to be punished; with the exception that he who denies that he is a Christian, and proves this by making supplication to our gods . . . shall secure pardon through penitence. No attention should be paid to anonymous charges, for they afford a bad precedent and are not worthy of our age.

Questions:

- *How does the structure of each source serve to carry its message?*
- *How does Paul use Græco-Roman culture to make his point?*
- *What is the most important result desired by the Roman government officials?*

Responses:

For more on these sources, go to http://www.concisewesternciv.com/sources/psc6 .html.

ROMA DELENDA EST

In another of those amazing ironies of history, just after Christians vanquished the Roman religions, invading Germans triumphed over the Roman armies. In AD 410, an army of the Visigoths (western Germans) invaded Italy and sacked Rome, the first time barbarians had attacked the city since the Celts had done so eight centuries before, in 390 BC. The Visigoth army then marched on to plunder other regions while more Germanic peoples crossed the weakened imperial borders. It seemed the Roman curse "Carthago delenda est" (Carthage must be destroyed) had come back against Rome itself. Many Romans who had not been thoroughly Christianized, still believing in the old gods, naturally blamed the Christians for this catastrophe. They accused Christians of having offended the Olympian gods, who then had withdrawn their heavenly protection. Calamities seemed a sure sign of divine wrath, as people often still believe in our own time.

To answer this charge against the Christians, Bishop **Augustine** of Hippo (d. AD 430) wrote the book *The City of God*. This book defended Christianity by presenting Augustine's view of God's working in history. Augustine said that people were divided into two groups who dwelt in metaphysical cities: those who lived for God and were bound for heaven and those who resided in this world and were doomed to hell. Every political state, such as the Roman Empire, contained both kinds of people. While Rome had been useful to help Christianity flourish, whether it fell or not was probably in the end irrelevant to God's plan. This argument emphasized the separation of church and state. God sanctioned no state, not even a Christian Roman Empire. Instead, individuals ought to live as faithful Christians, even while the so-called barbarians attacked. Indeed, shortly after Augustine's death, Germanic armies destroyed the city over which he was bishop, Hippo, near ancient Carthage.

How did the Germanic tribes and their allies come to conquer Hippo and so many other cities of the Roman Empire? Historians have proposed a number of explanations, some better than others. Reasons such as the poisoning of the Roman elites by lead water pipes are silly. It is likewise absurd, as some cultural critics do, to blame the fall of Rome on ungodly moral corruption. When it fell, Rome was as Christian and moral a state as there ever could be. The Christians, such as Bishop Augustine, were in control. Many Romans may have been imperfect sinners, but a closer cooperation of church and state could hardly be imagined. Despite this, the great historian of the fall of Rome, Edward Gibbon, blamed much of the Roman collapse on this rise of Christianity, saying that its values of **pacifism** undermined Rome's warrior spirit. Pacifists protested war, taking seriously Jesus's criticism of people who "live by the sword" and his title as Prince of Peace. According to Gibbon, the conflicts among orthodox Christians, heretic Arians, and lingering pagans also weakened the empire. Modern historians embrace neither Augustine's nor Gibbon's explanations.

The better explanations of Rome's fall focus on its economic troubles, which remained unsolved by imperial mandates. First, more plagues had reduced the numbers of Roman citizens. Rome was no longer strong enough to conquer and exploit new provinces. No expansion meant that taxes at home burdened the smaller population.

Second, the shortage of revenues also meant smaller armies. Therefore, the Romans began to recruit the unconquered Germanic peoples living on their borders, inviting them to settle inside imperial borders as groups classified as *foederati* or legal tribes. Yet troop levels still fell short despite the German reinforcements. Transfers of warriors from one part of the border to another left gaps in the defenses. The Roman superiority in strategy could not make up for the lack of manpower.

Imperial armies soon depended on these inexpensive barbarians to defend Rome from other barbarians. The *foederati* Germanic immigrants never became as integrated or romanized into Roman society as had other earlier-conquered peoples. As the Goths, for instance, increased their power and influence, they tended rather to barbarize the Romans, preferring their systems of politics based on personal relationships rather than written laws. Here, as with the Greeks, changes in military structures affected politics and society. Nevertheless, the Romans still stood a good chance of defending the empire against the outsider Germanic tribes and peoples, who had no serious reason to launch major assaults.

The military situation changed, however, when the **Huns**, nomadic pony-riding archers from the steppes of Central Asia, swept into Europe in the early fifth century. The impetus for this migration may have been drought in their traditional lands. The Huns reputedly slaughtered most people in their path, drank blood and ate babies, and enslaved the few survivors. Actually, they absorbed many tribes of various peoples along the way, especially the Iranian Alans, becoming a multiethnic but effective invading multitude. The terrified Germanic peoples in eastern and northern Europe fled from the Huns in the only direction possible: into the Roman Empire. Most historians think they entered as refugees, with the elderly, the women, and the young, as well as the warriors. Thus, these movements are sometimes called the **Germanic barbarian migrations**. Far from being uncountable hordes, the newcomers were comparatively few, each tribe numbering only in the tens of thousands. Even after they had moved into the Roman Empire, the Germanic tribes and nations themselves remained in flux. Under inspired warrior kings, the tribes absorbed and re-formed as different groups melded together or fell apart. Some tribes remained a force for decades or even centuries, while others broke up and rapidly re-formed with different tribes and nations. What changed history was the German migrants taking over the rule of Rome in the western half of the Roman Empire.

The transfer of power began when the group called Visigoths by later historians crossed imperial boundaries, with permission, in AD 376. The combined tribes of Thervingi, Greuthungi, and Alans (those who had not joined the Huns) wanted to settle down and be farmers. But two years of quarrels with corrupt imperial authorities culminated in the Battle of Adrianople where the Visigoths crushed the Roman army and killed the reckless eastern emperor Valens. Since the subsequent Roman emperors and commanders were both inexperienced and unwilling to risk another battle, the Visigoths briefly settled along the Danube. But pressure from plundering raids by the Huns continued to push more Goths against the borders, threatening both Romans and the Visigoths. A new Visigothic leader, Alaric, led his people across the empire looking for a permanent place to settle. As mentioned before, the Visigothic army carried out the sack of Rome in AD 410 after the Romans refused to negotiate about a homeland for them. Alaric died shortly after, but within a few years, the Visigoths had settled down into a kingdom that straddled the Pyrenees from the south of Gaul into Hispania, or the Iberian Peninsula.

Worse was to come. More barbarians poured across Rome's once well-defended borders. A frozen Rhine River allowed large numbers of Alans, Alemanni, Suebi, and Vandals simply to walk into Roman Gaul on the last night of December AD 406. The Vandals fought their way through the Franks, who were already setting up a claim to eastern and northern Gaul, then passed through the Visigothic kingdom, crossed the Mediterranean, and finally conquered North Africa (including Carthage and Augustine's Hippo) for a kingdom of their own. From there, the Vandals carried out one of the worst sacks of Rome in AD 455, lending their name to the word *vandalism*. By then Rome had left Britain defenseless by withdrawing troops to the mainland. As a result, Angles, Saxons, and Jutes sailed across the North Sea in the mid-fifth century. They conquered the island, despite a defense by a leader who later became known as the legendary King Arthur.

Finally, the long-feared Huns moved into the empire itself. Actually, they turned out to be not quite as monstrous as the tales spread about them. They were just one more collection of peoples seeking a place to live and grabbing as much power as they could. The Romans even negotiated with the Huns, surrendering territory along the Danube and paying tribute to them rather than fighting. For a time, it seemed that the leader of the Huns, Attila (r. 445–453), could conquer the Roman Empire. But when his Huns raided west into Gaul in 451 and south into Italy in 452, Roman legions allied with Germanic war bands defeated their common foe.[5] The allied Romans and Germans held off Hunnic conquest. The following year, Attila died of a nosebleed on his wedding night to his (perhaps) seventh bride. After Attila's unexpected death, no competent ruler followed. The Hunnic Empire dissolved, and the Huns disappeared as a people, retreating back to Asia or blending in among the diverse new Europeans.

Instead of a Roman recovery, the so-called **Germanic barbarian kingdoms** became supreme throughout western Europe. German chieftains and kings soon finished off the Roman imperial administration in the West. In AD 476, Odavacar (or Odoaker), the commander of Gothic and Roman armies, seized power by toppling the last emperor in the western half of the Roman Empire.[6] He declared himself king of Italy. This unwarranted deposition annoyed the current Roman emperor in the east, so he commissioned the Ostrogoths (eastern Germans) under their king Theodoric to attack Italy on his behalf. After several years of warfare, Odavacar surrendered. The victorious Theodoric assassinated Odavacar at dinner and then proclaimed himself ruler, backed up by his Ostrogothic warriors. Theodoric (r. 493–526) ruled with little restriction over an Ostrogothic kingdom in the Italian Peninsula and beyond. Although he remained a heretical Arian Christian, he tried to forge a society that tolerated religious and ethnic differences among Romans and Germans.

The western half of the Roman Empire fell because its armies could not defend it. What must not be forgotten, however, the Roman Empire continued for another thousand years. The barbarians' feet had trampled only the western portion of the empire. The eastern half continued to fight on and to preserve Roman civilization. For centuries the new capital of Constantinople was one of the greatest cities in the world. Later historians have designated that part of the Roman Empire as **Byzantium** or the **Byzantine Empire**, named after the Greek city Byzantion that Constantine had made his capital. The emperors maintained their roles as protector and promoter of the Christian Church, in the tradition of Constantine. Historians call this cooperation between imperial and ecclesiastical leaders *caesaro-papism*.

---

5. A popular legend says that the bishop of Rome, called Pope Leo, singlehandedly convinced Attila to turn back from another sack of the former Roman capital.

6. The last emperor had the myth-rich name of Romulus Augustus, which evoked the founder of Rome and the founder of the Principate government. Critical contemporaries added as an insult the suffix *-ulus* (meaning small) for the teenager who was a puppet of his father, Orestes. Roman leadership had become so weak that Orestes had been the commander of Roman armies in Gaul, despite being a German (Pannonian) who had worked with Attila. Orestes and his troops had toppled the previous Roman emperor in Ravenna only one year before Romulus Augustulus's own fall.

A "sacred" emperor appointed the bishops who worked with the unified Christian state. After the fall of the western half of the Roman Empire, the eastern half increasingly took on a Greek flavor, since ethnic Greeks filled all the leadership positions. Once more the Greeks ruled a powerful political empire.

The reign of **Emperor Justinian** (r. 527–565) marked the transition from the ancient Roman Empire to the medieval Byzantine Empire. Justinian has been considered both the last emperor of Rome and the first Byzantine emperor. He had several notable achievements. First, he ordered to be built in Constantinople one of the greatest churches of the world, the Hagia Sophia (Holy Wisdom) (see figure 6.4). Second, he had the old Roman laws reorganized into the Book of Civil Laws, often called the **Justinian Code**. This legal handbook not only secured the authority of Byzantine emperors for centuries to come; it also helped the West rebuild its governments after the twelfth century (see chapter 8).

Justinian's attempt to restore the Imperium Romanum in the west was less successful. His armies, led by brilliant generals such as Belisarius and Narses, managed some reconquests, including the Vandal kingdom in North Africa and much of the Ostrogothic kingdom in the Italian Peninsula. These victories notwithstanding, Byzantine intrigues at the court undermined the generals. Even worse were natural disasters. Volcanic eruptions far away clouded the atmosphere

Figure 6.4. Justinian's Hagia Sophia, the Church of Holy Wisdom, rose over Constantinople at the emperor's command. The minarets were added later, when it was converted into a mosque after the fall of the Byzantine Empire in 1453. Until recently it had been secularized as a museum, but is a mosque again.

with dust, producing climate change of a "year without summer." A "mini ice age" lasting a century and a half followed, with lower temperatures, a shorter growing season, and too much rain. Perhaps helped by the bad weather, a killer pandemic arrived in the empire from Asia. This "Justinian Plague," probably the bubonic plague, may have killed half the population of Constantinople alone and ravaged rural populations as well. The eastern empire barely survived, much less having the resources and power to hold on to the old western provinces of Rome. Shortly after Emperor Justinian's death, most of Italy fell back under the control of squabbling German kings. From then on, the German kings ignored Constantinople, and Byzantium ignored them right back.

Despite the shared inheritance of Greece and Rome, the Byzantine Empire increasingly shifted its interests to the Balkans and the Middle East, which had been part of the Roman Empire, and to eastern Europe which had not. The territory of the former Hunnic Empire was soon filled by two new peoples. The pony-riding archer Avars held the Danubian plains for several hundred years. They perhaps introduced the stirrup to Europeans. Another new people, the **Slavs**, invaded as well. Their diverse splinter groups settled from the Baltic Sea coast down through the Balkans after the collapse of the Hunnic and Avar Empires. For a time, so many of the Slavs were captured and sold in slave markets that a new word for "slave" in many European languages derived from their name. By the eighth century, missionaries from the Byzantine Empire had converted most of the Slavs in the Balkans to Christianity. The Cyrillic alphabet, modeled on Greek letters, became the written script of many southern Slavs.

But the Byzantine Empire still had to fight to gain direct rule over these Balkan Christians. For example, Emperor Basil II, the "Bulgar Slayer" (r. 976–1025), expanded dominion over the Albanians, Serbs, and Bulgars (an Asiatic people who had blended with some Slavs). Basil earned his harsh nickname not only by killing many Bulgarians in battle but also by allegedly blinding thousands of Bulgarian prisoners before sending them home. While the Byzantines enjoyed some success in dominating Slavic Serbs, and Bulgars, they would have more trouble with an unforeseen new civilization springing from the deserts of Arabia.

Review: How did the Roman Empire fall in the west, yet not in the east?

Response:

STRUGGLE FOR THE REALM OF SUBMISSION

The sudden rise of the Islamic civilization in the seventh century surprised every-one. The new religion of **Islam** (which means "submission" in Arabic) worshipped the same omnipotent God as Judaism and Christianity. All three are called the Abrahamic religions, since Abraham and his God figured in the scriptures of each. Islam originated in Arabia, an arid peninsula that had so far largely remained out-side the political domination of major civilizations. Muhammad (b. ca. 570–d. 632), an Arab merchant from Mecca, became Islam's founder and final prophet. At about the age of forty, he claimed that the angel Gabriel revealed to him the message of God (called Allah in Arabic).

He recorded these revelations in the Qur'an (meaning "Recitation"), the book containing the essentials of Islam. The tenets of Islam are usually summed up as five "pillars." The first is *shahadah*, the simple proclamation of faith that there is no God except Allah and that Muhammad is his last prophet. Second is *salat*, praying five times a day (at the beginning of the day, noon, afternoon, sunset, and before bed, always on one's knees and facing toward Mecca, whether in a mosque or not). Third is *zakat*, the obligation to pay alms to care for the poor. Fourth is *sawm*, to fast from sunrise to sunset every day during the lunar month of Rama-dan. Last is a pilgrimage (*hajj*) to Mecca that should be undertaken once in one's lifetime, if one can afford it. Everyone who keeps these pillars is a Muslim and is promised eternal life in paradise after death.

Other issues such as polygamy and restrictions on food and alcohol were less important but were added to the discipline of submission to divine commands. Islam was syncretic: it combined the Arabs' polytheistic religion centered on the moon (hence the crescent symbol), the Persian dualism of Zoroastrianism, a con-nection with Judaism via Abraham as a common ancestor, and even a recognition of Jesus as a prophet (although not God incarnate). Islamic scholars over the next decades developed rules of behavior or sets of laws called *shari'a*, based on their interpretation of what Muhammad wrote in the Qur'an.

Most in Mecca refused to believe in Muhammad's calls for submission to God's commands. In AD 622 he fled Mecca to a nearby city. The residents of his home-town had refused to listen to him. That flight (*Hegira* or *Hijra*) marks the found-ing year of the calendar still used today in Islam, namely 1 AH, from the Latin *anno Hegirae* (in the year of the flight). The place of his refuge became known as "the City of the Prophet," or Medina. There he successfully won converts called **Muslims**. His followers soon launched a series of conquests, starting with Mecca, to force their neighbors' submission to the commands of God's prophet.

The meaning of the term applied to these assaults, *jihad*, ranges from a "strug-gle" to a Muslim version of holy war. Clearly, his followers interpreted Muham-mad's message to mean that Islamic submission to Allah should reign everywhere. When peaceful, voluntary conversions failed, the alternative was war to establish political supremacy over non-Muslims. By the time of his death, Muhammad ruled over much of Arabia. His successors went on to conquer a third of what had been the Roman Empire (from the Iberian Peninsula, across North Africa, and over Palestine and Mesopotamia), as well as the Persian Empire. Within a hundred years of Muhammad's death, Muslim armies had won territories from the Atlantic Ocean to southern Asia and into the Indian subcontinent.

The Muslim conquest succeeded for several reasons. First, the fanaticism and skill of the nomadic Arab warriors from the desert overwhelmed many armies fighting for uninspiring emperors and kings. Second, the Eastern Roman/Byzantine Empire and the Sassanid Persian Empire had both exhausted themselves from their long and inconclusive wars over Mesopotamia. Third, many Muslim rulers were tolerant of the religious diversity among their new subjects. So long as Muslims ruled, they did not force those who believed in the same God to fully convert. Muslim rulers usually allowed Jews and Christians to keep their lives and their religions, burdening them only with paying extra taxes. So, while many individuals may have converted to Islam, the Christian, Jewish, and even Zoroastrian communities endured for centuries within Muslim states. Polytheistic adherents faced greater challenges.

Through their conquests, Arabs became a new cultural contender. Islam's domination of the Iberian Peninsula, North Africa, and Mesopotamia prevented those former areas of the Roman Empire from participating in developments in the rest of the West. Instead, the Muslims took the shared Græco-Roman heritage in another direction. Within their territories, the new Arab rulers carried out their own *islamization*, encouraging the faith and practices of Islam, as well as *arabization*, promoting Arabic culture and language among their new subjects. Since the faithful were supposed to read the Qur'an in the original language in which it was written, namely Arabic, most educated Muslims learned to read that language. In much of Mesopotamia and North Africa, Arabic became the dominant language, replacing the Greek, Latin, Coptic, Syriac, Aramaic, and other languages of the conquered peoples. Only in Persia did the natives resist linguistic conversion, although the Persians, henceforth called Iranians, shared their own rich civilized heritage with their fellow Muslims.

Islamic civilization drew on what the Greeks and Romans had united, adding in Iranian and other cultures. While Roman cities in western Europe crumbled under barbarian neglect, Muslim cities blossomed with learning and sophistication. They had paved streets and plumbing. Although their religion prohibited pictures and sculptures of people, Islamic civilization created impressive public buildings, especially mosques with lofty domes and towering minarets, decorated with elaborate calligraphy, patterns, and color. Communities of scholars studied in libraries both the Qur'an and other sources of knowledge. Some Muslims became Sufis, exploring the religious experience through *mysticism*, the idea that people can attain a direct experience with God. Philosophers expanded the fields of metaphysics, medicine, mathematics, and science. Al-Khwarizmi, for example, popularized "Arabic" numbers, which had been invented in non-Muslim India. His name is remembered today through the words *algebra* and *algorithm*. In commerce, merchants with their luxury goods of silks, ceramics, and spices ventured far into Asia and Africa, by land and by sea, to bargain and trade. Muslim pilgrims traveled hundreds of miles within the Muslim-Arabic Empire in safety.

This Arabic Empire surpassed Alexander's in size and civilization. Unfortunately for Islam, it did not last much longer. Muhammad and the Qur'an left little guidance about who should lead the Muslim community after Muhammad's death. Muslims split over the issue of Muhammad's successor, called the caliph (meaning "successor"), the ultimate judge in all matters political or religious. The vast majority of Muslims, or the Sunni (meaning "traditional"), were willing to accept any respectable dynasty, whether established in Medina, Damascus, Baghdad, Cairo, or Istanbul (as they were). Hence, Sunnis were open to competing rulers and political divisions. A minority, the Shia or Shi'i (meaning "sect"), thought the heirs of Muhammad's family (beginning with his cousin and son-in-law Ali) should unite all Muslims in Dar al-Islam (the realm of Submission to God). The death in battle of Muhammad's grandson and Ali's son, Hussein, in AD 680 (61 AH) sealed the breach in Islam. Shiites began seeking a holy figure, the Imam, who would miraculously unite Muslims again someday. Besides these ongoing disagreements between Shiites and Sunnis, ethnic differences among converted Arabs, Berbers, Egyptians, Mesopotamians, Iranians, and others also weakened solidarity and loyalty toward any one united empire. Islam thus lost its political unity and has been unable to regain it ever since.

In addition to internal fighting, Islam faced hostile borders with Christians in western Europe and in the Byzantine Empire. In particular, the Byzantine Empire successfully fended off multiple Muslim onslaughts, helped by "Greek fire," a liquid spray that burned sailors and ships, even on water. Although the Byzantine emperors lost substantial territory south of Asia Minor to Muslims, they managed a few compensatory gains over the southern Slavs in the Balkan Peninsula.

If the Roman Empire had survived intact or if the attempted Muslim conquest of Europe had succeeded, the West as we know it would never have existed. Civilization would have had a very different geographic foundation, centered, like the Roman Empire, on the Mediterranean. Byzantium or Islam could have bound western Europe together with the Balkans, North Africa, and the Middle East.

Instead, the collapse of Roman power in western Europe, combined with the rise and fall of the Byzantine and various Muslim empires, meant that eastern Europe, Africa, and Asia remained outside the main development of Western civilization for the next thousand years or more. In their regions of the former united Roman Empire, the Orthodox Christian Byzantine Empire and the various Muslim realms directly inherited a rich Græco-Roman culture of classical antiquity. Yet the Byzantines and Muslims flourished on the other side of a cultural divide that arose after the Germanic conquest of the western portion of the Roman Empire. Only in western Europe did various elements of Græco-Roman, Judeo-Christian, and Germanic cultures meld through many difficult centuries to become Western civilization.

Review: *How did Islam rise as a rival civilization?*

Response:

Make your own timeline.

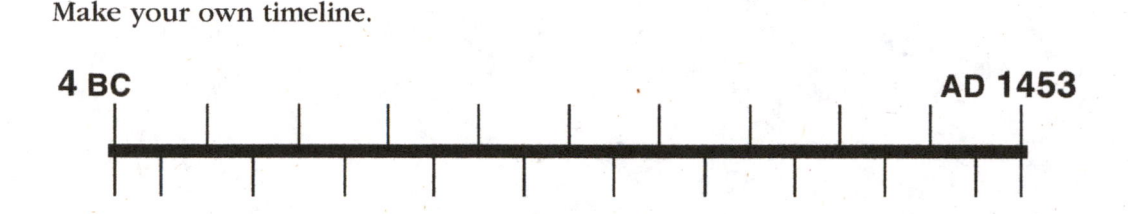

CHAPTER 7

From Old Rome to the New West

The Early Middle Ages, AD 500 to 1000

The collapse of the western half of the Roman Empire during the fifth century AD marked the end of "ancient" history and the beginning of "medieval" history (see timeline B). The intellectuals after the fifteenth century who coined the term *Middle Ages* (whose Latin form provides *medieval*) saw the thousand years of history between classical antiquity and their own (early modern) day as one horrible detour for civilization. For the intellectuals of the so-called Renaissance (see chapter 9), the previous thousand years seemed simply barbaric when compared to the glories of Greece and Rome. Even today, *medieval* often describes something backward, vicious, or stupid. These meanings do not actually reflect the full historical truth. Rather, much improved over the course of the Middle Ages, even if Europe's wealth and power lagged behind the civilizations in Asia. The term *medieval* does not really apply to history there. India saw the beginning of Islamic conquests and conversions, and a variety of new states arose in South and Southeast Asia. Chinese civilization flourished in a "golden age," despite changes in dynasties, while Japan asserted its independence. Nevertheless, for western Europe, modern historians divide the thousand years between AD 500 and 1500 into three medieval periods (early, high or central, and later), hence the use of the plural *Middle Ages*. First came the **early Middle Ages** (about 450–1050), during which Europe rebuilt after the collapse of Rome (see map 7.1).[1] During these centuries, three main cultures (Græco-Roman, Christian, and Germanic) wove together to give birth to and nurture the creative childhood of Western civilization.

GOTHS IN THE GARDEN

The Germans or Goths had dismantled the western half of the Roman Empire where they settled. To the remnants of Rome's Christianized Græco-Roman civilization,

---

1. If you noticed that the dates differ between the chapter headline and this sentence, good for you! Historians disagree about when exactly these time periods began or ended—there is no easily identifiable big event (like a war or a leader's death) to mark them.

Map 7.1. Dark Ages Europe. How was the former Roman cultural area divided up?

the new political masters added their Germanic culture. Like the term *medieval*, the Renaissance humanist admirers of classical antiquity applied the term *Gothic* as an insult describing the medieval period. "Barbarians" had ruined Roman civilization. Likewise, art historians denigrated the art and architecture of the High and later Middle Ages with the term *Gothic*. They preferred the svelte Corinthian columns and bleached-white calm nudes of antiquity to the pointed arches and the polychrome tortured crucifixions of late medieval art. In contrast, educated medieval people who noticed the difference between their own times and the ancient world often saw themselves much as we refer to ourselves: "modern."

The illiterate Germanic leaders of the new so-called barbarian kingdoms who replaced the officials of imperial Rome left few written records. Thus, the first few centuries after the fall of Rome might justifiably be called the **Dark Ages**. We are indeed in the dark about much that happened. Sadly, the term *Dark Ages* also too often insults the entire Middle Ages as being full of ignorance, cruelty, and superstition.

Although the Germans were uncivilized, they had not intended to destroy all the benefits of civilization. Rome's wealth and comforts were attractive. German regimes clumsily tried to continue the Roman system, but barbarians simply did not know how to manage urban life. They feared and avoided cities. Thus, towns lost populations, sports stadiums sat empty, libraries crumbled, and forums gave way to farmland. Much was lost just from neglect. Ancient technology, such as water mills and glassmaking, went forgotten. Until the new ruling elites learned the ways of civilization, the West lapsed into primitive rural conditions.

The barbarian conquest resulted in two large ethnic groups living side by side, the ruling Germans and the former Romans. The German kings took the best land for themselves. They preferred woodland and field for hunting and farming. Germanic lords lived in manor halls (large structures that housed warriors and dependents) situated in small villages throughout the countryside. The conquered Roman population often became servile dependents, working for the German warriors in charge. Actual slavery in western Europe slowly declined, since the uncivilized Germans were satisfied with peasants as workers rather than humans as property.

The Germans themselves were diverse, as shown by the numerous names of the peoples invading the western half of the Roman Empire: Visigoths (made up of Tervingi, Greuthungi, and some Asiatic Alans), Ostrogoths (who had freed themselves from the Huns), Vandals, Alemanni, Suebi, Franks (divided into Ripuarians and Salians), Angles, Saxons, Jutes, Gepids, Frisians, Batavians, Heruli, Rugians, Scirians, Burgundians, Bavarians, Thuringians, and Lombards. Some were not even distantly related to Germans, as other peoples entering Europe from Asia attached themselves to successful leaders. Constant warfare left some groups so weak that they either quickly joined a new ethnic conglomeration or disappeared altogether. The various tribes spoke in many different dialects and accents, each almost incomprehensible to the others. In western Europe they separated into many petty realms, regularly trying to conquer one another.

Within the borders of the old empire (except in Britain and near the Rhine and Danube Rivers), the Germans were actually an ethnic minority. Gradually, they stopped speaking their German language and adopted the ever-evolving language of the Romans. Thus, Latin slowly turned into vernacular "Romance" languages: Spanish and Italian (named after Roman geography) and French (named after the Germanic Franks). Over centuries, the distinctive German character of the ruling class also disappeared as they intermarried with the Roman descendants.

The Germans did not comprehend the Roman government with its ideas of laws and citizenship and the concept that only the government could use violence. Instead, Germanic rule was based on blood and oath. They thought of justice as personal rather than state controlled. Instead of loyalty to some distant ruler, impersonal regime, or abstract deity (whether the gods of Rome or the person of the emperor), Germans saw themselves connected to one another through ties of kinship. These bonds ranged from the nuclear family of parents and children to extended families, clans, tribes, "folk," and, finally, to the king as father of all. Kings as war leaders bound their warriors with oaths to dedicate their lives to fight for him. A Roman government built on an impersonal system of laws switched to German kinship of blood relations and personal oaths. Under this system, families preferred to take justice into their own hands, avenging wrongs by punishing wrongdoers themselves. So, if one family member was robbed, other family members hunted down the robber and exacted retribution (usually death, of course).

Thus, the natural tendency to want to punish those who had wronged oneself soon escalated into larger confrontations. For example, a robber killed in vengeance probably had a family of his own who did not take kindly to his death, so they would take justice into their own hands. After his family members killed the killers, yet another round of reciprocal vengeance might bring on vendettas or **feuds**. Families became trapped in escalating cycles of violence against one another. The German kings and lords tried to prevent feuds through *wergild* (literally "man gold," or having guilty parties pay families money in compensation for injuries or robberies). When guilt or innocence was still in doubt, the barbarians resorted to **trials by ordeal** instead of Roman criminal court procedures. Trial by combat pitted accuser and accused, or their champions, against one another. One typical ordeal, that of hot iron, required the accused to carry a red-hot metal bar for nine paces without dropping it. The burned hands would then be wrapped. If after three days the wounds were healing, the accused was innocent; if they festered with infection, the accused was guilty and subsequently hanged. The Germans believed that their Christian God guaranteed a just outcome.

Indeed, the Christian Church itself was the greatest institution to survive Rome's collapse in western Europe. Its institutions and beliefs helped to sustain whatever remained of civilization. By the time the Germans invaded Rome, many of them had already been converted to Christianity by missionaries. The invaders were usually respectful of holy places. The network of Christian bishops in the dioceses that had coexisted with Roman imperial provinces continued uninterrupted in many places. The Christian order, however, was somewhat complicated by the heretical Arian form of Christianity advocated by many of the ruling Germans. The Church managed only slowly to bring many Germans into catholic orthodoxy.

This new Christian society built on the ruins of the Roman Empire often defined itself as a universal realm of **Christendom**. Serious divisions throughout the Middle Ages, however, prevented Christendom from ever becoming more than a dream. Rivalries between rulers remained more powerful than cooperation toward a Christian commonwealth. Religious unity also suffered as a rift grew between west and east: Latin-speaking Christians in the kingdoms of western Europe versus Greek-speaking Christians in the eastern Byzantine Empire. In addition, kings in western Europe would soon be fighting with their own bishops and with the bishop of Rome over leadership. The idea of Christendom during the Middle Ages remained attractive but unrealized.

The troubles of the age led some Christians to withdraw from worldly cares so that they could better concentrate on God. This new way of life, called *monasticism*, organized a few people to bind themselves under strict rules. The monastic movement had already begun in the late Roman Empire, as some Christians in the East imitated Jesus's wanderings in the wilderness and isolated themselves to live as hermits. As this isolationist ideology migrated to the West, religious leaders instead promoted cenobitic, or group, monasticism. Its participants, communities of monks led by an abbot (or, for females, nuns under an abbess), gathered together apart from the bustling world to dedicate their life to prayer and meditation.

In the 520s, Benedict of Nursia became a most influential abbot when he set up the monastery of Monte Cassino in southern Italy. To guide his flock of monks, Benedict wrote down a set of rules or regulations for this special life-style. While life under the **Benedictine Rule** was not unduly harsh, it was not particularly comfortable either. The abbot (or abbess) exercised parental author-ity in leading monks (or nuns) in a life of work and prayer. Their basic princi-ple was *asceticism*, choosing to avoid material comforts and sensual pleasures. They came together daily to sing psalms eight times a day, from before dawn to long after sunset. They were to have no possessions, with limited clothing, food, and drink (see the Primary Source Project). They spent their days farming and, perhaps most important for the future of civilization, reading books. Under the Benedictine Rule, monks and nuns read the pagan classics of Greece and Rome in addition to the Bible and spiritual writings of the Church Fathers. They laboriously copied these texts by hand onto parchment bound into books, thus preserving much of the literature of the ancients in their small libraries. For a while, monasteries were isolated islands of learning in a sea of barbaric illiteracy. The only real progress in medieval medicine was the study of herbal remedies by monks and nuns. In time, these islands of learning would provide fertilizer and seed for the regrowth of civilization.

The rise of monasticism divided the ecclesiastical ministers into two groups: monks and nuns, known as **"regular" clergy** (those clerics guided by regulations and isolated from lay communities), separated from the previously established "secular" clergy (bishops and priests involved in the world). Of the two, monastics were the role models of the early Middle Ages for the laity as well as the rest of the population of lords and peasants. Cloisters seemed to create a heavenly com-munity here on earth. The lay magnates and lords who wanted to support monas-tical work donated land to them or sent their extra children (whose inheritance or dowry might drain the family landholdings) to join the cloistered communities. Even the roughest sinner, when he felt death's hand upon his neck, might join a monastery, renounce the world, and partake in a blessed community that seemed a sure path toward paradise.

It is unclear how much the secular and regular clergy succeeded at making the values of Christianity real in Christendom. Some bishops never abandoned the customs of the noble families from which they came (again, see the Primary Source Project). Kings and their Christian warriors continued to exert horrific vio-lence to defend and extend their power. Various kingdoms briefly rose in power, only to soon vanish into history. The Ostrogoths fell to the Lombards; the Visig-oths and Vandals to the Saracens; many to the Franks.

Ethnic differences, though, left traces in the *regionalism* that still flourishes in many provinces of Europe today. European regions inherited their diversity both from the peoples, such as Gauls and Celts, earlier romanized to varying degrees after Roman conquest, and from *germanization* following the new Ger-man conquerors. The integration and assimilation of former Roman citizens and enslaved workers with the new German warriors progressed slowly over centuries. The unified regime of Rome with its culture of Christian and Græco-Roman citizens under an emperor had been replaced by numerous kings who saw themselves and their peoples as more divided than united by their German ancestries. And on the fringes, realms of Celts (Picts, Irish, Bretons), Basques, Scandinavians, and Slavs were consolidating. The Jews also remained a barely tolerated minority. They lived scattered through the decaying cities, keeping their culture relatively segregated and intact as usual.

As an exception to this diversity, only two large groups of Germans who had invaded the Roman Empire rose to dominate these early medieval centuries and provide the political and social framework for Western civilization: the Anglo-Saxons and the Franks. Interestingly, both of these German peoples had entered the Roman Empire as pagans (not as Arian heretics, like many other Germans).

The name of the **Anglo-Saxons** reflects members of several different tribes, mostly Angles, Saxons, and Jutes, who invaded the island of Great Britain from across the North Sea beginning around 450. Since the Roman military had largely withdrawn from the island decades earlier, the Romano-Britons were easily overrun (although some trace of native resistance may be seen in the myths of King Arthur). By the sixth century, the Germans ruled most of the formerly Roman areas of Britain, except for the western fringes of Cornwall and Wales. The Picts who dwelt in the northern third of the island, beyond Hadrian's Wall, fought off the Anglo-Saxons, just as they had the Romans. These people soon became the Scots of Scotland, closely tied to the Irish of Ireland (who had likewise never been conquered by Rome, although they had been converted to Christianity by the Briton missionary Patrick and others in the fifth century). In the southern two-thirds of Great Britain, though, the Anglo-Saxons soon so outnumbered the Romano-Britons that the latter's Celtic and Latin languages disappeared (except in Wales and Cornwall). The Germanic conquerors established numerous small kingdoms, such as those of the Angles (Anglia), the West Saxons (Wessex), the East Saxons (Essex), Mercia (people of the marshes), and the lands in the north around the Humber River (Northumbria).

Christian missionaries from Ireland soon targeted the pagan Anglo-Saxons for conversion. Irish monk-missionaries arrived to preach throughout the northern realms. Meanwhile, other missionaries from the bishop of Rome succeeded in converting the king of Kent in the south by 600. Forced to choose between the Irish and Roman versions of Christianity, the majority of Anglo-Saxon kingdoms accepted unity with Rome at the **Council of Whitby** in 663. Energized with faith, Anglo-Saxon missionaries were soon both enforcing religious discipline and evangelizing other Germans on the Continent. Irish missionary monks joined them and slowly accepted obedience to Rome.

While the Anglo-Saxons gained religious unity, political divisions almost led to their downfall. Beginning in 789, the **Vikings** began raiding the British Isles. The Vikings, Norsemen, or Northmen were a new wave of Germanic peoples who had settled in Scandinavia (modern Denmark, Norway, and Sweden) outside the orbit of ancient Rome and the moderating influence of Christianity. Viking raiders have long been notorious for ruthless plundering. They also settled down, farmed, and traded. Viking emigrants succeeded in occupying most of the Anglo-Saxon kingdoms (as well as key portions of what would become Ireland, Normandy in northern France, and southern Italy and Sicily). Called Varangians in eastern Europe, Vikings united Finns, Balts, and Slavs as the "Rus'" and set up a kingdom around Novgorod and Kyiv. So Vikings began the political structures that would evolve into Ukraine and Russia. In all those distant places, Vikings soon assimilated into the culture of the local populations. They discovered and settled Iceland and briefly had colonies in Greenland and even North America.

Among the several Anglo-Saxon kingdoms, only Wessex barely survived Viking invasions. **King Alfred "the Great"** (r. 871–901) restored Wessex's power, setting it on the path to dominate the island. As a younger son of a king, Alfred originally wanted to take the vows of a monk. After the deaths of his brothers made him king, Alfred instead found himself at war. He led his armies to fight the Vikings to a standstill, confining them to a portion of the kingdom called the Danelaw. Secure from conquest, Alfred then tried to promote culture and literacy, especially with his translation of part of the Bible into Old English. Alfred's success established the unified and enduring Kingdom of **England** (taking its name from the Angles). Descendants of prehistoric Britons, Celtic conquerors, Roman victors, Anglo-Saxon invaders, and now Viking colonizers all blended together to become the English.

In the 990s, another wave of Viking invasions yet again almost destroyed the kingdom. This time the Danish king Canute fought his way to the English crown. As King Canute of England (r. 1016–1035), he converted to Christianity, paid off and sent home most of his Viking army, pacified the English realm, and briefly united it with his other possessions of Denmark and what would become Norway and Sweden. After Canute's death, England once more gained a dynasty separate from Denmark. Despite this shaky, vulnerable start, the English people melded together from this diverse prehistoric/Celtic/Roman/Anglo-Saxon/Viking heritage. Soon another invasion and ethnic clash would force England into the High Middle Ages and into a central role in the development of Western civilization.

Meanwhile, on the Continent, the **Franks** had shown themselves to be the second enduring group of Germans. They started out more united than the English by having a royal dynasty called the **Merovingians**, named after a legendary founder, Merovech. By the end of the fifth century, the Franks had expanded from their base across the northern Rhine River into northern Gaul. **King Clovis** (r. 481–511) won the support of the local Roman population and elites when he (and therefore his people) converted directly to orthodox catholic Christianity. He then used his blessing from the clergy to conquer many of his neighboring Germans, such as the Aquitainians, Burgundians, and Suebi, who were still pagans or heretical Arian Christians who rejected the Nicene Creed. The kingdom that Clovis established was ethnically diverse. It combined the various German tribes with the large population of Roman Gauls. Although Clovis and his successors committed murders, betrayals, and various atrocities, the clerics who chronicled their history thought that God specially blessed the Merovingian kings because they championed orthodox catholic Christianity and political unity. In such uncertain times, it seemed possible to honor God through the brutality of warfare.

Like the Anglo-Saxons, the Franks came close to vanishing into history by being conquered by advancing Muslims. In 711 (92 AH), a combined Arab and Berber army invaded Europe by landing near the southern tip of the Iberian Peninsula, which then became known as Gibraltar (or "Rock of Tarik," named after the Muslim commander). The Muslim army quickly crushed most of the three-hundred-year-old Visigothic kingdom. Then a force crossed the Pyrenees Mountains and attacked the Franks. In October 732 (113 AH), at the **Battle of Tours** or **Poitiers** (there has been some dispute about the location), a Frankish army led by Charles Martel ("the Hammer") stopped and turned back the Muslim invaders. The Muslims (who soon were called Moors or **Saracens** by the western Europeans) retreated into the Iberian Peninsula, most of which they continued to control for several centuries. Although it was unclear at the time, the Franks had halted the Muslim advance into Europe from the southwest.

The Franks had been able to stand strong only after dispensing with their other political danger: dividing up their kingdoms among numerous heirs. Many Germanic peoples did not use primogeniture, or inheritance by only the eldest surviving son. Instead, if the king died with more than one son as heir, the realm was split up among the male survivors. Before long, royal brothers and cousins, aided by some of their queens, were fighting against one another over the divisions of the fractured Frankish kingdoms. These kings grew weaker as they handed out lands and authorities to compensate those aristocrats and nobles who fought in their place. Within a few decades, the Merovingian dynasts gained the nickname of "do-nothing kings." They gloried in their semidivine royal authority but did little to govern for the benefit of the people.

Fortunately for the future of the Franks, ambitious royal servants kept Frankish power intact. Managers of the king's household soon seized the important reins of rulership. These mayors (from the Latin word *major*, meaning "greater") of the various royal palaces soon became the powers behind the thrones. One of them, the above-mentioned Charles Martel, managed by 720 to reunify the splintered Frankish kingdoms in the name of his Merovingian king. The successes of Mayor Charles Martel helped Western civilization to develop in western Europe.

Review: How did German rule combine with the Roman heritage in the West?

Response:

PRIMARY SOURCE PROJECT 7: BAD BISHOPS VERSUS BENEDICT ABOUT MORAL RULES

Some people in the Dark Ages could choose between religious and secular lifestyles. The first source, written by a bishop, illustrates the corrupt condition of some leaders of the Church who were supposed to be role models of Christian behavior. Instead, these bad bishops imitated the worst of the aristocracy. In contrast, Benedict of Nursia offered another way of life suitable for Christians. His rule for his monastic community in Monte Cassino provided structure for monks and nuns from then until today.

Source 1: *The History of the Franks* by Gregory of Tours (ca. 590)

An uproar arose against the bishops Salunius and Sagittarius. They . . . became their own masters and in a mad way began to seize property, wound, kill, commit adultery, and various other crimes. When king Gunthram [r. 561–592] learned of it he ordered a synod to meet in Lyons. The bishops assembled and after examining the case found that they were absolutely convicted of the crimes charged to them, and they ordered that men guilty of such acts should be removed from the office of bishop.

But since Salunius and Sagittarius knew that the king was still favorable to them, they went to him complaining that they were unjustly removed and asking for permission to go to the pope of the city of Rome. And [the pope] sent letters to the king in which he directed that they should be restored to their places. This the king did without delay, first rebuking them at length. But, what is worse, no improvement followed. . . . [T]hese men daily engaged in greater crimes and, as we have stated before, they armed themselves like laymen, and killed many with their own hands in the battles which Mummolus [Count of Auxerre] fought with the Lombards. And among their fellow citizens they were carried away by animosity and beat a number with clubs and let their fury carry them as far as the shedding of blood. Because of this the outcry of the people again reached the king. . . .

[T]he king was greatly aroused and took away from them horses, slaves, and whatever they had, and ordered them to be taken and shut up in distant monasteries to do penance there. . . .

Now the king's sons were living at this time, and the older of them began to be sick. And the king's friends went to him and said: "Beware lest perhaps these bishops be condemned to exile though innocent, and the king's sin be increased somewhat, and because of it the son of our master perish." . . . [T]he bishops were released and were so penitent that they apparently never ceased from psalm singing, fasting, almsgiving, reading the book of the songs of David through the day, and spending the night in singing hymns and meditating on the readings.

But this absolute piety did not last long, and they fell a second time and generally spent the nights in feasting and drinking, so that when the clergy were singing the matins in the church these were calling for cups and drinking wine. There was no mention at all of God, no services were observed. When morning came, they arose from dinner and covered themselves with soft coverings; and buried in drunken sleep they would lie till the third hour of the day. And there were women with whom they polluted themselves. And then they would rise and bathe and lie down to eat; in the evening they arose and later they devoted themselves greedily to dinner until the dawn. . . .

Source 2: *Benedictine Rule* by Benedict of Nursia (ca. 530)

33. Whether the Monks Should Have Anything of Their Own

More than anything else is this special vice to be cut off root and branch from the monastery, that one should presume to give or receive anything without the order of the abbot, or should have anything of his own. He should have absolutely nothing: neither a book, nor tablets, nor a pen—nothing at all. For indeed it is not allowed to the monks to have their own bodies or wills in their own power. But all things necessary they must expect from the abbot of the monastery; nor may they have anything which the abbot did not give or permit. . . .

39. Concerning the Amount of Food

We believe, moreover, that . . . two cooked dishes are enough for all tables: so that whoever, perchance, can not eat of one may partake of the other. [I]f it is possible to obtain apples or growing vegetables, a third may be added. One full pound of bread shall suffice for a day. But the eating of the flesh of quadrupeds shall be abstained from altogether by everyone, excepting alone the weak and the sick. . . .

40. Concerning the Amount of Drink

Each one has his own gift from God, the one in this way, the other in that. Therefore it is with some hesitation that we assign the amount of daily sustenance for others. Nevertheless, in view of the weakness of the infirm we believe that [about sixteen ounces] of wine a day is enough for each one. Those moreover to whom God gives the ability of bearing abstinence shall know that they will have their own reward. But the prior shall judge if either the needs of the place, or labor, or the heat of summer, requires more; considering in all things, lest satiety or drunkenness creep in. Indeed, we read that wine is not suitable for monks at all. But because, in our day, it is impossible to persuade the monks of this, let us at least agree that we should not drink until we are sated, but sparingly. For wine can make even the wise to go astray. . . .

48. Concerning the Daily Manual Labor

Idleness is the enemy of the soul. And therefore, at fixed times, the brothers ought to be occupied in manual labor; and again, at fixed times, in sacred reading. . . .

55. Concerning Clothes and Shoes

Vestments shall be given to the brothers according to the nature of the places where they dwell, or the temperature of the air. For in cold regions more is required; but in warm, less. This is for the abbot to decide. We nevertheless consider that for ordinary places there suffices for the monks a cowl and a gown apiece—the cowl, in winter hairy, in summer plain or old—and a working garment, on account of their labor.

Questions:

- *How does the structure of each source serve to carry its message?*
- *How did the bishops fail to meet expectations of Christian leaders?*
- *What rules did Benedict fashion to better regulate virtuous behavior?*

Responses:

For more on these sources, go to http://www.concisewesternciv.com/sources/psc7 .html.

SOURCES ON FAMILIES: TACITUS, *GERMANIA* (AD 98)

Although the historian Tacitus wrote his Germania *during the height of the Roman Empire, many scholars consider it to be a reasonably accurate view of Goths or early Germans. Others note that Tacitus may have been writing more to comment on Roman* mores *rather than on Germanic customs. Either way, this selection portrays Gothic marriage and family as Tacitus admired it.*

XVII . . . The women have the same dress as the men, except that they generally wrap themselves in linen garments, which they embroider with purple, and do not lengthen out the upper part of their clothing into sleeves. The upper and lower arm is thus bare, and the nearest part of the bosom is also exposed.

XVIII Their marriage code, however, is strict, and indeed no part of their manners is more praiseworthy. Almost alone among barbarians they are content with one wife, except a very few among them, and these not from sensuality, but because their noble birth procures for them many offers of alliance. The wife does not bring a dower to the husband but the husband to the wife. The parents and relatives are present, and pass judgment on the marriage-gifts, gifts not meant to suit a woman's taste, nor such as a bride would deck herself with, but oxen, a caparisoned steed, a shield, a lance, and a sword. With these presents the wife is espoused, and she herself in her turn brings her husband a gift of arms. This they count their strongest bond of union, these their sacred mysteries, these their gods of marriage. Lest the woman should think herself to stand apart from aspirations after noble deeds and from the perils of war, she is reminded by the ceremony which inaugurates marriage that she is her husband's partner in toil and danger, destined to suffer and to dare with him alike both in peace and in war. The yoked oxen, the harnessed steed, the gift of arms, proclaim this fact. She must live and die with the feeling that she is receiving what she must hand down to her children neither tarnished nor depreciated, what future daughters-in-law may receive, and may be so passed on to her grand-children.

XIX Thus with their virtue protected they live uncorrupted by the allurements of public shows or the stimulant of feastings. Clandestine correspondence is equally unknown to men and women. Very rare for so numerous a population is adultery, the punishment for which is prompt, and in the husband's power. Having cut off the hair of the adulteress and stripped her naked, he expels her from the house in the presence of her kinsfolk, and then flogs her through the whole village. The loss of chastity meets with no indulgence; neither beauty, youth, nor wealth will procure the culprit a husband. No one in Germany laughs at this vice, nor do they call it the fashion to corrupt and to be corrupted. Still better is the condition of those states in which only maidens are given in marriage, and where the hopes and expectations of a bride are then finally terminated. They receive one husband, as having one body and one life, that they may have no thoughts beyond, no further-reaching desires, that they may love not so much the husband as the married state. To limit the number of their children or to destroy any of their subsequent offspring is accounted infamous, and good habits are here more effectual than good laws elsewhere.

XX In every household the children, naked and filthy, grow up with those stout frames and limbs which we so much admire. Every mother suckles her own offspring, and never entrusts it to servants and nurses. The master is not distinguished from the slave by being brought up with greater delicacy. Both live amid the same flocks and lie on the same ground till the freeborn are distinguished by age and recognized by merit. The young men marry late, and their vigor is thus unimpaired. Nor are the maidens hurried into marriage; the same age and a similar stature is required; well-matched and vigorous they wed, and the offspring reproduce the strength of the parents. Sister's sons are held in as much esteem by their uncles as by their fathers; indeed, some regard the relation as even more sacred and binding, and prefer it in receiving hostages, thinking thus to secure a stronger hold on the affections and a wider bond for the family. But every man's own children are his heirs and successors, and there are no wills. Should there be no issue, the next in succession to the property are his brothers and his uncles on either side. The more relatives he has, the more numerous his connections, the more honored is his old age; nor are there any advantages in childlessness.

Questions:

- *What is the role of property in these German marriages and families?*
- *Compared to the problems of marriage in the Augustan Age (the previous chapter), how does Tacitus contrast those with German marriages?*
- *What specific characteristics do German wives have?*

Responses:

For more on this source, go to http://www.concisewesternciv.com/sources/sof7. html.

CHARLES IN CHARGE

Mayor Charles Martel, who won at Tours/Poitiers, belonged to one of the most important families in Western history. Historians call that dynasty the Carolingians, from Carolus, the Latin version of the name Charles. Members of this family rescued the Franks from infighting and made them a powerful force again. Having beaten back the Moors, Mayor Charles Martel handed his power to his two sons (although one quickly gave up and retired to a monastery). The remaining sole heir, Pepin or **Pippin "the Short"** (r. 741–768), soon grew dissatisfied with ruling as mayor in the name of the officially crowned King Childeric III of the Merovingian dynasty. Pippin appealed to the person whom he considered to have the best connection to the divine, the bishop of Rome, better known as the **pope**.

The institution of the popes, called the **papacy**, played a key role in the rise of the Carolingians and Western civilization. The name *pope* comes from *papa*, or "father," a title also often used for bishops. A number of bishops called either popes or patriarchs had risen to preeminence by the fifth century in Rome, Alexandria, Antioch, Jerusalem, and Constantinople. Together, in "ecumenical" councils, bishops and other Christians had declared orthodox doctrine and settled controversies. With the division of the Roman Empire into two halves and the collapse of Roman authority in the West, four patriarchs remained under the growing authority of the Byzantine emperors in the east. Meanwhile, the bishops of Rome adopted the title of pope for themselves alone and claimed a superior place (primacy) among the other bishops and patriarchs. These other patriarchs might have granted the bishops of Rome a primacy of honor, but not actual authority over them and their churches. In any case, the popes lived too far away to change developments in the Byzantine Empire. In western Europe, though, religious and political circumstances favored a unique role for the bishops of Rome.

The figure who first embodied the medieval papacy was **Gregory I "the Great"** (r. 590–604). The growing importance of the monastic movement is reflected in his being the first pope who had previously been a monk. Much more important, though, were Gregory's three areas of activity, which defined what later popes did. First, the pope provided spiritual leadership for the West. Since the West lacked a literate population in comparison to the East, Gregory's manuals (models of sermons for preachers and advice on being a good pastor) filled a practical need. His theological writings were so significant that the Roman Catholic Church later counted him as one of the four great Church Fathers, alongside Ambrose, Jerome, and Augustine (even though Gregory lived nearly two centuries after them). Second, Gregory acted to secure orthodox catholic Christianity all over the West, far outside his diocese in central Italy. Gregory sent missionaries to the Visigoths in the Iberian Peninsula, to Germany, and, perhaps most famously, to the British Isles. Third, the pope was a political leader. He helped organize and defend the lands around Rome from the invading Lombard Germans, consolidating the political power of the popes, which endures to this day in the Vatican City.

The necessity of papal political leadership increased when later popes disagreed with some Byzantine emperors in the eighth century. The eastern Christians were caught up in the **Iconoclastic Controversy**, which interpreted literally the Old Testament commandment against having graven images. Iconoclasts were those who physically sought to shatter religious pictures and sculptures. (Today the word figuratively refers to those seeking to overturn traditional ways). Eastern patriarchs and bishops increasingly began to support iconoclasm and actually destroyed art in churches. When the western popes refused to go along, the Byzantine emperor confiscated lands in southern Italy that had been used to support the papal troops. At the same time, the Germanic Lombard invaders again threatened Rome from the north.

At this pivotal moment, when the pope needed a new ally in the West, a letter came from the Frankish mayor of the palace, Pippin "the Short," son and heir of Charles Martel. In the letter, Pippin coolly inquired of the pope whether someone who wielded the power and authority of a king should not also hold the title of king. Needing Pippin's army, the pope agreed. So Pippin had the last Merovingian king shaved of his regal long hair and bundled him off to a monastery in 751. Then Pippin became the first king of the Franks from the Carolingian dynasty. In return for the papal favor, Pippin marched to Italy and defeated the Lombards in 754 and 756. His victories also made him king of the Lombards and gave him control of the northern half of the Italian Peninsula (while the southern part remained under nominal Byzantine authority for the next few centuries). In his gratitude, Pippin donated a large chunk of territory in central Italy to the pope. This **Donation of Pippin** eventually became known as the **Papal States**. These lands provided the basis for a papal principality that lasted for more than a thousand years. The arrangement also began a mutually supportive relationship, profitable for both the pope and Pippin, which historians call the **Frankish-Papal Alliance**.

The cooperation between the papacy and the Carolingians culminated under Pippin's son, Charles. He is known to history as **Charlemagne** (r. 768–814), which means "Charles the Great." As his father had before him, Charlemagne at first inherited the throne jointly with his brother, but the latter soon found himself deposited in a monastery. As sole ruler, Charles continued to support the popes. First he invaded Italy, utterly breaking the power of the Lombards. A few years later, after political rivals had roughed up the pope, Charlemagne marched to Rome to restore papal dignity.

On Christmas Day AD 800, the grateful pope crowned Charlemagne as emperor of the Romans. The circumstances and significance of this coronation have remained unclear. Did it merely recognize Charlemagne's actual authority or give it a new dimension? Was the pope, by placing the crown on Charlemagne's brow, trying to control the ceremony and the office? Did it insult the Byzantine emperor, who was, after all, the real Roman emperor (even if some alleged at the time that the eastern throne was vacant, since a mere woman, Empress Irene, ruled after deposing and blinding her son)? In any case, the coronation resulted in a brief enthusiasm for imitating ancient Rome. An emperor once again ruled the West in the name of Rome's civilization (see map 7.2).

In many ways, though, Charlemagne resembled his barbarian German ancestors more than a Roman Caesar Augustus. He dressed in Frankish clothing and enjoyed beer and beef (instead of wine and fish as the Romans had). A man of action, he led a military campaign almost every year to one portion of his

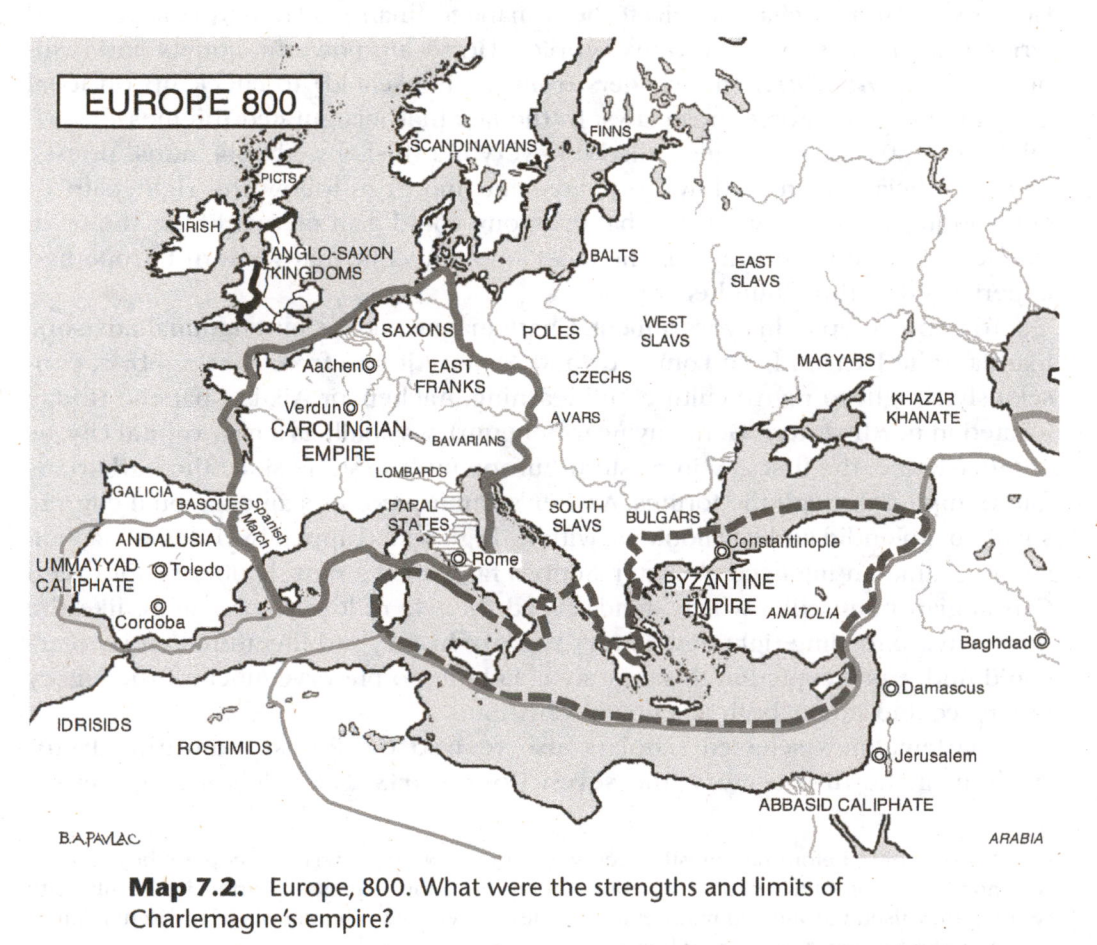

Map 7.2.   Europe, 800. What were the strengths and limits of Charlemagne's empire?

empire or another. Thus, he expanded his rulership and conquered the heartland of Europe, which became the core of the European Community more than a millennium afterward. He deposed the Bavarian duke and took over his duchy. He smashed rebellious Lombards as his father had. He also fought the Saxons in northern Germany (cousins of the long-since-Christianized Anglo-Saxons in Britain). The Christian king tried for thirty years to convert the pagan Saxons to both religious and political obedience. These Saxons faced two choices: either be washed in the water of holy baptism or be slaughtered in their own blood. Many died; survivors converted, then were forcibly migrated to other parts of the empire, where they assimilated. Charlemagne wiped out the Avars (Asiatic raiders who had settled along the Danube). The emperor successfully defended his empire's borders against Danes in the north and Moors in the south. Charlemagne's empire became bigger than any other political structure in the West since Emperor Romulus Augustulus lost his throne in AD 476.

Charlemagne was more than just a bloodthirsty barbarian king. He consciously tried to revive the Roman Empire and its civilization. Although the government still heavily depended on his person, he continued the efforts of his predecessors to expand governance into an institution centered on the palace. He had administrators, such as a chamberlain to help manage finances. He had collected and written down laws for his various peoples. He set up powerful counts and bishops as *missi dominici* (messengers from his household) to check up on local government and enforce those laws. In the law that inaugurated the messengers' mission in 802, Charlemagne called on everyone (bishops, abbots, nuns, priests, counts, officials, men, widows, orphans, and more) to follow the right path of law and justice in this world so that everyone could gain eternal life in the next. Charlemagne's government was the most ambitious one that western Europe had experienced in three hundred years.

To improve upon his government, Charlemagne and his international advisors, like Paul the Deacon from Lombardy and Alcuin Albinus from Northumbria, consciously sought to revive culture and learning. Aachen, or Aix-la-Chapelle (today located in northwestern Germany near Belgium), was built as a new capital city, as another Rome, the first city in western Europe built in stone since the barbarians had trampled through the forums. Aachen's centerpiece was an octagonal church, small but splendid and harmonious, with its high walls capped by a dome. Aachen soon became an intellectual center. Scribes fashioned a new, legible script called Carolingian minuscule, which standardized the use of lowercase letters, like the ones you are reading right now.[2] Every work of history and literature that scholars could find was recopied in this new style, helping to preserve much of the legacy of Greece and Rome, both pagan and Christian.

Charlemagne's selected scholars also revived the Roman educational curriculum of the fifth century: the **seven liberal arts**. The *trivium* of grammar,

---

2. Everything before had mostly been written ONLY IN CAPITAL LETTERS. People who text that way nowadays are interpreted as shouting. When the printing presses started in the fifteenth century, they used Carolingian minuscule, as rediscovered by the humanists of the Renaissance, as the model for new typefaces or fonts.

rhetoric, and logic with the *quadrivium* of arithmetic, geometry, music, and astronomy were taught once more, this time in schools attached to monasteries and cathedrals. This so-called **Carolingian Renaissance** (780–850) hoped to use education to revitalize a way of life that had disappeared in western Europe since the Germans had swept away Roman rule. The Frankish/German Charlemagne used the liberal learning of Greece and Rome to consolidate the new culture of Western civilization.

Regrettably for the cause of civilization, Charlemagne's revitalization attempt failed. The empire was too large and primitive for the weak institutions of government he was able to cobble together. First, he faced the difficulty of paying for art, literature, architecture, and schools with a poor agricultural economy that offered no functional taxation. Second, Frankish aristocrats saw little value in book learning. Third, Charlemagne's own codifications of laws, written for the Alemanni, Burgundians, or Saxons, preserved ethnic differences rather than binding together a new common imperial unity. A final difficulty for Charlemagne was his own mortality. He drove the system along by force of will and sword, but death was certain. His successors lacked his abilities.

Fortunately for imperial unity, Charlemagne's vast empire managed to hold together for a few years after his death because only one son survived him to inherit it all. Under Emperor Louis "the Pious" (r. 814–840), the Carolingian Renaissance peaked. Then Louis prematurely divided up his empire among his own three sons and invested them with authority during his own lifetime. Not surprisingly, they soon bickered with him and with one another. When Louis tried to carve out a share for a fourth son by another wife, civil war broke out. The ensuing hard-fought peace agreement shattered the political unity of western Europe for more than a thousand years.

The **Treaty of Verdun** in 843 officially broke apart Charlemagne's empire into three sections, each under its own Carolingian dynasty. The actual treaty was written in both early French and German, showing that a linguistic division matched the political one. The treaty established a kingdom of the West Franks, out of which grew **France**; a kingdom of the East Franks, out of which rose **Germany**; and a middle realm, Lotharingia (named after Louis's grandson, Lothar). At the time, Lotharingia was the heart of the empire, including not only today's small province of **Lorraine** on the border of France and Germany but also the Lowlands (modern Belgium, the Netherlands, and Luxembourg), south through Switzerland, and over the Alps into northern Italy. This mixed ethnic and linguistic middle realm had no geopolitical cohesion except its prosperity and its dynasty. Both the West Franks and the East Franks targeted Lorraine after its short-lived Carolingian dynasty died out. For the next eleven hundred years, the French and the Germans fought over possession of this middle territory.

As if all of these political divisions were not bad enough, foreign invaders killed any hope for a reunified and coherent empire. From the north, the Vikings or Norsemen sailed in on longships; from the east, the pagan/polytheist **Magyars** or Hungarians swept out of the steppes of Asia on swift ponies; and from the south, from North Africa and the Iberian Peninsula, Muslim Moors or Saracens raided by land and by sea. None of these invaders was Christian. Only the Saracens were civilized. They all murdered, plundered, raped, and burned at will. The feuding Carolingian kings could do little to stop these marauders. Fragile western Christendom nearly ended under these attacks.

Thus, Charlemagne's brief success at reviving civilization crashed. His quarreling descendants, resentful aristocrats, invading barbarians, and hostile non-Christians almost destroyed everything the Germanic kingdoms had achieved. Few empires could have survived such an assault from both within and without. The popes were of little help either, as petty Roman nobles fought each other over the papal throne. In 897, a vengeful pope, Stephen VI, even put on trial the corpse of his predecessor Pope Formosus. Such postmortem vengeance did little good, since Pope Stephen was himself soon deposed and strangled.

Even as the Carolingian Empire died, its corpse became the fertilizer for the future. The empire left a dream of reunification, reinforcing the longing for the onetime unity and cultural greatness of the Roman Empire. But the political reality that followed nonetheless divided West Franks and East Franks into France and Germany. These two realms, together with England, soon formed the core of the West. Despite limited resources, these westerners fought off the assaults from without and established a new order and hierarchy from within. The result was the blossoming of medieval Western civilization.

Review: How did the Carolingian family rise and fall?

Response:

THE CAVALRY TO THE RESCUE

Without a central government, the peoples of the collapsing Carolingian Empire needed to defend themselves. New leaders inspired others to follow them, whether through their own achievements or their claims of dynastic succession. To defend against Viking attacks, they built military fortresses called **castles** (see figure 7.1). These fortifications were not simply army bases with walls; they were family homes. The quaint saying "A man's home is his castle" quite literally came from this period. Castles were originally primitive stockades or wooden forts on hills. A castle became the home of a local leader who convinced others to build it and

Figure 7.1.   The square block of an early castle dominates the town of Loches in France.

help defend it. These castles became new centers of authority from which lords ruled over small areas, usually no larger than a day's ride.

Hiding out in castles was not a long-term solution, however. "The best defense is a good offense" is another saying appropriate to the time period. Fortunately for Western civilization, **knights** rode to the rescue before all could be lost in the onslaughts of Vikings, Magyars, and Saracens. The new stirrups imported from Asia fixed these warriors firmly in the saddles of their warhorses. Their armor for defense and lance and sword for offense made knights effective heavy cavalry when riding together in a charge. A large group of knights and horses, made up of several tons of flesh and iron, overpowered all opponents. Yet only a wealthy few who could afford the training, acquire the equipment, and command the loyalty of others became knights.

Already by 1050, knights had won Europe a respite from foreign invasions. The three external enemies ceased to be threats. The Norsemen stopped raiding, converted to Christianity, and set up the Scandinavian kingdoms of Denmark, Norway, and Sweden, along with the Icelandic Commonwealth. The adventurous spirit of the Norse was redirected to carry some of them across the Atlantic Ocean to settle in Greenland and even, briefly, North America. The Magyars, meanwhile, became Hungarians. Their successful migration settled them in the Pannonian plain along the middle Danube. Their King Stephen consolidated both his rule and the structure of the Kingdom of Hungary with his conversion and that of his people to Christianity in 1000. Only the Saracens remained hostile and unconverted. Rather than continuing to harass their Christian neighbors, they concentrated their efforts on developing their own civilization in the Iberian Peninsula, called Andalusia. There the descendants of Phoenicians, Celts, Romans, Jews, Visigoths, Arabs, and Berbers lived in relative peace.

Knights won in their own part of Europe because they were the best military technology of the age. Armored heavy cavalry dominated battlefields for the next five hundred years, long after the threats of Vikings, Magyars, and Saracens had dissipated. As we have seen before, a social group with a monopoly on the military can rule the rest of society. By 1100, the knights had closed their ranks and became an exclusive caste of nobility limited to those who inherited it. Their ethos of nobility meant that they lived the good life because they risked their lives to defend the women, children, clergy, and peasants of Christendom. They lived in the nicest homes, ate the most delicious food, and wore the most fashionable clothing. Meanwhile, the peasants paid for these comforts.

This closed social group of the nobility distinguished itself through **chivalry**, the code of the knights. The ceremonies for initiation to knighthood were surrounded with elaborate rituals. In their castles and courts, knights practiced courtesy and refined manners with one another and with courtly ladies, such as saying "please" and "thank you" and using napkins. At **tournaments**, they practiced fighting as a form of sport, entertaining crowds and winning prizes. On the battlefield, they applied rules to fight one another fairly, never attacking an unarmed knight, for example.

While there were many regional variations, the organization of these knights required new structures, or ***feudal politics***.[3] A vassal (a subordinate knight) promised fealty (loyalty) and homage (personal service on the battlefield or in the political courts) to a lord (a superior knight) in return for a fief (usually agricultural land sufficiently productive for the knight to live from). A lord was as powerful as the number of vassals he could call on. Lords began to take on new titles that reflected the number of vassals each could bind to himself with fiefs. Above the simple knight at the bottom of the hierarchy were, in ascending order, barons, counts (or earls in England), dukes, and, ultimately, the king. Rather than the kingdoms, however, the most important political units in the eleventh and twelfth centuries were baronies, counties, and duchies.

A network of mutual pledges of fidelity provided the glue for feudal politics. While governments are ultimately based on whether or not people uphold the rules, feudal politics meant keeping personal agreements to one's lord rather than about obeying public authority. Originally, a fief, being a lord's gift, was supposed to revert to the feudal lord upon a vassal's death. The powerful drive of family, however, where parents provided for their children, soon compelled fiefs to become virtually hereditary. Sometimes lords and vassals broke their oaths of service and loyalty. When vassals defied their lords, only fights among the knights could conclusively settle the dispute. Thus, the feudal age has been renowned for its constant warfare. Yet enough lords and vassals did uphold their oaths that medieval society largely remained stable. The web of mutual promises of loyalty, the gathering at court to give advice and pronounce judgments, the socializing at

---

3. The term *feudalism* carries too many different meanings to be useful as a historical concept anymore; it is best avoided. Likewise, the phrase *feudal system* makes these arrangements sound more organized than they were. Finally, do not confuse "feudal" politics with feuds or vendettas.

tournaments, and the shared risks of battle all forged a ruling class that held on to power for centuries. Power was based on promises.

Even the clergy could not avoid being drawn into the feudal network, since dioceses and abbeys possessed a great deal of land. Various lords demanded that the churches contribute to the common defense. Rather than share their wealth or have knights seize control and turn church-owned farms into fiefs, bishops and abbots became feudal lords themselves. Thus, clerics became responsible for building castles, commanding knights in battle, and presiding over courts. Some bishops and abbots became prince-bishops and prince-abbots who ruled in the same way as feudal dukes and counts. These political obligations recognized the Church's real power but often clashed with its spiritual aims.

To compensate somewhat for their involvement in feudal politics, ecclesiastical leaders tried to suggest that divinely inspired morality was part of the code of chivalry and the rules of war (see figure 7.2). In some regions, bishops and

Figure 7.2.   This sculpture in Magdeburg Cathedral of the ancient martyr and saint Maurice portrays him as a Black African in twelfth-century armor. Thus Christian values identify with knighthood, regardless of ethnicity.

princes proclaimed the **Peace of God**, which both classified clergy, women, and children as noncombatants and limited the reasons for going to war. Church leaders also tried to assert the **Truce of God**, which was supposed to constrain how often warfare could be conducted, especially banning it on Sundays, holidays (literally "holy days" then), and during planting and harvesting. Too often, though, fighting went unchecked.

The peasants who worked the fields—namely, the vast majority of the population—did not share in the same political relationships as the knights. Instead, the farmers participated in similar yet separate, private, sociopolitical arrangements called *manorial* or *seigneurial economics*. The term comes from *manor*, which referred to the medieval economic unit of a village and its fields, or the French word *seigneur* for the lord of that manor. The harsh conditions of the early Middle Ages had forced many manors into self-sufficiency. Trade had nearly vanished since the roads were too dangerous to travel. The peasants cooperated in their local communities to produce much of what everyone needed to survive, such as food, clothing, and tools.

Most of those who worked on medieval manors for manorial lords were **serfs**. Medieval serfs had servile status, although not as low as that of the enslaved in Greece or Rome. They were legally connected or bound to the land of their lords. Serfs had few rights to make decisions about their own lives (such as choice of marriage partners or where to live). They owed obedience, some work (on the lord's land or on roads or castles), and dues (usually payments in the form of portions of their crops) to the seigneurs who legally possessed the land. Peasants thus paid for knights' expensive armor, horses, and castles. These burdens kept them poor from generation to generation. Nevertheless, serfs did benefit from having use of the land. Parents and their children lived in the same villages and farmed the same lands, season after season, according to law and custom. These arrangements provided livelihoods, some security, and continuity, since the seigneurs could not throw serfs off the land as long as they fulfilled their customary obligations. Medieval peasants depended on their lords for justice and defense and relied on the parish church for salvation.

The practices of feudal politics and manorial economics intersected where the manorial seigneurs were likewise feudal lords and vassals. Knights as lords of fiefs also acted as lords of manors. The political promises they made with their noble and free equals as fief holders were distinct from their rule of the inferior serfs as manorial workers.

Soon a simple agricultural innovation on these manors helped Europe prosper as never before. Beginning in the dark times after the fall of the Carolingian Empire, someone came up with the idea of **three-field planting**. Previously, the custom in European farming had been a two-field system, which left half the farmland fallow (without crops) every year to recover its fertility. The new method involved planting one-third with one kind of crop in the spring (such as beans or oats), another third with another crop in the fall (such as wheat or rye), and letting only a third lie fallow. The following year they rotated which crop they planted in each part of the field. This crop rotation resulted in larger harvests for less work and an improved diet for everyone. A climatic improvement of weather patterns, called the "medieval warm period" (ca. 770–1275), also yielded more crops.

New technology, much of which had spread to Europe after being invented in Asia, further boosted what the manorial peasants could accomplish. The horse collar enabled horses to pull plows without strangling. Windmills ground grain into flour more easily than human or animal labor. These and other agricultural and technological advancements added to the wealth of Europe. The work by the peasants on farms continued to produce wealth at the lord's behest. The rule of the knights defended the fragile kingdoms of France, England, Germany, and the rest. The prayers and labors of the clergy made Christianity the supreme religion of the West. Western civilization appeared secure.

The fall of Rome in the West in the fifth century had initiated a troubled time about which much remains in the dark for historians. In those difficult days, little energy was spent on learning and intellectual endeavors. As most people struggled to survive, only a few could create culture that survived long term, such as the rituals of the Latin Church or the epic songs of the Germans. Over the next few centuries after the chaos of the barbarian invasions, powerful rulers such as Alfred in England or Charles Martel among the Franks consolidated numerous small barbarian kingdoms into great realms. For a while, it looked as if the Carolingian Empire might actually unify the West as a revived Roman Empire. Its failure nonetheless left the kingdoms of France and Germany strong enough to hold out against new invasions. A thousand years after Christ's birth, Western civilization was strong and stable. The successful, ordered medieval society of catholic clergy, feudal knights, and manorial peasants (with some of the Jews still living among them) seemed settled forever as God's plan for humanity. The success of Christendom soon led to change, however. More sophisticated political and social structures, together with new ideas, shook up accepted assumptions. As a result, the West passed from the early Middle Ages into the High or Central Middle Ages in the eleventh century between 1000 and 1100.

Review: *How did feudal politics and manorial economics help the West recover?*

Response:

Make your own timeline.

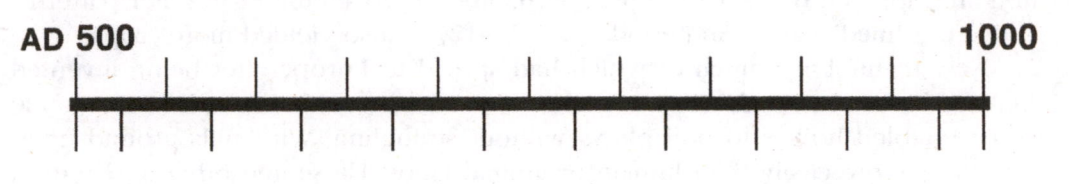

CHAPTER  8

The Medieval Mêlée

The High and Later Middle Ages, 1000 to 1500

Adistinctive form of Western civilization culminated in the **High** or **Central Middle Ages** (ca. 1000–1350). The early Middle Ages had combined the surviving remnants of Græco-Roman culture and Christianity (inspired by Judaism) with the rule of the German conquerors of the western half of the Roman Empire. Improved manorial agriculture raised the amount of wealth, while the stable feudal governments provided more security. As a result, medieval kingdoms became civilized, as towns and cities provided new avenues to riches (see map 8.1). At the same time, though, fighting took place everywhere, from the hand-to-hand mêlée of medieval knightly combat to vast wars about faith. Institutions and ideas fought with one another over which would master the minds, bodies, and souls of the diverse peoples in western Europe. Afterward, new environmental pressures would shape these conflicts in the **later Middle Ages** (ca. 1300–1500) (see map 8.1).

RETURN OF THE KINGS

After the danger of Vikings, Saracens, and Magyars had passed, the Christian knights waged war more and more against one another. These feudal lords could often ignore kings who failed to maintain order. Knights and vassals held their private interests to be more important than the general public welfare. Violence increased as private wars determined public policy. Kings clung precariously to their thrones, while sometimes able to pass dynastic power on from father to son. They could access fewer resources than the greater vassals in their realms. And civil war frequently followed when a dynasty failed to produce an heir. The old Germanic tradition that believed kings were semidivine, combined with the Christian Church's desire for a stable sociopolitical order, necessitated a new ruler. Often an aristocrat placed the crown on his own head—someone had to be king.

Despite this weakening of real royal power, the idea survived of kings as the focus for a state. The traditional roles of the king (warrior, lawgiver, symbol)

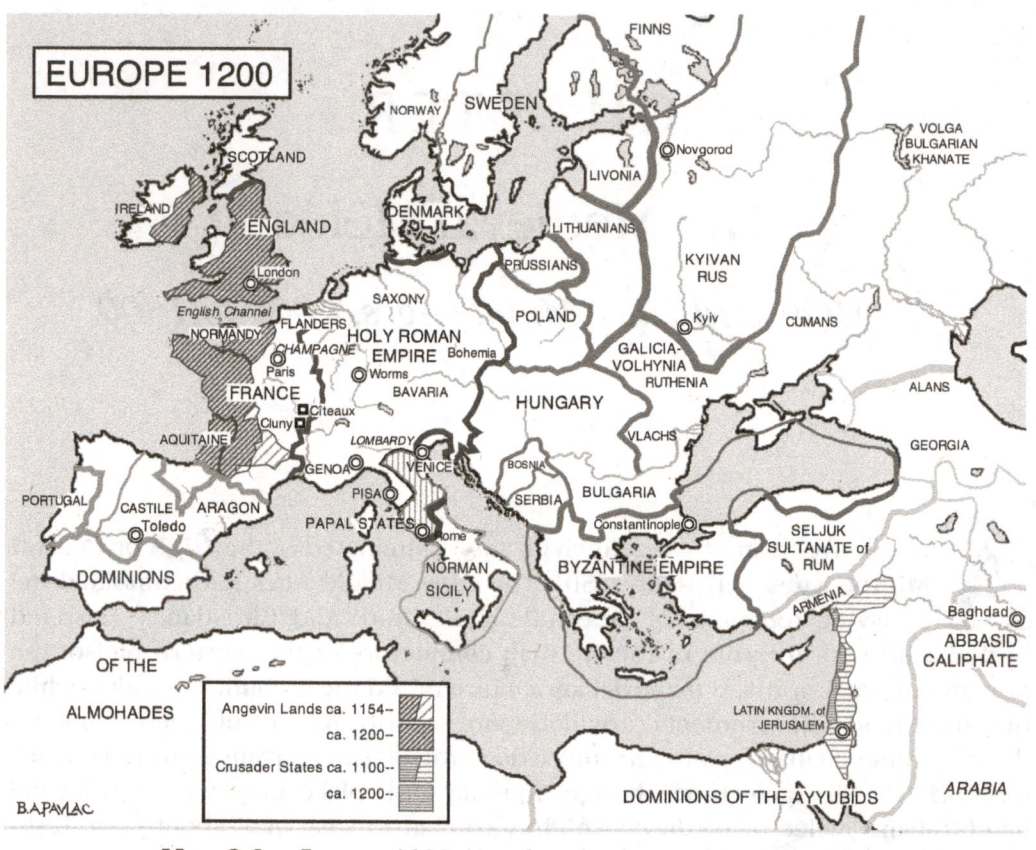

Map 8.1.   Europe, 1200. How fractured were the states of Europe?

and the new feudal structure offered certain advantages to kings. In the eleventh century, some kings took measures to reassert their authority by combining the fragmented feudal fiefs into a unified hierarchical structure and shifted from the personal oaths of fidelity to the rule of law. Most kings had attained the position of a *suzerain* (supreme lord), at the top of the hierarchy of feudal relationships. Kings pulled their unruly dukes, counts, barons, and knights together with their fiefs into a political system based on royal obedience, not personal promises. Their key difficulty became how to delegate royal authority without losing control to feudal competitors. The conflicts between kings and their rival aristocrats and nobles over deference to the throne shaped the various states of Europe.

The first kingdom to experience a reinvigorated royal power was that of the East Franks, which was soon renamed the Kingdom of the Germans. At first, when the Carolingian dynasty began to fail, dukes became more powerful. Dukes promoted feelings of regional unity under their own rule and soon gained greater authority than the nominal kings. As military commanders, local dukes also defended their various provinces against the Magyars and Vikings better than did the kings who lived far away. In 911, the last of the Carolingian dynasty, Louis "the Child," died and passed the kingship to the Duke of Franconia—ruler of the heartland of the East Franks. After a troubled reign, that duke in turn handed the kingship over to his strongest rival, the Duke of Saxony, Henry "the Fowler." The new king of the Germans was able to found a royal dynasty for Germany, passing power from father to son for several generations. The continuity of these Saxon kings reversed the trend toward divided duchies and instead helped to rebuild royal authority.

The most important king of this Saxon dynasty, **Otto I "the Great"** (r. 935–973), originally faced both rebellions and invasions. He managed to quell the revolts begun by his relatives by using both successful military campaigns and the support of the prince-bishops, to whom he granted lands and authority. Since bishops were supposed to be celibate, they had no heirs to whom they could pass on their power. Further, the king usually had the most important voice in selecting a successor bishop. The knights provided by these episcopal vassals bolstered royal leadership.

With this army, King Otto I defeated the Magyars at the Battle of Lechfeld in 955 (also allegedly helped by the Holy Lance that had pierced Christ's side during the crucifixion). Afterward, the Magyars ceased to invade, settled down to establish the Kingdom of Hungary, and converted to Christianity. Otto further conquered much of the Italian Peninsula. His pretext for invading the Kingdom of Italy was the rescue of the young Queen Adelaide, widow of King Lothair II, whom a usurper had locked up in a castle. Otto drove out the usurper, set free Adelaide, and made her his queen (which, of course, then supported his own claims as "king" of Italy).

Otto confirmed his rise in authority eleven years later in 962 when he had the pope crown him "Emperor of the Romans" in the tradition of Charlemagne. This act once again employed the name of the ancient Roman Empire, reviving what had first been lost to the West five centuries earlier, what had failed with the Carolingians just a century previously, and what technically still continued in Byzantium. The political state ruled by Emperor Otto I and his successors eventually came to be called the **Holy Roman Empire** (962–1806) both by its rulers and by later historians. At its height, this empire included all the lands of the Germans, Italy from the Papal States northward, much of the Lotharingian middle-realm territories of Burgundy and the Lowlands, Bohemia, and some Slavic lands on the northern plains of central Europe. The Holy Roman Empire dominated European politics for 150 years after Otto "the Great."

While the Germans were building the Holy Roman Empire, the Kingdom of England had just managed to survive another onslaught of Vikings in the tenth century. The short rule of King Canute's dynasty from Denmark settled matters briefly. After this dynasty died out at the beginning of the year 1066, civil war broke out. First, the native English earl Harold Godwinson claimed the English throne. Next, Harold fought off a Scandinavian invasion in the north led by his own brother allied with the king of Norway. Finally, Harold had to rush to the south to fight an invasion from Normandy. There he fell at the Battle of Hastings (14 October 1066), defeated by the army of the Norman duke, **William "the Conqueror"** (or "the Bastard" from another point of view). The victorious Duke William crowned himself King William I of England (r. 1066–1087) on Christmas

Figure 8.1. William "the Conqueror" started building a castle, the White Tower of the Tower of London, immediately after his conquest of England. Most of the windows were cut into the walls much later, once fear of invasion or rebellion had waned.

Day. William replaced virtually all the local magnates with his own loyal vassals after he crushed several rebellions by English nobles (see figure 8.1). The **Norman Conquest** of England changed the course of history.

The Normans were Vikings (Norsemen) who had seized and settled a province of France along the English Channel in the tenth century, calling it Normandy after themselves. They recognized the French king as *suzerain* and soon spoke only French. This combination of Viking immigrants and Frankish locals created an ethnic group that had an extraordinary influence on events. Some Normans later seized southern Italy and Sicily from the slackening grip of the Byzantine Empire and created a powerful and dynamic state there. In that kingdom, unique in the West, the Norman-French rulers fostered prosperity and peace among diverse populations of Italians, Greeks, and Arabs. The Normans also played a leading role in the Crusades (see below).

The Norman transformation of England, meanwhile, set that country on the path to world domination. Still possessing the Norman lands, the kings of England became less and less involved in the Scandinavian affairs of northern Europe and more tied to France and western Europe. Yet still England retained its distinct multicultural heritage. The French-speaking Normans slowly adopted the English language of the conquered subjects. As a result, the French/Viking influence of the Normans added to the previous Viking, Anglo-Saxon, Roman, Celtic, and pre-historic cultures.

William's military victories enabled him to assert a strong monarchical rule and to bind his new land under his law. One example was his command to have the ***Domesday Book*** written in 1086. It assessed the wealth of most of his new kingdom by counting the possessions of his subjects, from castles and plow land down to cattle and pigs. William used the knowledge of this book to tax everything more effectively. This assessment was the first such official catalog in the West since the time of ancient Rome.

William's dynasty ran into trouble, though, when his son Henry I died from eating too many lampreys in 1135. Henry had sired over twenty bastards, but his only legitimate male heir had drowned in a shipwreck. The result was, of course, civil war. On one side was Henry's daughter, the "Empress" Matilda, the widow of German Holy Roman emperor Henry V and current wife of the powerful Geoffrey, Count of Anjou, a territory just south of Normandy. On the other side, most barons of England supported her cousin, Stephen of Blois, from northern France. Yet Matilda and her husband's forces won Normandy in battle and negotiated a truce, stipulating that after Stephen's death the English throne would go to Geoffrey and Matilda's son, Henry. The young **King Henry II** (r. 1154–1189) thus founded the English royal dynasty of the **Angevins** (the adjective for Anjou), or **Plantagenets** (after a flower adopted as a symbol). The Plantagenets ruled England for the rest of the Middle Ages, from 1154 to 1485. In addition to England, Henry inherited Normandy and Anjou from his mother and father. Moreover, he gained Aquitaine through marriage to its duchess, Eleanor, whose marriage with King Louis VII of France had recently been annulled. He also began to achieve English dominance over Wales and Ireland. Thus, Henry II reigned over an empire that stretched from the Scottish border to the Mediterranean Sea.

Being crowned king and exercising real power were two different things, especially since many lords in Henry's vast territories had usurped royal prerogatives during the chaos of civil war. Henry used the widespread desire of many to return to the peace and prosperity of the "good ol' days" as a way to promote innovations in government, especially in England. In a campaign similar to that of Augustus Caesar to "restore" the republic, Henry claimed he wanted to revive the ways of his grandfather, the last Norman king, Henry I. By doing so, he actually concentrated rule in his own hands. Henry II pursued this through four means. First, he needed military domination, so he attacked and demolished all castles that did not have an explicit license from him. He built others in key locations, using the latest technology imported from the Crusades in Palestine (see the next section). He also preferred hired mercenaries to feudal levies. He asked his knights to pay "shield money" instead of providing their required feudal military service in person.

Second, he began a revision of royal finances to pay for this military might. His own treasurer had written that the power of rulers rose and fell according to how much wealth they had: rulers with few funds were vulnerable to foes, while rulers with cash preyed upon those without. Henry obtained good money through currency reform, creating the pound sterling: 120 pennies equaled a pound's worth of silver. If his minters made bad money, with less pure silver than as regulated, he had their hands chopped off. Circulating coins improved his people's ability to pay taxes. Further, he reinforced old sources of taxation, including the Danegeld tax imposed on the descendants of Viking invaders, who had long since become assimilated with the English. He raised crusading taxes to pay for a crusade he never took part in. All these funds were accounted for by the Office of the Exchequer, which took its name from the checkerboard cloth with which officials tracked credits and debits.

Third, in his role as law preserver and keeper, Henry improved the court system. He offered impartial judges as alternatives to the wide variety of local baronial courts. His judges had acquired a solid education at new universities in Oxford and Cambridge, where they trained in a revived study of Roman law based on the Justinian Code. These judges traveled around the country (literally on a circuit), hearing cases that grand juries determined were worthy of trial. For trials, judges often called on a **jury** of peers to examine evidence and decide guilt and innocence rather than relying only on the allegedly divinely guided trial by ordeal. Henry's subjects could also purchase writs, standardized forms where one had only to fill in the blanks of name, date, and so forth in order to bring complaints before the sheriff and thus the king. These innovations increased the jurisdiction of the king's law, making it relatively quick and available to many. At the same time, people became involved on the local level, holding themselves mutually responsible for justice. This system is still used today in many Western countries.

Fourth, Henry II needed a sound administration to organize all this activity, of which the Exchequer was a part. Since Henry spent two-thirds of his time across the English Channel in his French provinces, he needed loyal officials who would exercise authority in his name but without his constant attention. The result revived government by bureaucracy. Officials began to keep and store royal writs and records in bureaus and boxes, and perhaps even consulted them. Some appointed bureaucrats, such as the treasurer or the chancellor, stood in for the king, signing documents with the royal seal. London started to become a capital city, as it offered a permanent place for people to track down government officials. New personnel were hired from the literate people of the towns and universities rather than from the traditional ruling classes of clergy and nobles. The king held these officials accountable and hired or fired them at will, unlike nobles, who inherited offices almost as easily as they had fiefs. Henry paid the lower grades of officials with food, money, or even the leftover ends of candles, while he compensated higher-ranked ministers with Church lands and feudal titles. These civil servants made government more responsive both to change and to the will of the governed, or at least the crown.

The challenge any king faced in controlling appointed officials came to life in Henry's infamous quarrel with **Thomas Becket** (d. 1172). Becket had risen in Henry's service to the highest office of chancellor, all the while fighting for extended royal rights and prerogatives. Then Henry had Thomas Becket made archbishop of Canterbury, the highest-ranking churchman in England, believing that Becket would serve the royal will in both positions. Unfortunately for Henry, Archbishop Thomas experienced an unexpected religious conversion after his consecration. He became one of the reformers who resisted royal intervention in clerical affairs (see the next section). Years of dispute ended when four knights bashed Thomas's brains out in his own cathedral. Thomas Becket's martyrdom allowed the English clergy to appeal to Rome in spiritual affairs and to keep the benefit of clergy (that clerics be judged by Church courts, not secular ones). Still, many clerics remained loyal royal servants.

Despite bureaucratic innovations, government remained tied to the personality of the ruler. Rebellions by his sons marked the last years of Henry II's reign. His wife and their mother, Eleanor of Aquitaine, helped to organize the revolts. Henry locked up Queen Eleanor after she showed too much independence and resentment about his adulterous affairs. In return, she and her sons found support among barons who resented the king's supremacy. Nevertheless, the dynastic unity of Henry's lands survived for a few years after his demise, largely due to the sturdiness of his reforms. His immediate heir, King Richard I "the Lionheart" (r. 1189–1199), was away from England for all except ten months of his ten years of rule, yet the system functioned without him.[1] In contrast, Richard's heir, his younger brother King John (r. 1199–1216), pushed the royal power to its limit as he quarreled with King Philip II of France, Pope Innocent III, and his own barons, only to lose most of his Angevin territories in France (see below).

In 1215, John's unhappy subjects forced him to agree to the famous **Magna Carta** (Latin for "Great Charter"). This treaty between the king, the clergy, the barons, and the townspeople of England accepted royal authority, but limited its abuses. In principle, it made the king subject to law, not above it. This policy required the king to consult with representatives of the people on important issues, such as war and taxes. It became permanent mostly because John died soon after assenting to it, leaving a child as heir. Soon, the clergy, barons, and townspeople grew accustomed to meeting with the king and his representatives. In 1295, King Edward I summoned a model assembly of those who would speak with the king, called **Parliament** (from *parlez* in the French still spoken by the

---

1. Many modern versions of tales about Robin Hood are set during this time. The myth of the hero who robs from the rich and gives to the poor does date back to the Middle Ages, but historians have been unable definitively to connect legend to a historical time or person.

elites since the Norman Conquest). This body of representatives of the realm effectively realigned the rights of English kings and their subjects.

Meanwhile, the kings of France, who had started out in the tenth century weaker than those of England, became stronger by the thirteenth century. A French duke seized the throne from the last Carolingian king and founded a new Capetian dynasty that ruled from 987 to 1328. At first, the Capetians held only nominal power, effective merely over an area around Paris called the Île de France. With the rise of feudal politics, royal power had almost vanished. Only the king's position as *suzerain*, or keystone of the feudal hierarchy, barely preserved some respect for the crown. More powerful than these early kings were the dynastic nobles, especially the Count of Flanders, the Duke of Normandy, the Count of Anjou, and the Duke of Aquitaine.

Two particular medieval French kings instituted France's strong monarchy. First was **Philip II "Augustus"** (r. 1180–1223), whose nickname from the title of Roman emperors is the equivalent of "the Great." At the beginning of Philip's reign, Henry II's Angevin Empire seemed to doom the French monarchy, since Henry's territories in France of Normandy, Anjou, and Aquitaine overwhelmed the French king's lands. Fortunately for France, Henry's French possessions collapsed under his son John. Feudal complaints from the vassals enabled Philip to start a war against John. The Battle of Bouvines in 1214 sealed Philip's victory with the conquest of most of the continental possessions of the Plantagenets except for a sliver of Aquitaine called Guyenne. As conqueror (like William of Normandy in his conquest of England), Philip accumulated overwhelming authority. He then carried out reforms modeled on those of Henry II. His new administrative bureaucratic offices were settled in his chosen capital city, Paris. His only mistake was to break his first marriage to Ingeborg of Denmark and marry Agnes of Meran without the permission of a prelate. The papal interdict on France lasted four years. In the long run, though, Philip had guaranteed that the French king was the dominant power in France.

By the reign of his descendant **Philip IV "the Fair"** (r. 1285–1314), the king's power in France was supreme. Philip IV further strengthened royal authority with his own representative body, the **Estates-General**. Similar to the English Parliament, the Estates-General included representatives from the clergy, landed nobility, and commons or burghers from towns. These members gave their consent to and participated in enacting new royal taxes and laws, increasing the effectiveness of royal decisions. Philip IV also secured royal authority against even the papacy (see the next section).

Thus, the kings in Germany, France, and England had managed to restore authority and create the first three core states of Western civilization. Nevertheless, the West might still have been crushed by another invasion, by the Mongols or Tartars. These groups of pony-riding archers had come to dominate much of Asia under their leader Chengiz or Genghis Khan (r. 1206–1227). In 1241, the Golden Horde (polytheist Mongol and allied invaders under Genghis Khan's grandson Batu) moved westward. The horde first conquered the territory of the Kyivan Rus' and then smashed multinational Christian armies in both Poland and Hungary.

These defeats paved the way for a possible Mongol conquest of western Europe, which might have destroyed the young Western civilization. The next year, though, internal disputes over the Mongol dynasty ended the Golden Horde's interest in invading the little western corner of Eurasia. They retreated and only kept control of the Slavs on Europe's eastern fringe in their Khanate. The Mongols turned their attention to other parts of Asia. In the East, Mongols finally defeated the Sung dynasty in China, and Kublai Khan (r. 1260–1294) established the Yuan dynasty. In the southwest, the Mongol leader Hulagu smashed Iran, toppled the Abbasid Caliphate and flattened Baghdad in 1258. The Mamluks, former enslaved Turks and Circassians who had taken over Egypt, assumed the leadership of Islam in the Middle East. The Mamluk Caliphate pushed both the Mongols and Christian crusaders out of the Middle East by the early 1300s. Soon the polytheistic Mongols converted to Islam, yet their khanates fell apart under rival khans. As for Arab/Muslim civilization, many historians cite these devastating invasions as a turning point that ended a centuries-long "golden age."

Meanwhile, Christian states of northern and western Europe flourished, led by kings who worked closely with the wealth and influence of the clergy, defeated powerful enemies, and promoted the rule of law. These kings had taken primitive feudal authority and brought their nobles into order and structure, if not full obedience and subjugation. Their rivalries with one another also provided a dynamic of competition, both economic and military. Out of the diversity of these states and others to follow, Western civilization lurched forward in war and peace.

Review: *How did more centralized governments form in western Europe?*

Response:

DISCIPLINE AND DOMINATION

Feudal lords struggled to bind people together politically, while prelates attempted to unify the faithful religiously. The catholic orthodox Christian Church had survived both the fall of the Roman Empire in the West and the fall of the Carolingian Empire. Most people, peasant and noble, labored on in their roles of farming and administering, attending church services as best they could. Large numbers also retreated from the cares of the world to the haven of monasteries to become monks and nuns. Yet too often regular clergy had only taken vows because their families pushed them. Since many lacked sincere religious belief, religious dedication slipped. In numerous monasteries, the regulations of Benedict were either unheard of or unheeded.

One group of monks in the wild district of Burgundy decided to resist this neglectful attitude by founding the new monastery of Cluny in the year 910. First, the monks of the **Cluniac Reform** dedicated themselves to a strict observance of the Benedictine Rule, including a disciplined practice of the prayers of the Divine Office. Second, in order to maintain reform in their own cloister and in others that imitated it, they held regular meetings to inspire a proper tone and to correct abuses. Third, they exempted themselves from local supervision of either the nobility or the bishop, because both the nobility and ecclesiastical officials were too compromised by the rough-and-tumble feudal network to be trusted with faith. Instead, the monks placed themselves under the direct supervision of the distant bishop of Rome, the pope.

These reforms were done without either the knowledge or the permission of popes, but they reinforced a trend with enormous consequences for the Christians in the West. According to tradition and **canon law** (legal rules that governed the institutional Church), a local bishop or the king assumed supervision of a monastery. Local nobles might also intrude, using their power of patronage and family connections among the monks and nuns. To get around local interference, the supporters of bishops "found" a number of charters that documented an overarching authority by the distant pope in Rome. Later organizers of canon law accepted these forgeries as genuine. Hence, the pope assumed an exceptional superior authority in the canonical hierarchy. An appeal to Rome over any monastic issue ranging from ownership of a fishpond to possession of a benefice (a paying church position) might bring a local squabble directly to the pope's unique and supreme jurisdiction in a court of last resort, the pope's court in Rome, the Roman Curia.

Under the new reforms, aristocrats and nobles abandoned the pleasures and excitement of chivalry to accept the hard obedience and discipline of monasticism. Women suffering from the limitations of noble life under chivalry found independent living in nunneries. One of the children dedicated to the religious lifestyle was Abbess Hildegard of Bingen (b. 1098–d. 1179). Her history illustrates some of the options open to Benedictine nuns. Her noble family sent Hildegard, their tenth child, to join an anchoress when she was only eight years old. As an adult, she became abbess of the neighboring abbey and collected enough donations to found a new nunnery. Hildegard became famous for writings of her visions (which may have been caused by migraines) as well as for treatises on medicine, theology, and music.

The success of the Benedictine Cluniacs threatened to bring back the lack of devotion that had started the reform. Over the years, so many nobles donated land to monasteries and sent their children there that some worried the increasing wealth and influence might distract the Cluniacs from properly focusing on divine worship. By the late eleventh and early twelfth centuries, many male monastics supported a new **Cistercian Reform** that sought to go beyond the dedication of the Cluniacs. In monasteries like Chartreuse, Prémontré, and Cîteaux (which gave its name to the movement), these monks interpreted the Benedictine Rule as strictly as possible. In addition, the reformed monks only accepted novices older than sixteen years, refusing to accept the unwanted children of aristocrats. Chartreusians, Premonstratentians, and Cistercians also opened the cloisters to layman workers, who gained the benefits of communal life without being burdened with the obligations of education and prayer. The true calling of these new monks even inspired some diocesan clergy to reform as **canons regular**. Regular canons lived together in communities of prayer, and they also, like secular clergy, served the world as pastors and teachers. Thus, these monastic reforms opened various options for choosing the religious life, either among regular or secular clergy. Significantly, the brothers journeyed even farther into uninhabited hills, forests, and wastelands to build churches and farms to avoid secular temptations and concerns (see figure 8.2). This internal colonization increased the amount of farmland in the West and, therefore, its wealth.

Figure 8.2.   This sculpture of the sin of temptation on Strasbourg Cathedral warns about what lies behind a pretty face: poisonous snakes and toads.

Christians inspired by monastic reforms wanted a morally worthy spiritual leader. These reforms influenced the papacy to rise out of the depths of petty rivalry and become worthy and capable of leading all Christians. For centuries, the papal office had been the pawn of the rambunctious Roman nobility, as one family or another forced its candidate into St. Peter's Chair. Thus, the popes were too often men merely interested in the power and the wealth of the papal office. In 1046, after factional squabbles created three popes at once, Henry III, the king of Germany and Holy Roman emperor, arrived in Rome to restore order. Henry called the Synod of Sutri, which dismissed the three popes and then chose a new, universally recognized pope, Leo IX.

This pope and his successors believed that only an authoritarian papacy ruling from Rome could inspire more religious dedication of Christians. These attitudes initiated what historians call the **Hildebrandine** or **Gregorian Reform** (1050–1150), named after the monk Hildebrand, who later became **Pope Gregory VII** (r. 1073–1085).

One tragic consequence of this aggressive papal authority was a *schism*, or "tearing" or "splitting," of the orthodox catholic Christian Church into two parts: the Latin-speaking clerics in the West, who took the term *Catholic*, and the Greek-speaking ecclesiastics in the East, who came to be called *Orthodox*. Since the fall of the western half of the Roman Empire, Christians had slowly been separating on organizational, theological, and liturgical grounds. The eastern patriarchs, bishops, and abbots had kept a close relationship with Byzantine emperors. Although they had lost some dioceses to the Muslim advance in the Middle East and Africa, they had found new missionary success among the Slavic peoples of the Balkans and eastern Europe. The bishops of Rome, however, wanted recognition of papal primacy in authority over all other clergy. The Eastern primates, meanwhile, refused to recognize the popes as their superiors.

In 1054, arguments over relatively minor issues such as the supervision of churches, the addition to the Nicene Creed of the word *filioque* ("and the Son" when mentioning who sent the Holy Spirit), and the use of leavened or unleavened bread in the Eucharist brought on a crisis. Members of a papal commission to Constantinople aggravated the situation by excommunicating the patriarch there, who excommunicated them right back. Unity between Christians in East and West has never been able to recover from what is called the "Great Schism."[2] The Christian world divided between Western, "Latin," or Catholic Christianity (often called the "Church of Rome") and Eastern, "Greek," or **"Orthodox" Christianity**. The dividing line ran through eastern Europe, with Serbs, Montenegrins, Bulgarians, Macedonians, Ukrainians, Belarussians, and Russians affiliated with the Orthodox, while Croats, Slovenes, Slovaks, Czechs, and Poles submitted to Rome.

---

2. Many historians use the term the "Great Schism" to refer to the popes of the "Roman Church" splitting into separate lines between 1378 and 1417, which this text calls the "Great Western Schism." That minor and brief squabble among papal followers hardly compares to the ongoing separation since 1054 of "Eastern" and "Western" Christians.

For the reforming clerics in the West, though, the increasing papal supremacy justified the split. To help ensure the legitimacy of the pope, clergy in the diocese of Rome issued a unique election law in 1059 that revised the process for selecting the pope. Previously, the pope had been chosen in the same manner as other bishops, namely through election by the local clergy and laypersons of the diocese. Practically, though, powerful men, such as a king, actually did most of the choosing in the majority of cases. Reformers now entrusted a new role to churchmen called **cardinals**, who originally had been created as assistants to run the diocese of Rome. Under the new papal election law, only cardinals appointed by popes could vote for the next pope. This law removed the pope from being the plaything of the Roman nobility, but it also cut out the influence of the German king who was also Holy Roman emperor.

The reformers in Rome further hoped to encourage a higher quality of cleric by targeting what they considered the two worst problems in the Western Latin Church: **simony** and the sexual activity of clerics. First, simony, named after the figure Simon Magus in the New Testament, originally meant the sin of trying to purchase salvation. It had come to mean the crime of bribery, or even using political influence, to acquire a church office or benefice. Reformers wanted to take bribery out of the election process. The attack on clerical sexual activity was also partially related to the opposition to simony. Reformers thought that when clergy had children, the tendency to pass on to their heirs a priestly office (not to mention parish property) compromised the holiness of the priesthood (and the church's possessions).

Additionally, some reformers were squeamish about women and sex. Already in ancient times the male clergy had excluded women from leadership. With this new reform, clerical authorities in the West tried to restrict married priests from offices or sacraments, insisting on celibacy. They adopted misogynist attitudes from pagan philosophers and culture about female inferiority and corrupt sexuality, cringing at the thought that a priest might handle the holy body and blood of Christ in the mass after having touched the impure flesh of a woman. So reformers began a campaign against the many priests who were married and others who kept concubines or "house companions." Of all the reform efforts, people in the local parishes surely noticed this one the most, whether their priests obeyed or not.

To change clerical attitudes, the papacy began to intervene in local church affairs as never before. Legal scholars collected and commented on old and new canon law in support of the tighter ecclesiastical organization. Popes added lawyers and bureaucrats to their papal court, the Roman Curia. The popes often sent cardinals throughout western European realms as legates, the pope's official representatives who bore his full authority. The papal scribes issued bulls (named after the lead seal of authenticity hanging from them) in which the popes, on their own authority, codified law and moral issues. As a result, many thought the pope became less a spiritual leader than the head of a vast bureaucratic machine. While many of the popes over the next centuries were great lawyers and politicians, few had any inclination toward sanctity or sainthood.

Review: *How did reforms of monks lead to a reform of the Western Latin Church under the medieval papacy?*

Response:

SOURCES ON FAMILIES: JACOBUS DE VORAGINE, "THE LIFE OF SAINT ELIZABETH" (CA. 1260)

Religious life offered a powerful alternative to traditional marriage and family for medieval people. Elizabeth (b. 1207–d. 1231), daughter of the king of Hungary, became a popular saint, although few followed in her footsteps. A princess who married into a powerful family, she rejected the typical marriage and aristocratic lifestyle, devoting herself instead to helping the poor. Her husband supported her activities, which were supervised by her spiritual advisor, Conrad von Marburg (about whom much else could be written). Once widowed, Elizabeth transitioned to a monastic life of serving others.

. . . This holy virgin honored all the solemn feasts of the year with so great reverence that she would not suffer her sleeves to be laced on till the solemnity of the mass was finished, and she heard the office of the mass with so great reverence that when the gospel was read or the sacrament was lifted up, she would take off the brooches of gold and the adornments of her head, as circles or chaplets, and lay them down.

And when she had kept in innocence the degree of virginity, she was compelled to enter into the degree of marriage. And howbeit that she would not have been married, yet she dared not gainsay the commandment of her father. Therefore she consented to conjugal copulation, not in a libidinous fashion, but lest she disobey the command of her father, and to raise children for the service of God. Thus she submitted to the conjugal bed, but avoided sensual gratification. Then was she married to the landgrave of Thuringia, as the divine providence had ordained because she should bring many to the love of our Lord, and teach the ignorant. . . .

On a time when her husband the landgrave was gone to the court of the emperor, which was then at Cremona, she assembled from his granges all the wheat of the year, and administered to the needs of the poor who came from all sides, for at that time was great dearth in the country. And oft when she lacked money, she sold off her adornments for to give to the poor people. She did construct a great house under the castle, where she received and nourished a great multitude of poor people, and visited them every day, and she left not to visit them for any sickness or malady that they had, but she washed and wiped them with her own hands. . . . And moreover then she did so nourish in her house poor women's children so sweetly, that they all called her mother. . . .

And the blessed Saint Elizabeth had great desire that her husband should employ his puissance to defend the faith of God, and advised him, by salutary exhortations, that he should go visit the holy land and thither he went, and when he was there, this devout and noble prince, full of faith and of devotion rendered his spirit unto Almighty God, and so died, receiving the glorious fruit of his works. And then she received with devotion the state of widowhood. And when the death of her husband was published and known through all Thuringia, some of the vassals of her husband held her for a fool and wastrels of her goods, and threw her out of her heritage. . . .

And after this, one, her aunt, had great pity of her, and sent her wisely to her uncle, the bishop of Bamberg, who received her respectfully, and intended to marry her off again. [She said,] "and if mine uncle would marry me to any man I shall withstand it to my power and shall gainsay it with words. And if I may not so escape, I shall cut off my nose so that every man shall abhor me for my deformity." And then the bishop did send her to a castle against her will, for to abide there until some man should demand to have her in marriage. . . .

She took willful poverty, and her clothing was coarse and vile. She wore a russet mantle, her gown of another foul color, the sleeves of her coat were broken, and amended with pieces of other color.

Her father, king of Hungary, when he heard that his daughter was come to the estate of poverty, he sent a count to her for to bring her to her father; and when the count saw her sit in such a habit and spinning, he cried for sorrow, and said there was never a king's daughter seen that wore such a habit spinning wool. And when he had given his message and desired to have brought her to her father, she in no wise would agree to it. And she prayed our Lord that he would give to her grace to despise all earthly things and take away from her heart the love of her children, and to be firm and constant against the persecutions. And when she had accomplished her prayer, she heard our Lord saying: "Thy prayer is heard." . . .

And then this blessed Elizabeth received the habit of religion and put herself diligently to the works of mercy, for she received for her dower two hundred marks, whereof she gave a part to poor people, and of that other she constructed a large hospital in Marburg. Therefore she was called a wasteress and a fool, which all she suffered joyously. And when she had made this hospital, she became herself as an humble maid in the service of the poor. And she bore herself humbly in that service, that by night she carried the sick men in her arms for to let them do their necessities, and brought them again, and made clean their clothes and sheets that were foul. And when there were no poor, she would spin wool which was sent to her from an abbey, and from such she gave to the poor people.

And when she had been in much poverty she received five hundred marks of her dowry, much of which she gave unto the poor in an orderly fashion. . . .

Questions:

- *What does Elizabeth value most, beyond marriage and family?*
- *What difficulties does she face in living out her calling?*
- *How does Elizabeth build new family relationships through her ministry?*

Responses:

For more on this source, go to http://www.concisewesternciv.com/sources/sof8 .html.

PLENTY OF PAPAL POWER

As one of their unique prerogatives, the popes asserted the right to call **crusades** (1095–1492), the Christian version of holy war. Before the eleventh century, the Church recognized that war was sometimes necessary, but it was always sinful. Jesus's clear, explicit commands about nonviolence had even led many Christians in the Roman Empire to become pacifists. Augustine, however, had helped to establish what we call the ***just war theory***, which authorized wars to be fought if they were defensive, if they did not involve too much destruction or brutality, and if they aimed at establishing a more just peace. Although this theory could allow Christians to go to war under many circumstances, every act of killing nevertheless remained a sin that required confession, penance, and reconciliation.

But the concept of crusade actually turned the sin of war into a virtue. Instead of regretting the killing of another human being, the crusader could glory in it. Taking the lives of the enemies of God became a holy act, a good deed. No sin was committed—indeed, one got closer to heaven, just as if one were on a pilgrimage. The crusaders, then, were armed pilgrims. Instead of hiking to Santiago de Compostela to pray, they marched to Jerusalem to slay.

Many regions became the target of crusading activity. First, the popes gave their blessing on the crusading movement called the *Reconquista*, to reconquer Andalusia or Al-Andalus, ruled by the Islamic Moors since 711. Crusading armies from the kingdoms of Leon, Castile, and Aragon fought their way southward over centuries. A major Christian victory was Castile's taking of Toledo in 1085. Crusaders formed the Kingdom of Portugal in 1143. These kingdoms would wrangle with one another and the Moors until the end of the Middle Ages.

Second, the most famous crusades were those to liberate the Holy Land, Outremer (French for "across the sea"), or Palestine. These crusades started because of a misunderstanding with the Byzantine emperor. About AD 1040 (or 431 AH) the **Turks** seized power in Iran. The Turks were yet another horse-riding archer people who swept off the Asiatic steppes toward Europe, as the Huns and Avars had done before and as the Mongols would do later. The Turkish Seljuk dynasty converted to Islam, allowing it to win support among Muslims of other ethnicities. With surprising swiftness, the Seljuks conquered Mesopotamia and crossed the borders of the Byzantine Empire. They defeated, captured, and humiliated the Byzantine emperor of the Romans at the Battle of Manzikert (AD 1071; 453 AH). This decisive Turkish victory gained them Asia Minor, which became a new Turkish homeland, the basis of the country named Turkey in the twentieth century and Türkiye in the twenty-first. Many thousands of Turks migrated into Asia Minor, threatening the core of the Byzantine Empire.

The lands of Asia Minor had been some of the most important and prosperous areas for the Byzantines. Their loss further weakened the empire, leaving it less able to resist attack either by the Turks or others. The Byzantine emperor appealed to the pope to find mercenaries to help fight the Turkish Muslims. Pope Urban II used the request for his own purposes. In a speech at the Council of Clermont in France in November 1095, he spread myths of Muslim atrocities and exhorted knights and infantry to drive the "unclean" and "wicked" peoples from the lands of Christians, particularly from Jerusalem, which were actually under the control of Arab Egyptians, not the Turks (whom the pope called Persians). The inflamed Christians in France shouted, "God wills it!"

Surprisingly, or miraculously (as Western Christians believed), the First Crusade (1095–1099) achieved some success. At first, a ragtag horde of fervent outsiders and peasants marched toward Jerusalem, slaughtering along the way a few European Jews who refused to convert to Christianity. Unfortunately, the Turks then massacred or enslaved this rabble in Asia Minor before they ever reached Jerusalem. In 1099, however, a better-organized feudal army under various dukes and counts survived the difficult journey through Europe and Asia Minor. Their zeal overcame many losses brought on by battles, thirst, and hunger (the last sometimes solved by cannibalism). These crusaders then surprisingly conquered the Levantine coast, including Jerusalem itself, allegedly helped by the Holy Lance that had pierced Christ's side, as well as by fasting and processions. As they sacked the "holy city," the Christian crusaders waded up to their ankles in the blood of slaughtered Muslim men, women, and children in a mosque where they had taken refuge. The crusaders also burned Jews alive in their homes and synagogues. Then the rival crusading leaders set up several small principalities.

To survive, as it did for the next two centuries, the Latin Kingdom of Jerusalem and the crusading princedoms needed more than miracles. The new Western princes and knights in Outremer hardly cooperated either with one another or with the Byzantine Empire. They did make some efforts at cooperating with the Muslims who were their subjects and neighbors. They needed and received continued reinforcements from back in Europe. These zealous temporary conquerors disliked the civilizations of Byzantium and Islam, despite their shared Græco-Roman legacy. Their crusading mentality often prevented the Christians who had settled down in Palestine from working with the pragmatic Muslims or allowing peoples of different heritages to live together in peace.

Also complicating relations was a new clerical ideal inspired by crusading, namely, military monasticism. **Monk-knights** lived in organized Christian communities of chastity, obedience, and prayer like monastic monks, but they also fought as warriors on the battlefield against infidels. These militarized religious orders, like the Hospitallers or the Templars, provided much-needed resources of money, social service, and trained warriors.

The Middle East became a complicated jumble of diverse and competing elements. Although the Muslims called all Western Christians "Franks," the crusaders were actually deeply divided. The "Franks" rarely forgot that they came from England, Scotland, France, various provinces of the Holy Roman Empire, Italian merchant city-states, or Norman Sicily, all of whose governments quarreled with one another. Political loyalties, ethnic pride, and religious bickering often weakened their joint efforts in the Holy Land.

In turn, the "Franks" labeled all their Muslim opponents with the blanket term *Saracens*, which ignored the deep religious divisions of Sunni, Shiite, and even Assassin. This last, a secret sect of alleged hashish smokers, murdered its enemies, giving us the term ***assassination***. The Assassin murders of important Muslim leaders helped keep Islamic factions divided, terrorized, and at war with one another. Likewise, ethnic differences among Arabs, Egyptians, Iranians, Kurds, and Turks long delayed a united Islamic front. For decades, the disunion among Muslims allowed the crusaders to survive by playing one group off against the other. The Kurdish Saladin (Salah al-Din Yusuf ibn Ayb), who had taken control of the Egyptian caliphate, almost succeeded in defeating the crusaders in the 1180s. But the so-called Third Crusade of Richard "the Lionheart" of England reestablished a strong Christian foothold, even if Jerusalem remained under Muslim control.

Instead of strengthening Byzantium, the Crusades weakened that Christian empire, as western forces seized lands for themselves and increased Islamic fanaticism. In the Fourth Crusade of 1204, Latin crusaders actually attacked the Byzantine Empire itself. They seized and plundered the until-then unconquered Constantinople, briefly making it the center of a Latin Empire that lasted until 1261, when the Byzantines recaptured the city. Finally, in 1295, unified and zealous Muslims drove the crusaders back beyond the sea and reclaimed Palestine and the Levant.

The Holy Land had been lost, but other crusades continued. A third important region for crusading, after Palestine and the Iberian Peninsula, was in northeastern Europe, along the southern and eastern shores of the Baltic Sea. The **Teutonic Knights**, named after their common German ethnicity, were the most successful crusaders there. They had started as an order of crusading monk-knights in

Palestine. Meanwhile, various princes of the Holy Roman Empire were conquering the pagan peoples of eastern Europe and bringing in German immigrants to settle towns and farms in a movement called the *Drang-nach-Osten* (drive to the east). As part of these efforts, the Teutonic Knights gained a papal license to conquer the still-pagan Baltic people called Old Prussians. The Teutonic monk-knights founded their own principality, called **Prussia**, and henceforth ruled over the Prussian peasants, who were slowly converted to Christianity and assimilated into German culture. More crusading armies conquered and converted the last pagans of Europe, the Baltic peoples of Lithuanians, Estonians, and Latvians, although they managed to retain their languages and ethnicities.

The Crusades sprang from the conviction that Christians held the only answer to the meaning of life, combined with the military power to impose Christian beliefs beyond the heartland of Christian churches. The Crusades promoted little cultural exchange. The Muslims who interacted with the Franks considered them uncivilized, even barbaric. With few exceptions, political or intellectual leaders of East and West barely communicated with each other. Many westerners did develop a taste, though, for luxury goods, spices, rugs, porcelain, and silk that came from Muslim merchants, who themselves traded deep into Asia across the Silk Road or along the Arabian Sea. And even though the Crusades failed in Palestine, their successes on the borders of Europe, in the Iberian Peninsula and along the Baltic Sea, strengthened the supremacy of the Western Latin Church. In the few years since the schism between Eastern and Western Christianity in 1054, the latter had shown itself to be more dynamic and aggressive.

Soon, however, crusading fervor turned even against the Christian kings of the West. Popes began to use their power to call for crusades against internal foes within western Europe. The Gregorian Reform had created such a powerful papacy that it was even able to challenge royal governments such as that of the Holy Roman Empire. This was a shift away from the Frankish-Papal Alliance begun under the Carolingians. The papal coronations of Charlemagne in 800 and then Otto "the Great" in 962 as "emperors of the Romans" marked two high points of this bond. Otto I had also expanded the collaboration between church and state by relying on prince-bishops in Germany to help support his royal authority and military might. Furthermore, Otto's descendant, Henry III, reached a high point of royal influence over church affairs when he helped restore the disgraced papacy in 1046.

When Henry III died ten years later, however, the empire faced a crisis because his son and heir, **Henry IV** (r. 1056–1106), was only six years old. Many magnates used the long regency until Henry IV came of age to seize what they could from his royal rights and prerogatives. During this time the papacy also, as mentioned above, regained power and asserted its independence. Further, after a pope attacked the Normans in southern Italy and Sicily and lost, the victorious Normans actually formed an alliance with their recent enemy. Thus protected by Sicilian Normans, the popes no longer needed their traditional alliance with the German emperors.

When Henry IV became German king in his own right, he wanted to regain the power that his father Henry III had wielded. Henry IV's attempts unleashed a clash between church and state that changed the West. The **Investiture Struggle**, Contest, or Controversy (1075–1122) began because of the appointment of new bishops. Its name derives from the religious ceremony of investiture, which formally installs bishops in their office. Kings across Europe believed that they, by divine right, could install bishops. Against this practice, the radicals in the papal reform movement had expanded the definition of simony to include any royal involvement in the election of bishops, even when no money changed hands. Their extreme claim for "papal plenitude of power" threatened royal rights everywhere. In the Holy Roman Empire, where prince-bishops served as both vassals and spiritual leaders, the Investiture Struggle fueled civil war.

Disagreements between King Henry IV and Pope Gregory VII over who selected bishops in northern Italy sparked the first open fight over papal versus royal power (see figure 8.3). As King Henry IV's episcopal candidates clashed with

Figure 8.3. A Croatian king of the eleventh century, a contemporary of Emperor Henry IV. If this was King Zvonimir, he may have given obedience of his church to the authority of Pope Gregory VII. Yet the portrait shows someone prostrate at his feet, submitting to royal power. Note the attributes of kingship: crown, throne, robes, scepter (cross), and orb (ball representing the world).

papal nominees, Pope Gregory VII threatened Henry with excommunication. In the winter of 1076, Pope Gregory made good on his threat and also declared that Henry was no longer king.

Although the pope's legal claim to depose Henry was doubtful, Henry's enemies in Germany seized the opportunity to rise up against him. Even many of his loyal bishops abandoned him, although they had supported his denunciation of the pope. The Duke of Poland took the opportunity to declare himself king, with Gregory's approval. In a brilliant move, however, Henry rushed to Italy over frozen Alpine passes. The pope fled to the castle of Canossa, fearing an attack. Yet Henry arrived there with only a small retinue. Instead of raging in armor and ferocity, the king stood in sackcloth and repentance before the castle gates for three wintry days. Since the pope was in the job of forgiveness, he lifted Henry's excommunication. Although Henry remained, technically, deposed from his kingship, the confusion about his status gave him the opportunity to regroup his military forces and defeat most of his opponents.

Nonetheless, the war in the empire dragged on, as each side stuck to its interpretation of the role of bishops and their election. Gregory excommunicated Henry a futile second time. In turn, Henry's armies drove Gregory from Rome into exile with the Normans in southern Italy, where he died. Finally, Henry's own son rebelled against him to become Henry V (r. 1105–1125). Yet the pope excommunicated Henry V as well, because he relied on prince-bishops as his vassals. After two generations of open warfare, the Investiture Struggle between church and state finally ended with the **Concordat of Worms** in 1122. A concordat is an agreement between a state and the church, while Worms, a city on the upper Rhine River, ruled by a bishop, was where the treaty was agreed to by Henry V and the papacy. The treaty was a compromise. The principle that clergy and laypeople of dioceses were to elect their bishops was reasserted (except for Rome's bishop, of course). Still, the king could be present at each election in Germany (and thus exert an influence and even decide deadlocked elections). The German king gave up the right of investiture regarding a bishop's ecclesiastical office, but he could grant feudal possessions before a bishop's full consecration (at least within the German, if not in the Burgundian or Italian, parts of the empire). Similar compromises were eventually worked out in France and England.

While the Investiture Struggle was officially over, neither advocates of papal authority nor proponents of royal power were satisfied with this compromise. The Holy Roman Empire especially suffered from ongoing differences between emperors and popes. Emperor Henry V died without an heir in 1125, and, not surprisingly, a civil war erupted. Two major families took the lead in the competition for support from the magnates: the Welfs and the Staufens. Successive popes, using their influence and their recognized right to crown the German king as Holy Roman emperor, regularly played one side against the other over the next several generations.

By 1256, the Staufen dynasty had been extinguished, while the Welfs had shrunk to mere dukes again. Even worse for German power, the dynastic principle of succession within a family had been broken. Instead, seven powerful magnates (the archbishops of Cologne, Mainz, and Trier; the king of Bohemia; the Duke of Saxony; the Margrave of Brandenburg; and the Count Palatine by the Rhine) asserted themselves as "electoral princes." These seven claimed the sole right to select the next German king. As a result, the office of emperor/king of the Holy Roman Empire declined in power, if not prestige, while the actual rule of the local territorial magnates was magnified. Unfortunately for the popes, their obsession with weakening the Holy Roman emperor led them to ignore two new threats— the kings of England and France.

Review: How and why did the popes fight against their enemies?

Response:

PRIMARY SOURCE PROJECT 8: GREGORY VII VERSUS HENRY IV ABOUT CHURCH VERSUS STATE

Two different personalities inflamed the Investiture Struggle, a fight between religious and political leaders in the West. The first source presents a private list presumably drawn up by Pope Gregory VII, wherein he set a high bar for papal plenitude of power. The second source is German king Henry IV's public response to criticisms of his royal authority made by the pope.

Source 1: *Dictatus Papæ* by Pope Gregory VII (ca. 1075)

1. That the Roman Church was founded by God alone.
2. That the Roman bishop alone is properly called universal.
3. That [the pope] alone has the power to depose bishops and reinstate them.
4. That his legate, though of inferior rank, takes precedence of all bishops in council, and may give sentence of deposition against them.
5. That the pope has the power to depose [bishops] in their absence.
6. That we should not even stay in the same house with those who are excommunicated by [the pope].
7. That for [the pope] alone is it lawful, according to the needs of the time, to make new laws, to assemble together new congregations, to make an abbey of a canonry; and, on the other hand, to divide a rich bishopric and unite the poor ones.
8. That [the pope] alone may use the imperial insignia.

9. That the pope is the only person whose feet are kissed by all princes.
10. That his name alone shall be spoken in the churches.
11. That his name is unique in the world.
12. That he has the power to depose emperors.
13. That he may, if necessity require, transfer bishops from one see to another.
14. That he has power to ordain a clerk of any church he may wish.
15. That [the bishop] who is ordained by [the pope] may preside over another church, but may not hold a subordinate position; and that such a one may not receive a higher rank from any bishop.
16. That no general synod may be called without his consent.
17. That no action of a synod, and no book, may be considered canonical without his authority.
18. That his decree may be annulled by no one, and that he alone may annul the decrees of any one.
19. That he may be judged by no one else.
20. That no one shall dare to condemn a person who appeals to the apostolic see.
21. That to this See should be referred the more important cases of every church.
22. That the Roman Church has never erred, nor ever, by the testimony of Scripture, shall err, in perpetuity.
23. That the Roman pontiff, if he shall have been canonically ordained, is undoubtedly made a saint by the merits of blessed Peter, Saint Ennodius, bishop of Pavia, bearing witness, and many holy fathers agreeing with him, and as is contained in the decrees of blessed pope Symmachus.
24. That by his command and consent, it shall be lawful for subordinates to bring accusations.
25. That he may depose and reinstate bishops without assembling a synod.
26. That no one can be considered Catholic who does not agree with the Roman Church.
27. That [the pope] can absolve the subjects of unjust rulers from their oath of fidelity.

Source 2: Letter to Pope Gregory VII by King Henry IV of Germany (27 March 1076)

Henry, king not by usurpation, but by the holy ordination of God, to Hildebrand, not pope, but false monk.

This is the salutation which you deserve, for you have never held any office in the Church without making it a source of confusion and a curse to Christian men instead of an honor and a blessing. To mention only the most obvious cases out of many, you have not only dared to touch the Lord's anointed, the archbishops, bishops, and priests; but you have scorned them and abused them, as if they were ignorant servants not fit to know what their master was doing.

This you have done to gain favor with the vulgar crowd. You have declared that the bishops know nothing and that you know everything; but if you have such great wisdom you have used it not to build but to destroy. . . .

All this we have endured because of our respect for the papal office, but you have mistaken our humility for fear, and have dared to make an attack upon the royal and imperial authority which we received from God. You have even threatened to take it away, as if we had received it from you, and as if the empire and kingdom were in your disposal and not in the disposal of God. Our Lord Jesus Christ has called us to the government of the empire, but he never called you to the rule of the Church.

This is the way you have gained advancement in the Church: through craft you have obtained wealth; through wealth you have obtained favor; through favor, the power of the sword; and through the power of the sword, the papal seat, which is the seat of peace; and then from the seat of peace you have expelled peace. For you have incited subjects to rebel against their prelates by teaching them to despise the bishops, their rightful rulers. You have given to laymen the authority over priests, whereby they condemn and depose those whom the bishops have put over them to teach them. You have attacked me, who, unworthy as I am, have yet been anointed to rule among the anointed of God, and who, according to the teaching of the fathers, can be judged by no one save God alone, and can be deposed for no crime except infidelity. . . .

Come down, then, from that apostolic seat which you have obtained by violence; for you have been declared accursed by St. Paul for your false doctrines and have been condemned by us and our bishops for your evil rule. Let another ascend the throne of St. Peter, one who will not use religion as a cloak of violence, but will teach the life-giving doctrine of that prince of the apostles. I, Henry, king by the grace of God, with all my bishops, say unto you: "Come down, come down, and be accursed through all the ages."

Questions:

- *How does the structure of each source serve to carry its message?*
- *Which statements by Gregory would Henry find most or least objectionable?*
- *How does Henry personalize his argument?*

Responses:

For more on these sources, go to http://www.concisewesternciv.com/sources/psc8.html.

THE AGE OF FAITH AND REASON

The debates and writings provoked by the protracted conflict over papal authority helped to create a new literature of political theory, where individuals could speculate about the nature and purposes of government. Many of these new ideas came from an unexpected source, the Muslim-dominated Iberian Peninsula called Andalusia. When Christian crusaders liberated the city of Toledo in 1085, they found libraries full of books written in Arabic. Rather than burning them in fanatic zeal, they hired Jews who had long lived peacefully among the Arabs in Toledo to translate the books into Latin. In that city and soon in several more, the writings from the ancient Greeks and Romans as well as from more recent Muslims, such as Ibn Sina (Avicenna) and Ibn Rushd (Averroës), became available to medieval scholars. The books revealed the advancements Arab scholars and inventors had made in mathematics, astronomy, geography, science, and medicine. Much of this knowledge had been ignored in the West for centuries. More important for westerners was the rediscovery of the writings of Aristotle, whom the Arabs had long appreciated, studied, and interpreted. Aristotle's dialectic logic lit an intellectual fire in the monastic and cathedral schools that had survived the collapse of the Carolingian Empire. Students in the West leapt at the opportunity to learn.

Some of these schools blossomed into **universities**. The seven liberal arts continued as the basic curriculum for education. The new universities in turn provided advanced higher education, where students became "masters" and "doctors" (teachers) after studying the available subjects of canon law, secular law, medicine, theology, or philosophy. A now-familiar kind of person, the scholar, appeared in the West for the first time since the fall of Rome, inspired by the knowledge of antiquity and the scholarship that had continued to be pursued in the Byzantine and Muslim civilizations. The whole purpose of scholars in universities was to profess new knowledge (hence the title "professor"). They brought the light of education to what had been the darkness of ignorance. Secular rulers likewise recognized the value of these institutions of higher education and encouraged their foundation in places as diverse as Bologna, Salerno, Paris, Oxford, Cambridge, and Heidelberg. Yet academics formed an international guild, taking on themselves the responsibility to maintain quality in research and teaching.

The universities flourished under the protective umbrella of the Western Latin Church, even when secular princes founded them. Members of the academic system were technically clergy. Therefore, faculty and students fell under the special canon laws about universities and not under the laws of secular courts. The metaphor of the ivory tower used to describe higher education reflects the legal distinctions that separated universities from the urban communities in which they were located. Conflicts between townspeople and students were considered (and sometimes still are) "town" versus "gown" (although most students these days only wear academic gowns at graduation). Then, as now, youthful enthusiasm for extracurricular activities would sometimes annoy the neighbors. Then, as now, learning was difficult. Then, as now, some students preferred to study varieties of beer and wine rather than versions of Plato and Aristotle.

In the thirteenth century, donors and religious officials organized **colleges** as residential and educational spaces to help the young "bachelors" become more disciplined. The collegians might move on to the higher degrees of master or doctor, but many were satisfied with a "bachelor's degree," as they are today. The word *bachelor* also demonstrates that only men could study at these new, advanced schools. Women might receive some education in monastic schools, either as nuns or students of the nuns. Formal higher education, though, remained closed to women for centuries.

While the Western Latin Church was the cradle for this growing systematic legacy, it almost strangled that baby in the cradle. Once again, some Christians feared that ideas drawn from pagans were dangerous or irrelevant. Sources of knowledge from anything other than divine revelation frightened them. The use of human reason might lead to error, even heresy. The scholar **Peter Abelard** (b. 1080–d. 1142) seemed the perfect example. Through talent and sheer intellectual arrogance, he had become one of the leading academicians of his day. Then a scandalous affair with his pupil Heloïse almost ruined his career. He had arranged for himself to be her private tutor (since the canon law forbade women to attend schools and universities). After she had his illegitimate child, though, instead of properly marrying her, he seemed to want to put her away in a nunnery.[3] Her angry guardian hired some thugs who castrated Abelard. He recovered to resume his teaching at the university, where his ideas caused more problems for him. His celebrated definition of wisdom asserted that we must first doubt authority and ask questions; questioning will then lead us to the truth. Clearly, however, Abelard's questions led him into trouble, just as Socrates's had in ancient Athens. Their experiences suggest another basic principle:

Questioning authority is dangerous.

Abelard's opponents organized to silence him as a heretic. Those defenders of tradition seized upon his too-subtle explanation of the Trinity to get his ideas condemned at a local church council. They compelled him to stop teaching and even made him throw his own books into the flames.

A century later, though, Aristotle's dialectic method emerged victorious. Other clerics, notably **Thomas Aquinas** (b. 1225–d. 1274), used the tools of Aristotelian logic, as Abelard had, but were careful to make sure their answers were complete and orthodox. Aquinas thought that human reason, properly used, never conflicted with divine revelation. This *Scholasticism*, or philosophy "of the schools," is clearly expressed in Aquinas's book, *Summa Theologiae* (*Sum of Theology*). Therein he used dialectic arguments to answer everything a Christian could ever want to know about the universe. Aquinas allayed the fears about Aristotle by harnessing his logic for the Western Latin Church. Eventually Aquinas's logical

---

3. The influence of Arabic knowledge on these scholars is shown in Abelard's name for his child: Astrolabe, after a device that measures the positions of sun, planets, and stars to help in navigation.

explications seemed so solid and orthodox that later the Roman Catholic Church declared him its leading philosopher.

Despite Aquinas's success, the intellectual debate did not stop. Philosophers continued to argue about truth. Some drew on Plato's idealism that universal ideas shaped reality; others advocated **nominalism**, which proposed that only particular objects in the observable world existed. Another debate among scholars focused on politics, especially proposals about how best to regulate human society. Aquinas argued that the pope was the supreme human authority, but many others fought this idea with words and weapons. Kings sought out scholars and founded universities to argue for the supremacy of kingship and the royal connection to the divine, as had been done since the dawn of ancient civilizations.

Within these debates, the institution of the university further strengthened liberty for everyone by promoting new knowledge. Universities were not intended to convey merely the established dogmas and doctrines of the past or of powerful princes and popes. Instead, professors were, and are, supposed to expand upon inherited wisdom. Once the idea of learning new ideas became acceptable, it inevitably led to change. Nevertheless, popes continued to claim the allegiance of all humanity. Kings still tried to bind their clergy to them as servants to enforce the royal will. Neither of these attempts dominated in the West. By the end of the Middle Ages, no single power, whether the pope, king, one's own connection to God, or the independent human mind itself, would rule both the hearts and minds of mortals. Creative tensions between the demands of faith and the requirements of statehood enriched the choices available to peoples of the West.

During time off from intellectual pursuits, some scholars produced literature, which at the time was not studied at universities. Much of the literature of the Middle Ages was written in the language of scholarship, government, and faith, namely Latin. Student poets called Goliards were famous for their drinking songs, while other clergy produced histories, epic fantasies, mystical tracts, and religious hymns.

Modern universities today usually neglect to teach about this medieval Latin literature. They instead favor studying the literature from vernacular languages, those that people spoke at home and that later evolved into the European languages of today: Romance languages (French, Italian, Portuguese, Spanish, and Romanian), Germanic languages (German, Dutch, Norwegian, Danish, Swedish, and English), Celtic languages (which still survive as Irish Gaelic, Scots, Welsh, and Breton), and Slavic languages (Polish, Czech, Serbo-Croatian, Bulgarian, Russian, etc.). Vernaculars only slowly drove out Latin from government and universities. Eventually, languages that people spoke in their regular lives found validation in literary works that began to be written down after the twelfth century.

Romance became one of the most popular genres of vernacular literature. Works of romance prose or poetry often told of heroic adventures complicated by men and women facing challenges in their love. The most famous work of medieval literature is **Dante's _Divine Comedy_**, written in the vernacular dialect of Florence, which became the basis of modern Italian. The author had fallen for the ideal girl, Beatrice, but she had died young. In a vision, Dante journeys to hell (_Inferno_), where the Roman poet Vergil (also spelled Virgil) guides him through circles of punishment. Then Beatrice helps him through purgatory and finally to paradise to behold the ultimate love of God. Along the way, Dante sees and converses with many people whose stories and fates illustrate his view of good and evil, right choices and wrong choices.

In religious belief and practice in medieval western Europe, almost no one could choose their faith. While the few Jews and fewer Muslims could convert to Christianity, everyone else was baptized into the Western Latin Church. The structures built for worship, the cathedrals and parish churches, along with abbeys and monastery churches, remain as testimonies to the importance of faith in the Middle Ages. Believers replaced the simple and small churches of the early Middle Ages with such zeal that almost none survive today. Huge amounts of wealth, effort, and design went into constructing the new stone cathedrals, minsters, chapels, and parish churches of the High Middle Ages.

Church floor plans were usually based on the Latin cross or the ancient Roman basilica, which had a long central aisle (or nave, after the Latin word for "ship") with an altar for the Eucharist at the far end. The people gathered in the nave, while clergy carried out the sacrificial ceremonies around the altar. Music increasingly added decorative sound around the spoken word. We still have written copies of medieval music because monks invented a system of musical notation (no texts of Greek or Roman music have survived). Western music began with a simple plainsong, one simple line of notes called Gregorian chant, and evolved into complex polyphony, many notes sung alongside and around each other in harmony.

Two architectural styles of churches can be recognized as medieval.[4] The first style of stone churches we now call **Romanesque** because they inherited many of their design elements from ancient Roman buildings, especially the rounded arch (see figures 8.4 and 8.5). These churches, built between 1000 and 1300, tend

Figure 8.4. The blocky Romanesque Abbey of Maria Laach sits squarely on the earth, while its towers point to heaven.

---

4. For more on medieval art, go to http://www.concisewesternciv.com/arth/ar8.html.

Figure 8.5. The bright nave of the Romanesque Abbey of St. Godehard in Hildesheim illuminates the decorated paneled ceiling.

to have a blocky appearance, with thick walls necessary to hold up the roof. Still, they were built quite large, often airy, and full of light. The walls were frequently decorated with frescoes, and the capitals (tops) of columns were carved with sculptures illustrating key ideas of the faith. The second style of churches we now call **Gothic** (that insulting term mentioned at the beginning of chapter 7), although medieval builders called it the "modern" or the "French" style (see figures 8.6 and 8.7). After Western encounters with Islamic architecture in Andalusia, Sicily, and the Levant, Gothic cathedrals (built from about 1150 to 1500) adopted the pointed arches used there. The Gothic or pointed arch allowed architects to build even taller naves and open up the walls to more windows. They filled the windows with colored stained glass, designed in patterns and pictures of faith, pierced by light from heaven.

All these structures required highly skilled builders and a great deal of wealth. Townspeople competed with their neighbors in other communities to have the best possible church or cathedral. Sometimes their efforts to surpass one another led to disaster when improperly designed churches collapsed. Other times, sponsors ran out of resources, and construction remained idle for decades, centuries, or forever. Medieval skylines were sometimes defined by castles but always by churches, whose steeples people saw from far away and whose bells they heard throughout the surrounding countryside.

Figure 8.6.   The outside of the Gothic choir of the St. Vitus Cathedral in Prague highlights the flying buttresses holding up the walls, while their pinnacles reach toward heaven.

Figure 8.7. The high Gothic nave of Canterbury Cathedral opens a sacred space.

It made sense for the people under the authority of the high medieval Church of Rome to devote much time and energy to the religion of Christianity. The worldview that a moral life in this world prepared one for another life after death gave meaning to the troubles people faced as individuals and as a society. Kings might fight with popes, but that did not cast doubt on the meaning of the Gospels. Cluniac monks might live differently from Cistercians, who in turn did not act like Templars, but everyone observed rules put in place to conform their lives in obedience to the commands of the Church of Rome.

Review: *How did medieval culture reflect both religion and rationalism?*

Response:

A NEW ESTATE

While kings and popes quarreled over the leadership of the West, a revived social institution was growing that would overshadow them both: cities. Townspeople did not fit into the usual medieval classifications, typically divided into three estates: priests to pray for all, knights to fight for all, and peasants to work for all. No sooner had this trinitarian social division established itself in the popular imagination than the shock of economic development shattered its reality. By the twelfth century, the growing success and stability of medieval society had brought civilization to a new height. And by definition, towns and cities have always been synonymous with civilization.

The growth of these cities sprang directly from improvements in the economy and in political rule. Wealth from three-field farming and from monastic communities now financed those who did not themselves live on and work the land. The peace and order from the kings' feudal suzerainty offered opportunities for cities to organize. The Jews, forbidden from farming, also formed a core community of towns, as they had since Roman times. Some cities sprouted up from those originally founded by the Romans, especially where cathedrals and their clerics had maintained cores of religious communities. Since the time of the ancient Roman Empire, bishops had been obliged to live in their cathedral cities. Although bishops had been tempted to move away while cities were in decline during the early Middle Ages, boom times in the High Middle Ages made urban life attractive again. New cities also sprang up at the feet of castles, where feudal and manorial lords controlled a ready source of wealth. Some clever ecclesiastical and secular lords who saw the increasing importance of trade even planted new cities at crossroads and river crossings. Thus, cities such as Cambridge or Innsbruck arose, named after the bridges over their rivers.

Cities grew first and fastest in two regions, the Lowlands (modern Belgium, the Netherlands, and Luxembourg) and Lombardy in northern Italy (with nearby coastal cities such as **Venice**, Genoa, and Pisa). Both regions had dense populations and easy access to seaborne trading routes. By the twelfth century, merchants from those areas gathered at **fairs** in the French province of Champagne (long before the invention of the sparkling wine that has taken the province's name). These fairs were much more than a typical village market, since merchants from many communities competed with one another about price and quality. As farmers entered contests for their animals and produce, competition encouraged better and bigger specimens. The festive atmosphere entertained consumers with varieties of new goods to purchase. Today's county fairs across the United States and trade fairs in Europe are descendants of these medieval fairs. Then and now, fairs were engines of economic growth. The triad of the Lowlands, Champagne, and Lombardy became the core of new commerce in the High Middle Ages.

Traders from medieval Europe began to venture even farther abroad. The First Crusade to the Holy Land had founded new Western principalities in the Levant. Merchants followed right behind the military. The Lombard cities of Genoa, Pisa, and Venice exploited the Mediterranean sea routes, avoiding and soon outselling the Byzantine Empire. As the crusading states failed, the city-state of Venice in particular succeeded in becoming a significant maritime political power from the Adriatic to the Aegean. Venetians continued to oppose Muslim expansion while exploiting every commercial opportunity.

Some European merchants even ventured beyond the Eastern Mediterranean. A few traveled along the ancient Silk Road through Central Asia, which had long connected the Middle East with China. The most famous merchant was Marco Polo (b. 1254–d. 1324) from Venice, who with relatives and servants lived for a time in the Chinese Empire and East Asia in the second half of the thirteenth century. Upon his return to Europe, the Genoese jailed him as a prisoner of war. He used his time to write a book about his adventures. Many people scoffed at his tales (and some are scoffworthy), but he did accurately describe much of the wealth and glory of China, which far excelled that of Europe at the time.

Still, the Europeans kept gaining ground. Building on wealth produced from commerce, Europeans were starting to use machines to make products, a process called **industrialization**. Years ago, history textbooks credited European inventors with technological innovation. Clearly, though, Asians and North Africans used similar machines decades, if not centuries, before the westerners. Merchants brought back from the comparatively advanced Chinese, Indian, and Muslim civilizations useful iron plows, horse collars, drills, gears, and pumps. In the thirteenth century, Europeans did invent spectacles or eyeglasses, which enabled many more people to perform fine-detail work and even to read a book like this. In any case, after the twelfth century, industrialization further increased the availability of goods to Europeans. The word *manufacture*, which originally meant making something by hand, now described people working with machines.

A boom in textiles arose from a **cottage industry**, in which merchants traveled from home to home, door to door, "putting out" goods to be manufactured in individual houses and then picking up the finished products to be sold. Family members in one home might spin the raw wool into thread, down the lane they might weave the thread into cloth, and on the other side of the village they might sew the cloth into a tunic. Peasant wives and children had more time to devote to this new work because of labor saved in the farm fields through iron plows, horse collars, and three-field planting. Peasants thus earned extra income that allowed them to purchase still more new goods. An increasing spiral of growth followed. As some people's work became more specialized, they quit being peasants and became artisans and craftspeople who lived in towns, earning their living from the skills of their minds and hands, not from labor on the land. Towns needed this internal immigration to overcome the death rates from urban diseases.

As mentioned before, these commercial people of towns and cities did not easily fit into the medieval trifold conception of clergy, nobles, and commoners. With no other option, the townspeople became commoners, yet their social status shared little with that of the medieval serf. They gained a new status as burghers, burgesses, or **bourgeoisie** (drawn from the German word for castle). Burghers were free men (bourgeois women, of course, remained less free than their fathers, husbands, and sons). Unlike the subservient serfs, burgesses were not bound to the land but traveled freely. Indeed, the bourgeoisie held the freedom of ownership, buying and selling of property, and possessing it in peace. They were not responsible to the manorial courts. Instead, the townspeople exercised the freedom of self-government, creating laws and representative political institutions such as **mayors** and **town councils**. Many burghers even gained the right to bear arms (at this time, both swords and heraldic crests). Towns might be thought of as huge castles, although with a multitude of families living behind high stone walls instead of only one. Townspeople raised their own troops and defended their castle-like city walls. Many town patricians even gained entrance to the nobility and aristocracy with coats of arms, imitating the lords who dominated society. None imagined that the bourgeois way of life would one day dominate Western civilization.

These freedoms did not come easily. The townspeople often had to fight to have their liberties and rights respected by the well-born lords of society. They began to organize **communes**, meaning they sought to have the laws recognize them as a collective group of people who organized their own affairs separately from the rest of nobility-dominated Europe. The kings, dukes, bishops, and magnates often resisted and attacked the communal corporations at first, seeing them as a threat to their authority and social superiority. Eventually, however, the lords largely accepted the townspeople, recognizing the economic advantages of a flourishing urban life that created new wealth. The lords granted charters of liberty to the burghers, defining and affirming their self-government and civil rights.

The communal self-government of mayors and town councils slowly revived democratic government in the West.

Once again, though, democracy was difficult. Having successfully fought the lords, townspeople next fought one another over a share of the authority and wealth. Medieval citizens often mixed politics with violence. The rich and powerful wanted to exclude the poor and the powerless. The elite patricians fought against the middle-class artisans. Both tried to keep down the teeming rabble. If frustrated by loss in an election or by exclusion from any political participation at all, groups of townspeople might assassinate their rivals or riot to overthrow them.

Institutions called **guilds** often provided a peaceful framework for political, social, and economic interaction. These organizations allowed owners (the masters) and workers in a craft or trade (baking, shoemaking, cloth dyeing) to supervise the quality and quantity of production. Even universities (whose product was knowledge) structured themselves as guilds. Master artisans trained the next generations of apprentices and journeymen (day laborers, from the French *journée*, or day) in the proper skills. Guilds also became the vehicles for social and political cohesion, as they provided social welfare for their members, organized celebrations, and set up candidates for urban elections. Despite the instability that always accompanies democracy and economic change, cities and their civilization were a success in the West again. Towns soon began to grow in size and numbers comparable with the contemporary civilized societies of Islam, India, and China.

To minister to these new townspeople, new kinds of monks called **mendicants** began to appear in the thirteenth century. Their name comes from the Latin word for begging, and that is how they were supposed to receive their livelihood. The earlier Benedictine or Cistercian monks drew income from the production of the land. Mendicants were to live from the excess production of town commerce. The townspeople had become wealthy enough to have extra money that they devoted to charity. The mendicants were to preach and teach, living only from alms.

Appropriately, the mendicants preached against the popular values of city life. The new urban elites gloried in wealth and ostentation, imitating the nobility. This attitude was *materialism*, valuing goods and pleasures provided by wealth in this world. The most famous medieval Christian opponent of this materialism was the founder of the Franciscans, **Francis of Assisi** (b. 1181–d. 1226). Francis helped to promote the idea of *apostolic poverty*: that the original apostles were poor, and so modern clergy should be also. He set an example of rejecting the wealth of the patricians and reaching out to the new urban poor.

As took place with previous monastic reforms, the success of mendicant friars led later generations to stray from the original ideals. They acquired endowments, properties, and possessions. The Franciscans were soon split between those who sought apostolic poverty and those who observed obedience to the wealthy and politically powerful papacy. Another main group of mendicants, the Dominicans, focused on education and fighting new heresies that were already appearing in the twelfth century. Serious heresies had not been a problem since the German barbarians who were Arian Christians had converted to orthodox catholic Christianity at the beginning of the early Middle Ages. Since then, everyone in the West had to be Christian.

Everyone, that is, with the exception of the Jews. Christian authorities allowed Jews to retain their faith, honoring them as the original "chosen people" of their God. The Christian authorities nevertheless carefully and legally discriminated against the Jews, confining them to living in towns (and usually particular neighborhoods), prohibiting them from owning farmland, and allowing them only certain professions, such as moneylending. Christians periodically stole their wealth, falsely accused them of crimes, attacked them when things went wrong (such as during a plague), forced Jews to convert, then killed them if they would not. At any time, a king might expel the Jews from the kingdom, as happened in England in 1290 and France in 1306. Known as "Ashkenazi" Jews, they found refuge in the Holy Roman Empire, the Kingdom of Poland, and the Grand Duchy of Lithuania. Even had it been allowed, no Christian would have chosen to convert to Judaism.

The new heresies of the High Middle Ages were different from Judaism, since they offered real alternatives to catholic orthodox Christianity. They probably arose because of the increasing success of the European economy. More trade with the East (eastern Europe, the Middle East, Asia) transported new ideas from those distant places. As some merchants became wealthy, enjoying their own materialism, many decided that the priests and monks should not share in their rising economic comforts. Instead, they listened to advocates of apostolic poverty.

One of the first successful heretics was Pierre Valdès (or Peter Waldo), who lived in the late twelfth century. Like Francis of Assisi a generation later, Waldo rejected materialism and called for poverty and simplicity among the clergy. Bishops uncomfortable with Waldo's appeals tried to silence and punish him. Peter Waldo refused and escaped into the Alps, where he set up small groups, the **Waldensians**, some of which persist to this day. A few isolated Waldensian villages survived every effort by the official Church to kill or convert them.

The other major heretical movement was *Catharism* (which probably comes from a word meaning "the pure"), whose followers were also known as **Albigensians** (named after the southern French town of Albi). The Cathars' dualism alleged that God ruled the spirit while the devil claimed material things, a belief similar to the early Christian heresy of Gnosticism. Since in their view even the flesh was evil, Cathars resisted the pleasures of this world in order to gain heaven. They rejected the Western ecclesiastical hierarchy and set up their own counter-church. As they attracted members from the nobles, townspeople, and peasants, the Cathars broke the monopoly of the official Western Latin Church, especially in southern France.

The Western Christians struck back. First, the mendicants preached the Catholic faith, but soon words were not enough. Next, they revived the ancient Roman legal procedure known as the **inquisition**, which comes from the Latin word for "inquire" or "ask." Normally, someone had to submit a complaint before an investigation about a crime could be initiated. To maintain public order, however, the Romans occasionally used the inquisition as an alternative. In this procedure, the government commissioned a tribunal to uncover crimes committed in a certain region, even if no complaints had been officially registered. Traveling judges were empowered to investigate crimes, arrest people, prosecute alleged criminals, and punish them. Thus the modern legal powers that are today divided among police, district attorneys, judges, and juries were combined into one lethally effective instrument.

The Western religious authorities in the thirteenth century thought the situation serious enough to reinstate this method. When the majority of people in a region had converted to heresy, no complaints of the crime would come to authorities. So popes and bishops commissioned investigators, often Dominicans, to ferret out heretics. They could enter a province only with the explicit permission of the local political ruler. After finding heretics guilty, the clerical inquisition then handed them over to "the secular arm," namely the local political powers, which burned them to death at the stake. The use of torture during the investigations has disgraced the inquisition in the history of jurisprudence. At times, some historians and critics of religion have exaggerated the inquisition's excesses of brutality and injustice. Even so, unless one believes that any means is justified by ending sin, the "Holy Inquisition" remains a blight on Christianity.

Surprisingly, even the Holy Inquisition did not stamp out the Cathar heresy. So the Western Latin Church finally resorted to its highest level of violence: a crusade. In 1225, Pope Innocent III sanctioned a Catholic invasion of southern France to destroy the Cathars. The so-called Albigensian Crusade succeeded. One story goes that in a town in the south of France, everyone was massacred. Those who worried that some Catholic Christians might have been caught in the general slaughter were told that "God will know his own," bringing the righteous into heaven and sending the heretics to hell. The success of the Albigensian Crusade strengthened the French king by putting confiscated lands under his direct control. The crusade and subsequent royal rule destroyed a flourishing, distinctly southern French culture, along with the Cathars. In the next centuries, ecclesiastical leaders elsewhere in many provinces likewise called other crusades against several rebellious enemies, since by definition defying the Church's authority in any fashion was heretical.

Review: *How did the revival of trade and towns change the West?*

Response:

NOT THE END OF THE WORLD

The spread of heresy might have threatened people's souls, but the spread of disease surely plagued their bodies. Tragically, trade connections with Asia brought not just spices and silks but also the disaster called the **Black Death**. In 1347, contagions that had swarmed along trade routes from the East entered the crowded and dirty cities of Europe. For the next several years and regularly thereafter, plague sprawled through both urban and rural Eurasia. Most research now blames the plague on the bacterium *Yersinia pestis*, spread first from fleas on black rats to people, then from person to person. It manifested with increasingly lethal bubonic (showing swelled buboes or lumps), pneumonic (attacking the lungs), and septicemic symptoms (quick-killing fevers), suggesting that more than one disease was at work. Regardless, the Black Death swept through the population of western Europe, killing probably one out of three people. The impact varied, though, since some regions saw almost no sign of disease while other towns were nearly wiped out. Well into the eighteenth century, less virulent waves of plague returned to strike down tens of thousands of Europeans, over and over (and it still appears in recent times). One successful way to stop the spread of pestilence was the quarantine, or (as the name indicates) forty days of isolation to show that people were not infected. Otherwise, in their fear and ignorance, people acted as they often act in crises. Some tried to help others, some fled, some surrendered to despair, and some whooped it up as if it were their last day on earth.

Aiding the spread of disease was again a climate change of general cooling. What historians call a "mini ice age" began about 1300 and lasted until about 1700. The climate in Europe became a few degrees cooler. Winters lasted longer, and summers got shorter. This change shortened growing seasons and increased rainfall where it was not needed. The effects sharply reduced food production, and a hungry European population became even more susceptible to illness. A widespread famine broke out between 1315 and 1322.

Historians usually see the period between 1300 and 1350 as the transition from the High Middle Ages (ca. 1000–1350) to the later Middle Ages (ca. 1300–1500). The climatic change and increase in epidemics created what scholars call a demographic catastrophe that sent the gradually rising European population into a sharp decline. The high mortality rates and fear of death led at times to a breakdown of the fragile social order that had been created during the High Middle Ages. As the later Middle Ages followed, everyone had to cope with rougher natural circumstances, the continued political and social dominance of the clergy and knightly nobility, increasing competition with townspeople, and dissatisfaction among the peasants. The later Middle Ages was a time of increasing unrest and uncertainty.

The reduction in population also caused labor shortages that forced economic changes. Peasant farming shifted from lord-serf to landlord-tenant. Now peasants' uncertain livelihood depended on paying rent instead of long-standing customary obligations such as labor services and portions of crops. Post-plague, if a peasant failed to come up with the rent, he and his family might more easily be thrown off the land and left with nothing. Also, landlords tried to focus more on cash crops like wheat for export instead of vegetables for local consumption. The latter had traditionally been encouraged on the self-sufficient manor, when farmers grew what they needed to eat. While serfdom had limited social and political freedom, being tied to the land had allowed serfs a certain economic freedom—they could at least feed their families. Their new change in status left them more vulnerable to homelessness, hunger, and poverty.

Peasants began to rebel against both the restrictions of serfdom and, para-doxically, the insecurity caused by its decline. Some even thought of a religious justification, as shown in the rhyme, "When Adam delved and Eve span, who was then the gentleman?"[5] **Peasant revolts** started to happen with some regu-larity. The most famous are the Jacquerie, a rebellion in France in 1358, and the Wat Tyler Revolt in England in 1381. In the first stage of rebellions, peasants killed a few landlords, burned some buildings and records, and grabbed property for themselves. Sadly for the peasants, virtually all their revolts ended in defeat. Within weeks, royal or noble armies reorganized and slaughtered hundreds, if not thousands, of peasants. The traditional landholding clergy and nobility, joined by the bourgeoisie, were too well organized, too well armed, and too powerful. That these rebellions increasingly took place at all, though, showed that something was wrong with the order of society.

In France and England, the leadership of the clergy likewise eventually found itself challenged anew by powerful authoritarian kings, which Germany lacked. During the High Middle Ages, when popes had struggled with the Holy Roman emperors over leadership in "Christendom," the papacy seemed to have won. The constant change of royal dynasties because of elections made the Holy Roman emperor seem more of an annoyance than a puissant monarch. The German kings of the Holy Roman Empire declined in authority except in their own personal dynastic lands. In contrast, German dukes, counts, prince-bishops, and even bar-ons and some imperial knights ruled as near-sovereign territorial princes.

The kings of France and England, however, became strong monarchs with centralized authority over their realms. The kings of both of those countries drew on the power of dynasty, military might, and taxes on towns. They also relied on the advice and support of people through elected representative bodies, the Estates-General in France and the Parliament in England. Both kingdoms were expanding. England almost succeeded in conquering Scotland, held off only by the plucky heroics of William Wallace and Robert the Bruce in the early 1300s. The English did, however, increasingly dominate Ireland and Wales. The French, meanwhile, nibbled away at the Western borders of the Holy Roman Empire. Even more important, France and England offered renewed resistance to papal claims of authority.

A new power conflict appeared during the reign of Pope **Boniface VIII** (r. 1294–1303). Boniface resisted the kings of England and France, who wanted to

---

5. Or, reworded for modern sense: "When the first human beings worked, Adam dug in the ground and Eve spun thread like peasants; there existed then no class distinctions as they do now when nobles rule and profit from peasant labor."

tax their clergy to finance a war they were preparing to fight against each other. In two papal bulls (from 1296 and 1302), the pope decreed and commanded that papal permission was needed for kings to tax the clergy and Church lands. He reminded the monarchs that popes commanded kings, not the other way around. Furthermore, to be saved from hell, every Christian, king and commoner alike, needed to obey the Roman pontiff.

The pope's declarations notwithstanding, the kings of England and France had other ideas. The kings retaliated with economic sanctions, shutting down their borders and forbidding all export of precious metals and revenues to Rome. They convened their representative assemblies (Parliament and the Estates-General), many of whose clergy representatives sided with their nations against the pope. The most extreme reaction was from King Philip IV "the Fair" of France. He sent agents to Italy who tried to kidnap the pope while he was enjoying the summer in Anagni, away from the heat of Rome. Although freed by Anagni's townspeople, the shocked Boniface died a month later. If a German emperor had tried to do this fifty years earlier, the next pope would have proclaimed a crusade against him. In this case, the king of France escaped with impunity.

Indeed, Philip IV tried to grab hold of the papacy for himself and his dynasty. He helped to elect a Frenchman as pope, Clement V (r. 1305–1314), a man who not only favored the French king but also packed up and moved the Curia out of Rome to the city of **Avignon** on the southeastern border of France. There the papacy resided throughout the so-called **Babylonian Captivity** (1309–1377), named after the real Hebrew exile 1,800 years earlier. The popes were hardly captives. Actually, they expanded their administration of the Western Latin Church. They paid for their palace and power by collecting tithes and annates (the first year's income from important ecclesiastical offices such as bishop and abbot). Popes even took over provisions or reservations (the right to name men to church offices, especially bishoprics), although these appointments were often done in consultation with, and at the request of, the local princes.

Many Christians were properly aghast at this situation. The pope was, of course, the bishop of Rome, and by canon law a bishop was to reside in his cathedral city. It often seemed, as the number and influence of French-born cardinals increased, that the papacy had become a tool of the French king. Many called for the pope to return to Rome, including the famous inspirational religious figures Catherine of Siena and Bridget of Sweden.

Finally, Pope Gregory XI did return to Rome in 1377, only to die the next year. The cardinals, under pressure from the Roman mob, quickly elected an Italian, Urban VI (r. 1378–1389). To their dismay, the cardinals found him demanding, hot tempered, and cruel. Rather than deal with the situation forthrightly, most of the cardinals left Rome for the cooler temperatures of Anagni. There they declared that their election of Urban was invalid and elected a new pope of French descent, Clement VII (r. 1378–1394). They then blithely returned with their new pope to Avignon. Urban, meanwhile, refused to recognize his deposition and continued to reign in Rome. Thus the Western Latin Church was faced with a unique schism: two popes who had been elected by the same cardinals. Different princes chose allegiance to one pope or the other, often depending on whether they liked the French (and their Avignon puppet) or not.

This "Papal Schism of 1378" or **Great Western Schism** did not turn out as disastrous or long-lasting as the other "Great Schism" that separated Western catholic and Eastern orthodox Christianity back in 1054.[6] Theoretically, this division could have gone on forever, since both popes created cardinals, and each new college of cardinals elected its own papal successor after its pope had died. At one point, the majority of cardinals from both parties decided to end the schism by meeting at Pisa in 1409. In the shadow of the leaning tower, they deposed both the Avignon and Roman pontiffs and elected a new pope. Since the first two refused to recognize their depositions, the Western Latin Church now had three popes!

This Great Western Schism was healed by the old practice of *conciliarism*. The first councils dated back to the days of the Christians' liberation under Constantine. The ancient Church used councils to create hierarchy and to resolve differences. Important ecumenical councils of all Christians had then been held for centuries until the Great Schism in 1054 between the "Catholics" and "Orthodox" ended the possibility of truly universal Christian cooperation. As popes revived "universal" councils (for the West only) in the eleventh century, they used them to dominate the Western Latin Church. Now, however, a council saved the papacy. Supported by the Holy Roman emperor, Sigismund of Bohemia, all parties attended the **Council of Constance** (1414–1417). The council first gained the resignation or deposition of the three popes based in Pisa, Avignon, and Rome and then successfully elected a new, universally recognized pope, Martin V.

The representatives to the Council of Constance understood the advantages of representative assemblies such as Parliament in England, the Estates-General in France, the Cortes in Castile, and the Diet in Germany. Therefore, they wrote a constitutional role for councils within the Western Latin Church's governance which required that new councils be called at regularly set intervals. Nevertheless, the recovered papal monarchy stamped out that idea, which would have diluted the popes' absolute authority. Popes delayed and dissolved later councils until they declared as a heresy any appeal to a future council. The papacy in Rome settled onto its seemingly secure foundations.

Nonetheless, times were changing. The pope's victory faded as the structures of civilization ended the Middle Ages and began the early modern period. The Middle Ages had begun with Christendom, but its body of faith had fragmented into the Western Latin and Eastern Orthodox Churches. In much of Europe, popes of the Church in Rome strained to rule both their own clergy and the secular lords, while alternate forms of religious life began to sprout up. The three early medieval divisions of society (the clergy who prayed, the knights who fought, and the serfs who worked for both) adapted to a fourth (the townspeople who manufactured and traded). Before long, old ideas and new practices further fractured what had once been Christendom, transforming it into our modern West.

---

6. A few history books label this schism of multiple popes from 1378 to 1417 as the "Great Schism," without the qualifying terms *papal* or *Western*. That exaggerates its significance compared to the separation of Western and Eastern Christians, which still endures.

Review: *How do the later Middle Ages expose the problems of medieval institutions?*

Response:

Make your own timeline.

1000   **1500**

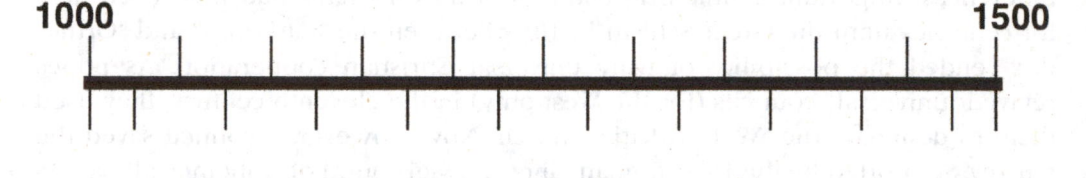

CHAPTER 9

Making the Modern World

The Renaissance and Reformation, 1400 to 1648

A lready in the fifteenth century, some intellectuals had begun to claim that centuries of backwardness had given way to a new "modern" age (see timeline D). All people, of course, believe they live in modern times, and they do. For historians, this transition to a "modern" time period, or even "early modern," reflects the changing elements of society, state, and culture compared with those of the Middle Ages and before. One key to this transition was a new appreciation for classical antiquity, the culture of ancient Greece and Rome. Historians have named that perception the **Renaissance**, meaning a rebirth of attitudes toward Græco-Roman culture. Classical antiquity had, of course, been appreciated to one degree or another since its collapse in the West a thousand years before. Beginning around 1400, however, a renewed interest in ancient history intertwined with economic, political, and religious developments. The Renaissance was the first of a series of modern "revolutions" during which Europeans decided to remake their culture based on ideas. Reflecting on the past while sailing into the unknown, the Europeans traveled out of the later Middle Ages (ca. 1300–1500) and landed in the early modern period of history (ca. 1400–1815) (see timeline C).

THE PURSE OF PRINCES

As the Europeans recovered from the onslaught of the Black Death, the resurging economics of the towns propelled them into undreamed-of wealth and success. Amid plague and peasant rebellion, a dynamic idea later called *capitalism* began to catch on. Capitalism was a new form of economic practice that went beyond the markets of farmers or fairs. The "capital" of capitalism refers to a substantial amount of wealth that is available, and necessary, for investment. Many businesses require capital to begin operation or to maintain themselves. One form of capital is profit, wealth left over after all expenses have been paid. When profits could be obtained, the practice of capitalism dictated what to do with them: reinvest.

In its simplest form, then, capitalism means to invest capital, make profits, then reinvest those profits. The usual human inclination is to spend excess wealth on showiness: fine homes, gourmet foods, extravagant parties, designer fashions, and grand edifices. One can, of course, give money away or bury it in the ground. Investing profit in one's own operations or in providing start-up and operating funds for another business, however, promoted long-term growth. Thus, capitalism became an engine for economic progress: wealth bred more wealth. Likewise, capitalism encouraged innovation. Clever investors looked for a new enterprise, a novel endeavor, which, if successful, would bring an even greater profit.

Only much later did historians and theorists use the exact term *capitalism*. Some historians also argue that other civilizations, either Muslim, Indian, or Chinese, practiced capitalism first and that westerners learned its techniques from them. Wherever it came from, more problematic is that people today often misunderstand the term *capitalism*. Many people often confuse capitalism with free markets. While capitalism requires markets (a space for people to exchange goods and services), they do not have to be entirely free (without restrictions imposed by authorities). This leads to another basic principle:

> **There is no such thing as an entirely free market; all markets have rules and costs.**

One of the key arguments among market participants, then and now, is over how many regulations or fees there should be. The number of rules and expenses imposed on markets makes them more or less free or fair. If the market is an actual place, there are expenses for rent, cleaning, and upkeep. Many fees are taken by middlemen. One of the most important rules determines how much honesty is required between buyer and seller. And breaking certain rules sometimes can mean punishment by law (see figure 9.1).

Another ongoing difficulty with capitalism has been when people lost their capital in financial markets. If a business venture failed, not only was there no profit, but the original capital could also disappear as well. Risk has always existed with capitalism—wealth can simply vanish into thin air. On the one hand, luck, creativity, and business acumen can create huge funds from a small incentive. On the other hand, irrational exuberance, misfortune, stupidity, and economic ignorance can just as easily destroy riches. Poor investors have lost vast assets. For example, a sudden mania for tulips in the Netherlands during the 1630s drove up prices many times their previous worth. At the most extreme, one exotic bulb for a garden cost the equivalent price of a mansion. When the bubble burst, tulip bulbs once again became merely potential flowers, that is, very affordable. Yet since early capitalists succeeded more often than they failed, the European economy grew over the long term. Capitalists may have accumulated most of the new wealth, but they also provided employment and opportunities for others to become wealthier. Indeed, capitalism helped make Western civilization the most

Figure 9.1.   This woodcut from a legal handbook (ca. 1500) shows the various punishments monarchs inflicted on criminals. Top row: cutting off an ear, preparation for dunking, disembowelment, burning alive at the stake, eye gouging, hanging. Bottom row: flaying, beheading, breaking with the wheel, cutting off a hand. (University of Pennsylvania)

powerful culture the world has ever known, during what historians have called the **Commercial Revolution** (1350–1600).

The encouragement of innovation and the increase in wealth after the Black Death made medieval economic methods obsolete. The guild's hierarchical, regulated structure stifled progress, as measured by the creation of new forms of business. By definition, the guild promoted one kind of industry and opposed others. The masters who ran guilds increasingly seemed to want only to hold on to their power rather than seek improvements. While guilds had served to help medieval towns thrive, they were too inflexible to adapt to capitalism's drive for change.

The Commercial Revolution put in place more modern economic methods. The partnership or firm replaced the guild as the important structure for business. Usually this involved a family or several families pooling their resources to provide capital. As a business evolved, different members or alliances might come and go, which also encouraged creativity.

In the fourteenth century, families began to establish **banks**, the premier capitalist institution. The new banks evolved from benches of money changers into organizations that housed money and earned profits through finance. While bankers paid interest to attract depositors, the collection and safeguarding of deposits was merely a means to accumulate capital. Bankers invested assets as loans. A system of banks also allowed money to flow more easily from one part of Europe to another without anyone actually lugging around boxes of gold bars and bags of silver coins. Instead, banks issued bills of exchange, the forerunner of the modern check (an idea probably borrowed from Muslim trading partners). Commencing in Italy, bank branches sprang up in cities all over Europe.

This rise of finance as a major economic activity required some religious reform. Up to this time, most moneylending in the medieval West had been carried out by Jews, since Christians interpreted holy scripture as declaring that making profit from money was sinful usury. So they let Jews make loans. Jews held the same belief in not making profit from other Jews, but they allowed loans to Christians. By the close of the Middle Ages, Christian leaders interested in profit redefined the sin of usury to allow more lending so that they could finance palaces and church building without borrowing from Jews.

To keep track of all this wealth, Italian money counters invented double-entry bookkeeping (borrowing some ideas from Hindu merchants). Since ancient times, businesses had simply entered a running tally of incomes and expenses in paragraph form, if they kept records at all. This new method, much like any modern checkbook or bank statement, arranged the moneys into two columns, which could be easily added or subtracted; a third column tracked the running sum of overall credit or debt. Most important was the replacement of Roman numerals of letters (I, V, X, L, etc.) with "Arabic" numbers, which Muslims had borrowed from Hindus. Thus, a merchant could better account for how much the business had on reserve or owed.

As in most economic revolutions, benefits and costs distributed themselves unevenly among varied social groups. People still earned wealth through agriculture, commerce, and manufacturing, but finance began its rise to predominance. As happens so often, the rich became richer while the poor became poorer. Women were encouraged to work, although in lower-status jobs at lower wages than men were paid for the same work. Women workers' low cost and the ease with which they could be fired helped businesses maintain their profit levels. A growing class of menial laborers piled up at the bottom of the social scale as well-paid family artisans lost out to cheap labor. The wealthiest merchants began to merge with the nobility, becoming indistinguishable in their manner of living if not in the family trees of their noble ancestors. As a whole, though, the overall affluence and standard of living in Western society rose.

Princes who took advantage of this economic boom became the monarchs of the later Middle Ages and early modern times. The practice of **public debt**, allowed by the new banking system, financed princely proliferation of power. Before capitalism, a prince's debts were considered his own—he had to finance them from his dynastic revenues. Although a prince's incomes were often quite substantial, they were limited by agricultural production and a few taxes levied on trade. The new idea of public debt meant that bankers could finance loans to the princes, and then all of the prince's subjects had to pay the loans off through taxes and customs duties on imports and exports. Throughout history, governments have had the ability to raise taxes and pile on debt as much as they could get away with. If governments raised taxes beyond what taxpayers could tolerate, however, reaction ranged from political concessions to revolution. Capitalism offered a safer alternative to simply demanding more contributions, since the money came from bankers, who usually supported growing debt because they profited off interest on loans. Sometimes a prince's debts grew too large, and through bankruptcy he defaulted on his debts. Then capital disappeared, followed by business failures and unemployment. More often, however, governments settled up their loans with interest, the bankers got their profits, and the princes became more powerful while the common people paid the price in the end. A prince might also try to raise revenues by plundering a neighboring country, but that was shortsighted. Best was to annex another province, help it prosper, and tax it.

Such control over territories caused the **Hundred Years War** (1338–1453) between France and England. King Edward III of England's Plantagenet dynasty wanted to protect some independence for Flanders (for wool) and preserve what few English territories remained in the southwest of France (for wine). The latter region, called Guyenne, was the last remaining French province of Henry II's Angevin Empire (most of which his son John had lost in the thirteenth century). The kings of France wanted both Guyenne and Flanders for their own. A French dynastic crisis provided King Edward a pretext for war. King Philip IV "the Fair" had died in 1314, leaving three young sons. Within a few years, they had all died without leaving any male heirs in the Capetian dynasty—a situation France had not faced for more than three hundred years. The French aristocracy, without too much fighting, decided on Philip's grandnephew, who succeeded as King Philip VI, the first king of the Valois dynasty (1328–1589). Meanwhile, however, Edward III of England claimed the throne of France as a grandson of Philip IV (although through Philip's daughter).

As the name implies, the Hundred Years War took generations to grind its way toward a conclusion. Along the way, war and politics changed decisively from medieval to modern. When the war began, knights still reigned supreme on the battlefield, as they had for centuries. Over time, however, weapon makers had concocted better ways both of killing knights and of protecting them. They had also devised new ways to storm castles, while architects planned better ways to defend them. At the time of the Norman Conquest in 1066, knights wore chain mail (heavy coats of linked iron rings). By the middle of the Hundred Years War, jointed plate armor enveloped knights from head to toe. Castles in the eleventh century had been simple wooden forts on hills. By the fourteenth century, they had become elaborate stone fortresses with massive towers and high walls built in concentric circles and surrounded by deep ditches.

England perfected the use of two medieval weapons in its wars with its immediate neighbors. By the fifteenth century, the English had conquered the Welsh but continued to fight off and on in the north against the Scots. These border wars changed English military technology and tactics. The English adopted a unique weapon, the **longbow**. Originally used by the Welsh, the longbow was as tall as a man and required long training and practice to pull. It could pierce armor at four hundred paces and be reloaded more quickly than its only competitor, the crossbow. English skills with the longbow were so important that in 1349 the king banned all sports other than archery. English knights had also learned from fighting the Scottish William Wallace and Robert the Bruce to dismount from vulnerable horses and defend themselves and their archers with **pikes**, long spears of two or three times a man's height. Thus, foot soldiers once more returned as a powerful force on the battlefield, as had been the Greek phalanx.

During the Hundred Years War, the English raided France, devastating the countryside. French knights who tried to stop the raids took a while to realize that they no longer dominated combat. The English archers and dismounted knights wreaked havoc on French armored cavalry in three mighty battles: Crécy (1346), Poitiers (1356), and Agincourt (1415). Each battle turned the tide for the English and nearly led to the destruction of the French monarchy and kingdom. In the Treaty of Troyes (1420), King Henry V of England forced the French king to skip over the legitimate royal heir, who held the title of "dauphin," and instead grant the succession to the future child of Henry V and his French princess-bride.

Henry's sudden death, however, saved the French. Royal and noble families fought over the guardianship of the infant heir, Henry VI (r. 1422–1461). The English advantage might still have prevailed over the divided and demoralized French, but then the unique **Joan of Arc** (b. 1412–d. 1431) arrived to save the French kingdom. This lowborn teenager believed that the voices of saints and angels told her to help the uncrowned French prince, the Dauphin Charles. In 1429, Charles put her in shining armor at the head of a French army, which she "miraculously" led to victories over the English. Shortly after the Dauphin gained his crown as King Charles VII (r. 1429–1461), Joan was captured in battle. The French did nothing to rescue Joan, while the English put her on trial as a heretic. The crime of wearing men's clothing doomed her, because it meant she defied the authority of inquisitors to control her. The English burned her alive at the stake and scattered her ashes.

Meanwhile, Charles VII cleverly used the ongoing English occupation of northern France to extort power from the French nobles and townspeople. In 1438, the Estates-General gave him the right to regularly collect taxes, such as those on salt and hearths. Everyone paid the salt tax, while the rich paid more of the hearth tax since their larger homes had more fireplaces. These revenues enabled Charles VII to raise a national, professional army paid by the government rather than one composed of feudal vassals, or hired mercenaries. Such a force had not fought in Europe since the time of the Roman legions. He also invested in the new-to-Europe technology of **gunpowder**, which had found its way from China by the fourteenth century. Charles VII's armies shot guns to punch holes in knights' armor and fired cannons to pound castles to rubble. The French finally drove the English back across the Channel (see map 9.1).

The English did not cope well with this defeat. They become more English, as the elites stopped speaking French, their language of choice since the Norman invasion of 1066. Their government, meanwhile, briefly spun out of control. When Henry VI turned out to be mentally unbalanced, factions formed to control him. These opposing groups eventually came to blows in civil wars called the **Wars**

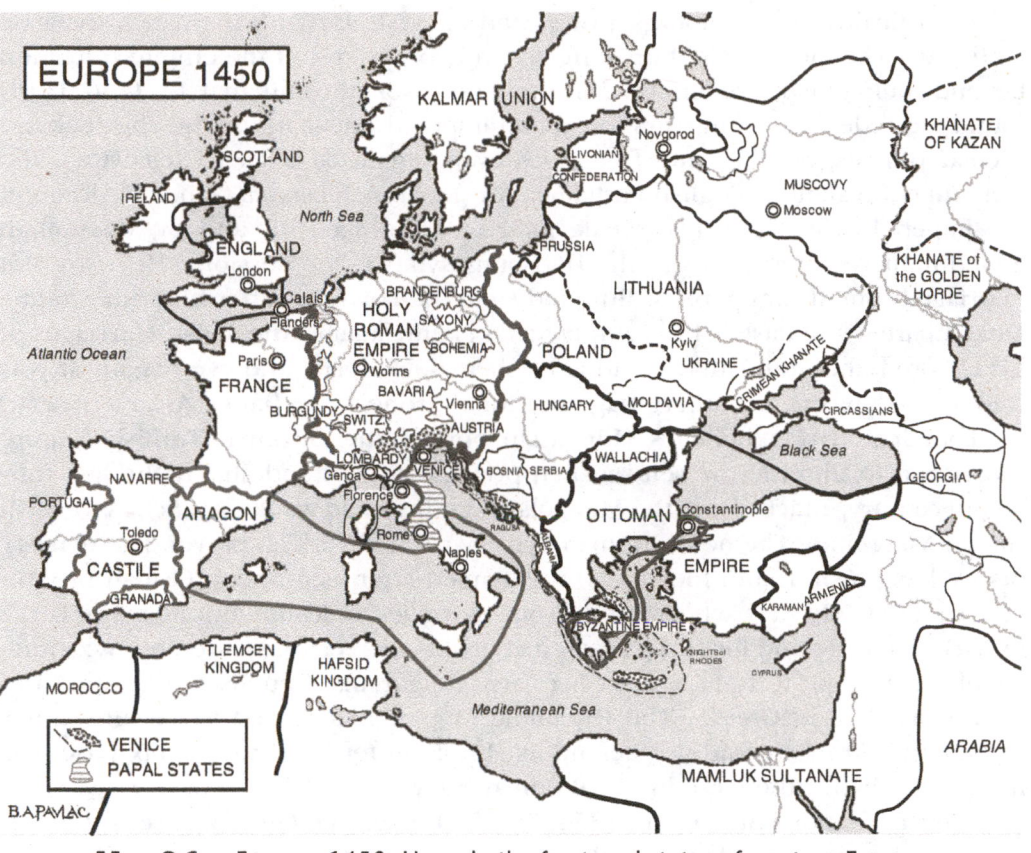

Map 9.1.   Europe, 1450. How do the fractured states of western Europe compare to those of the map of the year 1200 (map 8.1)?

of the Roses (1455–1487). During these, one aristocratic alliance (Lancaster) lost to another (York), which in turn lost to a third (Tudor) in 1485. King Henry VII (r. 1485–1509) of the new **Tudor dynasty** (1485–1603) provided England with a strong monarchy, exploiting the desire of the English to return to political stability in alliance with the English Parliament. In Parliament's House of Commons, Henry bonded the English monarchy with the English middle class. The Tudor kings working with Parliament gave England a strong and flexible government, able to adapt to changing times.

While English and French kings reaffirmed their ascendance, the Holy Roman emperors slipped even further into impotence. Since the end of the Staufen dynasty in 1256, powerful families had fought over who would succeed as Roman king and emperor, officially chosen by seven electoral princes. The Golden Bull of 1356 confirmed an elective monarchy for the empire. This law strengthened the territorial princes, leaving the Holy Roman emperors more as figureheads than authoritarian monarchs. The election of Frederick III in 1438 offered some stability, although no one realized it at the time. His **Habsburg dynasty** (1438–1918) monopolized the royal and imperial title, with the briefest of interruptions, until the Holy Roman Empire's end in 1806.

Realistically, the Habsburgs' power and interests lay with their own dynastic lands: **Austria** and its neighbors. Effective rule of the rest of the empire remained beyond their grasp. Frederick's son and successor Maximilian I (r. 1486–1519) found too little success in wars to expand imperial domination. The spiritual and secular princes, nobility, and free cities even organized a Diet (Reichstag), the German equivalent of English Parliament or the French Estates-General. Although the imperial office remained weak, marriages arranged for and by Maximilian added numerous territories to the Habsburg dynasty's possessions. His own first marriage brought him parts of Burgundy and the Lowlands after his father-in-law Duke Charles "the Rash" of Burgundy died in battle against the Swiss. Marriages of his children and grandchildren added Bohemia, Hungary, and even Spain. It was said of his dynasty, "Let others wage war for a throne—you, happy Austria, marry."

Looming on Maximilian's Hungarian border, the Ottoman Turkish Empire threatened to unsettle the self-satisfied princes of Christendom. By the late thirteenth century, attacks from the Mongols and others had weakened Seljuk Turkish rule in Asia Minor. The new Ottoman dynasty revived Turkish power. The dynasty (as well as plush, round footstools) was named after its founder, Osman or Othman (d. 1324, 724 AH), who started as one more *bey*, or leader among many Turks in Asia Minor. He and his troops served at first as mercenaries, hired by Byzantine Greeks in Europe to fight against Serbians, Bulgarians, Genoese, Venetians, and Latin Crusaders in Greece. The Byzantine Empire had ceased to be innovative. Byzantium's armies could not defend its shrinking territory, whose tax base was needed to pay for the large imperial bureaucracy.

A decisive moment came in 1354 (755 AH) when the Ottomans seized a permanent base for themselves in Gallipoli on the European side of the Dardanelles, south of Constantinople. From there, Ottoman armies with *ghazis* (religious warriors) expanded in two directions: into southeastern Europe and across Asia Minor. The Ottomans soon took the title of sultan (meaning "authority"), given to powerful Muslim rulers second in rank only to the caliph, the religious and political leader of all (Sunni) Muslims.

Southeastern Europe fell under the rule of Turkish Muslims. One conquest was the dual province Bosnia-Herzegovina, where the Bogomils had built up a heretical kingdom united by the dualistic religion of Catharism. Once the Turks had taken Bosnia-Herzegovina, many Slavs there converted to Islam. Next the Turks crushed the Serbian kingdom at the Battle of Kosovo Polje (28 June 1389, 791 AH), a site also called the Field of the Blackbirds (after the winged scavengers who fed on the innumerable corpses of Christian warriors). Most of the divided Bulgarian Empire quickly collapsed. Crusading armies with troops from western Europe actually tried to confront the Ottoman danger. The Turks slaughtered those crusaders at Nicopolis in Bulgaria (1396, 798 AH). The fleeing Christian knights cut off the fashionably long tips of their shoes in order to run away more quickly.

The few remaining unconquered Byzantine territories gained a respite when the great conqueror Tamerlane, or Timur "the Lame," of Samarkand in Central Asia (b. 1336–d. 1405) attacked the Ottomans. His reputation for slaughter surpassed even that of the Huns or the Mongols. Timur's defeat of the Ottoman armies in

1402 (805 AH) almost ended the dynasty. Three years later, however, Timur was dead, and his empire crumbled.

The Ottoman dynasty reconsolidated and expanded their empire. Jews, Orthodox Christians, Muslims, Greeks, Turks, Slavs, Arabs, and Armenians were arranged into efficient groups that provided troops and taxes. The Ottomans organized interconnected bureaucracies to manage the diverse peoples and widespread territories. Their armies relied on a new kind of professional warrior, the janissaries, who had been taken as young Christian boys from the conquered lands and trained to be loyal Muslim soldiers.

After crushing another crusading army at Varna on the Black Sea in 1444 (850 AH), the Turks besieged Constantinople, the last remnant of the once-mighty Roman Empire. The massive cannons of Mohammed or Mehmet II "the Conqueror" (r. 1451–1481) shelled the city for weeks. Defeat was only a matter of time as the walls became rubble. A Byzantine soldier who forgot to close a door through the walls, though, opened the way to a speedy defeat. The last "Roman" emperor died among his handful of troops defending Constantinople's once-impregnable walls. Thus fell the Byzantine or Roman Empire, once and for all, in AD 1453 (857 AH). The Greeks were a defeated people once more.

Mehmet II made Constantinople, renamed as Istanbul (possibly from the Greek phrase "to the city"), his new imperial capital. He rebuilt and repopulated the metropolis (although no one told the Turks about the many underground cisterns that had been used to supply the city with water since Roman times). The Ottomans continued to overpower diverse peoples in the Middle East and North Africa. After the conquest of Mamluk Egypt, the Ottoman sultans finally assumed the title of caliph. In 1526 (932 AH), the Turks then seized much of Hungary from the Austrian Habsburgs. With this victory, the Ottomans were ready to advance into the Holy Roman Empire itself and perhaps from there subdue all of Christendom.

By 1600, the Ottomans were equal in power, wealth, and creativity to any of the Europeans (see figure 9.2). Their empire proved its success by conquering huge swaths of territory in the Middle East and North Africa. On the one hand, they allowed people to keep their ethnic identities while welcoming conversions to Islam or assimilation to Turkish ethnicity. On the other hand, they sometimes exploited ethnic conflicts to maintain their rule, encouraging minorities to dislike one another rather than their Turkish overlords. Either way, the Ottoman Empire provided a powerful rival to the West.

The victories of the Ottomans ended any lingering medieval dream of a united Christendom. Meager attempts by crusaders to help the Byzantine Empire and other Balkan Christians failed miserably. Western popes and princes worked against one another rather than against the common enemy. The various monarchs were looking out for their own narrow dynastic interests first. Western civilization remained in the hands of diverse petty and grand states of Europe.

Once the notion of a universal Christendom was gone, so was a key component of what had defined the Middle Ages. No one precise moment, event, or battle marks the transition when medieval became modern history. Today, some

Figure 9.2.   The Blue Mosque dominating the skyline of Istanbul reflects the glory of the Ottoman Empire around 1600.

historians even argue that medieval times lingered into the seventeenth and eighteenth centuries. Transformations in thought and belief, however, further turned the West away from the medieval construct of priests, knights, and peasants. Rivalry of European states with the Ottomans and between one another would soon make Western civilization the most powerful society in world history.

Review: *How did late medieval monarchs concentrate still more power?*

Response:

MAN AS THE MEASURE

Urban centers in the Italian Peninsula led the way in ending the Middle Ages. Rich cities in the northern half had long been prizes for foreign powers, especially German kings and emperors ever since Pippin "the Short" and Otto "the Great." The economic revival of the High Middle Ages allowed cities such as Genoa, Pisa, and Venice to expand and flourish even more. They prospered from trade and capitalistic finance, persevered through politics and warfare, and won independence from both German emperors and Roman popes. They had intensified their dealings with Byzantines, Turks, Arabs, and even Mongols.

Self-government was difficult, however. Strained by economic change, citizens easily fought among themselves over control of elections and laws. Class warfare between wealthy merchants, prosperous artisans, and the poor strained the peace of the towns. In desperation for some order, tyrants known as despots seized power in many Italian towns during the later Middle Ages. These despots started as local nobles, merchants, or even mercenaries (called *condottieri* in Italian). Since these dictators removed at least one source of strife—namely, the struggle for leadership—the citizens often tolerated them, just as had happened in ancient Greece and Rome. Some despots managed to establish dynasties. Thus, these new Italian princes often cut short the towns' initial experiments in democratic, republican government.

A successful despot might provoke war across the Italian Peninsula, seeking for his city-state to dominate others. Ambitious princes began to conquer their neighboring towns, urged on by merchants wanting to eliminate competitors. The Peace of Lodi in 1454, however, granted the entire peninsula a brief respite. For the next four decades, five great powers upheld a fragile peace. In the south, the Kingdom of Naples was the largest in area, but it was weakened by struggles over the throne between the foreign houses of Anjou (from France) and Aragon (from the Iberian Peninsula). In the center of the Italian Peninsula, the Papal States were bound together loosely under the authority of the pope. Just north of Rome, in Tuscany, **Florence** dominated all its immediate neighbors (see figure 9.3). In the northwest, Milan ruled the plains of Lombardy. Finally, in the northeast, the

Figure 9.3. The Renaissance dome of Florence's medieval cathedral rises above the rest of the city.

maritime power of Venice put down a strong foothold on the mainland, adding to its other possessions stretching along the eastern coast of the Adriatic and into the Aegean Sea. Venice's unique government was an oligarchy of the most powerful merchants, who dominated their elected ruler, called the doge.

This balance of power in the Italian Peninsula ended in 1494, when the French king Charles VIII as heir of Anjou invaded to claim the Kingdom of Naples. Charles's invasion sparked decades of war throughout the peninsula (and spread a new, nasty form of the sexually transmitted disease syphilis, which may have come from the Americas, although it was commonly called the "French" disease). Wars proliferated while French kings, German emperors, Spanish monarchs, and Italian despots fought for supremacy. In the midst of these wars, over several generations, European culture left the Middle Ages and entered the early modern period of history.

The cultural shift called the Renaissance (ca. 1400–1600) also helped push Europe into modernity. The Renaissance started in Florence. While figuring out how best to succeed in their political challenges, the Florentines sought inspiration from the Greeks and Romans of ages past. They could afford spending the time and money to revive humanism from classical antiquity because of the wealth generated from their new capitalist banks. At first, humanism had merely meant an interest in "humane letters" or the reading of classical writers. Inspired by the poet Petrarch (b. 1304–d. 1374), intellectuals had begun to scour old monastic libraries for ancient manuscripts. They edited what they found, creating the intellectual tool of **textual criticism**—comparing different versions of an author's writings found in manuscripts written by hand at different times in different places in order to recover the best, most accurate text. One famous example is Lorenzo Valla's discourse disproving the so-called Donation of Constantine, allegedly recording the Roman emperor's gift of secular power to the papacy. To the disgruntlement of popes, Valla demonstrated that the document was a forgery.

Enthusiasm for the Latin literature of Rome soon prompted these humanists to appreciate the importance of the Greek language and literature. During the Middle Ages, knowledge of Greek had been virtually lost. The phrase "It's all Greek to me" probably was coined because medieval readers could not decipher passages of Greek frequently quoted by ancient Roman writers. Western scholars exploited scholars who were fleeing with their manuscripts from the collapsing Byzantine Empire. Soon the Western curriculum expanded to include the literature of ancient Greece. While today literary texts in the vernacular (the language spoken by the common people), like the Italian poetry of Petrarch, are more highly valued, the ancient classics in "dead" Greek and Latin were the focus of Renaissance intellectuals and educators well into the nineteenth century.

Florence's **Medici** family played a key role in supporting this intellectual revival after they took over that city's leadership. The Medicis had risen to power in local government financed by their family banking business. Over time, they began their own aristocratic dynasty after surviving urban rebellions, assassination plots, invasions, and banishment. Along the way, they also aspired to be patrons of the arts, those who fostered creative interaction with Greece and Rome.

On a metaphysical level, Renaissance Neoplatonic philosophers reinterpreted the ideas of Plato. On a visual level, artists drew inspiration from styles of classical art and created the new painting, architecture, and sculpture of Renaissance art. Artists such as Leonardo da Vinci, Michelangelo, and Raphael pioneered a new naturalism in painting and sculpture that emphasized a realistic view of the world and the human body (see figure 9.4).[1] The one error they made was assuming that the ancients left their marble statues unpainted and white. As a result, the polychromy so popular in medieval sculpture vanished. On a literary level, intellectuals eagerly sought and read authors from classical antiquity.

One such intellectual was Niccolò **Machiavelli**. At the beginning of the sixteenth century, Machiavelli had himself been tortured and exiled from Florence for supporting the wrong political faction. In those times, suspicion of disloyalty to rulers meant having one's arms jerked out of the sockets on a torture device

Figure 9.4. In this selection from the fresco of the School of Athens in the Vatican, Raphael portrays Leonardo da Vinci as Plato in the center left and Michelangelo as the architect leaning on the block in the foreground. The majestic setting and the many other great thinkers from classical antiquity reflect the Renaissance fascination with Greece and Rome.

1. For more on Renaissance art, go to http://www.concisewesternciv.com/arth/ar9.html.

called the *strappado*, a modified pulley. During his exile from the city, Machiavelli consoled himself every night by reading ancient writers of Greece and Rome. Inspired by them (and to win the favor of the Medicis), he wrote **The Prince** (1513). This book combined examples of classical antiquity and contemporary politics. It offered advice on how a prince should hold on to power in an occupied territory, suggesting that a ruler's primary goal ought not to be virtue, as political writers had been propounding through the Middle Ages. Instead, a prince was to wield power, using force and fear, lying or largesse, as long as he did not become hated. Many readers claimed to be shocked by this "Machiavellian" advice for amoral political behavior freed from the constraints of Christian morality. In secret, though, most princes and politicians have admired how Machiavelli accurately described brutal power politics. He aimed to end the diversity of Italian principalities by uniting them under one powerful prince. All his practical suggestions were grounded in his humanist scholarship of antiquity.

A major boost to the humanist scholarly enterprise was the invention of the **printing press** in Germany around 1450. Using a few hundred molded pieces of movable type, any sheet of text could be reproduced much more cheaply, easily, and quickly than the laboriously handwritten page of every single book in Europe up to that moment.[2] The multiplication of books further encouraged the expansion of literacy, since more publications gave more people more writing to read.

This flood of printed materials also helped spur a change in education, giving rise to new kinds of schools. The sons of nobles and wealthy townspeople, after getting an education in a primary or "grammar" school, then attended secondary schools. These advanced institutions went beyond the primary education of reading, writing, and arithmetic, but not so far as the serious scholarly study offered by the "higher education" of colleges and universities. In secondary schools (the forerunners of American high schools), students further refined their knowledge of the classical curriculum of the liberal arts. Through reading ancient Latin and Greek authors, a student was supposed to learn how to be worthy of liberty. The well-rounded Renaissance gentleman, an individual fit in mind and body, became the ideal.

Compared to that of men, the place of women, genteel or not, remained much more restricted. Ladies were to be respected, but few opportunities opened for their advancement. Lack of access to schools and the inability to control property remained the norm. Only a rare individual like **Christine de Pisan** (b. 1363–d. ca. 1430) could make her living from writing. Widowed and with children to support, Christine managed to market her books on history, manners, and poetry to rich male patrons in France and England. She remained an isolated example of the successful woman, unfairly forgotten soon after her death. Society still measured success by a man's achieving his material best, crafting for himself a place of honor in this world. Some intellectuals began to ask the "Woman Question":

---

2. Printing with woodblocks, and even movable type made of wood, clay, or bronze, began centuries earlier in China and Korea. The thousands of ideograms necessary for printing, however, limited the usefulness of the technology compared to the flexibility and cost saving offered by Western alphabets, which only had a few dozen letters and punctuation symbols.

whether women were in any fashion to be considered equal to men. The usual answer persisted that females remained inferior to males.

Perhaps the greatest writer of the Renaissance, if not of all time, was the English actor, poet, and playwright **William Shakespeare** (b. 1564–d. 1616). The subjects of his plays ranged over histories (such as *Henry IV* and *Henry V*), comedies (such as *Twelfth Night* and *A Midsummer Night's Dream*), and tragedies (such as *Hamlet* and *Macbeth*). His writing captures in poetry and action a sense of universal human drama and character, drawing heavily on the classics. During his lifetime, acting companies built the first public theaters since classical antiquity, including his Globe Theater in London. Theaters soon appeared in other European cities, where actors revived plays from ancient writers, adapted to new audiences.

With all this focus on success in the world, the humble path of Christ seemed somehow less attractive. Yet, as Renaissance ideas spread from Italy to northern Europe, many scholars in England, the Lowlands, and Germany did bend humanism to a more Christian view. This **Christian humanism** still emphasized the classics, using one's critical mind, and taking action in the world, but it added an interest in the writings of the Christian faith. Thus, along with Latin and Greek, Christian humanists learned Hebrew in order to read both the Old Testament in its original language and the writings of rabbi commentators.

The most famous Christian humanist was **Erasmus** (b. 1466–d. 1536). He sought to promote the best, most pure form of Christianity as he understood it from his reading in the New Testament and the writings of the early Church Fathers. His humanist outlook gave him a mocking attitude to authority. In *The Praise of Folly* (1509), Erasmus satirized all the problems of his contemporaries, especially the hypocrisies and failures of the Western Latin Church. Questioning authority became an important intellectual tradition, although the powers that be have never taken kindly to it.

Although Renaissance humanists encouraged a more critical look at the world, Erasmus and many of his contemporaries credulously accepted and promoted dangerous changes in beliefs about witches and witchcraft (see Primary Source Project 9). Historians have yet to fully understand how and why the fear of witchcraft began during the Renaissance. Prior to 1400, the usual position of the ecclesiastical hierarchy had been that witches did not exist. The theologians taught that anyone claiming to be a witch was a dupe of the devil, and any supposed magic spells were meaningless deceptions. After 1400, however, many authorities in the Western Latin Church changed their opinions to say that a real conspiracy of witches existed, organized by the devil as a vital threat to Christian society. Actually, no reliable evidence remains that any such organized plot existed or that any magic spells have ever succeeded against anyone, anywhere.

Regardless, many ecclesiastical and secular leaders began the **witch hunts** (1400–1800), actively seeking out suspected witches, torturing them into confessing impossible crimes, and then executing them. Like the ancient Roman persecution of Christians, the hunts were sporadic, intermittent, and geographically scattered: worst in the Holy Roman Empire; moderate in France, Scotland, and England; and rare in the rest of Europe. Nevertheless, tens of thousands died, with more untold numbers submitting to false accusations, having loved ones persecuted, or suffering from pervasive fear. Authorities most often accused older women living on the margins of society, yet also younger women, men, and even children fell victim to suspicions.

These witch hunts ended once leaders no longer believed in the reality of diabolic magic. Fewer bouts of bad weather, the rising power of the state, improving economies, and more rational attitudes promoted by the Renaissance, the Scientific Revolution, and the Enlightenment (see below and chapter 11) all contributed. By the eighteenth century, most leaders, both religious and political, had once more come to the sensible view that witches and witchcraft were imaginary and no threat.

While scholars studied the classics and certain magistrates hunted witches, religious leaders began to rethink the accepted tenets of medieval faith. The new, more worldly emphasis of humanism deviated from the basics of medieval Christianity. Humanism prioritized this world; Christianity, the next. The ongoing need of many people for metaphysical certainty soon broke the unified religious system of the Middle Ages. Just as westerners accepted and fought for separate political states, they embraced and died for divided religious sects.

Review: *How did the Renaissance promote the West's transition into modernity?*

Response:

PRIMARY SOURCE PROJECT 9: WITCH HUNTER VERSUS CONFESSOR ABOUT BELIEF IN WITCHES

The age of the Renaissance and Scientific Revolution was also the time of the witch hunts. In the first source, an ecclesiastical official involved in hunting describes how far persecutions had gone in a German princedom. In contrast, a priest who heard the last confessions of people condemned for witchcraft came to a very different conclusion. In his book titled in Latin Cautio Criminalis *(Warning about Criminal Procedure), Friedrich Spee harshly criticizes the process and belief system. While he had to publish his book anonymously out of fear of retribution, his arguments soon helped stop the hunts.*

Source 1: "Report on Witch-Hunts" by the Chancellor of the Prince-Bishop of Würzburg (1629)

As to the affair of the witches, which Your Grace thinks brought to an end before this, it has started up afresh, and no words can do justice to it. Ah, the woe and the misery of it—there are still four hundred in the city, high and low, of every rank and sex, nay, even clerics, so strongly accused that they may be arrested at any hour. It is true that, of the people of my Gracious Prince here, some out of all offices and faculties must be executed: clerics, electoral councilors and doctors, city officials, court assessors, several of whom Your Grace knows.

There are law students to be arrested. The Prince-Bishop has over forty students who are soon to be pastors; among them thirteen or fourteen are said to be witches. A few days ago a Dean was arrested; two others who were summoned have fled. The notary of our Church consistory, a very learned man, was yesterday arrested and put to the torture. In a word, a third part of the city is surely involved. The richest, most attractive, most prominent, of the clergy are already executed. A week ago a maiden of nineteen was executed, of whom it is everywhere said that she was the fairest in the whole city, and was held by everybody a girl of singular modesty and purity. She will be followed by seven or eight others of the best and most attractive persons. . . . And thus many are put to death for renouncing God and being at the witch-dances, against whom nobody has ever else spoken a word.

To conclude this wretched matter, there are children of three and four years, to the number of three hundred, who are said to have had intercourse with the Devil. I have seen put to death children of seven, promising students of ten, twelve, fourteen, and fifteen. Of the nobles—but I cannot and must not write more of this misery. There are persons of yet higher rank, whom you know, and would marvel to hear of, nay, would scarcely believe it; let justice be done. . . .

P.S.—Though there are many wonderful and terrible things happening, it is beyond doubt that, at a place called the Fraw-Rengberg, the Devil in person, with eight thousand of his followers, held an assembly and celebrated mass before them all, administering to his audience (that is, the witches) turnip-rinds and parings in place of the Holy Eucharist.

There took place not only foul but most horrible and hideous blasphemies, whereof I shudder to write. It is also true that they all vowed not to be enrolled in the Book of Life, but all agreed to be inscribed by a notary who is well known to me and my colleagues. We hope, too, that the book in which they are enrolled will yet be found, and there is no little search being made for it.

Source 2: Selection from *Cautio Criminalis* by Friedrich Spee (1631)

1. Incredible among us Germans and especially (I blush to say it) among Catholics are the popular superstition, envy, libels, calumnies, insinuations, and the like, which, being neither punished by the magistrates nor refuted by the pulpit, first stir up suspicion of witchcraft. All the divine judgments which God

has threatened in Holy Writ are now ascribed to witches. No longer does God or nature do anything, but witches everything.

2. Hence it comes that all at once everybody is clamoring that the magistrates proceed against the witches—those witches whom only their own clamor has made seem so many.

3. Princes, therefore, bid their judges and counselors to begin proceedings against the witches.

4. These at first do not know where to begin, since they have no testimony or proofs, and since their conscience clearly tells them that they ought not to proceed in this rashly. . . .

7. At last, therefore, the Judges yield to their wishes, and in some way contrive at length a starting-point for the trials. . . .

10. And yet, lest it appear that [Gaia, a name for the accused] is indicted on the basis of rumor alone, without other proofs, as the phrase goes, lo a certain presumption is at once obtained against her by posing the following dilemma: Either Gaia has led a bad and improper life, or she has led a good proper one. If a bad one, then, say they, the proof is cogent against her; for from malice to malice the presumption is strong. If, however, she has led a good one, this also is none the less a proof; for thus, they say, are witches wont to cloak themselves and try to seem especially proper.

11. Therefore it is ordered that Gaia be haled away to prison. And lo now a new proof is gained against her by this other dilemma: Either she then shows fear or she does not show it. If she does show it (hearing forsooth of the grievous tortures wont to be used in this matter), this is of itself a proof; for conscience, they say, accuses her. If she does not show it (trusting forsooth in her innocence), this too is a proof; for it is most characteristic of witches, they say, to pretend themselves peculiarly innocent and wear a bold front.

12. Lest, however, further proofs against her should be lacking, the Commissioner has his own creatures, often depraved and notorious, who question into all her past life. This, of course, cannot be done without coming upon some saying or doing of hers which evil-minded men can easily twist or distort into ground for suspicion of witchcraft.

If, too, there are any who have borne her ill will, these, having now a fine opportunity to do her harm, bring against her such charges as it may please them to devise; and on every side there is a clamor that the evidence is heavy against her. . . .

14. And so, as soon as possible, she is hurried to the torture, if indeed she be not subjected to it on the very day of her arrest, as often happens.

15. For in these trials there is granted to nobody an advocate or any means of fair defense, for the cry is that the crime is an exceptional one, and whoever ventures to defend the prisoner is brought into suspicion of the crime—as are all those who dare to utter a protest in these cases and to urge the judges to caution; for they are forthwith dubbed patrons of the witches. Thus all mouths are closed and all pens blunted, lest they speak or write. . . .

19. Before she is tortured, however, she is led aside by the executioner, and, lest she may by magical means have fortified herself against pain, she is searched,

her whole body being shaved, although up to this time nothing of the sort was ever found. . . .

21. Then, when Gaia has thus been searched and shaved, she is tortured that she may confess the truth, that is to say, that she may simply declare herself guilty; for whatever else she may say will not be the truth and cannot be. . . .

24. Without any scruples, therefore, after this confession she is executed. Yet she would have been executed, nevertheless, even though she had not confessed; for, when once a beginning has been made with the torture, the die is already cast—she cannot escape, she must die.

25. So, whether she confesses or does not confess, the result is the same. . . .

31. . . . It would be a disgrace to her examiners if when once arrested she should thus go free. Guilty must she be, by fair means or foul, whom they have once but thrown into bonds. . . .

37. Wherefore the judges themselves are obliged at last either to break off the trials and so condemn their own work or else to burn their own folk, aye themselves and everybody. For on all soon or late false accusations fall, and, if only followed by the torture, all are proved guilty.

38. And so at last those are brought into question who at the outset most loudly clamored for the constant feeding of the flames. For the fools rashly failed to foresee that their turn, too, must inevitably come—and by a just verdict of Heaven, since with their poisonous tongues they created us so many witches and sent so many innocents to the flames. . . .

46. From all this there follows this result, worthy to be noted in red ink: that, if only the trials be steadily pushed on with, there is nobody in our day, of whatsoever sex, fortune, rank, or dignity, who is safe, if he have but an enemy and slanderer to bring him into suspicion of witchcraft. . . .

Questions:

- *How does each writer define the problem about witches?*
- *What specific details does each writer use to explain the problem with witches?*
- *How does each writer hope to solve the problem?*

Responses:

For more on these sources, go to http://www.concisewesternciv.com/sources/psc9a .html.

HEAVEN KNOWS

A religious revolution called the **Reformation** (1517–1648) fractured the medieval unity of Christians in the West beyond recovery. The Reformation first addressed the Church's institutional role in the plan for salvation. Yet the Reformation also reflected the ongoing political, economic, and social changes created by Europe's growing wealth and power. The calls for reform in the Church of Rome had been long and loud since the Great Western Schism had divided the papacy between 1378 and 1417. With the concept of conciliarism crushed, calls for reform went unheeded. The papacy's long avoidance of reform made the Reformation more divisive than it might have been.

Some believers still found comfort and hope in many of the rituals and practices of the medieval Western Latin Church: sacraments (from baptism through the mass to final unction), pilgrimages and shrines, saints' days, the daily office, hospices, and hospitals. An increasingly popular mysticism led some to question the value of a priestly hierarchy. Religious women such as the recluse Julian of Norwich (d. 1416) or the wandering housewife Margery Kempe (d. 1438) continued the practice of Hildegard of Bingen by sharing vivid and novel visions of their interactions with God.

And the Church of Rome's worldly interventions also alienated many. Popes had not lived down the scandals of the Avignon exile and three rival popes. Even worse, the Renaissance wars in Italy led many to consider the pope to be a typical petty prince rather than a potent moral force and spiritual leader. Christendom watched scandalized as the popes deepened their political rule over the Papal States in central Italy. Cesare Borgia for his father, Pope Alexander VI (r. 1492–1503), and then Pope Julius II (r. 1503–1513) personally led papal armies into battle. Popes played power politics and lived in profane pomp. Thus, many Christians gradually grew disillusioned with a papal monarchy. The bishop of Rome seemed to represent the obstacle to reform.

A successful call for reform rose in an obscure and unexpected place: the small college town of Wittenberg in the Holy Roman Empire. There, **Martin Luther** (b. 1483–d. 1546), the simple son of prosperous Saxon peasants, had risen to be a professor at the university. Additionally, Luther dedicated himself to monastic discipline in a house of Augustinian canons regular (sometimes called Austin Friars). Finally, Luther served as the pastor of a local parish church.

As a pastor, Luther grew increasingly disturbed when his poor parishioners bought **indulgences** from traveling salesmen. Indulgences had originally developed out of the Western Latin Church's sacramental system of penance. When one committed sin, confessors taught, one had to do penance, such as some good deed, prayers, or a pilgrimage. During the later Middle Ages, some clever clerics suggested that instead of having a penitent take the time and trouble for a complicated and expensive pilgrimage to Rome, why not just have that person pay the comparable amount of cash instead? Consequently, the Western Latin Church gained money, which it could use for anything it wished. Sin thus became a tool of capitalist investment. Granted, theologians did officially insist that indulgences could not forgive sin unless the purchaser was truly contrite. Nevertheless, the sales pitch by indulgence sellers often overlooked that quibble. Encouraged to buy these fill-in-the-blank forms, people believed that their sins (or those of their dead friends or relatives) were instantly pardoned: a popular saying went, "When the coin in the coffer rings, the soul from purgatory springs."

In Luther's home province of Saxony, the local prince-archbishop of Magdeburg had authorized a vigorous sale of indulgences. The archbishop's share of the profits paid off his debts to the pope, who had suspended canon law so that the archbishop could take possession of more than one prince-bishopric. At the same time, the pope needed these funds to help build the new Renaissance-style St. Peter's Basilica on the Vatican Hill. This new edifice, the largest church building the world had yet seen, designed by the great artist Michelangelo, replaced the crumbling twelve-hundred-year-old structure built under Constantine.

Ignorant of these backdoor financial deals, Martin Luther nevertheless developed his own objections to indulgences. In his theological study and experience of faith versus works, he began to question the entire concept of indulgences being useful for salvation. For Luther, sin seemed so pervasive and powerful that he felt any normal means of penance could not erase its stain on the soul. No matter how many good works he undertook or how much he attended the mass, Luther worried that sin made him unworthy to enter the perfection of heaven. In comparison, he felt like a ripe lump of manure. Luther broke through his dilemma with a revelation upon reading Romans 1:17: "The just shall live by faith." He proposed that a person is assuredly saved, or justified, simply by the belief in the death and resurrection of Jesus Christ. And if faith alone justified sinners, then the sacraments provided by the ordained priestly hierarchy were unnecessary. Hence, Luther's declaration of "justification by faith alone" undermined the dominant position of the chief priest, the pope, as an arbiter of salvation.

Luther offered his **Ninety-Five Theses**, or arguments, about his developing theological point of view. According to tradition, he posted a copy of them on the door of the Wittenberg church on 31 October 1517. Publishers printed these theses and spread them with amazing rapidity across the realms of Europe. Luther became the hero and voice for those who wanted to reform the Western Latin Church.

The ecclesiastical hierarchy largely dismissed his ideas and sought to shut him up. When the pope finally excommunicated Luther in June 1520, the defiant reformer publicly burned the papal bull along with books of canon law, thus dismissing the entire structure of the Church of Rome. The newly elected Holy Roman emperor **Charles V** Habsburg (r. 1519–1556) then convened a Diet in the city of Worms to consider the situation. At the 1521 **Diet of Worms**, Luther refused to recant, asserting his own understanding of scripture and reason and his own conscience. He held his position with the legendary words, "Here I stand; I can do no other." The emperor allowed Luther to leave the Diet, whereupon his supporters spirited him away into hiding. Charles concluded the Diet by declaring Luther an outlaw and by pledging to kill him in order to stamp out his heretical ideas.

Since Emperor Charles V ruled over the most wide-ranging empire in history up to that time, such a threat carried weight. As the head of the Habsburg dynasty,

Charles V had inherited the lands of Austria and most of the lands of Burgundy (including much of Flanders) from his grandfather, Emperor Maximilian. From his mother he received Naples and Spain, which by this time also included much of the New World (see the section "God, Greed, and Glory"), and soon possessions in Asia. The sun never set on Charles V's empire. Having become Holy Roman emperor by divine grace, Charles also decided to defend the Holy Roman Church.

Surprisingly, this powerful emperor never concentrated enough power to crush Luther and his allies. First, he was weaker in reality than on parchment. The office of Holy Roman emperor had been wasting away during centuries of conflict with the popes and the German princes. Second, Charles faced turmoil in the lands he controlled as a dynast. Both Bohemia and Hungary opposed Habsburg rule. Even some nobles in Spain, regardless of wealth from its new colonial possessions, rebelled against Charles's authority. Third, King Francis I of France started a Habsburg-Valois dynastic conflict to weaken Charles's encircling France from the southwest and the east. Even though he enjoyed the title "Most Christian King," Francis even encouraged the Muslim sultan of the Ottoman Empire to conquer Charles's ally Hungary in 1526 and then besiege the Austrian capital of Vienna in 1529.

Meanwhile, the outlawed former monk set up a new Christian denomination called ***Lutheranism***. While in hiding, Luther translated the Bible into simple German. In doing so, he both set the style of modern German and promoted literacy. He simplified the worship ceremonials, emphasizing more preaching, prayer, and music. Luther closed monasteries, ending monasticism and clerical celibacy for his followers. That action complicated his personal life, however. Several nuns, both inspired by Luther's writings and disappointed with religious life, escaped from their nunnery by hiding in fish barrels. One of them, Katherine von Bora, complained to Luther that since the single, celibate life of a monastic was no longer an option, nuns needed to be married and have children. So he married Katherine and started a family (see the Source on Families).

Ultimately, Luther relied on the power of Lutheran princes who protected him after the Diet of Worms. Starting with Luther's own Duke of Saxony, many other northern German princes and kings in Scandinavia welcomed the Lutheran Church. The new structures allowed the princes to act as popes in their own provinces.

When the Habsburg Charles V tried to ban Lutheranism at a Diet in 1529, Lutheran princes protested. From that event onward, **Protestantism** came to include all Christians who adhered neither to Eastern Orthodoxy nor to the pope in Rome. Once debate failed, the Protestants resorted to weapons against Catholics, and wars of religion (1546–1648) sporadically erupted throughout western Europe. Charles never achieved the military victory needed to crush Luther's princely supporters. With the **Treaty of Augsburg** in 1555, Charles V capitulated to the right of princes to maintain their Lutheran churches. He resigned his throne the next year and died shortly thereafter.

Luther's successful defiance of ecclesiastical and political authority raised a question for Christianity: who had the authority to interpret and define faith? The original, traditional answer had been the Church councils. Such was still the position of the Orthodox churches in eastern Europe, although they had not held a council since long before the Great Schism with the Western Latin Church in 1054. The Church of Rome had rejected conciliarism and instead granted the papacy a monarchical authority to determine the faith.

In contrast, Luther relied solely on his own conscience, as guided by holy scripture. Yet how was his conscience necessarily better than anyone else's? Could not anyone claim to be guided by the Holy Spirit and use individual judgment to assert doctrine? Such is what happened. Religious leaders formed new sects and denominations.

Already in opposition to Luther, some bourgeoisie wanted more asceticism from the clergy (although the burghers themselves often spent their wealth on conspicuous consumption). Even more radical, many German peasants had seized on Luther's rhetoric on the defiance of authority and applied it to their social and political obligations. They rebelled against their lords in 1525. As was typical of peasant revolts during the later Middle Ages, the peasants killed a few hundred landlords; the nobles then regrouped and avenged the deaths by hanging many thousands of rebels. Luther disassociated himself from the peasants, calling them "thievish, murderous hordes."[3]

Some successful reformers in the sixteenth century collectively formed the denomination of **Anabaptism**. Anabaptists consisted of many different groups lumped together by enemies who disagreed with their common refusal to accept infant baptism. For Anabaptists, only mature adults ought to be baptized. These groups often drew their followers from the lower classes, who rejected religious hierarchy and ecclesiastical wealth.

Both Lutherans and Catholics joined in exterminating most of the Anabaptists through such traditional methods as torture and war. A notorious example was the siege and destruction of Münster in 1535. There the allied Lutherans and Catholics killed thousands of Anabaptists as they retook the city. The victors tortured the survivors, executed them, and then hung their remains on a church tower in cages that remain there today. Only a few groups of Anabaptists survived, often by fleeing to the New World, especially Pennsylvania, which was founded in the late seventeenth century on a principle of religious tolerance. Their successors exist today in such denominations as the Mennonites, Moravians, Hutterites, and Amish or Pennsylvania Dutch.

Various reform ideas soon spread from Germany to France, one of the most powerful nations in Europe. The kings of the Valois dynasty held the Concordat of 1516, which authorized them to appoint most of the bishops, abbots, and abbesses, while the pope got a large cut of the revenues. One Frenchman, however, found himself more sympathetic to Luther's reforms than the structures of kings and prelates. **Jean (or John) Calvin** (b. 1509–d. 1564) learned of Luther's ideas in school. Inspired by them, he created his own new religious framework, called **Calvinism**, which he refined after being called to be the leading preacher in Geneva, Switzerland. Geneva became the center of a theocracy, a government based on divine commands. While elected leaders still ran the town council, they

---

3. See the Primary Source Project at http://www.concisewesternciv.com/sources/psc9b.html.

passed laws that tried to make the townspeople conform to Calvin's beliefs. From Geneva, Calvin then sent missionaries throughout Europe.

Calvin differed from Luther in two main ways. First, Calvinism focused on **predestination** or *determinism*: the belief that God determined in advance, for all of time, who was saved and who was damned. Nothing any person did could influence God's preordained, omniscient decision. This idea went back to Augustine and had a certain logic to it: if God knows everything, then he surely knows who is going to heaven and who is going to hell. While some complained that this belief removed free will, Calvinism called believers to choose to live the exemplary life of saints, participating in baptism and the Lord's Supper. In doing so, they hoped to re-create God's kingdom on earth, which would indicate their deserving of salvation.

A second difference in Calvinism was its democratic tendency; members of a church were supposed to be involved in running it. The congregation itself approved ministers or appointed the preacher instead of a distant pope or prince from above. Calvinism expanded through much of the West under the title of Reformed churches in the northern Lowlands (the Netherlands) and much of the Rhineland. In France, Calvinists were called Huguenots. In Scotland they formed Presbyterian churches, and in Wales, Congregationalist churches. In England and its colonies, most Calvinists were labeled Puritans.

When Luther first called for reform, no one thought that the authority of the pope could be overthrown by religious ideas. Yet Lutherans, Calvinists, small groups of Anabaptists, and other sects successfully defied papal control. And papal supremacy would suffer yet another loss before it reorganized and redefined itself. Amid all this religious diversity, killing for reasons of faith continued.

Review: On what issues did the different Protestants carry out reforms?

Response:

SOURCES ON FAMILIES: MARTIN LUTHER, *TABLE TALK* (1566)

While the great reformer Martin Luther preached and wrote about marriage and family, he also talked about it informally with students and visitors around a table in his residence. Many quotes from these informal conversations on a wide variety of subjects were compiled by recorders over the years and eventually published as his Table Talk. *The source presented here collects a variety of quotes. Of his and Katherine, or Katie, von Bora's six children together, Elizabeth died in infancy; their other daughter, Magdalene, or Lena, is featured here at about two years old and at her death at thirteen.*

"My boy Hans is now entering his seventh year. Every seven years a person changes; the first period is infancy, the second childhood. At fourteen they begin to see the world and lay the foundations of education, at twenty-one the young men seek marriage, at twenty-eight they are house-holders and *patres-familias*, at thirty-five they are magistrates in church and state, until forty-two when they are kings. After that the senses begin to decline. Thus every seven years brings a new condition in body and character, as has happened to me and to us all." . . .

"To have peace and love in marriage is a gift, for a good woman deserves a good husband. To have peace and love in marriage is a gift which is next to the knowledge of the Gospel. There are heartless wretches who love neither their children nor their wives; such beings are not human."

"The greatest blessing is to have a wife to whom you may entrust your affairs and by whom you may have children. Katie, you have a good husband who loves you. Let another be empress, but you give thanks to God."

"The faith and life of young children are the best because they have simply the Word. We old fools have hell and hell-fire; we dispute concerning the Word, which they accept with pure faith without question; and yet at the last we must hold simply to the Word as they do. It is moreover a trick of the devil, that we are drawn by our business affairs away from the Word in such a manner that we do not know ourselves how it happens. There it is best to die young."

To his infant child Luther said: "You are our Lord's little fool. Grace and remission of sins are yours and you fear nothing from the law. Whatever you do is uncorrupted; you are in a state of grace and you have remission of sins, whatever happens."

Playing with his child, Magdalene, he asked her: "Little Lena, what will the Holy Christ give you for Christmas?" and then he added: "The little children have such fine thoughts about God, that he is in heaven and that he is their God and father: for they do not philosophize about him."

As Magdalene lay in the agony of death, her father fell down before the bed on his knees and wept bitterly and prayed that God might free her. Then she departed and fell asleep in her father's arms. Her mother was also in the room but farther from the bed because of her grief. As they laid her in the coffin he said: "Darling Lena, it is well with you. You will rise and shine like a star, yea like the sun. I am happy in spirit but the flesh is sorrowful and will not be content; the departing grieves me beyond measure. It is strange that she is certainly in peace and happy and yet I so sorrowful. I have sent a saint to heaven."

"We should care for our children, and especially for poor little girls. I do not pity boys; they can support themselves in any place if they will only work, and if they are lazy they are rascals. But the poor little race of girls must have a staff to lean upon. A boy can go to school and become a fine man if he will. But a girl cannot learn so much and may go to shame to get bread to eat."

As his wife was still sorrowful and wept and cried aloud, he said to her: "Dear Katie, think how it is with her, and how well off she is. But flesh is flesh and blood blood and they do as their manner is: the spirit lives and is willing. Children doubt not, but believe as we tell them: all is simple with them; they die without pain or anguish or doubt or fear of death just as though they were falling asleep." . . .

When one day Luther's wife was upholding her authority pretty insistently he said to her with feeling: "You may claim for yourself the control over affairs of the house, saving nevertheless, my just rights. Female government has accomplished no good since the world began. When God constituted Adam master of all creatures, they were safe and governed in the best way, but the intervention of woman spoiled all: for that we have you women to thank, and therefore I am not willing to endure your rule."

Questions:

- *What are the differences between males and females within families?*
- *How does faith serve the young and old?*
- *How does husband Luther interact with his wife Katherine?*

Responses:

For more on this source, go to http://www.concisewesternciv.com/sources/sof9 .html.

FATAL BELIEFS

Although Calvinism gained popularity in England, the **English Reformation** (1534–1559) originated uniquely due to matters of state. The reigning king, **Henry VIII** (r. 1509–1547), had strongly supported the views of the pope against Luther. The pope had even awarded King Henry the title of "Defender of the Faith," still sported by English monarchs today. A higher priority for Henry, however, was the security of the Tudor dynasty, for which he thought he needed a male heir. After twenty years of marriage to Catherine of Aragon and six births, only one child had survived, a daughter, Mary. Although a daughter could legally inherit the throne in

England, Henry believed, like most monarchs of his time, that he needed a son. So he asked the pope to end his marriage, as many kings before and since have done. Contrary to the common version of history, Henry did not want a divorce (the breakup of a genuine marriage). He actually sought an annulment (the declaration that a marriage never had existed). Catherine steadfastly resisted, backed up by her nephew and Luther's overlord, Emperor Charles V. Charles just happened to have an army outside of Rome. Fearing the nearby Holy Roman emperor more than the distant English king, the pope refused to support Henry's annulment.

Still determined to father a legitimate male heir, Henry decided to break with the pope. In 1534, Parliament's passing of the Act of Supremacy made Henry head of the **Church of England**. His bishops then legally and willingly annulled his first marriage and blessed his second with his courtier Anne Boleyn, who was already pregnant. The pope's excommunication of Henry and declaration that his new marriage was void hardly bothered the monarch or the great majority of the English people. Both the king and many of his subjects had long disliked what they saw as Roman interference in English affairs. Moreover, many of the members of Parliament profited nicely from the subsequent dissolution of the monasteries, whose properties they bought up at bargain rates. Despite the schism, Henry remained religiously conservative, so Calvinist and Lutheran ideas gained very little influence.

Unfortunately for Henry, he did not achieve his sought-after heir with his second wife, Anne Boleyn; she managed to give birth only to a healthy daughter, Elizabeth. To make way for a new wife, Henry had Anne executed on trumped-up charges of adultery. The third wife, Jane Seymour, gave birth to his heir, Edward, but she died soon after, possibly of puerperal fever. Three more marriages followed. Henry had the fourth marriage annulled and the fifth wife legitimately executed for adultery. His sixth wife managed to outlive him. Despite this rather unseemly string of marriages, most of the English people did not oppose their king. Henry had to chop off the heads of relatively few who resisted his religious transformation.

A genuinely distinctive Church of England, or *Anglicanism*, grew after Henry's death. The nine-year-old King Edward VI (r. 1547–1553) and his advisors began to push the Church of England further away from the Church of Rome. They began to alter significantly the interpretations of the sacraments and methods of worship to be more in line with simplifications introduced by Calvinist, Lutheran, and other Protestant reformers from the Continent.

These policies abruptly reversed when the young Edward died after a reign of only six years. A brief effort failed to put his cousin, the Protestant Lady Jane Grey, on the throne. Henry's daughter by his first marriage, Mary I (r. 1553–1558), won the day. Having remained faithful to the religion of her mother, Mary forced the English Church back under the authority of the pope. To do so, she persecuted clergy and laypeople, many of whom, surprisingly, were willing to die rather than go back to obedience to Rome. She burned several hundred "heretics." For these efforts, the English have dubbed her "**Bloody Mary**." Her disastrous marriage to her cousin King Philip II of Spain did not help, either. Many English people hated him both as a Spaniard and as a "papist." Philip also avoided both the country and his wife. When Mary died without an heir, Henry's daughter by Anne Boleyn, Queen **Elizabeth I** (r. 1558–1603), inherited the crown.

Elizabeth, who had managed to survive the turbulent political and religious policies, now faced a choice herself: should she maintain obedience to Rome or revive the Church of England? In 1559, with a new Act of Supremacy enacted in Parliament, she chose the latter course. Henceforward, the English monarch occupied a ceremonial role as "Supreme Governor" of the Church of England. Anglicanism defined itself as Protestant while still Catholic, trying to maintain the best of both those versions of Christianity. The *Book of Common Prayer* (1549) laid out how worship was to be carried out, but it said little about belief. One's conscience was up to oneself—a fairly tolerant attitude. Fortunately for Elizabeth, most English embraced her religious compromise.

In fact, Elizabeth became one of England's greatest monarchs. The late sixteenth century saw a number of powerful and effective women on or behind the thrones of Europe, provoking the Calvinist preacher John Knox in Scotland to rail against such a "Monstrous Regiment of Women," as he titled a pamphlet against them. Although the others ruled quite competently, Elizabeth outshone them all. England flourished during her reign, culturally, economically, and politically. Renaissance culture reached its high point with Shakespeare's plays. Meanwhile, the English navy began to help its countrymen explore and start to dominate the rest of the world, taking the first steps toward founding the British Empire. Ironically, Henry VIII thought he needed a male heir to be king of England. Instead, a "weak and feeble woman," Elizabeth, surpassed her father's and half-brother's accomplishments.

But Elizabeth still had to reckon with the ***Roman Catholicism*** of her enemies. By the beginning of her reign, newly devout and energetic popes had begun what historians call either the "Counter-Reformation" or the "Catholic Reformation." Putting behind them the distractions of the Renaissance, Roman pontiffs now sought to recover believers in lands recently lost from obedience to them. They redefined their leadership over what now became the Roman Catholic Church as the only true Christianity. The papacy called the **Council of Trent** (1545–1563) to reform and institutionalize its faith for the future. Leaders chose the obscure cathedral city at the southern edge of the Alps for a general council because it satisfied Charles V (it was in the empire), the king of France (it was not German), and the pope (its residents spoke Italian).

Some clergy at the Council of Trent wanted to compromise or adopt some ideas of the Protestants, but the council rejected that path. Instead, the Roman Catholic Church of the popes insisted on salvation or justification by faith supported by good works (not the Protestant doctrine of faith alone). Celibate Roman Catholic priests administered most of the seven sacraments. The Tridentine Reform (named after the Latin word for Trent) limited some abuses and corruptions and established seminary schools for a better-educated priesthood. The council affirmed that their true church, through the papacy, had the final authority to define belief and interpret scripture—not Luther's conscience, or Anabaptist interpretations, or Calvin's scholarship, or anyone's literal reading of the Bible. The popes increased their interest in organizing and clarifying the smallest details of belief and practice.

New monastic orders and improvement of older ones aided the popes in reform. The Ursulines dedicated themselves to the education of girls and women. Most importantly, the Society of Jesus, or the **Jesuits**, gained sway in European affairs. Ignatius Loyola founded the Jesuits after suffering wounds as a soldier in Charles V's Spanish army. During the painful recovery from a shattered leg, he envisioned a new kind of monastic order. Instead of being confined to the cloister, Jesuits dedicated themselves to religious vocation (formed through the *Spiritual Exercises*), education (becoming teachers and guides), and missionary work (both in Europe and the world). Loyola saw his order as a spiritual army for the Roman Catholic Church, with a so-called fourth vow (after poverty, chastity, and obedience) of absolute dedication to the pope.

The Tridentine Reform set a militant tone for Roman Catholicism during the next two hundred years. Roman Catholicism aimed to recapture the allegiance of lost followers and gain more new converts. A new Roman Inquisition began its work in 1542, partly inspired by the Spanish Inquisition of Ferdinand and Isabella. The Spanish Inquisition policed converted Jews and Muslims; this new Roman version hunted Protestants as heretics since they rejected papal teaching. An **Index of Forbidden Books** declared the reading of certain authors to be sinful. First issued in 1559 by the Holy Office in Rome and regularly revised thereafter for four hundred years, the list restricted the circulation of banned works in Roman Catholic countries and forbade Roman Catholics from reading those prohibited books. This censorship even included all the works of Erasmus, so fearful had the papacy become of any criticism.

The renewed Roman Catholic vigor also expressed itself in a series of wars of religion that lasted until 1648. Traditionally, territorial, dynastic, and economic reasons shaped decisions for fighting wars. In this period, however, ideological differences between adherents of branches of Christianity incited warfare. For a few decades, people were ready to kill and die for Lutheranism, Anabaptism, Calvinism, Anglicanism, or Roman Catholicism. Monarchs thought that their subjects needed to conform to their own dogmas as a matter of both public order and divine virtue. Armies killed in the belief that their neighbors should worship the same way they themselves did. Some soldiers also enlisted simply as a way to earn a living—the military was a growth industry.

In the vanguard of militant Roman Catholicism was Elizabeth's former brother-in-law, King **Philip II** of Spain (r. 1556–1598). Philip had inherited most of his Habsburg father Charles V's possessions (except the Austrian ones, which, along with the elected title of Holy Roman emperor, came to his uncle Ferdinand). In Philip's domains, Spain had one of the world's best armies, Flanders was the textile manufacturing center of Europe, and the Americas poured silver into his treasuries. Philip also briefly united Spain with Portugal, making him the ruler of the sole global power. He built a new, modern capital for himself in Madrid. While Madrid was not conveniently connected to the waterways that bound Philip's empire together, it was easily accessible from his palace of El Escorial, a massive, gray religious retreat (see figure 9.5). Philip was hardworking but perhaps too focused on small details. He saw himself as a divinely appointed monarch obliged

Figure 9.5.   King Philip II of Spain often retreated to the gray abbey of El Escorial, which served also as a second palace, away from Madrid.

to attend to every corner of his empire. At the head of a vast bureaucracy, he regulated the lace on court costumes, ordered murders of political enemies, corrected the spelling of secretaries, and held *autos-da-fé* (public burnings of heretics at which he might serve as master of ceremonies).

Above all, the king of Spain sent armies to fight for his vision of the Roman Catholic faith. His navy's victory over the Ottoman Turks at the Battle of Lepanto (1571) cheered the Christian West, showing that the Ottomans were not invincible. At the time, the Muslim sultan claimed the defeat meant nothing—he would just build another fleet, which he did. Despite this boast, historians have seen the defeat at Lepanto as an obvious turning point toward the long, slow decline of Ottoman dominion. Similarly, however, Philip's power also began to diminish. He could not manage his empire from Madrid, as his territories were far too large for the available means of communication. He could not afford his government either. All the silver from the Americas caused ruinous inflation. He declared bankruptcy three times and thereby impoverished many of the bankers and merchants whose finances he needed so badly.

In particular, some of those capitalists, namely the prosperous Calvinist Dutch in the northern part of the Lowlands, resented paying for Philip's dreams of a Roman Catholic empire. In 1581, they declared independence from his rule and formed the **Dutch Netherlands** (often called Holland after the main province). They even began to construct their own democratic government (see the next chapter). The Dutch fought on and off for eighty years before they gained full independence for themselves. To stop this rebellion, Philip first sent in the

Duke of Parma, whose army earned infamy for its brutality against the civilian population. In turn, Dutch and Huguenot merchants harassed Spanish shipping. Philip next turned his attention to England, which had been supporting the upstart Dutch after the death of Philip's wife Queen Mary I. Hostilities simmered for several years as English sea dogs or privateers (informal pirates with permission from a government to raid shipping) preyed on Spanish possessions. Riches looted by the Spanish from the American natives wound up being plundered by the English instead.

Philip retaliated by instigating plots against Elizabeth's life and throne. The pope declared her an illegitimate, excommunicated heretic and encouraged the faithful to overthrow her rule. Philip and the pope supported Elizabeth's cousin, Mary Stuart, Queen of Scots (not to be confused with Elizabeth's half-sister "Bloody Mary" Tudor, the late queen of England), as the true English monarch. The unfortunate Mary Stuart had lost her Scottish Highlands kingdom through her own folly, falling under a legitimate suspicion of blowing up her husband. She fled from her own people to England. Elizabeth kept her in comfortable confinement until Mary got herself implicated in a treasonous Roman Catholic plot. Elizabeth finally ordered Mary's beheading, although it took the headsman three whacks of his axe to succeed.

Seizing upon Elizabeth's execution of Mary in 1587 as an excuse, Philip assembled the **Spanish Armada**. This fleet of 130 ships aimed to sail from Spain to the Lowlands and then ferry Parma's troops across the North Sea to invade England. It all went terribly wrong. The most famous English sea dog, Sir Francis Drake, destroyed most of the fleet in its harbor before it could set sail. A rebuilt fleet launched in 1588, but adverse weather slowed its progress. That the commanding admiral had never been to sea was not helpful, either. Easily repulsing the English in the Channel, the admiral did finally anchor his fleet off the coast of the Lowlands, only to be told, quite reasonably, that if troops there were diverted to England, the Netherlands might succeed in their rebellion. Then the English broke up the armada by pushing fireships (empty, burning hulls) among the fleet. The panicked Spanish broke formation and came under English guns. Storms sank most of the rest.

Philip at first wrote off this defeat, much as the Ottoman sultan had his own at Lepanto. Notwithstanding Spain's appearance of strength over the next decades, it sank to a second-rank power. England, however, continued its ascendancy, becoming stronger than ever as its national patriotism became bound with its religion and its burgeoning imperialist ventures.

Meanwhile, France had not been able to help Philip II fight Spain's traditional enemy, England, since France itself almost broke apart in religious warfare. The Huguenots (the name for French Calvinists) had grown to about 10 percent of the population. Their numbers were particularly strong in the productive artisan and business classes. King Henry II might have moved against them once France's long conflict with the Habsburgs ended in 1559, but that same year the Valois dynasty plummeted into crisis with the unexpected death of King Henry II during a joust. A piece of splintered lance had thrust through his eye into his brain. The last of the Valois dynasty, Henry's three young sons with their mother, Queen Catherine de Medici (b. 1519–d. 1589), were trapped between two powerful aristocratic families: the Huguenot Bourbons and the Roman Catholic de Guises. Fighting over the throne using betrayal, assassination, and war, these powerful families nearly destroyed both the monarchy and the country.

The Roman Catholic party almost triumphed with the **St. Bartholomew's Day massacre** (14 August 1572), during which they viciously murdered thousands of Protestants, nobles and commoners, men, women, and children, in the streets of Paris. Henry of Bourbon survived that slaughter and was soon able to gain military domination over most of the country. After the death of the last Valois in 1589, he became officially recognized as the French king **Henry IV "of Navarre"** (r. 1589–1610), founding the Bourbon dynasty. Hostility to his Protestantism still stood in the way of his acceptance by some Roman Catholics. So, in 1593, Henry converted to Roman Catholicism, allegedly saying, "Paris is worth a mass." He continued to protect the Protestants, though, with the proclamation of the **Edict of Nantes** (1598). This act mandated a certain level of religious tolerance. It allowed Protestants to worship freely and to fortify fifty-one cities for their own self-defense. Official recognition of diversity brought some peace and security.

The last of the religious wars, the **Thirty Years' War** (1618–1648), engulfed the Holy Roman Empire and eventually drew in the entire continent. The conflict began in Bohemia, as the Austrian branch of the Habsburgs labored to convert that province back to Roman Catholicism. Leaders in Prague "defenestrated" the emperor's representatives—meaning they actually tossed them out the window.[4] Habsburg armies quickly crushed the rebellious Bohemians, but other German princes who feared losing autonomy to a resurgent imperial power soon took up arms against Austria. Two foreign Lutheran monarchs invaded the empire—first the king of Denmark, then the king of Sweden. The Protestant armies gained brief advantages through their use of well-drilled and coordinated cavalry, artillery, and infantry units, setting the tone of military tactics for the next centuries. Regardless, the Roman Catholic Austrian Habsburgs continued to win, fortified by the resources of their Spanish cousins.

Eventually, what began as a religious war ended as a purely political conflict. France had long feared being surrounded by the Habsburg territories of Spain in the south and the Holy Roman Empire in the east. So Roman Catholic France entered the war against Roman Catholic Austria. Dynastic and national politics overruled religious fraternity. Thus, religion faded as a motive to go to war in the West.

Indeed, the **Peace of Westphalia**, which was signed in 1648, forced Europe into new, modern, international political relationships (see map 9.2). With religious diversity now irreversible, the medieval ideal of a unified Christendom had vanished. Instead, the numerous independent states of Europe lived in an uncertain rivalry. Each became a sovereign state, free from the influence of higher authorities, although able to agree on international principles if necessary. The

---

4. Depending on the point of view, contemporaries said their lives were spared by angels bringing them gently to ground, or their landing on a garbage heap.

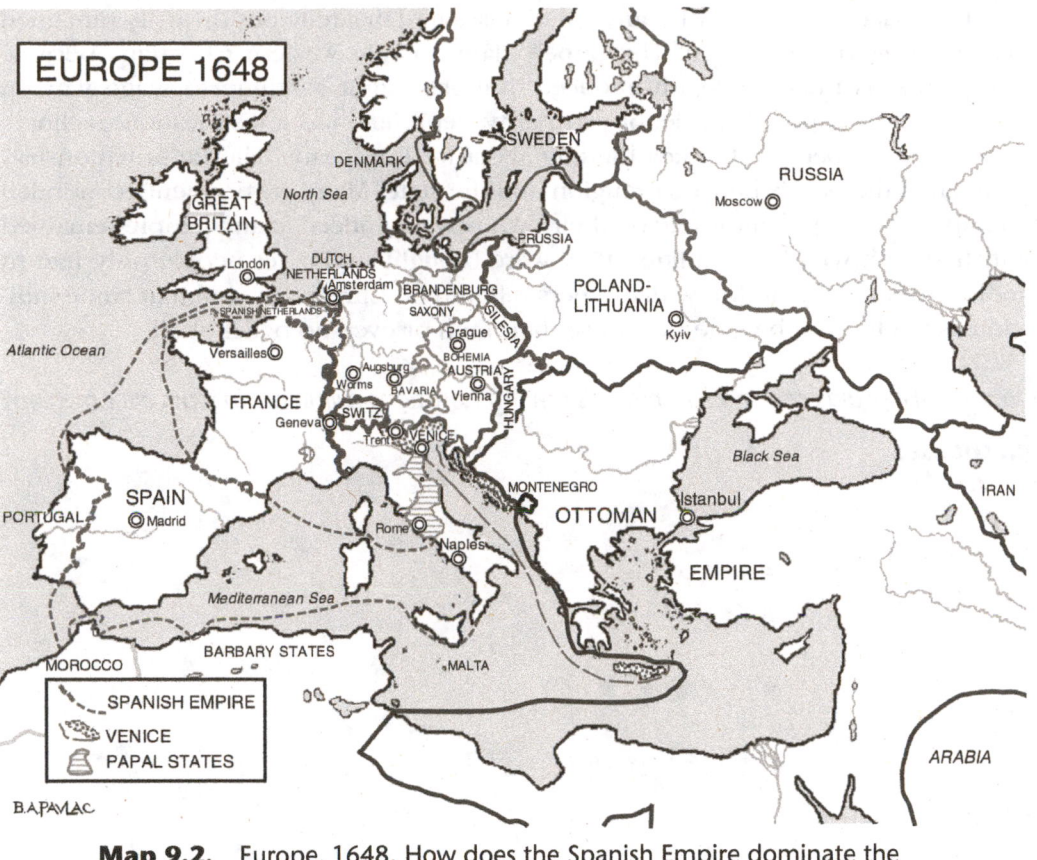

Map 9.2. Europe, 1648. How does the Spanish Empire dominate the western fringe of Europe?

most important principle created and then maintained a ***balance of power***, ensuring that the countries should join together against any single state that tried to dominate Europe. This alliance principle kept the great powers in check and left the middle-ranked and small buffer states free to prosper.

The rest of the treaty redrew some political borders to establish a rough balance of power. Spain held on to the southern "Spanish" part of the Netherlands (soon to be known as Belgium) but lost the northern Dutch Netherlands, which everyone henceforth recognized as an independent, sovereign state. The Swiss had their independence affirmed. The Holy Roman Empire became a mere geographical expression as a synonym for Germany. The petty principalities within the empire were more sovereign than the empire itself. The Holy Roman emperor became even less relevant, a yet still weaker figurehead. While the Austrian Habsburgs kept control of the imperial office, they drew most of their power from their varied collection of hereditary territories on the empire's southeastern borders. Meanwhile, France chewed away a few bits of the empire, bringing its border eastward to the upper Rhine River. Of course, neither the balance of power nor religious toleration stopped war altogether. States continued to try to expand at the expense of their neighbors.

The lack of total victory for any one side assured that religious diversity remained part of Western civilization. The pope's claim to rule Western Christians became irrelevant, his prestige greatly reduced. Nations might continue to wage war on one another, for power, pride, or prosperity, yet religion as a justification declined. Instead, states became the key binding agent for Europeans. The Reformation had weakened the bonds between religion and the state. Many governments continued to impose religious uniformity on their own people. Indeed, many people remained satisfied with whatever tradition they were brought up in. Yet people only had to look across borders to know that others differed on Christianity and that some individuals might even be able to choose their faith or even no belief at all.

Review: *How did early modern reforms among Christians culminate in wars over religion?*

Response:

GOD, GREED, AND GLORY

Another change from the medieval to the modern in European history was **Western colonial imperialism**, when various kingdoms built empires based on overseas colonies. Historians today argue about what exactly made the Europeans strong enough to take the lead in a new global history after 1500. Answers used to imply, if not outright argue, ***Western exceptionalism***, the idea that Europeans were somehow different from (and better than) peoples in other civilizations. More recent historians object to that characterization, especially considering the brutality with which Europeans "civilized" the world.

Comparative historians who measure the relative accumulation of wealth, strength of government, level of cultural sophistication, status of technological development, and impulse toward creativity of various civilizations around the world over the centuries note that Europe did not rank near the top when European countries began their conquests. Historians used to call their imperialism "voyages of discovery." The explorers, of course, only "discovered" what the indigenous peoples in these faraway lands knew all along. The difference was that Europeans could exploit these foreign peoples and places as never before in their history. They declared their own Doctrine of Discovery, making up a theory to justify their invasions. Europeans "legally" declared lands new to them as "empty,"

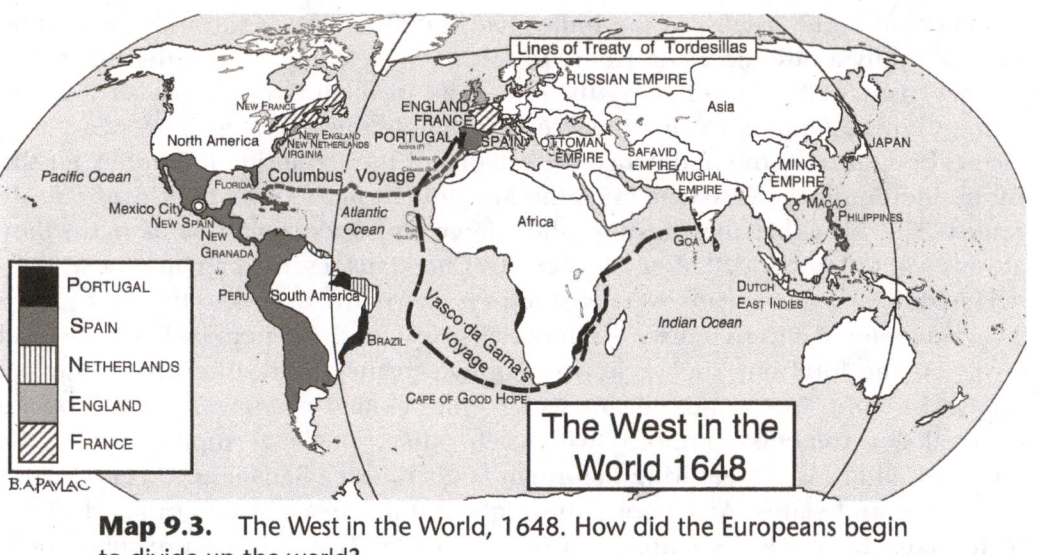

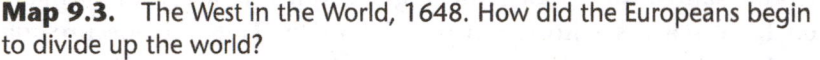

Map 9.3.   The West in the World, 1648. How did the Europeans begin to divide up the world?

ignoring the indigenous humans whose cultures in those places had existed for centuries, if not millennia. These expeditions allowed Europeans to take profit from preexisting trade networks that incorporated much of Asia and Africa, adding on the *terra incognita* or unknown lands of the Americas and in the Pacific Ocean (see map 9.3).

Europeans had three desires that fed their drive to go abroad. The first came from Christianity's own evangelistic and crusading impulses, which had already driven Western culture beyond the borders of Europe. Even before Latin Christianity began to split apart, westerners urged the gospel of Christ on "heathens," as seen in the Crusades. The Reformation likewise encouraged the divided Christians to convert the world, to prove their own version of Christianity as the most successful and, therefore, most divinely sanctioned. Some Europeans ventured on a path of world domination in the name of eternal salvation. Would Jesus, the Prince of Peace, have approved that his message came at the point of a sword and with the price of plundering? His followers thought so, and they had the power to do it.

God provided a spiritual motivation, while money afforded a material one. The capitalism that sprouted from the Commercial Revolution had transformed Europe from a poor offshoot on the fringes of a world trade system centered in Asia to a mainstay of economic dynamism. Financial investments from capitalists further pushed these "voyages of discovery" forward. Instead of being barriers, the deep seas and oceans soon became highways of commerce, much as rivers and coastal waters had long been.

A second motive for colonialism, then, was the opportunity for profit. Europeans wanted to travel to "the Indies," regions in distant Asia known to possess fantastic wealth in the form of spices, such as pepper, cinnamon, and nutmeg. The difficulty of transport to Europe and the high demand for the spices meant that what today sits on our shelves in small jars costing pennies was worth more than its weight in gold in 1500.

The main trade routes to the Indies had traditionally run through the Middle East. But only a rare merchant from Europe, such as Marco Polo in the thirteenth century, managed to travel along the Silk Road through Central Asia all the way to the Chinese Empire. During much of the Middle Ages, western European merchants bought from the middleman merchants of the Byzantine Empire. After the Byzantine Empire's demise in 1453, the Muslim Ottoman Turks took over supply routes. The idea that the Muslims shut down the trade routes is a myth; they always wanted to trade. Rather, the Western Christians resented paying these "infidel" middlemen. Europeans were looking for alternative access to the East.

Pride offered a third motive for imperialism, on both the personal and national levels. At the forefront, monarchs were drawn to the glorification that conquest always brought. New lands meant wider empires and revenues. The European national governments competed with each other for global supremacy. At the lower social levels, adventuring in foreign lands raised a Renaissance gentleman's reputation and status. Any poor man might acquire treasure or farmland of his own, taken from natives who could not defend it. Thus an obscure man could rise to prominence, whether by lording it over foreigners or by bringing immense wealth back home to Europe. All these contradictory motives, winning fame, fortune, and souls for Jesus, tempted Europeans out across the wide oceans.

Surprisingly, the new imperialism began with the little country of **Portugal**, founded in the twelfth century as part of a crusade during the *Reconquista* of the Iberian Peninsula (see chapter 8). Over the years, Portugal had fought against the Muslims, but its armies were soon cut off from confronting the enemy by neighboring Castile's successful expansion in the Iberian Peninsula. Unable to combat the Moors in Europe, little Portugal sought another outlet for its crusading zealotry. It channeled its expansionism toward Africa, hoping both to convert the Africans and to profit from trade on that continent. Prince Henry the Navigator (d. 1460), one of the main proponents of African expeditions, also wished to find enough gold to maintain his court in proper style. The voyages that he sponsored discovered and colonized the uninhabited islands of the Azores and the Madeiras in the Atlantic. Colonists found the latter islands so heavily forested that they set a fire that burned for seven years, leaving the land covered in ash. From the new, fertile soil they grew a new wine, Madeira. Heavily populated Africa was a different matter. Instead of converting and conquering, the Portuguese only wrested away small chunks of African coastline, where they built forts to defend harbors and trading outposts. From these bases, the Portuguese began to deal in slavery, enslaving Africans from the mainland to work on sugarcane plantations in the Madeiras.

Explorers soon thought that it might be possible to sail around the continent of Africa to reach the Indies. Yet sailors faced some serious challenges. First, ocean travel in the Atlantic was far more dangerous than in the Mediterranean and coastal waters. So the Portuguese adapted sailing technology from Muslim civilization in Africa and the Middle East to build ships called caravels, sturdy enough to handle the high seas. Second, navigation was aided by other Muslim achievements, such as the compass, astrolabe, and maps and charts. In this way, European voyagers used the Arabs' own ingenuity against them.

On the western edge of Europe, the Portuguese were well located to launch such voyages. In 1468, the Portuguese explorer Bartolomeu Diaz succeeded in rounding the optimistically named Cape of Good Hope, the southernmost point of Africa. It took another thirty years before **Vasco da Gama** traveled beyond that cape. In 1498, he sailed up the east coast of Africa and then ventured across the Arabian Sea to reach India, guided by Arabian pilots. He did not have much of value to trade with the Indians, but the spices he brought back profited his expedition thirty times the amount of its cost. On da Gama's next voyage, the Portuguese military technology of guns overpowered the natives. Da Gama plundered foreign merchant cargoes, blew the Arab ships out of the water, shelled cities, exploited rivalries between states, and intimidated princes. Other Portuguese followed. Soon they dominated all seagoing trade and commerce in the Arabian Sea and the Indian Ocean.

Portugal was too small to grab and keep vast territories. For five hundred years, though, the Portuguese held on to many fortified coastal enclaves: Angola, Guinea, and Mozambique in Africa; Goa in India; Timor in the Indies; and Macao in China. Only in Brazil, in the Americas, did they establish a large colony with European immigrants. Despite its overseas imperial success, Portugal itself remained on the periphery of European affairs, only rarely participating in the approaching wars among European states disputing who would dominate the world.

Even before Vasco da Gama had begun exploiting and killing Indians in India, Portugal's neighbor **Spain** had hoped to beat its rival to the Indies. Spain was a young country, founded only in 1479 when King Ferdinand came to the throne of Aragon, adding his wife Isabella's Kingdom of Castile which they had co-ruled since 1475. Through their marriage, husband and wife united their two kingdoms to create Spain, centralizing power in both their hands while weakening the nobles and other estates. Ferdinand's wars in the southern Italian Peninsula secured Spanish possessions there.

Ferdinand and Isabella rounded out their immediate realm on the Iberian Peninsula by finishing the *Reconquista* crusade begun in the eleventh century. In 1492 they defeated Granada, the last Muslim principality in western Europe. Then, to impose uniformity and conformity on their tidy kingdom, they kicked out of the country all Muslims and Jews who refused to convert to Christianity. Portugal expelled them also in 1497. These "Sephardi" Jews settled throughout the Mediterranean countries, Christian and Muslim, especially the Ottoman Empire. Meanwhile, Spanish authorities worried about the sincerity of conversions by those Muslims and Jews who stayed behind, called, respectively, Moriscos (after the old term *Moors*) and Marranos (a word for "pig"). The monarchs set up the infamous **Spanish Inquisition** (1478–1834) to deal with their suspicions. The Spanish Inquisition investigated and punished cases of people who secretly practiced Islam or Judaism, as well as some cases of witchcraft and sodomy.[5] Over the

---

5. The crime of sodomy could involve a wide number of sexual activities, from bestiality to oral sex, depending on the particular legal system. Most often sodomy has meant sexual activity between people of the same sex. The name comes from the Bible story of Sodom and Gomorrah, although many biblical scholars suggest the crimes the biblical people of Sodom were actually guilty of range from attempted rape to inhospitality.

centuries, the inquisitors ferreted out, tortured, and burned many people to death. By the early 1600s, Spain gave up worrying about whether Moriscos had been converted or not and simply expelled tens of thousands of them to North Africa. Spain's authorities enforced cultural uniformity as they built their new nation.

While Queen Isabella presided over the defeat of Muslim Granada, she gambled on an unusual plan to reach the lavish Indies. In 1492, an eccentric Italian ship captain, **Christopher Columbus**, proposed sailing westward across the Atlantic Ocean, rather than to the south around Africa (which would not succeed for six more years). Isabella's advisors were correct to warn her that Columbus's voyage should fail. Contrary to a popular yet incorrect myth, their advice was not based on a mistaken belief that the world was flat—since the time of the ancient Greeks, every educated person knew that the world was round or, more properly, a globe. Instead, Isabella's advisors were correct to point out that Columbus had underestimated the distance from his last supply point in the Canary Islands to Japan.[6] While Columbus thought that he needed to travel a mere 2,400 miles, Isabella's advisors knew, in fact, the distance to be more than 8,000 miles. Columbus would have died at sea had he not stumbled upon the "New World." For most of his life, Columbus believed that what he had claimed for Spain was part of the true Indies of the East, just as he read in Marco Polo's book. He did not want to give up that belief. Instead, other explorers, like Amerigo Vespucci, quickly recognized that the islands of the Caribbean were the "West" Indies and that new continents lay just beyond. Therefore, mapmakers labeled the continents **North** and **South America** after Amerigo Vespucci, not Christopheria or Columbia after Christopher Columbus.

Columbus discovered the Americas at exactly the right moment for Europeans to exploit their advantages. There had been, of course, earlier contacts between the Old World of Eurasia and Africa with the New World of the Americas, going back even to the Vikings. In all these earlier interactions, however, the travelers lacked the interest or ability to dominate the "native" Americans who had been living there for tens of thousands of years. By 1492, however, Spain was ready to commit resources for conquest and was lucky enough to have them succeed beyond expectation.

Columbus's legacy has been tarnished by his domination of the indigenous peoples (mistakenly, of course, called Indians, after Columbus's goal of reaching the East Indies). He kidnapped locals and killed to seize land at will. In his desire to acquire gold, Columbus had the hands cut off of Indians who failed to turn in his quotas. Those who fled he had hunted down with huge hounds who tore off their limbs while still alive. His soldiers forcibly took native women for themselves. Following Columbus, other Spanish adventurers called **conquistadors** conquered much of the Americas, supported by a firm conviction in God's blessing

---

6. The Spanish were just finishing up their conquest of the Canary Islands in 1492. The conquerors killed off most of the native Guanche people and extinguished their culture. Immigrants from Spain became the new masters of the islands, profiting from sugar plantations worked by newly imported enslaved Africans from the continent. Many historians see this Spanish policy as beginning colonial imperialist genocide.

for their cause, rich financial backing, and a well-drilled military equipped with horses and guns (see the Primary Source Project only online at http://www.con cisewesternciv.com/sources/psc9c.html).[7]

Historians call the European takeover of the Americas and its consequences the Columbian Exchange, a mutual transfer of goods and ideas between the "Old World" and the "New." The rate of exchange mostly added up to be in Europe's favor, however. European settlers rushed into the Americas, grabbing control of vast expanses of land and essentially enslaving native peoples. Wealth in precious metals and food products flowed into Europe, having been produced by the native peoples. Europeans ate better with foods transplanted from the New World, including peanuts, maize, sunflowers, chilis, pineapples, and tomatoes (although tomatoes were originally suspected of being poisonous because of their bright red color). The potato in particular, because of its high caloric content, would improve the health of European peasants. It took a long time for its cultivation to spread, however, since people were suspicious of the strange root vegetable. Cocoa and vanilla delivered new flavors, soon enhanced with plentiful sugar. Tobacco smoking proffered a new social pastime (even if addictive and deadly). In turn, both native and immigrant Americans fed on cattle, pigs, chickens, sugarcane, coffee, rice, oranges, bananas, and even the honey of honeybees brought from the Old World to the New. Cats, dogs, donkeys, and horses offered companionship and working animals for Americans. Along with these new agricultural resources, the original inhabitants gained new rulers and a new religion.

The European conquest came surprisingly easily, within a few decades after Columbus's discovery. Caribbean island dwellers could not organize a strong military resistance since the islanders were still at the socioeconomic level of hunter-gatherers or simple agriculturalists. No indigenous people in the Americas used metal tools and weapons, the wheel, or beasts of burden (except llamas in the Andes). Even so, millions of American Indians on the mainland were quite civilized and organized. Two recently formed empires maintained societies based in cities as sophisticated as any in the Old World. One of the peoples who ruled the so-called Aztec Empire, the Mexica, gave their name to modern-day Mexico. Their political power reached southward toward Central America. The Aztec capital of Tenochtitlan (today, Mexico City) arguably possessed more comforts, and certainly more people, than any one city in Spain. At the same time, the Incan Empire based in Peru controlled much of the west coast of South America. Each empire coordinated agriculture, war, and peace for millions of people, with armies well trained in conquest. These civilized societies were, ironically, even more vulnerable to conquest. They shared three serious disadvantages for competition with the Spanish: deification, ethnic conflicts, and vulnerable immune systems.

First, deification hurt the natives because they expected too much from their own human rulers, who were considered to be gods. The Aztec practice of sacrificing humans for religious reasons, carving out beating hearts with obsidian knives, also upset many subject peoples who did not believe in the Aztec gods. Even worse, the natives too often incorrectly believed the Europeans were gods

---

7. Only online at http://www.concisewesternciv.com/sources/psc9c.html.

Figure 9.6.   The Spanish conquistadors are the new lords of the palace as they order the Incan ruler Atahualpa strangled by his own people. (NYPL Digital Collection)

themselves. The newcomers' pale skins, shiny armor, and unfamiliar horses contributed to this falsehood, which the lying conquistadors exploited to the utmost. This sham allowed Hernán Cortés in Mexico and Francisco Pizarro in Peru to get close to, capture, and then execute the native emperors (see figure 9.6). Therefore, the embodiment of both church and state collapsed with one blow. Murdered emperors left the natives disorganized and doubting their own gods.

Second, the diversity of the Native Americans helped the Spanish defeat the native political states. The Incan and Aztec Empires, like many empires, centered on specific ethnic groups that dominated others through warfare. Enemies of these empires, tribes that remained unconquered or had been recently subjugated, readily cooperated with the Spanish against the native imperial supremacy. The Spanish played various tribal groups against one another. Then the conquistadors replaced every native civilized political structure that oversaw good farmland. Only on the fringes of the Spanish Empire did Indians retain some self-rule. They usually survived as hunter-gatherer societies, protected by mountains, deserts, or jungles.

The third and worst problem for the natives was their vulnerability to diseases carried from Europe. We understand now how many diseases are caused by germs (see chapter 11). In the sixteenth century, though, many people felt that disease was a punishment from God. Such had been the case with the Black Death, which killed a third of the European population within a few years. Little knowledge existed on how to prevent or cure illnesses. The Spanish, naturally and unintentionally, brought with them various germs from Europe, from diseases as harmless as the common cold to the more lethal measles, mumps, whooping cough, chicken pox, and the very deadly smallpox. The Europeans bore substantial immunities to these diseases, but the Native Americans had never been exposed to them. In contrast, perhaps the only illness that the Europeans brought back from the Americas may have been the sexually transmitted disease of syphilis. It first appeared in Europe at about this time and for the next few centuries disproportionately afflicted sexually promiscuous people, especially prostitutes, soldiers, and aristocrats.

The Spanish conquistadors suffered comparatively few deaths from the pandemics they started. The natives of the Americas were not so fortunate. Millions of them became sick and died. Disease spread rapidly along imperial roads, completely depopulating large regions and breaking down local sociopolitical networks. Natives lost faith in their own gods, seeing how the divine seemed to favor the invaders with fewer deaths and more recovery.

Through exploitation of political rivalries, military tactics, and disease, Spain quickly came to dominate the Americas, wiping out much of the indigenous cultures and civilization and replacing them with its version of Western civilization. At the time, the Spanish did not realize the total extent of the devastation or fully comprehend their own role in the plagues. But they knew how to take advantage of the situation. Empty land was theirs for the taking. Over the next three centuries, perhaps close to two million Spaniards migrated to what would become known as Latin America (from the linguistic origins of Spanish and Portuguese). The Spanish reduced to servitude and enslavement those natives who survived disease and slaughter. They imposed the *encomienda* system of peonage on the natives, reducing their status to one similar to medieval serfs. Only insufficient numbers of colonial settlers prevented the Spanish from expanding farther into North America than they did.

The Spanish masters exploited the defeated. Natives dug in the silver mines (of which there were plenty, but disappointingly few sources of gold). Or they labored in the fields for long hours under the southern sun. Many died from overwork and lack of care, exploited worse than animals. Only a few voices protested, notably Bartolomé de Las Casas, the first priest ordained in the Americas. He spoke out to claim human and Christian dignity for the Indians. He and others won the argument that Indians had souls and were human, capable of entry into heaven after death. But many continued to die. Within a few decades, the native population of the Americas fell from what was probably eleven million to only two and a half million.

While this depopulation guaranteed European domination, it also threatened the Western exploitation. Who would produce the silver and food that the Europeans desired and needed? How could they replace all the dead miners and peasants?

The Portuguese offered a solution with the **Atlantic-African slave trade**. In the year 1400, slavery hardly existed in Europe, although it was common in most other civilizations. Soon thereafter, the Portuguese gained an interest in slavery, which they had seen operating among the Africans. Beginning in 1444 they began to buy and sell black Africans, with the official excuse of the need to convert heathens to Christianity. In reality, they wanted cheap, expendable labor for their sugarcane plantations in the Azores and Madeiras. Producing sugar, which everyone's sweet tooth craved, promoted inhumane labor practices. The cane crop required hard, nasty, and dangerous harvesting in dank thickets, where workers hacked away at rough, sharp stalks with machetes. Over the next few centuries, Europeans of various nationalities captured and shipped millions of diverse ethnic Africans to be enslaved in the Americas. The first boatload arrived by 1510, not even two decades after Columbus's discovery. By the time the Atlantic-African slave trade ended in the nineteenth century, about ten million Africans had been shipped to the Americas, most unloaded in the Caribbean islands and Brazil, but about a fifth going to British colonies. Millions more died before ever reaching the American slave markets, of disease and in the fetid holds of slave ships (see figure 9.7). Such losses were just part of the cost of doing business.

An improved method of investing capital, the bourse or **stock exchange**, soon financed this slave trade and other colonial ventures. First appearing in Antwerp in 1485, the stock exchange provided an alternative to banks as a place for capital to be gathered and invested. Previously investors risked all of their possessions if investments in a business failed. By 1600, joint-stock companies provided a better way to protect investments by selling shares of stock to many investors. And if a business failed, losses were restricted only to the number of shares any individual

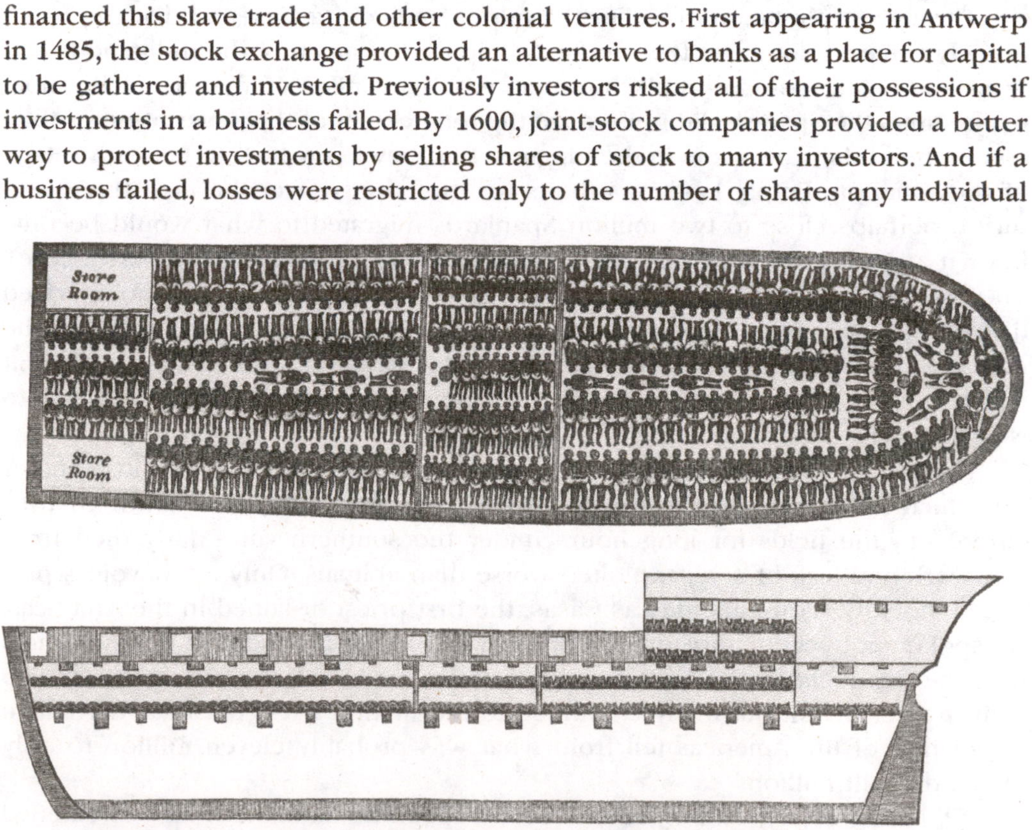

Figure 9.7. These cross sections of the decks of a slave ship, from above and from the side, show how human beings were packed for transatlantic transport. (NYPL Digital Collection)

owned. This limited liability meant that someone who prudently invested only a portion of their wealth through stock in any single venture could not be ruined. Remember, risk was always part of capitalism. Just like any form of property, precious metals, or currency, the value of any stock anytime, anywhere depends on what people believe it to be. In a marketplace, if participants see worth, the cost rises; if they do not, the price falls. Over the centuries, despite some economic disasters, the overall economy dominated by the West has grown.

Although the New World looked like a profitable investment, it had a mixed impact on the European economy. American silver mines added tons of bullion to the treasuries of Spain, which then filtered out to the other nations of Europe and even to China through world trade. But so much silver also led to quick and devastating inflation. A "price revolution," where inflation swiftly drove up the costs of goods and services, hurt the middle and poorer classes of Spain, eventually weakening the Spanish Empire. The history of capitalism is rife with both growth in wealth and suffering caused by crises in investments.

The original simple idea of capitalism (reinvesting profits) offered no real guidelines on how to best keep those profits flowing to everyone's benefit. Some intellectuals attempted to figure out how to prevent economic disaster and promote economic growth. As part of the Commercial Revolution, they began to propose one of the first "economic theories," sets of ideas that offered comprehensive explanations for how people could best carry out economic activity (see diagram 14.2). Since then, many theories have tried to suggest ways to best harness capitalism. Unlike scientific theories (see chapter 10), however, no economic theory has as yet sufficiently explained human economic activity.

The early *economic theory of mercantilism* linked the growing early modern nation-states to their new colonial empires. Theorists emphasized that the accumulation of wealth in precious metals (bullion) within a country's own borders was the best measure of economic success. Mercantilist theory favored government intervention in the economy, since it was in governments' self-interest that their economies succeed. The theory argued that a regime should cultivate a favorable balance of trade as a sign of economic success. Since most international exchange took place in actual gold and silver, monarchs tried to make sure that other countries bought more from their country than they themselves bought from other monarchs' countries. By these means, the bullion in a country's treasury continued to increase. Monarchs then obsessed about discovering mines of gold and silver, a practically cost-free method of acquiring bullion.

Because of this tangible wealth, governments frequently intervened by trying to promote certain enterprises to strengthen the economy. State-sponsored monopolies had clear advantages for a monarch. A state-licensed enterprise, such as importing tea leaves from China or sable furs from Siberia, could easily be supervised and taxed. Diligent inspections and regulation ensured that monopolies' goods and services were of a high quality. The government could then promote and protect that business both overseas and domestically.

Fueled by burgeoning capital and inspired by developing theory, both accredited and unsanctioned adventurers sailed off to exploit the riches of Asia, Africa, and the Americas. Unfortunately for European imperialists, the world was already fairly crowded with other powerful peoples. Various kingdoms and states in East Asia (the Chinese Empire, Japan), the Indian subcontinent (the Mughal Empire), and Africa (Morocco, the Songhai Empire, Abyssinia/Ethiopia) had long histories, rich economies, sophisticated cultures, and intimidating armies that kept Europeans at arm's length, for a while. Conversion efforts by Jesuits in Japan and China would meet with little success. In Asia, the Spanish only managed to conquer various principalities in the archipelago they renamed the Philippines after King Philip II, who had ordered the expeditions. Tropical diseases in Africa and Asia also killed many Europeans who ventured there. The European powers ruled the oceans but could only nibble at the fringes of Asia and Africa.

Even so, Spain and Portugal boldly divided up the world between them in 1494 with the **Treaty of Tordesillas** (see map 9.2). The full ramifications of Columbus's voyage remained unclear, and Vasco da Gama had not yet reached the Indies. Nevertheless, both kingdoms claimed dominion over half of the globe each, with the pope's blessing.

People of other Western nations did not let the Spanish and Portuguese enjoy their fat empires in peace for long. Outside the law, pirates in the Caribbean along the Spanish Main (the Central and South American coastline) and in the Indies plundered whatever they could. Some captains became legalized pirates, licensed by governments with "letters of marque." For example, raids by the English Sir Francis Drake and his sea dogs helped provoke the Spanish Armada. Smugglers snuck products to markets, avoiding tariffs while supplying customers with cheaper or forbidden products.

By 1600, the Dutch, the English, and the French had launched their own overseas ventures, with navies and armies grabbing and defending provinces across the oceans. They all began to drive out natives in the Americas, and to a lesser degree in Africa and Asia. They also turned on one another. In Asia and Africa, the Dutch grabbed Portuguese bases in South Africa and the East Indies. The English, in turn, seized Dutch possessions in Africa, Malaysia, and North America (turning New Holland into New York and New Jersey). The English planted their own colonists along the Atlantic seacoast of North America. The French settled farther inland in Quebec. Likewise, in the Caribbean, India, and the Pacific, the French and English faced each other in disputes about islands and principalities while the native peoples were caught in the middle.

From the Europeans' point of view, they brought the benefits of Western civilization. Of course, actual material benefits went mostly to the European masters. These European "illegal immigrants" seized power from the original native rulers and owners. The colonizers ravaged the native cultures, often with cruelty (scalping was invented by Europeans) and carelessness (smashing sculptures and pulverizing written works). Priceless cultural riches vanished forever. Land grabbing displaced the local native farmers and dismantled socioeconomic structures. Where social bonds did not snap apart, European immigrants ignored and discriminated, trying to weaken the hold of native religions, languages, and even clothing styles. Robbed of their homes and livelihoods, most non-European subjects found resistance to be futile against the weight of European power.

As a result of the westerners' expansion around the world, the name "Europe" became a binding agent for the West. At the same time, Europeans remained very diverse. Christianity had broken down into increasingly numerous sects. The Holy Roman Empire was a shadow with no ability to unify Europeans. What was left were numerous ethnicities. Various Europeans hurled insults and launched wars against one another, which they justified using grotesque ethnic stereotypes. While the people of one's own nation were invariably perceived as kind, generous, sober, straight, loyal, honest, and intelligent, they might allege that the Spanish were cruel, the Scots stingy, the Dutch greedy, the French perverted, the Italians deceptive, the English smug, or the Germans boorish. So, Europeans remained pluralistic in their perceptions of one another while united in their desire to dominate the globe over foreign "others."

The elites also recognized certain common bonds in how they practiced their gentlemanly manners in ruling over the lower classes. They expanded government authority, grew their increasingly national economies, and revered the Christian religion (no matter how fractured). Missionaries preached the alleged love and hope of Christianity, while global natives found themselves confronted by new crimes brought in by the westerners, such as prostitution and vagrancy. A few Europeans adopted a notion of the morally pure "noble savage" as a critique on their own culture. Most others legitimized their supremacy over all global peoples because of Western exceptionalism. Europeans were "civilized," and everyone else was "barbaric" and primitive. They increasingly viewed humans through racist lenses of skin color. "White" Europeans were superior, justified by virtue of their power and technology. The other "colored" peoples were inferior, whether "red" American Indians; "brown" North Africans, South Asian Indians, Southeast Asians, and Pacific Islanders; "yellow" Chinese; or "black" sub-Saharan Africans and Australians. These "colors," of course, do not accurately reflect the actual skin tones of any human being. To have a "white" complexion is not actually white, of course, even for albinos. Colors are simplified labels for the supremacy of one kind of person over another. Through increasing contacts with other peoples, the rest of the world seemed truly "foreign."

The sub-Saharan "black" Africans suffered the most under these racist paradigms because of modern slavery. Of course, through most of history, in most civilizations, the masses, both free and enslaved, have supported the few at the top. Many Asians, Muslims, Native Americans, and Africans themselves practiced slavery. Ancient Greece and Rome were slave societies. But in those societies, most of those enslaved were ethnically the same as or similar to the masters. The Atlantic-African slave owner, in contrast, often practiced the worst kind of "chattel" slavery, considering the lives of those enslaved to be unhuman and expendable as furniture. African heritage and darker-pigmented skin became synonymous with inferiority and suitability for being enslaved. The legacy would be an enduring institutionalized racism in the Americas.

This Eurocentric attitude is reflected in the early maps of the globe. Medieval maps had usually given pride of place in the center to Jerusalem. By the sixteenth century, geographers had a more accurate picture of the globe and could distinguish other continents as connected to one another by at most a narrow isthmus (such as Panama for the Americas, or Sinai between Eurasia and Africa). Nonetheless, they "split" the continent of Eurasia into "Asia" and "Europe," arbitrarily deciding on the Ural Mountains as a dividing point (although these hills hardly created a barrier—as the Avars, Huns, Magyars, and Mongols had demonstrated). Westerners saw vast stretches of eastern Europe as hardly civilized at all, a tempting target for building empires. The maps had changed to show that Europeans had moved from being located in one small corner of the map to the center. The explorers who led the voyages of discovery showed audacity and heroism, added to the geographic knowledge of Europeans, and allowed some mutually beneficial cultural exchange. Wielding a newfound global power, Western civilization had conquered bits of the Old World and most of the New by the mid-seventeenth century. Much more was to come in the nineteenth century.

Review: *How did the "voyages of discovery" begin colonial imperialism by Europeans?*

Response:

Make your own timeline.

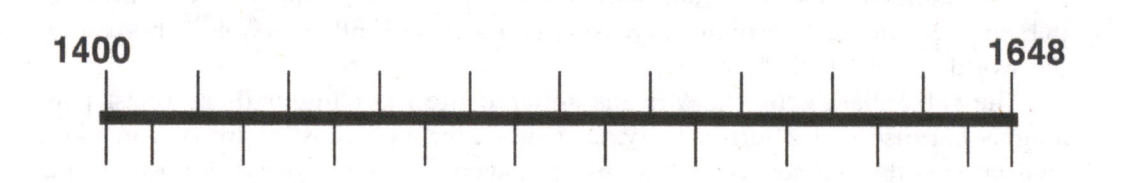

1400   **1648**

CHAPTER 10

Liberation of Mind and Body

Early Modern Europe, 1543 to 1815

While fighting over forms of faith, people also pondered their place in God's creation. Was each person's position ordained and unchangeable, or could people achieve something higher than the status into which they were born? The increasing use of the mind, as advocated by the humanists of the Renaissance, supported the latter attitude. Yet the more humanists examined the writings of the Greeks and Romans, the more they discovered flaws and mistakes about the natural world. If the philosophy of antiquity could be so wrong, then how could one find truth? Western civilization provided a new method with the so-called **Scientific Revolution** (1543–1687), which unleashed an ongoing force for change and power. Ideas that freed people from ignorance about nature would in time lead them to question social hierarchies and transform political systems.

LOST IN THE STARS

A religious problem unexpectedly triggered the invention of modern science. The Julian calendar, established in 45 BC, had become seriously out of sync with nature. As mentioned in chapter 5, Julius Caesar had reformed the calendar by adding a leap day every fourth year to compensate for the estimated 365¼ days of the solar year. According to the Julian calendar, the first day of spring (the vernal equinox, when the hours of day exactly equal those of night) should occur around 21 March. But since the solar year is several minutes less than the estimate, extra days had accumulated over the centuries. By the fifteenth century, the vernal equinox fell in early April. The church feared that this delay jeopardized the sanctity of Easter (which was celebrated on the first Sunday after the first full moon following the vernal equinox). The Counter-Reformation papacy, eager to have its structures improved and reformed, called on intellectuals to come up with both an explanation about the Julian calendar's errors and a solution.

Previously, in the Middle Ages, the study of the processes of nature took the name of natural philosophy. Natural philosophy included the mystical and supernatural in order to contemplate and interact with divine creation. By the Renaissance, the dominant views on nature were shaped by the ancient Greek Aristotle, as adapted and transmitted by medieval Muslim philosophers and then the victory of Scholasticism. Most intellectuals accepted Aristotle's logical assertion that the earth sat at the center of the universe. According to Aristotle, the sun, the moon, the other planets, and the stars (attached to giant crystalline spheres) revolved around the earth (which every educated person knew was a globe). The Greek natural philosopher Ptolemy had elaborated on this idea in the second century AD. Aristotle and Ptolemy's earth-centered universe was labeled the Ptolemaic or **geocentric theory**. After the success of Aquinas and the Scholastics, the Western Latin Church endorsed this Aristotelian view. It liked the argument that proximity to the center of the earth (hell's presumed location) corresponded with imperfection and evil, while distance from earth (toward heaven) equaled goodness and perfection.

The geocentric theory was not the only reasonable view of the universe, however. A few ancient Greeks had disagreed with Aristotle's concept and argued instead that the sun was the center of the universe, with the earth revolving around it (and the moon revolving around the earth). This sun-centered universe was called the **heliocentric theory** (see diagram 10.1).

Without any winning evidence either way, Renaissance intellectuals could, at first, reasonably see both the geocentric and the heliocentric as valid scientific theories. Many people today misunderstand the meaning of a **scientific theory**,

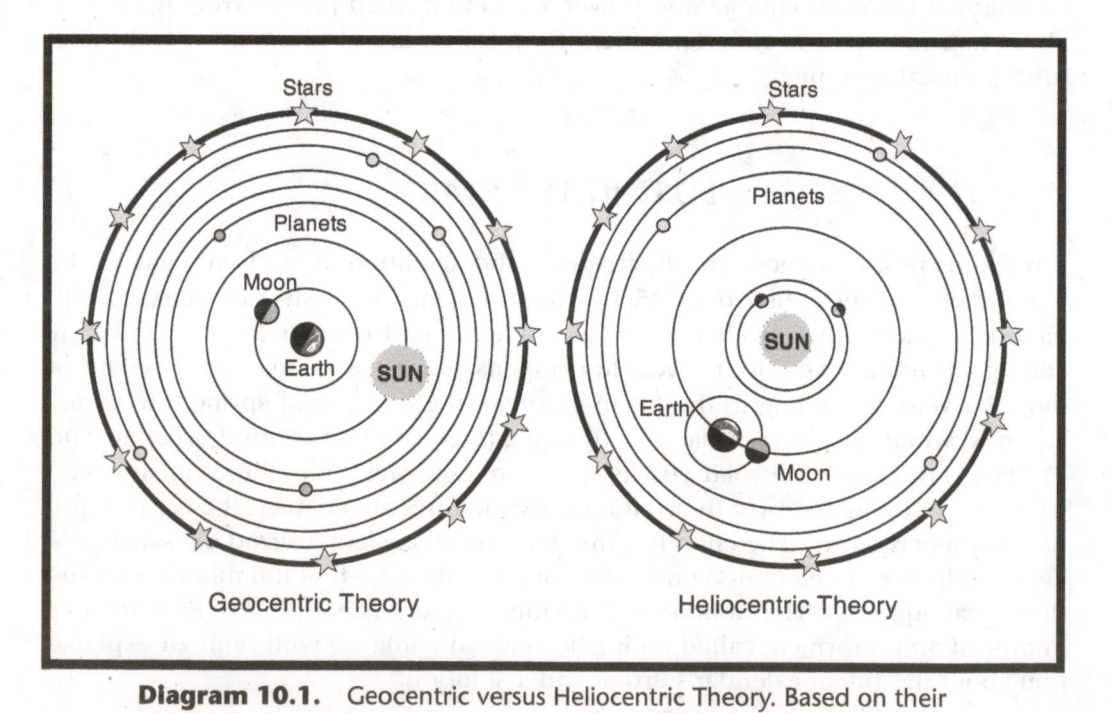

Diagram 10.1. Geocentric versus Heliocentric Theory. Based on their observations and perspectives, ancient Greek philosophers had first proposed these theories for the structure of the universe.

probably because the word *theory* has multiple definitions. In science, a theory does not mean something "theoretical" in the sense of a possible guess that is far from certain (that would be a hypothesis). Rather, a valid scientific theory explains how the universe actually works and is supported by most of the available facts and contradicted by very few, if any. If not much is known, then several opposing theories may well be acceptable. After scientists have asked new questions and new facts have been discovered, a scientific theory may either be invalidated and discounted or supported and strengthened. In this way, as scientists discovered new information, the geocentric theory eventually failed to explain the heavens, while the heliocentric theory won support.

As sixteenth-century astronomers looked at the heavens, they discovered the information that they needed to correct the calendar. They measured and calculated the movement of the stars and planets. They figured out that the year is actually 365.2422 days, a fraction less than the 365¼ used by the Julian calendar.

Therefore, a new calendar was proposed, one that did not add a leap day in century years that were not evenly divisible by four hundred. For example, 1900 would not have a leap day, but 2000 would.[1] Pope Gregory XIII adopted these changes in 1582, giving Western civilization the **Gregorian calendar** to replace the Julian. He dropped ten days from that year to set the calendar back on track with the seasons: thus the day after 5 October 1582 became 15 October 1582, at least in those areas that accepted papal authority. Anglican England and Orthodox Russia waited a few centuries to conform to the papal view, partly because they were suspicious about anything that came from the Roman Catholic Church.

In spite of the changes to the calendar, however, the papacy fought against embracing the scientific theory that the earth revolved around the sun. In 1543, the canon and astronomer Mikolaj Kopernig in Poland (who used the Latinized name **Nicolaus Copernicus**) published a book, *Concerning the Revolutions of the Celestial Bodies*, which argued convincingly for the heliocentric theory. Copernicus knew the controversy this position would provoke and had waited to publish it until he was on his deathbed. As he expected, the Roman Catholic Church rejected his argument out of hand and put his study onto the *Index of Forbidden Books*. The papacy told astronomers they had to support the geocentric theory because it conformed to their preferred reading of the Bible and the belief system of Aristotle and Scholasticism.

The Roman Catholics notwithstanding, new evidence continued to undermine the geocentric theory and support the heliocentric theory. The best facts were presented by **Galileo Galilei** (b. 1564–d. 1642) of Florence. In 1609, he improved a Dutch spyglass and fashioned the first functional telescope, which he turned toward the heavens. Galileo discovered moons around Jupiter, mountains and craters on the moon, sunspots, and other phenomena that convinced him that the heavens were far from Aristotelian perfection. His publication the next year, *The Starry Messenger*, supported the Copernican theory. It sparked a sensation among intellectuals, while it also angered leaders of the Roman Catholic Church. Clergy warned Galileo that his ideas were dangerous. Therefore, he kept silent until he

---

1. The calendar today is adjusted by fractions of seconds every year using data from atomic clocks kept accurate by measuring the oscillations of radioactive elements.

thought a pope had been elected who would support his inquiries. Cautiously, he framed his next book, *Dialogue on the Chief World Systems* (1636), as a debate in which the Copernican view technically lost but the Aristotelian view looked indefensibly stupid.

The papacy saw through the device. The Roman Inquisition called in the seventy-year-old and questioned him, using forged evidence. The inquisitors threatened Galileo with the instruments of torture, probably including pincers, thumbscrews, leg screws, and the rack. They defined disagreement with the Roman Church as heresy, and thus Galileo was automatically a heretic. Galileo pled guilty, and the Inquisition sentenced him to house arrest for the rest of his life.[2] The aged scientist nonetheless continued experiments that helped lay the foundation of modern physics. His studies increasingly showed that Aristotle was incorrect about many things, not only the location of the earth in the universe.

A person born in far-off England during the year Galileo died, **Isaac Newton** (b. 1642–d. 1727), assured the doom of Aristotle's views about nature. Newton first studied the properties of light (founding modern optics) and built an improved reflector telescope, which he also turned to the heavens. Like most scientists of his era, Newton accepted the Copernican/heliocentric theory, but he still wanted to find an explanation for how the moon, planets, and stars stayed in their orbits while apples dropped from trees to the ground.

Supposedly inspired by an apple that fell off a tree onto his head, Newton worked to measure moving bodies, in the process inventing calculus as a tool. He finally arrived at an explanation for how the universe works, published in the book *Principia* (1687). In that treatise, Newton's theory of universal gravitation accounted for the movements of the heavenly bodies. He showed that all objects of substance, all things with the quality of "mass," possess gravitational attraction toward one another. So the moon and the earth, just as an apple and the earth, are being drawn toward each other. The apple drops because it has no other force acting upon it. The moon stays spinning around the earth because it is moving fast enough; its motion balances out the earth's gravitational pull. The delicate opposition of gravity and velocity keeps the heavens whirling.

With the publication of the *Principia*, many historians consider the Scientific Revolution to have triumphed, having created the modern, Western idea of science. Some recent historians note here the "disenchantment" of nature: instead of natural philosophy's embrace of the mystical and supernatural to contemplate and interact with divine creation, science focused on cold, hard facts. Traditional authorities, such as Aristotle, were to be doubted until proven. No longer relying on divine revelation or reason (the big debate of the Middle Ages), trustworthy knowledge was now to be obtained through a specific tool of reason called the **scientific method**. Between the years of Copernicus and Newton's books, other intellectuals such as Francis Bacon and René Descartes had worked out this basic set of scientific principles (see table 10.1).

The scientific method also compensated for the human frailties of individual scientists. For example, Newton wrote serious commentaries about the biblical book of Revelation, tried vindictively to destroy the careers of academic rivals,

---

2. For his plea, go to http://www.concisewesternciv.com/sources/galileo.html.

Table 10.1.   The Scientific Method

1. Find a problem.
2. Form a hypothesis (a reasonable or educated guess to the solution).
3. Conduct experiments (repeatedly) and/or observations (extensively).
4. Make the argument and conclusions, usually in written form.
5. Share the knowledge, usually through publication.
6. Others repeat the experiments and/or observations and share confirmations, modifications, or refutations.
7. Form scientific theories based on overwhelming evidence or laws proven by universal evidence.

Note: The step-by-step process of the scientific method rigorously uses experimentation and observation to explain how nature works.

and fudged some of the data in his *Principia*. With the scientific process, however, human scientists applied the method to test their conclusions and produced better information about the natural world than had ever before been available in history. As a result, the Scientific Revolution had enormous consequences for Western civilization and then the world. Science became such an essential part of the Western worldview that it forms another basic principle:

> **Science is the only testable and generally accessible method of understanding facts about the universe; every other means of explanation is opinion.**

That does not mean that all science is always correct. Many assumptions (especially about human nature) can be affected by bias or can change due to new information. Even mistakes can be useful tools to push investigations toward a more accurate understanding of nature.

As they experimented, scientists invented tools to help them (see figure 10.1). One result was an acceleration in the invention of technology, which made life easier, safer, and more productive. Most people in the world around 1600 lived much the same way as they had for several thousand years. By the late seventeenth century, though, **scientific academies** (such as the British Royal Society) had institutionalized scientific inquiry and its application to economic growth. Scientists were not mere theoreticians but innovators and inventors, from thermometers to timepieces, pumps to pins. These inventions were soon translated into the physical power used to dominate the globe. Medical and agricultural advances based on science followed. By 1800, westerners were living much more prosperous and comfortable lives, largely because of science.

The success of the Scientific Revolution was not complete or universal. Its attitudes only slowly spread from the elites through the population. Many westerners rejected the scientific mind-set of skepticism because they preferred specific religious doctrines or general superstitious attitudes. Moreover, science is not perfect. Honest scientists cannot proclaim certainty about the permanence of their discoveries: when presented with new information, true scientists should change their

Figure 10.1.   A seventeenth-century scientist, fashionably dressed and armed with a sword, examines a barometer that measures air pressure to help forecast the weather. (Treasures of the NOAA Library Collection)

minds. Theories can come and go. Long ago the heliocentric theory was severely modified—while the sun *is* the center of our solar system, it is certainly *not* the center of the universe. In time, new science led Newton's own theory of universal gravitation to be overturned (see chapter 13). And ultimately, science cannot answer basic questions about the meaning of life and death. Nevertheless, with its discoveries and revisions, science constantly changes life in Western civilization.

Review: *How did the Scientific Revolution change traditional views about nature?*

Response:

FROM THE SALONS TO THE STREETS

Historians have decided that the year of Newton's *Principia* marks the beginning of a major intellectual movement known as **the Enlightenment** (1687–1789). During this time, scientific academies and universities adapted and spread many scientific ideas. Some men chattered about these ideas in the new coffeehouses. In addition, a few wealthy and curious women gathered a variety of interesting people to discuss the issues of the day in their **salons** (pleasant rooms in their fine homes, not beauty parlors). Beginning in Paris, salon hostesses such as Madame Goffrin or Madame Rambouillet guided the witty conversation of clergymen, politicians, businessmen, scientists, and amateur philosophers, writers, and popularizers known as ***philosophes*** (French for philosopher). The *philosophes* took what they learned, especially the lessons of science, and publicized it.

Philosophes made Paris the cultural capital of Western civilization in the eighteenth century. During those decades, French culture reigned supreme among the elites of the West. The French language (*lingua franca*) took over intellectual life and international communication, replacing the Latin of the Middle Ages and the Renaissance. Europeans who wanted to seem sophisticated imitated French styles of cuisine, clothing, furnishings, luxury goods, and architecture. From their salons, intellectuals explained to society how the new science and economics impacted life. Four major concepts summarize their Enlightenment views: **empiricism**, **skepticism**, **humanitarianism**, and **progress**.

The first of these concepts, ***empiricism***, came from the starting point of science: observations by our senses are both accurate and reasonable. Knowledge obtained from studies of the natural world could consequently help explain human activities. This effective idea contradicted many past religious authorities, who had depended on divine revelation for their knowledge. Those supernatural, metaphysical, or spiritual answers were too open to dispute, too difficult to prove. Of course, humans do not always draw the correct conclusions from their observations, nor does the natural world always correspond to human experience. Regardless, *philosophes* were convinced that applying the tools of science to human character would help improve society.

One proponent of empirical thinking was John Locke of England. He proposed that the human mind was like a *tabula rasa* (blank slate) on which all learned information was written. His most famous empirical argument justified England's Glorious Revolution (see below) toward more democratic politics. Locke argued against books such as Thomas Hobbes's *Leviathan*, in which large sections on a Christian Commonwealth and the Kingdom of Darkness argued for absolutism.

Another famous example of an empirical argument became the ***theory of classical liberal economics***. This theory contradicted the prevailing theory of mercantilism, arguing instead for making capitalism "free market" or **laissez-faire** (a term coined by contemporary French economists). Classical liberal theorists justified their case using observations of the behavior of peoples and institutions, from smugglers to ministers of state, from banks to empires. They argued against the theory of mercantilism, where government officials made key economic decisions by granting monopolies and raising tariffs. Instead, they theorized that rational individuals looking out for their own "enlightened" self-interest would make better economic choices. The most famous formulation came from the Scotsman Adam Smith in his book *The Wealth of Nations* published in 1776. He saw that individual actions would accumulate to push the economy forward, as if collectively by a giant "invisible hand." Like all economic theories, classical liberal economics has serious flaws, as later history showed. For a long time, though, it made more sense than the likewise flawed theory of mercantilism.

The second Enlightenment concept, *skepticism*, followed from Descartes's principle of doubting everything and trusting only what could be tested by reason. A popular subject for skepticism was Christianity, with all its contradictions, superstitions, and schisms. Skepticism soon promoted the fashionable belief of *deism*. This creed diverged from classic catholic orthodox Christianity. Deists saw God as more of a creator, maker, or author of the universe, and not so much as the incarnate Christ who redeemed sinful man through his death and resurrection. It was as if God had constructed the universe like a giant clock and left it running according to well-organized principles of nature. Thus, for many deists, Christianity became more of a moral philosophy and a guide for behavior than the overriding concern of all existence.

Many leading intellectuals embraced *agnosticism*, thus going even further down the road of doubt. Agnostics considered the existence of God impossible to prove, since God was beyond empirical observation and experimentation. Agnostics were and are concerned about this life, ignoring any possible afterlife. A few among the elites, such as the Scottish philosopher and historian David Hume, journeyed all the way to *atheism* and denied outright the existence of God. Many agnostics and atheists, moreover, attacked Christianity as a failed religion of misinformation, exploitation, and slaughter.

For the first time since the Roman Empire's conversion, Christianity was not the belief of all the leading figures of Western civilization. This trend would only continue. A natural result was that *toleration* became an increasingly widespread ideal. The most famous *philosophe*, Voltaire (François-Marie Arouet, b. 1694–d. 1778), thought religion useful, but he condemned using cruelty on earth in the name of saving souls for heaven. The spread of toleration meant that people of one faith would less often torture and execute others for having the "wrong" religion. Christian doctrine went from being compulsory to providing one more option among many. Religion became a private matter, not a public requirement.

Nonetheless, while many elites were turning away from traditional religion during the eighteenth century, most of the masses experienced a religious revival. Following a lull after the upheaval of the Reformation, large numbers of westerners embraced their Christian beliefs even more passionately. At the same time, Christianity continued to fragment into even more denominations. During the "Great Awakening" in America of the 1730s and 1740s, revivalist Methodists broke off from the Church of England, which they considered too conservative or moderate. New religious groups such as the Society of Friends, nicknamed Quakers, expressed their faith in meetings of quiet association. Quakers left Europe to settle in the new American colony of Pennsylvania, founded explicitly for religious toleration. In Germany, followers of **Pietism** sought to inspire a new fervent faith in Lutheranism, dedicating themselves to prayer and charity. Ironically, if one counted believing Christians and compared the numbers to those of nonbelieving rationalists, the Enlightenment remained more an age of faith than of reason. These numbers lead to another basic principle:

> **Every religion has elements that are nonsensical to a rational outsider; nonsense or not, belief in some form of religion fulfills a vital need for most people.**

Enlightenment *philosophes* clearly stated the first part of the principle; the historical record proves the second part.

Religious toleration reflected the Enlightenment's third big concept, **humanitarianism**, the attitude that humans should treat other humans decently. Ostensibly, the Christian faith and Christ's command about loving one's neighbor had a strong humanitarian component. Throughout history, however, Christian society clearly fell short of that ideal with, for example, crusades, inquisitions, witch hunts, slavery, and cooperation with warmongers. Some Christian preachers had even claimed that suffering was a virtue, calling on the faithful to wait until they died before they received any reward of paradise.

Beyond the suffering of hard conditions, active cruelty saturated eighteenth-century Western society. People visited insane asylums to watch inmates as if they were zoo exhibits. Curiously, zoos also started at that time out of scientific interest; they likewise cruelly confined wild animals in unnatural, small, bare cages. Popular sports included animal fights where bulls, dogs, or roosters ripped each other to bloody shreds. The wealthy ignored the sufferings of the poor, worsened through economic upheavals and natural disasters. Public executions frequently offered Sunday pastimes for large crowds, who watched as criminals were beheaded, burned, disemboweled (intestines pulled out and thrown on a fire), drawn and quartered (either pulled apart by horses or the dead body chopped into four pieces after partial strangulation and disembowelment), beaten by the wheel (and then the crippled body tied to a wheel and hung up on a pole), or simply hanged (usually to die by slow strangulation) (see figure 9.1). The corpses dangled for weeks, months, or even years, until they rotted and fell in pieces from their gibbets.

With the Enlightenment, the elites began to abolish such inhumanity. The new humanitarianism's virtue did not require divine commandments as its foundation. Instead, this principle of morality declared that human beings, simply because they were observably human, should be respected. Rulers passed laws to end the practices of torture and to eliminate the death penalty, or at least to impose it only for the most heinous of crimes. Soon, long-term imprisonment became the common, if expensive, method of punishing criminals. Some reformers actually thought that prisons might even rehabilitate convicts away from their criminal behavior.

Even more novel, leaders began to use social reforms to prevent crime in the first place. They reasoned that poverty and ignorance contributed to the motivations of criminals, so by attacking those social ills, crime rates could be expected to decline. The idea of promoting a good life in this world, summed up in Thomas Jefferson's famous phrase, "life, liberty and the pursuit of happiness," came, for some, to be considered a basic human right.

Although those noble words came from a plantation owner who enslaved people his entire life, another radical agenda of humanitarianism was the abolition of slavery. In the Enlightenment, for the first time in history, leaders of society actually began to feel guilty about enslaving other human beings. The Atlantic-African slave trade had made human beings so expendable that as much as a quarter of the enslaved bought from slavers in Africa did not live through the Atlantic crossing, as they were chained and stacked in the filthy holds of tiny ships (see figure 9.7). Abolitionists argued for human rights for all people of whatever "color" and against the enormous profits made by those who traded in enslaved persons and those who used them on plantations and in households. Western powers slowly abolished formal, state-sanctioned slavery during the nineteenth century, such as Prussia in 1807, Spain in 1811, and France in 1848. It was not always a moral victory, however. Some historians argue that growing industrialization (see the next chapter) made traditional slavery less necessary. Most slaveholders only freed their enslaved people when forced to by authority, and even then governments often compensated them for their financial loss. Unfortunately for the newly freed, they did not receive much land to farm, money to start businesses, or education to succeed in the cities. Enduring racism also inhibited their acceptance and ability to prosper.

In spite of this liberation of enslaved humans, half of the species, namely women, continued to suffer subordination because of sexism. A handful of reformers did suggest that wives should not be under the thumb of their husbands. **Mary Wollstonecraft**'s book *A Vindication of the Rights of Woman* (1792) put forth well-reasoned demands for better education of the "weaker" sex. Her notoriously unconventional lifestyle, however, undermined her call for justice. She conducted an unhappy and notoriously public love affair that produced an illegitimate daughter. As a result, many scandalized people dismissed her propositions. Long after the Enlightenment had ended, few opportunities had opened for women. Effective women's rights in politics, the economy, and society would have to wait many decades.

In any case, the notion that human conditions should improve, namely *progress*, was the fourth big concept of the Enlightenment. In contrast, the Judeo-Christian concept of history had direction, but not necessarily any sense that life would improve. Christians thought that at some point, either today or in the distant future, the natural world would end and humanity would be divided into those sent to hell and those united with God in heaven. The *philosophes* argued instead for a betterment of people's lives in this world, as soon as feasible, based on sound scientific conclusions drawn from empiricism. They argued that material and moral development should even happen in their own lifetimes.

As one form of progress, the Enlightenment promoted new forms of communication and fought against government censorship. Free thought was useless without free speech and a free press. **Encyclopedias**, such as the *Britannica* (first published in 1760 and still going today) or the French *Encyclopedia, or a Systematic Dictionary of the Sciences, Arts and Crafts* (begun in 1751 and finished with its first edition in 1780), offered a bulwark against lapsing back into ignorance. In thirty-five volumes, the French *Encyclopedia* provided a handbook of all human knowledge, indeed, a summary of the Enlightenment. According to its editor, Denis Diderot, the project was supposed to bring together all knowledge, especially about technology, so that humanity could be both happy and more virtuous. Progress became reality as more people learned to read and more written materials appeared for them to read. The new literary form of **novels** (which means "new") also entertained people about the possibilities of change. Novels are book-length, fictional stories in prose about individuals who can pursue their own destinies, often against difficult odds. Samuel Richardson's *Pamela, or Virtue Rewarded* and Daniel Defoe's *Robinson Crusoe* told such tales. **Newspapers** also began publication. They informed people of recent developments in politics, economics, and culture. Armed with these foundations of information, society could only move forward.

Not everyone agreed on these four principles. Two contrasting views of history and human nature rose out of the Enlightenment to be debated ever since. Thomas Hobbes in his book *Leviathan* (1651) argued that defenseless people in the original state of nature, before civilization, suffered danger and violence from each other. As he put it, lives were "solitary, poor, nasty, brutish, and short" without strong government and restrictive social rules. Jean-Jacques Rousseau (b. 1712–d. 1778) in various works argued the opposite. He thought pre-civilized people lived peacefully with one another until civilization's invention of property rights ruined everything. His famous dictum, "Man is born free and everywhere is in chains," promoted revolution against the status quo. Which view is correct?

Progress, humanitarianism, skepticism, and empiricism were agents for change in Western civilization. The *philosophes* wrote about new expectations for human beings in this world, not necessarily connected to traditional Christianity. Building on Renaissance humanism, the Enlightenment offered a rational alternative to the Christian emphasis on life after death. Actions based on reason, science, and kindness could perhaps transform this globe, despite the flaws of human nature. The question was, who could turn the words into action and actually advance the Enlightenment agenda?

Review: *What improvements did Enlightenment thinkers propose for human society?*

Response:

SOURCES ON FAMILIES: JEAN-JACQUES ROUSSEAU, *ÉMILE, OR ON EDUCATION* (1762)

Rather than write another philosophical tract, the philosophe *Jean-Jacques Rousseau presented his theories about education, marriage, and love in the form of a novel. He describes in detail how his protagonist, the orphan Émile, should be brought up. In the last chapter, Rousseau extensively discusses the nature of women and the best way they should be raised, before describing how his hero meets and marries his designated helpmeet, Sophy. Some of his contemporaries criticized Rousseau because he lived with a woman out of wedlock and sent their children to an orphanage rather than raise them himself.*

Sophy should be as truly a woman as Émile is a man, i.e., she must possess all those characters of her sex which are required to enable her to play her part in the physical and moral order. Let us inquire to begin with in what respects her sex differs from our own.

But for her sex, a woman is a man; she has the same organs, the same needs, the same faculties. The machine is the same in its construction; its parts, its working, and its appearance are similar. Regard it as you will, the difference is only in degree.

Yet where sex is concerned man and woman are unlike; each is the complement of the other; the difficulty in comparing them lies in our inability to decide, in either case, what is a matter of sex, and what is not. . . .

In the union of the sexes each alike contributes to the common end, but in different ways. From this diversity springs the first difference which may be observed between man and woman in their moral relations. The man should be strong and active; the woman should be weak and passive; the one must have both the power and the will; it is enough that the other should offer little resistance.

When this principle is admitted, it follows that woman is specially made for man's delight. If man in his turn ought to be pleasing in her eyes, the necessity is less urgent, his virtue is in his strength, he pleases because he is strong. I grant you this is not the law of love, but it is the law of nature, which is older than love itself.

If woman is made to please and to be in subjection to man, she ought to make herself pleasing in his eyes and not provoke him to anger; her strength is in her charms, by their means she should compel him to discover and use his strength. The surest way of arousing this strength is to make it necessary by resistance. . . . This is the origin of attack and defense, of the boldness of one sex and the timidity of the other, and even of the shame and modesty with which nature has armed the weak for the conquest of the strong. . . .

The Most High has deigned to do honor to mankind; he has endowed man with boundless passions, together with a law to guide them, so that man may be alike free and self-controlled; though swayed by these passions man is endowed with reason by which to control them. Woman is also endowed with boundless passions; God has given her modesty to restrain them. . . .

Thus the different constitution of the two sexes leads us to a third conclusion, that the stronger party seems to be master, but is as a matter of fact dependent on the weaker, and that, not by any foolish custom of gallantry, but by an inexorable law of nature. For nature has endowed woman with a power of stimulating man's passions in excess of man's power of satisfying those passions, and has thus made him dependent on her goodwill, and compelled him in his turn to endeavor to please her, so that she may be willing to yield to his superior strength. Is it weakness which yields to force, or is it voluntary self-surrender? . . .

The experience we have gained through our vices has considerably modified the views held in older times; we rarely hear of violence for which there is so little occasion that it would hardly be credited. Yet such stories are common enough among the Jews and ancient Greeks. If fewer deeds of violence are quoted in our days, it is not that men are more temperate, but because they are less credulous, and a complaint which would have been believed among a simple people would only excite laughter among ourselves; therefore silence is the better course. There is a law in Deuteronomy, under which the outraged maiden was punished, along with her assailant, if the crime were committed in a town; but if in the country or in a lonely place, the latter alone was punished. "For," says the law, "the maiden cried for help, and there was none to hear." From this merciful interpretation of the law, girls learnt not to let themselves be surprised in lonely places.

This change in public opinion has . . . produced our modern gallantry. Men have found that their pleasures depend, more than they expected, on the goodwill of the fair sex, and have secured this goodwill by attentions which have had their reward. . . .

The consequences of sex are wholly unlike for man and woman. The male is only a male now and again, the female is always a female, or at least all her youth; everything reminds her of her sex; the performance of her functions requires a special constitution. She needs care during pregnancy and freedom from work when her child is born; she must have a quiet, easy life while she nurses her children; their education calls for patience and gentleness, for a zeal and love which nothing can dismay; she forms a bond between father and child, she alone can win the father's love for his children and convince him that they are indeed his own. What loving care is required to preserve a united family! And there should be no question of virtue in all this, it must be a labor of love, without which the human race would be doomed to extinction. . . .

Questions:

- *What does the source assert as the main differences between men and women?*
- *How does the source claim that "violence" against women (or sexual assault) has changed from ancient times to the author's?*
- *What does the source say are conditions necessary for women to raise families?*

Responses:

For more on this source, go to http://www.concisewesternciv.com/sources/sof10 .html.

THE STATE IS HE (OR SHE)

Since the late sixteenth century, various works by political theorists had been proposing how government could contribute to progress. Some intellectuals suggested rather radical ideas, which are explained in the next section. Most, however, justified the increasing powers of **absolute monarchy**. These arguments reflected new intensity of royal power, the most effective form of absolutism to date.[3] Political theorists and *philosophes* asked how people should be ruled in a fashion that improved society. Many, such as Thomas Hobbes and Jean Bodin, answered that as much power as possible should be put in the hands of a dynastic prince. Diets and parliaments were seen as chaotic and inefficient.

While the term *absolutism* is embedded in the seventeenth and eighteenth centuries, the basic concept dates back almost to the beginning of civilization. Rulers had always been naturally inclined to claim as much authority as possible. Yet ancient and medieval rulers lacked the capacity for effective absolutism. A king like Charlemagne sought to order society, but other forces—the aristocracy, the weak economy, primitive transportation and communication, the low level of education, as well as foes he needed to slaughter—made society too resistant and slow to feel the power of government.

Early modern arguments for absolutism relied on two main justifications. The first one, popular from the late fifteenth to the early eighteenth centuries, was rule by **divine right**. This idea drew on ancient beliefs that kings had special connections to the supernatural. Even the early medieval Germanic kings like the Merovingians appealed to their divine blood to justify their dynasty. The Carolingians and other Christian dynasties afterward based their views on Old Testament kings like David and Solomon. It was a comforting thought that God had selected monarchs through royal bloodlines. Kings mirrored the God who

---

3. The famous phrase from Lord Acton, "Power tends to corrupt, and absolute power corrupts absolutely," leaps to mind. But he was writing decades later.

ruled the universe: as he reigned in heaven completely, so monarchs on earth had the right to unconditional domination. The pomp and God-given prestige of kings sometimes made the papacy and religion less important. This dynastic argument was so strong that even women were allowed to inherit the throne in many countries.

With the rising skepticism of the Enlightenment, the justification for absolutism eventually changed. Once deists doubted God's active intervention in our planetary affairs, justifying monarchy by divine selection lost its resonance. Therefore, the second argument sanctioning royal absolutism turned on rational utility. This *enlightened despotism* asserted that one person should rule because, logically, unity encouraged simplicity and efficiency. Moreover, this autocratic rule should benefit most of the subjects within the state, not merely enhance the monarch's own personal comfort or vanity.

Historians usually credit France with becoming the first modern European state because of its revival of royal absolutism. By ending the civil wars of the late sixteenth century, King Henry IV rode a tide of goodwill and a widespread desire for peace to become an absolute monarch. He revised the taxes, built public works, promoted businesses, balanced the budget, and encouraged culture. He allegedly originated the famous political promise that there would be a chicken in every pot (at least on Sunday). In an age when most peasants rarely ate meat, that was quite a goal. Living well in this world was becoming more important than living well for the next.

Henry's assassination by a mad monk in 1610 threatened France's stability once again. Henry left only a child, Louis XIII, on the throne. As illustrated before, a child ruler has often sparked civil wars as factions sought to replace or control the minor. This consequence highlighted a major flaw of monarchical regimes dependent upon one person: what if the king were incompetent or a child? The system could easily break down.

Appointing competent and empowered bureaucrats to rule in the king's name solved this weakness. Louis XIII gained such a significant and capable minister with **Cardinal Richelieu** (d. 1642).[4] Instead of serving the papacy, as his title would suggest, Richelieu became the first minister to his king. As such, he worked tirelessly to strengthen absolute government in France. As a royal servant, the cardinal ruled in the king's name. Also, because as a cleric he was required to live in celibacy, there was no danger he would create his own rival dynasty, as the Carolingian mayors of the palace had done under the Merovingians. When Louis XIII came of age, he continued to relish all the privileges of being a king while Richelieu did all the hard work.

Therefore, the king's minister continued to deepen the roots of monarchical authority. Richelieu strengthened the government with more laws, more taxes, a better army, and a streamlined administration. By executing select nobles for

---

4. Cinematic versions of Alexandre Dumas's *The Three Musketeers* often portray Richelieu as a villain who seeks the throne for himself. Realistically, it would have been impossible for him to become king. Historical evidence, and the novel, shows him to be a Machiavellian manipulator, but for the benefit of the French crown.

treason, he intimidated all of the nobility. Although he was a Roman Catholic cardinal, Richelieu made decisions for reasons of state, not faith. He helped the German Protestants during the Thirty Years' War because weakening the Habsburg emperors benefited France. While he withdrew some of the privileges granted to French Huguenot Protestants by the Edict of Nantes, his motivation was political. He interpreted the rights of Protestants to self-defense and fortified cities as impinging on the king's claim to a monopoly on force—only agents of the king could kill. In a notorious example of manipulation, the cardinal deliberately manipulated a panic about demon-possessed nuns in order to interfere in the Huguenot town of Loudun.

Both Richelieu and his king died within a year of each other, again leaving a child as heir, **Louis XIV** (r. 1643–1715). Once more, the crown almost plunged into a crisis over an underage king. Nevertheless, Louis XIV managed to hold on to the throne under the protection of another clerical minister, Cardinal Mazarin. Once he reached maturity, Louis XIV became the most powerful king France had ever known. Louis XIV differed from Louis XIII in that he himself actually wanted to rule. He took charge, depicting himself as shining over France as the "Sun King." According to Louis's vision, if the land did not have the sunlight of his royal person, it would die in darkness. He allegedly claimed, "L'État, c'est moi" (I am the state).

Louis XIV's modernizations were numerous. He met with his chief ministers in a small chamber called a **cabinet**, thus coining a name for executive meetings. These cabinet ministers then carried out the royal will through the bureaucracy. Instead of relying on mercenaries, France raised one of the first modern professional armies, which meant that paid soldiers were uniformed and permanently housed in barracks. Since so many troops were recruited from the common classes, this army continued the decline of the traditional responsibilities of medieval knights for warfare. Being a noble no longer meant military service. To pay for these royal troops, Louis intervened in the economy with the intention of helping it grow. His ministers adopted a version of the economic theory of mercantilism, whose advocacy of government intervention naturally pleased the absolute monarch. The government targeted industries for aid and both licensed and financed the founding of colonies.

Louis XIV's most noticeable legacy (especially for the modern tourist) was his construction of the palace of **Versailles**, which became a whole new capital located a few miles from crowded, dirty Paris. There he collected his bureaucracy and government and projected a grand image of himself. Actually, the palace was rather uncomfortable to live in. The chimneys were too short to draw smoke properly, so rooms were smoky and drafty. The kitchens were a great distance from the dining room, so the various courses, soup, fish, poultry, and so on, got cold before they could be eaten. Yet Louis nourished a palace culture, with himself as the royal center of attention. Aristocrats and nobles clamored to reside in his palace, maneuvering to attend to both the intimate and public needs of the most important person in the country. They dressed him, emptied his chamber pots, danced at his balls, bowed down at his entrances, and gossiped behind his back.

Naturally, this luxurious living required huge amounts of money from the nobles and the taxpayers. Likewise, the brilliance of the court did not entirely blind the members of the aristocracy to their long-standing prerogatives; but for a moment, absolutely, Louis was king.

Historians usually qualify Louis's greatness because of two ambivalent decisions. For one, Louis XIV revoked the Edict of Nantes. He did not comprehend the advantage of tolerating religious diversity in his realm. His view was *un roi, une loi, une foi* (one king, one law, one faith). This action raised fewer outcries than it might have decades earlier; many people had transferred their desire for religion into loyalty to the state. Still, outlawing Protestantism in France hurt the economy, since many productive Huguenots left for more tolerant countries, especially the Netherlands and Brandenburg-Prussia. For his own purposes, though, Louis XIV achieved more religious uniformity for Roman Catholicism.

The second troublesome choice of Louis's reign was his desire for military glory, *la gloire*. He thought he should wage war to make his country, and consequently himself, bigger and stronger. He aimed to expand France's borders to the Rhine River. Such a move would have taken territories away from the Holy Roman Empire. Other tempting targets were the rich Lowlands, both the Spanish Netherlands held by the Habsburgs and the free Dutch Netherlands. Yet Louis was no great general himself; he entrusted that role to others. He himself stayed far away from the battlefront even while he committed France to a series of risky wars. Unfortunately for his grand plans, other European powers, particularly Britain and Habsburg Austria, resolutely opposed France, fearing a threat to the balance of power.

By the time Louis XIV died in 1715, France had sunk deeply into debt and lay exhausted. This situation reveals another flaw of absolutism: if anyone disagreed with government policies, little could be done to change the monarch's mind. In France, the Estates-General, the representative parliamentarian body created in the fourteenth century, had not met in more than a century. At most, people could request change by presenting a petition to the monarch. Furthermore, Louis and other absolute monarchs easily tired of criticism. They tended to insulate themselves and heard advice only from handpicked, obsequious bureaucrats and self-seeking sycophantic courtiers. Despite this limitation, Louis set the tone for other princes, kings, and emperors. Any prince who wanted respect needed new palaces, parties at court, and military victories. Princes all across Europe imitated the Sun King.

One of the Sun King's most interesting imitators came from a place that seemed insignificant at the beginning of Louis's reign. Far off eastward, where Europe turns into Asia, a new power called **Russia** was rising. Western Europeans had not taken much note of Russia up to this point. A principality around Kyiv had flourished in the Middle Ages, but then the **Mongols** conquered it. During the 1400s, the dukes of Moscow managed to throw off the Mongol yoke and slowly freed neighboring people from Mongol domination, replacing it with their own.

By 1600, the Duchy of Moscow controlled various peoples to become the Russian Empire, ruled by the **tsars** (sometimes spelled *czar*, the Russian word for emperor, derived from *Caesar*). Russia was already a huge, if sparsely populated, territory by 1613 when the Romanov dynasty came to power. The Romanovs provided continuity and stability after a period of turmoil. Like other imperialist European powers, the Russians conquered peoples outside of Europe who were less technologically advanced. Unlike the other European powers, though, Russians did not need to cross oceans; they only had to traverse the Ural Mountains eastward into Asia. Thus began the notable reversal of a historical trend. Up until 1600, horse-riding archers from the vast steppes of Central Asia, whether Huns, Avars, Turks, or Mongols, had periodically invaded Europe. Now Europeans began to invade Asia. By 1648, Russians had already crossed Siberia to reach the Pacific Ocean. Then they pushed southward, taking over the Muslim Turkish peoples of Central Asia. Their empire transformed Russia into a great power, although western Europeans did not recognize it at first, since Russia was so far away.

The first ruler who made Europeans take notice was **Tsar Peter I "the Great"** (r. 1682–1725). Peter saw that Russia could become greater by inaugurating a policy of ***westernization*** (conforming local institutions and attitudes to those of western Europe). Thus, Russia became more and more part of Western civilization (see figure 10.2). Before Peter, the main cultural influences had come from Byzantium and Asia. Since the Byzantine Empire's collapse in 1453, Moscow's rulers had proclaimed themselves as the successors of Rome and Constantinople who would defend Eastern Orthodox Christianity. Protecting Orthodoxy looked to the past, while Peter's promoting the Enlightenment moved Russia into the future. Peter's tour of England, France, the Netherlands, and Germany in 1697 and 1698 taught him the power of the Commercial and Scientific Revolutions. He also admired the culture flaunted by Louis XIV. In pursuit of that last goal, he

Figure 10.2.   A modern statue honors Tsar Peter "the Great" of Russia (and his wild-eyed horse) in the city he founded, St. Petersburg.

legislated that Russian nobles speak French, shave off their bushy beards, wear powdered wigs, and dress in silk knee pants like the courtiers of Versailles. Such fashions were impractical in a cold Russian winter, but if the tsar commanded, no one said *"Non,"* much less *"Nyet."*

Tsar Peter's new capital of **St. Petersburg** surpassed even Louis XIV's Versailles. Peter built not only a palace but a whole city (naming it after the saint with whom the tsar shared a name was no coincidence). First, he had needed to conquer the land, defeating Sweden in the crucial Great Northern War (1700–1721). Before the war, Sweden had claimed great power status based on its key role in the Thirty Years' War. Afterward, Sweden was no more than a minor power, while Russia rivaled other great powers. Then at enormous expense, forty thousand workers struggled for fourteen years to build a city on what had once been swampland. Thousands paid the price of their lives. Located on an arm of the Baltic Sea, the new Russian capital was connected by sea routes to the world. St. Petersburg perfectly symbolized the Enlightenment's confidence that the natural wilderness could be tamed into order. Peter also considered St. Petersburg his "window on the West," his connection to the rest of Europe. As much as they might wish, Europeans could never again ignore Russia after Peter; by force of imperial will, he had made his empire part of the Western balance of power.

Besides the rulers of France and Russia, many other monarchs aspired to greatness through absolutism. One of the most interesting appeared in the empire of Austria, whose rulers of the Habsburg dynasty were also consistently elected Holy Roman emperors. The ethnically German Habsburgs had assembled a multiethnic empire of Germans, Czechs, Slovaks, Hungarians, Croatians, Italians, and many other smaller groups. The dynasty alone, not tradition or affection, held these diverse peoples together. In 1740, many feared a crisis when **Maria Theresa** (r. 1740–1780), an unprepared twenty-three-year-old princess who was pregnant with her fourth child, inherited the Austrian territories.

Although her imperial father had issued a law called the Pragmatic Sanction to recognize her right, as a mere woman, to inherit, he had never trained her for rulership. Instead, Maria Theresa's husband, Francis of Habsburg-Lorraine (who was also her cousin), was expected to take over Austria as archduke and become elected as emperor. Maria Theresa loved her husband (literally—she gave birth sixteen times), but Francis showed no talent for politics. Other European rulers also knew this. When Maria Theresa's father died in 1740, France, Prussia, and others attacked in the War of Austrian Succession (1740–1748). Her enemies seized several of the diverse Austrian territories and by 1742 crowned the Duke of Bavaria as Holy Roman emperor—the first prince other than a Habsburg to hold the title in three hundred years.

Surprisingly, Maria Theresa took charge of the situation, becoming one of the best rulers Austria has ever had. Showing courage and resolve, she appealed to honor, tradition, and chivalry, which convinced her subjects to obey and her armies to fight. To support her warriors properly, she initiated a modern military in Austria, with standardized supply and uniforms as well as officer training schools. She reformed the economy, collecting new revenues such as the income tax and introducing paper money. This last innovation showed a growing trust of government: otherwise, why would people accept money that for the first time in Western civilization was not made of precious metal? The move boosted the economy, since conveniently carried paper money made it easier to invest and to buy things. Maria Theresa's confident bureaucracy reorganized the administration of her widespread lands. She also devoted attention to social welfare, leading to her declaration that every child should have a basic education, including girls. Thus, schools were built and maintained at public expense. Her revised legal codes eliminated torture, stopped the witch hunts, and investigated crime through rational methods (see figure 10.3). Her imposition of uniformity and consistency promoted the best of modern government. Admittedly, Maria Theresa did build an imitation Versailles at Schönbrunn and did live the privileged life considered appropriate to an empress. Yet people were willing to support an enlightened monarchy that also did something for them. In the end, Maria Theresa's competent reign safeguarded Austria's great power status and its people's prosperity.

Maria Theresa's great rival was Prussia's King **Frederick II "the Great"** Hohenzollern (r. 1740–1786). Prussia had only become a significant power since the Reformation. At that time Prussia's rulers, the Teutonic Knights, converted to Lutheranism and established themselves as a secular dynasty to rule their principality. Their line did not last long, though, and Prussia passed to the Hohenzollern dynasty of the neighboring Electoral March of Brandenburg in 1618. The Hohenzollerns survived the Thirty Years' War and slowly built Brandenburg-Prussia up to a middle-ranked status, becoming "kings in Prussia" by 1715. Frederick II himself had some reluctance about assuming the throne, and as a young man he tried to flee his overbearing father. The king captured Prince Frederick, forced him to watch his best friend shot for treason, and threatened to do the same to Frederick. The young Frederick bowed to the will of his father and became much more serious about his future kingship.

Frederick's father died in 1740, in the same year as Maria Theresa's. In addition to the royal crown, he inherited from his father a well-drilled army and a well-supplied treasury. Frederick used them to grab the rich province of Silesia from Maria Theresa, thus starting the War of Austrian Succession. Frederick's greatest success was having Prussia survive both the War of Austrian Succession and the Seven Years' War that followed, with the prize of Silesia intact. As the actual general in command of his armies, much of the credit for this went to him personally. Aside from his conquests, King Frederick II also ruled in an enlightened manner, improving finances, justice, administration, and social welfare. Therefore, by the end of his reign, Prussia was a great power, competitive with England, France, Austria, and Russia.

Maria Theresa and Frederick found another enlightened despotic rival in their younger contemporary, **Tsar Catherine II "the Great"** (r. 1762–1796). She was actually a German princess, Sophie Friederike Auguste von Anhalt-Zerbst-Dornburg, brought to Russia to marry the heir to the imperial throne. Once her husband became tsar, Catherine gained her lover's help to remove and execute her husband; then she took over herself. Despite this ruthless start to her reign,

Figure 10.3. In the manner of the Enlightenment, reason applied even to torture. A legal handbook written for Maria Theresa shows the most efficient means of questioning someone, using a ladder for torture. She outlawed such methods soon after the handbook was published. (University of Pennsylvania)

Figure 10.4.   This satirical British cartoon mocks the various rulers of Europe, centering on a boxing match between King Frederick William II of Prussia and a bare-chested Tsar Catherine II of Russia. The other rulers excuse their lack of participation, while wishing for the worst for Catherine. On the left, Sultan Selim III and Emperor Leopold II chat about recent conflicts with Russia. The Dutch burgher and King George III stare. Underneath the Prussian king's legs, little Poland laments being partitioned. Behind Catherine is the British prime minister, who is sorry his country is involved. In the distance little Louis XVI of France and Charles IV of Spain complain that revolution has made then irrelevant. On the right, Christian VII of Denmark and Gustavus III of Sweden prepare for future conflicts. (NYPL Digital Collection)

Catherine largely ruled in the fashion of enlightened despotism, maintaining her personal absolute rule, despite taking a number of male lovers. Voltaire corresponded with and Diderot visited her. She promoted the arts, some schooling, orphanages, hospitals, and a method of inoculation to prevent epidemics. The tsarina's armies expanded Russia's southern border to the Black Sea, taking Crimea from the Ottoman Empire (see figure 10.4). Yet she allowed some toleration for the Islam of her new subjects.

Austrian, Prussian, and Russian despots sealed their enlightened cooperation with the notorious **Partitions of Poland** (1772–1795). In 1772, the Polish-Lithuanian Commonwealth was the second-largest European nation in square miles, next to Russia. Yet its elected kings had almost no power. The nobility claimed to run the country through their parliament, the Sejm. Nevertheless, their self-confidence had gone too far, since any one noble in the body could veto any attempt at legislation. Consequently, few laws or reforms passed, and Poland could not keep pace with the innovations of its enlightened neighbors. Considering this incompetence of the Polish government, the enlightened sovereigns argued that it would be better if Austrian, Prussian, or Russian monarchs ruled the Poles. Polish forces were unable to defend and resist the occupation of their country, which only proved the point of their government's ineffectiveness. In several stages, Austria, Prussia, and Russia carved up the country. By 1795, rationalizations by absolutists had wiped Poland and Lithuania from the map.

Review: *How did absolutism gain ascendancy in early modern Europe?*

Response:

(PROSPEROUS) PEOPLE POWER

Fundamentally, debates about political structures are about who should decide when and how governments can interfere in the affairs of their own people and of those of neighboring states. Governments decide important issues of law (about private property and taxes, private violence and public safety, personal versus public morality and religion) and war. With absolutism, the prince (or the reigning emperor, king, queen, archduchess, prince-bishop, duke, etc.) represented the entire state, while all people therein were subjects. Monarchs reigned above the law or were themselves, in essence, the law. Everything circled around the ruler.

While absolutism flourished, some began fighting for another view: that power should flow upward from the citizens, who needed to participate in decision making. In the Western heritage, the notion that the people should rule themselves goes back to the democracies of the ancient Greece *poleis* and the Roman Republic. Citizens had organized into factions that collectively argued about a variety of policies, leaning toward tradition or innovation regarding government intervention (greater or lesser) and participation by people (the rich or poor, the fewer or the many). Those systems had failed long ago, but they were not forgotten. Then, in the Middle Ages, elected governments in towns and cities or in communes reasserted democratic principles. Yet self-government had not actually expanded beyond the size of a local government.

The one exception was the **Swiss Confederation**. In the late thirteenth century, Swiss townspeople and peasants had the audacity to claim self-rule, without any aristocracy. The legends of Wilhelm Tell and his archery date to this period of liberation from the Habsburg dynasty. Contemporaries, however, saw the Swiss success as an unusual circumstance brought about by the Swiss pikemen's ability to defend Alpine passes. Few gave Switzerland much respect. After a brief attempt at becoming a dominant regional power, the confederation retreated into neutrality and nonintervention after defeat in a war over Italy in 1515. Even then, few understood how the Swiss state held together, divided by four languages

(German, French, Italian, and Rhaeto-Romansch) and several versions of Christianity (Roman Catholicism, Calvinism, Zwinglism, Waldensianism, etc.). For all other countries, monarchy based on a subservient aristocracy and nobility seemed the superior method of rule.

Around 1600, though, a few countries began to explore democracy as an alternative structure for political power. The two basic components of all modern democracies have been *republicanism* and *constitutionalism*. As in ancient Rome, republicanism was government by elected representatives, where office seekers competed for votes, served limited terms, and then were replaced, even by their political opponents. Constitutionalism meant that law limited a government's powers, whether formally written in an explicit document or merely collected as traditions and practices. Constitutional law prohibited government from violating certain specified rights of citizens. For such a democracy to function, therefore, broad obedience to standards of law and willingness to compromise with others of differing ideologies were required.

In 1581, the **United Provinces of the Netherlands** became the first modern country to give up on kings. As seen in the Reformation, the various provinces of the Calvinist Dutch Netherlands (of which the most famous was **Holland**) had declared their freedom from the Roman Catholic Habsburg king of Spain. Fighting for religious freedom for themselves, they also soon extended it to others. The majority of the Dutch were reformed Calvinists, but they also tolerated English Puritans (including the Pilgrims), Mennonites, Lutherans, and even Roman Catholics.

The industrious Dutch merchants behind the successful rebellion against the Spanish monarchy created a new form of national government. They did not simply replace one monarch with another (although the noble dynasty of Orange was interested). Instead, the great merchants, or Hooge Moogende (High Mightinesses), pooled their resources and ran the state. The new Dutch regime was an oligarchy or, perhaps, a *plutocracy*, with rule based on wealth. Only male members of the propertied classes held political offices, much like the oligarchic patricians in ancient Rome. Although the Dutch people sometimes turned to the aristocratic House of Orange for leadership, the elected representatives usually ran the country, making the key decisions in war and peace. They also spent money on artists such as Rembrandt, Hals, and Vermeer, creating a "golden age" of northern Baroque culture.

Under this democratic government, Holland became Europe's greatest economic power for several decades of the seventeenth century. Possessing few natural resources and only a tiny territory with no hope for expansion in Europe, the Dutch pursued economic power through trade. Dutch investors and politicians founded the Bank of Amsterdam in 1609 to provide capital. Cheap fly-boats hauled cargo at the best price and speed.

The Netherlands even became a world power, creating a colonial empire to rival those of the Spanish and Portuguese. The Dutch Empire stretched from the East Indies to South Africa, to the Caribbean, to the "New" Netherlands in North America along the Hudson River. A government-chartered monopoly for Asian trade, the United East India Company (using the initials VOC) paved the way for

Figure 10.5.   An early version of a corporate logo, the "VOC" of the
Dutch East India Company (Vereenigde Oost-Indische Compagnie) marks
a cannon, one of the artillery pieces with which the Netherlands took
over trade in the East Indies.

joint-stock corporations in 1602 (see figure 10.5). As colonial masters, the Dutch
were less harsh than others toward the natives. The Dutch even encouraged a
vibrant trading network within East Asia, unlike other Europeans whose trade
exploited the colonies solely for the mother country's benefit. Still, Dutch armed
merchants crushed any attempts by Asians that might threaten their monopoly on
nutmeg (and other spices). They committed arson, killed, or enslaved when they
thought necessary. Not for the first time, the benefits of democracy at home did
not extend to colonized native territories around the world.

Nevertheless, their economic advantage did not last long. Dutch economic
supremacy ended by 1700. The Dutch were too small in population, too vulnerable to French invasion, and too easily cut off from the Atlantic by the English, who
could close the Channel and patrol the North Sea. In several wars, the Dutch managed to defeat or hold off the English Royal Navy. But when a prince of Orange
and his spouse became King William III and Queen Mary of Great Britain in 1688,
their policies against France actually benefited the English more than the Dutch.

While the Netherlands lost supremacy of the seas, they maintained a vital role
in the international economy. A state did not have to be mighty to prosper. While

Holland was no longer a great power after 1700, the Dutch Republic nevertheless remained richer and freer than most countries of Europe.

By 1700 then, England had taken Holland's place as the major maritime power. The accession of the Stuart dynasty of Scotland to the throne of England (1603–1714) had helped England surpass Holland. When the Tudor dynasty ended with the death of the "Virgin Queen" Elizabeth, a quick decision by English leaders settled the crown peacefully on her cousin, King James VI of Scotland, who became King James I of England. These combined realms were officially renamed the **United Kingdom of Great Britain** a century later. The unification of these traditional enemies did not always go smoothly, especially because the English certainly dominated the arrangement. Yet the combined British energies (throwing in Wales and occupied Ireland) slowly advanced science, technology, exploration, and profit. Soon, the British controlled the largest empire in world history.

On the path to becoming a world empire, the English stumbled through the **English Revolution** (1642–1689), which democratized their politics. The revolution's roots went back to the Reformation and deep into the Middle Ages. The many medieval kings and princes had founded representative bodies of clergy, nobles, and townspeople to consult with them about taxes and laws. The English body, Parliament, was originally no stronger than any other medieval political body. The English Reformation then bestowed on Parliament decisive power as it made the laws that established the Church of England. Parliament also made decisions about the dynasty, endorsing different heirs as Henry VIII went through his wives and as his children were crowned and subsequently died. These historic decisions ensured that Parliament's elected representatives enjoyed a real partnership with the royal government.

The new Stuart dynasty at first lacked an appreciation for this development. That was odd, since the first Stuart monarch, James VI of Scotland, had minimal power in his own homeland, being hemmed in by rambunctious nobles who had thrown out his mother, Mary Stuart, Queen of Scots. Yet when James VI of Scotland became James I of England (r. 1603–1625) through an act of Parliament, he became infatuated with the divine-right theories of absolutism. He even tried to lecture the body that made him king about his God-granted prerogatives.

The delicate Anglican compromise that had created a national church unintentionally helped prevent absolutism in England. While the government required that everyone worship in the Church of England using *The Book of Common Prayer*, many believers disagreed about how that worship should be done. At one end of the spectrum, English Calvinists, called Puritans, wanted a more reformed church. At the other end, supporters of bishops wanted worship and belief similar to Roman Catholicism, although without the papacy.

Not even allowed into the debate were extreme Protestant sects and fervent Roman Catholics, whose beliefs remained illegal. Some Puritans felt so oppressed by being forced to worship in the Anglican style that they became **separatists**, rejecting not only the English faith but also England itself. One group settled briefly in the tolerant Netherlands before getting permission to settle in the New

World; they became the Pilgrims of Plymouth Colony, Massachusetts, in 1620 (the ones who originated the American holiday of Thanksgiving).

The first Stuart king, James I, usually supported the Anglican compromise, even though many Puritans suspected him of being too Roman Catholic. James I's commission of a translation of the Bible into English, the King James Bible, helped to overcome suspicions concerning his religious leanings (although his favor toward certain male courtiers continued to provoke gossip and anger about his sexual inclinations).

Suspicions about the religious convictions of the Stuarts increased under Charles I (r. 1625–1649), James I's son and successor. Charles relished autocracy even more than his father and tried to rule without Parliament for several years. His effort at divine right failed him, because of religion. On one hand he was too Catholic, unwisely provoking hostility by allowing his French queen to hold Roman Catholic masses in the royal palaces. On the other hand, he was too authoritarian as supreme governor of the Church of England. He insisted that all of his Protestant subjects worship the same way. In 1640, he tried to impose the Anglican *Book of Common Prayer* on the Scottish Calvinist Presbyterians. The Scots rebelled.

Charles did not have the funds to fight a civil war with his usual revenues, and tradition required Parliament to participate in raising taxes. Reluctantly, Charles held elections and called Parliament into session. The parliamentarians proceeded to insist on their prerogatives to share power with the king. Charles resisted. By 1642, the king (supported by many of the nobility, great landowners, and conservative and moderate Anglicans) was at war with many of the parliamentarians (supported by lesser gentry and yeomen, the merchant classes, the large cities, and the Puritans). The **English Civil War** (1642–1651) consequently broke out.

Unexpectedly, the country gentleman **Oliver Cromwell** (d. 1658) became the commander of the parliamentarians. Cromwell mastered recruiting, commanding, supplying, and inspiring armies to victory. His New Model Army—using the latest military technology of combining cavalry, pikes, and muskets—reinforced the increasing role of common people in the armed forces at the expense of the nobility. Just as in ancient Greece and Rome as well as in the Middle Ages, military change transformed politics. Parliament's armies defeated the royal forces and captured the king. Parliament convicted King Charles I of treason and had him beheaded on 30 January 1649 (see the Primary Source Project http://www .concisewesternciv.com/sources/psc10a.html).

The English parliamentarians decided to form a government without a monarch, namely a republic, or as they called it, the **Commonwealth**. Of course, democracy was difficult. Cromwell quickly became discouraged with all the infighting and quarreling among the country's leaders, so he took harsh action. He purged the government of those representatives he did not like and took over himself. Basing his authority on the command of the armed forces, he turned the Commonwealth into the first modern *dictatorship*, called the Protectorate. Modern dictators belong not to some noble or royal dynasty but rise from the people to autocracy, often because of military success, unique charisma, or political intrigue. Using absolutism, Cromwell suppressed Roman Catholics and rebellious sentiment in Ireland by conducting severe reprisals. He then encouraged the settlement of Protestants from Scotland and Wales into the northern counties of Ulster and also led a trade war against the Dutch. In spite of these harsh measures, many of the English saw Cromwell as a "benevolent" dictator.

Most modern dictatorships lack the traditional prestige conferred by royalty, so, like the ancient Greek tyrannies, they often do not last in the same family more than a generation or two. And like Augustus Caesar, Cromwell did not properly plan for a means of succession. After Cromwell died, the British had to decide how to secure stability and responsibility without the dictator's strong hand. Cromwell's son and heir lacked the ability of the father, and he willingly resigned. Unwilling to revive the short-lived republic, Parliament finally recalled the Stuart royal dynasty, asking for the **Restoration** of the monarchy. King Charles II (r. 1660–1685) eagerly accepted. While he had the same Roman Catholic and autocratic sympathies as his father, Charles II was at least clever enough not to let those views get in the way of being king. Instead of fighting political battles with Parliament over power, Charles II relished a sumptuous court life and many mistresses. Ironically, despite all his promiscuity, Charles II had no legitimate children. Parliament conceded that, according to dynastic habit, upon Charles's death the British throne would go to his brother James II (r. 1685–1688). The second James began acting like an absolute monarch. Even worse, he openly converted to Roman Catholicism and had his son and heir baptized in that faith. Unwilling to tolerate a Roman Catholic as king, many English had had enough.

In the **Glorious Revolution** of 1688, the English established their enduring democratic system. With little bloodshed, they forced James to flee to France. As noted above, Parliament then invited James's Protestant daughter Mary to be their queen, and as co-ruling king, her husband, Prince William of Orange from the Netherlands. Although James attempted to win back the throne with an invasion of Ireland, he lost at the Battle of the Boyne in July 1689.[5] Thereafter, the English substantially subdued Ireland, and Irish independence vanished for centuries.

Other Scots, meanwhile, especially those in the Highlands, disputed the claims of William and Mary and wanted their own Stuart dynasty back. Large parts of Scotland rebelled in 1715 and again in 1745 in the name of Stuart pretenders to the throne (including Bonnie Prince Charlie). Following the Battle of Culloden in 1746, the English crushed Scottish hopes for independence. Curiously, the English were so worried about Scottish resistance that they also banned the Scots from wearing tartan plaids or kilts for several decades. As a consolation prize, the victorious Parliament generously approved a small measure of toleration for religious dissenters, both Roman Catholics and Presbyterian Calvinists.

---

5. England was still under the Julian calendar when the battle was fought on what then was dated "Old Style" 1 July 1689. When England converted to the Gregorian "New Style" calendar, the date should have been recalculated as 11 July 1689. Irish Protestants in Northern Ireland, however, celebrate the Boyne annually on the "Twelfth" of July, partly because of another victory on that date over Irish Roman Catholics.

Most importantly, Parliament affirmed through the Glorious Revolution that it was in charge, not the monarch, although it took several more decades for Parliament to reach its full authority. The idea of *parliamentarianism* meant that an elected representative body ran the government. This system used a cabinet, where the important state officials met in a small conference room to make the important decisions. Under absolutism, these cabinet members were appointees of the king; under parliamentarianism, they were elected by voters. The member who got the most support in the Parliament and who led the cabinet became the **prime minister** (in some countries later called a chancellor). Prime ministers held on to power as long as they had a majority of votes, either in parliament or the next election. The prime minister increasingly took on actual leadership of the nation, as the cabinet met more and more often without the monarch. The prime minister's faction made policy and appointed the bureaucrats and civil servants. The British kings and queens faded into figureheads, representing that old ideal of parents of the country rather than actual war leaders and lawgivers. By keeping a royal dynasty and using it as a stabilizing force, Britain became the most important Western *constitutional monarchy*. Such a system uses both constitutionalism (even if there is no one single document, laws limit government authority) and republicanism (even if there is a hereditary crowned head, elected representatives wield the power).

It is surprising that having suffered so much for the sake of establishing democratic government at home, the British were unwilling to grant it to their fellow countrymen abroad. Once the British acquired an empire, they lost the perspective of the ruled and relished the supremacy of the ruler. By 1763, Britain had the most significant world empire of all the European nations. The first clash among these European empires was the **Seven Years' War** (1756–1763), which could be considered the first world war. Armed forces fought three simultaneous campaigns: in Europe (especially Maria Theresa of Austria versus Frederick II of Prussia), in India (where the British called it the Third Carnatic War), and in the Americas (where the American colonists called it the **French and Indian War**). In the last two theaters, the British victory was decisive. The British drove the French out of India, leaving the British as the only significant Western power there. In North America the British tried biological warfare against France's Native American allies, intentionally giving them blankets infected with smallpox. The French lost Quebec and only managed to hold on to a few islands in the Caribbean and French Guyana on the north coast of South America. For the next two centuries, the British Empire was the greatest empire of the world, surpassing all previous empires.

Nevertheless, wars and empires are expensive. Despite their victory, the British needed to figure out both how to pay for and how to defend their world empire. One obvious choice for revenue was the American colonists, who had gained security with the loss of the French threat to their north. The British wanted the Americans to contribute their fair share to the economic well-being of the mother country. Many Americans instead wanted to look after their own welfare, and they clearly did not want to pay any taxes. If they did, they at least wanted a voice in parliamentary decisions—thus a slogan of their rebellion became "No taxation without representation." The **American Revolution** (1775–1789) basically was fought about taxes: who pays, how much, and who decides? The English had no desire to give the American colonists any sort of representation, even though the Americans were just as sophisticated with their technology, politics, society, and even culture as the English themselves. The American lands were rich with potential, especially since the native "Indian" peoples were so easily and quickly being eliminated after losing their French allies as a result of the Seven Years' War.

Additional acts of Parliament affecting the Americans spurred them to create a national self-government. The Second Continental Congress brought together representatives from the thirteen colonies. More importantly, the colonists organized their own military forces. First, the American minutemen militias skirmished with British troops at Lexington and Concord in April 1775, sparking the **American War of Independence** (1775–1783), the military contest that ensured the success of the Revolution. With proper financing and with George Washington (d. 1799) in charge, the Americans soon had an army almost able to win European-style set-piece battles. On 2 July 1776, the Congress declared independence from Britain. Two days later, the adoption of a Declaration of Independence immortalized American independence. In that document, the **United States of America**, as the joined colonies called themselves, provided a clear justification for their actions: resistance to tyranny. Of course, the Americans knew that labeling the king a tyrant was mere propaganda. Ever since the English Revolution, Parliament was actually responsible for the governance of the British Empire. Whatever the king's role, the Americans argued that governments were responsible to the governed and that people had a right to change their government, even by force, when it became tyranny.

Ultimately, force decided the destiny of the United States. Facing the strongest empire in world history, the American revolt seemed doomed to fail. Americans were divided against themselves, with many loyalists refusing to become patriots. The British were able to attract many enslaved Blacks to their side by promising freedom. They offered material support to Native Americans as well. To break the Indians' power, Americans launched brutal campaigns, such as Sullivan's March, which destroyed every native village they found in New York and Pennsylvania. It worked. Canadians, however, refused to join the USA. In reaction, the United States tried to invade and conquer British provinces there. That failed. And the idea that backwoods American sharpshooters with their Kentucky long rifles regularly picked off the British redcoats is a myth.

What ultimately won the War of Independence was help from diverse foreigners. Some volunteers, like Thaddeus Kosciuszko and Casimir Pulaski from partitioned Poland, or Baron von Steuben from Prussia and the Marquis de Lafayette from France, fought alongside the Americans because they were inspired by the United States' claims to liberty. Most important, countries whose worldwide empires had suffered from British attacks and competition allied with the Americans: the Dutch, the Spanish, and, most importantly, the French. These powers harassed the British at sea and sent supplies and money. Without the decisive help of these foreign states, Americans would probably have lost the war for independence and would still be drinking tea and eating crumpets. Instead, after signing the Treaty of Paris in 1783, the Americans found themselves free and independent.

The difficulty of defeating the British then gave way to the challenge of creating permanent institutions of government. Fearing the "rabble," elites of wealth and property remained in charge in America—there was no argument about that. Nevertheless, they decided against an American monarchy (Washington's lack of legitimate children certainly discouraged dynastic thoughts). Americans needed to construct a political system that recognized the diverse needs of so many different colonies and colonialists. At first, the Americans created a weak central government. This attempt, the Articles of Confederation, lasted only a few years before the solution proved unworkable.

So, in a rather radical step, the politicians decided to start over and inaugurated a strong central government. The leaders of the revolution, especially Washington, Benjamin Franklin, Alexander Hamilton, and James Madison, decided on the principle of *federalism* and the office of the **presidency**, which were embodied in the US Constitution taking effect in 1789. Federalism meant that the dominant national government shared authority with the powerful state governments, while reserving many freedoms to individual citizens themselves. In other words, the stronger federal regime interacted with strong state administrations while a Bill of Rights sheltered the people.

The federal government itself separated its powers into legislative, executive, and judicial branches. The legislature, called Congress, enacted the laws, decided on taxes, declared war, made peace, and consented to (or blocked) important bureaucratic and judicial appointments. The president commanded the armed forces and enforced the laws as head of the executive branch and independent of the legislature. This authority differed from the parliamentarianism of other modern democracies, where the prime minister or chancellor served as both leader of the legislature and chief executive official. The third branch, the judiciary, resolved civil legal disputes, convicted criminals, and, through judicial review, came to interpret the laws.

The big problem of US history and politics ever since has been about the competing interests of what the federal government can impose on states or the people, what state governments can ignore from the national government and can themselves enforce on their own state residents, and what the people (citizens, immigrants, natives, others, individually and collectively) can assent to or resist from either federal or state governments. Nearly every serious issue since the foundation of the American republic has revolved around this tough juggling of competing powers and freedoms.

Historians have argued about whether the American Revolution was really revolutionary. American society before independence hardly differed from that afterward. The prosperous people with property still dominated economic, political, and social affairs, although Americans got rid of inherited titles of nobility. Still, the wealthy Americans who had been in charge before the revolution remained largely in charge after it—only the overstated threat of tyranny from across the

Atlantic had been eliminated. Perhaps the new system that enabled reform of the original founding model was the most revolutionary accomplishment. Certainly, the political system slowly welcomed more people into the process. White males without property attained suffrage by the early nineteenth century, decades before their British counterparts. Other inhabitants remained excluded far longer. Women did not gain the right to vote until 1920, Native Americans until 1924, and most African Americans until 1965.

Geography helped the United States become powerful. First, America's location in the Western Hemisphere protected the country from the warfare waged by European states against one another. Yet at the same time, advanced sailing ships eased cultural exchange, so science, trade, and ideas flowed easily back and forth across the Atlantic. The United States of America remained firmly connected to Western traditions. Second, America's vast unconquered wilderness offered ample opportunities for expansion and occupation, unlike in Europe, where most agricultural land had been divided up and claimed for centuries.

The available land in America, of course, had been and would be stolen from the native "Indians." In grabbing this land, "immigrant" Americans imitated other colonizing Europeans, both absolutist and democratic. Without any sense of irony or embarrassment, the Netherlands, Great Britain, and the United States fought for the right of their own citizens to participate in government while not hesitating to wield violence to seize rulership over non-Europeans in Asia and the Americas.

Review: *How did democratic forms of government spread in the early modern West?*

Response:

THE DECLARATION OF LIBERTY, EQUALITY, AND FRATERNITY

The clash of republican and absolutist politics peaked in the **French Revolution** (1789–1815). British and American ideals of liberty inspired the French *philosophes* to criticize their own absolutist government, called the ***ancien régime*** by historians. If the Americans could overthrow royal "tyranny," then why couldn't the French? The American War of Independence provided an immediate example. France had helped America partly through a desire to hurt Great Britain. In doing so, France paid enormous sums for military endeavors while acquiring almost nothing in return from the Treaty of Paris in 1783. France won no territories, in contrast to the vast continental possessions allotted to the United States. The huge French war debts helped to drive the French government toward a crisis of bankruptcy. Because of the worsening economic situation, all social classes became dissatisfied with the government. Poor harvests in 1787 and 1788 yielded peasant anger against Versailles. The middle classes also resented their heavy tax burden and limited social mobility. The nobility and clergy objected to how the absolute monarchy had usurped many of their once-numerous privileges.

The growing grumbling targeted the monarch personally. Despite France's role in the Enlightenment, the Bourbon dynasty had never produced an enlightened despot to reform its regime. **King Louis XVI** (r. 1774–1792) was a nice man, but he showed no particular talent for governing. He was actually more interested in being a locksmith than a king. This would not have been a problem if some able bureaucrat had ruled for him, as Richelieu had for Louis XIII. Sadly, Louis XVI was neither able to find competent ministers nor able to support them for long against palace intrigues.

Remarkably faithful in his marriage vows (for a Bourbon), Louis likewise lacked an able woman to rule from behind the scenes, as Louis XV's mistress Madame Pompadour had done. Louis XVI's spouse, the notorious **Queen Marie Antoinette**, contributed to the growing contempt for the monarchy. Although Marie Antoinette was the daughter of Maria Theresa Habsburg, she inherited none of her mother's talents for governance. She instead preferred parties, balls, masquerades, and the life of luxury that absolute monarchs enjoyed. There is no evidence, however, that she said something so callous as, "Let them eat cake [*brioche*]," when she heard that peasants were begging for bread; the quote actually came from a fictional character in a novel by Rousseau. Yet people readily believed that Marie Antoinette could have said it. Her actions and reputation hurt her royal husband's position. Louis XVI's reign again exposed both the enduring strength and the fatal flaw of absolutism: everything depended on one person.

As Louis confronted his shortage of funds, he naturally thought of the basic ways governments raised money: conquest, loans, and taxes. The first choice of war was risky, and it required money up front to equip the troops. Besides, he had no readily available excuse to attack anyone. As for the second alternative, the French banks were tapped out, while foreign banks did not want to take on the risk of French credit. That left only raising taxes. When Louis tried to raise taxes, however, the nobles who ran the courts, the *parlements*, judged that he could not do so. The nobles hoped to use this financial crisis for their own gain, restoring some of their long-lost influence. They insisted that the king would have to call the Estates-General, as Philip IV had done four and a half centuries earlier. Certainly, as an absolute monarch, Louis could have just raised taxes. Instead of acting firmly and risking some civil disturbance, the king gave in.

Since no living person remembered the Estates-General (which had last met in 1614), public officials quickly cobbled together a process from dusty legal tomes. About nine hundred representatives would be elected, three hundred from each of the three estates: first, the clergy; second, the nobility; and third, the common people (although only the top 20 percent of the bourgeoisie, such as doctors and lawyers, were actually eligible to run for election). Some members of the Third Estate complained that their vastly greater numbers compared to the size of the other two estates deserved more representation. The king gave in, again, and conceded that they were allowed to have about six hundred representatives (see diagram 10.2). While this concession might seem more equitable, it preserved the predominance of the first two estates. For one, the members of the upper two estates were often related to and connected to each other, so they shared the same views. For another, each estate voted in a bloc—thus the three hundred clergy had one vote, the three hundred nobles had one vote, and the six hundred commoners had one vote. Therefore, the Third Estate would probably always be outvoted two to one.

Shortly after the representatives to the Estates-General arrived at Versailles for the opening ceremonies on 5 May 1789, the Third Estate began to agitate for voting by individual representatives rather than by bloc, aiming to at least even

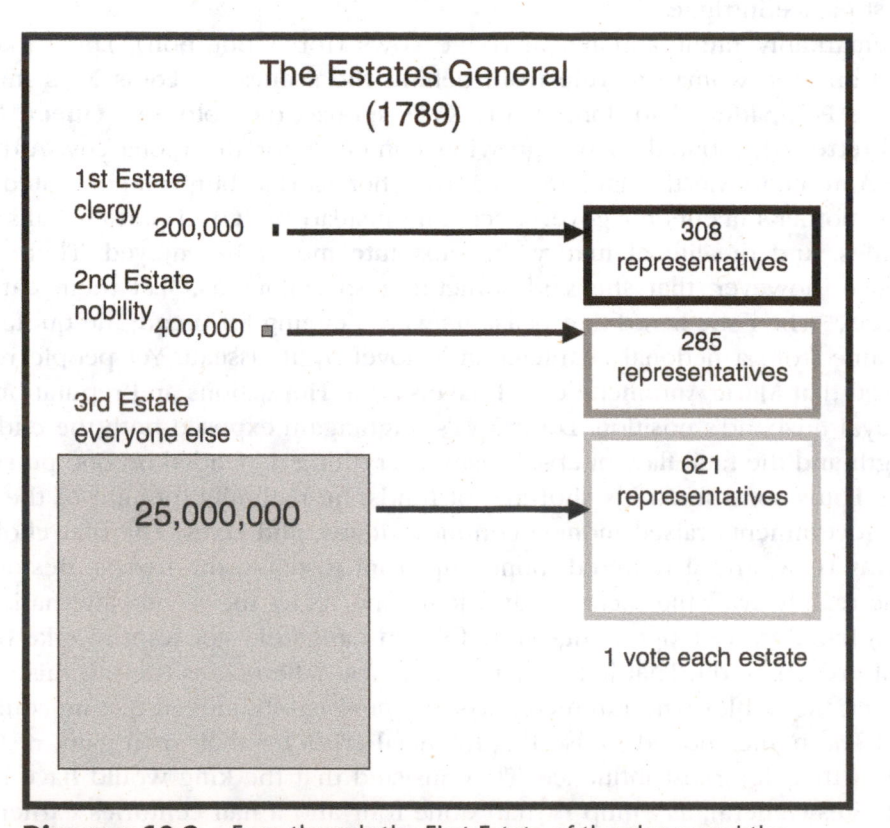

Diagram 10.2. Even though the First Estate of the clergy and the Second Estate of the nobility comprised only a tiny proportion of the population (the small boxes as compared to the huge box of the Third Estate), each estate elected about an equal number of representatives. Since each estate voted as a bloc, the first two could always easily outvote the third. The quarrel over voting by estate versus by representative paralyzed the Estates-General.

out the votes to 600–600. They also tried to declare themselves as a new legislature, the National Assembly. The king was upset by this wrangling and tried to discourage any more meetings by locking up the meeting hall on the morning of 20 June. Many representatives, mostly those from the Third Estate along with a few sympathizers from the other two, proceeded to a nearby indoor tennis court. There they swore the **Tennis Court Oath**, pledging not to go home until they had written a constitution. In fact and in law, a constitution meant the end of an absolute monarchy. Instead of sending in the troops and disbanding this illegal assembly, Louis once more gave in. Thus the bourgeoisie seized control and began a true revolution.

Things soon got out of control, as so often happens in political revolutions. While the politicians in Versailles quibbled about the wording of constitutional clauses, the populace of Paris recognized that change was at hand. They naturally feared its destructive potential. To protect themselves and their property, some Parisians began to organize militias, or bands of citizen-soldiers like the minutemen of America. Yet the Parisians lacked weapons. On 14 July 1789, a semiorganized mob approached the Bastille, a massive royal fortress and prison in the heart of the city. The crowd demanded that the Bastille release its prisoners (whom they believed were unjustly held for political reasons) and hand over its weapons to the Parisian militias.

The fortress was completely secure from the militia and accompanying rabble, so the name given to this event, the **storming of the Bastille**, is quite exaggerated. In the hope of calming the situation and avoiding too much bloodshed from violence in the neighborhood, the fortress commander opened the gates. The mob rewarded him by beating him to death and parading his head on a pike. While the liberators gained some weapons, they found inside only a few petty criminal prisoners. Nevertheless, the attack symbolized the power of the people over the monarch. The people had openly and clearly defied royal authority and used violence on their own initiative for their own interests. The citizens of Paris tore down the fortress, stone by stone, actually selling the rubble as souvenirs. A more forceful and ruthless monarch would have mobilized his troops, declared martial law, and snuffed out this insurrection with notable bloodshed. What did Louis do? He gave in again.

Events were soon beyond any possible royal intervention. As the peasants in the countryside heard about the storming of the Bastille, they also decided to rebel. The "Great Fear" spread as peasants attacked their landlords. The peasants killed seigneurs and burned the records that documented their social and economic bondage. The National Assembly panicked, since its members owned much of the land that the peasants were appropriating. They acted to calm things down on 4 August 1789, abolishing the *ancien régime* with its absolute monarchy and feudal privileges. A few weeks later, the National Assembly issued a **Declaration of the Rights of Man and of the Citizen** (see Primary Source Project 10). Similar to the American Bill of Rights, this document declared "liberty, property, security and resistance to oppression" for all Frenchmen. It guaranteed liberties to citizens and restrained government. This document worked as planned: it calmed passions and allowed the forces of order to restore moderation. It also originated the phrase "Liberty, Equality, Fraternity," which became the motto of the revolution.

Much more would need to be done for these goals to be realized, but the revolution had issued a clarion call for justice. Sadly, these gains did not apply to women, as is illustrated by the masculine term *fraternité* (fraternity/brotherhood). Revolutionary men in France (just as they had in England and America) excluded females from the benefits of Enlightenment ideals. In response, Olympe de Gouges proposed a **Declaration of the Rights of Woman and of the Female Citizen**, in which she rewrote the original as a manifesto supportive of women (see Primary Source Project 10). For this and other writings questioning the republic, the government soon sliced her head off. A woman might be a "citizen," but the male citizens enjoyed the real protections and liberties of the law.

The royal family likewise lost their liberty and independence. In October, women who became angry at the bread shortage marched from the city of Paris out to Versailles. Thousands of marchers killed a few guards, ransacked the palace, and escorted the royal family back to Paris, to the palace of the Tuileries (near the Louvre). The people made Paris once more the capital. This action shattered any remaining royal authority. On the first anniversary of the storming of the Bastille the following summer, the king gave in and swore loyalty to the new constitution.

Two days before that oath, the National Assembly had secularized the Roman Catholic Church in France in the spirit of the Enlightenment. The government also needed cash. In autumn 1789, the regime had already nationalized and begun confiscating church property, especially that of monastic orders not involved in education or hospitals. On 12 July 1790, the Civil Constitution of the Clergy restructured all the dioceses and parishes and turned the remaining clergy into civil servants. Bishops, priests, and the last few monks and nuns would henceforth be paid by the state and required to take an oath to France. Many did not, preserving their loyalty to papal authority and thus becoming liable to arrest and prison as enemies of the revolution. Two groups benefited from these restrictions on the Roman Catholic Church in France. Protestants gained freedom of worship with the Declaration of Rights, while Jews became equal citizens by 1791.

Louis never reconciled himself to limited authority and the church's humiliation. A year after his constitutional oath, on the night of 20–21 June 1791, he finally stopped giving in and took decisive action. He and his family fled from their palatial house arrest. Unfortunately for him, a combination of bad luck, incompetence, and the king's own hesitant nature allowed revolutionary forces to catch the royals at Varennes. With the humiliated royal family imprisoned and back in Paris, itself disturbed by anti-royal mob violence, many elected representatives eventually decided they needed a monarch no longer. The National Convention unanimously proclaimed the republic on 21 September 1792. The legislature then convicted King Louis XVI of treason (by 361 to 360 votes) and had him beheaded on 21 January 1793. He met his death on the new, lethally efficient killing machine, the guillotine, which became symbolic of the revolution. In October, Marie Antoinette followed her husband to beheading on the scaffold. While their daughter survived into old age, their son the dauphin, or Louis XVII, disappeared and was presumed dead. Other members of the royal family fled the country. The French Bourbon dynasty seemed to have ended in humiliation.

The elected bourgeois politicians now running the French Republic faced other grave problems not easily solved by chopping off heads. The first challenge was how to make political decisions. In a fashion appropriate to democracy, they accidentally established a model of political debate and diversity. When the representatives gathered in the new republic's National Convention, their seating arrangement gave us the terminology of modern political discourse. Those to the **right** of the speaker or president of the body opposed change. Those to the **left** of the speaker embraced change. Those in the middle were the **moderates**, who needed convincing to go one way or the other. Extremists on the right were **reactionaries**, and extremists on the left were **radicals** (which today is more used for any extremist of any political leaning). This vocabulary of *left* and *right* suggests that all political disagreements are about promoting or resisting change. These labels may have simplified issues, but they enabled politicians to start organizing groups around ideologies and specific policy proposals.

Review: *How did the revolutionaries in France execute political changes?*

Response:

PRIMARY SOURCE PROJECT 10: DECLARATION OF THE RIGHTS OF MAN VERSUS DECLARATION OF THE RIGHTS OF WOMAN ABOUT HUMAN RIGHTS

Historians usually see the Declaration of the Rights of Man as a foundational document for human rights. Issued by the French revolutionary government to calm civil disturbances, its basic principles embody many of the ideals of the Enlightenment. The manifesto by Olympe de Gouges points out how the rights of "Man" presumes male dominance while ignoring women's views. In 1748, Olympe de Gouges had been born Marie Gouze, in a bourgeois family, yet became a writer and antislavery activist in Paris. The radical Jacobins arrested and then guillotined her as a counterrevolutionary on 3 November 1793.

Source 1: Declaration of the Rights of Man and the Citizen by the National Convention (26 August 1789)

The representatives of the French people, organized as a National Assembly, believing that the ignorance, neglect, or contempt of the rights of man are the sole cause of public calamities and of the corruption of governments, have determined to set forth in a solemn declaration the natural, unalienable, and sacred rights of man. Therefore the National Assembly recognizes and proclaims, in the presence and under the auspices of the Supreme Being, the following rights of man and of the citizen:

Article I. Men are born and remain free and equal in rights. Social distinctions may be founded only upon the general good. . . .

IV. Liberty consists of the freedom to do everything which injures no one else; hence the exercise of the natural rights of each man has no limits except those which assure to the other members of the society the enjoyment of the same rights. These limits can only be determined by law. . . .

VI. Law is the expression of the general will. Every citizen has a right to participate personally, or through his representative, in its foundation. It must be the same for all, whether it protects or punishes. All citizens, being equal in the eyes of the law, are equally eligible to all dignities and to all public positions and occupations, according to their abilities, and without distinction except that of their virtues and talents. . . .

X. No one shall be disquieted on account of his opinions, including his religious views, provided their manifestation does not disturb the public order established by law.

XI. The free communication of ideas and opinions is one of the most precious of the rights of man. Every citizen may, accordingly, speak, write, and print with freedom. . . .

XIV. All the citizens have a right to decide, either personally or by their representatives, as to the necessity of the public contribution; to grant this freely; to know to what uses it is put; and to fix the proportion, the mode of assessment and of collection and the duration of the taxes. . . .

Source 2: *Declaration of the Rights of Woman and the Female Citizen* by Olympe de Gouges (1791)

Mothers, daughters, sisters, female representatives of the nation, organized as a National Assembly, believing that the ignorance, neglect, or contempt of the rights of woman are the sole cause of public calamities and of the corruption of governments, have determined to set forth in a solemn declaration the natural, unalienable, and sacred rights of woman. Therefore the sex that is superior in both beauty and courage during the sufferings of maternity recognizes and proclaims, in the presence and under the auspices of the Supreme Being, the following rights of woman and of the female citizen:

Article I. Woman is born free and remains equal in rights to man. . . .

IV. Liberty and justice consists of the freedom to do everything which injures no one else; hence the exercise of the natural rights of woman has no limits except those which the perpetual tyranny of man opposes to them. . . .

VI. Law is the expression of the general will. Every female and male citizen has a right to participate personally, or through their representative, in its foundation. It must be the same for all, whether it protects or punishes. All female and male citizens, being equal in the eyes of the law, are equally eligible to all dignities. . . .

X. No one shall be disquieted on account of his fundamental opinions; woman has the right to mount the scaffold, she should have the same right equally to mount the tribune. . . .

XI. The free communication of ideas and opinions is one of the most precious of the rights of woman, especially since this liberty assures that fathers acknowledge the legitimacy of children. Every female citizen may, accordingly, speak with freedom, "I am the mother of a child who belongs to you," without being forced by a barbaric prejudice to conceal the truth. . . .

XIV. The female and male citizens have a right to decide, either personally or by their representatives, as to the necessity of the public contribution; to grant this freely; the female citizens can accept this only when an equal division is admitted, not only in wealth, but also in the public administration. . . .

Questions:

- *About which rights are the two sources essentially in agreement?*
- *Which rights does de Gouge critique most strongly?*
- *How do both of these documents challenge the established order?*

Responses:

For more on these sources, go to http://www.concisewesternciv.com/sources /psc10.html.

BLOOD AND EMPIRES

War was the second problem facing the French elected representatives. After the French arrested their king, Louis's royal relatives and aristocrats called for an invasion to restore their fellow absolutist to power. The French government, however, declared war first. In reaction, an alliance of small and great powers formed against the French. A series of conflicts, called the **Wars of the Coalitions** (1792–1815), burdened Europe for the next generation. Ironically, considering its own democratic revolutions and empire building, Great Britain became the head of the coalition and the French Republic's most determined opponent. England feared the growth of French power more than it approved France's democratic and republican trappings. Great Britain sought to maintain the traditional balance of power among the states of Europe against a hegemonic France.

The revolution enabled France to create a new kind of war. During the *ancien régime*, many of the French officers in the royal army had been "blue bloods," aristocrats and nobles so named because one saw the veins through their fair, pale skin. But many nobles had fled the country once revolution began. France's aristocratic enemies then expected that without God-given elite leadership, the rabble republican army would readily collapse. On the contrary, the French were inspired to shed their red blood in defense of their nation more fervently and ferociously than ever before, since it was *theirs* now, not the monarch's. They managed to turn back the first invading forces in a skirmish at Valmy on 19 August 1792. As the war ground on, talented officers rose through the ranks based on their ability, not blue-blooded favoritism.

The new regime called all the people to war, whatever their status. As ordered by the government, young men fought, married men supported the troops with supplies, young and old women sewed tents and uniforms or nursed the sick, children turned rags into lint for making bandages, and old men cheered on everyone else. Modern "total war" began. The huge new armies of inspired countrymen provided the key to victory. The problem of feeding such large numbers of soldiers led to the invention of ways to preserve food. Scientists discovered that food boiled and then sealed in bottles and tin cans would not spoil. This invention for wartime would later help feed many civilians in peacetime.

Under pressure of war and revolutionary fervor, the government became more radical and took extreme steps in changing society. This phase of the French Revolution has earned the name the **Reign of Terror** (June 1793–July 1794), or simply the Terror, an extremist period that lasted only thirteen months. The radical Jacobins (named after a club where they met) and their leader, Maximilien Robespierre, decided that they needed to purge the republic of its internal enemies. They formed the infamous **Committee of Public Safety**, which held tribunals to arrest, try, and condemn French reactionaries, even though that violated previously guaranteed civil liberties. As often happens during perceived national emergencies, the government excused itself for its drastic measures. Actually, the death toll of the Terror was comparatively small (at least compared with the subsequent war casualties). In Paris, fewer than 1,300 people were guillotined. In the countryside, however, death tolls piled higher, with perhaps as many as 25,000 executed in the troublesome province of the Vendée, mostly through mass drownings.

During the Terror, radicals implemented Enlightenment ideals with a vengeance. The radicals' new Republic of Virtue threw out everything that the *philosophes* considered backward, especially if it was based on Christianity. They replaced the Gregorian calendar: the new year I dated from the declaration of the republic; weeks were lengthened to ten days; and the names of the months were changed to reflect their character, like "Windy" (*Ventôse*) or "Snowy" (*Nivôse*). Some radicals tried to abolish Christianity, turning churches into "temples of reason." Palaces, such as the Louvre, were remodeled into museums. Education was provided for all children at taxpayer expense. Slavery was abolished. Perhaps most radical of all, the government required the metric system of measurements. Tradition and custom were supplanted by the ideas of *philosophes*.

In the end, the Terror gained a bad reputation because its leaders became too extreme. They even began to arrest and execute one another, accusing their former compatriots of less-than-sufficient revolutionary passion. Moderates naturally feared that they would be next. So in the month "Hot" (*Thermidor*) in the republican year II (or on the night of 27–28 July 1794), moderates carried out a coup d'état (an illegal seizure of power that kills few) called the Thermidor Reaction. The moderates arrested the radical Jacobin leaders and sent them quickly to the guillotine. The politicians set up a new, more bourgeois government, restricting voting and power to those of wealth. The new regime, called the Directorate, was a reasonably competent oligarchy, but uninspired and uninspiring.

Meanwhile, military decisions forced change. The republican French armies repeatedly gained victory in battle due to competent commanders, vast numbers, and inspired morale. Therefore, instead of relying on loans or taxes, the Directorate used conquest to help pay the bills in 1796–1797. In a series of campaigns invading parts of Italy and the Rhineland, one general in particular gained the greatest fame: **Napoleon Bonaparte** (b. 1769–d. 1821). The dashing General Bonaparte soon surpassed the bland politicians in popularity, proving again that people are easily seduced by military successes. While most contemporary monarchs found it safer to stay away from the battle lines, Napoleon's generalship provided inspirational passion for the French.

Had it not been for the Revolution, Napoleon would not have amounted to anything noteworthy in history. As a Corsican and a member of a low-ranking family, he could never have risen very high in the ranks of the *ancien régime*.[6] The revolutionary transformation of the officer corps and the increased size of the

---

6. The idea that Napoleon was short was a myth largely created by British propaganda. It has given rise to many jokes and the label "Napoleon complex" for a small person compensating for lack of height with oversized aggression. In reality, he was about five feet seven inches in height (170 cm), average for those times and taller than his opponent Lord Nelson. Historians suggest that the origins of his mythical small size lie with the artistic license of cartoonists, misuse of the French term of affection "the little corporal," the contrast with the very tall imperial guards, and the difference between the length of inches in the French and English measurement systems. The "Napoleon complex" also gave rise to the idea that insane people often imagined themselves to be as powerful as Napoleon.

French army, however, provided Napoleon an opportunity to shine. With military brilliance he maneuvered huge armies, negotiated them through foreign lands, and combined his troops to crush enemy forces in decisive blows. Soon the French dreamed not only of dominating Europe but also of restoring France's world empire. In 1798, Napoleon sailed off to invade Egypt, aiming to damage British imperial interests in the Eastern Mediterranean and the Middle East. His only success there was the discovery of the Rosetta Stone, whose inscriptions in Greek and hieroglyphics allowed modern scholars to finally translate ancient Egyptian (see figure 2.3). Soon the British navy decisively crushed Napoleon's hopes for conquest in Egypt (and seized the Rosetta Stone for the British Museum).

Napoleon nevertheless managed to rush back to France before news of his defeats could spread. Back in Paris, he seized control of the government in a coup d'état on 18 Brumaire VIII (or 9 November 1799). Imitating the Roman Republic, Napoleon declared himself as first consul and proclaimed (with about as much sincerity as Augustus Caesar had) that his leadership would restore the "French Revolutionary Republic." In a brilliant move, he held a **plebiscite** for the French people to endorse his seizure of the state. Named after the ancient Roman plebeians, plebiscites are votes with no binding power. So even if the French people had voted against his constitutional changes, Napoleon could have gone ahead anyway. Napoleon's real power was based on his military command. His army could have put down any opposition.

Nevertheless, the French people felt involved merely by being allowed to vote, and they indeed voted overwhelmingly for him. Many a dictator would later resort to the same method of opinion management. Plebiscites preserved the façade of popular endorsement. The trappings of republican government decorated Napoleon's absolutism. Napoleon's rise to dictatorship showed again (as with Oliver Cromwell) that a relatively obscure, simple person could become the leader of a great power through talent, luck, and ruthlessness rather than dynastic birth. As in ancient Greece and Rome, people were willing to sacrifice their democratic participation in government in exchange for victories against neighboring states.

The lure of dynasty was too powerful for Napoleon to ignore, however. He crowned himself emperor in 1804, abandoning the titles of the republic. A few years later he divorced his wife Josephine, who was too old to bear his children, so that he could wed the Habsburg emperor's young daughter Marie Louise. By marrying a Habsburg princess, the once-obscure Napoleon joined the most prestigious bloodline in Europe. Furthermore, the new French empress Marie Louise soon bore her newly imperial husband an imperial son and heir.

For a time, Napoleon's political activities as ruler of France helped to cement his positive popular and historical reputation. His foundation of the Bank of France aimed to finance a strong economy. Napoleon appeased the spiritual needs of many French citizens by allowing the Roman Catholic Church to set up operations again (although without much of its property, power, or monopoly on belief). He restored the Gregorian calendar. Napoleon himself felt that his greatest achievement was the **Napoleonic Code**, a legal codification comparable to the Justinian Code in the sixth century. Beyond simply organizing laws as Justinian had, Napoleon's lawyers tossed out the whole previous system and reassembled a new one based on rationalist principles and the equality of all adult male citizens. These laws were a bit like window dressing, considering Napoleon's dictatorship, and, as usual, women were granted few rights at all. Nevertheless, Napoleon provided a rationalized system that has remained the foundation of French law as well as that of many other countries today in Europe (Holland, Italy) and Latin America. The code even influenced the laws of Louisiana in the United States (which belonged to France until 1803). On the basis of these reforms, some historians have said that France gained an enlightened despot in Napoleon, at last.

Napoleon's military talent forged a massive empire that might have united the Continent under French power and culture. With his victory at the Battle of Austerlitz on 2 December 1805, he defeated an alliance of Austria, Prussia, and Russia. He redrew the map of Europe and reduced the size of those three great powers. With the annexation of the Lowlands, Switzerland, and much of northern Italy, France itself bloated into an empire virtually the size Charlemagne's had been. In 1806, the Holy Roman Empire vanished into history, although the Habsburgs conjured up a separate imperial title as emperors of their hereditary lands in Austria. Bonaparte controlled much of the rest of Europe through puppets, usually his relatives propped up on thrones. He ruled over the largest collection of Europeans up to that point in history.

Great Britain, however, refused to concede Europe to Napoleonic supremacy. Britain's worldwide possessions and growing economy gave it the ability to maintain hostilities with France until a means could be found to break up Napoleon's empire. Napoleon himself recognized the difficulty of maintaining overseas colonies. In 1803, Napoleon sold France's claims on the huge Louisiana Territory to the United States (the indigenous peoples who lived there were not consulted, of course). French armies also failed to crush a rebellion in Haiti, leading to that country's independence by 1804. And the British navy decisively crushed the French fleet on the Atlantic side of the Straits of Gibraltar at the Battle of Trafalgar on 21 October 1805. At that point, France was blockaded by the British navy and could not even control the waters off its own coast. This naval victory notwithstanding, Britain lacked the forces to invade France directly, as frustrated as naval Athens had been versus infantry Sparta during the Peloponnesian Wars.

Thus, Napoleon dominated the land, the British the sea. Neither could or would end the conflict. Instead, indirectly, the British supported a festering revolt in Spain after 1808. In turn, Napoleon tried to damage the British economy with his "Continental System," which established an embargo prohibiting all trade between his empire and any allies of the British Empire. Too many Europeans, however, had become addicted to the products of the global economy (including tobacco and coffee) that usually came through British middlemen. Napoleon's higher prices, heavy taxes, and French chauvinism (arrogant nationalism) alienated many Europeans.

Moreover, the empires of Prussia, Austria, and Russia had merely been defeated, not destroyed. They waited for an opportunity to strike back. In 1812, Russia's refusal to uphold the embargo broke the Continental System. In reaction,

Napoleon decided to teach that country a lesson: he invaded with the largest army yet assembled in human history—probably half a million men. Unfortunately for his grand plans, the Russians avoided a decisive battle. Napoleon found himself and his huge army stranded in a burned-out Moscow with winter approaching. As Napoleon retreated back to France, his forces suffered disaster. Only a few tens of thousands survived to return from the Russian campaign.

Although Napoleon rapidly raised another army, his dominance was doomed. Other generals had learned his strategy and tactics too well. Peoples all over Europe rebelled, aided by British money and troops. The insignificant War of 1812 declared by the Americans did not distract the British enough to do Napoleon any good at all. At the Battle of Nations near Leipzig, about half a million soldiers fought inconclusively over French domination for three days in October 1813. More than one hundred thousand men died there in one of the largest battles in history. While Napoleon remained unbeaten, he had to retreat from Germany. By March 1814, coalition armies had invaded France and finally forced Napoleon to abdicate.

Incredibly, Napoleon managed to overcome even this major defeat. For a few short months, Napoleon sat in imprisonment on the island of Elba off the coast of Tuscany. Then one night he escaped, and for "Napoleon's Hundred Days" he once again ruled France as *l'Empereur*. The countries that had so recently triumphed over him refused to accept Bonaparte back as the leader of France. British and Prussian forces finally, ultimately, once and for all overthrew Napoleon at the **Battle of Waterloo** (18 June 1815) in Belgium. This time the British shipped the captured emperor off to exile on the barren island of St. Helena in the South Atlantic, where he died a few years later of a stomach ulcer.

The French Revolution reaffirmed the basic principle that democracy is difficult. In trying to establish a republican government, the French stumbled through several failed regimes, finally unleashing a dictatorship, as had the English under Cromwell. They were not the first to experience this, nor would they be the last. Sadly, the human tendency to want simple answers and strong leaders would repeat itself in other revolutions that quickly took the same sharp turns toward autocracy.

But with Napoleon's final downfall, everyone knew that an era had ended. Millions of lives and vast amounts of property had been lost in rebellion, repression, and wars, causing the suffering of whole societies. The victors faced the questions of what should be retained and what should be revised (see map 10.1). The leaders of the French Revolution had proclaimed their inspiration from previous intellectual and political revolutions. Their ideas of liberty, equality, and fraternity continued to challenge and inspire despite the French Empire's collapse. The Scientific Revolution granted Europeans new power to understand and control nature. The Enlightenment freed them to play with new ideas that overthrew authority. New governments, both absolutist and democratic, gave Western states still greater abilities to fight with one another and conquer foreign peoples. Revolutions in Britain, America, and France provided examples of how to change regimes. The legacies of scientists, *philosophes*, monarchs, republicans, and radicals worked themselves out on the ruins of Napoleon's empire. Few suspected at that time how the next century would transform the West more than any previous century had.

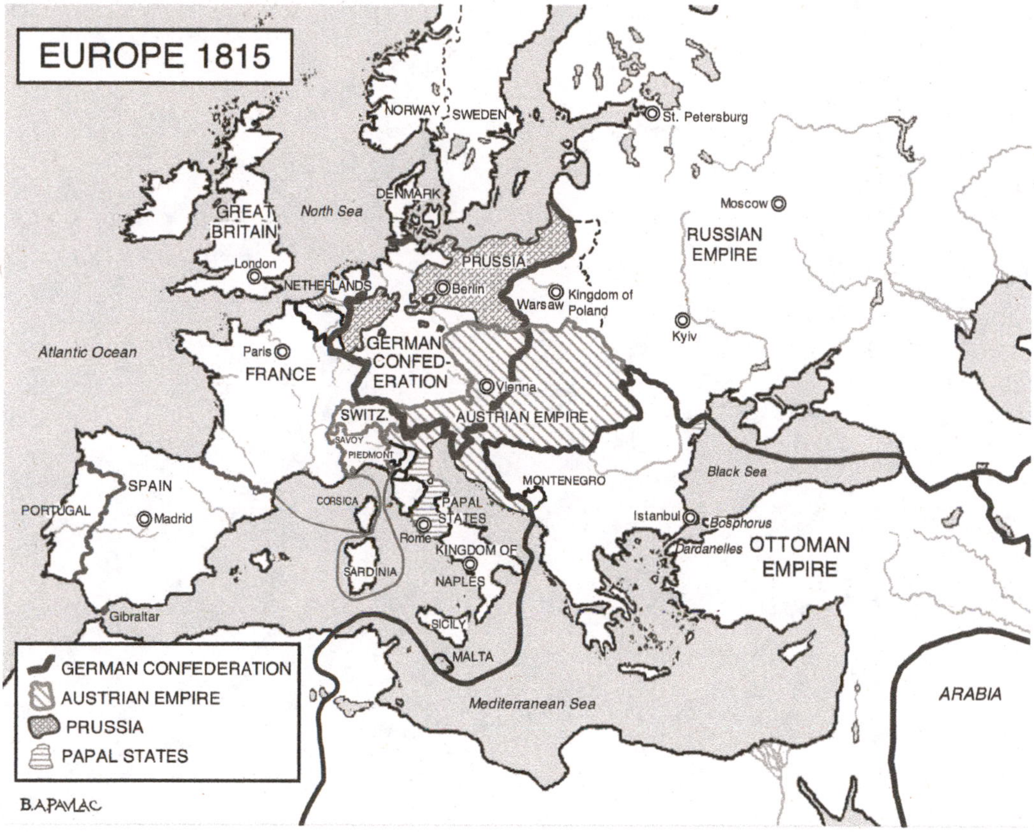

EUROPE 1815

NORWAY   SWEDEN   St. Petersburg

DENMARK   Moscow

GREAT   North Sea   RUSSIAN
BRITAIN   EMPIRE

London   PRUSSIA
NETHERLANDS   Berlin   Kingdom of
Warsaw   Poland

Atlantic Ocean   Paris   Kyiv
FRANCE   GERMAN
CONFED-
ERATION   Vienna

SWITZ.   AUSTRIAN EMPIRE
SAVOY
PIEDMONT

SPAIN   MONTENEGRO   Black Sea

PORTUGAL   CORSICA   PAPAL   Istanbul   Bosphorus
Madrid   STATES   Dardanelles   OTTOMAN
Rome   EMPIRE
KINGDOM OF
SARDINIA   NAPLES

Gibraltar   SICILY   ARABIA

MALTA   Mediterranean Sea

GERMAN CONFEDERATION
AUSTRIAN EMPIRE
PRUSSIA
PAPAL STATES

B.A.PAVLAC

Map 10.1.   Europe, 1815. How does the center of Europe show instability?

Review: *How did war alter the French Revolution and cause Napoleon's rise and fall?*

Response:

Make your own timeline.

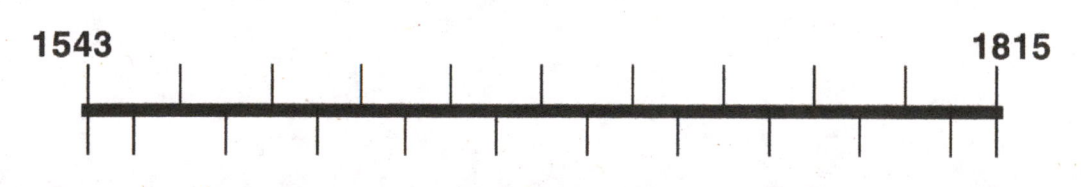

1543   1815

CHAPTER 11

Mastery of the Machine

The Industrial Revolution, 1764 to 1914

Historians call the rough hundred years after the fall of Napoleon the **nineteenth century** (1815–1914). The period forms a convenient unit between the Wars of the Coalitions and World War I. Between those two worldwide conflicts, Western civilization went through numerous changes in its economic practices, political ideologies, social structures, and scientific ideas. Probably the most important change was the one brought about by the **Industrial Revolution** (1764–1914), during which economies became dominated by manufacturing via machines in factories. Just as the French Revolution opened up new possibilities, so did the Industrial Revolution. The rise of new technologies and business practices fashioned the most profound economic change in human history since the invention of agriculture. The increasing sophistication of machines both supplied more power to the masters of those devices and dominated the lives of those who worked with them. Machinery also pushed Western civilization to further heights of prosperity and power. Under the leadership of new political ideologies, people increasingly abandoned the quaint agricultural ways of the past and forged the now-familiar industrialized society of our modern world.

FACTS OF FACTORIES

The basic structures of civilization had been fairly stable since the prehistoric Neolithic Agricultural Revolution. For thousands of years, the overwhelming majority of people, the lower classes, carried out their assigned task of producing enough food for themselves, plus a little more for their betters who did not farm. Only the few privileged people of the upper and middle classes did not get their hands dirty in tilling the land or raising animals. The environment—insects and rodents, drought, flood, storm, and frost—often threatened to destroy the farmers' crops. Whole families labored from dawn to dusk much of the year with few material comforts to enjoy.

Farming started to become much easier with the **Scientific Agricultural Revolution**. This revolution began around 1650 in England. Science transformed farming life, offering more control over the environment than ever before. Scientists recommended different crops to plant, such as potatoes and maize (corn), because they grew more efficiently and were more nutritious. They developed new kinds of fertilizer (improving on manure) and new methods of land management (improving crop rotation and irrigation), reducing the amount of fallow land. Fences went up as landlords enclosed their fields, consolidating them into more manageable units.

Thus, fewer farmers could produce more food than before. But with fewer jobs in agriculture to keep everyone employed, a huge social crisis threatened to overwhelm England. The last traditional protections for peasants of the medieval manor disappeared. Landlords threw tenants off land that their families had worked for centuries, severing long-standing social and economic relationships. The agricultural working class broke up. Even independent family farmers with small plots of land lost out because they could not compete against the improved larger estates.

At the same time, more food and better medical science stimulated rapid population growth. As in ancient Rome after the Punic Wars, large numbers of people without land began to move to the cities, hoping for work. Others left England, emigrating to find farmland, especially in the British colonies of North America. Another open field was a new colony in Australia, which Captain Cook had explored in 1770. The Aborigines who had inhabited the continent for over fifty thousand years were hunter-gatherers with Stone Age technology. The British brushed them aside and designated the continent as a penal colony for their own criminals. The first shipload of undesirables landed in Botany Bay in 1788. Yet exporting people could not solve Britain's unemployment rates and a threatening rebellion. Arriving in the nick of time was the Industrial Revolution, whose new technologies turned many of the landless rural peasants into urban factory workers.

The revolution began in England, which possessed a number of inherent advantages. First, its promotion of science launched the Scientific Agricultural Revolution. Second, Britain's political system of elected representatives quickly adapted to the new economic options. Third, Non-Conformists (mostly firm Calvinists who refused to join the Church of England) put their efforts into commerce, finance, and industry because lingering religious discrimination excluded them from civil service jobs and universities. So instead, the Calvinists' diligent "Protestant work ethic" (as later coined by sociologist Max Weber) drove the economy.

A fourth advantage for England was its diverse possessions. In the immediate vicinity, England bound Scotland, Wales, and Ireland into the United Kingdom of Great Britain. Great Britain ruled the world's largest empire in the eighteenth century, despite the loss in 1783 of the colonies that became the United States. Across the oceans, Britain held Canada, Egypt, South Africa, Australia, islands in the Caribbean (the "West Indies"), and parts of India. These far-flung territories provided many raw materials and goods, like sugar, cotton, and tobacco. Slave labor made these products especially profitable. The slave trade also encouraged shipbuilding and weaponry industries. The British navy, so successful in the Wars of the Coalitions against Napoleon, protected British merchant ships as they traded their cargoes around the globe with many native peoples (and seized some of them to be sold as slaves).

Financial innovations gave the English yet more advantages over competitors. One was the invention of **insurance**, such as policies offered by Lloyd's of London, then and today. Insurance companies would calculate risk to business enterprises, charge according to the odds that those risks would come to pass, and generally make substantial profits. By covering losses caused by natural disasters, theft, and piracy, insurance made investing less risky and more profitable. After 1694, the Bank of England also provided a secure and ready source of capital, which was backed by the government itself. The large number of trading opportunities within the empire minimized each individual capitalist's risk. Altogether, Britain possessed the best chance to seize upon the new industries.

Lastly, three new developments in energy, transportation, and machinery combined to produce the Industrial Revolution. First, improved energy came from harnessing the power of falling water with water mills. The second development, transportation, overcame the constant problem of bad roads. The technology for paved roads had been neglected since ancient Roman times. After the fall of Rome, most roads in Europe were dirt paths that became impassable mud trenches whenever it rained. Travel became significantly easier, however, with the building of **canals**, or water roads. During the eighteenth century, many canals were excavated to connect towns within the country. These canals were highly suitable in soggy England because they actually became more passable with rainy weather. Since barges were buoyant in water, one mule on a towpath could pull many more times the tonnage of goods than a horse with a wagon on a muddy trail. While most canals have long since been filled in or forgotten, for a few decades they were the best mode of technologically efficient transport.

The third improvement, new machines, vastly increased the power of human beings. The first mechanical devices were invented to make textiles, a huge market considering that all Europeans needed clothing for warmth, comfort, decency, and dignity. At the beginning of the Industrial Revolution, the best technology for making thread was the single spindle on a spinning wheel, as known from fairy tales. Weaving cloth was done by hand on a loom, pushing thread through weft and warp.

A series of inventions through the eighteenth century multiplied the efficiency of one weaver at the spinning wheel and loom. The breakthrough occurred with James Hargreaves's **spinning jenny** (1764). Instead of one woman making one thread at a time, the new machine enabled one person to manufacture many dozens of threads at once, at lower cost per piece. Fights over the ownership of technology soon complicated competition. Hargreaves certainly "borrowed" important concepts from other inventors and businessmen, who in turn took his jenny and made money off of it. Richard Arkwright, a former wigmaker, combined his own and others' inventions into the best powered spinning and weaving machines. Concerned with theft of ideas, inventors protected their inventions with patents, namely government-backed certificates. Nevertheless, claims often came down to lawsuits. Hargreaves died a pauper, Arkwright a wealthy knight. The bold, lucky, and unscrupulous often succeeded in making fortunes, while rightful inventors died in poverty and obscurity. Entrepreneurs like Arkwright simplified the manufacturing process by combining all the innovations in energy, transportation, and machinery. The **factory** or (in British) the **mill system** brought workers and raw materials together with machines in specialized buildings called by those names.

This Industrial Revolution was controlled by men, but it also transformed women's lives. Men did most of the inventing of and investing in machines, ran the factories, and pocketed the profits. Men forbade women from apprenticeships, education, training, and even getting advanced technological jobs. Political, economic, and social structures continued to exclude women from positions of authority and influence. Such had been the status of most women since the beginning of civilization. As machines became more important, men claimed that women lacked a mechanically capable mind, while men alone were suited for tinkering with technology. In the nineteenth century, men remained masters of both women and the machines.

Nevertheless, the machines affected every woman's life, inside and outside the home. Since the twelfth century, women and children had earned extra income by making goods by hand through the cottage industry or putting-out method. After the eighteenth century, factory-made products cut into what women had earned this way. Losing that income soon drove women and children to work in factories, where they were often hired because owners could pay them lower wages than men. Adding in the cheap labor of women and children, industrial production increased efficiency and lowered prices. As prices went down, demand went up, since more people could afford the machine-manufactured goods, from linen tablecloths to teacups. Moreover, as new industrial forms of artificial lighting such as the arc lamp were invented, production could go on around the clock to get the maximum use out of the machines, which never slept. Thus, capitalist industrial manufacturing emerged as investors funded the building of factories for profit.

A second wave of industrialization hit with the invention of the **steam engine**. In 1769, James Watt and Matthew Boulton adapted their machine from mechanical pumps used to remove water from coal and iron mines, then to lift the rock to the surface (see figure 11.1). In turn, coal became the main fuel source for these engines. Coal outmatched previous materials that people burned for energy, such as plant and animal oils, wood, or peat. The switch to the fossil fuel coal gave Europeans a decisive advantage in power over other peoples of the world. With innovation, the coal-fired steam engines vastly increased their energy output while their physical size shrank. By the 1830s, small steam engines on wagons with metal wheels running on tracks called **railroads** were transporting both goods and people (see figure 11.2). Trains on such railways soon eclipsed canals as the most efficient transportation, since they were cheaper to build and could run in places without plentiful water. Water travel remained important, though. Steam engines in ships meant faster, more certain transit across seas and oceans, further tying together markets of raw materials and factories for manufacturing. Europeans sped up.

Some people resisted the rise of these machines, most famously the **Luddites**. Today, that label applies to anyone who is suspicious of, or hostile to, technology. The term originated from the name of a (possibly) mythical leader of out-of-work

Figure 11.1.   A massive coal breaker looms over an industrial wasteland. Inside, the coal from deep underground was broken down into smaller sizes for transport. (Luzerne County Historical Society)

artisans. The artisans' jobs of making artifacts by hand were now obsolete. In the cold English winter of 1811–1812, bands of artisans broke into mills, destroyed the machines, and threatened the owners. The government, of course, arrested, shot, or hanged the troublemakers. Great Britain had a war to win against France and was not going to let a few unemployed louts threaten enormous potential profits for the nation.

Nevertheless, the Luddite fear was a natural and foreseeable reaction to a change that left workers vulnerable. At the beginning of the nineteenth century, classical liberal economics (as described by Adam Smith) had increasingly been adopted by both business and government. Industrialization meant that only the entrepreneurial class who controlled large amounts of capital could create most jobs. Neither factory owners nor politicians felt much responsibility for those paid very little or even thrown out of work (see Primary Source Project 11). Even Adam Smith had observed that capitalists would conspire to keep wages low, if workers were prohibited from organizing to increase their wages. Some economists, such as the English banker David Ricardo, told the poor that they should just work harder and be more thrifty. **Ricardo's "iron law of wages"** exploited even those who had jobs. This economic theory advised factory owners to pay workers the bare minimum that allowed survival. Otherwise, Ricardo argued, workers might have too many children, only increasing the numbers of the poor and unemployed. The dominant economic theories at the beginning of the Industrial Revolution favored the new industrial capitalists over the new factory workers.

Figure 11.2. Steam engines on railways (with windmills to pump water from far underground to store in a tank) enabled expansion across the American continent by the mid-nineteenth century. (Treasures of the NOAA Library Collection)

Review: *How did inventions and capitalism produce the Industrial Revolution?*

Response:

LIFE IN THE JUNGLE

The division of society into capitalists and workers led Western civilization to become more dependent on cities than ever before. The populations of industrialized cities rapidly rose upward in a process called *urbanization*. By definition, cities had been central to civilization since its beginnings, but only a small minority of people had ever lived in them. Most people needed to be close to the land, where they could raise the food on which the few urban dwellers depended. After 1800, modern machines helped consolidate more people into urban life. Fewer jobs on the land meant that more people looked for work in the factories. Cities swelled into metropolitan urban complexes. The old culture of the small village where everyone knew everyone increasingly waned. This new urban living required people to abandon outmoded traditions and adopt new ways of thinking and acting.

At first, the cities grew haphazardly, in fits and starts, with little planning or social cohesion. In many districts, people did not know their neighbors, and residents could only find low-paying jobs, if any. The result was slums of badly built and managed housing. Slums became dangerous places of increased drug use, crime, filth, and disease.

Concerned citizens founded public health and safety organizations to manage these dangers. Firefighters became more professional. Likewise, modern **police** forces formed as a new kind of guardian to manage the lower classes. Law enforcement on the scale at which our modern urban police forces function had been unnecessary in earlier rural society. In small, stable rural villages, people had known all their neighbors, and therefore crime was limited by familiarity. In the anonymous urban neighborhood afflicted with poverty, though, crime by strangers inevitably increased. Of necessity, crime investigations required more care and scientific support. During the 1820s, Sir Robert Peel's "bobbies" (nicknamed after their founder) and their headquarters in Scotland Yard (named after the location) in London were merely the first of these new civil servants. Police forces insisted that only they were authorized to use violence within the urban community.

The concentrated numbers of new urban dwellers, which rose from hundreds of thousands into millions, also spewed out levels of pollution unknown to earlier civilization. Streets became putrid swamps, piled high with dumped rotting food and excrement. Major cities had tens of thousands of horses as the main mode of transportation, each producing at least twenty pounds of manure a day. Air became smog, saturated with the noxious fumes of factory furnaces, coal stoves, and burning trash. Infectious diseases such as dysentery, typhoid, and cholera (newly imported from India) plagued Western cities because of unsanitary habitats. Urban populations died by the thousands from new plagues fostered by industrialization.

Since disease was not confined only to the poorer districts, politicians found themselves pressured to look after public health. Cemeteries were relocated from their traditional settings near churches to parklike settings on the city's fringes. In Paris, the bones dug up from cemeteries around the city were stacked in huge underground caverns. Regulations prohibited raising certain animals or burning specific materials. The government paved roads, especially with the cheap innovative material of tar and gravel called asphalt or macadam (after its inventor, John McAdam). City officials created **sanitation** organizations. Upton Sinclair's novel *The Jungle* (1906) about horrid urban living and working conditions actually led the US government to improve the regulation of food quality. Employees called garbagemen, refuse collectors, waste management professionals, or sanitation engineers took trash to dumps. Freshwater supply networks replaced the old-fashioned wells, piping in clean, drinkable water from reservoirs, while networks of sewers whisked dirty water away.

In this process, Western civilization perfected the greatest invention in human history: **indoor plumbing**, namely, hot and cold running water and a toilet (or water closet) (see figure 11.3). Such mundane items are often taken for granted

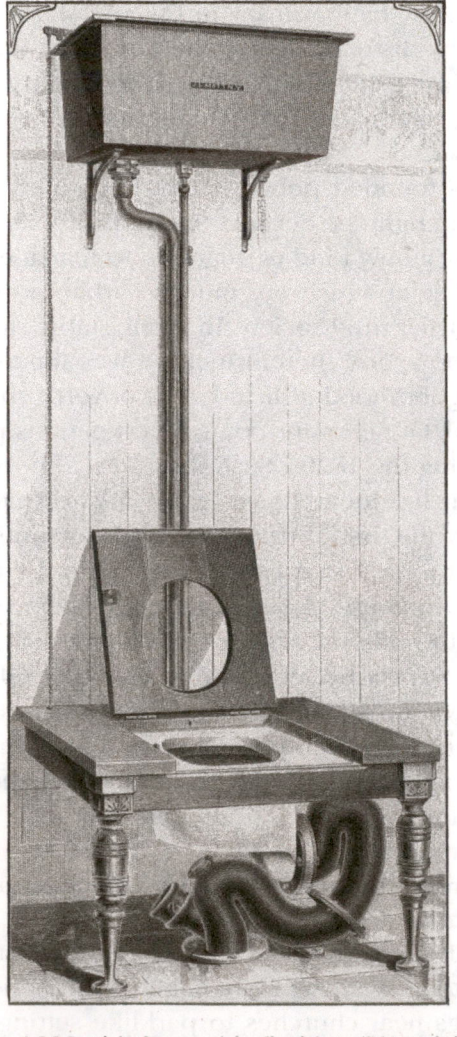

Figure 11.3. In 1888, this fancy side-flushing "Warwick" water closet offered a wood seat made of cherry, black walnut, or ash with bronzed iron legs and a cast iron "slop safe." (NYPL Digital Collection)

by both historians and ordinary people. The Romans had public lavatories and baths, some medieval monasteries had interesting systems of water supply, and a few monarchs and aristocrats had unique plumbing built into a palace here or there. But since the fall of Rome, cleanliness had been too expensive for most Europeans to bother with. Whether rich or poor, most people literally stank and crawled with vermin. In the nineteenth century, free-flowing water from public waterworks, copper pipes, gas heaters, valves, and porcelain bowls brought the values of hygienic cleanliness to people at all levels of wealth. Of course, not all worries could go down the drain or vanish with a flush; the waste merely accumulated somewhere else in the environment. Most people, unconcerned, have easily ignored such messy realities. Regardless, more and more nineteenth-century westerners enjoyed the cleanliness and comforts of lavatories. With the new plumbing, plagues like cholera, typhoid, and dysentery began to diminish and even disappear in the West.

As industrialized cities grew in size and safety, their inhabitants accumulated wealth previously unimagined in human history. Some of those riches were spent on culture: literature, art, and music. Some were spent on showing off: bigger houses, fancier fashion, and fine dining. Because a few earned so much more than the rest, the Industrial Revolution initiated a major transition of class structures in Western society. At the bottom, supporting the upper and middle classes, was the hard labor of the **working class** (also called the proletariat after the ancient Roman underclass), made up of fewer and fewer farmers and more and more factory workers. The upper classes became less defined by birth after landownership ceased to be the most productive way to gain wealth. A successful businessman could create a fortune that dwarfed the lands and rents of a titled aristocrat. The *nouveau riche* (newly wealthy) set the tone for the new upper crust.

Meanwhile, the middle class became less that of merchants and artisans and more of managers and professionals: the white-collar worker who supervised the blue-collar workers in the factories. The colors reflect class distinctions: white for more expensive, bleached and pressed fabric, blue for cheaper and darker cloth that showed less dirt. Physicians, lawyers, and professors likewise earned enough to qualify for the "upper"-middle-class way of life. Most people came to idealize middle-class values: a separate home as a refuge from the rough everyday world; a wife who did not have to work outside the home, if at all; the freedom to afford vacations; and comfortable retirement in old age.

Essentially, these middle-class values were new, unusual, and limited only to a small portion of the population. These so-called **family values** were not in the least traditional, as some social conservatives today would like people to think. Throughout civilized history, most men and women had both worked at home or on the land close to home, in shops or on farms. And the entire family worked together: husband, wife, and children, perhaps with a few others in servile status. Most people never thought of vacation trips, only restful religious holidays. Those who survived into old age usually had to keep working to earn their keep. For a model of actual traditional family life, look to the Old Order Amish or Pennsylvania Dutch, who live today in communities stretching from Pennsylvania to

Missouri, Iowa, and Wisconsin. These people have consciously rejected the Industrial Revolution and its technologies. They cannot ignore it, as their young people are tempted toward the ease that the wealth of modern life provides. Nonetheless, their values of hardworking farm families reflect the family values actually passed down through the millennia of civilizations before the Industrial Revolution.

By moving people away from farm communities, the Industrial Revolution generated serious tensions within society that few people wanted to recognize. The domestic sphere was damaged, as people worked outside the home. Social mobility became more volatile, as it was easier to rise but also to fall in class status. One major business failure could send not just the capitalist owner but also many thousands of workers into the poorhouse. For workers at the bottom of society there were few protections. Businesses rotated through boom and bust, good times and bad times, hirings and firings. Whole societies became subject to market cycles, which economists have never been able to predict or prevent, despite their supposedly expert studies.

Over time, though, the Industrial Revolution did seem to confirm the Western notion of progress. Some people continued to suffer, and still suffer, under the system. But by and large, things for most people usually got better enough to prevent social collapse. The quality of life improved. More people had more possessions, filling their kitchens with cookware and tableware. More people became free from ignorance and disease. More people had access to more opportunities than ever before in human history. Before the Industrial Revolution, most people stayed at the level at which they were born. Capitalist industrial manufacturing, it seemed, had unleashed the possibility for anyone to achieve the good life, at least as far as creature comforts went. The only questions seemed to be: What did those at the bottom need to do in order to move up, and how long would they need to wait for their chance at the good life?

The new **consumer economy**, where unknown distant workers manufactured most products that people purchased and used, only stoked impatience. Gone were the neighborhood shoemaker, blacksmith, and farmer. Instead, distant capitalists encouraged consumers to acquire goods, even if they did not need them. To accomplish this, **advertising** became a significant tool for economic innovation. It began with simple signs in stores where people shopped. Soon, promotions were on every package and on the side of every road and byway. Advertisers began to create needs to stimulate consumer consumption and grow the economy. They defined new forms of proper usage for the various classes, in hygiene, fashion, and leisure. Businesses with mail-order catalogs, such as those by Montgomery Ward (1872) or Sears, Roebuck and Co. (1886), delivered thousands of products, from watches to prefabricated homes, through modern postal services. By the end of the nineteenth century, majestic department stores, such as Harrods (1849) in London, Le Bon Marché (1852) in Paris, and Macy's (1858) in New York, served as shopping meccas for the rich and middle classes in urban centers, while the lower classes could buy merchandise at the "five-and-dime" discount chains, Woolworth's (1879) or Kresge's (1899) in the United States. Even Christian holidays felt the impact, as Christmas (the celebration of Jesus's birth) began to outshine Easter (the celebration of Jesus's resurrection) because its ritual of buying and giving gifts suited consumerism. Charles Dickens's novella *A Christmas Carol* (1843) tells this tale.

Also by the late nineteenth century, a second wave of innovation intensified the revolution across much of Western civilization. The mastery of electricity and steelmaking allowed cities to grow even larger, not only across the landscape but also up into the sky. Church steeples had been the tallest urban structures since the Middle Ages. Business towers of the early **skyscrapers** began to define the modern city skyline. Previously, most residential and business buildings were limited to five stories because builders were unable to engineer useful load-bearing walls, and people were unwilling to climb too many stairs. With steel-girder skeletons (1884), electric safety elevators (1887), and lightbulbs (1879), buildings could be erected to ten, twenty, even sixty stories![1] Below the earth, subways (London in the 1860s, Budapest in 1896, New York in 1904) propelled workers to and from their homes and factories. Communication through telegraph (1830s), then telephone (1876), and finally radio (1906) tied the world more tightly together.

Western economies also needed more energy to function. Coal gained a competitor in another mineral, petroleum. This "rock oil" has since become so important to human beings that it has been abbreviated to the word "**oil**." The first crude oil well in Titusville, Pennsylvania (1859), led the way in supplying industrial society with this power source. People first valued oil as a fuel that was refined into kerosene for lamps. Kerosene replaced whale oil, which had itself replaced other plant and animal oils. Petroleum's associated by-product, natural gas, in turn fueled lighting, heating, and cooking. Oil could be made into a grease for lubrication. Oil also became the foundation of a new **petrochemicals** industry. The first petrochemical businesses made dyes for coloring fabric, soon followed by fertilizers and medicines. By 1900, researchers formulated petroleum into Bakelite, the first plastic. Bakelite could take on new shapes, forms, strengths, and even colors. Plastic continued to unleash waves of inventiveness. At the time, no one worried about how the burning, refining, or disposing of petroleum products might create their own problems.

Finally, oil's combustible properties began to replace coal to power engines. For steamships and steam locomotives, that meant burning oil instead of burning coal to boil the water for steam. At the nineteenth century's end came an invention that would transform industrial people's mobility: the **internal combustion engine**. Oil refined into diesel or gasoline fueled this new, stronger, smaller, and therefore more mobile motor. Karl Benz, who worked with bicycle shop owners in Germany, bolted an engine onto a frame to rotate pneumatic tires and created the **automobile** (1886). The two Wright brothers, who owned a bicycle shop in Dayton, Ohio, placed the engine among large airfoils to spin a propeller and launched the **airplane** (1903). Both the car and the airplane would revolutionize travel in the twentieth century, outpacing the success of the train. Western civilization was now on the move, faster than ever, by land, sea, and air.

---

1. These early skyscrapers included the Home Insurance Building (1884) in Chicago, the Flatiron Building (1902) in New York (with twenty-one stories plus a penthouse), and the Woolworth Building (1913), also in New York.

Review: How did urbanization develop a modern society?

Response:

SOURCES ON FAMILIES: GEORGE SAND ON THE END OF HER MARRIAGE (1835)

The French writer Amandine-Aurore-Lucile Dupin (b. 1804–d. 1876) is better known by her adopted nom de plume*: George Sand. She is famous for defying gender expectations by her using a male name; dressing in men's clothing; writing novels, memoirs, and literary criticism; smoking; and carrying on numerous affairs, most famously with the pianist and composer Chopin. At only eighteen she had conventionally married François Casimir Dudevant, the illegitimate son of a baron, and soon bore a son and a daughter. In 1831, however, she began to explore Paris dressed as a man, publish professionally, and have affairs. In these two letters she describes the circumstances of domestic violence in 1835 that led her to separate from her husband. The courts dissolved the marriage the following year and awarded her custody of the children (although Dudevant did briefly abduct their daughter).*

To Hippolyte Chatiron [her half-brother],

My friend, I am about to tell you some news which will reach you indirectly, and that you had better hear first from me. Instead of carrying out our agreement pleasantly and loyally, Casimir is acting with the most insane animosity towards me. Without my giving him any reason for such a thing, either by my conduct or my manner of treating him, he endeavored to strike me. He was prevented by five persons, one of whom was Dutheil, and he then fetched his gun to shoot me. As you can imagine, he was not allowed to do this.

On account of such treatment and of his hatred, which amounts to madness, there is no safety for me in a house to which he always has the right to come. I have no guarantee, except his own will and pleasure, that he will keep our agreement, and I cannot remain at the mercy of a man who behaves so unreasonably and indelicately to me. I have therefore decided to ask for a legal separation, and I shall no doubt obtain this. Casimir made this frightful scene the evening before leaving for Paris. On his return here, he found the house empty, and me staying at Dutheil's, by permission of the President of La Chatre [a small town]. He also found a summons awaiting him on the mantelshelf. He had to make the best of it, for he knew it was no use attempting to fight against the result of his own folly, and that, by holding out, the scandal would all fall on him. He made the following stipulations, promising to adhere to them. Dutheil was our intermediary. I am to allow him a pension of 3,800 francs, which, with the 1,200 francs income that he now has, will make 5,000 francs a year for him. I think this is all straightforward, as I am paying for the education of the two children. My daughter will remain under my guidance, as I understand. My son will remain at the college where he now is until he has finished his education. During the holidays he will spend a month with his father and a month with me. In this way, there will be no contest. Dudevant will return to Paris very soon, without making any opposition, and the Court will pronounce the separation in default.

Dear Hydrogen [friend and neighbor Adolphe Duplomb],

You have been misinformed about what took place at La Chatre. Dutheil never quarreled with the Baron of Nohant-Vic. This is the true story. The baron took it into his head to strike me. Dutheil objected. Fleury and Papet also objected. The baron went to search for his gun to kill every one. Every one did not want to be killed, and so the baron said: "Well, that's enough then," and began to drink again. That was how it all happened. No one quarreled with him. But I had had enough. As I do not care to earn my living and then leave my substance in the hands of the devil and be bowed out of the house every year, while the village hussies sleep in my beds and bring their fleas into my house, I just said: "I ain't going to have any more of that," and I went and found the big judge of La Chatre, and I says, says I: "That's how it is." And then he says, says he: "All right." And so he unmarried us. And I am not sorry. They say that the baron will make an appeal. I ain't knowin'. We shall see. If he does, he'll lose everything. And that's the whole story.

Questions:

- *What is the difference of tone and content in the two letters and why?*
- *About what does Sand seem most concerned?*
- *What involvement do various people outside the marriage have within the married relationship?*

Responses:

For more on this source, go to http://www.concisewesternciv.com/sources/sof11 .html.

CLEANING UP THE MESS

Politically, the nineteenth century began not with a leap forward but with a step backward. Elites sought to tidy up the political disorders left by the Wars of the Coalitions during the French Revolution. After Napoleon's final defeat in 1815, many of the victors thought that the revolutionary ideas of liberty, equality, and fraternity had met their own Waterloo. The French and Industrial Revolutions together brought too much change too fast. A retreat to nature seemed preferable to the dirty, seething cities. The **Romantic movement** rejected the stark results of the Enlightenment's rationality and of industrial technology's advance. The romantics produced poetry, stories, and art that expressed a longing for a simpler time, whether a reimagined past or a fantasy fairyland. Additionally, traditional ruling dynasts seemed better than crude upstarts like Bonaparte. Many traditionalists hoped that all would return to their version of normal.

The victors over Napoleon convened the **Congress of Vienna** (1814–1815) to reorder the chaos left by France's conquest of Europe. Over the course of nine months, hundreds of leaders and diplomats from all of Europe discussed the future (even while dancing and drinking at the many parties). Leading the assembly in its deliberations was Prince **Clemens von Metternich** (b. 1773–d. 1859), first minister for the absolutist Habsburg emperor of Austria. Metternich and others developed the political concept of **conservatism**, namely, the policy that advocated preserving as much as possible of traditional political, social, and cultural structures. Under Metternich's leadership, the congress allowed only such alterations in the old system as were necessary for European stability. It restored most of the old dynasties to power, dumping Bonaparte's relatives and puppets and sending them into exile or retirement. The restorations ranged from the beheaded Louis XVI's brother as the new king of France to the pope ruling once more over the Papal States. A few citizens protested, but all over Europe princes reaffirmed absolutism by shredding constitutions.

The Congress of Vienna also reasserted the balance of power between the great powers of Europe: Britain, France, Austria, Prussia, and Russia (see map 10.1). France had too often tried to conquer Europe, so the victors strengthened states on France's borders to help prevent any further aggression. Along the northeastern border of France, the United Kingdom of the Netherlands combined the Dutch and the Belgians under the aristocratic dynasty of Orange, newly elevated to royalty. Along the southeastern border, the melded Kingdom of Sardinia-Savoy-Piedmont barred the Alpine access to Italy. Austria held sway over the rest of northern Italy. Directly east of France, Prussia acquired a conglomeration of territories in the Rhineland. Prussia and Austria took joint leadership of a new, albeit weakened, German Confederation that merged the hundreds of small principalities of the dead Holy Roman Empire into a mere few dozen. These measures effectively hemmed in France. No one cared to ask whether the peoples of these newly drawn states wanted their assigned roles in the balance of power.

In an attempt to prevent further warfare and revolutions, the Congress of Vienna also tried two new alliance mechanisms. Previously, alliances had lasted for only the duration of wartime. After 1815, nations tried to use alliances to prevent war. First was the **Holy Alliance**, binding together the absolute rulers of Orthodox Russia, Roman Catholic Austria, and Lutheran Prussia in a pragmatic burst of religious cooperation. This agreement called for the promotion of Christian charity and peace, yet it failed due to the power politics of tsar, emperor, and king.

The innovative **Quadruple Alliance** of Austria, Prussia, Russia, and Britain better maintained the reestablished order. For the first time, **collective security** provided an ongoing peacetime mechanism to prevent reckless wars between states. According to the doctrine of balance of power, states organized against one another only when one or more threatened the status quo. In contrast, collective security meant that all nations worked together regularly to maintain peace. After 1815, the recurrent meetings of great powers to uphold international harmony became known as the "Concert of Europe." The Quadruple Alliance provided the first multinational peacekeeping structure to solve civil disturbances in the lesser states of Europe and to prevent dangerous unrest among the peoples.

Although the Quadruple Alliance worked relatively well, Britain slowly began to withdraw. As the only great power with a substantial overseas empire, England was uncertain about its growing rivalry with Russia, the dominant Eurasian power. Meanwhile, the restored Bourbon dynasty in France regained respectability among other European nations as it resisted reform and revolution. Thus, France gradually took England's place within the Concert of Europe. Europe settled into a few rare decades of peace.

No Western ruler even contemplated including the distant United States of America. Yet America's example of republican government also showed many that an alternative to absolutism was still possible. While strict social hierarchies reasserted themselves in Europe, the commoners remembered their access to power under the French revolutionary regime, however brief or illusory. Proclamations of liberty and equality had not been well implemented under Napoleon's dictatorship, but the lower classes liked those ideas all the same. The bourgeoisie continued to accumulate wealth and demand more power for themselves. The aristocracy increasingly lost its purposeful social function. Even absolute monarchs adopted many of Napoleon's and revolutionary France's methods precisely because they were so successful.

The idea of revolution simply would not disappear: people had already seen for themselves that political action could topple incompetent authoritarian regimes. Those in the nineteenth century who supported revolutions were usually categorized as liberals. The political concept of *liberalism* stood for embracing change in order to broaden, as much as reasonable, people's political, social, and cultural opportunities. Liberalism appealed to the middle classes whose fortunes were rising with the Industrial Revolution. Its ideas promised the expansion of their political and economic power and influence.

It is important to note that the specific beliefs held decades ago by liberals on the left and conservatives on the right of the political spectrum were quite different from what they are today (see table 11.1). The nineteenth-century conservatives embraced absolute monarchy with its strong interventionist bureaucracy,

Table 11.1. Views of Western Political Parties in the Nineteenth Century

Conservatism	Liberalism
Absolute monarchy	Parliamentarianism
Social class distinctions	Equality of citizens
Aristocratic and upper-class support	Capitalist and middle-class support
Mercantilism	Laissez-faire/classical liberal economics
Multiethnic states	Nationalism
Union of throne and altar	Separation of church and state

Note: The issues important in the nineteenth century are not necessarily those that matter today. Then and now, conservatism tends to resist change, while liberalism promotes it.

economic theory of mercantilism, distinctions among social classes (with aristocrats at the top), and a close cooperation of state and church (called the union of throne and altar). In contrast, the nineteenth-century liberals called for constitutional and republican government, laissez-faire economic theory, equality before the law for all citizens (perhaps even including women), and separation of church and state with religious toleration. Conservatives cobbled together multiethnic states bound together by dynastic loyalty, while liberals called for nations with ethnic uniformity (about which see chapter 12). These dichotomies do not necessarily fit well with today's issues. In general, only the basic attitudes of a leftist acceptance of change and a right-wing resistance to change are still true today. In general, conservatism is pessimistic, doubting that anything new will work; liberalism is optimistic, proposing change, and if it doesn't work, trying something else. But in lives lived today, political identification should always focus on specific policies, not misleading labels.

Nevertheless, the basic **political parties** of modern Western democracies became organized around these two competing ideologies. Political parties offered structure both to win in elections and, once elected, to cast votes in representative bodies. As more people accumulated substantial wealth and property, they wanted to influence political decisions that could affect their ability to make more money. Taxation, regulations, and monetary strength became issues of national debate. As a result, both sides in many countries used the methods of parliamentarianism. Liberals tried to reduce government regulations, while conservatives sought to preserve advantageous taxation. In the cities, political parties that controlled the levers of power and patronage operated so smoothly for their constituents that they themselves earned the name "machines." Political parties with their permanent leadership, mass membership, and enforcement of discipline at the polls became essential to the functioning of modern government.

Throughout the nineteenth century, the conservatives retained their dominance in most places. The propertied people of lineage wanted to stay in charge, sharing power only with the new rich capitalists. But politics changed with more frequency and without too much violence in England, which already had basic constitutional and republican structures. Majorities in Parliament bounced back and forth between the first two significant political parties, aptly named Liberals (nicknamed Whigs in England and America) and Conservatives (called Tories even

Figure 11.4. The British Parliament buildings were built during the nineteenth century in a romantic style imitating Gothic architecture. (Nicole Mares)

today in Britain). The Whig **Reform Bill of 1832**, for instance, appeased the middle classes by removing some of the worst antiquated structures for parliamentary elections and doubling the electorate to about 20 percent of the population. Working-class citizens then launched the Chartist movement, in which they petitioned, marched, and demonstrated to get representation for themselves. Although the Chartist movement largely failed and vanished after 1848, Parliament slowly legislated reforms to further open up political participation (see figure 11.4). By 1884, the British had reached universal suffrage for men, meaning all adult male citizens had the right to vote. Despite fears about social revolution, voting and democratic institutions still left the privileged wealthy in charge, much as they always had been since the beginning of civilization. Politics opened access to power to only a few more people.

On the European continent, meanwhile, liberals resorted to revolutionary action as a force for political change. France in particular kept breaking out in revolutionary fervor. Without the same traditions and institutions as Britain had to channel the violence of political change through the ballot box, criticism of the regime all too easily escalated first into riots and then into rebellion. Armed clashes flashed on the barricades, with soldiers on one side and bourgeoisie, workers, and students on the other. This violence recast the regimes, even if it did not always improve them. And once France had erupted into revolution, more outbreaks exploded throughout the rest of Europe in 1830, 1848, and 1870.

The **Revolutions of 1830** were the first to significantly affect European politics. In July, the French people deposed the absolutist-inclined King Charles X and replaced him with the more liberal King Louis-Philippe. The United Netherlands split into the separate countries of the Netherlands and **Belgium**.[2] Even though the conservative Metternich wanted to force the new countries to reunite, the other members of the Quadruple Alliance overruled him. They recognized Belgium as a sovereign state and signed a treaty that guaranteed its inviolable neutrality. This meant that any country's attack on Belgium would violate international law and trigger war with the other great powers. In eastern Europe, the Congress of Vienna had granted some autonomy to small Poland as a "kingdom" technically separate from, yet still ruled by, the Russian tsar. When the Poles tried to free themselves from Russian domination in 1830, they lost miserably. The Russian reprisal erased any political liberty the Polish people had enjoyed. Other efforts by Germans and Italians in certain principalities, as well as the Spanish and Portuguese, managed to secure a handful of liberal reforms.

The **Revolutions of 1848** sparked by France were even more widespread and, initially, successful (see map 11.1). In February of that year, the French, who had grown weary of the Bourbons, with their tendencies to incompetence and tyranny, tossed Louis-Philippe off the throne and proclaimed the Second Republic (1848–1852). The French Bourbon dynasty ended in humiliation. Elsewhere in Europe, many rulers capitulated to revolutionary demands. The Prussian king accepted a constitution. In Austria, Metternich and his mentally impaired emperor, Ferdinand I, both resigned. The new eighteen-year-old Emperor Francis-Joseph I (r. 1848–1916) promised a constitution. Different regions of his empire seized the moment to declare independence. Czechs, Hungarians, and Italians took up arms against Habsburg absolutism. People in the German Confederation came together at a parliament in Frankfurt to better unify the German people under constitutional authority. Unfortunately for German liberals, a lack of leadership and squabbling over methods and goals slowed progress. Furthermore, European rulers soon realized that most of their military remained obedient, while liberal politicians held the allegiance of very few armed forces. By the summer of 1849, royal armies commanded by loyal generals had restored most monarchs to their absolutist thrones at the cost of much bloodshed. Despite so many failures, many people still hoped to unite and influence their state's politics.

For example, the French found it difficult to arrange political stability. The hastily arranged democracy of the Second Republic in 1848 quickly degenerated into the Second Empire (1852–1871) under the dictatorship of Louis Napoleon, the nephew of Napoleon Bonaparte. Louis took the name Emperor Napoleon III (whose number recognized the "reign" of Napoleon's son, who had died years earlier as a pampered prisoner in the Schönbrunn Palace outside Vienna). One of Napoleon III's few major innovations was to rebuild Paris with broad boulevards. His original intention was that the wide streets would allow his troops to move

---

2. The new Belgium remained divided between French and Dutch (Flemish) speakers. Recently ethnic factions have sought to further subdivide the country, taking sixteen months after the 2019 elections to form a coalition government.

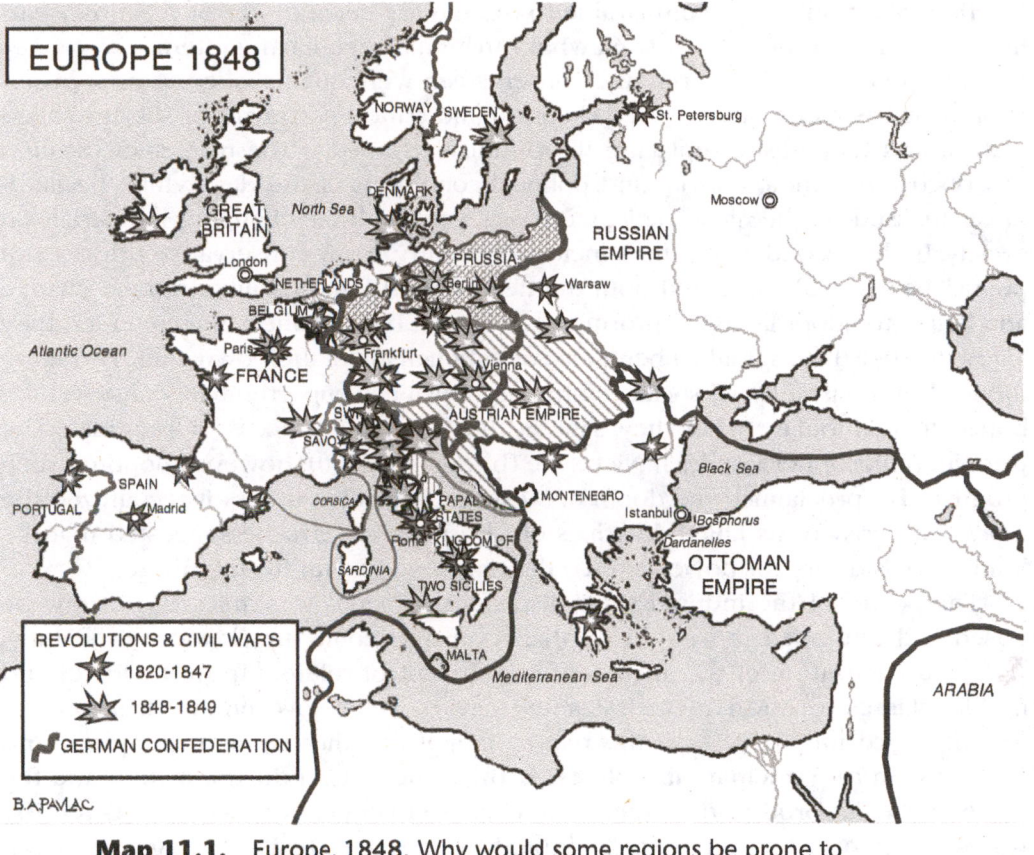

Map 11.1. Europe, 1848. Why would some regions be prone to revolution and not others?

quickly through the city and, if necessary, break any bourgeois barricades. The unintended consequence was to open up Paris for growth and development as one of the leading urban centers in Europe. Yet Napoleon III's imperial rule did not bring lasting peace and stability. Failed foreign policy rather than domestic insurrection, however, ended his reign.

In 1870, Napoleon III recklessly declared war on Prussia, which began the Franco-Prussian War (see chapter 12). France's swift and humiliating defeat led to a brief struggle over the nation's political destiny. Most of the country recognized a moderate-conservative **Third Republic** (1871–1945). At the same time, an organized group of liberals and radicals in the capital proclaimed the **Paris Commune** (March–May 1871). The commune tried to establish a socialist state of complete equality and justice (on socialism, see below). Instead, the national government's forces of moderation and conservatism crushed this effort, using Napoleon III's new wide boulevards to successfully invade the city. Frustrated Communards burned down the Tuileries Palace, which had been the residence of kings and emperors. They also almost destroyed the adjoining Louvre Museum and all its precious art. The victorious Third Republican government killed or executed more than twenty thousand Communards and exiled another seven thousand. After this

reactionary bloodletting, comparable to the radical Reign of Terror a century earlier, the French settled into a somewhat functional republican system.

After 1848, both liberalism and conservatism were quite shaken. A new generation of artists and writers offered skeptical and critical portrayals of society, called
realism and naturalism, replacing the optimistic hopes of the romantics. Realists
described the common social and political conditions of the day, while the natu-
ralists focused on the most tragic and harsh aspects of the changing industrialized
society. In the second half of the nineteenth century, many conservative princes and
politicians shrewdly accepted both the necessity and inevitability of some change
and began to adopt liberal platforms. Also, as will be explained in chapter 12, they
learned to use the originally liberal idea of nationalism for their own aims. By taking
the lead on constitutions, social reform, and business opportunities, conservatives
hoped to manipulate what they saw as the inevitable process of progress. The
German philosopher Friedrich Nietzsche (b. 1844–d. 1900), however, doubted such
progress. He proclaimed the doom of Western civilization unless it recognized the
moral hypocrisy of its failed doctrines of Christianity. Nietzsche suggested that the
human will's desire for power offered the only certain path for the future.

The power of the industrial age also transformed war. Armies could now be
raised and equipped more quickly than ever and could attack more efficiently.
The industrialization of war increased recruitment of soldiers from the lower and
middle classes for the larger armies and navies. Since government decisions on
war or peace might increase the risk to their lives, the common people found
more reason to participate in politics. At the same time, industrialization and the
resultant wealth produced smaller-scale violence over political disputes. **Guerrilla
warfare** (Spanish for "little war," adopted from Spain's resistance against Napoleon) became more common. Guerrillas were irregular forces, neither recruited
nor drafted, neither trained nor uniformed like the professional soldiers of modern industrial armies. Instead, guerrillas were usually volunteers defending their
homeland, moving easily in and out of civilian populations. With their smaller
and less-well-equipped numbers, guerrilla bands were too weak and too few to
survive open battle against well-armed and drilled armies. They succeeded best
in sneak attacks. For the first time, guerrillas easily acquired more weapons and
supplies through the manufacturing capacity and the transportation options introduced by the Industrial Revolution.

The other form of political violence enabled by the Industrial Revolution was
terrorism. Terrorists used lethal violence in the name of a political ideology. Since
terrorist organizations were not powerful enough to have armies or even guerrilla
forces, they resorted to murder and mayhem on a small scale to change politics. Their targets were often civilians (mostly because noncombatants are easier
to kill than trained, equipped, and alert armed forces). Industrialization enabled
terrorists to travel, both to acquire their weapons and training and then to reach
their intended victims. They saw themselves as champions of the downtrodden.
Civilized regimes treated them as criminals, claiming the use of violence as their
own unique privilege. Yet a successful terrorist could transcend into a respected
statesman of a body politic, just like usurpers of old.

Bombings and assassinations, consequently, multiplied in the nineteenth century. The most famous terrorists in the nineteenth century were those who believed in **anarchism**, the idea that if the growing industrialized and bureaucratized societies were destroyed, a utopian agricultural society would appear. Anarchists blew up government offices and killed leaders to undermine the structures of political trust and obedience that held societies together. Within a few years of the turn of the twentieth century, anarchists had killed a president of the United States, a prime minister of Spain, a tsar of Russia, a king of Italy, and an empress of Austria, among others. Despite these successful murders, anarchists' promise of unrestrained freedom failed to attract much support from industrialized peoples. Anarchism has faded into being noted for its graffiti rather than its influence.

Review: How did competing political ideologies offer alternatives in the nineteenth century?

Response:

FOR THE WORKERS

Conservatives and liberals frequently confused anarchism with **socialism**, a very different movement. Many of them intentionally promoted this confusion, hoping to associate the terrorist anarchists with the socialists. They insinuated that both movements advocated violence, where in reality most socialism of the nineteenth century was nonviolent. Socialists' diversity left them vulnerable to misunderstanding (see diagram 11.1). There existed, and still exist, many varieties of socialism, although many Americans today often lump them all together as one collective bad thing: a dictatorship that confiscates all private property. To the contrary, what socialist movements shared in common was the desire to improve workers' rights and lives. They differed widely, though, in their approach to accomplishing their goal of helping the working class. Whatever their disagreements with each other, different kinds of socialism offered alternatives to the liberalism of the middle classes and the conservatism of the upper classes. What could be bad about helping industrial and agricultural workers and their families?

Well, neither liberals nor conservatives wanted to share power with or redistribute wealth to the masses. They feared that giving more votes and money to

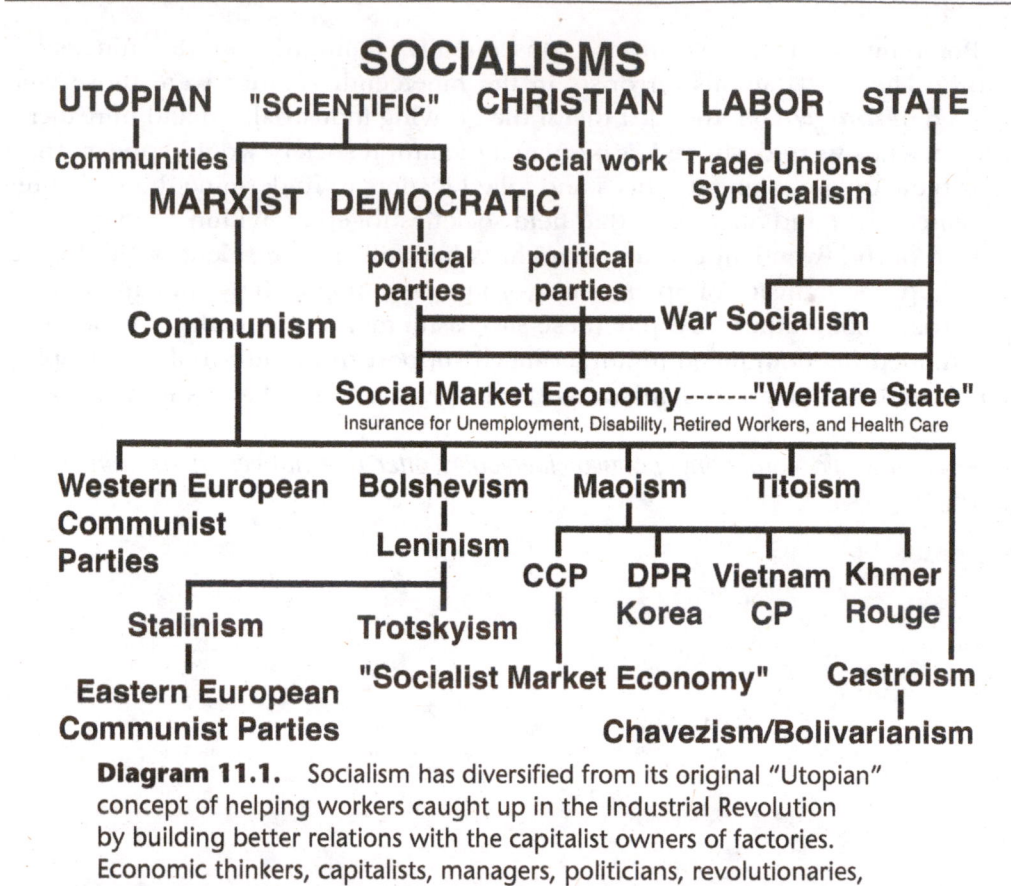

SOCIALISMS

UTOPIAN   "SCIENTIFIC"   CHRISTIAN   LABOR   STATE

communities   social work   Trade Unions

MARXIST   DEMOCRATIC   Syndicalism

political   political
parties   parties

Communism   War Socialism

Social Market Economy ------- "Welfare State"
Insurance for Unemployment, Disability, Retired Workers, and Health Care

Western European   Bolshevism   Maoism   Titoism
Communist
Parties   Leninism
         CCP   DPR   Vietnam   Khmer
Stalinism   Trotskyism   Korea   CP   Rouge

"Socialist Market Economy"   Castroism
Eastern European
Communist Parties   Chavezism/Bolivarianism

Diagram 11.1.   Socialism has diversified from its original "Utopian" concept of helping workers caught up in the Industrial Revolution by building better relations with the capitalist owners of factories. Economic thinkers, capitalists, managers, politicians, revolutionaries, religious leaders, and workers have all contributed to these varieties of programs that have spread from the West around the world. The role of government, marketplaces, nationalism, private property, and worker autonomy varies in each system, many of which are hostile to one another. When labeling someone or some system "socialist," be sure to apply relevant specifics from the wide range of ideas held under the umbrella term "socialism."

the working classes would mean less for themselves. If workers had an effective voice, the freedom of the middle and upper classes to do what they wanted to do would be constricted. Wealthier elites might have to pay higher taxes; they might make fewer profits; they might have to rub shoulders with social inferiors in shops and churches; they might have to grovel for the votes of the majority of all adults.

So both liberal and conservative governments of the nineteenth century tried to prevent class conflict by resisting socialism in any form. Governments have protected ownership of property since the beginning of civilization, originally to benefit the few who possessed most of the farmland. Meanwhile, peasants called for land reform, claiming that all humanity deserved a share in creation. In the industrial age, factories became the most important places of wealth creation. Factories more obviously belonged to those whose investments financed their construction. As a result, politicians and managers passed laws and used force to intimidate workers, with firings, busting heads, arrests, and executions. They excused these policies as "law and order" or "protection of property rights." Workers called for a fair share of wealth, even if they lacked access to capital. Workers organized, demonstrated, and used violence to change the industrial system, calling it "people's justice." For workers, the exploitation suffered under the factory system excused vandalism, murders, and bombings.

The Industrial Revolution was transforming society regardless. Social roles were in flux, and traditional roles based on rural relationships were disappearing. People lost a sense of "knowing their place." Then along came the socialists, advocating social justice and trying to create a more equitable society based on a more fair distribution of wealth. Many socialists also argued for granting equal rights to women and for protecting women and children from being harmed by economic necessity. Socialists rejected both mercantilism and classical liberal economics and argued for better ways to invest capital and reap profit.

Many workers found socialism more attractive than either liberalism or conservatism because it promised to relieve their misery. Factory owners and managers vigorously exploited workers, especially at the beginning of the Industrial Revolution. Workers sweated away in shifts lasting between ten and fifteen hours, with few breaks. Holidays were rare and weekends nonexistent. Lack of education or connections prevented laborers from finding better work than in factories or mines. Ricardo's "iron law of wages," where owners paid workers as little as possible, resulted in whole families toiling away in factories just to make ends meet. Also, because women and children were paid less for the same work done by men, factory owners employed larger numbers of them. The lives of worker families focused on the capitalist's factory, not the domestic fireplace. Indeed, the hearth vanished entirely for most, since available housing was in crowded, unsafe, and unsanitary tenements, ramshackle collections of small rooms.

Between the home and factory, even wretched homes were often better than the dangerous workplaces. Stale air and loud noise were common health hazards for workers. Whirring gears and belts crushed slow fingers and tore off errant arms. Long days only increased the fatigue and carelessness that caused accidents. Injuries on the job were the victim's responsibility, since workers' compensation, health insurance, and even the ability to sue owners for negligence did not exist. The only alternative to working in a factory was being arrested for the "crime" of poverty and being forced to work in poorhouses or debtors' prisons. Various works by Charles Dickens chronicle many of the awful conditions faced by the working class.

The domination of machines became more relentless at the beginning of the twentieth century. The Industrial Revolution culminated in the perfection of the conveyor-belt system and the invention of interchangeable parts. This innovation led to modern mass manufacturing with **assembly-line production**. Henry Ford made it famous when his workers began manufacturing his Model T car in 1905. Workers focused on narrow, repetitive tasks that reduced the time to make a car from a day and a half to an hour and a half. The myth put forward and often believed even today is that Ford increased his workers' pay so that they could all afford the cars. Actually, he raised the wages because the workers needed the incentive to work through the mindless repetition of modern production. Ford's policies at his auto factories notwithstanding, he began a trend toward increased wages and benefits for workers.

Such concessions were too little, too late for many workers, who turned instead to socialism. Socialists proposed their own solutions to solve the workers' plight, since in the century and a half from the spinning jenny to the Model T, most factory owners and capitalists had been unwilling to help workers prosper. Six separate socialist trends competed against the laissez-faire attitudes of the industrial capitalist manufacturers.

The first, **utopian socialism**, called for business leaders to improve working conditions, often explicitly based on economic facts, historical trends, and even moral visions. Historians have labeled it "utopian" because these socialists dreamed of an ideal society, along the lines described in literature about imaginary states called utopias. In 1825, the French nobleman Count Henry de Saint-Simon published his call for socialism, *The New Christianity*, which appealed to the commands of Jesus. His followers originally gave voice to the phrase "From each according to his capacities, to each according to his work." He also called for production to be done for the general welfare, not private profit.

Perhaps the most famous utopian socialist was **Robert Owen** (b. 1771–d. 1858), a Welshman who rose from poverty to become a wealthy capitalist factory owner in Scotland. The "dark Satanic mills" disturbed Owen.[3] In reaction, he began to argue that employers should treat their workers as humanely as possible. They should provide secure housing, good pay, shorter working hours, schools, banks, and shops, while children should be properly educated (see Primary Source Project 11). In consequence, he claimed, productivity would increase. Although Owen continued to make a profit, his attempts to build model socialist communities, such as at New Harmony, Indiana, were less than successful. His ideas did lead, however, to modern co-ops. Few businessmen or politicians paid attention.

The second variant of socialism, whether called **"scientific" socialism**, **Marxism**, or **communism**, would become enormously influential and creatively destructive. Karl Marx and Friedrich Engels initiated their ideology in 1848, the year of so many liberal and nationalist revolutions. Their publication of **The Communist Manifesto** began with the phrase, "A specter is haunting Europe—the specter of Communism." At the time, few knew what these two theorists were writing about. The *Manifesto* called for a proletarian (working-class) revolution. First, the communist revolutionaries would destroy the current regimes, abolishing capitalist private property and bourgeois sexist laws. Then, workers would control the "means of production" (factories, offices, farms) and construct a society of equality and prosperity.

In subsequent years, Marx expanded on this program and soon conceived a whole new way of understanding history. He expounded upon "scientific" laws

---

3. The line comes from "Jerusalem," a poem by William Blake (1804), who calls on the English to do better and create a heaven on earth in their land. Later set to music, it has become an alternate national anthem for England.

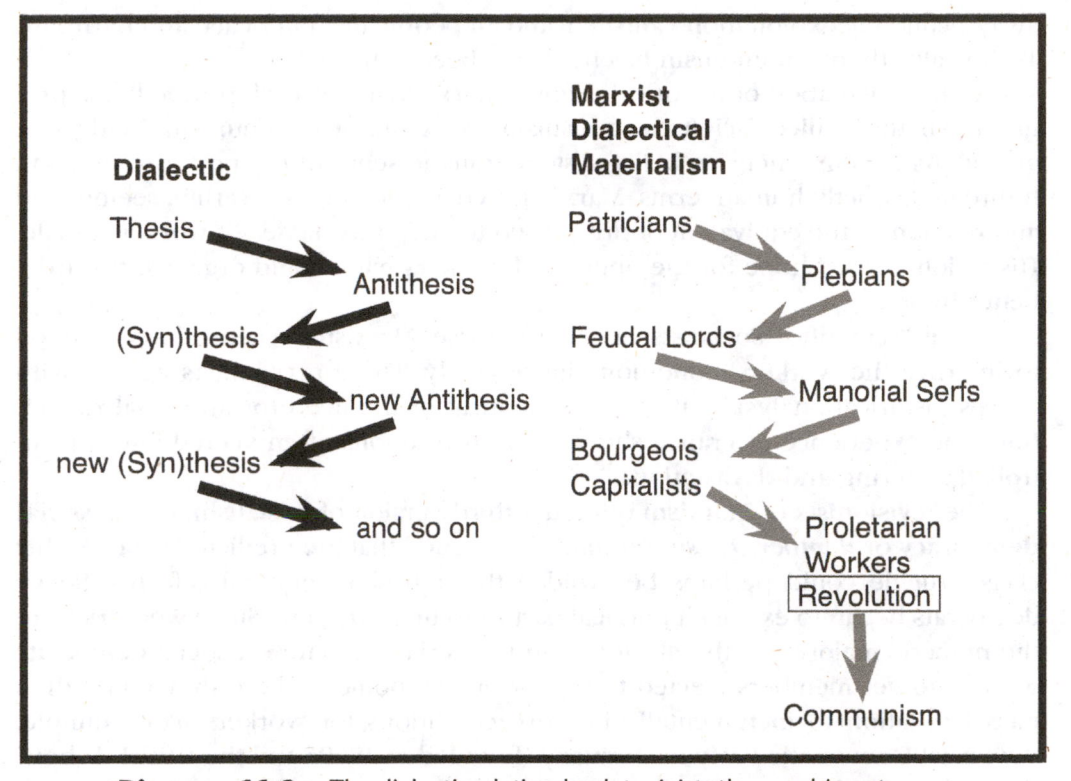

Diagram 11.2. The dialectic, dating back to Aristotle, combines two pieces of information to create a third. The German philosopher Hegel applied this process to the history of ideas, suggesting that a dominant ideology (a thesis) provoked its opposite (an antithesis), and the two clashed to combine into a new synthesis. That synthesis thus became the new thesis, which generated its own antithesis, continuing the process through history. Marx applied the concept to the classes that controlled the means of production. He predicted that his contemporary situation, capitalists against the workers, would lead to a new utopia of communism and the end of history.

that explained the past and the future. Borrowing from the dialectic syllogism applied to history by the German philosopher Hegel, Marx argued that all change in civilization had been the result of class struggle, a process he called *dialectical materialism* (see diagram 11.2). In each historical period, a dominant class (such as the patricians in ancient Rome) had controlled the means of production. An opposite, or antithetical, group then rose in response (such as the rebellious class of the plebeians). Their clash over economic power generated a new ruling and new subservient class. Marx claimed that this "scientific" study of history could be used in his own contemporary age to understand the dominant bourgeoisie and the exploited proletariat. A violent class conflict was inevitable, but this time the downtrodden would seize control of their destiny. The proletarians were to organize themselves for the forthcoming revolution and guide humanity to a new, more just society. Using "scientific" socialism, Marx claimed that humanity would attain communism, defined as a condition in which the state withered away, economic exploitation vanished, and all people lived in peace and harmony. Technically, then, communism has never yet been achieved.

As an explanation of historical change, Marx's vision was sloppy. Still, his program, whether called "scientific" socialism, Marxism, or communism, held great appeal. As a comprehensive belief system, it made sense of the past, present, and future in distinctly human terms. Marx rejected a belief in the afterlife, seeing God and religion as the equivalent of drugs used to keep the masses of workers docile. His vision offered hope for the oppressed workers who would organize toward a better future.

Some "scientific" socialists began to revise Marxism because they wanted to improve the workers' conditions immediately. These revisionists agreed with Marx's historical analysis but became skeptical of the need for an actual revolution. The experience of France showed that revolutions often veered into uncontrolled suffering and devastation.

The revisionists of Marxism offered a third version of socialism, called **social democracy** or *democratic socialism*. They argued that the predicted catastrophic class struggle could perhaps be avoided through slow, gradual reforms. Social democrats began to establish political parties to help workers. Since workers were the numeric majority of the electorate in industrialized nations, social democrats worked to get members elected to representative bodies, where they could then pass legislation to incrementally improve conditions for workers. For example, the Social Democratic Party in Germany (founded in 1869) and the British Labour Party (founded between 1881 and 1906) were the result of this revisionist socialism. Most Western nations, with the notable exception of the United States of America, have prominent and competitive social democratic parties.

The atheism of most "scientific" socialists contrasted with the fourth socialist movement, namely, *Christian socialism*. These socialists based their efforts on the Christian call to "love thy neighbor." Jesus constantly preached about helping the poor and powerless and avoiding the sins of wealth. Pope Leo XIII in *Rerum Novarum* (*Of New Things*, 1891) specifically tried to find a middle ground between the private property absolutists and the more radical socialists. The Roman Catholic Church declared that while private property ought to be protected, owners bore responsibility for the workers. The pope described contemporary workers as miserably exploited by the unchecked greed of capitalism. He proclaimed that the dignity of human beings requires that workers be paid a fair wage (not just a barely livable one). Christian socialists rejected the utopian dreams of new communities and the atheistic historical views of Marxists and social democrats and instead offered a more moderate, even conservative, alternative. They founded organizations for distributing charity to the poor, for helping workers reach a decent living wage, and even for forming political parties (such as the Christian Social Union in Bavaria).

Some Christian socialists joined in a fifth kind of socialism, which was to organize **labor unions** (called *trade unionism* in Britain and syndicalism in France). Labor unions originated out of self-help—workers themselves offering care for sick and old workers. Soon they tried to demand better working conditions and

Figure 11.5. This sign from a Pennsylvania coal mine illustrates the diversity of nationalities brought to build America's industry. (Luzerne County Historical Society)

pay. At first, liberals and conservatives passed laws prohibiting unions from protecting workers' interests. In America, companies hired workers from many different nations so that they could not converse with one another and organize into unions (see figure 11.5).

Workers organized anyway. A widespread movement begun as the First International (Working Man's Association) brought together unions, various socialists, and, with difficulty, anarchists in London in 1864. Disagreements, especially about support for the Paris Commune, ended the organization just a few years later. The Second International in 1889 tried to take up leadership of worker movements, yet accomplished little. Those socialists did break with anarchists, particularly over the issue of violence. Anarchists, ironically, organized their own congress and continued assassinations and bombings. Many in the International actually wanted the workers' lot to get worse, hoping to spark rebellion by driving the proletariat to desperation. Only the collapse of bourgeois dominance, they believed, would begin the revolution. In the meantime, workers still suffered.

By the end of the century, national and local unions had become the most effective means of improving workers' livelihoods. Their use of the strike (work stoppage) sometimes forced managers into giving workers better contracts. Unions carried out tens of thousands of strikes in industrialized nations in the last decades of the nineteenth century. The strikers hoped to gain public sympathy (through marches and picketing), instigate boycotts (refusal to buy the company's products), and prevent companies from hiring non-union replacement workers (called "scabs" by the unionists).

Of those tens of thousands of strikes, most were peaceful. When death and destruction followed, it was usually from the harsh policies of owners and their government allies. In 1897 a parade of unarmed striking miners in Lattimer, Pennsylvania, marched to encourage strikers to join a union. The local sheriff and deputies shot to death nineteen unarmed workers and wounded dozens more. In 1913–1914, intervention by the Colorado National Guard provoked the "Colorado Coalfield War" as strikers tried to get an eight-hour workday from mines partly owned by the monopolist millionaire John D. Rockefeller. Tensions climaxed on 20 April 1914 with a shooting battle called the "Ludlow Massacre," with eighteen workers shot and two women and eleven children dead in a fire. As more workers attacked strikebreakers, federal troops intervened and ended this virtual war by killing dozens more miners. Before World War I, governments almost always sided with the capitalist factory owners when fighting erupted.

A sixth variant, ***state socialism***, came from the liberals and conservatives who had so long and so well represented the desires of the capitalists. Both parties sought to stop the flow of voters onto the rolls of socialist political parties by addressing the workers' needs. The archconservative Chancellor Bismarck in Germany, who wanted economic stability and political order (see chapter 12), took the greatest measures. In the 1880s, while still vigorously opposing the growing Social Democratic Party, Bismarck passed laws that helped German workers (and attracted their votes) by providing for national health insurance, work accident insurance, and even retirement pensions (social security). His opponents attacked these policies by calling them "state socialism." But Bismarck turned the insult into a point of pride. In turn, England ended its inhumane poor laws and legalized labor unions with their right to strike and picket. Poverty came to be regarded as less of a crime or a private failure and more of a social need to be addressed by legislation. Some decades later, state socialism, social democracy, and labor unions would work together to form what would be called the modern welfare state.

In many industrialized states, the passing of child labor laws (prohibiting them from working and sending them to school) revolutionized Western society (see figure 11.6). Ironically, many commoners had actually resisted earlier efforts of enlightened despots to provide universal education. Schooling increased the economic burden of children for their parents because they could not contribute to the family labor force until their teen years. Nineteenth-century elites also discouraged education for all people, perfectly aware that workers with education did not often want to do dirty, hard labor. They feared that workers would aspire to rise above their "assigned" social level. That is why, even in the West today, a university education is considered a ticket to a middle-class lifestyle. While education was not an immediate cure-all, a compulsory, basic grade-school education at taxpayer expense in state schools soon became the norm in the West. Literacy approached 100 percent in many Western industrialized countries by 1900.

Meanwhile, improved production through worker efficiency and new technology made **corporations** more and more powerful. Until the modern corporation, most businesses had been small, local institutions based on families or the partnerships of a few individuals. The corporation became a business where a

Figure 11.6. These boys worked in and around the coal mines rather than going to school. Note that one is missing an arm, probably from an industrial accident. (Luzerne County Historical Society)

multitude of people could pool their capital resources (stockholders) and elect representatives (a board of directors), who then appointed a chief manager (president or chief executive officer) to run the company. The corporation was an artificial legal construction: like a person, it could own property, incur debt, sue, and be sued. Meanwhile, the people who owned that corporation were immune from bankruptcy—only vulnerable for the amount of stock that they held. This legal status granted corporations a huge advantage over mere mortal citizens, since corporations could theoretically "live" forever (only "dying" through bankruptcy). This was, of course, blatant hypocrisy by the ruling elites. They could form corporations that represented and united the voice of thousands of stockholders, but they would not allow unions to represent and unite thousands of workers? These corporations, fed by huge flows of capital, soon came to dominate Western economies both within their home nations and around the world.

Corporations were so successful that many quickly bloated into burgeoning conglomerates, combining several together to be known as **cartels** or **trusts**. These associations conspired to establish monopolies, the control of prices and production of whole economic sectors, reducing or completely eliminating competition. Railroads, steel, oil, and even sugar came under monopolistic control in many nations. While critics in the United States called the owners "robber barons," unfairly enriched by exploited workers, tycoons saw themselves as sharp businessmen justly compensated with unimaginable wealth. Some governments became concerned at this concentration of economic power in a few hands. The dominant "free market" economic theory of laissez-faire (or classical liberal economics) required competition to keep the system fair and efficient. Since cartels crushed competition, governments soon felt compelled to enact antitrust laws to break up the monopolies. Some capitalists cried that this intervention would ruin economic growth, but governments responded by citing the need to protect their citizens from exploitation.

In America some reformers adopted the approach of *populism*, which held that the masses of people have more wisdom and worthiness than the few elites. Populists resented intellectuals as "know-it-alls," capitalists as greedy manipulating predators, career politicians as corrupt, city folk as stuck up, and the Roman Catholic Church as foreign and not Protestant. These ideas increased class friction.

The question of whether making a profit necessarily excludes fair treatment of workers and consumers has been a challenge faced by citizens of the West ever since the nineteenth century. What actions should citizens or their governments take to regulate or promote the rights of human individuals against legal corporations? The bundle of ideas advocated by diverse socialists still provides answers to the world today. Socialism's concept of equality originated in the suffering of the workers early in the Industrial Revolution. Therein lay its appeal, even as versions of socialism underwent varied successes and many failures in the twentieth century.

Review: *How did socialists address problems manufactured by the Industrial Revolution?*

Response:

PRIMARY SOURCE PROJECT 11:
SMILES VERSUS OWEN ABOUT THE GOOD LIFE

Two British reformers during the height of the Industrial Revolution offer different advice on how to create a just society. Samuel Smiles was a Scottish writer and editor who also briefly worked for a railroad company. The success of his advice manual, Self-Help *(1859), led him to go on lecture tours in support of his classical liberal proposals. A generation earlier, Robert Owen rose from modest circumstances in Wales to become manager and part owner of a cotton mill in New Lanark, Scotland. He wrote* A New View of Society *(1813) and began to lecture and call for socialist reform based on his experiences.*

Source 1: *Self-Help* by Samuel Smiles (1866)

"Heaven helps those who help themselves" is a well-tried maxim, embodying in a small compass the results of vast human experience. The spirit of self-help is the root of all genuine growth in the individual; and, exhibited in the lives of many, it constitutes the true source of national vigor and strength. Help from without is often enfeebling in its effects, but help from within invariably invigorates. Whatever is done for men or classes to a certain extent takes away the stimulus and necessity of doing for themselves; and where men are subjected to over-guidance and over-government, the inevitable tendency is to render them comparatively helpless.

Even the best institutions can give a man no active help. Perhaps the utmost they can do is, to leave him free to develop himself and improve his individual condition. But in all times men have been prone to believe that their happiness and well-being were to be secured by means of institutions rather than by their own conduct. Hence the value of legislation as an agent in human advancement has usually been much over-estimated. . . . Moreover, it is every day becoming more clearly understood, that the function of government is negative and restrictive, rather than positive and active; being resolvable principally into protection— protection of life, liberty, and property. But there is no power of the law that can make the idle man industrious, the thriftless provident, or the drunken sober; though every individual can be each and all of these if he will, by the exercise of his own free powers of action and self-denial. . . .

It may be of comparatively little consequence how a man is governed from without, whilst everything depends upon how he governs himself from within. The greatest slave is not he who is ruled by a despot, great though that evil be, but he who is the thrall of his own moral ignorance, selfishness, and vice. The solid foundations of liberty must rest upon individual character; which is also the only sure guarantee for social security and national progress. In this consists the real strength of English liberty. . . .

It is this energy of individual life and example acting throughout society, which constitutes the best practical education of Englishmen. Schools, academies, and colleges, give but the merest beginnings of culture in comparison with it. Far higher and more practical is the life-education daily given in our homes, in the streets, behind counters, in workshops, at the loom and the plough, in counting-houses and manufactories, and in the busy haunts of men. This is the education that fits Englishmen for doing the work and acting the part of free men. This is that final construction consisting in action, conduct, self-culture, self-control,—all that tends to discipline a man truly, and fit him for the proper performance of the duties and business of life,—a kind of education not to be learnt from books, or acquired by any amount of mere literary training.

Source 2: *A New View of Society* by Robert Owen (1817)

According to the last returns under the Population Act, the poor and working classes of Great Britain and Ireland have been found to exceed fifteen millions of persons, or nearly three-fourths of the population of the British Islands.

The characters of these persons are now permitted to be very generally formed without proper guidance or direction, and, in many cases, under circumstances which directly impel them to a course of extreme vice and misery; thus rendering them the worst and most dangerous subjects in the empire; while the far greater part of the remainder of the community are educated upon the most mistaken principles of human nature, such, indeed, as cannot fail to produce a general conduct throughout society, totally unworthy of the character of rational beings.

The first thus unhappily situated are the poor and the uneducated profligate among the working classes, who are now trained to commit crimes, for the commission of which they are afterwards punished.

The second is the remaining mass of the population, who are now instructed to believe, or at least to acknowledge, that certain principles are unerringly true, and to act as though they were grossly false; thus filling the world with folly and inconsistency, and making society, throughout all its ramifications, a scene of insincerity and counteraction.

In this state the world has continued to the present time; its evils have been and are continually increasing; they cry aloud for efficient corrective measures, which if we longer delay, general disorder must ensue. . . .

For such has been our education, that we hesitate not to devote years and expend millions in the detection and punishment of crimes, and in the attainment of objects whose ultimate results are, in comparison with this, insignificancy itself: and yet we have not moved one step in the true path to prevent crimes, and to diminish the innumerable evils with which mankind are now afflicted. . . .

In those characters which now exhibit crime, the fault is obviously not in the individual, but the defects proceed from the system in which the individual was trained. Withdraw those circumstances which tend to create crime in the human character, and crime will not be created. Replace them with such as are calculated to form habits of order, regularity, temperance, industry; and these qualities will be formed. Adopt measures of fair equity and justice, and you will readily acquire the full and complete confidence of the lower orders: proceed systematically on principles of undeviating persevering kindness, yet retaining and using, with the least possible severity, the means of restraining crime from immediately injuring society; and by degrees even the crimes now existing in the adults will also gradually disappear; for the worst formed disposition, short of incurable insanity, will not long resist a firm, determined, well-directed, persevering kindness. Such a proceeding, whenever practiced, will be found the most powerful and effective corrector of crime, and of all injurious and improper habits.

Questions:

- *What are the institutions that affect human lives mentioned by each author?*
- *What kind of personal character and attributes are mentioned by each author?*
- *What room is there for cooperation between individuals and institutions?*

Responses:

For more on these sources, go to http://www.concisewesternciv.com/sources /psc11.html.

THE MACHINERY OF NATURE

The technology that powered the Industrial Revolution was, of course, based on scientific principles established by the Scientific Revolution. Throughout the nineteenth century, science continued to advance in areas other than those focused on profits. Scientists wanted to know more about how the universe worked. While Newton had supplied many answers about the movements of the planets, scientists began investigating other aspects of the earth itself, life upon it, and even people themselves. How did nature function, especially if science left God out of the equation? Scientists were determined to find out by using observable and experimental data to explain the mechanics of nature.

First, another phase of the Scientific Revolution crystallized, as the new science of geology studied our planet Earth. The traditional Western explanation for the earth's history had been drawn from the biblical book of Genesis. Many Jews began their calendar with their calculated date of the beginning of creation, equivalent to 3761 BC. In the seventeenth century, Irish bishop James Ussher recalculated the earth's age from biblical genealogies: he concluded that God created angels and the globe of the earth on 23 October 4004 BC. At first, the influence of scripture inclined scientists to think along the lines of a ***theory of catastrophism*** to explain geology. According to this theory, rare and unusual events of enormous power, resembling divine intervention, explained the features of the earth. While the theory of catastrophism provided some understanding of the earth's past, new discoveries soon called it into question.

Charles Lyell's book *Principles of Geology* provided a new theory in 1829. Lyell proposed the ***theory of uniformitarianism*** to explain the history of the earth, saying that the same (uniform) processes shaping the earth today have always acted to mold the planet. Thus, erosion and deposition; uplift and subsidence of landmasses; deformation by volcanoes, earthquakes, glaciers, and so on have formed every existing landscape. He concluded that the earth was not fixed but in flux. Since many of these processes move infinitesimally slowly, the theory required that earth be at least millions of years old.

Many Christians who interpreted the Bible literally opposed this new theory, since these numbers contradicted calculations based on Genesis. Nonetheless, the practice of science increasingly left biblical explanation out of the equation. Indeed, most scientific evidence collected over the nineteenth century clearly supported uniformitarianism, while almost none backed up catastrophism. Uniformitarianism could, by measurable natural processes, account for the highest mountain and the deepest valley. Just as scientists had come to accept the theories of heliocentrism and universal gravitation, they now embraced the theory of uniformitarianism because it had explanatory power and conformed to the evidence of nature.

Fossils provided much of the evidence for research into the earth's history. Scientists found petrified remains both of contemporary-looking organisms and of strange creatures that did not seem to exist anymore. Excavations dug to build mines, canals, and foundations unearthed more and more fossils. Scientists began to organize these fossilized bones and called the large creatures dinosaurs ("terrible lizards"). As geologists compared layers of rock in which fossils were found, science showed that dinosaurs had lived many millions of years ago before becoming extinct. But how had those monsters, and many other life-forms, died out, while other just-as-ancient species still lived on the earth and under the seas?

Biologists, scientists who studied living things, tried to solve that mystery. The oldest layers of rock showed a few simple life-forms, such as algae. More recent rock layers showed a connected diversity of life, as evidenced by the appearance of new species (namely a scientific category of living things that could reproduce with each other). As eons wore on, some species, like the dozens of kinds of dinosaurs, had clearly gone extinct. Others, like ferns, clams, and cockroaches, had survived into the present with little change. The fossil record showed that overall, life had become increasingly diverse and complex over time. Scientists called this process of biological change ***evolution***.

Christian religious literalists opposed evolution as vehemently as they earlier had denied the age of the earth or, going back to Copernicus, the location of the earth at other than the center of the universe. Evolution, the age of the earth, and the earth's noncentral place in the universe, nonetheless, are scientific facts.

Many nonscientists complained (and still complain) that the idea of evolution is a theory, meaning a mere guess with little supporting evidence. These people apparently misunderstand science. Scientific theories are not just good guesses; they offer comprehensive explanations of the facts. Gravity is a scientific fact, once best explained by Newton's theory of gravitation (and since modified by other theories). Evolution is a scientific fact. Nineteenth-century scientists sought a theory that explained how life on earth had become more diverse and complex over the eons.

Then **Charles Darwin** (b. 1809–d. 1882) provided a scientific theory to explain the fact of evolution. He pondered the issue for years after investigating the unique species of finches, iguanas, and tortoises on the Galapagos Islands off the western coast of South America, which he had visited during his voyage on the ship *Beagle* in the 1830s. Darwin finally published his book ***The Origin of Species*** (1859) only after a fellow naturalist, Alfred Wallace, had puzzled out the same theory. Darwin's ***theory of natural selection***, also called "survival of the fittest," proposed that the struggle of creatures for food and reproduction encouraged change. As living things adapted to their environment and competed with other living things, certain advantageous characteristics enabled them to survive. Whether by stealth, strength, speed, size, or intelligence, some organisms outlived others and lasted long enough to pass those favorable characteristics on to their own viable offspring. Over millions of millennia, small, incremental variations slowly separated offspring into more complex and more diverse species. Species that did not compete successfully, especially when a climate changed, became extinct. The theory of natural selection relies on the natural drives for food and sex as a mechanism for diversity. Thus, Darwin outlined a means whereby scientists could frame their study of life on earth. While modifications have been made to Darwin's theory, all subsequent science has served only to confirm and support the scientific fact of evolution.

This science notwithstanding, some Christians became even more outraged when Darwin's second significant book, *The Descent of Man* (1871), argued that humans were descended from the same apelike ancestors as chimpanzees and baboons. Many Christians were offended by a human connection to beasts and worried what that would imply about the human soul. Without God's creation, nothing differentiated us from other soulless living things. Religious leaders preached that this godless view of nature would lead to immorality.

Their point seemed proven when social theorists used humanity's connections to animals to argue that the "survival of the fittest" was how human societies should be run. This ideology came to be called ***Social Darwinism***, which argued that human ethics should reflect selfishness, greed, and exploitation of the weak because of inherited differences. Thus, the poor deserved their poverty, or the defeated were properly conquered, while the acquisition of wealth and power proved the superiority of the upper class. This skewed rationalization encouraged laissez-faire capitalism, nationalism, imperialism, and racism. The millionaire oil magnate John D. Rockefeller himself pronounced that ruthless competition in business was not evil, but instead reflected the laws of nature and God. His rise from a simple farm boy through hard work, frugality, and secret deals surely proved his superiority. These ideas in turn invigorated materialism and secularism.

Social Darwinism, though, significantly conflicted with the theory of natural selection. Evolution is about adaptation, not dominance. A despised creature like the cockroach survived with speed, stealth, and the ability to eat garbage. Meanwhile, a dinosaur like *Tyrannosaurus rex*, the biggest and meanest carnivore, went extinct because it could not adapt. Evolution has no moral direction—it is merely the description of nature's work over eons of time. Social Darwinists, however, saw social supremacy as the main survival virtue and bruising competition as the means.

Social Darwinists were only one part of a larger movement to apply science to human activity. A third advance in science during the nineteenth century emerged as intellectuals invented the scholarly subjects of the **social sciences**. These fields sought to analyze human beings and then propose theories and laws to explain them. The study of history was tossed into this new category after being bolstered with statistical studies. The new subject of political science clarified the multiplying electoral systems of Western democracies. Sociology studied modern societies, while anthropology examined ancient or primitive cultures. The West's new domination of foreign cultures provided new opportunities for social scientists to investigate and compare diverse peoples.

Of great consequence was the decision of sociologists and anthropologists to scrutinize Christianity. They applied the same methodology of textual criticism originated in the Renaissance to assemble the best versions of ancient texts. The Bible was clearly a collection of ancient writings, similar to those of many other faiths around the world. *Higher criticism* dissected the Bible, instead of viewing it as a perfect product of instantaneously inspired creation by the God of Jews and Christians. Scholars began to read the Bible as a flawed compilation composed by human beings over hundreds of years. This method reasonably explained many of the Bible's contradictions, inconsistencies, and obscurities. From the Book of Genesis alone, odd passages such as two versions of the creation of humans, different numbers of animals Noah took into the ark, and the unusually long lives of the first humans could be attributed to imperfect human editing.

As a result, the growing explanatory power of science and social sciences further weakened the hold of Christianity among the educated elites of Western civilization. In reaction, Christians of all denominations, whether Orthodox, Roman Catholic, or Protestant, began to split into two large factions with two basic attitudes toward the Bible. *Fundamentalism* reasserted standard Christian beliefs that those who did not accept the divine Jesus as their savior were going to hell after death. Their interpretation of inerrancy about the Bible claims that original biblical texts have been divinely created, without error of any kind, and can be clearly understood under guidance of the Holy Spirit. Meanwhile, *modernism* embraced textual and higher criticism to better understand a divinely inspired Bible composed by fallible humans. Modernist scholars accepted science in its worldview and ambiguity in its faith. Nevertheless, Christianity continued its decline as a belief system, although most people in the West remained practicing Christians.

Criticisms of religious belief were made by the founder of psychiatry, **Sigmund Freud** (b. 1856–d. 1939), who focused on religion's incompatibility with science. Freud abandoned much of his Jewish heritage for a more rational look at culture's interaction with individuals. As a psychiatrist, Freud brought new insights into the debate on the origins of and treatments for mental illness. He famously argued that when a person's subconscious drives (id) conflicted with social expectations (superego) and internalized lessons (ego), then neurosis and even psychosis could result. While this scheme is not specifically accepted today by the psychiatric community, it had enormous impact at the turn of the twentieth century. Freud also shocked the "decent" society of his turn-of-the-century Vienna when he unveiled how the human sex drive (libido) could affect mental health. As a result, sex became a part of public discourse instead of being confined behind closed doors.

Through the study of biology, science discovered more practical applications for public health, largely thanks to **Louis Pasteur** (b. 1822–d. 1895) of France. First, Pasteur explained the process of fermentation, which rescued the French wine industry. Additionally, his pasteurization process saved milk from spoiling. Finally, his ***germ theory of disease*** helped save lives. Pasteur's science proved that microscopic organisms, such as bacteria (which are alive) and viruses (which mechanically multiply), caused many illnesses. Many scientists thought the idea ridiculous. But science-based research proved him right. Of course, the germ theory does not explain all diseases, such as most cancers or the illnesses of old age. Still, it has led to a huge advancement in medical cures and disease prevention.

Pasteur's studies also proved the efficacy of immunization through both the old practice of inoculations (giving people a live form of a disease) and new vaccinations (giving a dead or related form). Inoculations (or variolations) had been introduced to England by Lady Wortley Montagu in 1721 after she observed the Turks using them to prevent smallpox. In 1796, Edward Jenner discovered vaccinations after observing that milkmaids got mild cowpox but not lethal smallpox. Many leaders argued against vaccinations as demonic intervention in God's will to kill by disease. Nevertheless, boards of health began to set public policies to bring epidemics under control, especially by mandating vaccinations as well as hygiene. Even so, some objected to such measures based on what they believed were their God-given right not to be told what to do, even if it saved lives (see figure 11.7).

Modern scientific medicine really began after 1850. Antiseptics (which killed germs on the outside of the body) were soon followed by antibiotics (which killed germs inside the body). Those medicines together with anesthesia enabled people to survive surgeries (and difficult childbirth), whose pain and infections had easily killed throughout history. Western medical practices actually succeeded at improving the health and survival of people to a degree unknown by any previous society. Cities that had become more befouled by disease because of industrialized urbanization became more livable. They grew rapidly in population from the increased birth rates of their citizens, instead of the previous movement to town of displaced rural farmers.

Figure 11.7.   British satirist James Gillray produced this cartoon in 1802 as smallpox vaccinations were being encouraged throughout Britain. Because the medicine was based on cowpox, Gillray shows how some people thought they might become infected with cow parts. (NYPL Digital Collection)

Finally, physicists were also busy unlocking the secrets of the universe at the smallest level. Scientists such as Pierre and Marie Sklodowska Curie in France and J. J. Thomson and Ernest Rutherford in England formulated *atomic theory*. Drawing on ideas of the ancient Greeks, modern physicists confirmed that atoms (from the Greek for "not able to be cut") were the smallest part of matter that possesses the properties of an element. At the time, no one could have guessed that the atomic force that bound an atom together could be unleashed to enable humans to destroy all of civilization.

Overall, the nineteenth century had rapidly multiplied the options open to the citizens of Western civilization. The Industrial Revolution drove the economy, with its varied goods, services, and ideologies available to consumers of the upper, middle, and lower classes. Conservatives, liberals, anarchists, and the several flavors of socialists argued for different kinds of political economy, if not revolution. New scientific ideas and inventions opened the doors to the future, while romantics and many people of faith found comfort in the past. Christianity continued to fragment. Despite and because of these internal differences, however, Western civilization would soon reign supreme over most other peoples around the globe.

Review: *How did modern science generate new and unsettling knowledge?*

Response:

Make your own timeline.

1764   **1914**

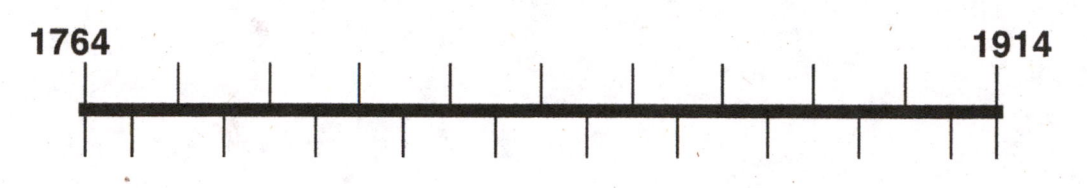

CHAPTER

The Westerner's Burden

Imperialism and Nationalism, 1810 to 1918

By building on the superiority in industrialization and technology achieved during the nineteenth century, Western civilization gained mastery over the world as never before. Western advances dominated the globe through a revival of colonial imperialism and a new sense of self-identity called nationalism. The West's collisions with diverse world cultures both vindicated and challenged its own cultural assumptions. The British poet Rudyard Kipling's acceptance of "The White Man's Burden" (bringing civilization to primitive natives) illustrates the culture's dialogue with itself. Race, sex roles, and nationalism became linked to political control over those perceived as inferiors. Fateful decisions led the West on a path toward the most destructive war the world had ever experienced.

"NEW AND IMPROVED" IMPERIALISM

As covered in chapter 9, Western nations had begun having success with colonial imperialism outside Europe in the late 1400s and early 1500s. The "voyages of discovery" by Portugal and Spain, followed by the Netherlands, France, and England, ended in conquests of distant foreign peoples and seizure of their lands. Disease had given the Europeans a decisive advantage in their conquest of the New World, since the natives of the "Americas" lacked immunities and were killed more often by germs than by guns. On the other hand, many peoples in the Old World of Africa and Asia had resistance to disease, which meant that westerners could gain only small footholds along the coastlines. Many of these peoples enjoyed their own civilizations, which for many centuries had been more advanced technologically, politically, militarily, and culturally than the West. By the early nineteenth century, the Portuguese, Spanish, French, and Dutch controlled only scattered remnants of their once-vast overseas possessions in Asia, Africa, and the Americas. Western colonialism's ruling over distant territories seemed destined to decline.

Only the British Empire reigned over a substantial overseas colonial empire, waving its imperial glory in all the corners of the world, despite the loss of the

BARBARIE   —   CIVILISATION.

Figure 12.1.   The Boxer Rebellion is critiqued by this illustration by René Georges Herman Paul for a magazine. The (here unprinted) caption reads, "It's a matter of perspective. When a Chinese coolie strikes a French soldier the public cry 'Barbarity!' But when a French soldier strikes a coolie, it's a proper blow for civilization." (*Le Cri de Paris*, 10 July 1899)

colonies that became the United States of America. Many British saw their imperial rule as benevolent, promoting peace and prosperity both at home and around the world (see figure 12.1). Their reputation for less violence and cruelty was burnished by propaganda (and destruction of incriminating documents in archives).

Of course, some Western nations were jealous of Britain's success with its colonies. By 1830, Britain's old rival France became particularly resentful of this empire on which the sun never set. The French began to invade new lands across the seas to acquire their own colonies again. In response, the British expanded their overseas possessions. As others joined in, a revived and more powerful wave of colonial conquest, or ***neo-imperialism*** (1830–1914), rolled around the world (see map 12.1).

Most westerners remained confident in their own progress. Because industrial technology had increased their power over nature, most Europeans more than ever believed that their own "civilized" cultures surpassed those of "primitive," "ignorant," and "superstitious" "barbarian" peoples. And still, Christianity needed to replace native beliefs for the natives' own good, even if many Western leaders were hardly religious. They could appeal, though, to Christian voters by supporting missionary work to convert "heathens." Naturally, these missionaries needed protection from headhunters, cannibals, and fierce natives who held their own religious beliefs. So European governments sent in troops. They carried out "pacification" by force. The West's nationalistic pride, smug cultural superiority, and international security demanded global empires.

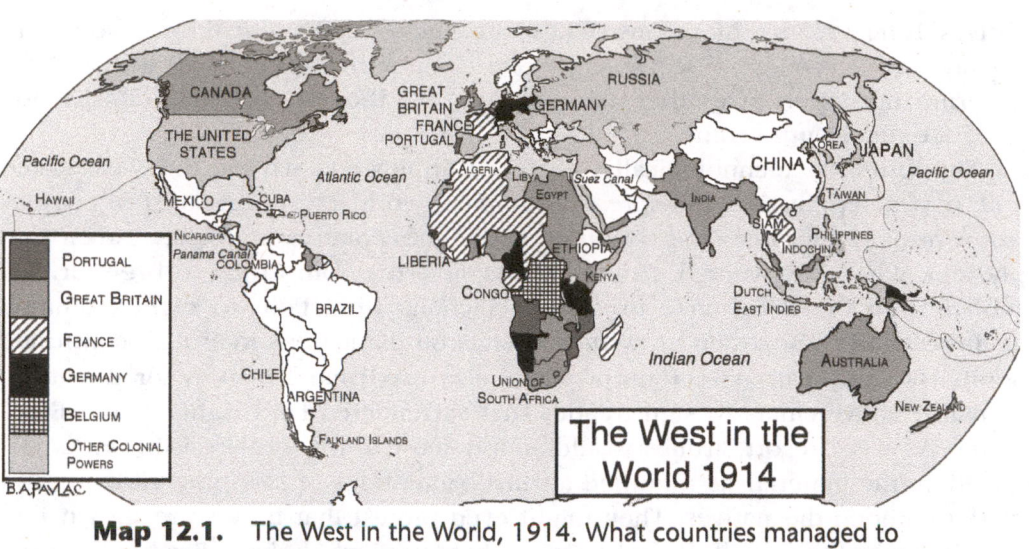

Map 12.1. The West in the World, 1914. What countries managed to remain free of Western imperialism?

The Scientific and Industrial Revolutions empowered this new burst of Western imperialism. First, scientific medicine enabled westerners to better survive foreign climates and their diseases, such as malaria or sleeping sickness. Knowledge about germs and infection, inoculation and vaccination, and the discovery that taking quinine (made from cinchona in Peru) prevented malaria all increased westerners' ability to ward off or cure previously lethal diseases.[1] Second, modern Western military force and technology outmatched indigenous Africans and Asian armies. Even in the previous century, Asians and Africans armed with bow, spear, and machete could barely compete with Western soldiers shooting muskets. By 1850, a few thousand well-trained modern troops equipped with quick-loading rifles and artillery could crush sizeable tribal armies. Third, the new industrial economy demanded new resources to feed the round-the-clock machines and consumer appetites. Businessmen and the politicians who backed them thought that empires would provide both. Additionally, emigrants settling on the vast tracts of underused farmland in distant colonies provided another outlet for the excess population of Europe, easing social tensions at home.

In reaction, economists revised the old economic theory of mercantilism for the new circumstances. While the mercantilism of the seventeenth century had asked for government intervention to foster a favorable balance of trade, the economic *theory of neo-mercantilism* of the nineteenth century restricted itself to asking for government intervention in order to help build empires and open foreign markets. At home, the government was to continue its laissez-faire policy and allow businessmen free use of their private property. But as merchants wandered into the dangerous outlands, they wanted the muscle of Western military forces to protect both their persons and their newly "acquired" possessions from the

---

1. In the British Empire they put the quinine into tonic water and mixed it with gin (alcohol flavored with juniper oil) to create the gin and tonic. Decades earlier, cheap gin had produced a serious intoxication problem among the lower classes. The new gin and tonic made the drink respectable. Modern tonic water, though, does not contain enough quinine to prevent malaria.

natives. It may seem a bit inconsistent for business leaders to call for government to stay out of economic decisions in one circumstance (domestic) and call for government support in another (international), but they have done so consistently since the nineteenth century.

Supported by technologically advanced armies and navies, the West sailed with new determination and spread around the world. Most non-Western peoples lost control of their lives and countries. Sometimes enterprising businessmen simply took what they wanted. British agents stole tea from China to brew drinks, rubber from Brazil to make tires, and cinchona from Peru to extract quinine against malaria. They then grew these plants on plantations in British-controlled South and Southeast Asia. Entrepreneurs also used fraud, bribery, or threats to convince native chiefs to sign treaties that surrendered land rights to the Europeans. As a last resort, armies would simply mow down local resistance. As justification, the imperialists mouthed altruistic intentions of stopping violence and warfare among the natives. They might even protest that they were drawn into empire against their will, forced to make hard, violent choices. Further, Europeans often exploited native ethnic differences, exaggerating them to set the ethnic groups against one another. Such tactics revived the classic method of divide-and-rule. The westerners almost always profited and prevailed.

The intensity of domination varied in three degrees. First, in **spheres of influence**, the natives remained ultimately in charge. In these areas, one Western state would form an alliance and a close working relationship with the native regime, keeping other Europeans out and arranging the best deals for itself. Second, in **protectorates**, the native leaders still held a great deal of authority, at least when it came to running their own society. The Western power became decisive only in foreign affairs and in many economic decisions. Third, in complete colonization, native structures and societies were substantially eliminated, and Western people ruthlessly moved in and took over.

This had been the case centuries before during the colonization of the Latin American states, the United States, Canada, Australia, and New Zealand. Immigrant Europeans shoved the comparatively few aboriginals onto the worst lands. The Dutch colony of **South Africa**, located on the Cape of Good Hope since 1652, also saw Europeans seize from the local peoples the best pasture and farmland. The descendants of the Dutch colonialists even began calling themselves **Afrikaaners**. They saw themselves as Africans, just as the descendants of English colonialists in America viewed themselves as Americans. Meanwhile, the original natives in that region of Africa, San and Khoekhoe, were weakened by smallpox, war, and enslavement.[2]

In most new colonies formed under neo-imperialism after 1830, the natives similarly retained little power and little hope that conditions would improve. In

---

2. How various peoples adopt or are given names determines their status. The San (meaning foragers) were hunter-gatherers, similar to other bushmen or pygmies elsewhere in Africa. The Khoekhoe, whose name means "people people," were pastoralists who often took on a paternalistic and exploitative position over the San. The Dutch insultingly named both Hottentots, probably after their common "clicking" language, now called Khoesan.

most of Africa, the Pacific Islands, and parts of Asia, the minority population of Europeans who possessed the majority of the land and authority restricted the natives to a subservient role—foreigners in their own country. Recent historians, however, see native peoples acting as subalterns, officially subservient to the westerners yet subversive beneath the surface. Westerners at the time merely interpreted natives' lack of enthusiasm for empire as laziness and stupidity.

Some nineteenth-century science supported Western supremacy through racism, supported by poorly thought-out science. Anthropologists divided up the human species into several "races" based on what they thought were shared bloodlines (a special, imagined quality inherited from common ancestors), as demonstrated by such anatomical differences as eye shape, nose length, or skin color. Their studies also "proved" that some races were superior to others. All this science has since been proven to be bogus. Humans belong to the same species, and "racial" differences are insignificant. But the Europeans who believed in racism constructed the idea that they were at the top, part of the "Caucasian race" (named both because some scientists considered that the people who lived in the Caucasus Mountains were the "prettiest" and because many believed humans first appeared there). The British and their colonial offshoots in Canada, the United States, South Africa, New Zealand, and Australia emphasized their "Anglo-Saxon" heritage as notably superior among other "whites" and Caucasians.[3] Social Darwinism argued that the dominance by Europeans allegedly proved their racial superiority. Thus, no matter how hardworking or educated colonized races could become, their unchangeable skin color and "racial heritage" meant they would always be inferior.

The transformation of South Africa opened the door for neo-imperialism. After some interventions during the wars of the French Revolution, the British took over the colony from the Dutch after the Congress of Vienna in 1815. British settlers moved in among the Dutch, confirming a mixed society where the few European colonists dominated the large numbers of transported Asian workers and the many native Africans who still lived there. But the Dutch and English did not get along. When the British outlawed slavery in the South African colony in 1835, thousands of Dutch Afrikaaners left on the Great Trek. They journeyed hundreds of miles inland to escape what they saw as British oppression. The Afrikaaners seized new fertile land and enslaved the native black Africans who had survived recent wars against one another. The Dutch Afrikaaners set up the Transvaal and the Orange Free State as two sovereign Western countries in southern Africa. The Western technology and methodology of these farmers (called Boers) made the land produce great wealth.

The South African conflicts focused the attention of Britain's rivals upon the continent. At the beginning of the nineteenth century, only a few European imperial possessions clung to Africa's fringes, many originating as bases for the Atlantic-African slave trade to the Americas. The French led the new wave. Their

---

3. The concept is also nonsense considering that modern DNA studies show that the average English genes are only about a third from Anglo-Saxons, another fifth from Celts, a tenth from Vikings, and much of the rest from ancient Europeans.

neo-imperialism began in 1830 with "the flyswatter incident." When a French diplomat arrogantly refused to discuss repaying a debt owed to Algerians, the Ottoman governor slapped him in the face with a flyswatter. Outraged by this insult to French *honneur*, France conquered the Algerian provinces and made them part of France. Thousands of French immigrants then began buying land and settling in. They declared a "*mission civilisatrice*," or undertaking to civilize the "barbarians." In reality, most of the Africans who lived north of the Sahara Desert, along the Mediterranean coast, had been civilized for thousands of years without suffering the several centuries of collapse the Europeans had during the Middle Ages. Egypt was one of the oldest civilizations, while Islamic Arab-speaking states had preserved and built on the heritage of ancient Greek and Roman colonization. European imperialists preferred to ignore those heritages, and now had the military power to do so.

It took a few more years for Europeans to penetrate into the interior of Africa. At the beginning of the nineteenth century, the Europeans called Africa the "Dark Continent," partly because they held so little knowledge beyond their coastal bases. They neither knew of nor cared about the rise and fall of many African empires (Ashanti, Mali, Zimbabwe) and kingdoms (Benin, Dahomey) and urban civilizations (Timbuktu, Kano) over the centuries. These political states were often vulnerable to war and conquest from their neighbors with ambition because of the wide ethnic diversity in Africa, home to over fifteen hundred languages (from Afar to Zulu). Economies ranged from hunter-gatherers (Hadza, !Kung, Mbuti) to pastoralists (Maasai, Dinka, Fulani) to agriculturalists (Azande, Abyssinians, Yoruba). Commerce routes, dominated by Arab Muslim traders, crisscrossed the continent, although the closing of Western slave markets had reduced demand for that human product. Diverse ecosystems ranged from the large arid deserts of Sahara and Kalahari to vast savannas and grasslands full of animals, high alpine pastures, and florid tropical rainforests. Tropical diseases spread by mosquito (malaria, dengue, yellow fever) and tsetse fly (sleeping sickness), and worm (you don't want to know) weakened native societies (although they had also kept Europeans out).

Nevertheless, Christians in the early nineteenth century were eager to convert sub-Saharan Africans from a multiplicity of animist and polytheistic religions. Missionaries and explorers began bringing back fascinating accounts. Most famous were dispatches from the journalist Henry Stanley as he searched for the Scottish explorer, missionary, and humanitarian Dr. David Livingstone, allegedly lost in the Congo in 1871. Stanley's dry remark upon finding him, "Doctor Livingstone, I presume," is a statement of the obvious (finding the only European man amid so many Africans). More important, Stanley published exotic tales of African riches apparently free for the taking. Stanley laid the foundation for the seizure of the Congo River basin by King Leopold of Belgium. Dr. Livingstone had wanted to minister to the spiritual and physical needs of the natives; Leopold desired to exploit the region as his own pet colony, plundering it of rubber and ivory. To deal with Congolese who did not cooperate, the Belgians hacked off their hands, following the example of Columbus. Others they raped, terrorized, or shot. Over the next few decades, the Belgians' brutal treatment of natives reduced the population from more than thirty million to less than ten million (see the Primary Source Project at http://www.concisewesternciv.com/sources/psc11a.html).

Western neo-imperialism soon overwhelmed the rest of Africa as other leaders began to follow Leopold's example. The fate of one hundred million Africans changed with the stroke of a pen in 1884. The leaders of Europe convened a meeting in Berlin to discuss the recent Belgian takeover of the Congo. At this Congress of Berlin they defined the ground rules for their **Partition of Africa** (1884–1914). Each interested power was permitted to move in from a specific area of coastline and stake claims to whatever territories it could. During this "Scramble for Africa," the invading nation was to notify other European governments so that they did not stumble into war with one another. The conquest of more than ten million square miles of African lands quickly followed.

Even the traditional rivals France and Britain managed to forget many of their ancient grievances with each other. The French were crossing the African continent from west to east, while the British linked a chain of territories from north to south. This competition intersected in the Sudan and almost sparked a larger war. The French had begun to dig the **Suez Canal**, an artificial waterway to link the Mediterranean and the Red Sea. After the French investors ran into difficulties, the British rushed into Egypt in 1882. They wanted to finish the Suez Canal, which offered a much shorter route to British India than sailing all the way around Africa. Then, in 1885, a Muslim revolt led by the "Mad Mahdi" drove the British out of Egyptian-dominated Sudan. The British General Gordon and his troops died defending Khartoum, Sudan's capital. After the French showed some interest in claiming the Sudan, the British invaded again in 1898. They avenged Gordon by killing thousands of Muslims with machine guns and retook the country. A small French force (mostly of Senegalese troops) slogged across the continent to confront the British at Fashoda on the Nile (today Kodok in the South Sudan). Instead of fighting, the two commanders toasted each other and parted on friendly terms; diplomats then carved up the region for France and Great Britain. This cooperation in Africa soon led to the Entente Cordiale, a British-French alliance.

While the British ended up with the best share of Africa, they faced an unanticipated challenge to their new supremacy in South Africa. The discovery of diamonds in 1867 brought in many new European settlers to the British colony, looking to make quick and easy fortunes. In 1877, the British felt bold enough to seize bankrupt Transvaal (also known as the South African Republic by its Boer citizens of Dutch ancestry). The Boers submitted partly out of fear of the neighboring Zulu kingdom. After the British victory in the Anglo-Zulu War (1879) removed that threat, the Boers fought back against British occupation and won Transvaal's independence by 1881.

Then, in 1886, the discovery of gold in Transvaal unleashed yet another crisis. Many *uitlanders* (European foreigners) flooded into Boer territories in a gold rush. As the British adventurers and then British officials threatened to take over Transvaal and its ally the Orange Free State, Afrikaaners preemptively launched the **Boer War** (1899–1902), which unexpectedly challenged British military supremacy. The Boers fought an effective guerrilla campaign until the British defeated them with a new radical measure, the **concentration camp**. The British rounded up large numbers of civilians whose only crime was being the wrong kind of person (in this case, an Afrikaaner) and confined these men, women, and children in barracks under guard and surrounded by barbed wire. The British thus perfected the concentration camp as a technique of social conquest, which others would later imitate. Tens of thousands of camp residents, young and old, male and female, died from disease and hunger. The British also burned farms and armed native Africans (at least until victory had been achieved). The British won the Boer War, but at the cost of many lives and sharp international criticism. Thus, the Boer War marked the dangerous precedent of westerners fighting other westerners over foreign plots of land.

Despite this crushing defeat, the large population of Afrikaaners still resisted British domination. So the British and the Afrikaaners compromised a few years later with the creation of the **Union of South Africa**. South Africa developed into a Western industrialized nation, although its British and Afrikaaner populations remained a minority. The 80 percent majority of the population (a few immigrants from India, some "coloreds" of mixed heritage, and the large numbers of black Africans) tried to organize their own political participation by founding the (South) African National Congress (1912). Joint British and Afrikaaner rule, however, effectively excluded peoples of non-European ancestry.

In the Scramble for Africa, other Western powers managed to grab different slices to appease their appetites for the moment. While Western civilization had ended the international slave trade, many millions of Africans lived in slave-like conditions under these new European masters in what had been their own countries. France appeared to hold the next-largest share after Britain, yet much was a wasteland of forbidding desert or impassable jungle. The Germans won a couple of key colonies, but they grumbled that theirs did not compare well enough with those of the French and English. They nearly exterminated the indigenous Herero, Khoekhoe, and Nama peoples in their colony of Southwest Africa (today Namibia). Even little Portugal beefed up its colonial presence. Portuguese armies marched inland from centuries-old coastal bases to kill and conquer. The newly unified Kingdom of Italy grabbed a few pieces of Somalia on the eastern Horn of Africa. Regrettably for Italian pride, the Italians tried to invade Abyssinia (now called Ethiopia), which was actually predominantly Christian. The native army armed with arrows and spears decisively trounced the Italian invaders at the Battle of Adwa (or Adowa, 1896). Italians were the only westerners to be defeated by Africans during this wave of imperialism. Indeed, by 1914, native Africans governed only in Abyssinia and to some extent in Liberia. That country was an American protectorate run by Africans whose ancestors had, for a time, been slaves in the United States. Even if very few people from the West migrated to Africa, westerners ruled almost all of Africa for the next half century.

While Africans succumbed relatively quickly to Western supremacy, the Asians experienced more varied levels of resistance. Europeans had been confined to small trading posts in most of Asia since the first contacts by Vasco da Gama of

Portugal in 1498. Only the Dutch control of most of the islands in the East Indies and the Spanish of the Philippines were significant acquisitions.

The first major Asian region to fall was the Indian subcontinent. The Mughal Empire (1526–1857) had dominated most of South Asia after the conquests of Babur (r. 1526–1530), a Turkic-Mongol from Central Asia. Although the rulers were Muslims, they promoted a degree of religious tolerance for Hindus, Parsees, Jesuits, Buddhists, and others. They supported education, literature, and the arts (most famously the Taj Mahal). Later rulers abandoned religious toleration. When the Mughals began to persecute the new monotheistic religious sect of the Sikhs, they in turn organized militarily against the emperors. Then in 1707 a civil war between rivals for the "Peacock Throne" broke out, resulting in many rebellions by local rajahs.

The British took the most advantage of the internecine violence. With Great Britain's victories in the Seven Years' War, it had been the supreme western power in the subcontinent. It ruled indirectly through the East India Trading Company from cities such as Madras (Chennai), Bombay (Mumbai), and Calcutta (Kolkata). British businessmen increasingly decided economic policies in the fractured Mughal Empire.

An odd incident in 1857, however, provided the means and opportunity for British imperialists to gain ascendancy over most of South Asia. A rebellion broke out when the British military introduced the latest Enfield rifle and its cartridges to their native troops, called sepoys. This ammunition was more efficient than the ball and powder of muzzle-loaded muskets. The bullet and explosive charge were wrapped together in greased paper, and a soldier needed only to bite off the paper and load the powder and cartridge in the rifle. Suddenly, the rumor spread among the natives that the grease on the paper was either beef fat or pig fat. The former was abhorrent to Hindus, who believed that cows were sacred, and the latter was repulsive to Muslims, who held that swine were unclean. Thus began the so-called **Sepoy Mutiny** (1857) or, as some Indians call it, the "First War for Independence." Sadly for an independent India, the British quickly rallied and used their superior organization, technology, and Sikh and Gurkha battalions to crush the rebels. The vengeful British destroyed dozens of temples and mosques and killed or injured thousands of innocent civilians. One favorite death penalty was "blowing from a gun," namely binding a rebel across the mouth of a cannon and then firing it.

From then on, the British "Raj" treated most of India as an outright colony, while only a few rajahs managed to preserve their states as protectorates. The British also aggravated the traditional differences among religious groups. They set Hindu, Muslim, Sikh, and others against one another: the classic divide-and-rule routine used by imperialists in all ages. And no matter how much the Indians tried to emulate the British, they could never measure up to snooty school breeding. In their intellectual arrogance the colonial civil servants tried to "improve" agriculture through European practices, which only upset the ancient ecological balance. The result was epidemics and famines. In 1876, Parliament granted Queen

Victoria (r. 1837–1901) the title of empress of India. She reigned over a land she never visited and, like her countrymen, little understood.

Farther east, most of the inhabited islands scattered across the South Pacific became colonies in the second half of the nineteenth century. Europeans wanted these islands as safe harbors to store and provide food, water, and coal for their steamships. Also, many islands were mountains of guano, or bird poop, that was useful as fertilizer. Most islanders could defend themselves only with Stone Age technology and thus quickly lost.

In East Asia, powerful states that in a previous century had possessed sufficient military technology to defend their borders now found themselves outmatched by the West. The most powerful Asian state, the Chinese Empire, had endured many invasions and rebellions since its foundation two millennia before, in 221 BC. The Manchu or Qing dynasty (r. 1644–1911) still had a tight hold on China in the eighteenth century. But many Chinese resented the dynasty because they were "foreigners" from Manchuria, as their name indicates. But the emperors perpetuated the rule of preceding dynasties dating back centuries. Their highly educated "mandarin" bureaucrats managed laws, taxes, and trade, all promoted with public works of roads, canals, and harbors. The peasants had very little power or wealth, but such had been their status in most countries through most of history. The Manchus had also dominated Tibet, Mongolia, and Taiwan (called Formosa by European colonists who were driven out). Yet the Chinese Empire preferred *isolationism*: their foreign policy avoided friendship and trade with nations not under their power. From the cultivated Chinese point of view, the westerners were barbarians who lacked the sophistication of Chinese culture. Chinese merchants wanted very little from the outside world, although they were willing to sell their tea, silks, and porcelain for cold, hard Western silver and gold.

The British and the Americans, meanwhile, tried to find a product that the Chinese would be willing to buy. They worried that the neo-mercantilist balance of trade tilted too much to the Chinese advantage. Ultimately, they found a product that would break open the Chinese markets: illegal drugs, in particular, opium. This highly addictive narcotic damaged the Chinese economy, health, and morality. Nevertheless, Western merchants smuggled opium into China from the fields of western and Central Asia where it grew best. Pursuit of profit surpassed obedience to Chinese law. When the Chinese authorities justifiably confiscated and destroyed this dangerous drug, British merchants complained to their own regime about property rights. The British Empire declared war on China to protect the British right to sell addictive opiates. In the short **Opium Wars** (1839–1842), the Chinese sustained humiliating and decisive defeats by modern British military technology.

The triumphant British imposed "unequal treaties" that opened up China to Western exploitation. Under the concept of **extraterritoriality**, British people and possessions were exempted from native laws and authority (much as foreign diplomats and embassies still are today). Therefore, British merchants and missionaries could do what they wanted. The treaties also forced the Chinese to hand over parts of several key ports, allowing British warships and troops to move at will throughout China to defend British citizens and interests. In the next few years, other Western great powers also bullied the Chinese into handing over these same privileges to them as well. Westerners out to make a profit attacked and under-mined Chinese society.

By 1900, the United States feared that the Europeans might carve up the weak-ened Chinese Empire into distinct economic and political zones. To keep access to markets as free as possible, the United States advocated an "open door" policy throughout China: promising mutual cooperation and no trade barriers among Western imperialists. The open-door policy merely meant that China was open to being bought and sold in little bits by westerners rather than all at once. The Chinese imperial government lacked the ability to resist. The idea of **nativism**, though, provided a rallying point. Nativists argued that current inhabitants needed to be protected against more recent immigrants and foreigners.

In China such opposition to westerners led to the **Boxer Rebellion** (1900). The name *Boxer* came from an anti-Western Chinese association whose symbol was the raised fist. The insurgents attacked foreigners all over China and laid siege to hundreds of diplomats, soldiers, missionaries, and merchants in the foreigners' quarter of the capital city of Peking (today called Beijing). After only fifty-five days, Western troops smashed the revolt and imposed more humiliating treaties on China (see figure 12.2). Shortly afterward, in 1903, the incompetent empress who had managed Chinese affairs for decades died, leaving only a child to inherit the crumbling mechanisms of power. Without leadership, the empire fell to a republican revolt in 1911. Western imperialists stayed and provoked terrible con-sequences in the developing twentieth century (as explained in later chapters).

In Southeast Asia between India and China, **Siam** (modern-day Thailand) managed to negotiate for itself a sphere of influence rather than a more serious takeover. The British had conquered Burma (modern-day Myanmar) to the west, as the French seized Indochina (what would become Vietnam, Laos, and Cambo-dia) to the east. Yet neither side was sure how to dominate the powerful little state of Siam, which was likely to put up a fight. Instead, Siam became a buffer between French and British colonies. It learned from both, although the westernizing influ-ence of the governess Anna Leonowens on Kings Mongkut (r. 1851–1868) and Chulalongkorn (r. 1868–1910) has been exaggerated by modern musicals and films. Siam's forward-looking kings slowly brought Western ways into the country.

By this time, Europeans confidently predicted that their humanitarian burden of looking after the less-advanced peoples of the world would last far into the future. This "caretaking," however, was two-sided. On the one hand, Europeans could point with pride to the construction of a few railroads, roads, harbors, large colonial administration buildings, schools, hospitals, and military bases. Their laws and economics brought a Western order and growth to places once considered by Europeans to be violent, barbaric, and stagnant. Christian missionaries were win-ning converts. And to its everlasting credit, the West ended the international trade

Figure 12.2. "China—the cake of kings and emperors" is a satiric cartoon by Henri Meyer observing how the imperialist Western powers ignore the Chinese as they carve up China. A caricature of a mandarin, a highly trained bureaucratic official, is helplessly gesturing in the background. Considering the cake are Queen Victoria of England, a German general, Russian Tsar Nicholas II, Marianne (a symbol of France), and a Japanese samurai. (*Le Petit Journal*, 16 January 1898/Art Resource)

in African slaves and did much to stop most other slavery.[4] All humans became more connected, for good or ill, than they ever had been before in history. The Europeans even drew on the culture of the new lands and showed appreciation for some of the "exotic" art, artifacts, and literature of "Orientals" and Africans.

On the other hand, Europeans blithely ignored the exploitation, cruelty, and hopelessness created by their supremacy. Many native peoples suffered humiliation, defeat, and death. Although worldwide health and standards of living often improved because of Western medical practices, few noticed how modern transportation helped spread diseases such as cholera and even the bubonic plague. Colonial peoples also lost control of their livelihoods due to business decisions made in distant lands. These global economic bonds only intensified with time. Natives often felt like prisoners in their own countries, as traditional social status and customs vanished. Europeans justifiably outlawed *suttee* (the custom of widow burning in India) while ignoring how their own policies impoverished many other widows and families. Most of the peoples of the world had been fine without Western colonialism before the nineteenth century. No sooner had they been subjugated than they began working to regain their autonomy. Within a few decades, they would succeed.

Review: *How did the Europeans come to dominate Africa and Asia?*

Response:

FROM SEA TO SHINING SEA

While Europeans added to their empires, a new Western power was rising, unsuspected, in the Western Hemisphere. The United States of America, like Russia before it, initially aimed its imperialism not across oceans, but across its own continental landmass. The peace agreement with Britain after the War of Independence granted the Americans most lands east of the Mississippi River and south of the Great Lakes, giving the United States a size comparable to western Europe.

---

4. Very few countries allow slavery as legal, but too many ignore the practice. Interestingly, the Thirteenth Amendment in the United States still permits "penal servitude," namely treating criminals as enslaved.

Yet many Americans believed it was their obvious national purpose, or **manifest destiny**, to dominate all of North America.

Some acquisitions came relatively peacefully. No "Americans" lived west of the Mississippi in 1803. In that year, the new nation practically doubled its size with the stroke of a pen. Napoleon, after losing Haiti, gave up on his own New World empire and sold the Louisiana Purchase to the United States. Neither government in Paris or Washington, DC, of course, consulted with the indigenous peoples about who owned the land. After a second attempt to conquer Canada in the War of 1812 failed, the Americans peacefully negotiated away any rivalry with Britain over mutual borders in the north with Maine or the Oregon Territory. The United States also bought Florida from Spain. To fully control these new territories, however, the Americans would have to relocate or kill many of the natives, who continued their resistance throughout the nineteenth century.

The next large acquisition, from the newly independent Mexico, did not come peacefully. Even before Mexican independence from Spain, American immigrants had been moving into Mexico's province of Tejas, most of whose population was Native American, especially Comanche. These immigrants, called Texians, swore to learn Spanish and obey Mexican laws. But when the Mexicans created a stronger federal government and outlawed slavery, the Texians successfully rebelled in 1836. At first, the United States was reluctant to annex the new independent Texas. A decade later, though, the activist President Polk did so. Armed troops shooting at one another over disputed borders triggered the **Mexican-American War** (1846–1848). The United States was quickly victorious and briefly considered, but decided against, taking over all of Mexico. Instead, the Yankees only confiscated a third of Mexico's territory, leaving the rest of the country as the United States' weak southern neighbor.

Meanwhile, the Indians, or Native American peoples, stood in the way of the United States' unquestioned supremacy of America. Most Indians had been killed or relocated from the original thirteen colonies before the American War of Independence. In the 1830s, **Indian removals** forced nearly all of those who had remained east of the Mississippi River onto reservations on the western side, even though some tried to defend their treaty rights in US courts. While courts upheld their rights, American power expelled them. Next, the California Gold Rush (1848–1859) tempted Americans westward to the Pacific Coast across the Great Plains, which had been acquired in the Louisiana Purchase, and the Southwest, which had been won from Mexico. The natives who lived there fought against the newcomers, whom they saw as trespassers. Rather than honor and enforce its own legal agreements, again the US government rapidly and repeatedly broke all treaties signed with Indian tribes. In a series of **Plains Indian Wars** (1862–1890), superior Western technology and numbers gave the "cowboys" victory over the Indians.

In the popular imagination of Western civilization, images of these conflicts were colored with contradictions. "Noble savages" might seem to be either tragic heroes or barbaric "redskin" murderers. Were "civilized" men and women on the frontier heroes who embodied liberty and self-reliance as they tamed the wilderness, or were they ruthless exterminators of women and children as they stole Indian land? Either way, by the end of the nineteenth century, European Americans in the United States and Canada had killed most Native Americans or the First Nations peoples and confined the remnants to reservations with near-worthless land. Only the "closing" of the American frontier meant that settlers could no longer simply take land from the original inhabitants.

For the time being, though, with both so much good farmland available and new factories being built, immigration swelled America's population. The rapid arrival of so many immigrants fed feelings of populism, which claimed to promote simple virtues through connections to the land and "traditional" culture. Some populists adopted nativist policies that were actively hostile to immigrants, fearing that new foreigners would steal land and jobs.

As Americans completed their domination of the Indians, some began to consider whether opportunities of manifest destiny could be extended beyond the shores of North America. Since 1823, the United States (with the support of the United Kingdom of Great Britain) had upheld the Monroe Doctrine, which prevented the Europeans from reintroducing colonial imperialism to Latin America (see the next section). Increasingly, though, the United States began to see the Western Hemisphere as its own imperialist economic sphere.

The United States gained strength through its industrialization, while Latin America had remained largely agricultural, which suited the British whose trade dominated the region. Soon US merchants and politicians intervened with their own "dollar diplomacy," using American economic power, whether through bribery, awarding of contracts, or extorting trade agreements, to influence the decisions of Latin American elites. Subservience to Western capitalists earned Central American governments the nickname "banana republics," coined by the writer O. Henry in 1904. At the end of the nineteenth century, American corporations transplanted bananas, which originated in Southeast Asia, to cultivate in Central America. Under the American business plan, peasants who had grown corn to feed their families instead became laborers who harvested bananas to feed foreigners. If workers in Caribbean or Central American states resisted, the northern giant would send troops to occupy their country and protect American property and trade. As a result of these "Banana Wars," US marines occupied countries like the Dominican Republic, Haiti, and Nicaragua, then propped up corrupt dictators who exploited their people but maintained friendly relations with the "big brother" to the north.

At the same time, US interests looked westward to possibilities for profit in the Pacific. Even before the Civil War, Americans began grabbing small islands (see map 12.2). America's first major victim was **Japan**, which almost suffered the same fate as its exploited Asian neighbor, China. The cluster of islands that the Japanese themselves called the Land of the Rising Sun had maintained an isolationism policy for centuries. Since the early 1600s, the Tokugawa dynasty (hereditary military dictators, called shoguns) had lorded over a well-ordered, stable, closed society in the name of powerless figurehead emperors. Samurai warriors ruled as nobles over peasants. In the first age of imperialism, Japan had tentatively

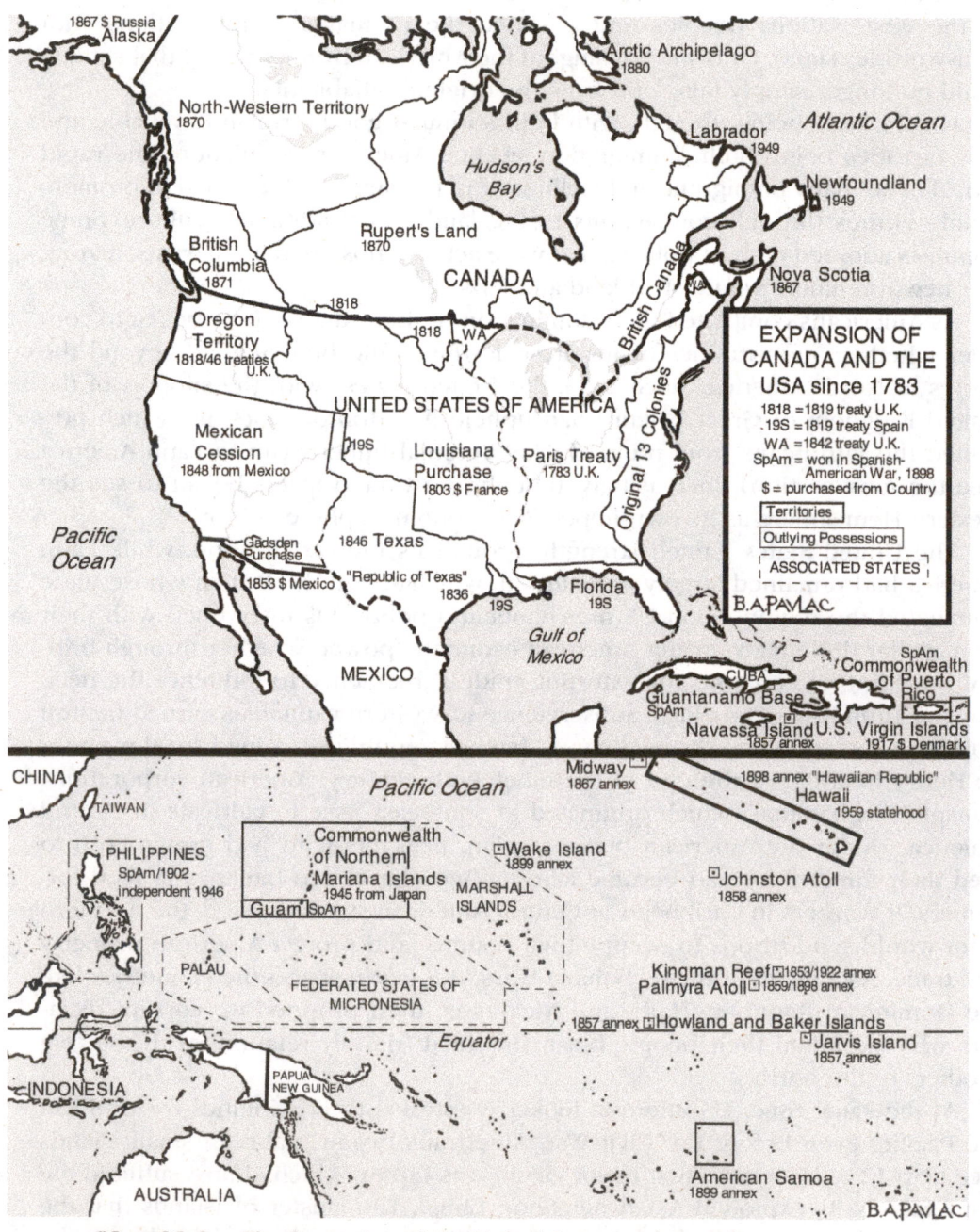

Map 12.2. The Expansion of the United States and Canada.

welcomed contact with Western explorers, traders, and missionaries. By the late 1600s, though, the shoguns killed and expelled Europeans, then shut the borders to Western influence. After that, the Japanese permitted only one Dutch ship once a year to enter the port of Nagasaki for international trade. Otherwise, the Japanese wanted to be left alone.

That isolation ended in 1853 when American warships under the command of Commodore Matthew C. Perry steamed into Tokyo Harbor. Perry demanded the Japanese open trading relations with the United States or else he would open fire with his modern cannons. Ironically, the government of the Tokugawa shogun had destroyed most firearms, leaving Japan defenseless. Fearful Japan submitted to a treaty loaded with extraterritorial exploitation, just as had China. The British, French, Russians, and all the others soon followed the Americans to share in the spoils.

Despite this forced opening of its borders, Japan ended up doing something few other non-Western countries could: it rapidly westernized. The Japanese replaced the discredited Tokugawa shogun with the figurehead emperor during the **Meiji Restoration or Revolution** (1868). Then the Japanese traveled out into the world in droves and learned from the West about what made its civilization so powerful. The British taught the Japanese about constitutional monarchy and the navy. The Americans trained them in modern business practices. The French enlightened them about Western music and culture. The Germans drilled them on modern armies. Within a generation, the Japanese revolutionized their country to make it almost like any other Western power.

The name *Meiji Restoration* is a misnomer, however, since the Meiji dynasty was not so much restored to power as transformed in purpose. Before the restoration, the emperors had drifted through a shadowy, ineffectual existence under the shoguns (like the "Mikado" of the contemporary Gilbert and Sullivan operetta). Now the emperor became a godlike figure who united Japanese religion with Japanese patriotism, much as Alexander or Augustus had done for the Greeks and Romans. This deified monarchy was the only unmodern move made by the Japanese. Otherwise, Japan plunged into a relatively smooth Western revolution, easily crushing the few samurai who resisted. Japan's equivalent of the commercial, intellectual, scientific, industrial, and English/American/French political revolutions was all accomplished in short order. The emperor's subjects soon sought to honor him with an empire, imitating what the British had done for their kings and queens. Thus, the westernization of Japan had enormous consequences for the twentieth century.

At the turn of the twentieth century, the United States went on an imperialistic spree. Looking for an excuse, the Americans seized upon the explosion of the US battleship *Maine* in Havana Harbor to start the **Spanish-American War** (1898).[5]

---

5. The American battle cry of "Remember the *Maine*" expressed a feeling of vengeance similar to the Texan "Remember the Alamo." Unfortunately, the *Maine* should properly be remembered as an example of yellow journalism where the government and media together sensationalized the incident to whip up war fever. Studies of the wreck have shown that its destruction happened by accident, not a nefarious Spanish conspiracy (which made no sense anyhow).

American victories added Puerto Rico and the Philippines as colonies and Cuba almost as a protectorate. President William McKinley partly justified the seizure of the Philippines with the need to convert the native islanders to Christianity. Ignorant Americans apparently did not know that most Filipinos were already Roman Catholic. When many Filipinos fought back with a guerrilla war, US forces ended resistance by resorting to concentration camps. Hundreds of thousands of Filipinos died of disease and malnutrition in the badly managed camps. McKinley also annexed Hawaii, where American pineapple and sugarcane corporations had seized power from the native Queen Liliuokalani (r. 1891–1893).

The next president, Theodore Roosevelt (r. 1901–1909), suggested a corollary to the Monroe Doctrine, that the United States would use force to counter European economic claims in Latin America (thus keeping the European imperialists out). In 1903, when Colombia refused the American offer to build a canal through its province of Panama, the United States helped provincial leaders stage a rebellion. The grateful leaders of Panama gave control of a canal zone to the United States. American know-how finished the Panama Canal by 1914, although that extraordinary effort killed over five thousand workers brought in from the Caribbean and Europe. Many died from yellow fever, until science explained its spread by mosquitoes. Medical corps then fought the disease with protective nets for sleeping and draining stagnant water sources.

Such expansionist efforts showed how Americans could behave just as badly as the rest of the westerners. Most Americans, however, have usually seen themselves as somehow different, confident in their rugged individualism, creative opportunism, compassionate humanitarianism, and eager mobility. This concept of moral superiority to the other Western and world cultures is called ***American exceptionalism***. This idea resembles the common Western exceptionalism that had supported imperialism since the Renaissance, where the stronger deserved to rule over the weak. The American version asserts that manifest destiny reflects a God-given calling and that American motives and democratic institutions are more pure and generous than those of contemporary imperialist powers. Some historians have suggested that the United States does indeed differ from European states due to its origins as a society of immigrants seeking freedom and economic opportunities in an empty place with plenty of land and natural resources (although Canada, Australia, and New Zealand offer comparable histories).

History shows, however, that American success too often came from brutal methods to dominate that land and seize resources, a record that most Americans do not acknowledge. It is no coincidence that the United States began its global imperialism right after the Plains Indian Wars had finally ended with the total defeat of the Native Americans. Most American pioneers were unaware of the consequences of acquiring so much influence over so many peoples, first at home and then abroad; they noticed only the benefits of growing wealth and prosperity. American imperialism had made the United States one of the leading Western powers by 1914, poised to become the most powerful country in the world. But with power comes responsibility, and the United States would only slowly come to learn this lesson in the twentieth century.

Review: How did the United States of America become a world power?

Response:

NATIONALISM'S CURSE

While imperialism cobbled together widespread empires, a new idea was transforming politics in Europe. As seen in the experience of the United States, Western imperialism merged with the new ideology of *nationalism*. This idea decreed that states should be organized exclusively around ethnic groups. Nationalists believed that a collection of people sharing ethnicity, called a nationality, is best served by having its own sovereign state. The Industrial Revolution's empowerment of the masses further affected the choices of dividing people into states. Many nationalists argued that the masses of people from the bottom up should define what makes a country, especially since the aristocratic and royal dynasties who ruled from the top down often came from foreign ethnic groups. Some dynasties, though, took the lead in promoting nationalism, themselves setting the criteria for determining nationalist characteristics. Nationalism's earliest proponents hoped that it would usher in an era of fraternal peace, as different nations learned to respect one another despite their cultural differences.

Tragically, the emphasis on nationalism has instead more often resulted in increased international conflict. These clashes derive from a basic principle:

> **The greatest problem for nationalism is how to define exactly who belongs and who does not.**

Including some people in a group while throwing out others created tensions. Each ethnic identity varies according to its definers. Ethnicity may be constructed using geographic location, shared history, ancestry, physical characteristics, political loyalty, language, religion, fashion, or any combination thereof. Language was often the starting point, as cultural builders collected fairy tales and songs that contributed to a unique legacy. The increasing level of literacy meant that education reformers imposed one dialect on all people in the "nation," enforcing linguistic conformity.

Even many historians wrote to support the creation of national identities. History books specified the heroes and villains, military victories and defeats on the road to the nineteenth-century nation-state. If their nation was successful, historians could celebrate all the virtues that led to national unity. If their ethnic nationality had failed to achieve statehood, historians would explain all the reasons for failure, usually blaming foreign nationalities. In these endeavors, scholarship became propaganda supporting patriotism and nation forming. As one historian has noted, nationalities are "imagined communities," where people pick and choose criteria that define belonging. In schools and academic institutes, in the theater and novels, nationalists transmitted the supposed identity of a particular nationality.

Any or all ethnic groups exist as long as either its members or outsiders say they do. Of course, the same could be said of other social constructs such as caste, class, gender, nationality, or being human. At its most extreme, nationalism blended with racism. People thought of ethnic traits, like race, as something inherited and therefore unchangeable. Interest groups and political parties often organized around nationalist and racist ideas, embracing those who belonged and hating those who did not, without any possibility of finding common ground. Having an "other," an enemy, helped to build social cohesion around what one's own ethnicity was not. Nationalist political histories of nation building became illustrious stories of destined greatness for the victors or tragic tales of grievance for the losers.

At the beginning of the nineteenth century, Metternich's conservative decisions at the Congress of Vienna had dismissed nationalist dreams. Each of the five great powers present at the congress included many people who did not fit the "ethnic" name of the state. Centuries of conquest and migration had left a very jumbled Europe. In the Austrian Empire, no one ethnic group was in a majority, as Germans, Magyars, Italians, Slavs (most importantly Czechs, Slovaks, Croats, and Poles), and others vied for the attention of the Habsburg emperor. Russia also included many different ethnic groups, including the Asians in Siberia in the east, Turks in the southeast, and Balts in the northwest, as well as the Slavic Poles and Ukrainians in the west. Prussia did have a majority population of Germans, but Roman Catholics of the Rhineland felt no sense of "Prussianness," nor did most Danes in the north and the large numbers of Poles and Wends (non-Polish Slavs in eastern Germany). Great Britain locked many disgruntled Scots, Irish, and Welsh into a "United Kingdom" with the English. Even France, which might seem the most cohesive, had Basques in the southwest, Bretons in the northwest, and Alsatian Germans in the east, as well as speakers of various dialects and "*langues*," none of whom wanted to learn the mandated word for *patrie* (fatherland). Most of the smaller countries of Europe likewise lacked absolute ethnic homogeneity.

Liberals supported nationalism early in the nineteenth century. They neither noticed the ethnic tensions in Great Britain (with the Scots, Welsh, and Irish preserving their distinctive traits) nor acknowledged the chauvinist oppression of French patriots. The decisions made at the Congress of Vienna; the clumsy German Confederation; and the backward multiethnic absolutist Austrian, Russian, and Ottoman Empires contradicted the bourgeois values of political participation and moneymaking opportunities. So liberal nationalists drew a simple conclusion:

If the French have France, the English have England, and even the Portuguese have Portugal, why shouldn't our ethnic group have their own Ethnicgroupland?

Surprisingly, the nationalist spirit first coalesced into reality across the Atlantic Ocean. On the French colony of Saint-Domingue on the Caribbean island of Hispaniola, enslaved people led a nationalist revolt between 1789 and 1804 to found an independent **Haiti**. In 1825, sore loser France blockaded the island nation, despite the Monroe Doctrine. They forced Haitians to pay an indemnity. Payments totaling $560 million were only completed in 1947. Recent scholars estimate that if the money had stayed and been invested in-country, it would have been worth over $115 billion.

While Western powers long refused to recognize Haiti, its successful rebellion (and Napoleon's invasion of Spain in 1808) helped inspire the **liberation of Latin America** (1810–1825) from Spanish and Portuguese colonial imperialism. The descendants of European conquistadors and colonizers, known as Creoles (or *criollos*), slowly found their interests diverging from either the distant imperial mother countries of Spain and Portugal or the annoying and arrogant new arrivals called *peninsulares*. Many Creoles formed juntas, groups of elites who seized power from colonial administrators. In 1811, the most famous liberator, Simón Bolívar (b. 1783–d. 1830), fought for a free Gran Colombia (which later broke up into Venezuela, Colombia, Panama, and Ecuador. Meanwhile, José de San Martín, "the Liberator," freed his homeland of Argentina along with Chile and began to fight for Peru. San Martín then retired, leaving Bolívar to complete the independence of Peru and Bolivia (later named after him). The success of other freedom fighters helped create Mexico, the United Provinces of Central America, Paraguay, Uruguay, and Brazil. By 1825, only a few islands in the Caribbean Sea remained of what had once been Spain and Portugal's vast empires in the Americas (see map 12.3).

The newly independent countries claimed to aspire to democracy, but their presidential systems (modeled on the US Constitution) often instead led to strongmen called *caudillos* who generally favored a few powerful interest groups to the disadvantage of both others and the citizens as a whole. Some political violence continued, usually confined to civil wars or insurgencies. Notably, the United Provinces of Central America broke up by 1841 into the separate states of Honduras, Guatemala, Nicaragua, El Salvador, and Costa Rica.

The leaders of these new Latin American nations possessed no significant ethnic differences from one another, except for geographic location. The elites all still spoke the Spanish of the mother country (or Portuguese in Brazil), wore similar styles of clothing, practiced the same politics and economics, and worshiped as Roman Catholics. People of diverse ancestry lived lower down the political and social hierarchies. People placed at the bottom were usually the native "Indian" inhabitants and the "Black" peoples imported from Africa to be enslaved.[6] In the middle of the social scale were large numbers of *mestizos* (meaning of "mixed"

---

6. The great majority of the millions of enslaved people in the Atlantic-African slave trade were shipped to Caribbean islands and Brazil. Abolition of slavery in the Americas began in the 1820s and ended with Cuba in 1886 and Brazil in 1888.

Map 12.3. The Liberation of Latin America, Early Nineteenth Century. Only some of the many still-independent native peoples are named on the map. What prevented their conquest and assimilation by Westerners?

Indian and European lineage) in countries such as Mexico, while other countries had "mulattoes" (a term of unknown origin and best avoided today) of "mixed" African and European ancestry. Brazil's government eventually defined people according to five categories: white, brown, black, Asian, and indigenous. Each of the new Latin American countries had to deal with these ethnic diversities and fabricate nationalist patriotic identities different from neighboring states.

To the north, the United States endured its own major nationalist ethnic conflict with the **American Civil War** (1861–1865). This war decided whether the United States would survive united as one nation or divide into two or more countries. The country's very name, "United States," revealed the ethnic divisions at its origin. While some citizens called themselves American, more were likely to identify with their state, as a Virginian or a New Yorker. Regional differences concerning slavery sharpened these distinctions. Southerners, even those who were not slaveholders, defended their "peculiar institution" because that was how Southerners defined themselves. Under this pressure, the delicate balance among federal, state, and individual rights broke down.

In the war that followed, the northern Union defeated the southern Confederacy because of the North's superior numbers, technology, and President Abraham Lincoln's determination. Even so, people emancipated by the war were supposed to get forty acres of farmland and a mule. Few did. Even worse, the reaffirmed federal unity did not entirely eliminate Southern ethnicity, since resentment still festered long after defeat. "Jim Crow" laws reduced Blacks to second-class citizens. Even a century after the war, sympathizers of the Confederacy flew flags and raised statues to honor the rebellion and to intimidate African American descendants of slavery. Only after 2016 did protests about some of these memorials lead to the removal of many such symbols.

Back in Europe, the failures of the revolutions of 1848 weakened the liberal alliance with nationalism, but conservatives then adopted the idea. Nationalism appealed to the conservatives' inclination to look to the past for guidance. Indeed, nineteenth-century historians began to collect and assemble imaginative histories of ethnic groups that they argued were the forebears of modern nationalities. They collected source documents and organized them. Historians in those countries that represented a nationalist victory (for example, England or France) attributed success to cultural or racial superiority. Even historians of ethnic groups excluded from power (for example, the Irish and the Basques) adopted nationalistic perspectives, since they could glorify some distant heroic freedom that had been squelched by political tragedy or unjust conquest. The Romantic movement heavily contributed to these efforts. In addition, conservatives saw how exploiting the passion growing from nationalism could empower themselves. Conservative leaders applied **Realpolitik**, or pragmatic politics, doing whatever was necessary to achieve a stronger state.

Italy was an early success for nationalism in Europe. Of course, there had never really been a country called Italy, at least not like the one envisioned by its nationalist proponents. Italian history began with Rome and its city-state, which quickly became a multiethnic empire. In the Middle Ages, no single kingdom ever included the entire Italian Peninsula. Since 1494, various principalities there had

Kingdom of Sardinia-Savoy-Piedmont	Kingdom of Prussia
Revolutions of 1848-1849	
King Victor Emmanuel II Savoy-Carignano 1849-1878 Prime Minister Camillo di Cavour 1852-1861	
Austro-Piedmontese War 1859-1860 Garibaldi conquers Kingdom of Two Sicilies 1860 **Kingdom of Italy** Turin becomes capital 1861	King Wilhelm I Hohenzollern 1861-1888 Minister President Otto von Bismarck 1862-1890
Florence becomes new capital 1865	Danish War 1864
Seven Weeks War 1866 adds Venice	excludes Austria **North German Confederation**
Franco-Prussian War 1870-1871 adds Rome which becomes new capital 1871	adds southern German states **Second German Empire** Berlin becomes capital 1871

Diagram 12.1. The national unifications of Italy and Germany in the nineteenth century share similar developments and certain wars.

been dominated by foreign dynasties—the French, the Spanish, and the Austrians—while the popes clung desperately to their Papal States.

In the wake of the failed revolutions of 1848, many Italian nationalists called for a Risorgimento (resurgence and revival) of an Italian nation-state. From 1848 to 1871, the Kingdom of Sardinia-Savoy-Piedmont spearheaded unification. Conservative prime minister **Count Camillo di Cavour** (r. 1852–1861) proposed a scheme for unification to his absolutist monarch, King Victor Emmanuel II. First, they would modernize and liberalize Sardinia-Savoy-Piedmont. Then several well-planned military actions would topple both Habsburgs in the north and the petty regimes in the rest of the Italian Peninsula (see diagram 12.1).[7]

The scheme succeeded. The king graciously granted his own Kingdom of Sardinia-Savoy-Piedmont a constitution and founded a parliament, which, weak as it was, surpassed what most Italians had had before (namely, no legislatures at all). The Piedmontese government built roads, schools, and hospitals. Other Italians began to admire the little northern kingdom. Yet Cavour's sponsorship of the republican mercenary **Giuseppe Garibaldi** almost derailed the plan. In 1861, Garibaldi

---

7. The worst battle of the Austro-Piedmontese War was Solferino (24 June 1859), where clashed two armies commanded by emperors: Emperor Francis-Joseph of Austria against Allied French-Piedmontese forces led by Emperor Napoleon III. The evening after the slaughter, Jean-Henri Dunant, a Swiss citizen who had been trying to run a business in colonial Algeria, came across the tens of thousands of unattended dead and wounded. To better aid victims of disaster and war, he founded the International Red Cross (1863) and got the first Geneva Convention (1864) signed to create more civilized rules of warfare.

and his thousand volunteers, the "Red Shirts" (named after their minimalist uniform), were supposed to invade Sicily and cause disturbances that would illustrate the need for Piedmontese leadership in Italian politics. But Garibaldi swiftly conquered the entire island. Then he sailed to the mainland, where he took control of the Kingdom of Naples and even marched on Rome itself. Piedmontese armies rushed south to meet him, and Cavour managed to convince Garibaldi to hand over his winnings to a united Kingdom of Italy ruled by King Victor Immanuel.

From there, a few more stratagems were required to round out the new kingdom. Cavour prevented French intervention by bribing France with the provinces of Savoy and Nice. Then in 1866, Italy, France, and Prussia defeated the Habsburgs and forced them to surrender Lombardy and Venice. The last major obstacle to Italian unity was the papacy. Popes had possessed political power in central Italy since the fall of Rome in the fifth century, a control further consolidated by the Donation of Pippin and Charlemagne in the ninth century. A thousand years later, the popes lost their political rule. In 1870, necessities of the Franco-Prussian War required the French troops protecting the Papal States to return home. The royal Italian government seized control and made Rome the kingdom's capital. The resentful pope forbade Roman Catholics to cooperate with the Kingdom of Italy. Nonetheless, a united Italy soon took its place among the great powers (see map 12.4).

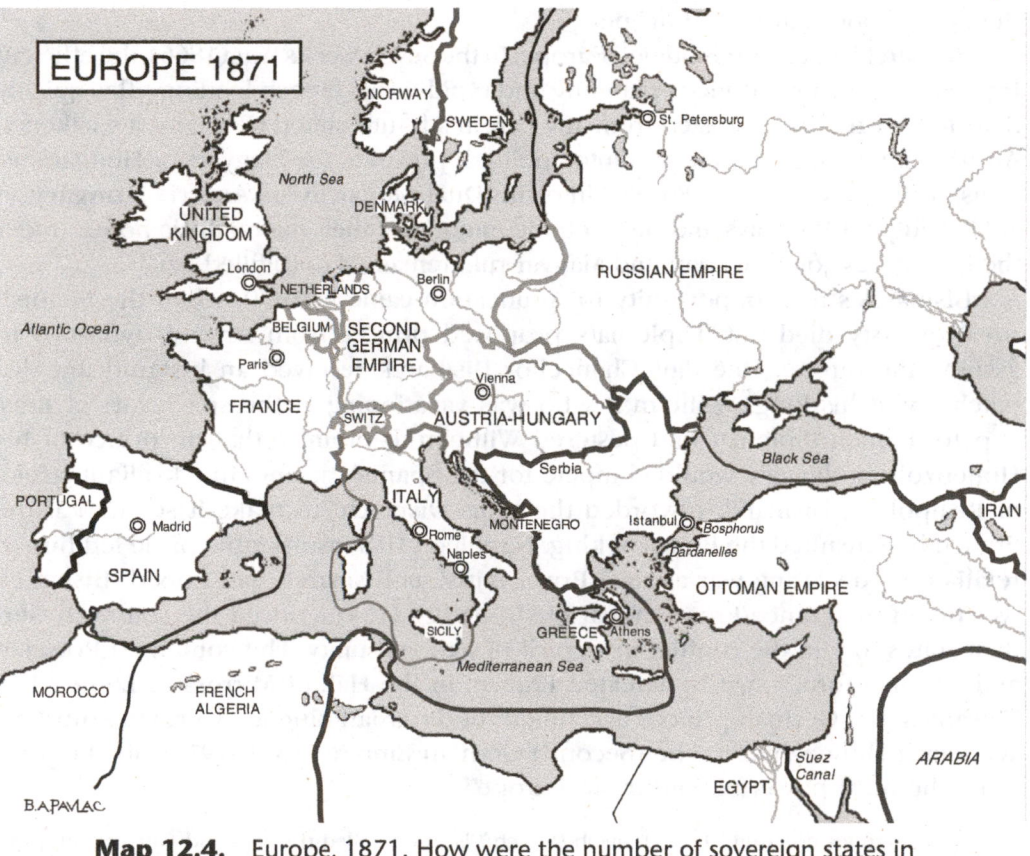

Map 12.4. Europe, 1871. How were the number of sovereign states in Europe being reduced?

The unification of **Germany** (1862–1871) saw a similar process. Unlike Italy, there had actually been a united Germany back in the early Middle Ages, but it had quickly expanded into the loose union of the Holy Roman Empire, which also included northern Italy, Burgundy, Bohemia, and the Lowlands. After the Wars of the Coalitions against revolutionary France had shattered the Holy Roman Empire, the German Confederation replaced it in 1815. This fragile union never functioned well, largely because of the rivalry over leadership between Prussia and Austria. The liberal attempt to create a unified Germany through the Frankfurt Parliament in 1848 failed completely. In turn, a conservative leader succeeded.

From 1862 to 1890, Otto von Bismarck served the king of Prussia as chancellor (prime minister). The Junker (or Prussian aristocrat) had liked neither the Frankfurt Parliament nor the Confederation. Imitating Cavour, Bismarck planned and carried out the unification of Germany in service to the Hohenzollern dynasty of Prussia, purposefully excluding the Habsburgs of Austria. First, he molded Prussia into a more modern, liberal state, albeit with a weaker parliament and a stronger executive power than in Britain. Yet his policy of power politics, called Realpolitik, emphasized warfare, which he called decision by "blood and iron." Bismarck knew he had to fight, especially against Austria, to overcome the resistance of other great powers to German unity under Prussia. He therefore tricked his opponents into declaring wars and then defeated them one after another with the most modern army in Europe.

Bismarck's success remodeled Europe. In the Seven Weeks War (1866), the efficient Prussian army with advanced planning and rapid-firing, breech-loading rifles quickly defeated Austria. Once ousted from any part in a future united Germany, a weakened Austrian imperial government granted political power to the Magyars or Hungarians, transforming the Austrian Empire into the Dual Monarchy of **Austria-Hungary** in 1867. Sadly for the Slavs and other ethnic minorities, their nationalistic hopes under the Habsburgs' joint Austrian and Magyar rule remained unfulfilled.

Bismarck's next opportunity for unification came in 1870, when the Spanish royal dynasty died out. Diplomats proposed princes from several dynasties to assume the throne. One day, Chancellor Bismarck received an insignificant dispatch about his king, Wilhelm I, who was vacationing at the spa resort of Ems. A petty French diplomat had pestered Wilhelm to promise that no prince of his Hohenzollern dynasty would compete for the Spanish throne. In a brilliant stroke of Realpolitik, Bismarck reworded the "Ems Dispatch" to make it seem as if the French had insulted the Prussian king. Napoleon III's insufferable pride led him to retaliate by declaring war against Prussia, just as Bismarck had hoped. Bismarck welcomed the Franco-Prussian War (1870–1871). He convinced the southern German states to join the conflict in a spirit of national unity. The combined Prussian and German forces swiftly defeated France. In the Hall of Mirrors of Louis XIV's Versailles, the German princes acclaimed the Prussian king as "German emperor" Wilhelm I Hohenzollern. The (Second) German Empire (1871–1918) quickly rose to be the most powerful country in Europe.[8]

---

8. Bismarck's creation, "Das Deutsche Reich," is often called the "Second German Empire" by historians because (spoiler alert) it would fail. The Holy Roman Empire is considered the first German empire. And you may have heard about the "Third Reich." If not, see chapter 13.

European nationalism, however, found difficulty including the Jews who had lived in Germany, Italy, and many other older European countries for centuries. Jewish life had almost never been easy, since many Christians of the Middle Ages and Renaissance were antisemites. Their animosity took the form of denying Jews civil rights; prohibiting them from most jobs; confining them in ghettoes (named after the neighborhood where since the early sixteenth century authorities in Venice had locked Jews in every night); expelling all of them from countries such as England, France, Spain, and Portugal; and killing many of them in pogroms (from the Russian word for destroying Jews, coined in the late nineteenth century).

Following the increased tolerance of the Enlightenment, Jews actually gained civil rights during the nineteenth century. They could participate in politics and freely choose professions. After they were allowed entrance to universities, many Jews rose to prosperity and prominence in law, education, and medicine. Jews themselves decided how much to assimilate, or act like their Western neighbors. Jews had three main ethnic divisions: Sephardi Jews were those who settled in North Africa and the Ottoman Empire, Ashkenazi Jews found homes in central and eastern Europe, and Mizrahi Jews had remained in southwest Asia. Judaism had also split into three main movements: orthodox, conservative, and reformed. Many Jews even ceased to keep a distinctly Jewish culture and became "secular."

Not unexpectedly, the Jews' sudden success and prominence in the nineteenth century inflamed antisemitism. The worst occurred in Russia, where the government oppressed Jews directly. In reaction to the assassination of Tsar Alexander II in 1881 by a terrorist bomb, the government imposed the harsh May Laws (1882) even though Jews had nothing to do with the attack. Russia forcibly relocated millions of Jews and stripped them of many economic and civil rights. Adding to Jewish suffering, a wave of pogroms broke out, namely mob attacks that brutally tortured and murdered Jews and burned their homes. While the regime did not organize pogroms, it did little to stop them or punish the aggressors.

In western Europe, the most notorious example of antisemitism was the **Dreyfus Affair** (1894–1906) in France. The French government tried and convicted a Jew, Captain Alfred Dreyfus, of treason for turning over secrets to the Germans. They imprisoned him on Devil's Island, a sweltering penal colony located off the coast of South America. In truth, Dreyfus was innocent. Further investigation soon found the real traitor, a well-born aristocrat named Ferdinand Esterházy. Astoundingly, a trial found Esterházy innocent in 1899. The subsequent arguments over Dreyfus's guilt or innocence exposed the fractures in France's unified national façade. After a second trial wrongly convicted Dreyfus again in 1899, only presidential intervention in 1906 freed him.

As a consequence of the hostility toward Jews that was exposed by this affair, some Jews invented their own form of nationalism, called *Zionism*. In 1897, the first World Zionist Congress convened in Basel, Switzerland. The delegates faced a real difficulty: how could the Jews have their own country if other ethnic groups already occupied every livable space in the whole world? Although some Jews suggested forming a homeland in South America or Africa, most aimed for the traditional homeland of Palestine, which was at the time a province of the Turkish Ottoman Empire. The Ottomans did permit some Jewish immigration at first, since the Jews were a source of revenue. But how many Jews could poor Palestine accommodate as more continued to arrive?

The issue of the Jews and their attempt at nationalism exposed the most difficult flaw in nationalism: how should nation-states deal with people who did not conform to nationalist standards? Every border drawn left aggrieved minorities on the other side. Diverse people lived next to one another everywhere, more than ever since the rise of mobility in modern society. Once nationalists gave up on tolerance of ethnic differences, only three choices remained: forcing conformity in outward cultural behavior, imposing confinement to certain parts of the country, or eliminating the "foreign" people through exile or death. Any one of these choices, though, provoked conflict. Nationalism has often encouraged domination but too rarely cooperation.

Paradoxically and tragically, nationalism allied with imperialism. While nationalist political theorists were asserting rigidly defined states along ethnic lines, they also encouraged cobbling together multiethnic overseas empires. Of course, this imperialism was a contradiction in itself. As conquered peoples everywhere learned of nationalism, they then aspired to run their own lives along ethnic principles, apart from their masters. Today, while imperialism has diminished, nationalism still prevails to both unite and divide people.

Review: *How did various nationalisms unify and divide Western nations?*

Response:

SOURCES ON FAMILIES: ETHEL HOWARD, *POTSDAM PRINCES* (1915)

The years before World War I were the last heyday of many royal dynasties, who lived in a special kind of family. This memoir by Ethel Howard relates her experiences as an English governess raising the young children of Kaiser Wilhelm II of the Hohenzollern dynasty of Prussia. Her charges ranged from the crown prince at fourteen, followed by five younger boys, down to the baby princess Victoria Luise, or "Sissy," age three. This selection describes Howard's appointment, then her early duties and experiences. She later went on to be a governess for the imperial family of Japan.

I was quite young at the time, and the thought of the coming parting was a nightmare to me. We were more closely knit than is common amongst most families, so much so that my father always compared us to a bundle of sticks. I had never gone abroad before, and the thought of leaving the simple and happy shelter of home for the cold and rigid ceremonial and unknown difficulties of a foreign Court appalled me. I knew little or no German, and as the hour of my departure approached I felt more and more nervous.

When, in December 1895, the dread moment arrived, my courage failed me, and I actually jumped out of the railway carriage, exclaiming, "No, I can't go so far from home, not for any Emperor!" My mother, whom I worshipped, gently pushed me in again; and so, amid blinding tears, I set forth to my new life. . . .

I was shown at once to my bedroom, which though not large was a most palatial apartment, everything in it being very beautiful, the Berlin china-ware bearing the Royal Crown, and all the linen being embroidered in the same manner.

This room was set somewhat apart from the others in the main Palace, being in fact in the visitors' wing. I was not very much impressed by the fact at the time, though I did rather wonder why (since I was obviously not a visitor) I had been put in this wing. Later I was told that it was done purposely, for the reason that the sudden introduction into the fullness of Court grandeur had frequently unbalanced people's minds—in fact, they had become temporarily insane through it. . . .

I learnt that each Prince had a military governor. My work as English governess was mapped out for me, and I was given a time-table, which, however, was liable to alteration at a moment's notice, especially in the Potsdam Palace. When my duties with the Princes did not claim me, I was to act as a sort of extra lady-in-waiting, attending on odd Royalties who happened to be visiting, or even on the Empress herself. . . .

I was given the early morning work, which necessitated my finishing breakfast and being ready to go out walking at 8 a.m. It was winter when I got there, and anyone who knows the intense cold of Berlin will appreciate how severe I found this morning exercise. It lasted from 8 a.m. until just before 12:30, when one had ten minutes or so to change for luncheon. . . .

The whole morning I used to spend walking with each Prince in turn, half running, as it was too cold to sit down or walk slowly; the reason for their walk and talk alone with me being that their English conversation should have my individual attention, and that they should thus perfect their knowledge of the language without too much realizing that they were doing so. . . .

In Potsdam the Princes used to be present at the terrible and formal midday meal, usually at 12:30 or 1 o'clock, but subject, like everything else, to the vagaries of circumstances. I, for one, never enjoyed it, nor, I think, did they. To this meal numerous guests were invited daily, and I often met and conversed with gorgeously arrayed officers and diplomats whose names are now household words in every land. . . .

There was nearly an hour of eating, drinking, and talking, and then we would all adjourn together, ladies first, into the room where we took coffee. Here we were often compelled to drag out another hour—a weary one to me, I must confess, as it did not seem to be correct to sit down, and after a whole morning on one's feet, and a heavy midday meal, one simply longed for a chair.

The Princes would stay talking until such time as they were carried off by their respective governors for study, and I did not see them again as a rule until after tea. . . . Then I took the Princes again for recreation, often playing games with them in the Palace garden. Supper alone with them at seven o'clock, after which I would read English story-books to them until eight o'clock, when they went to bed . . . and by that time so tired, I often went to bed very early. . . .

[I]t seemed to me that courtiers, whatever their rank, were but servants, and that wheels within wheels and petty endeavors to gain Royal favor were worth but little. I made the excellent resolution, therefore, to do what I believed to be best for the Princes, regardless of whom I might annoy. . . .

Questions:

- *What is unique about the family life of the imperial family?*
- *What made the imperial family so different from her own?*
- *What were the priorities for rearing the princes?*

Responses:

For more on this source, go to http://www.concisewesternciv.com/sources/sof12.html.

THE BALKAN CAULDRON

The center of nationalist and imperialist conflict at the beginning of the twentieth century was the Balkan Peninsula, that large triangle of land roughly south of a line drawn from the north of the Adriatic to the north of the Black Sea. The ethnic divisions of western Europe really seemed quite simple compared with those of the Balkans, where the migration of multiple ethnicities had left many different peoples living cheek by jowl with one another. Along the eastern coast of the Adriatic, the Albanians may be one of the oldest surviving peoples to settle in Europe. Then the ancient Greeks became dominant in the far south, after which the Romans conquered the area as far as the Danube. At the collapse of the western Roman Empire in the fifth century AD, many Romans left, but some Latin survivors in the region became known as the Vlachs, while others may have been ancestors of those called Romanians. Migrating Germanic tribes briefly dominated the peninsula, but most of them eventually moved on into central and western Europe, a few to return a millennium later in small enclaves near the Danube and in Transylvania. The Slavic peoples migrated next, including Serbs, Croats, Slovenes, Macedonians, and Montenegrins. In the seventh century, out of Central Asia came the Bulgars, followed in the ninth century by the Magyars (Hungarians). By the later Middle Ages, Romany (or Gypsy folk) from South Asia wandered through the peninsula. And, as always, there were some Jews in the cities. Finally, in the later Middle Ages, the Turkish Ottoman Empire imposed its own order on the region, converting many to Islam (especially Bosnians, Albanians, Pomaks, and Torbeshes) and leaving governance to a relatively few immigrant Turks.

The Ottoman Empire had once been a powerful rival to the West but had declined after 1600. That multinational state did not experience anything similar to the commercial, scientific, industrial, religious, and intellectual revolutions of the Renaissance, Reformation, and Enlightenment, nor the English/American/French political revolutions. Indeed, many of its religious leaders, both Muslim and Orthodox Christian, preached against Western ways. The sultans too often came to power through conspiracies carried out by the wives and eunuch custodians of the harem. The empire's bureaucracy operated according to complexity rather than efficiency. Its armies practiced tradition rather than innovation. The Ottoman Empire soon lacked the ability to defend itself and earned the nickname "the Sick Man of Europe."

After the failed Turkish siege of Vienna in 1683, the Habsburgs reclaimed all of Hungary, Croatia, and bits of other provinces in the Balkans from the Turks. By the eighteenth century, though, Austria was unable or unwilling to liberate the rest of the Balkans from Turkish rule. Although the Congress of Vienna in 1815 Austria had grudgingly accepted the Ottoman Empire as a necessary part of the European state system, others saw it as ripe to be challenged.

The first nationalist movement to upset the status quo came from one of the founding peoples of Western civilization, the Greeks. Of course, there had never before been a unified state actually called Greece. Historical precedent notwithstanding, modern descendants of Spartans and Athenians decided in the early nineteenth century that they wanted their own country. They organized the nationalist **Greek Revolt** (1821–1829) against the Ottomans.

At first, the Western great powers supported the absolutist Muslim monarchy's war against the Greek rebels, obedient to the conservative principle of preserving political stability. Many of the common people of Europe, however, saw the Greeks as romantic heroes, if not fellow westerners, and they sent aid. Some, like the poet Lord Byron, even went off to fight for them (although he died there quite unromantically of dysentery). With pressure from their own people, the great powers stepped in to provide a conservative, not a nationalist, solution. The great powers of Great Britain and France graciously gifted the new Kingdom of Greece with its own absolute monarchy, but not with an ethnic Greek king; rather with a prince borrowed from Germany. The traditional role of a king as symbolic parent and unifier of the people did not require the monarch to share the ethnicity of his subjects.

Greece's Balkan neighbors, still under Ottoman rule, could not help noticing its precedent. They also began to embrace nationalistic ideas. **Pan-slavism**, promoted by Russians, called for all Slavs everywhere to live together. A more focused attitude of Slavic nationalism, called **yugo-slavism**, promoted the idea that the southern Slavs of the Balkans should unite. The Serbians, the largest group among these Slavs, advocated this policy.

Meanwhile, the swelling Romanov Russian Empire decided to expand southward. The Russians built forts, sent in armies, and destroyed the Kazakh Khanate on the steppes of Central Asia by the mid-nineteenth century. In the next years, Russians built more forts, sent in more armies, and incorporated "Turkistan," the ancient homeland of Turkish peoples. They and their nomadic livelihood were pushed aside in favor of Russian immigrant farmers. In the Caucasus Mountains, they conquered Azerbaijanis, Georgians, and Chechens after wars where both sides committed atrocities. Those peoples were ethnically Turkic, Kartvelian, and Northeast Caucasian respectively, and mostly Muslims. Since they were neither Slavs nor Orthodox Christians, Russia started to russify them.

Russia also targeted the Ottoman Turkish Empire in the name of Orthodox Christian unity, pan-slavism, and imperialism. This Russian objective alarmed the other Western powers. Great Britain especially feared Russia approaching their colonies in the Indian subcontinent. Also, if Istanbul fell, Russian fleets could gain access to the Mediterranean from the Black Sea through the Bosphorus and the Dardanelles, thereby complicating British naval power. When a dispute broke out about protecting Orthodox Christians in Jerusalem, which was under Ottoman rule, Russia provoked the **Crimean War** (1853–1856). Russian troops invaded the Ottoman provinces of Moldavia and Wallachia (the latter a part of Romania today). The British and French Empires sided with the Ottoman Empire and sent troops to the Crimean Peninsula on the Black Sea.

This small war is remarkably memorable. First, the traditional enemies England and France cooperated. Second, they learned to overcome the logistical difficulties of fighting so far from their homelands. Third, the work of Florence Nightingale (b. 1820–d. 1910) with the wounded started to promote modern nursing. She instructed the medical men in charge about the benefits of hygiene, rest, and kind attention for soldiers recovering from camp diseases and modern explosive weapons. Fourth, the British poet Tennyson's poem "The Charge of the Light Brigade" tried to stir up an ideal of courage, even in the face of futile cavalry attacks against deadly cannon fire. And finally, soldiers brought back to Europe the habit of cigarette smoking as a more popular means of consuming tobacco than chewing or smoking cigars and pipes.

Russia's defeat in the Crimean War slowed its aggression against the Ottoman Empire only for a few decades. In 1876, Muslim Ottoman troops slaughtered several thousand Orthodox Christian Bulgarians while crushing a rebellion against the dynasty. Russia seized the opportunity to declare war, both to avenge those massacred and to help the Serbs and Montenegrins who were fighting the

Ottomans. Russian armies marched toward Istanbul. This time Russia quickly won a resounding victory, and Russian diplomats began to redraw the borders of the Balkans, hoping to fulfill Russia's pan-slavist hopes. The other great powers, however, again stepped in and brought the Russians to the Congress of Berlin in 1878 (not to be confused with the Congress of Berlin in 1884, which dealt with Africa). This congress forced the Russians to renounce their gains. In doing so, it created the new countries of **Serbia**, **Bulgaria**, and **Romania**, each stabilized with conservative monarchies (the latter two with princes again borrowed from Germany).

More than ever, it seemed the Ottoman Empire was teetering on the brink of total collapse. The new states of Serbia, Bulgaria, and Romania were dissatisfied with their new borders. Each looked across its frontiers into neighboring states and saw people of the same nationality "trapped" in other countries. In Ottoman-ruled Macedonia, some of those people formed one of the first modern terrorist groups, the IMRO (Internal Macedonian Revolutionary Organization). Swearing loyalty over a gun and a Bible, its members fought against both Muslim rule and the territory-hungry desires of Serbia, Romania, and Bulgaria. Meanwhile, Austria-Hungary was supposed to preserve **Bosnia-Herzegovina** as a protectorate. Instead, Austrian politicians annexed Bosnia outright in 1908; Austrian bureaucrats presented the dual province as a gift for the aged Habsburg emperor Francis-Joseph to celebrate the sixtieth anniversary of his accession to the throne.

Some Turks tried to slow the momentum toward dismemberment of their Ottoman Empire. A coup d'état in 1908 by a group of westernizing nationalists called the "**Young Turks**" encouraged *pan-turkism*, or using Turkish nationalism to strengthen the empire. Before such a policy could take effect, Italy launched the Italo-Turkish War (1911) to seize the large Ottoman province of Tripoli (modern Libya), just across the Mediterranean in North Africa. Interestingly, Italy's venture into modern war provided the first experimental use of both airplanes and poison gas as weapons. Italy's armies managed to defeat those of the "Sick Man of Europe" in Africa.

Italy's unjustified attack on the Turks in turn encouraged the other Balkan states to imitate its success. In October 1912, Serbia, Romania, Bulgaria, Montenegro, and Greece pounced on Macedonia, beginning the First Balkan War (1912–1913). The success of the Balkan states immediately raised the concern of the European powers. They convened a conference at London in the spring of 1913 to settle matters. While at the negotiating table, the greedy Bulgarians decided to try to secure what they could on their own. In June, Bulgaria launched a preemptive strike on its recent allies, beginning the Second Balkan War (1913).[9]

When the fighting stopped in August 1913, a peace conference set up new borders (see map 12.5). Bulgaria yielded to some losses, most importantly its Mediterranean coastline. Romania and Greece benefited nicely. Serbia ended up with the key chunk of Macedonia. Austria also encouraged the creation of **Albania** as an independent country. This move followed nationalist principles, since the ethnic Albanians were not closely related to the Serbs—they were not even Slavs.

---

9. For a report of Christian atrocities against Muslims, go to http://www.concisewesternciv .com/sources/plight.html.

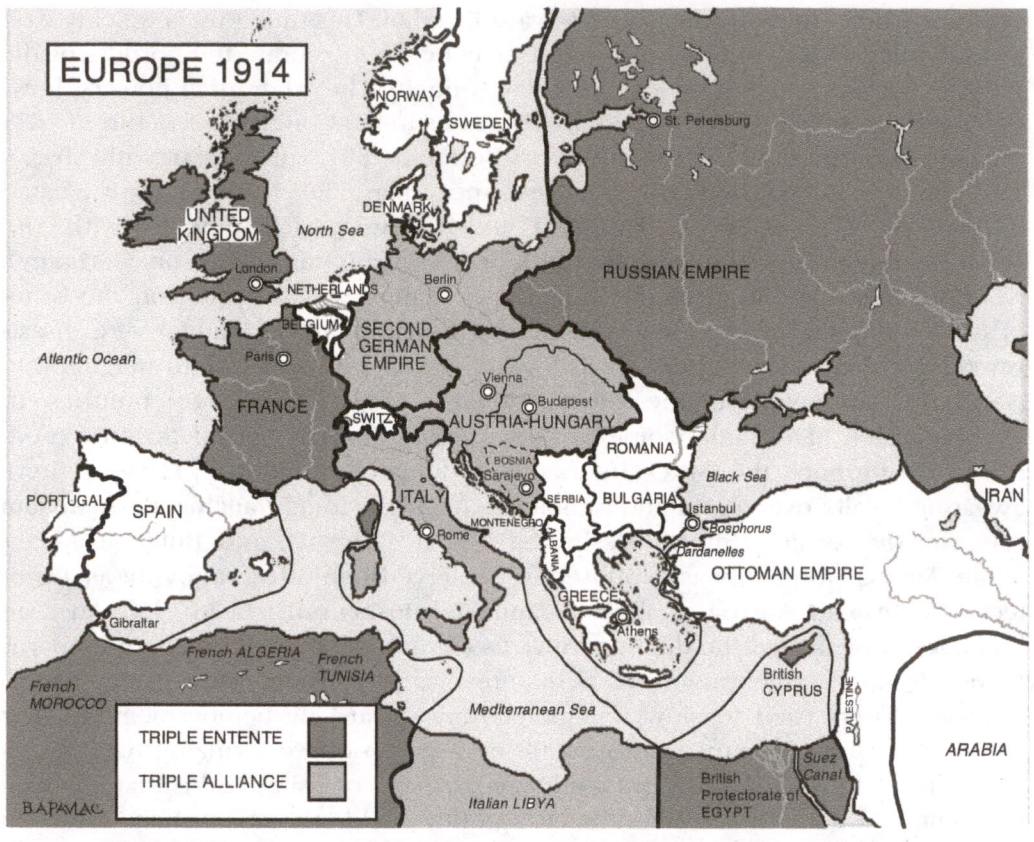

Map 12.5. Europe, 1915. What geographical factors led to joining or avoiding the large alliance systems?

Nevertheless, Serbia had wanted to rule over the Albanians, especially to gain a coastline and seaports on the Adriatic Sea.

Frustrated, Serbian nationalists focused much of their anger on Austria-Hungary. Conspiratorial military officers formed a secret organization called the Black Hand. Having assassinated the king and queen of Serbia in 1903, it next turned its attention against the Habsburgs. They recruited ethnic Serbian college students from Bosnia and trained them in small arms to carry out assassinations, a method of terrorism made popular by anarchists.

The terrorists struck on 28 June 1914, as the heir to the Austro-Hungarian throne, Archduke **Franz Ferdinand**, and his wife, Sophie, visited the Bosnian capital of Sarajevo. The amateurish assassins had been less than successful at first. A bomb thrown at the archduke's car bounced off, only injuring some soldiers and civilians. Astoundingly, security remained lax. Later that day, the archduke's car made a wrong turn and stopped right in front of where another assassin, Gavrilo Princip, was getting a sandwich. The nineteen-year-old terrorist shot Franz Ferdinand and Sophie at point-blank range. They were dead within minutes, their three young children orphaned.

The political leadership of Austria-Hungary pounced on this incident as a pretext for war against Serbia. Emperor Francis-Joseph, who did not much care for his heir, was not motivated by grief or anger. Furthermore, no firm evidence at the time linked the Serbian government to the terrorists. But the Austrians thought war would solve their ongoing annoyance with Serbia. Decisively, the Austrians' only dependable ally, the Germans, backed them up with a virtual blank check, a promise to support Austria in whatever action it might take. A month after the assassination, the cautious Austrians finally sent an ultimatum to Serbia, long after the tragedy and ensuing sympathy had faded from the front pages of newspapers. The Serbians, as expected, could not accept the whole ultimatum and mobilized their military in preparation for the expected war. On 1 August 1914, Austria-Hungary declared war on Serbia. That lit the fuse for World War I.

Overall, the nineteenth century's experience of nationalism was mixed. It did indeed promote some major peaceful arts. Nationalists identified, categorized, and recorded the language and literature, song and dance, costume and custom of the myriad ethnic groups that resided in Europe. Turning ethnicity into nationality, however, had required wars ranging from such diverse locations as the Alps and the Andes, the Rhine and the Rio Grande, and the islands in the Caribbean and the Aegean. Even worse, what should have been no more than a petty third Balkan war between Austria-Hungary and Serbia instead metastasized into the worst conflict in human history up to that point.

Review: *How did nationalism and the decline of the Ottoman Empire destabilize the Balkans?*

Response:

THE GREAT WAR

Both imperialism and nationalism came together to provide the fuel for the Great War, now known as **World War I** (1914–1918). This first of the three great global conflicts of the twentieth century deserves the global part of its title mostly because of the enormous damage it inflicted and the worldwide reach of its consequences. Although some battles took place in Africa, the Middle East, the South American coast, and the Pacific, the overwhelming bulk of the fighting happened in Europe, in the heart of Western civilization.

Everyone expected Franz Ferdinand's assassination to spark a war between Austria-Hungary and Serbia, yet few anticipated the conflagration that resulted. Each participant who joined in envisioned a short, sharp war, where the "guns of August" would be silenced by Christmas. Each nation confidently believed that civilization and/or God stood with them alone. Each felt aggrieved by the actions of the others. Serbia wanted to dominate the Balkans. Austria wanted a reckoning with Serbia. Russia wanted revenge against Austria. France wanted revenge against Germany. Britain wanted to maintain its international supremacy. The Ottoman Empire wanted to survive. Italy wanted an empire. Few got what they wanted.

Historians have particularly debated how Germany's war aims shaped the origins of World War I. Many German nationalists had called for a larger overseas empire to gain the Second German Empire its place in the sun. The clumsy efforts of Kaiser Wilhelm II (r. 1888–1918) to promote German prestige (such as comparing them to the Huns) had other Europeans viewing this latecomer to geopolitics as a bumbling upstart.

Much more responsible for so many nations entering the war, however, were the alliances that had been forged during the previous decades. On one side was the **Triple Alliance**, begun by Chancellor Bismarck to preserve the newly united Germany from French revenge for its losses in the Franco-Prussian War. His alliance bound Austria-Hungary and Italy in a mutual defense agreement with Germany. On the other side was the **Triple Entente**, which France had slowly pulled together in reaction to the Triple Alliance. France cautiously bound itself with Great Britain and Russia, although all three had many traditional and contemporary rivalries with one another. Their combined mistrust and fear of Germany, however, ultimately proved greater than their suspicions about each other (see map 12.5).

These alliances had originally been intended to prevent war by making conflict too risky. Instead, they turned into mutually supportive military cooperatives, twisting the delicate balance of power into two hostile blocs. Intensifying the alliances were military strategies connected to **mobilization**, or getting armed forces from peacetime standing to wartime footing. The vast armies supported by modern industrialization, transportation, and communication required complex timetables to get troops where they were needed either to attack or defend. Generals thus pressured politicians to declare war hastily, in time for mobilization to be effective.

Alliances and mobilization plans together escalated the war from a minor Balkan brawl to a clash that involved almost all of Western civilization. After Austria declared war on Serbia, Russia mobilized against Austria, wanting to support its Slavic brothers' defense. Realistically, Russia's claim to mobilize only against Austria was absurd, since the Germans knew that Russian plans were aimed against both Germany and Austria. Hence the Germans immediately demanded both that the Russians stop mobilization and that the French declare their neutrality in the conflict. These measures would have prevented a general war, but at the sacrifice of

Serbia. Ideally, German war plans expected, even desired, that the Russians and French would continue their mobilizations.

The Germans' own strategy (called the Schlieffen Plan after the general who first proposed it) predicted a slow Russian attack in the East, which would allow a German first strike against France in the West. Then, after taking out Paris within a few weeks, according to the Schlieffen Plan, the Germans would eliminate the Russian forces at leisure. Accordingly, when the French hesitated to declare themselves neutral, the Germans declared war against France. The German plan to capture Paris failed to properly take into account Belgium. The Germans expected their armies to rush through Belgium, even though the country had been officially neutral by treaty since its creation in 1830. But when German troops began invading Belgium, both the Belgians and the British objected to the violation of neutrality. When the Germans refused to withdraw, the British reluctantly declared war. So by the end of the first week of August, the Allied Powers or **Allies** of Serbia, Russia, France (and its colonies), Belgium (and the Congo), and Great Britain (with its "dominions" of Canada, Newfoundland, Australia, New Zealand, and South Africa and other colonies) were fighting the **Central Powers** of Germany and Austria-Hungary, so named because they were surrounded by their enemies.

Unfortunately for all the well-made plans on both sides, general staffs failed to account for the huge numbers of troops as well as variations caused by both commanders and dumb luck. German forces were distracted as Belgian resistance bogged down their invasion, the British landed troops more quickly than expected in France, the Russians moved rapidly into eastern Prussia, and French forces pushed swiftly into the Alsace. When the Germans turned southward toward Paris earlier than planned, Parisians rushed enough troops to the front, some in taxicabs, to halt the German advance. Neither side on this western front could attack the other's flank since the armies were so huge in a small area. So the Germans pulled back a few miles and dug in. Swiftness transformed into stalemate as both sides huddled in trenches along a combat zone stretching over four hundred miles, all the way from the North Sea to the Swiss border.

Thus, the fighting on the western front unexpectedly developed into **trench warfare**. The Crimean War and the American Civil War had already pointed in this direction, but few commanders had learned from those conflicts. A few soldiers dug in and armed with machine guns could pulverize thousands of approaching enemy infantry, especially when assisted by barbed wire, land mines, and artillery. Now millions of troops faced one another, alternating between tedious, aimless boredom in the muddy, filthy, reeking trenches versus terrifying, bloody, explosive combat of frontal assaults (see Primary Source Project 12). Soldiers fell ill because of vermin and infections, including the notorious trench foot. The noise and concussive force of exploding munitions caused a new malady among the troops called shell shock (today classified as posttraumatic stress disorder). The German attempt to storm the fortifications around Verdun alone cost hundreds of thousands of lives on both sides over several months of constant bombardment. Although the French managed to repulse the German attacks, the Battle of Verdun weakened the French so much that they could hardly begin any further offensives themselves. The British launched the Battle of the Somme in the north to help relieve the pressure on the French at Verdun. On the first morning of that assault, thirty thousand British soldiers were slaughtered in about an hour. Both sides introduced new weapons to break the stalemate. But airplanes, poisonous gas, and even tanks (armored vehicles) proved unable to capture victory for either side.

The western front got most of the press, while massive destruction afflicted other fronts as well. Great armies raging back and forth across hundreds of miles of territory on the eastern front against Russia and Serbia ravaged Poland and the Balkans. Allied forces quickly occupied most German colonies in Africa and the Pacific. Only in East Africa did some German forces hold out for the entire war. Meanwhile, in the fall of 1914, the Germans pressured the Ottoman Empire into joining their side.

Instead of opening up decisive fronts against Russia, however, the Ottoman Empire found itself vulnerable. A British army mostly of Australians and New Zealanders (ANZACs) landed at Gallipoli on the Dardanelles in April 1915, threatening the capital of Istanbul and the sea passage of the Dardanelles. Turkish defenses forced the Allies to withdraw with heavy casualties by the end of the year. Concurrently, an Ottoman invasion of Russia and Iran in the Caucasus had failed disastrously. Leading Muslim Turkish commanders blamed Armenian Christians for allegedly collaborating with the Orthodox Christian Russians. Beginning in April 1915, the Turks forcibly relocated the Armenians, marching them hundreds of miles across barren landscapes without proper supplies. The **Armenian massacres** led to hundreds of thousands of deaths from exhaustion, starvation, exposure, drowning, and shooting. Such horrors later led to the invention of the word "genocide"—the killing off of an entire ethnic group (although today's government of Türkiye continues to dispute this interpretation). Whatever one calls these atrocities, the men, women, and children remain dead.

Ultimately, the acquisition of allies became the key to victory. The Central Powers of Germany, Austria-Hungary, and the Ottoman Empire convinced only one more country to join their side. Italy had refused to honor the Triple Alliance and at first stayed neutral. Only Bulgaria joined the Central Powers in October 1915, hoping to recoup its losses from the Second Balkan War. German military skill and industrial efficiency might have won the war for its side if the war had been short, as the Schlieffen Plan had assumed. Instead, the Central Powers' inability to find more allies doomed them in the long run.

The weight of the world slowly massed against the Central Powers as the Allies of Serbia, Russia, France, Belgium, and Great Britain won more nations to their side. In the fall of 1914, Japan eagerly declared war on Germany and occupied most of its Asian and Pacific possessions. By 1915, the Allies had tempted Italy to attack Austria with territory to be confiscated from its former Triple Alliance partner. The Allies also seduced the Romanians with possessions from Austria-Hungary, while they offered Greeks lands from the Bulgarians and the Ottomans. The British tried to win the support of both Arabs in the Ottoman Empire and international Jews. By 1917, the British officer T. E. Lawrence (Lawrence of Arabia) had inspired an Arab revolt against the Ottomans in the Arabian Peninsula, based on the assurance that they could have their own nation-states after the war. Arabs did not know that the Sykes-Picot Agreement between the British and the French planned to divide up the Ottoman Empire among themselves. At the same time, the **Balfour Declaration** supported a Jewish homeland in Palestine. The Allies did not care that such promises were mutually exclusive.

On the high seas, British naval superiority hoped for a decisive blow against the German fleet. Short of that, the British intended that a blockade would starve out the Central Powers. In turn, the Germans tried to seal off the British Isles with another new weapon of war: U-boats or submarines. To neutral nations, submarines seemed more cruel than traditional surface warships, since large numbers of survivors after a torpedoing could not be rescued by the small, vulnerable, undersea warships.

The Germans especially annoyed the neutral Americans with their submarine warfare on commercial ships. Most notorious was a German U-boat's sinking of the passenger ship *Lusitania* (1915), which went down so swiftly that hundreds of people drowned within sight of the Irish coast. Even though the *Lusitania* was a legitimate target that was carrying contraband (weapons and military supplies) in a war zone, the many civilian deaths violated the American sense of fair play. To appease the Americans, for a little over a year the Germans limited their U-boat attacks to warships.

Early in 1917 the Germans further angered Americans with the infamous Zimmermann Telegram. In it the German government tried to convince Mexico to invade the United States. The Germans were foolish to think Mexico could have attacked the United States, since Mexicans were fighting their own civil war.[10] The British intercepted Zimmermann's telegram by tapping into the transatlantic undersea cable line and handed the telegram over to the Americans. As a result, in April 1917 the United States opened hostilities against Germany. Over the next year more than a dozen other countries, including Thailand, China, and many in Latin America, declared war against one or more of the Central Powers.

The American men, materiel, and money came just in time to sustain the Allied armies. For three years, the European nations had been exhausting themselves trying to win on their own. Drained of men and resources, the home front became the last crucial area of war efforts toward victory. Out of necessity, most industrialized states had adopted *war socialism*, under which governments took control of large sectors of the economy, creating a new military-industrial complex. Central planning by government bureaucrats working with leaders of industry ensured access to raw materials and production for the armed forces. Workers gained better wages and benefits to keep up their production of munitions and provisions without striking. Safety concerns were less important. If workers were injured or

---

10. Actually, the United States had been intervening in the Mexican Revolution (1910–1920) for several years. Americans briefly supported the rebel Pancho Villa with arms and money but then abruptly stopped. In retaliation, Villa organized several raids against the United States. American troops pursued him until the United States entered World War I. A victorious authoritarian and socialist regime under the Institutional Revolutionary Party (PRI) soon dominated Mexico for most of the century.

killed on the job, that was the cost of victory, just like losses on the battlefield. Many women also entered the public workforce in offices and factories to replace manpower serving with the armies. Consumers tolerated shortages of goods and services in order to help the troops.

To keep up flagging morale, regimes used the modern media for the spread of **propaganda**—information slanted to support a specific political cause. Exaggerated British disinformation convinced many Allies and Americans that the Germans were entirely monstrous "Huns," despoilers and murderers of innocent women and children. Protestors against the war ended up silenced or in jail. At the time, one could insightfully observe that the first casualty of war is truth.[11]

By the autumn of 1918, the peoples of the Central Powers were surprised to discover that they had lost the war, although their governments had always assured them that victory was within grasp. They had briefly hoped for victory when Russia fell out of the war in 1917, convulsed by revolution (see the next chapter). But America's finances, industrial might, and even its quickly trained armies more than made up for the loss of Russia to the Allies. The Central Powers lost the war because they could not overcome the numerical advantages of the Allies. Exhausted by late October and early November, the Ottoman Empire, Bulgaria, Austria-Hungary, and finally Germany got caught up in their own revolutions, and their armies collapsed. They surrendered, one after the other.

When the killing stopped at 11 a.m. on the eleventh day of the eleventh month of 1918, more than eleven million victims of combat and disease were dead. Millions more had been wounded, some suffering vicious, horrible mutilations made possible by modern poisonous and explosive chemicals. Billions of dollars of capital had been spent and blown up. Millions of acres of territories had been ravaged; untold thousands of families had been made homeless. Dynasties had been toppled and states shattered: the Romanovs in Russia, the Hohenzollerns in Germany, the Habsburgs in Austria-Hungary, and the Ottomans in their Muslim empire all lost their thrones. Whole populations were demoralized and on the edge of disintegration. Many thought—hoped—that this would be the war to end all wars (see figure 12.3). Sadly, it was only a prelude to worse conflicts.

Review: *What made World War I more destructive and transformative than all previous wars?*

Response:

---

11. These words have often been attributed to the isolationist-minded opponent of the war, American senator Hiram Johnson, who allegedly said them in a speech in 1917. No reliable source to the senator has yet been identified. Ironically, truth is also a casualty of wanting good quotations.

THOSE WHO WITH PATIENT TOIL BUILT UP THE STATELY PILES OF MEDIAEVAL ART ARE GONE · THEIR NAMES ARE FORGOTTEN THEIR WORK IS IN RUINS ·· BUT TO-DAY IS BUILD-ING A NOBLER STRUCTURE · THE TEMPLE OF HUMAN RIGHTS ·· THAT WILL ENDURE FOR THOSE WHO HAVE LAID ITS FOUNDATIONS HAVE LAID THEM IN GOOD WILL TOWARD MEN AND HAVE LABORED FOR PEACE ON EARTH

CHRISTMAS NUMBER
1 9 1 8

Figure 12.3. The Cathedral of Rheims is portrayed as heavily damaged by shelling from German artillery in the Christmas issue of a magazine, right after war's end. Its stated expectation of better days based on human rights still has not been met. (*The Youth's Companion*, vol. 92, no. 49, 5 December 1918)

PRIMARY SOURCE PROJECT 12: "IN FLANDERS FIELDS" VERSUS "DULCE ET DECORUM EST" ABOUT DEATH IN WAR

The horrors of trench warfare during World War I still allowed moments of reflection, as shown by these two poems written by soldiers who had been at the front. One reaction was by the Canadian John McCrae, who calls on the living to remember the cause for which soldiers had died. The English Wilfred Owen questions the legitimacy of the war. His poem's title comes from its last two lines (translated as "It is sweet and proper to die for the fatherland"). Owen is quoting the ancient Roman poet Horace, who encouraged young men to train for the imperial legions. Both soldier-poets died on the western front.

Source 1: "In Flanders Fields" by John McCrae (1915)

In Flanders fields the poppies blow
Between the crosses, row on row
That mark our place; and in the sky
The larks, still bravely singing, fly
Scarce heard amid the guns below.
We are the Dead. Short days ago
We lived, felt dawn, saw sunset glow,
Loved and were loved, and now we lie
In Flanders fields.
Take up our quarrel with the foe:
To you from failing hands we throw
The torch; be yours to hold it high!
If ye break faith with us who die
We shall not sleep, though poppies grow
In Flanders fields.

Source 2: "Dulce et Decorum Est" by Wilfred Owen (1917)

Bent double, like old beggars under sacks,
Knock-kneed, coughing like hags, we cursed through sludge,
Till on the haunting flares we turned our backs
And towards our distant rest began to trudge.
Men marched asleep. Many had lost their boots
But limped on, blood-shod. All went lame; all blind;
Drunk with fatigue; deaf even to the hoots
Of gas-shells dropping softly behind.
Gas! GAS! Quick, boys!—An ecstasy of fumbling
Fitting the clumsy helmets just in time,
But someone still was yelling out and stumbling
And flound'ring like a man in fire or lime.—
Dim, through the misty panes and thick green light,
As under a green sea, I saw him drowning.
In all my dreams before my helpless sight
He plunges at me, guttering, choking, drowning.
If in some smothering dreams you too could pace
Behind the wagon that we flung him in,
And watch the white eyes writhing in his face,
His hanging face, like a devil's sick of sin,
If you could hear, at every jolt, the blood
Come gargling from the froth-corrupted lungs,
Obscene as cancer, bitter as the cud
Of vile, incurable sores on innocent tongues,—
My friend, you would not tell with such high zest
To children ardent for some desperate glory,
The old Lie: *Dulce et decorum est*
Pro patria mori.

Questions:

- *What are the different perspectives of the poems' "narrators"?*
- *How do the poems use different imagery to convey meaning?*
- *Upon reflection, what attitudes should soldiers and civilians hold about war?*

Responses:

Make your own timeline.

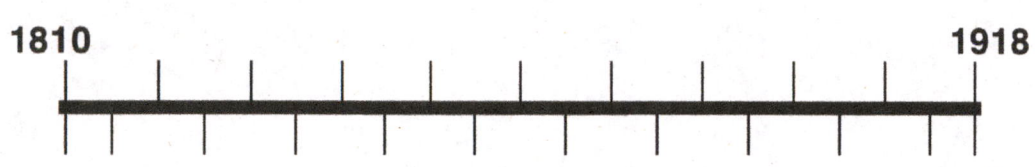

1810   **1918**

For more on these sources, go to http://www.concisewesternciv.com/sources/psc12.html.

CHAPTER  13

Rejections of Democracy

The Interwar Years and World War II, 1917 to 1945

Many people in the West thought they had won the Great War in the name of democracy. Western civilization increasingly promoted the idea that most adults in a nation should share in governance. Further, a majority of voters chose representatives to make decisions collaboratively within legal and moral boundaries of behavior in established parliaments and other representative bodies. While such participatory politics had been growing in power and influence since the seventeenth century, democracy remained difficult. Democratic governments were undermined by the Great War's loss of life, economic destruction, high-handed government policies, shattering of old morals and traditions, and flawed peace process. The "war to end all wars" led to the even worse World War II.

DECLINE OF THE WEST?

The Scientific Revolution had offered science as the vehicle for humanity's progress toward peace and prosperity. In the early twentieth century, the virtues of science seemed less certain (see timeline E). The chemical explosives, poison gasses, and machined weapons of the Great War showed how science could instead drive nations toward death and destruction. Nor could science help much with a worldwide plague, the "Spanish" **influenza pandemic** (1918–1919).[1] This version of the flu killed perhaps as many as forty million people worldwide, far more than the deaths caused by the recent war and perhaps more than any other such disease in history. The virus variants swept around the globe with amazing velocity and lethality, despite quarantines and masking. Scientists did not have time to develop vaccines before the natural mutation of the germ and increasing resistance of the human immune system stopped the spread. Once the Spanish flu had ceased to infect, it also faded from memory.

---

1. While called the Spanish flu, because physicians first studied it in Spain, the disease probably originated in Kansas or France.

New scientific conclusions further weakened confidence that the world could be understood and improved. Einstein's complex **theory of relativity** (1916) replaced the logical simplicity and sensible familiarity of Newton's clockwork universe. According to this new theory, a person's position of observation, or point of view, could affect such facts as the measure of time or distance. Even matter and energy were interchangeable, according to the famous formula $E = mc^2$ (energy equals mass times the speed of light squared). The physicist Heisenberg's uncertainty principle (1927) stated that one could know either the location or the direction of an atom's electron, but not both simultaneously. Another theoretical experiment for understanding the atom, Schrödinger's cat, suggests that states of matter are only determined by observation (one can only know whether a cat in a box is alive or dead if the box is opened). These additions to atomic theory seemed to make the universe more confusing.

The future of world peace also grew uncertain as the Allied Powers tried to clean up the mess left by the Great War in the Paris Peace Treaties of 1919. In January 1918, while the war was still raging, American President Woodrow Wilson had already set the tone for peace proposals with the declaration of his **Fourteen Points**. These ideals proposed a world of international cooperation with open and honest diplomacy, support for nationalistic principles, and avoidance of warfare. The European peoples embraced the common sense and decency of the Fourteen Points. Indeed, many of the new countries created out of the peace treaties drew up democratic constitutions with reasonable attempts at responsible self-government. Participation of all adult citizens—with laws and amendments even finally granting the vote to women—reached its high point in most modern industrialized states just after the Great War.

It was too much to hope that a few months of negotiations could easily overcome the grudges and disagreements amassed during a thousand years of European conflict since the Treaty of Verdun in 847. As the first sitting US president ever to travel abroad, Wilson hoped to guide the peace process, since America's power had won the war for the Allies. The other leaders of the "Big Four" allies (Lloyd George of Britain, Clemenceau of France, and Orlando of Italy) only grudgingly accepted his preeminence. But their grievances against the Central Powers and their imperialist self-interest undermined the conference.

Wilson's vision of a new international institution, the **League of Nations**, might have helped. This organization was meant to replace the obviously failed practice of sovereign nations facing off in a balance of power, with or without alliances. Instead, the League was to promote collective security in a fashion similar to the Concert of Europe conducted by the Congress of Vienna a century before. Its standing forum of delegates would replace the need for emergency congresses or conferences convened every time an international crisis broke out. The League offered the possibility for diverse nations with divergent interests to work together rather than against one another. Another world war, people rightfully feared, could doom civilization as they knew it.

Instead of forging a new beginning for cooperation in Europe, those who wanted to punish the Central Powers outmaneuvered Wilson's good intentions. In the **Treaty of Versailles**, signed in Louis XIV's baroque palace, the Allies forced the Germans to accept primary blame for the war. That treaty also pointedly excluded Germany from the new organization of "free" peoples. Thus, one of the most important great powers was deliberately left out. The victorious Allies also shut out their former great power ally Russia because of its new communist government (see below). The winners hardly considered admitting representatives of oppressed colonial peoples all over the world.

The worst blow to League membership was the refusal of the United States to join. Many Americans had never shared Wilson's vision of international participation; they instead thought the United States should return to isolationism. These Americans tried to ignore the reality that the United States was inextricably tied up in world affairs with its colonies in the Pacific, its grip on the Caribbean and Latin America, and its worldwide economic reach. Additionally, partisan politics poisoned the process. Wilson was a Democrat, and both houses of Congress were held by Republican majorities. The Republican leaders of the Senate, which constitutionally ratified all treaties, suggested a few changes they thought would preserve American independence of action and control over its own armed forces. Wilson refused to compromise and embarked on a whirlwind campaign to win popular support for "his" treaty. The stress of traveling thousands of miles in just a few weeks brought on a stroke, which incapacitated him. His wife, Edith, practically ran the White House for months as she interpreted the bedridden president's feeble attempts at communication.

Wilson's removal from politics meant that the United States of America signed a separate peace with Germany, without the covenant concerning the League of Nations. So, the United States turned its back on collective security and drifted into isolationism. Great Britain and France, nervous about the growing influence of American power, were glad at first to see the Americans leave. For the next two decades, the United States retreated behind the shelter of the Arctic, Pacific, and Atlantic Oceans. The defensive value of bodies of water, however, shrank in an age of motorized ships and aircraft.

In reality, the United States had become essential to Western civilization even as it withdrew its political interests. Before World War I, most cultural, widespread economic, and social influence came from Europe. After the war, European society seemed stagnant compared to the creativity coming from Americans. During the **Roaring Twenties**, America swelled with the artistic creativity of the Jazz Age.[2] The "Lost Generation" of American writers, disillusioned by both World War I and American materialism, led the literary elites of the West even while they drank past midnight in Paris. Since America became the main creditor nation of European war debts, New York replaced London as the capital of global finance (see figure 13.1). This cultural and economic shift to the New World remained unthreatening to the Old World because of the United States' reluctance to maintain large armed forces or to throw around its diplomatic weight. American jazz music, however, hit Europe hard, thrilling those who were moved by its African- and

---

2. For more on the art of this period, go to http://www.concisewesternciv.com/arth/ar13.html.

Figure 13.1. New York City. A construction worker on a skyscraper in Manhattan admires the nighttime skyline. (National Archives and Records Administration)

Caribbean-based rhythms and horrifying those who could not hear its beauty or appreciate its complexity.

Millions first heard jazz music over the new invention of **radio**, which tied the world's cultures together as never before. Although invented before the war, radio as a medium came into its own in the 1920s. Radio stations were built all over the industrialized nations. Although usage taxes (paid by owners of radio sets) supported public broadcasting in many European countries, radio's expansion in the United States was mostly financed through paid advertising. Either way, radio signals reached around the globe, especially thanks to the British Broadcasting Corporation's growth throughout the British Empire.

When not gathered at home around their radios for entertainment, Western audiences also flocked to the **movies**. Motion pictures, like radio, had started in industrialized countries before the war but became wildly popular afterward. Movie theaters or cinemas, specially built or remodeled from performance halls, showed a variety of films: reports on current events, travelogues, cartoons, adaptations from classic plays and literature, or comedies and dramas newly created for the silver screen. American filmmakers in the sunshine of Hollywood became the most prolific creators of that medium worldwide, soon outproducing the Europeans.

Movies became a dominant feature of Western culture. One of the first movie stars, the British-born Charlie Chaplin with his "Little Tramp" character, became an iconic figure around the globe. For the first few years, movies had no sound except as provided by local musicians in the theaters. The first movie with synchronized sound, *The Jazz Singer* (1929), portrayed the clash of old culture (a Jewish cantor) with his modernized and Americanized son (the jazz singer of the title). It symbolized the new age replacing the traditional past. Because of the success radio and movies had in English-speaking countries, English increasingly became the language of international media and culture.

The new world tied together by radio and movies seemed even smaller because of new innovations in transportation. Airplanes soared across oceans. Lindbergh captured the public imagination with the first solo flight from New York to Paris (1927). His instant fame demonstrated how radio and newsreels rapidly spread information and invented celebrities. Airlines soon began to fly paying passengers across all barriers of land and sea. The most popular and affordable transport, however, was the motorcar or automobile, symbolic of the movement and force of the twentieth century. As the car became the backbone of industrial production, the demand for paved roads and parking began to radically transform the urban and rural landscape. Automobiles also allowed more young people to escape parental supervision, making the "backseat" a byword for sexual opportunity.

The standards of living rose briskly in most of the industrialized West during the 1920s. At first, the costs and destruction of the Great War had drained the resources of many European nations, but it only took a few years to realign their economies back to peacetime production. Soon, consumer consumption became the great engine for economic growth of modern economies. More manufacturing meant better pay and benefits for production workers. While advertising enticed westerners to purchase more goods and services, easier access to credit lent them the means to do it quickly and conveniently. A rising level of prosperity nurtured an irresistible tendency toward materialism. Refrigerators and washing machines were soon not just novel modern conveniences but necessities. Even factory workers expected leisure time and vacations. By the late 1920s, members of the widening Western middle classes were enjoying themselves as never before.

For some people, that enjoyment included consuming mood-altering chemicals. Psychoactive substances such as opium (increasingly purified into morphine and heroin), cocaine, and marijuana became more accessible due to modern agriculture, processing, and transportation. As authorities in Western nations grew concerned over increasing rates of addiction and the resultant social destruction, they began to regulate and outlaw such recreational drugs. The United States went furthest, outlawing the manufacture and sale of alcohol with a law declaring Prohibition (1920–1933). Alcohol has been, of course, the most widespread recreational drug since civilization began, whether in the form of beer, wine, or distilled liquor. The American experiment with controlling alcohol consumption was unusual and ultimately unsuccessful. Unsurprisingly, recreational drug use remained prevalent in Western nations despite their official restrictions or prohibitions.

Despite seeming prosperity, for some the rising materialism, increasing drug use, and spreading popular culture fueled pessimism. For them, the war had killed or damaged too many promising youths, weakened traditional elites, and led to a decline in churchgoing. Oswald Spengler, in *The Decline of the West* (1922–1926), summed up people's fears. Although his book was more discussed than actually read, Spengler claimed in dense prose that Western civilization had become senile. The events of the 1930s would seem to prove his point.

The troubles began with the **Wall Street crash** (1929), which then triggered the worldwide economic collapse called the **Great Depression** (1929–1941). In the 1920s, the stock exchanges on Wall Street, the financial district of New York City, had been pushing people to invest more money than ever before. The eagerness to own stock, even in companies that were overvalued, pushed the prices higher. Many people, both rich and middle class, were buying stock on credit, believing that prices would keep rising forever. Thus, billions of dollars in stock values had accumulated out of sheer optimism and greed. One Thursday morning, 24 October 1929, some investors began to doubt the alleged worth of these stocks and sold them while the market was high, hoping to cash out with big profits. As other investors noticed and tried to bail out as well, the market plunged. Inevitably, financial institutions began to collapse, and wealth disappeared. Within a few weeks, the value of the market had fallen by 50 percent, and it continued to fall for the next three years. Billions of dollars of capital simply vanished into thin air.

Since New York had become the pivotal center for the investment of capital, the Wall Street crash smashed other Western economies. Banks called in their loans, but borrowers had little with which to pay them back. Even when banks confiscated collateral, such as homes or real estate, they still had too little cash on hand when frightened investors demanded their deposits. Forced into bankruptcy, banks failed, and the life savings of millions of people disappeared. Many businesses could not meet payrolls, saw their capital resources drained, and closed their doors. As consumers had too little disposable wealth to buy goods and services, businesses shut down because new orders dried up. On that account, more workers had no paychecks, further weakening demand and consumption. Governments tried to shore up their countries' factories and farms by erecting protectionist trade barriers of high taxes or bans on imports. These measures only damaged international trade and did little to help the domestic economies. Even food prices fell, forcing one out of every four farms into foreclosure in the United States. Millions of people went on the move looking for jobs, but too few could be found.

These effects spread through the industrialized West, hitting hardest in the United States, Japan, Germany, and Austria. The worldwide economic depression of the 1930s accelerated the abandonment of parliamentarianism in countries where they had had too little time to take root. People began to question their government's competency or whether democracy could work at all. Great Britain, France, and a few others clung to their parliamentary democracies, while communist and socialist parties gained in elections in nearly all Western nations.

The only place where organized socialist and communist movements remained weak was in the United States. In America, the administration of President **Franklin Delano Roosevelt** (r. 1933–1945) found other solutions to the economic collapse. When FDR (as he was commonly called) ran for president in 1932, he revitalized the Democratic Party with a coalition of intellectuals, Southerners (both white and Black), Jews, farmers, immigrants, and workers—all joined together in getting the economy moving. Roosevelt's advisors declared laissez-faire classical liberal economics to be a fraud, since its free rein to the capitalists had brought on the economic collapse. Instead, he proposed a "New Deal" for Americans, with massive government intervention in the economy and society.

The heart of the New Deal program was ***Keynesian economic theory***, which suggested a revision to the long-dominant theory of laissez-faire or classical liberal economics. Laissez-faire theory assumed that capital would always be available for investment. But the economic worldwide collapse of 1929 had eliminated many banks and much capital. To get out of such a serious economic collapse, when private capital was in short supply, British economist John Maynard Keynes recommended that governments spend money they borrowed from themselves. Such government spending could help fuel a recovery, which could then revive private capital investments. Governments could later pay off the massive public debt created by deficit spending through normal taxation and borrowing from banks after people were working and investing again. Most Western governments began to adopt and use this deficit-spending practice.

Deficit spending by Roosevelt's administration put Americans to work at government expense at jobs that ranged from planting trees to writing plays, building bridges to digging ditches. Nevertheless, the American economy failed to fully recover during the 1930s. Majorities of Americans, however, cheered by these efforts and FDR's image of sunny and determined optimism, voted him into office four times, more times than any other US president. Meanwhile, Roosevelt's political and economic enemies hated the growing power of the federal government and accused FDR of socialism and dictatorship.

Leaders of other democracies in the West did not enjoy the kind of popularity FDR did in America, although they did share his inability to end the Depression. Those leaders who did gain popular followings actually became dictators and often carried out real socialist policies. One after another, many westerners turned away from the enlightened participatory politics of liberal democratic parliamentarianism and handed their fates over to dictators. These dictators then tried to reshape the world according to their own visions.

Review: How did the West suffer cultural confusion in the wake of war?

Response:

RUSSIANS IN REVOLT

The first great modern political alternative to the Western democracies arose during World War I with the **Russian Revolution** (1917–1922). Before the Great War, the Russian Empire had already been playing catch-up as it ponderously industrialized in imitation of its European rivals. In politics, though, the absolute monarchy of Tsar Nicholas II (r. 1894–1917) had shown little interest in democratic institutions. Revolution then forced change, as it had in France a century earlier, with results that were equally unexpected. The Russian Revolution's overpowering ideology pioneered new forms of government: the modern autocracies of *totalitarianism* and *authoritarianism*.

These types of dictatorial regimes became commonplace after World War I. Although authoritarianism was somewhat less intrusive and effective than totalitarianism, both types adapted absolutism to a democratic age. As in an absolute monarchy, one person took charge of the state. Yet unlike the monarchies of old, the new dictators did not descend from some special god-linked dynasty but rather claimed to be singled out by "historical destiny." Often, the lower-class birth of a dictator worked to his advantage, allowing a portrayal as a man of the people, a member of the masses who had become important and empowered with industrialization. The authoritarian leader's clothing helped to cement this new image. Gone were the crowns, ermine robes, and scepters of kings. Instead, the business suit, antiquated traditional costume, or worker's overalls and cap linked the dictator with average citizens; as an alternative, a military uniform asserted the values of discipline, obedience, and force.

As opposed to monarchs, who relied on tradition, dynasty, nobility, and religion, the modern dictator maintained power through the modern mechanism of a political party—elite followers who willingly and diligently served the leader. The party embodied the "will" of the people, who were only asked to participate in rigged elections and plebiscites. The party structure also channeled the will of the dictator down to the local level. Control of the media, adding radio and film to the traditional theater, pamphlets, posters, books, and newspapers of previous eras, enabled propaganda to sway opinion even more effectively. Coordinated with the military, judiciary, bureaucracy, and law enforcement, autocracy could mobilize the masses to achieve national goals as never before in history.

The authoritarian and totalitarian regimes of the twentieth century sprang from both the nationalism and socialism that had arisen in the nineteenth century. Karl Marx died in 1883, never thinking that the first successful proletarian revolution might take place in Russia because of its minimal industrialization. The Russian regime had always lumbered on under the sheer weight of its conjoined rule of tsar, Orthodox Church, and landed aristocracy.

Defeat in wars, however, triggered drastic change for Russia. The empire first showed its vulnerability when it lost the **Russo-Japanese War** (1905–1906). First, the Japanese surprise attack on Russian positions in East Asia humiliated the tsarist regime. Critics of the monarchy seized the opportunity to begin the **1905 Revolution**. Soviets (or councils) of Workers and Soldiers organized by the socialist **Leon Trotsky** provided real muscle to the revolt. At first, Tsar Nicholas II made concessions, at least to middle-class demands for a representative and limited government. After the defeated yet loyal troops returned from the front, however, he realized he had the power to crush the rebellion after all. Consequently, Tsar Nicholas acted on a basic principle:

> **No revolution can succeed against a relatively competent government.**

The tsar broke his promises to liberalize his government, revoked the constitution, and repressed the radicals, executing some and sending many others to prison in Siberia. Yet some survived, to keep plotting.

The enormous costs of World War I offered a second opportunity for revolution, as the tsar's governance failed in the crucible of that brutal conflict. The Russian front, as mentioned in the previous chapter, is often ignored in histories, which prefer to concentrate on the dreadful trench warfare of the western front. Yet the vast ebb and flow of armies from the mountainous Balkans to the frigid Baltic ravaged eastern Europe more horribly than the battles of Verdun or the Somme had in western Europe. The Russians had some successes against the hapless Austrians, but the German high command soon took over operations on the eastern front. Their efficient command ground up Russian troops. Tsar Nicholas himself foolishly went to the front to take command of the troops, but he lacked any skills beyond his limited ability to inspire.

Meanwhile, the capital of Petrograd (the new name for St. Petersburg, which sounded too Germanic) remained in the hands of the tsar's dilettante wife, Tsarina Alexandra. She fell under the spell of the charismatic charlatan Rasputin. That mad "monk" had convinced her that he could cure their son, the Tsarevitch Alexei, of hemophilia. People suspected that Rasputin exercised a baleful influence over Alexandra, ruling from behind the scenes. Even after a group of nobles brutally murdered Rasputin, the government still seemed adrift. The high casualties among the soldiers and increasing food shortages for the common people made Russia ripe for collapse.

The spark that sent the dynasty up in flames came from the Russian women, or "*babushkas*" (named after their headscarves). On International Women's Day, 8 March 1917, women trying to provide food for their families became fed up with government incompetence in bread rationing and took to the streets in protest.[3] Troops sent in to put down the riots with force instead joined the *babushkas*. Within a week, Tsar Nicholas was talked into abdication. The Romanov dynasty ended; the first, and brief, Russian Republic (1917) began.

This new liberal democratic parliamentarian government was a revolutionary success in itself. Its fate, however, foreshadowed what would happen to so many other regimes after the Great War, as the newly responsible politicians failed to solve their nations' problems. Three serious issues faced Russia's new leader, Alexander Kerensky, a leftist Socialist-Revolutionary. First, the elected government shared power with a shadow regime made up of the revived Soviets of Workers and Soldiers. Second, the wrangling political parties failed to unite on a common policy either to solve issues of land reform or to energize the economy. Consequently, food shortages worsened. Third, and worst of all, the government continued fighting Germany after being urged, bribed, and bullied by the other Allied Powers to stay in the war.

A cunning move by the Germans guaranteed that Russia's fragile republic would fail. They sent **Lenin** (b. 1870–d. 1924) on a sealed military train from Switzerland through Germany to Russia in April 1917. Born as Vladimir Ilyich Ulanov, this revolutionary had taken on the pseudonym "Lenin" (whose meaning is unclear) and at the turn of the century had become leader of the Bolsheviks, a faction of the Russian Social Democratic Party. **Bolshevik** means the "majority," and Lenin claimed the name for his followers after winning a minor issue during a party congress held in exile in London in 1903. Actually, the other Social Democrats, the Mensheviks, or "minority," were usually in the majority on most issues. Still, Lenin knew the value of a good label. The term **Bolshevism** gave a Russian name to Lenin's strict, hard-line Marxism: the belief that an elite party of dedicated revolutionaries would carry out a violent revolution. Lenin had no patience with the desire of other revisionist Mensheviks and their social democracy to work with the bourgeoisie and change society gradually by applying constitutional methods. Nevertheless, until 1917 Lenin had merely offered words and ideas, having spent some of his adult career in Siberia and the rest in exile in western Europe. By sending Lenin back to Russia, the Germans hoped that his revolutionary activities would destabilize their enemy. Lenin seized the opportunity for the long-awaited proletarian revolution and fulfilled German hopes, to their later regret.

Lenin laid out his program to the masses with beautiful simplicity: "Peace, bread, and land!" He promised to end the war, feed the people, and let the peasants have the land they worked. He was not interested in winning elections. In

---

3. Russia still operated under the Julian calendar, so what the rest of the West counted as taking place in March was called the "February" Revolution by the Russians.

mid-July, his Bolsheviks tried to seize control of the government. Although that uprising failed, Lenin had converted to his cause Leon Trotsky, who had wavered over the years between Menshevik social democracy, Bolshevism, and his own version of Trotskyism. Trotsky then provided more power through the Soviets of Workers and Soldiers. The better-planned October Revolution succeeded with barely a hitch during the night of 6–7 November 1917.[4] A large number of leftists, including Socialist-Revolutionaries, Mensheviks, and Bolsheviks, seized key public buildings. The warship *Aurora* in the Petrograd harbor fired the shot that launched the assault on the government sitting in the Winter Palace. After a few more shots, the revolutionaries basically strolled right into the palace, which was defended by few soldiers, including some in the grandly named Women's Battalion of Death. Later films showing heroic battles were mere propaganda. Kerensky himself had already left and eventually ended up in New York, where he died in 1970.

On the morning after Lenin's coup, the leftists elected him as head of the provisional government. Now Lenin put into actual practice his version of Marxism, soon called **Leninism**. Bolshevism moved from theory to practice. First, Lenin's dictatorship began with disbanding the new representative assembly the day after it opened in January. Second, he quickly outlawed and destroyed all the other political parties who had helped in the October Revolution. Terror and violence by secret police and revolution-inspired informers kept people in line. Third, Lenin declared a policy of **war communism**, which nationalized business and industry, both domestic and foreign owned. The land reform went through, at least by taking properties away from the bourgeoisie and the Orthodox Church. Fourth, he reduced the workday to eight hours. Fifth, Lenin relocated the capital from Petrograd to Moscow, seeing Petrograd as too exposed to foreign intervention.

At the time, the forces of opposition were indeed dangerous. The first problem was Germany. Lenin ended Russian participation in World War I with the Treaty of Brest-Litovsk in March 1918. It gave away one-third of the Russian Empire's European possessions, although most of those areas (Finland, the Baltic states, Poland, and the Ukraine) were mostly inhabited by people who were not ethnic Russians. Then the "Whites" (a loose alliance of nationalists, monarchists, republicans, and socialists) counterattacked the "Reds" (the Bolsheviks and their fellow travelers) from all directions of the compass. The Bolsheviks in turn murdered the imperial family, who had been under house arrest in the distant Ural Mountains. They shot in cold blood the former tsar, his wife, and their five children (including little Anastasia, contrary to the claims of later pretenders and cartoons).

For a while, it seemed as if the Whites might succeed in their counterrevolution, especially as they were briefly helped by foreign intervention. The Poles provoked their own war, hoping to expand their border to include territories once belonging to the greater Poland-Lithuania. Even more dangerously, Allied armies (British, French, Japanese, and American troops) seized Russian ports in the north along the western Arctic coast, in the south along the Black Sea coast, and in the

---

4. Again, because of the Julian calendar, Russia's "October" Revolution took place in what the rest of the West called November.

east on the Pacific coast of Siberia. Their ostensible reasons were, first, to help fight Germany; second, to prevent munitions sent to the Russian Republic from falling into Bolshevik hands; and, finally, simply to crush the Bolsheviks themselves. At one point, five thousand American troops occupied the northwestern ports of Russia, while nine thousand were in eastern Siberia. American soldiers invaded Russia, shot at Russians, and killed some.

Still, the Bolsheviks won the civil war by 1920, despite Allied intervention. The counterrevolutionary Whites lacked any common political program, military coordination, or revolutionary fervor. The Reds had better lines of internal communication, the support of many of the peasants, and united, strong resolve under the leadership of Lenin and Trotsky, who had commanded the Red Army.

Following the first Bolshevik victory, the country lay in ruins, with millions dead, millions more threatened with famine and disease, and the economic structures in shambles. Here Lenin showed his true genius by introducing the New Economic Policy in 1921. This policy reversed the extreme nationalization program of war communism. The NEP allowed most businesses to be privately owned again and to generate private profits in relatively free markets. By the mid-1920s, Russia had gained stability and caught up with its prewar economic status.

The new success of the country was reinforced in 1922 when Lenin declared Russia to be the **Union of Soviet Socialist Republics**, or **USSR** (1922–1991). At the core of this new political structure was the Russian Federative Soviet Republic. It included much of the old Russian Empire, including Siberia. Some of the other socialist republics contributed some ethnic diversity, such as Ukrainians, Belarusians, Moldavians, Uzbeks, Turkmen, Kazakhs, Chechens, Georgians, Azerbaijanis, and Armenians. The collective state of the USSR defied and, indeed, superseded nationality with a new ideology based on proletarian revolution. The central Communist Party controlled the government bureaucracy and elections, while the Politburo, its highest organ, directed the people in a socialist transition to the utopia of communism prophesied by Karl Marx. Most inhabitants accepted the new stability of their self-proclaimed "workers' paradise."

The victory of the communists in the Russian Revolution inspired imitators and raised alarm in Western nations. In the chaos of the Great War's end, communist insurgents rose up in parts of Germany at the beginning of 1919. For a few months communists briefly seized power in Hungary. In 1920, the Party of Institutionalized Revolution settled Mexico's decades of political instability. This Mexican socialist regime carried out land reform on forty million acres and nationalized foreign companies. In 1921, Lenin organized the Third International or Comintern to promote communism abroad. Western nations feared that more Bolshevik revolutions could threaten their own status.

During this first **Red scare** (1918–1922), Western politics became their own dominated by nativism, a fear of foreigners and immigrants. Western nations controlled their borders, suppressed radical political parties, arrested and deported suspected subversives, and fired left-wing teachers and civil servants. In 1919, the US government founded a new national police agency, the Federal Bureau of Investigation (FBI), to fight domestic communism. In hindsight, such fears were unrealistic. By the mid-1920s, communism had gained hardly any additional believers.

In communist Russia, meanwhile, the man who had guided the revolution to its success was also faltering. Lenin ruled in a modest fashion, often out of the public eye. He began to fall ill from a series of strokes in 1922. His wife, Krupskaya, did her best to convey the increasingly debilitated leader's wishes (as Edith Wilson had done for her husband Woodrow after his stroke). Lenin was dead by January 1924. His mummified corpse, displayed in a glass case within a tomb in Red Square, became the sacred shrine for his Bolshevik revolutionary cause. The Bolsheviks now had to find a replacement for Lenin while lacking a political mechanism for choosing a successor.

The logical choice was Leon Trotsky, a key figure in the revolutions since 1905. He had much practical experience as an organizer of the Soviets and the Red Army. He was energetic, intellectually brilliant, and rhetorically inspiring. Yet some criticized Trotsky for arrogance, his Jewish heritage, and his ideological impurity: he had only converted late to Bolshevism. Strangely enough, others deemed him too radical as he pushed a program to start communist revolutions around the world.

In the end, Lenin's successor was a man called "Steel" or **Stalin** (b. 1879–d. 1953). Born Joseph Vissarionovich Dzugashvily in Georgia in the Caucasus Mountains, Stalin had played only a marginal role in the early revolutionary period. In the new Soviet Union, though, he rose to become general secretary for the Communist Party. In that position, Stalin directed the hard drudgery of bureaucracy necessary for the functioning of any complex modern state. He also found jobs and arranged promotions for his own friends and supporters. Stalin appeared more moderate than Trotsky because he advocated socialism in one state, Russia, rather than world revolution.

Stalin quickly secured his dictatorship. As general secretary of the Communist Party since 1922, Stalin wrote the constitution in 1924, then took control of both party and state by 1927. He convinced the Politburo to throw Trotsky out of the party and even exile him from Russia. Trotsky fled to socialist Mexico City, where in 1940 an assassin, on Stalin's orders, bashed in Trotsky's head with an ice axe.

Once in complete control, Stalin added his own variant to the communist systems Marx and Lenin had implemented before him. **Stalinism** probably would have horrified both of them. The tentative experimentation of the early years abruptly ended. Instead, Stalin established an absolute personal dictatorship, supported by the cult of his own personality. The dictator eliminated all his rivals, culminating in the **Great Terror** (1936–1938), an era that resembled the Reign of Terror of the French Revolution. Stalin arrested tens of thousands of "Old Bolsheviks," those who had fought alongside Lenin and Trotsky. All women, who under socialist principles of equality had risen to positions of authority, were removed. He liquidated half of his officer corps. Many of these victims were purged through show trials, where they publicly confessed to crimes of espionage or counterrevolutionary activity of which they could not possibly have been guilty. Stalin had many victims officially executed; others simply "disappeared." Stalin sent thousands to internal exile, into prison labor camps in Siberia called gulags.

The propagandized benevolent image of Stalin countered this campaign of fear. Stalin made sure that his own face, name, and reputation shone brighter than those of anyone else, including Marx and Lenin. The entire history of the revolution was rewritten to emphasize Stalin's alleged central role. Numerous holidays, ceremonies, and programs were dedicated to Comrade Stalin, who, with paternal caring similar to that of the tsars of old, looked after his proletarian flock.

People put up with this egotistical side of Stalin's regime partly because of his success with another key part of Stalinism: modernization. In just a few years, the Soviet Union's economic power had already advanced further than it had under the tsars. But even that achievement was not good enough for Stalin (see figure 13.2). He felt that his state was decades behind other advanced countries, and he wanted to make up the difference quickly. In 1928, he ended the New Economic Policy, Lenin's experiment with free-market capitalism and private ownership. Instead, a series of **Five-Year Plans** revived central planning of the economy to

Figure 13.2.   A Red Army soldier warns the Russians to "Be on Guard!" as European neighbors glare and grasp toward their lands. (NYPL Digital Collection)

a degree never before experienced. The government bureaucracies regulated the economy down to the minutest detail, emphasizing heavy industry. Forced laborers hastily built new cities in Siberia, such as the poorly planned Magnitogorsk, which went from a population of a few bears to two hundred thousand people in a mere ten years.

Stalin freely borrowed ideas from the United States. The steelworks in Magnitogorsk were modeled on those of Gary, Cleveland, and Pittsburgh, along with their freely flowing industrial pollution into air and water. Large-scale, mechanized, industrial farming in the American heartland inspired *collectivization* of agriculture in Russia. The state confiscated the peasants' land, and communal groups then farmed the land. Many peasants resisted surrendering the land they had only recently gained. Stalin targeted prosperous peasants, called kulaks, as class enemies to be liquidated. The regime machine-gunned such opponents or sent them to prison camps. In turn, many peasants slaughtered their own animals or burned their own crops in retaliation, thus contributing to a major famine. Ukrainians regard the "terror-famine" or Holodomor that devastated their republic as a Soviet attempt at genocide. In all, the application of the Five-Year Plans killed perhaps ten million people and caused suffering for many millions more.

In the long term, though, Stalin saw positive results. The land was cleared; homes grew out of wilderness; factories hummed with machinery. Stalin's policies also provided access to education and health care for almost all citizens. The standard of living for most Soviet comrades far surpassed that of the tsar's subjects. Stalin had transformed a weary, second-rate great power into the second most powerful nation in the world, next only to the United States of America. Many westerners, disillusioned by their own infighting of splintered parties and the failures of capitalism in depression and inflations, admired what Stalin had accomplished. They joined socialist and communist organizations in their own countries, confident that these ideas embodied the future. It was easy to ignore the millions of dead: the pointless World War I, the heartless flu—death had taken so many in the past decades. At least these Russians, some said, had died for the worthwhile cause of progress. Unfortunately, no one could ask the dead for their opinion.

Review: *How did the Bolsheviks establish a new kind of state and society?*

Response:

LOSING THEIR GRIP

During the years after World War I, the colonial empires of the Western powers began to weaken. Exhausted by the efforts of global war, the European powers did not even realize that the strength of their imperial grip was wavering. In reality, profits and tax revenues from maintaining empires failed to cover the costs of investments and government payments. Leaders slowly came to realize that modern colonialism was not worth the costs in taxes and lives. Meanwhile, their distant subjects were also growing restless, and stronger.

At war's end, though, the European leaders still clung to continuing their own empires, and the new League of Nations helped them with that effort. The League took charge of the colonial territories of the defeated Central Powers and handed them out to the victorious Allies, calling them **mandates**. The British and French Empires received most of the former German colonies in Africa and the southern Pacific, as well as much of the non-Turkish regions of the dismantled Ottoman Empire. The Belgians took over Rwanda and Burundi, near King Leopold's original colony of the Congo. The Belgian colonial rulers pitted the very similar Hutu and Tutsi peoples against one another in order to better control the colony. As far as the imperialist planners of Western nations were concerned, it seemed at first that the twentieth century would continue just as the nineteenth had.

Colonial peoples saw this sharing of the spoils as a betrayal of President Wilson's idea of self-determination in the Fourteen Points. The West believed itself to have exported its glorious Western civilization to peoples who still lived in darkness. Those peoples who lived in the allegedly dark places of the globe did not see it that way. The victors callously ignored delegations from colonial areas. The Wafd (or "Delegation") Party from Egypt could not make its plea for independence heard. The Chinese argued in vain for concessions on extraterritoriality. Western leaders even snubbed Japan, their ally in the Great War.

For the next few decades, westerners remained certain they could hold on to and continue to convert the rest of the world to their way of life. Even though profits from colonial areas were slim to nonexistent, optimistic investors still hoped to make money. They believed they could adapt the colonial lands to the world economy, mostly to benefit the various mother countries. For example, confident British imperialists thought a handful of Oxford-educated civil servants and trained police officers could handle populations in South Asia that outnumbered them by thousands to one.

This imbalance in numbers tilted ever more against the West. Europe's own prosperity had caused a **population explosion** in the nineteenth century, when the inhabitants doubled in number even after immigration to the Americas and to colonial possessions. By 1914, however, imperialism had brought these industrial and scientific advantages to the four corners of the world. Soon the peoples of Asia and Africa also underwent their own population explosions (which to some extent still continue). In contrast, modern industrial society in the West after the war encouraged smaller families, with compulsory education and better workers' benefits. So population growth slowed, stopped, and even began to recede in

European countries throughout the twentieth century. Soon the "white" portion of world population began to shrink, as it is still shrinking today, compared with the "colored" portion. Europeans already in the 1920s noticed the trend and began to fear a Yellow Peril, a threat that Asians might regain their independence or even come to dominate the West. These fears found expression in suspense novels about the inscrutable evil genius Fu Manchu or the conquering "Yellow hordes" in the *Buck Rogers in the 25th Century* comic strip.

Contrary to Western stereotypes, the colored peoples of the world were neither stupid nor evil. Certainly, they had not gone through a commercial revolution, a scientific revolution, or an industrial revolution on their own. With imperialism, however, the lessons learned from those advancements were available to anyone with an open mind (and at less risk and lower costs). Once colonized peoples had recovered from the initial shock of the Western invasions and subjugations, they began to wield the westerners' own ideas against them, especially the idea of nationalism. They learned that self-government was not only for Belgians or Italians but also for Chinese or Congolese. Meanwhile, the Bolsheviks in Russia promoted themselves as the friends of "oppressed peoples" (avoiding mention of their own russification of non-Russian subjects). Soviet calls to resist capitalist and imperialist exploitation found willing listeners. Thus, pressures from the native peoples for self-government grew relentlessly.

The British Empire, which set the example for imperialism in the nineteenth century, led the way in its decline in the twentieth. Immediately after the Great War, its imperial structure began to crumble. The trouble began closest to home as the "**Irish Problem**" flared up for the British. In Ireland, the political party **Sinn Fein** ("Ourselves Alone") had worked toward independence from Britain since the turn of the century. In 1916, their Easter Rising in Dublin had been bloodily crushed. As soon as the war was over, many Irish formed the so-called Irish Republican Army (IRA). At first, the IRA used terrorism, but soon it organized enough to fight a civil war against the special British police troops, the "Black and Tans." The growing violence convinced Great Britain to withdraw. Both sides agreed to a semi-independent Irish state in 1920. In 1938 this state became the completely sovereign Republic of Ireland.

The fighting did not stop, however, as some Irish thought the victory incomplete. The sore spot remained the counties of **Northern Ireland**, also called Ulster, which stayed part of the United Kingdom of Great Britain. Back in the 1600s, Protestant Scotch-Irish families had settled there and ever afterward formed the majority. Since they had been in Ireland as long as white people had in North America (or Afrikaaners in South Africa), they considered themselves Irish, even if they identified with the Protestant English and Scots more than the Roman Catholic Irish. The moderate majority throughout Ireland accepted this division of the island, but a few demanded that the whole island be under one independent government. So some Irish Catholics began killing other Irish Catholics over this disagreement. The Irish Republican Army broke apart in this second civil war. By 1922, the moderates' acceptance of a divided island had won. Over the next five decades, only a few underground terrorists occasionally and ineffectively surfaced with a bombing or assassination to protest the ongoing political division of the island.

Of greater consequence to the decline of British power (although less violent) was the breakaway of the empire's four self-governing white **dominions**. Great Britain had colonized the three most important dominions, Canada, Australia, and New Zealand, in the same way as they had the American colonies. British immigrants stole the land from the natives, whether they were called the First Nations and the Inuit of Canada, the Aborigines of Australia, or the Maori of New Zealand. For those they did not slaughter, the British imposed fraudulent treaties, forced the natives from their lands, confined them to reservations, tried to drill the "savage" out of indigenous children in residential schools, and discriminated against them in the towns of "white" society. By 1900, populations of European descent had transformed these dominions into Western, modern, industrialized states that were comparable economically and socially to any nation in Europe. In the fourth significant dominion, the Union of South Africa, the white ethnic British and Dutch Afrikaaners co-ruled the land, even though they were in a small minority compared to the various tribes of black Africans.

All four of these states were tired of being bossed around by a Parliament sitting in London. As British dominions, they had been automatically drawn into World War I, where too much of their own people's precious blood had been spilled far from home on the battlefields of Europe. The dominions saw too many differences in economic policy as well, especially as the Great Depression overwhelmed the globe. In 1932, these four states negotiated an equal partnership in the newly formed **British Commonwealth**. This new structure offered its members economic cooperation, rather than political compulsion. As for the United Kingdom, the British Empire clearly dropped in its status as the ranking world power after losing direct and immediate access to the resources of Canada, Australia, New Zealand, and South Africa.

The British Empire suffered still more setbacks in the Middle East and South Asia. In 1922 the British finally granted independence to Egypt, a territory they had snatched from the Ottomans in the late nineteenth century. The British kept ownership, though, of the crucial Suez Canal until 1956. To compensate for the loss of Egypt, the British grabbed on to mandates carved out of the destroyed Ottoman Empire. Drawing arbitrary borders of straight lines on the map, British geographers contrived the countries of **Iraq** and Transjordan. They put in charge new kings, Faisal and Abdullah of the Hashemite dynasty. These two Arab sheiks had been allies of the British during the Great War but were virtually unknown to the peoples of Iraq or Transjordan.

The appointed King Faisal of newly created Iraq ruled over diverse peoples: a handful of Jews and Christians, and the Sunni Arabs in the center of the country, who traditionally hated the Shiite Arabs in the south. Also, the non-Arab Kurds in the north were frustrated that they had not gained their own country of Kurdistan (which would have taken parts of Turkey and Iran as well). The British helped Faisal fight insurgencies, using airplanes with poison gas against rebel Kurds and Arabs. By 1926 they had tired of fighting. The British withdrew, although they kept key military and economic privileges. The very next year, petroleum was discovered under Iraq's sands. Although modern British technology was necessary to pump the oil from the ground and refine it, Iraq was ultimately sole master of this resource, which made it a power to be respected and feared in the region.

Britain's other mandates in the Middle East were as troublesome as Iraq. The British split the Ottoman province of Jordan into two parts, Transjordan and **Palestine**. The latter was beginning to receive the Jewish immigrants encouraged by the Balfour Declaration made during the Great War, which had committed Britain to accepting a Jewish "homeland" there. The native Arabs quickly grew resentful at the growing numbers of new Jewish neighbors. By 1936, violence between Jews and Palestinian Arabs had intensified into a near civil war, with the British caught in the middle. By 1939, a fateful year, the British stopped all Jewish immigration in order to keep the peace with the Arab majority.

Meanwhile, the "jewel in the crown" of the British Empire, the Indian subcontinent, was increasingly hostile to continuing English rule. The British mistakenly believed their regime was doing the Indians a favor. Often Indians had been ruled by foreign conquerors, of which the British were merely the benevolent latest. Instead of being grateful, however, Indians resisted with their own version of Western nationalism. The **Indian National Congress**, founded in 1886, began as a body to help maintain British dominion but soon worked to expel it.

After 1915, the British Empire was shaken to its roots by the return to India of **Mohandas Karamchand Gandhi** (b. 1869–d. 1948). In his youth Gandhi had tried to assimilate. After studying law in London, he first tried to practice law in South Africa. Originally, Gandhi had been just one more Indian trying to make himself over as British. Then the injustice of being thrown off a train because he was not a white European radicalized him. Gandhi learned that for people of color, the Western ideals of liberty and equality were empty promises. After he organized the Indian community in South Africa to fight for civil rights, he returned to his native India in 1915.

By then, Gandhi had rejected westernization as materialistic, immoral, and godless. He began his transformation into a traditional Indian holy man, with enough success to earn him the honorific title "Mahatma" (Great Soul). He discarded Western pin-striped suits, starched collars, and ties and instead wore loose, homespun robes and shaved his head. He cultivated asceticism and simplicity. Certainly, some aspects of his life took on a touch of the unusual, such as his concern with vegetarianism and his practice of resisting sexual temptation by (literally) sleeping alongside naked young women. Most importantly, though, Gandhi took Indian religious ideas and turned them into a political philosophy. He claimed that *satyagraha* (soul force) could defeat the greatest empire in history, and his soul force was based on peaceful civil disobedience. Indians, he felt, would wake up British sensibilities by using their own ideals of decency and fair play.

A massacre by the British of hundreds of peaceful protesters in 1919 at Amritsar (or Jallianwala Bagh), boycotts of manufactured goods, protests of taxes on salt, and peaceful marches against discrimination all worked to Gandhi's advantage. In response, the British periodically imprisoned him. That only added to Gandhi's aura of righteousness. His nonviolence left him immune to criticism about means, while his fasts, simplicity, and eccentricity made him resistant to personal attacks. News spread by the global press made Gandhi a popular hero. Only the most stubborn of the British, like Winston Churchill, thought that England could hold on to India for much longer.

Meanwhile, the other European imperialist powers failed to recognize the precariousness of their own situations. France continued to hope to "civilize" its Caribbean, African, and Asian subjects. Belgium continued to exploit the Congo. The Italian, Dutch, Portuguese, and Spanish outposts limped along. Ignoring calls to recognize humanity in all people, certain westerners began to glorify attitudes of imperialism even more than the rabid nationalists had in the nineteenth century. These beliefs brought forth an alarming new ideology based on racism and violence.

Review: How were the Western empires slowly weakening?

Response:

FASCIST FURY

The crucible of World War I had obviously failed to reconcile the tensions between nationalism and imperialism. A new political ideology, *fascism*, fused those two ideas, offering an alternative to both communism and liberalism. Like the Bolsheviks, fascists rejected the actual practice of parliamentarian government, which they thought merely allowed political opponents to quarrel instead of solving serious problems. Despite their mutual hostility to liberal democracy, both Marxists and fascists differed from one another in their fundamental understanding of history. Marxists yelled that class conflict drove historical change, and only the unified workers could forge the ideal society. Fascists shouted that ethnic conflict explained the past, and only domination by a nationalist leader could make a better future.

In the fascist point of view, stronger people should dominate while the weaker individuals died out. The fascists cited the **eugenics** movement, which warped scientists' discoveries about heredity. Supporters of eugenics called for breeding policies that eliminated undesirables from the human gene pool.

Fascist ideology also called for a **corporate state** that bonded together the leader and people of one ethnic group. Fascists believed that since both workers and property owners belonged to the same ethnic people, they should cooperate in harmony under the beneficial guidance of the leader of the corporate state. The fascist protection of private property (properly used) made allies of the economic elites, while socialist language won over the workers. Even the old aristocrats and nobility were welcomed back as guardians of the national heritage.

Fascists also exalted violence. They embraced militarism, displayed in their love of uniforms, banners, and parades. Other militaristic virtues such as obedience, discipline, and endurance of hardships replaced liberal ideals such as creativity, freedom of conscience, and expanding opportunity. Fascism went beyond typical militarism and praised violence as the greatest glory of man, whether applied to the conquest of other peoples or to the forceful repression of domestic differences. Fascist bullies frequently hurt others just to prove their own superiority, even if it disturbed law and order.

Postwar Italy gave birth to this ideology of racism and violence. The country's imperial inferiority complex had deepened with embarrassment over its lackluster performance in World War I. At the war's end, Italians found their "victory" to be hollow and bitter. They had never really won any great battles. Their few acquisitions of territory from the dismembered Austrian Empire caused more problems than they were worth, since they actually acquired troublesome ethnic minorities from German South Tyrol and Slavic Istria. Italy had failed to gain anything from the Ottoman Empire as their Allies had promised. And the papacy, still bitter over the loss of the Papal States, continued to frustrate national politics. In addition, postwar economic readjustment caused unemployment and strikes, while the traditional socialist, liberal, and conservative parties could not cooperate with one another.

Out of this swamp, a former anarchist and socialist, **Benito Mussolini** (b. 1883–d. 1945), rose to become the first theorist and practitioner of fascism. Mussolini declared that he had the answer to Italy's civil disorders, even while his fascist thugs added to the turmoil. When the fascists staged a massive March on Rome in October 1922, Mussolini waited in the background, ready to flee the country if anything went wrong. He need not have worried. The democratic parties simply abandoned responsibility when confronted by the bold assertions of the fascists, as republicans had done when faced by the Bolsheviks in Russia during 1917–1918. The king of Italy readily appointed Mussolini as prime minister. Mussolini used this position to become "Il Duce" (the Leader) of both his party and all Italy.

It took several years, however, for the Italian fascists to reach their goal of authoritarian power. They bullied, assaulted, and murdered their opponents. They stripped Italians of civil liberties and political responsibility. Meanwhile, their propaganda showcased their job programs, swamp drainage, housing construction, and arrests of undesirables. Many people even came to believe that Mussolini made the notoriously late Italian trains run on time. He did not. Yet hopeful Italians and optimistic foreign observers convinced themselves that Italy was on the rise. Mussolini even reconciled the pope to modern Italy by signing the Lateran Concordat, establishing the Vatican City along with a few other palaces and properties as an independent territory under papal sovereignty. Italians achieved a certain perverse pride in their revived national standing. By 1927, Mussolini could do whatever he wished.

What Il Duce wished was to revive the Roman Empire. His fascist version, though, lacked the original's tolerance for diversity. Instead, Mussolini wanted Italians to impose their culture on all their subjects. On the European continent, he was already forcing Slavs in Istria and Germans in the South Tyrol to become Italians by forbidding their languages and even translating their family names into Italian. On the continent of Africa, he harshly repressed independence efforts in Italy's colonies of Libya and Somalia. Then some Italian troops stationed in Somalia violated the border of neighboring Abyssinia (more often called Ethiopia) in December 1934. Mussolini could not tolerate black Africans shooting at white Italians. He also sought to avenge the humiliating defeat of Adwa, where Italy had lost to the Abyssinians in 1898. Thus, in October 1935, Mussolini launched the **Italo-Abyssinian War** (1935–1937).

In response, Haile Selassie, the emperor of Abyssinia, appealed to the League of Nations to stop this aggression against one of its own members. The only action the League made in Abyssinia's defense was to impose economic sanctions against Italy with a trade embargo on many products. These sanctions, however, neither included oil, which powered Italy's modern military machines, nor curtailed the United States (not a member of the League), which continued to trade with Italy. As a result, with modern trucks, tanks, and planes, the Italian forces decisively defeated Abyssinia's less mechanized forces. By the summer of 1937, with all of Ethiopia occupied, the League lifted the insignificant sanctions, thus essentially endorsing Mussolini's aggression. When the League dared to disapprove, Italy withdrew its membership.

Fascism might have remained confined to Italy (and its empire), just as Bolshevism had been stuck in Russia, if not for the Great Depression. The apparent failure of democratic leaders to cope compared unfavorably with Mussolini's apparent success. Imitators seized power throughout eastern and southern Europe. These areas were particularly vulnerable to fascism. The Paris Peace Treaties had created many small states out of the former empires of Romanovs, Habsburgs, and Ottomans. This **balkanization** meant that small states struggled with national identity and ethnic minorities, economic competition with neighbors, and lack of investment capital, all with little tradition of democracy. Many welcomed the simplistic nationalism of hatred and exclusion pitched by fascists.

For example, the **Kingdom of Serbs, Croats, and Slovenes** founded at war's end soon succumbed to fascist yugo-slavism. Numerous other ethnic groups, however, such as Montenegrins, Bosnians, Germans, Italians, Magyars (Hungarians), Bulgars, Turks, Albanians, Macedonians, Pomaks, Vlachs, and Romany (Gypsies), resided among the dominant Serbs, Croats, and Slovenes within the borders of the kingdom. Both ancient and new disagreements among these ethnic groups frustrated cooperation and effective political action. In 1929, a bitter King Alexander dissolved the parliament, suspended the constitution, and abandoned democracy.

In his renamed **Kingdom of Yugoslavia**, Alexander enforced a royal dictatorship based on Serbian fascism. Rather than meekly accepting the dominance of Serbs, other ethnic groups organized an opposition. The Macedonians revived the IMRO, and the Croatians formed the new Ustaša (Insurrectionist) terrorist organizations. Working together as assassins where they had not as politicians, they blew up King Alexander on 9 October 1934 while he visited Marseilles. Nevertheless, his Serbian successor stuck with the fascist royal dictatorship for several more years.

In the far western part of southern Europe, the Iberian Peninsula also knuckled under to fascist dictatorships. Generals seized power in Portugal in 1926, and their military successors continued to rule there until 1974. In contrast, neighboring Spain briefly experienced an expansion of democracy. In 1931, a peaceful revolution had thrown out the capricious and arbitrary king and established the Republic of Spain. At first, liberals and democratic socialists presided over the government. Then anarchists and communists (influenced either by Trotsky or by Stalin) won elections and formed a coalition called the "Popular Front." These reform-minded leftists soon encroached on the traditional prerogatives of the Roman Catholic Church and Spanish aristocrats. They called on Generalissimo Francisco Franco to overthrow the legitimate government. Franco began the **Spanish Civil War** (1936–1939) by leaving his outpost in the Canary Islands, first to invade Spanish possessions in North Africa and then on mainland Spain itself. Franco next outmaneuvered his conservative allies and founded a fascist movement under his personal control, which he called the Falange (phalanx). Both fascist Italy and Germany helped him with money, supplies, seventy thousand Italian "volunteer" soldiers, and planes and pilots from the German Luftwaffe (air force).

Surprisingly, the legitimate Spanish republican government was able to slow the advance of Franco's fascist armies. A few foreign believers in democracy and socialism, such as the writers George Orwell and Ernest Hemingway, volunteered to aid the republicans, served in their militias, and publicized their cause. Even the Soviet Union aided the republicans with money and advisors. Such help by Bolsheviks, however, probably hurt more than it helped the Spanish republicans. No Western democratic government supported the Spanish Republic if it relied on Stalin.

Desperate for support, the republicans made a deal with the Basques, a people who have claimed to be the longest-standing residents of Europe. Through centuries of domination by Romans, Visigoths, Moors, Castilians, and modern Spaniards, the Basques had managed to maintain their language and culture despite having little political power. In October 1936, the Republic of Spain allowed the establishment of the "Republic of Euzkadi," an autonomous region of Basque self-government. To the fascistic nationalists under Franco, such diversity in Spain was intolerable. On 27 April 1937, German bombers unleashed the first successful strategic bombing raid in modern history on the Basque capital. By the end of the day, the city was in ruins, with more than two thousand dead. The terror felt by the people, if not the world, was expressed in Picasso's famous painting, named after the Basque capital: *Guernica*. The Republicans hurt their own cause by disagreements along ideological and ethnic lines. And without allies, they could not hold off the fascist onslaught. In March 1939, Franco finally

Figure 13.3.   The Valley of the Fallen. Franco's fascist memorial to
the dead of the Spanish Civil War was built with the forced labor of the
republican and socialist defeated. Disagreements between supporters
of the left and right or nationalism and regionalism about whether
the monument overly memorializes fascism continue to disturb politics
in Spain.

took Madrid and established a dictatorship that would last for the rest of his life,
thirty-six more years (see figure 13.3).

By 1939, only two countries in southern and eastern Europe remained democratic. The first country was **Turkey** (now spelled *Türkiye*), on the southeastern
fringe of Europe. The Paris Peace Treaty with the defeated Ottoman Empire left
only a weak and small Turkish state. Alone among the losers of World War I, however, the Turks resisted the treaty imposed upon them. An army officer, Mustafa
Kemal, overthrew the Ottoman sultan and abolished the sultanate on 1 November
1922, ending the one cultural institution that claimed to unite all Muslims. He
renamed himself **Atatürk** (b. 1881–d. 1938), which meant "father of the Turks," to

symbolize his role as a new founder for the Turkish people. He led Turkish armies to drive out invading Italians and Greeks while the British and French dithered. Atatürk then westernized his nation and set up a secular state.

While Atatürk largely succeeded at founding a stable democratic government, nationalistic resentments led the Turks to solve some ethnic conflicts by expulsion. Turkey banished most of its Greek and Bulgarian citizens, while Greece and Bulgaria returned the favor by deporting many of their Turks. Greeks had been living in Asia Minor since the sixth century BC. With these forced removals, twenty-five centuries of Greek civilization in the important region of Ionia ended abruptly. Nearly two million people were exchanged with much hardship, although fortunately few massacres. At the time, few other countries followed this relatively bloodless, if brutal, model of solving ethnic claims.

The brand-new country of **Czecho-slovakia** remained the only other state in southern and eastern Europe to resist authoritarianism.[5] Czecho-slovakia itself seemed like a miniature version of the vast multiethnic Habsburg Austro-Hungarian Empire, out of which it had been carved and then cobbled together. The rivalry between the two dominant ethnic groups of Czechs and Slovaks mirrored the conflict between Austria-Hungary's Germans and Magyars, while the Sudeten Germans mirrored the place of the Croats as a large third force. A minority of Magyars along the Hungarian border wanted to join Hungary, as Serbs had wanted to leave Austria and join Serbia. Nevertheless, Czecho-slovakia provided democratic representation and relatively fair treatment for all ethnic groups. The Sudeten Germans' fascination with fascism, however, would later destroy Czecho-slovakia (see below).

Thus, by 1939, all of southern and eastern Europe had come under authoritarian or totalitarian regimes: Latvia, Estonia, Lithuania, Poland, Austria, Hungary, Romania, Bulgaria, Yugoslavia, Albania, Greece, Italy, Spain, and Portugal. Those countries in Europe that did not have fascist regimes at least had fascist political parties. Even distant Japan (see below) prostrated itself before a clique of fascist generals. The tide of history clearly seemed to be rising for dictatorship, not democracy. Soon enough, the most fascistic of all fascists would begin a war intending to dominate Europe, if not the world.

Review: How did fascism spread across the West?

Response:

---

5. The Czecho-Slovak State, as the peace treaties named it, had been organized by exiles in Cleveland, Ohio, and Pittsburgh, Pennsylvania. The official name of the country between the wars often used the hyphen to separate the two dominant ethnic groups.

HITLER'S HATREDS

The most notorious and successful of fascists was, of course, **Adolf Hitler** (b. 1889–d. 1945). In 1933 he became "Der Führer" (the Leader) of the **Third Reich** (Third Empire), supposedly succeeding the Holy Roman emperors and the Hohenzollern kaisers. At first, Hitler peacefully extended the borders of his German state to its largest expanse since the fifteenth century. Then, in 1939, he launched a war that conquered most of the heartland of Western civilization.

Today it seems incomprehensible that Hitler could have attained such great power so quickly. Indeed, no one who had known Hitler during the Great War would have expected his later achievements. As the son of an insignificant Austrian civil servant, a reject from art school, and a mediocre painter of postcards, Hitler held in contempt the diverse ethnic groups of cosmopolitan Vienna. Ultra-nationalist ideas of *pan-germanism*, that all Germans should unite and dominate, entered his ideology. He fled his native Austria when the Habsburg regime called him to compulsory military service expected of all able-bodied male citizens. Shortly after Hitler arrived in Germany, however, he applauded the outbreak of the Great War, volunteered for the German army, and served on the front lines. Against all odds, he survived four years. During this time, he failed to distinguish himself with any leadership ability and rose only to the lowly rank of corporal.

Hitler's leadership only appeared as World War I ended and revolution threatened to tear Germany apart. During the last few years of the war, the Generals Hindenburg and Ludendorff had become military dictators, but they had failed to come up with a winning strategy. They realized the war was irrevocably lost even before the Allied armies broke through German lines in the fall of 1918. Revolutions began breaking out all over Germany (see figure 13.4). The Social Democrats attempted to bring stability and to prevent a communist takeover by proclaiming a new republic. This republican Germany, governed by its elected representatives, has since become known as the **Weimar Republic**, after the city where politicians hammered out its constitution.

Gravely threatening the fragile Weimar Republic were the peace terms imposed by the victorious Allies. As mentioned at the beginning of the chapter, the whole first part of the Treaty of Versailles, which established the League of Nations, was an insult to the excluded Germans. The Germans could have expected to lose Alsace-Lorraine and a few bits of land to Belgium, but they also lost a chunk of territory to Denmark, which had not even participated in the war. In the west, they lost the Saar region to France for fifteen years. In the northeast, the city of Danzig fell under unique League control. Poland gained a section of German people along the Baltic. This Polish Corridor gave it access to the Baltic Sea but cut off the province of East Prussia from the rest of Germany. Even worse, the Germans were to disarm: no navy, no air force, and an army of only one hundred thousand men without tanks or heavy artillery.

As intended, such a small force was insufficient to defend Germany, much less begin a war. A demilitarized Germany suited France. To further Germany's vulnerability, the western bank of the Rhineland (that side bordering France) was

By Claude Shafer in the *Cincinnati Post.*

DOG-GONE IT.

Figure 13.4. The editorial cartoon "Dog-gone it!" by Claude Shafer illustrates the dangers of unforeseen consequences. Germany did send the dog of revolution, namely the Bolshevik Lenin, to Russia. The Russian Revolution took that country out of the war, but the dog of revolution can go anywhere. After World War I, numerous revolutionary attempts broke out in Germany and elsewhere.

to be permanently demilitarized: devoid of troops or military installations. Thus, Germany could not easily invade France or Belgium, while France could march into Germany without trouble. To enforce these provisions, Allied troops were to occupy the Rhineland for fifteen years.

Worst of all, the Allies forced the Germans in part VIII, article 231, to accept the entire guilt for the war and responsibility for causing all the war's destruction. As a consequence, the Allies felt justified in making the Germans pay reparations in compensation. The costs of the war had been so high, though, that it took two years for the Allies to add up and present their bill. In the meantime, under threat of a renewal of armed conflict and with a blockade still starving Germany, the Allies forced the reluctant German representatives to sign the treaty on 28 June 1919, five years to the day after the assassination of Archduke Franz Ferdinand of Austria.

Paying close attention to these developments was the former corporal Adolf Hitler. After the war he stayed with the military, working for its intelligence agencies, gathering information on the numerous political parties that were springing up in the new Weimar Republic. One day Hitler attended the disorganized meeting of a group calling itself the German Workers' Party. He soon seized control of the party, changing its name to the National Socialist German Workers' Party, or the **Nazis**. Hitler then reshaped the party's platform into *Naziism* or *national socialism*, weaving together a powerful fascism with elements of racism, antisemitism, pan-germanism, nationalism, socialism, sexism, militarism, conservatism, and many other ideologies.

Hitler's love for Germany inspired a hatred for anything that he thought would weaken his nation in his eyes. He spelled out his chief goals in his 1924 autobiography, *Mein Kampf* (*My Struggle*). In his book Hitler argued that cultural diversity endangered Germany. He thought that Jews and Marxists threatened the superiority of the German or Aryan race.[6] He especially blamed Jews for Germany's defeat in the Great War, namely the "stabbed-in-the-back" myth.

In *Mein Kampf*, Hitler coined the term the "Big Lie" when he asserted that Jews were lying when they blamed the German commander General Ludendorff for Germany's collapse. Hitler explained how most people are more easily fooled by a fantastic falsehood than by a small fib. The masses could not conceive that anyone would have such audacious impudence to tell such a bald-faced lie. But historians consider that the Nazis themselves were the actual traffickers in the Big Lie. Ludendorff was at fault; the Jews had nothing to do with Germany's defeat. The Nazi propaganda "facts" and accusations against their opponents were vicious and wrong. People rarely want to accept blame for their own personal, communal, or national failure.

To overcome both the Jewish and Bolshevik threat, Hitler believed that he needed to become the dictator of Germany. A true German culture would then

---

6. The label *Aryan* comes from a pseudo-scholarly name for ancient Indo-Europeans who had settled Europe. Depending on the theorist, Aryans included all "whites" or "Caucasians," or just the more Nordic or northern Europeans (including the Dutch and Scandinavians), or just pure-blood Germans. The Aryan "race" is not to be confused with the Arian heresy of Christianity.

unify and strengthen the Germans as never before. Since other nations threatened German purity, Germany needed to expand into eastern Europe and acquire sufficient *Lebensraum* (living space). In *Mein Kampf* and in speeches and writings throughout the 1920s and 1930s, Hitler laid out a vision of national revolution and foreign conquest. Who could not have seen his desire for war?

Nevertheless, many both in Germany and abroad did not, even when Hitler's first attempt to seize political power involved force. The opportunity seemed ideal when Germany was racked by horrible inflation. In 1921, the bill for war reparations totaled 269 billion marks (worth ninety-six thousand tons of gold or over 770 billion of today's US dollars). When the German government briefly stopped paying the reparations in 1923, the French marched across the Rhine and occupied the Ruhr, the industrial heartland of Germany. German workers went on strike, and the Berlin government simply kept printing money to keep the economy functioning. Without either gold reserves or industrial production to back it up, however, the mark fell in value. This disastrous inflation meant that one dollar, which in 1914 had bought about four marks, would buy four trillion marks in 1923. To stop the disaster, the rich Americans stepped in with the Dawes Plan: US banks would loan the money to recapitalize Germany, which would then pay the reparations to France, which could then use the money to pay back what it had borrowed from the United States during World War I. Thus, a stream of capital flowed through the economic veins of the West. The plan worked, ending the ruinous inflation.[7]

This inflation had already provoked political uprisings all over Germany. Among others, Hitler himself attempted a *putsch* (German for coup d'état), having organized a march from a Munich beer hall to take over the province of Bavaria. The attempted coup failed miserably. Instead of executing Hitler for treason, however, the conservative court merely sentenced him to five years in prison. He served only nine months, using the time to write *Mein Kampf*. After his release from prison with his party banned, nothing more should have been heard of Hitler.

But then the Great Depression brought a return of the economic collapse. The American capital necessary for the Dawes Plan disappeared. Economic collapse spread around the world as banks shut down, businesses went bankrupt, and unemployment skyrocketed. Germany suffered most of all. Hitler used the disruptions to revive his party and establish it as the center of political discourse. His Nazi party went from the ninth largest in 1930 to the single largest in parliament (the Reichstag) by 1932 (although still in the minority). Soon democracy had ceased to function in the Weimar Republic. One chancellor with emergency powers followed another as each failed to solve the economic crisis.

---

7. Much of the original reparations were written off, and during the Great Depression, Germany stopped paying anything for years. But after World War II and even more after reunification, Germany finally paid off some of the bonds used to finance reparations. The final payment that closed Germany's books on the Great War was made on 3 October 2010. Other bonds owed by other countries for war debts have still not yet been redeemed. Debt endures.

On 30 January 1933, a coalition of nationalists and conservatives arranged for Hitler's appointment as chancellor.

Hitler then made sure that no remnants of parliamentary democracy would trouble him. He frightened the parliamentary majority into removing his rivals after a mentally imbalanced Dutch socialist committed arson on the Reichstag building. Once in Nazi hands, Hitler's Reichstag first outlawed the Communist Party (which, of course, had nothing to do with the arson but was the greatest rival to the Nazi party). In the next few months, the rump Reichstag outlawed every other political party. As for the remaining enemies of the new Nazi order? Within a few months, the Nazis opened their first concentration camp at Dachau, near Munich. Into this camp, and many others that followed, the Nazis sent political prisoners (communists, socialists, and pacifists), religious prisoners (Roman Catholics, Lutherans, and Jehovah's Witnesses), behavioral prisoners (sex offenders, homosexuals), and racial prisoners (foreigners, Romany [Gypsies], and Jews). Most Germans embraced the Nazi propaganda that Hitler would revive Germany's greatness, even, or especially, if it cost the freedom and lives of some of their fellow citizens. By 1939, eugenic fanaticism even led Nazis to murder thousands of ill, disabled, and neurodivergent children and adults in the very medical institutions that had been meant to help them.

After the communists and other political enemies had been dealt with, Hitler then had the chance to solve his "Jewish Problem." Nazi antisemitism saw Jews as a devious "race," which they determined based on bloodlines, not some concrete religious community or ethnicity. In the Nazi view, "the eternal Jew" was a subhuman conniver intent on destroying the superior Aryans and the rest of humanity. So, how to get rid of them? The solution started with some initial firings from government jobs, a few boycotts of Jewish businesses, and some assaults on Jews. Then punitive Nazi policies against Jews paused for two years. Many Jews thought that perhaps they had seen the extent of Nazi discrimination. The more prudent Jews emigrated.

Worse did come. First, in September 1935, new laws from the party center in Nuremberg revoked Jewish citizenship and with it many civil rights. In the next few years, more restrictions reduced more options for normal lives. Nazi propaganda exaggerated the Jews' ethnic differences, preventing any possible assimilation. Jewish businesses were marked, then closed; Jewish physicians could not practice on Germans; Jewish lawyers were dismissed from courts; all male Jews had to adopt the name "Israel" and female Jews the name "Sarah." During the night of 9–10 November 1938, thereafter remembered as Kristallnacht (Night of the Broken Glass) or the November pogrom, an organized Nazi assault smashed Jewish businesses, burned synagogues, looted homes, desecrated cemeteries, and murdered hundreds of Jews (although many of the deaths were officially listed as suicides). Those Jews who still wished to emigrate were allowed—if they could pay and if they could find a place to go. Few other countries wanted Jews. Even the British invitation to Palestine was withdrawn in 1939. The global outcry was minimal. The great powers were more concerned with Hitler's other plans that were slowly becoming more obvious.

Review: *How did Hitler rise to power and change Germany?*

Response:

SOURCES ON FAMILIES: JOSEPH GOEBBELS, "GERMAN WOMANHOOD" (1933)

The Nazis considered their takeover of the German government at the end of January 1933 as a revolution that ended the so-called Weimar regime and began a national revival along racist principles. On March 18, the propaganda minister Joseph Goebbels opened an exhibit in Berlin on "Die Frau" (which can be translated as the "Mrs.," "wife," or "woman"). In his speech, Goebbels laid out the Nazi vision for the role of women in the new Third Reich.

German Women, German Men!

I would like to see this moment as a fortunate coincidence, that I should present my first public speech directly to German women since taking over the Ministry of the People's Enlightenment and Propaganda. If I should acknowledge [the historian] Treitschke's saying, that "men make history," I do not thereby forget, that it is the women who raise our youngsters to be men. It is certainly known to you: the national-socialistic movement, as the only party, keeps women far from being directly involved in daily politics. The party has, as a result, been in many ways bitterly attacked and demonized, and all that is an injustice. It is not because we do not respect women, but rather because we respect them so much, that we have kept them far from the parliamentarian/democratic quarrels which have shaped politics for the last fourteen years in Germany. Not because we see in women something useless, but rather because we see in her and her mission something useful for a different purpose, than that which men fulfill.

. . . Nobody, who understands modern times, could conceive of the ridiculous idea to drive women out of public life, out of jobs, professions, being breadwinners. But it must not be left unsaid, that matters which are appropriate to men, must stay with men. And to such belongs politics and the military. . . .

If we took a fleeting glance at the last few years of German decline, then we would come to the fruitful, almost overwhelming conclusion, that so little were German men determined to prove themselves in public life as men, so much more did it fall to women to take on man's duty instead. A feminization of the man always leads to a masculinization of the woman. . . .

At the risk of sounding reactionary and traditionalistic, let me say it clearly and baldly: the first, best, and most suitable place for a woman is in the family, and the most wonderful task which she can fulfill, is to give children to her country and people, children, who carry forward the generations and the immortality of the nation. . . .

The liberal attitude toward family and child is complicit in Germany sinking so low within a few years, so that already today one can speak of the impending extinction of our people. While in the year 1900 one mature person had seven children, today one can expect only four children. If such birth rates remain the same, the ratio in the year 1988 would be one-to-one.

We are not willing to stare blankly and with crossed arms at the collapse of our culture and the destruction of our genetic substance passed on through our bloodlines. . . .

The new German women's movement begins here. If the nation again has mothers, who profess themselves freely and proudly to motherhood, then the nation cannot perish. If the woman is healthy, so are the people healthy. Woe to the state which forgets to care for the wife and mother.

Questions:

- *What does the source declare as the main role of women within society?*
- *What evidence does the source bring to support this need?*
- *How much are these values based in tradition or racism?*

Responses:

For more on this source, go to http://www.concisewesternciv.com/sources/sof13.html.

THE ROADS TO GLOBAL WAR

World War II can easily be seen as a continuation of World War I. That first great conflict did not resolve the pesky "German problem": how do you cope with a powerful, aggressive united Germany in the heart of Europe? Legacies of imperialism and nationalism remained roadblocks to peace. The nationalist aspirations of many peoples in Europe and around the world remained unfulfilled. The harsh competition produced by industrial manufacturing continued to set nations against one another. War still remained a popular solution for resolving differences.

Not surprisingly, many democratic peoples around the world did not want another world war. The potential death and destruction brought on by several great powers fighting again transformed many thoughtful people into pacifists. The two democratic European great powers, Great Britain and France, had been badly frightened by the horrors of that first Great War and the realization of their own fragility.

Meanwhile, westernization in East Asia was laying the foundations for a new, greater war. Imperialism's intervention had destabilized the two-thousand-year-old Chinese Empire. Uprisings against the imperial regime continued after the Boxer Rebellion in 1901. By the end of 1911, rebels had toppled the last emperor of China (which the child did not even notice, as he was so isolated inside the Forbidden City). The first president of the Republic of China was the Western-educated and trained **Sun Yatsen** (b. 1886–d. 1925). Sun had for years been planting the seeds for a democratic China, organizing the **Nationalist Party** (abbreviated as GMD or KMT).[8] He had designed the party along Western lines by incorporating ideals of nationalism, republicanism, and socialism. His democratically inclined methods proved too fragile, however. A few weeks after Sun was sworn in on 1 January 1912, a general forced him out of the presidency and seized power. Even so, the new military dictator could not prevent more uprisings, leaving much of China under the sway of local warlords.

Japan saw an opportunity to replace Western imperialism in China, deciding on a call to rule East Asia and the Pacific themselves. The Japanese had learned from the West about the importance of colonial possessions. Their joining the Allies at the beginning of World War I had enabled the Japanese to get hold of the German extraterritorial privileges in China. Japanese imperialists soon wanted to make all of China its special protectorate.

The Japanese quickly grew tired of the international community dominated by Western powers. They resented the disarmament conference held in Washington, DC (1921–1922), which restricted the Japanese navy to being at a lower rank than the British and American navies. The Japanese were offended by racist American laws limiting Japanese immigration. Then the Great Depression struck Japan in 1930 with all the fury that had wiped out businesses in the United States. Many Japanese blamed the resultant unemployment and social disorder on their European-style parliamentarianism. Consequently, many Japanese devised their version of fascism. Japanese fascists wanted to establish a new, revived, glorious Japan, this time with imperial domination over Asia. Intimidation and assassination silenced the critics as the Japanese military forcibly intimidated the government.

---

8. Chinese and Japanese personal and family names are traditionally in reverse order compared with Western names. Thus Sun was his family name and Yatsen his personal or given name. Also, the difference between GMD and KMT or other names comes from a change in the late twentieth century in how to transliterate Chinese characters into the Latin alphabet. In this text, the more modern is listed first, although the second version is still frequently seen.

Japan's fascists knew their opportunity to dominate China was limited, since China had begun to achieve stability under the leadership of Sun's Nationalists. After being ousted from the presidency, Sun rebuilt his own political base against the warlords by using the Nationalist Party, together with some new allies. One ally was Russia, which Sun's protégé, **Jiang Jei-shei** or **Chiang Kai-shek** (b. 1886–d. 1975), had visited in order to learn about modern Soviet military organization. The Nationalist Party also allied itself with the fledgling Chinese Communist Party. Founded in 1921 and inspired by the Bolsheviks, Chinese communism was another successful Western export to Asia. In 1927, after Sun's death, Jiang became leader of the GMD, attacked many warlords, and, unexpectedly, defeated most of them. Along the way, he also attacked his former allies, the communists, driving the survivors into a distant province in the southeast. By 1928, Jiang began to urge the Western powers to give up their oppressive extraterritoriality treaties and recognize China as an equal, sovereign great power.

The interaction of nationalism, imperialism, and communism complicated China's politics. After the Chinese communists had withdrawn to rural southern China, one of their leaders, **Mao Zedong** (b. 1893–d. 1976), began to adapt the party to the needs of the Chinese peasants, especially focusing on land reform. Jiang's Nationalists attacked a second time, which the communists survived through their legendary "Long March" of 1934–1945. The communists retreated for thousands of miles until they reached a haven in the far north.

Meanwhile, the Japanese seized the province of Manchuria from China. After Jiang's government appealed to the League of Nations, an investigatory committee looked into the matter and weakly criticized the Japanese aggression. In reaction, Japan only became more belligerent. In 1937, a minor incident at Beijing's Marco Polo Bridge (named after the medieval Italian traveler to China) prompted the Japanese to launch a full-scale invasion. Japan's attack on the city of Nanking in December 1937 viciously slaughtered almost half the city's population of six hundred thousand. The violation of tens of thousands of Chinese women gave the assault its name: the Rape of Nanking. The rest of the world, including the Western powers, watched and did nothing. They did not realize that this war between two Asian great powers was the beginning of **World War II** (1937–1945), which was soon to engulf them all.

Britain and France were more concerned with German aggression in Europe, although even there they took no decisive action. The French hoped that their Maginot Line, a series of complex and expensive fortifications begun even before Hitler came to power, would stop any possible German attack. In 1935, Hitler began to openly rearm Germany, directly violating the Treaty of Versailles. In 1936, he remilitarized the Rhineland, completely ending the imposed restrictions of the treaty. In March 1938, he bullied fascist Austria into agreeing to annexation, or **Anschluß**. When Austria's chancellor tried to hold a referendum to preserve Austrian independence, German troops simply marched into the country. Most people in Austria and abroad accepted the fait accompli. Austrians who openly objected wound up dead or in concentration camps. Then in the fall of 1938 at the **Munich Conference**, Hitler got the British, French, and Italians to sign off on his annexation of the Sudetenland, an ethnic German part of Czecho-slovakia. After that agreement, most ethnic Germans in Europe lived under Hitler's authority. The "rump" Czecho-slovakia meanwhile had lost the ability to defend itself.

People have often criticized the inaction of the great powers concerning the events both in Asia and in Europe as **appeasement**. The word simply describes a policy of giving in to an aggressive government's demands rather than fighting. It has become a term implying weakness and failure because, with hindsight, these actions allowed Japan and Germany to be better prepared for war. At the time, though, Western leaders saw appeasement as a reasonable approach. Not every issue is worth a war. When it came to Hitler's demands, why should Germany not be armed as every other nation was? Why should Germany not reasonably defend its own territory? How could anyone say that Germany should not include all ethnic Germans?

After the easy annexation of the Sudetenland, though, Hitler's demands ceased being reasonable, even under nationalist principles. Western leaders finally recognized Hitler's desire for *Lebensraum*, despite promises of peace (see Primary Source Project 13). In the spring of 1939, Hitler enticed or coerced the Slovaks into declaring independence from Czecho-slovakia. That act provided his excuse to occupy the territory controlled by the remaining Czechs. For the first time he had annexed substantial numbers of non-Germans, acting as an imperialist instead of a nationalist. This action finally woke up France and Britain to Hitler's expansionism. While France and Britain were not prepared to go to war for Czecho-slovakia, they did pledge their support to Poland, which seemed Hitler's next likely target (because of the Polish Corridor and Danzig). Not many noticed or cared about Mussolini's conquest of Albania in April 1939.

Hitler laid the foundation for further acquisitions in eastern Europe in a brilliant diplomatic maneuver. The deadly rivals Nazi Germany and communist Russia signed a nonaggression pact in late summer 1939. These newfound allies secretly divided eastern Europe into spheres of influence between them. Free from worrying about a possible two-front war, which had hurt Germany in World War I, Hitler could now do what he wanted. He invaded Poland on 1 September 1939, beginning the European phase of World War II.

Although Britain and France declared war two days later, there was little they could do to save Poland. Hitler's generals were able to test their *Blitzkrieg* (lightning war) tactics to great success (see diagram 13.1). Coordination of air power and tanks solved the problem of maneuvering large armies. Drugging soldiers with methamphetamines (today used in the form of "crystal meth") spiked their energy to fight long and hard. These tactics (and Russia's attack from the east) eliminated Polish defenses in a matter of weeks.

Germany at first seemed to have all the advantages. Britain and France sat through the "Sitzkrieg" (meaning "sitting war," a word play on *Blitzkrieg*) of the winter of 1939–1940, while Russia defeated plucky Finland to grab key defensive positions. With the spring thaw, Hitler surprised everyone with an attack on Denmark and Norway. Victory came quickly, first because effective use of paratroops enabled the Nazis to seize key locations. Second, native fascists,

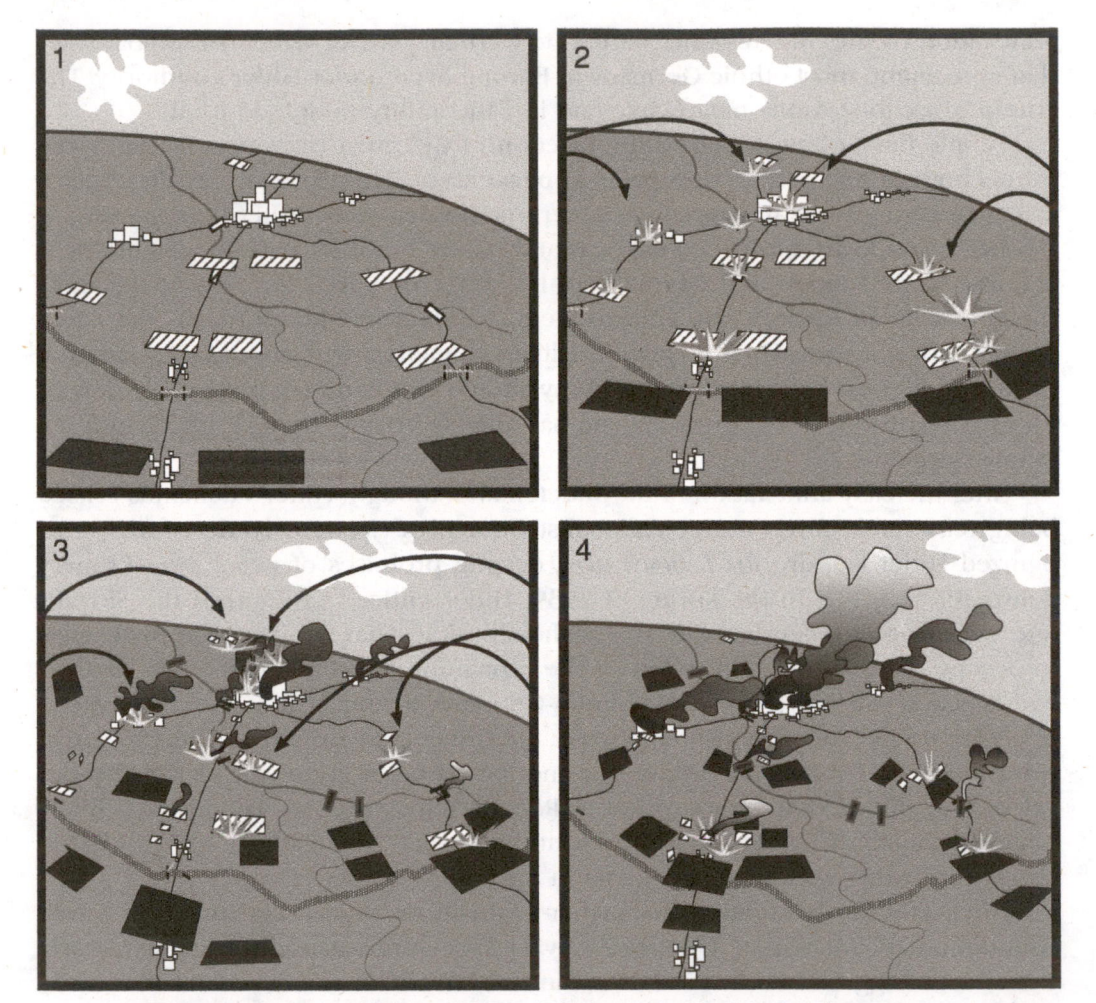

Diagram 13.1. Blitzkrieg! Phase 1: Before the Blitzkrieg-style warfare begins, black and striped military units face each other across a border. Phase 2: As attacking black ground forces advance, black's bombers strike far behind the lines to break up enemy units, disrupt lines of transportation and communication, and even bomb civilians in the cities, causing panic and confusion. Phase 3: Attacking black tank forces both confront enemy forces and go around them cross-country. Small commando units seize or build river crossings to enable larger armies to cross. Phase 4: Aerial bombing, artillery shelling, and flanking and encirclement by black armies have fragmented the defending striped forces. Infantry mops up the remains.

sympathetic with Nazi Aryan ideology, operated as "fifth columnists" (implying an extra group of troops on the inside) or "quislings" (named after the Norwegian fascist leader) to help the Nazis into their countries. Hitler thus solved another problem of World War I: Norway's ports on the Atlantic this time ensured that Germany could not be successfully blockaded, while its U-boats (submarines) could attempt to blockade Britain.

The new British prime minister, **Winston Churchill** (r. 1940–1945, 1951–1955), was barely in office when German armies attacked Holland, Belgium, France, and Luxembourg. The Germans evaded France's Maginot Line by punching tanks through the ill-defended Ardennes Forest. Like Poland, France fell in weeks. The British and a handful of allied forces managed to flee from Dunkirk on the French coast back to England, leaving much of their weaponry behind. By the fall of 1940, Hitler tried to soften up England for invasion with the **Battle of Britain**, the first decisive air campaign in history. Britain won this battle (partly due to the new invention of radar). Since Germany lacked the air cover to protect a sea-to-land assault, Britain gained time to recover and rearm. The prospect of defeating Germany alone, however, seemed bleak.

By this time, Hitler ruled most of Europe, with the largest empire since Napoleon's. If he had remained satisfied with these gains, the course of world history would have been much different. Nothing less would satisfy him, however, than German mastery of all Eurasia. Impatient and confident in his previous successes, Hitler betrayed and attacked his secret ally, the USSR, on 22 June 1941. His surprise attack was at first brilliantly successful.

With Britain still at his rear, Hitler launched a two-front war. Regrettably for Hitler, serious errors slowed his invasion of the Soviet Union. First, Britain was strong enough to help Russia with supplies. The vastness of Russia, as Napoleon had learned, also made it nearly impossible for armies to find and defeat all the Russian forces. At first, many peoples in Russia actually welcomed the German armies as liberators from the brutality of Stalin. Quickly, though, the Germans showed that they were Nazis, dedicated to enslaving or killing all non-Aryans. The peoples of the Soviet Union realized that there was something worse than Stalinism.

As the German offensive against Russia bogged down in the muddy autumn of 1941, several eager Nazis returned to their obsession about the Jewish Problem. They came up with a **Final Solution**: killing all Jews. To achieve this goal, the Nazis built several special camps in occupied Poland to which they shipped the Jews from their ghettoes. In Auschwitz, Treblinka, and Sobibor, the Nazis stole the Jews' last possessions, killed them in gas chambers, and burned their corpses in crematoria. The resulting death of millions of Jews has been named the **Holocaust** (Greek for burnt sacrifice) or **Shoah** (Hebrew for disaster). Some people these days, calling themselves "revisionist historians," deny the reality of this slaughter. They say it didn't happen; the Nazis did not try to execute all the Jews. Such people are either fools or liars. The Final Solution was as real as the rest of World War II. It is an indisputable fact of history. Given enough time, the Nazis would have killed every Jew they could have laid their hands on, followed by the extermination of other racial and social enemies. The only thing that stopped this Nazi genocide was losing the war.

Germany lost this war because, just as during World War I, its opponents built alliances to outnumber and outfight it. Before the war, Hitler had arranged superior alliances. Germany had named itself and its allies the Axis Powers, including hapless Italy, energetic Japan, and reactionary Spain, which, however, stayed out of the war. During the war, the only truly willing allies were the resentful states of Hungary (angry about its small size after World War I), Bulgaria (still simmering over its losses in the Balkan Wars), and Finland (having suffered Stalin's attack in 1939). In the end, the lack of cooperation among the Axis Powers doomed them. If Japan had invaded Russia, a two-front war might have brought down the Soviet Union. Instead, Japan decided to attack Great Britain and the United States of America.

Axis attacks made building a coalition of opposing Allies much easier. After Hitler had treacherously attacked Russia, Churchill quickly allied with Stalin, despite concern about communism. Churchill also successfully cultivated the American president, Roosevelt (see Primary Source Project 13). Churchill and FDR went so far as to sign the **Atlantic Charter** in the fall of 1941. This document proclaimed their mutual support and set generous goals for a postwar world, even though the United States was not yet in the war. Indeed, most Americans were isolationist, thinking it just fine if communists and fascists and Asians fought each other.

Then, on 7 December 1941, the Japanese launched planes from aircraft carriers and bombed the American military base at **Pearl Harbor** in Hawaii. They also attacked other British and American bases in the western Pacific. The attack on Pearl Harbor, though bold and successful in its immediate goal, was a strategic blunder. Attacking Britain made some sense: England could barely defend itself, much less its worldwide possessions. Bringing the United States into the war, however, doomed Japan. Americans saw the planes flown against Pearl Harbor as unjustified, especially since the bombing had taken place before a formal declaration of war. In the words of one of their own commanders, the Japanese had awakened a sleeping giant. The outraged Americans would never have stopped fighting to avenge the deaths of 2,600 soldiers and sailors until Japan was utterly defeated.

Just as in World War I, the entry of the United States into World War II was the beginning of the end. The vast industrial potential of the country and its determination to avenge Pearl Harbor guaranteed an Allied victory. Then, a few days after Pearl Harbor, Hitler made the worst mistake of his career. Without any real necessity, he declared war on the United States. This relieved Roosevelt of a huge dilemma. He had wanted to help Britain in Europe but could not easily ask Congress to authorize what would be a two-front war. Thus, even though America was committed to the War in the Pacific because of Pearl Harbor, Hitler's overconfident declaration brought the United States into the European conflict as well.

America was strong enough to fight, and win, a global war alongside the other Allies (see map 13.1). The United States fully unfolded its vast economic power, helping to equip the Allies and fighting major conflicts both in Europe and in Asia at the same time. By the summer of 1942, the Japanese were overstretched by their conquest of most British, Dutch, and American possessions in the Pacific. Counterattacking American forces began hopping from island group to island group, learning their own jungle combat tactics and using aircraft carriers to help cut Japanese communications and supplies. The battles in the Pacific were small in scale compared with the hundreds of thousands of men on the Russian front, but the fighting was brutal and nasty. Jungle heat and tropical disease sorely afflicted

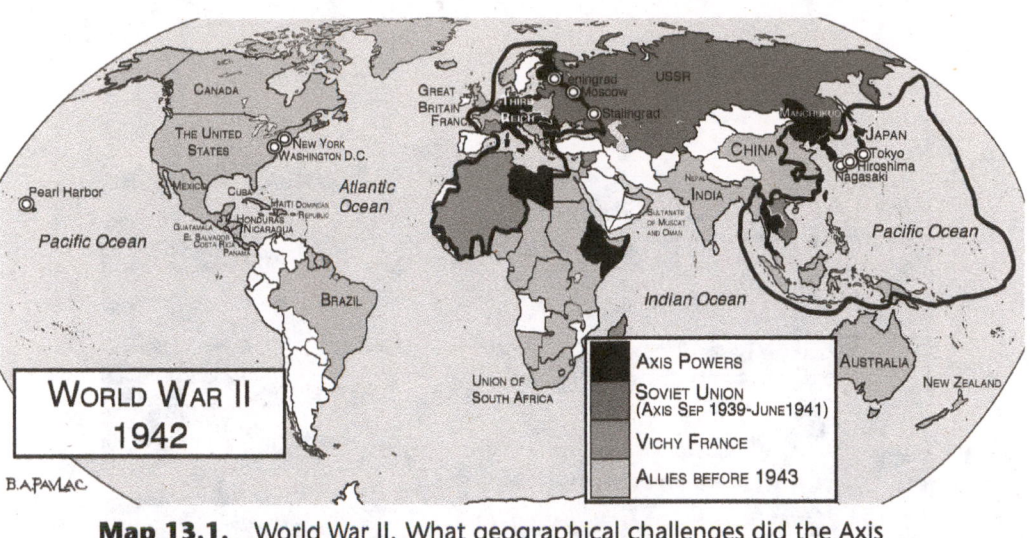

Map 13.1. World War II. What geographical challenges did the Axis Powers face in their quest for world domination?

both sides. Still, defeat was inevitable, even though the Japanese resisted to the last soldier on almost every island.

In the fall of 1943, the tide turned in Europe, as American forces began to liberate North Africa and the Russians enmeshed the Germans in the Battle of Stalingrad. By early 1944, German armies were in slow yet inevitable retreat. D-Day, or the Normandy invasion by the Allies (6 June 1944), saw the largest sea-to-land assault in human history. Meanwhile, Allied heavy bombers, the British by night and the Americans by day, were sparking firestorms, setting entire German cities on fire. In one night of bombing, a modern city could be reduced to rubble, while tens of thousands of civilians, including old men, women, and children, died in their bomb shelters from heat or suffocation. It is a myth, though, that carpet bombing broke the will of the Germans and significantly helped end the war. Actually, most civilians continued to support the regime. Only as Axis factories lost access to fuel and raw materials did their crucial armaments industries fail.

Nazi scientists had, for a while, hoped for "wonder weapons" to bring victory. Jets and rockets were put into action, but too little, too late. Another possibility had been a city-destroying device: an **atomic bomb**. German leadership in the study of physics had given the Nazis a great head start in the science for such a weapon. Instead, America built the bomb first. The most brilliant physicist of the century, Albert Einstein, had fled from Nazi Germany to America because of Hitler's persecution of Jews. Einstein wrote to President Roosevelt to encourage America to construct an atomic bomb before the Nazis could. The Nazis never came close to building such a weapon. By May 1945, Germany had been conquered. Hitler was dead from suicide, his body only partially cremated in a ditch because his last followers lacked enough gasoline.

After the defeat of Germany, Japan still fought on. In July 1945, American scientists successfully tested their "Trinity" atomic device, applying a divine name to a weapon of mass destruction. On 6 August, America dropped one bomb on

Figure 13.5.   A broken Roman Catholic church, St. Mary's or Urakami Cathedral, on a hill remains from the devastated city of Nagasaki after the second atomic bomb was dropped on Japan by the United States.

Hiroshima; on 9 August, another bomb on Nagasaki followed (see figure 13.5). The bombs accomplished what previously had taken hundreds of bombers dropping thousands of bombs. The two cities were incinerated in a flash: tens of thousands of people killed, many thousands more wounded, suffering from the little-known phenomenon of radiation. Japan finally surrendered on 14 August 1945.[9] Thus, the worst instantaneous destruction in human history ended the worst war in human history. The United States stood at the helm of Western civilization, now poised to lead it into the rest of the century.

Review: How did the German and Japanese desire for world empires shape World War II?

Response:

---

9. Several dozen Japanese soldiers continued to hold out, having not heard or refusing to believe that the war was over. The last two surrendered in 1974.

PRIMARY SOURCE PROJECT 13: HITLER VERSUS FRANKLIN D. ROOSEVELT ABOUT THE JUST SOCIETY

As nations prepared for World War II, leaders offered their ideological perspectives on fighting. Chancellor and Führer Adolf Hitler of Germany asserted his peaceful intentions but noted threats to his people (eight months before his invasion of Poland). Once the war had begun, President Franklin Delano Roosevelt called on Americans to support nations fighting against Hitler (eleven months before Pearl Harbor). He also set forth his view of measures needed for a just society.

Source 1: Speech to the Reichstag by Adolf Hitler (30 January 1939)

When, six years ago this evening, tens of thousands of National Socialist fighters marched through the Brandenburg Gate in the light of their torches to express to me, who had just been appointed Chancellor of the Reich, their feeling of overwhelming joy and their vows as faithful followers, countless anxious eyes all over Germany and in Berlin gazed upon the beginning of a development, the end of which still seemed unknown and unpredictable. . . .

But one thing remains unforgotten: It seemed that only a miracle in the twelfth hour could save Germany. We National Socialists believed in this miracle. Our opponents ridiculed our belief in it. The idea of redeeming the nation from a decline extending over fifteen years simply by the power of a new idea seemed to the non-National Socialists fantastic nonsense. . . .

To the Jews and the other enemies of the State, however, it appeared to be the last flicker of the national power of resistance. And they felt that when it had disappeared, then they would be able to destroy not only Germany but all Europe as well. Had the German Reich sunk into Bolshevik chaos, it would at that very moment have plunged the whole of Western civilization into a crisis of inconceivable magnitude. . . .

Gentlemen, we are faced with enormous and stupendous tasks. A new history of the leadership of our nation must be constructed. Its composition is dependent on race. . . .

What is the root cause of all our economic difficulties? It is the overpopulation of our territory. . . .

But to assume that God has permitted some nations first to acquire a world by force and then to defend this robbery with moralizing theories is perhaps comforting and above all comfortable for the "haves," but not for the "have-nots." Nor is the problem solved by the fact that a most important statesman simply declares with a scornful grin that there are nations which are "haves" and that the others on that account must always be "have-nots." . . .

[I]n connection with the Jewish question, I have this to say: It is a shameful spectacle to see how the whole democratic world is oozing sympathy for the poor tormented Jewish people, but remains hard-hearted and obdurate when it comes to helping them, which is surely, in view of its attitude, an obvious duty. The arguments that are brought up as an excuse for not helping them actually speak for us as Germans and Italians. . . .

Today I will once more be a prophet. If the international Jewish financiers in and outside Europe should succeed in plunging the nations once more into a world war, then the result will not be the bolshevization of the earth, and this the victory of Jewry, but the annihilation of the Jewish race in Europe! At the moment Jews in certain countries may be fomenting hatred under the protection of the press, of the film, of wireless propaganda, of the theater, of literature, etc., all of which they control. . . .

Source 2: Annual State of the Union Report to Congress by Franklin Delano Roosevelt (6 January 1941)

I have recently pointed out how quickly the tempo of modern warfare could bring into our very midst the physical attack which we must eventually expect if the dictator nations win this war.

That is why the future of all the American Republics is today in serious danger.

That is why this Annual Message to the Congress is unique in our history. . . .

The need of the moment is that our actions and our policy should be devoted primarily—almost exclusively—to meeting this foreign peril. For all our domestic problems are now a part of the great emergency. . . .

I also ask this Congress for authority and for funds sufficient to manufacture additional munitions and war supplies of many kinds, to be turned over to those nations which are now in actual war with aggressor nations.

Our most useful and immediate role is to act as an arsenal for them as well as for ourselves. They do not need man power, but they do need billions of dollars worth of the weapons of defense. . . .

Certainly this is no time for any of us to stop thinking about the social and economic problems which are the root cause of the social revolution which is today a supreme factor in the world.

For there is nothing mysterious about the foundations of a healthy and strong democracy. The basic things expected by our people of their political and economic systems are simple. They are:

Equality of opportunity for youth and for others.

Jobs for those who can work.

Security for those who need it.

The ending of special privilege for the few.

The preservation of civil liberties for all.

The enjoyment of the fruits of scientific progress in a wider and constantly rising standard of living . . .

In the future days, which we seek to make secure, we look forward to a world founded upon four essential human freedoms.

The first is freedom of speech and expression—everywhere in the world.

The second is freedom of every person to worship God in his own way—everywhere in the world.

The third is freedom from want—which, translated into world terms, means economic understandings which will secure to every nation a healthy peacetime life for its inhabitants—everywhere in the world.

The fourth is freedom from fear—which, translated into world terms, means a worldwide reduction of armaments to such a point and in such a thorough fashion that no nation will be in a position to commit an act of physical aggression against any neighbor—anywhere in the world.

That is no vision of a distant millennium. It is a definite basis for a kind of world attainable in our own time and generation. That kind of world is the very antithesis of the so-called new order of tyranny which the dictators seek to create with the crash of a bomb.

To that new order we oppose the greater conception—the moral order. A good society is able to face schemes of world domination and foreign revolutions alike without fear.

Since the beginning of our American history, we have been engaged in change—in a perpetual peaceful revolution—a revolution which goes on steadily, quietly adjusting itself to changing conditions—without the concentration camp or the quick-lime in the ditch. The world order which we seek is the cooperation of free countries, working together in a friendly, civilized society.

Questions:

- *According to the speakers, what are the dangers facing their nations?*
- *How does each speaker propose to overcome those dangers?*
- *How do the speakers see themselves and their nations at turning points?*

Responses:

Make your own timeline.

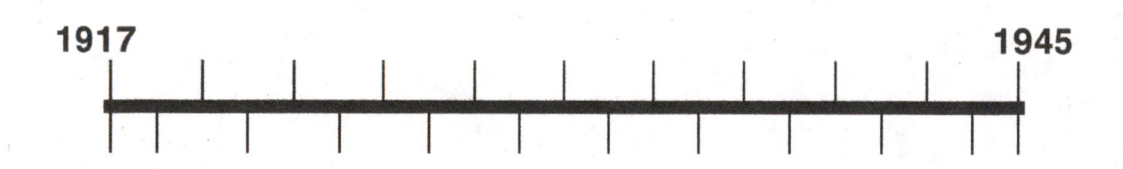

1917   **1945**

For more on these sources, go to http://www.concisewesternciv.com/sources /psc13.html.

CHAPTER 14

A World Divided

The Cold War, 1945 to 1993

The resounding victory of the Allies in World War II did not lead to international stability, as expected and hoped for. Instead, a new kind of conflict, the **Cold War** (1948–1991), dominated most of the latter half of the twentieth century. The Cold War resembled the long geopolitical competition between France and England that had lasted from the fourteenth to the nineteenth century. This time, two new primary enemies, the United States and the USSR, wrestled for world domination and threatened everyone else as never before. Their ideological points of view made it difficult to compromise or cooperate. During this colossal conflict between different aspects of Western civilization, the Cold War drew nearly every person on the planet into the influence of Western science, politics, economics, and culture.

FROM FRIENDS TO FOES

After the devastation of World War II, the first challenge for all states was the restoration of order and the reconstruction of economies. Much of Europe and Asia lay in ruins. Among the survivors, tens of millions of people had been displaced as soldiers, prisoners, forced laborers, or refugees. The millions of Germans who fled or were forcibly ejected from areas subsequently occupied by Russia, Poland, or Czechoslovakia gained little sympathy. Some nations again began to carry out ethnic removals to bring about nationalistic conformity. Yugoslavia kicked out Italians. Even Bulgaria and Greece seized the opportunity to expel thousands of Turks, even though Turkey had remained neutral during the war. Never before had such numbers of people been forced to migrate. Most displaced persons lacked homes and jobs, while states became much more ethnically uniform, as nationalistic ideals demanded. For their part, the Allied armies that occupied the defeated nations organized the slow rebuilding of those societies and suppressed the fascist policies that had caused the war.

The victorious Allies showcased the defeat of the fascists by conducting trials for war crimes against humanity. The slaughter and genocide of civilians during the war were considered so horrific that the victors undertook the unusual measure of convening international courts. As a result of the **Nuremberg Trials** in Germany, twenty-five captured Nazi leaders were hanged. Over the next several years a few dozen lower-ranking Nazis also faced judgment and execution.

Not all fascist criminals came to justice, however. Some Nazi sympathizers, collaborators, and even high-ranking officials managed to escape, many fleeing to sympathetic fascist regimes in Latin America, sometimes with the knowledge of local governments and Roman Catholic clergy. In particular, Nazi scientists, especially those responsible for work on rockets and jets, were smuggled to one victor or another. In Asia, the trials for Japanese war criminals were much less thorough. Emperor Hirohito of Japan had declared himself no longer a god, so the American occupiers retained him in office and absolved him of all responsibility for the war and atrocities committed by Japanese soldiers. Comparatively few Japanese war crimes were exposed or punished, especially since the United States was becoming less concerned about its wartime enemy, Japan, than about its wartime ally, Russia.

That the victorious wartime alliance fell apart so quickly surprised and confused many. Certainly, the victory in World War II created a unique geopolitical situation. The great powers, powerful countries who could assert military action around the world, had dominated international politics since the nineteenth century. By the end of World War II, though, England and its British Empire were clearly exhausted by the effort. France needed to rebuild, as did China, after suffering hard occupations. Of course, defeated Germany, Italy, and Japan lay in ruins and were occupied by the Allies. Only the United States and the Soviet Union remained capable of effective global action. Indeed, they had risen to the status of **superpowers**. They had large populations (over a hundred million), were industrialized, occupied vast continental landmasses, were rich in agricultural land and natural resources, and possessed massive military forces. The other declining great powers could not hope to match them.

Although they shared the attributes of superpowers, the United States and the USSR were extremely divided by opposing ideologies (see diagram 14.1). The Soviet Union was a totalitarian dictatorship with a secret police, the KGB; the United States worked along more republican and constitutionalist principles. The USSR used centralized state planning for its economy (often called communism); the United States practiced capitalism in a mixed economy of some socialistic regulation and competitive, semi-free markets.[1] Russia proclaimed itself to have outgrown nationalistic and class divisions (although its party elites led a substantially better life than its common workers); the United States, despite

---

1. As part of this ideological war, the term *capitalism* was redefined to oppose the "communism" of central planning of the economy by government. Thus, today many people define capitalism as the private ownership of the means of production instead of its simpler definition as the practice of reinvesting profits. Soviet-style "communism" likewise differed from Marx's ideal of common ownership.

	Politics	Economy	Society	Culture	Belief
USSR	totalitarian soviet one party	centralized, state-planned economy communism	classless society (party elites vs. masses) free public education	rigid censorship state-controlled press and arts	atheism persecuted Russian Orthodox
USA	democratic vs republican two parties	mixed economy: laissez-faire capitalism & socialism	upper middle lower classes private & public education	limited censorship free press profit-making arts	religious toleration separation of church & state nominally Christian

Diagram 14.1. This comparison and contrast between the United States of America and the Union of Soviet Socialist Republics notes how they represented different aspects of the Western heritage, which competed for people's allegiance during the Cold War.

a growing middle class, remained divided into significant economic disparities between rich and poor, often based on sex, ethnicity, and race. The Russian government rigidly controlled and censored its media; businesses, through their advertising dollars, influenced the American media. The Union of Soviet Socialist Republics proudly proclaimed itself to be atheistic (ostensibly believing in the dogmas of Marx, Lenin, and Stalin) and restricted worship by Orthodox Christians; the United States of America asserted religious freedom and toleration, while the majority of citizens attended diverse Christian churches. Communist Russia lost sight of the individual in its mania for the collective—many suffered so that the group might succeed; capitalist America awkwardly juggled individual rights and communal responsibility.

The differences in these practices and ideologies did not necessarily mean that a conflict was inevitable. Both sides could have decided to live and let live. Yet both sides envisioned their own path as the only suitable way of life for everyone on earth. Each state tried to dominate the world with its own vision of order, echoing the clashes of the past, whether between the Athenian creative individualism versus Spartan disciplined egalitarianism of the Peloponnesian Wars or revolutionary France against commercial Great Britain during the Wars of the Coalitions. The world split up between them.

The United States and its allies often called themselves "the West." The Soviet Union and its allies were often called the "Eastern bloc" because of their center in eastern Europe or from their association with China in East Asia. A more accurate terminology arose of the "First World" (the nations associated with the United States), the "Second World" (the nations associated with the Soviet Union), and the "Third World" (Latin America and the soon to be newly liberated colonial areas of Asia and Africa). A bloc of nonaligned nations who wanted to avoid taking sides never gained much significance.

The writings of the British author George Orwell (the pen name of Eric Blair, b. 1903–d. 1950) illuminated the ideological conflicts of the modern age. His non-fiction works counseled a gentle socialism while also attacking Western capitalism and imperialism, based on his experiences as a British police officer in colonial

Burma (now Myanmar), a vagrant in Paris and London, a combatant for the Spanish Republic, and a participant of life among downtrodden English workers. His fictional *Animal Farm* (1945) satirized totalitarianism in the Russian Revolution, while *1984* (1949) described a dystopian future of constant wars and lies. Especially *1984* warns of how people can easily accept propaganda that is inherently false and contradictory: "War is peace. Freedom is slavery. Ignorance is strength." A more dire warning about truth is the line "Who controls the past controls the future. Who controls the present controls the past." How fragile is history in the hands of ideologues, whether capitalist or communist?

The splits between East and West widened during Allied conferences as World War II wound down. First, in February 1945 at the Soviet Black Sea resort of **Yalta**, the "Big Three"—Stalin for the Soviet Union, Roosevelt for the United States, and Churchill for Britain—began to seriously plan for the postwar world after their inevitable victory. They agreed in principle that Europe would be divided into spheres of influence, thus applying the language of imperialism to Europe itself. Southern Europe went to the British, while much of eastern Europe came under the Russian sphere. Under the guidance of the British and Russians, self-government in different nations was supposed to be restored. The only sphere the United States committed itself to was joining Britain and Russia in occupying Germany.

After Germany's defeat but before Japan's surrender, the Big Three met again at **Potsdam** near Berlin in July 1945, although two of the leaders had been replaced. Stalin still represented the USSR, but Churchill had been voted out as prime minister and replaced by Labour Party leader Clement Attlee. In the United States, **Harry Truman** (r. 1945–1953) succeeded to the American presidency following the death of FDR in April. These three men shaped plans for the occupation of Germany (later adding France as a fourth occupier), *denazification* and the war crimes trials, restoration and occupation of a separate Austria, and peace treaties for the minor Axis members. While many questions remained open, the settlements seemed to be going well.

To provide for a more peaceful and unified global future, the United States and other victorious Allies created the **United Nations Organization** (UN). Fifty members signed the charter of the United Nations in San Francisco on 26 June 1945, as war still raged in Asia. The five victors of World War II (the United States, the USSR, Great Britain, France, and, generously, China), became the permanent members of the Security Council, with veto power over the organization's actions. The UN could provide some international regulations and help with health-care issues. More importantly, when the Security Council agreed, the UN's members could quickly and easily commit military forces. Its hope was to use collective security to maintain peace. The UN's peacekeeping role has indeed managed to keep many wars and rebellions from growing worse around the world. From the Congo to Cyprus, peacekeepers have saved lives. But the UN can solve an issue only if and when all five permanent members of the Security Council agree unanimously.

Soon enough, the superpowers diverged, as the temptations of occupation proved too strong for Stalin. Stalin soon began *sovietization* of the states in his sphere of influence (Poland, Czechoslovakia, Hungary, Romania, Bulgaria, and its occupied zones of Germany). Believing it his right to have friendly neighbors in eastern Europe, Stalin helped communist parties take over governments, which then claimed to be people's democratic republics. As in the Soviet Union, these regimes lacked opposition parties but still conducted feigned elections. The new communist leaders terrorized their people into fearful obedience. They reeducated, arrested, or executed "class enemies" such as fascists, but also liberals, conservatives, and socialists. They even purged their own followers, putting communist comrades in show trials just to prove that no one was safe. Using the excuse of rebuilding from the war's devastation, communist governments confiscated private property and nationalized businesses. As the occupying Soviet armies stayed and the new leaders of eastern European states took direction from Moscow, these "satellite" or "puppet" states were becoming protectorates rather than merely falling under a sphere of influence. These changes led the retired British prime minister Winston Churchill to use the metaphor of an "Iron Curtain" separating communist oppression from "Christian civilization" (see map 14.1).

At first, Americans ignored Churchill's warning. Nonetheless, growing communist-backed insurgencies in Greece and Turkey encouraged the Americans to share

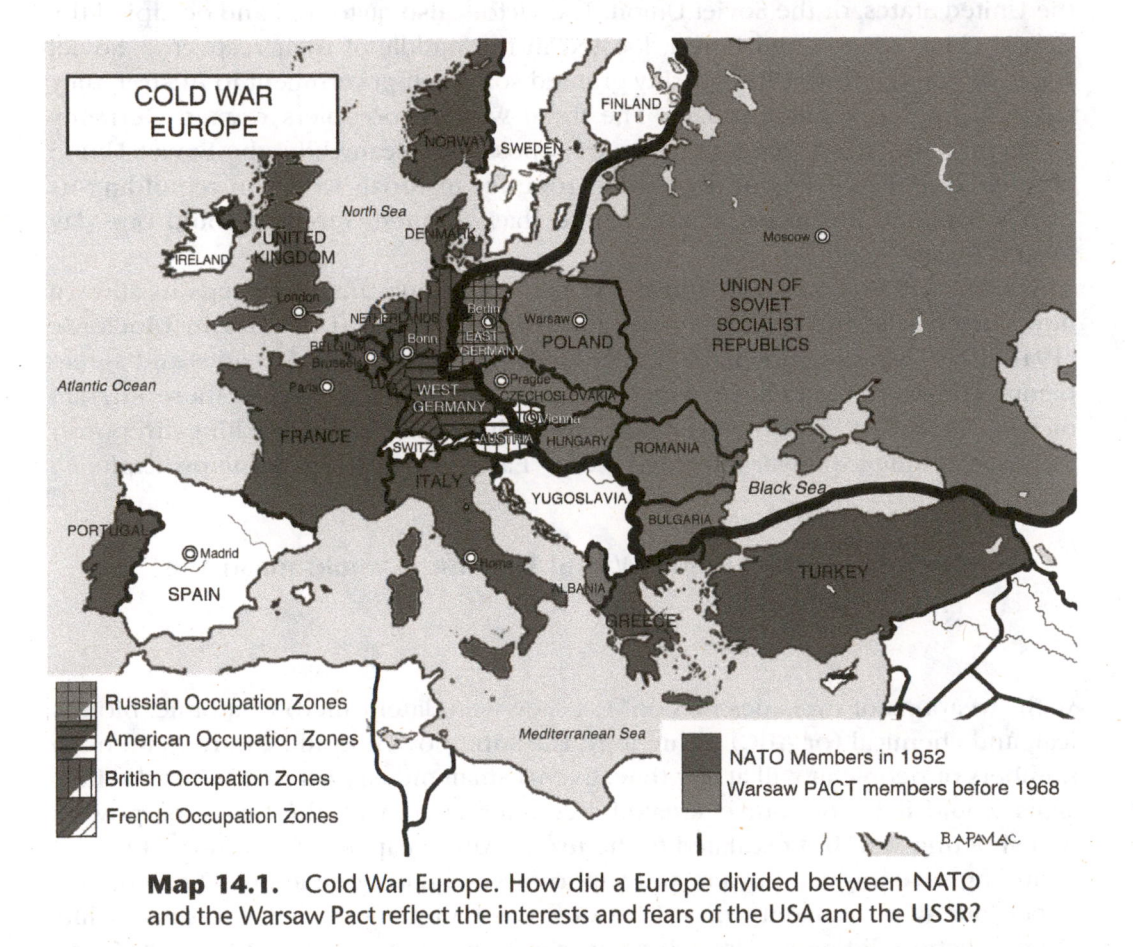

Map 14.1. Cold War Europe. How did a Europe divided between NATO and the Warsaw Pact reflect the interests and fears of the USA and the USSR?

Churchill's concerns. Soviet intervention in these new areas convinced American leaders that Stalin was expanding beyond the provisions of Yalta and Potsdam. President Truman decided to carry out a policy called **containment** to try to limit the influence of the Soviet Union in several ways. In his speech creating the **Truman Doctrine**, he promised aid to governments resisting hostile seizures of power by foreigners or even by armed minorities of natives. He explicitly contrasted the freedom of the United States with the tyranny of Russia. The United States followed up with military aid to the Greeks and Turks, who crushed the insurgencies. Through the Marshall Plan (or European Recovery Program), the United States also provided money to European states struggling with a lack of capital in the wake of the war. A small (compared to the total cost of the war) American investment of $13 billion helped rebuild Europe and weaken the appeal of communism. To further combat communism, a new American **Central Intelligence Agency (CIA)** gathered information and carried out covert operations outside the United States (including supporting armed intervention, sabotage, and assassination).

These heightening tensions solidified into an enduring dispute centered on occupied Germany. As the war ended, both Germany and Austria had been divided into four zones, each run by one of the victorious powers, Britain, France, the United States, or the Soviet Union. The victors also quartered and occupied the capital cities, Vienna and Berlin, located in the middle of their respective Soviet zones. While the four Allies quickly granted some self-government to Austria, they could not agree about Germany. The three Western occupiers wanted Germany to become more independent as soon as possible. Meanwhile, the Soviet Union plundered its East German occupation zone for materials to use in rebuilding its own devastated territories. It also feared that a united Germany could one day invade Russia again.

In June 1948, when the British, French, and Americans took steps to allow a new currency in the western zones, the Russians initiated the **Berlin blockade** (1948–1949), shutting down the border crossings in violation of treaties and agreements. The Allies could have, with legitimacy, used force to oppose these Russian moves. Instead of becoming a "hot" war, with each side unleashing firepower against the other, the war remained "cold." Each side held to a basic principle:

> **Nobody wanted World War III because it would mean the end of the world.**

With "weapons of mass destruction" (as they were later called) of atomic, biological, and chemical (or ABC) technology, the superpowers could exterminate huge numbers of people at will at any time. Even a small military action against the Russians would have, of course, created a counterattack, with the two superpowers in a shooting war. If it escalated to the use of ABC weapons, World War III (a war including several great powers and superpowers against one another) could have wiped out all of humanity, or at least destroyed all modern civilized ways of life. Only in fiction did people launch nuclear war, whether realistically predicting the catastrophic results as in the movie *On the Beach* or in James Bond movies where evil madmen plot world destruction.

A nonconfrontational solution to the blockaded city, the **Berlin airlift**, succeeded in the short term. The Western allies supplied the city, using airplanes to fly over the Russian barricades. Over nine hundred flights per day provided seven thousand tons of food and fuel to keep the modern city of two million people going for over a year. Enormous sums of money were spent, and men died (in several plane crashes), but no shots were fired. Then one day, the Russians opened the border again. Soon afterward, the Allied occupied zones became the new Federal Republic of Germany, or West Germany, based on the capitalist and democratic values of the Western allies. Subsequently, the Russians turned their sovietized occupation zone into the German Democratic Republic, or East Germany (see figure 14.1).

Both sides built new alliance systems. The **North Atlantic Treaty Organization (NATO)** bound together most western European states, along with Canada and the United States, in a mutual defense pact. Sweden and Switzerland retained their neutrality. Russia arranged the **Warsaw Pact** with its satellite states (Poland, East Germany, Czechoslovakia, Hungary, Romania, and Bulgaria) to better coordinate their military forces in opposition to NATO. These military alliances, ready to fight World War III, faced one another across the barbed wire and barricades that ran through the heart of German field and forest. Still, the divisions solved the "German problem," at least temporarily.

Figure 14.1. The glass stone mural *The Way of the Red Flag* of 1969, by a collective led by Gerhard Bondzin and placed on the side of the Culture Palace in Dresden, proclaims the values of the communist German Democratic Republic. A heroic female victory figure strides forward in front of various workers. At the top, the words read, "Despite everything, we are the victors of history."

Nevertheless, an arms race continued to threaten the world. By 1949, the Russians had their own atomic bomb. Then, by 1952, the United States developed the hydrogen or **H-bomb**, on which most modern thermonuclear weapons are based. Each H-bomb carried the explosive power of hundreds of times the Hiroshima and Nagasaki atom bombs (each of which destroyed an entire city). Aided by information gained through espionage, however, the Russians soon tested a thermonuclear weapon of their own. With or without spying, nuclear proliferation remained inevitable. With enough time, effort, money, and access to supplies, any nation can harness science to build nuclear as well as biological, chemical, or any number of conventional weapons. Throughout the Cold War, both sides kept shortsightedly relying on some fleeting technological advantage, only to see it vanish with the next application of scientific effort by the other side.

At first, complexity and cost usually meant that nuclear weapons remained in the hands of great powers. The British were next with nuclear bombs in the 1960s, quickly followed by the French. Soviet ally China came next. By the 1990s, India tested its prototype bomb, which prompted Pakistan to produce its own. It is unclear when South Africa and Israel got theirs, probably sometime in the 1970s, although South Africa has given up its technology, as have former Soviet republics such as Ukraine. Recently, North Korea has built atomic weapons and increasingly far-reaching missiles to carry them, while diplomats and inspectors have been trying to keep Iran from joining the "nuclear club."

These smaller states, though, possessed only a handful of nuclear weapons. In comparison, the two superpowers each held enough to destroy their enemies many times over. As technicians perfected **ICBMs** (intercontinental ballistic missiles) by the late 1950s, any target on the globe was vulnerable to vaporization. By 1977, the superpowers had stockpiled tens of thousands of nuclear devices—with the equivalent of about fifteen tons of TNT per person on the planet.

During the Cold War, the superpowers never pressed the button to end human history with the explosion of nuclear weapons. Instead, they relied on **deterrence** (preventing war through the fear that if one side started nuclear war, the other would finish it). The American policy of deterrence was aptly called MAD, the acronym for "mutually assured destruction." Both sides did play at brinksmanship (threatening to go to war in order to get your opponent to back down on some political point). In reaction to this periodic threat to civilization, some citizens of Western states began calling for nuclear disarmament. Governments also realized that they could not endlessly build risk into global politics. As a result, some areas became off-limits for weapons (Antarctica, the ocean floors, and outer space). Other countries were discouraged from acquiring their own weapons through nonproliferation treaties beginning in 1968. Throughout the 1960s and into the 1980s, the two superpowers negotiated on limits or mutual inspections of numbers and use of arms.

For the next several decades after the Berlin blockade, the Cold War was on. This third great world war of the twentieth century was unique in the history of politics. Like its predecessors, World Wars I and II, the Cold War cost enormous amounts of money, destroyed a lot of territory, cost many lives, and changed the destinies of nations. Unlike those other two conflicts, the main opponents, the

Soviet Union and the United States, never did actually fight each other, despite a string of international crises. Instead, they encouraged other people to do the killing, sometimes supplying intelligence, equipment, advice, and even soldiers to client states. These proxy wars killed perhaps fifteen million people over several decades. Although the Cold War was an ideological civil war of the West, it weighed on every international and many a domestic decision for almost all countries in the world.

Review: How did the winning alliance of World War II split into the mutual hostility of the Cold War?

Response:

PRIMARY SOURCE PROJECT 14: KHRUSHCHEV VERSUS NIXON ABOUT COMPETITION

Vice President Richard Nixon helped to open an American exhibit at a trade fair in Moscow in 1959. He and the Soviet premier Nikita Khrushchev engaged in spontaneous conversations about the different worldviews of America and the Soviet Union. Because some of the discussions took place around consumer products such as refrigerators and dishwashers, the exchanges became known as the "Kitchen Debate." The news conference was shown on American and Soviet television a few days later.

Source: The Kitchen Debate between Khrushchev and Nixon (24 July 1959)

Khrushchev: Regarding our wishes, we wish America the very best to show its goods, products, and abilities, great abilities and we will gladly look and learn. Not only will we learn but we also can show you what we do. This will contribute to improved relations between our countries and among all countries to assure peace throughout the world. We want only to live in peace and friendship with Americans, because we are the most powerful nations. If we are friends then other countries will be friends. If someone tries to be a little bellicose then we can tug his ear a little and say "Don't you dare." We can't be at war. These are times of atomic armament. A fool may start this war and a wise man won't be able to end that war. Hence these are our guiding principles in policy domestic and international. We wish you success in demonstrating America's capabilities, and then we will be impressed.

This is what America is capable of? And how long has she existed? 300 years? 150 years of independence and this is her level of achievement. We haven't quite reached 42 years, and in another 7 years, we'll be at the same level as America, and after that we'll go farther. As we pass you by, we'll wave "Hi" to you. [He waves and laughs.] And then if you want, we'll stop and say, "Please come along behind us." . . .

Another speaker: Mr. Vice President, from what you have seen of our exhibition, how do you think it's going to impress the people of the Soviet Union? . . .

Nixon: I, very early in the morning, went down to visit a market, and where the farmers from various outskirts of the city bring in their items to sell. I can only say that there was a great deal of interest among these people, who were workers and farmers, etc. I would imagine that the exhibition from that standpoint will, therefore, be a considerable success. As far as Mr. Khrushchev's comments just now, they are in the tradition we learned to expect from him of speaking extemporaneously and frankly whenever he has an opportunity.

And I am glad, and I am glad that he did so on our color television at such a time as this. [T]his, Mr. Khrushchev, is one of the, one of the most advanced developments in communication that we have, at least in our country. It is color television of course. It is, as you will see in a few minutes, when we will see the very picture of your speech and of my comments that has been transmitted. It's one of the best means of communication that has been developed.

And I can only say that if this competition which you have described so effectively, in which you plan to outstrip us, and particularly in the production of consumer goods, if this competition is to do the best for both of our peoples and for people everywhere, there must be a free exchange of ideas. There are some instances where you may be ahead of us—for example in the development of your, of the thrust of your rockets for the investigation of outer space. There may be some instances, for example, color television, where we're ahead of you. But in order for both of us [Khrushchev starts to speak] for both of us, for both of us to benefit, for both of us to benefit. . . .

Khrushchev: What do you mean ahead? No, never. We've beaten you in rockets and in this technology.

Nixon: You see, you never concede anything.

Khrushchev: We're ahead of you, too.

Nixon: Wait'll you see the picture.

Khrushchev: Good. We always knew that Americans were smart people. Stupid people could not have risen to the economic level that they've reached. But as you know, we are not fools. "We don't beat flies with our nostrils!" [Laughter.] In 42 years we've made progress. So let's compete! Let's compete. We can produce the most goods for the people. That system is better and it will win.

Nixon: Good. Let's have a, let's have a far more communication and exchange in this very area that we speak of. We should hear you more on our televisions. You should hear us more on yours. . . .

Nixon: You must not be afraid of ideas.

Khrushchev: We are telling you not to be afraid of ideas! We have no reason to
   be afraid. We have already broken free from such a situation, and we are not
   afraid of ideas.

Nixon: Well, then, let's have more exchange of them. We all agree on that, right? . . .

Khrushchev: Yes, I agree. But first I want to clarify what I'm agreeing on. Don't I
   have that right? I know that I'm dealing with a very good lawyer. Therefore, I
   want to be unwavering in my coalminer's girth, so our miners will say, "He's
   ours and he doesn't give in to an American lawyer."

Nixon: No question about that.

Khrushchev: You're a lawyer of Capitalism, I'm a lawyer for Communism. So let's
   compete.

Nixon: All that I can say, from the way you talk and the way you dominate the
   conversation, you would have made a good lawyer yourself. But what I mean
   is this: here you, here you can see the type of tape which will be trans—which
   will transmit this conversation immediately and this indicates the possibilities
   of increasing communication. And this increase in communication will teach
   us some things, and it will teach you some things, too. Because, after all, you
   don't know everything.

Khrushchev: If I don't know everything, then you know absolutely nothing about
   Communism, except for fear! I want you, the Vice President, to give your word
   that this speech of mine will be heard by the American people, reported and
   telecast on the TV in English. Will it be?

Nixon: Certainly it will . . . [shaking hands on it]. And . . . everything that I say
   will be recorded, and translated and will be carried all over the Soviet Union.
   That's a fair bargain.

Khrushchev: That's agreed! All your words will be recorded in Russian. We're businessmen. We came together on this immediately.

Questions:

  • *What details does Khrushchev use to support his ideology?*
  • *How do the speakers express ideas of competition?*
  • *How do the speakers use and understand processes of communication?*

Responses:

For more on this source, go to http://www.concisewesternciv.com/sources/psc14
.html.

MAKING MONEY

Rather than fight the Cold War, most Americans would probably have preferred to concentrate on expanding the US economy. But traditional American isolationism was doomed not only by the events of World War II but also by the worldwide economy led by the United States after the war. Some Western economies grew so fast that they needed to import immigrant workers for their factories. Western capitalists regularly took advantage of these workers by paying them less than they would union-organized Western laborers, but even so, such low wages far exceeded what the foreigners could have earned in their own native lands. Notably, West Germany's *Gastarbeiter* (guest workers) from the Balkans helped the German economy boom. Their labor served both West Germany and their home countries. Guest workers typically sent money back to families in their homelands, building capital for those economies. Their lives in Germany remained isolated, however, segregated from the main German culture. For a long time the Germans thought the workers would eventually go home again, and so they ignored issues of integrating the *Gastarbeiter*. Instead, many stayed from one generation to the next. Economic necessity, rather than defeat in World War II, created an ethnically mixed Germany.

Other European nations also accepted immigrants from their colonies as cheap labor. So many came to England in the 1960s that the British Parliament began restricting holders of British passports from moving from other parts of the Commonwealth to the mother country. Nevertheless, the numbers of foreign-born residents in western European states began to surpass the number of comparable immigrants in the United States, a nation traditionally much more favorable to immigration. Throughout Europe, the guest workers too often lived in shabby, crowded apartments lacking services and facilities, isolated from the main ethnic groups of the nation. This segregation allowed foreign workers and their families to maintain many of their own cultural traditions. Since many Europeans long ignored these new residents as an invisible underclass, the lack of integration and acculturation practically guaranteed eventual social disruptions of clashing cultures.

Coming out of World War II, the United States had the strongest internationally oriented economy, with dominant influence in the International Monetary Fund (IMF) and General Agreement on Tariffs and Trade (GATT). By the 1960s, though, the other great powers, especially Germany and Japan, had recovered from the devastation of the war. They then began to offer serious economic competition to the Americans. Both Germany and Japan used a socialistic cooperation of government, management, and workers to a degree that the Americans, with their deep-rooted antagonism between the interests of owners and unions, could not.

The rapid increase of wealth in the West was a significant victory for certain socialist ideas. After World War II, social democratic and Christian socialist parties came to power in many Western countries. Their gradual, legal, revisionist, state socialism created the modern **welfare state**. Germany rebuilt itself in record time, using the idea of a social-market economy. As in a free-market economy, German businesses were regulated as little as possible. At the same time, the German state enforced socialist welfare programs, which provided workers with protections for illness, health, old age, and joblessness, while labor unions gained representation on the boards of corporations. Sweden had also been building an egalitarian welfare state since the 1930s. By the 1970s it reached the high point of its "Swedish model" of generous pensions and unemployment compensation, plentiful public housing, strong trade unions, and some nationalization of industries, all paid for with high taxes.

For a while, Great Britain went furthest along the road toward the modern welfare state, although its loss of empire made adjustments difficult. The British swept away "poor laws" (which had condemned poor people to prison for debt) and instead initiated programs to provide a minimum decent standard of living for most people. Government support and regulation established national health-care programs, pensions, and unemployment insurance. Public education of high quality, through the university level, was available for free or at modest cost. Programs sent aid for housing and food directly to families. Many essential businesses, especially coal, steel, and public transportation, were nationalized and taken over by the government, to be run for the benefit of everyone, not just stockholders. Unfortunately for economic growth, government management did not provide efficiency, and some of these firms could not compete well in world markets.

All over the West, standards of living rose. The social "safety net" provided more chances for the poor to rise out of poverty. Reliable supplies of electricity and the installation of indoor plumbing became nearly universal. The middle class broadened out to include many of the working class, because social welfare legislation and union contracts gave workers decent wages and benefits. More people gained access to labor-saving appliances such as washing machines and automatic dishwashers. Homeownership increased. Meanwhile, the well-to-do continued to prosper (even if they disliked paying high taxes that were redistributed by the government to help the middle and poor classes).

This vast increase in wealth also led to an amazing lifestyle change in industrialized nations, especially the United States. Instead of the duality of city and countryside that had marked the living patterns of civilization since its beginning, most people began to live in a novel kind of place, the suburbs. **Suburbanization** blended traditional urban living with rural landscapes. The wannabes of the middle class sought open space (the yard with lawn) and separate dwellings (the standalone home), as well as shopping amenities (the shopping mall). Many jobs, however, continued to be located in the cities (see figure 14.2). Thus, commutes multiplied over vast miles of roads. To meet this need, production of motor vehicles in the United States soon reached the equivalent of one car for every man, woman, and child. Huge amounts of new construction catered to automobiles, from superhighways to parking lots. Europe also suburbanized, although more slowly, as it lacked open spaces that could be developed. Europeans also tended to favor mass transportation by bus, tram, or train over commuting by private automobile. Both western and eastern European societies aimed to provide consumer products, whether through capitalistic or communistic means of production.

Figure 14.2.   Railroads brought acres of cows to the stockyards in Chicago (here in 1947), where workers slaughtered meat for America. Better truck transportation and refrigeration would soon allow owners to build slaughterhouses outside of cities in rural areas.

While suburbs had many admirable comforts, their cost tore at the social fabric of the West, especially in the United States. Racial tensions in particular grew worse. Local zoning laws enforced a middle-class and white racial exclusivity on suburbs, "red-lining" Blacks into less desirable neighborhoods. American inner cities of the East and Midwest to which Blacks had migrated from the rural South before and after World War II became virtual ghettoes as whites fled to live in suburbs. "Urban" became a synonym for the culture of African Americans. European cities also became home to peoples from their former empires.

Suburbs also stressed the "traditional" family. By definition, living in suburbs required a good income. White men, both middle and working class, could earn enough in the 1950s and 1960s to allow their wives to stay home as domestic managers. Meanwhile, many stay-at-home women felt isolated in their suburban luxury. The economic shift of the 1970s (see below), however, soon forced women to find jobs, since two incomes became necessary to support the suburban lifestyle, and that meant absentee parents. Increasingly, children were left home alone. Television provided mindless entertainment for some. Along with the traditional consumption of alcohol, drugs such as marijuana, cocaine, heroin, and psychedelics were bought and then consumed behind closed doors. In dealing with increased drug use, many governments decided to take a criminal direction rather than a medicinal one, leading to larger and larger numbers of incarcerated. In America the "war" on drugs fell most heavily on Black Americans, while white suburbanites often got a pass. And organized crime increased its wealth and power by supplying mind- and mood-altering substances to people throughout the West. Various "wars" on drugs failed to achieve victory. How can a country defeat its own people who want to buy narcotics, stimulants, and psychedelics? By the twenty-first century, in contrast, governments such as those of Switzerland and the Netherlands, as well as several US states, were experimenting with decriminalization, legalization, and toleration of some recreational drugs, especially marijuana.

An expanded middle class and suburbanization had enormous consequences. The incredible affluence of the West led to a cultural revolution as the children born after the World War II generation started to come of age. Often called "baby boomers" in the United States, these large numbers of young people had more education, opportunities, and wealth than ever before. They criticized the elites of the "establishment" as hypocritically too interested in power, wealth, and the status quo rather than social justice. In turn, the "establishment" criticized young people as too obsessed with sex, drugs, and rock and roll. The popularity of movies, television, and recorded music gratified trends toward an "anti-establishment" counterculture. Rock and roll provided a new international youth culture that gained momentum with the worldwide sensation of the British music group the **Beatles** (1962–1970). On the one hand, some Western cultural conservatives worried that the long-haired rockers were as bad as communists. On the other hand, communists condemned the Beatles as sex-crazed capitalists.

A **sexual revolution** arose as part of the new counterculture. Greater freedom in sexual activity became possible with improvements in preventing pregnancy. In the late 1950s, pharmaceutical companies introduced reliable contraceptives in the form of an oral tablet for women. "The Pill" allowed more people to have sex without the risk of pregnancy And medically supervised abortions could end pregnancy with relative safety for a woman. The revolution also encouraged more sex outside the confines of traditional marriage. Sex became a more noticeable part of literature instead of being sold under the table. Courts refused to enforce censorship laws against serious novels like Henry Miller's *Tropic of Cancer* or art films like *I Am Curious, Yellow*. Everything from girlie magazines like *Playboy* to explicit pornography became more accessible.

This increasing extramarital sexual activity brought unforeseen medical risks. The Pill could have side effects for women's health, such as blood clots and hormonal imbalance. Even more serious were venereal or sexually transmitted diseases (STDs). For a few years in the middle of the century, the traditional sexual diseases of syphilis and gonorrhea had become treatable with modern antibiotics, so people did not have to worry about sexually transmitted diseases. But new diseases soon began to develop as multitudes of human bodies came into more frequent intimate contact. Acquired immune deficiency syndrome (AIDS) became a worldwide scourge in the 1980s. Since it was spread in the West at first by male homosexual sex, AIDS became a target of cultural conservatives, who saw the disease as a divine retribution against homosexuals. Despite these prejudices, persons attracted to the same sex, gays and lesbians, began to seek acceptance in Western society instead of being confined to the "closet."

The sexual revolution also spurred Western women to claim legal and economic equality with men. As mentioned above, greater numbers of married women were already moving into the workforce as middle-class standards became more difficult to afford on one income. Women were also progressively more dissatisfied with the title of "housewife," which held little respect in the culture at large. The *women's liberation* movement of the 1960s addressed important issues, such as the rights of women to go to university, serve on juries, own property, and be free from legal obedience to their husbands' commands. Despite the notable defeat of the Equal Rights Amendment in the United States, most women in the West achieved substantial equality before the law and opportunity for economic access in the 1970s.

Women's liberation, however, faltered after these initial successes. The women's movement fragmented as women of color, or religion, or class, or different sexual orientation disagreed with and held different goals from the white middle-class women who had first led the reforms. Around the world today, families and societies still deny women education or force them into marriage or prostitution according to long traditions of "civilization." In spite of this continued subjugation of women, the term *feminism* has often become associated with hatred of men rather than its true definition of advocating women's equal access to political, economic, and social power structures.

In the United States of America, the struggle for **civil rights** for minorities coincided with the struggle for women's rights. The "race issue," oversimplified as "black" versus "white," divided Americans. The population of African origin, the former slaves and their descendants, lived under nominally "separate but equal" policies, which in reality imposed second-class status on Blacks in the United States. Beginning in the 1950s, court challenges, demonstrations, marches, sit-ins, boycotts, and the nonviolence of Dr. Martin Luther King Jr. (b. 1929–d. 1968) challenged segregation laws. The Civil Rights Acts of 1957, 1960, and 1964 gave Blacks real political participation not seen since the brief Reconstruction era after the American Civil War. Sadly, right after these gains, more riots burst out in American cities, and King himself was assassinated. But the possibility for Americans of African heritage to achieve the "American dream" was finally, at least officially, possible.

The inhumane horrors of World War II further motivated some westerners to try to make human rights a permanent part of the international social agenda. Eleanor Roosevelt, the widow of FDR, had pushed the United Nations in that direction already in 1948 with the Universal Declaration of Human Rights. Enforcing the noble goals of equality presented a still unfinished task.

The Union of South Africa, with its minority of "whites" (those descended from British or Dutch settlers) and majority of "coloreds" (Indian and mixed ancestry) and "blacks" (native African) offered a contrast. At the beginning of the Cold War, the ruling party had intensified racist discrimination through a legal system called **apartheid** (1948–1993). This set of laws deprived the darker-skinned peoples of their right to vote, choose work, and live or even socialize with anyone of the wrong "race." Fear of the natives' long-standing political organization, the African National Congress, encouraged the South African government to imprison and persecute their leaders, including Nelson Mandela. Worldwide criticism, boycotts, divestment, and sanctions had somewhat isolated the racist regime by the 1970s. Still, many Western governments, in the name of Cold War solidarity, ignored appeals by human rights groups.

Just as some westerners were concerned about the rights of their fellow humans, others focused on the "rights" of the planet itself. Since the beginning of the twentieth century, petroleum, usually just called oil, provided the most convenient source of power. Refined into either diesel fuel or gasoline, it was cheaper and easier to use than coal. Natural gas, a by-product of drilling for oil, also found numerous uses because of its efficiency in combustion. Burning coal or oil, though, added noticeably to worsening air pollution. Petrochemicals were also fouling the waters of rivers and coastlines and killing wildlife. The heavily populated and highly industrialized West produced more waste and garbage than had all the humans in all of previous history put together. A growing awareness of the dirty results of urbanization and industrialization spawned *environmentalism*, or looking after the earth's best interests. An annual Earth Day was first celebrated on 22 April 1971. Political parties usually called **Greens** were organized chiefly around environmental issues, winning representation in parliaments in some European countries by the end of the century. Meanwhile, many governments responded to environmental degradation by regulating waste management and encouraging recycling. The damage to nature slowed its pace, and in a few areas the environment even improved.

As an alternative to oil, some suggested **nuclear energy**, power based on the same physics that had created atomic and nuclear weapons. Nuclear power plants used a controlled chain reaction to create steam, which drove turbines and dynamos to generate electricity. Many Western nations began building nuclear power plants, hoping for a cleaner, more efficient, and cheaper form of power that did not depend on Middle Eastern oil sheiks. Disasters, however, helped to reduce enthusiasm for the technology. First, at **Three Mile Island** in Pennsylvania (1979), a malfunctioning valve cut off coolant water to the hot reactor, causing part of the radioactive pile to melt down. If the situation had not been solved, a catastrophic explosion might have created the equivalent of an atomic bomb. Still today, hundreds of thousands of tons of highly radioactive debris remain to be cleaned up. Then, at **Chernobyl** in the Ukraine on 26 April 1986, two out of four reactors at a nuclear complex did explode. Only a handful of people were killed outright, but thousands needed to be evacuated and were forbidden to return to their now-contaminated homes. Hundreds of children subsequently developed birth defects, thyroid diseases, and immune system damage. While none of these accidents was a worst-case disaster, they were enough to discourage the construction of more nuclear power plants in many Western nations. Finally, the huge problem of how to safely dispose of nuclear waste products, dangerously radioactive for generations to come, remains unsolved.

Concern about the physical world mirrored a continued interest in the human spirit. Religious divisions, sects, and options multiplied. Perhaps the nuclear arms race, which had created a situation in which the world could end with the press of a few buttons, made people appreciate the fragility of human existence.

Indian-inspired sects and practices such as yoga, Hare Krishna, and Transcendental Meditation made their way into Western belief systems. Other leaders reached into the ancient polytheistic religions or combined Christianity with hopes about space aliens. The ability of some cults to convince their members to commit mass suicide regularly shocked the public. At the same time, established world religions other than Christianity took root in the West. Muslim immigrants set up mosques in every major city. The first traditional Hindu temple in Europe was dedicated in London in 1995. The variety of concepts available to individuals and communities seeking supernatural answers to the meaning of life reached into the thousands. In the United States, televangelists took to the airwaves and raised millions of tax-free dollars from people who felt closer to God through their televisions than at a neighborhood church.

In contrast, attendance in Christian churches declined in western Europe. Religiously inspired laws, such as enforced prayer in public schools or no sales on Sunday, disappeared in most Western nations. In eastern Europe, communist regimes shut down Orthodox churches, turning them into museums, storehouses, or abandoned ruins. The Roman Catholic Church, which had once dominated Western civilization, seemed to be drifting toward irrelevance. The Second Vatican Council (1963–1965) briefly encouraged many with its new *ecumenism* and liturgy in the common language of the people rather than Latin. But soon quarrels over how much the Roman Catholic Church should modernize sapped away momentum. Pope John Paul II (r. 1978–2005) and his compelling personality briefly inspired Roman Catholics and others. The first non-Italian pope since the Renaissance, John Paul II traveled the world and revitalized the international standing of Roman Catholicism. Even his efforts, though, could not reverse the trends in Europe toward unbelief.

In wealth, opportunities, and creativity, the West held its own in the Cold War conflict with "godless communism." The standard of living in communist states seemed meager in comparison, despite the advantages of basic health care, education, and job security for those loyal to the approved ideology. Both sides had used their industrialized economies to pay for the ongoing conflict of the Cold War. As it stretched into decades, the decisive question became one of who could afford to "fight" the longest.

Review: *How did the postwar economic growth produce unprecedented prosperity and cultural change?*

Response:

SOURCES ON FAMILIES: SHIRLEY CHISHOLM, SPEECH ON EQUAL RIGHTS (1969)

The proposed Equal Rights Amendment to the US Constitution was an attempt to change the fundamental law of America in response to women's rights. In this address to the House of Representatives, Congresswoman Shirley Chisholm (r. 1969–1983) explains why the amendment is necessary. Chisholm was the first African American woman to win a congressional seat and the first to run for president within a major party. The amendment was approved by Congress in 1972 but failed to receive enough ratifications from states to become law.

Mr. Speaker, when a young woman graduates from college and starts looking for a job, she is likely to have a frustrating and even demeaning experience ahead of her. If she walks into an office for an interview, the first question she will be asked is, "Do you type?"

There is a calculated system of prejudice that lies unspoken behind that question. Why is it acceptable for women to be secretaries, librarians, and teachers, but totally unacceptable for them to be managers, administrators, doctors, lawyers, and Members of Congress?

The unspoken assumption is that women are different. They do not have executive ability, orderly minds, stability, leadership skills, and they are too emotional.

It has been observed before, that society for a long time discriminated against another minority, the blacks, on the same basis—that they were different and inferior. The happy little homemaker and the contented "old darkey" on the plantation were both produced by prejudice.

As a black person, I am no stranger to race prejudice. But the truth is that in the political world I have been far oftener discriminated against because I am a woman than because I am black.

Prejudice against blacks is becoming unacceptable, although it will take years to eliminate it. But it is doomed because, slowly, white America is beginning to admit that it exists. Prejudice against women is still acceptable. There is very little understanding yet of the immorality involved in double pay scales and the classification of most of the better jobs as "for men only."

More than half of the population of the United States is female. But women occupy only two percent of the managerial positions. They have not even reached the level of tokenism yet. No women sit on the AFL-CIO council or Supreme Court. There have been only two women who have held Cabinet rank, and at present there are none. Only two women now hold ambassadorial rank in the diplomatic corps. In Congress, we are down to one Senator and ten Representatives.

Considering that there are about 3½ million more women in the United States than men, this situation is outrageous.

It is true that part of the problem has been that women have not been aggressive in demanding their rights. This was also true of the black population for many years. They submitted to oppression and even cooperated with it. Women have done the same thing. But now there is an awareness of this situation, particularly among the younger segment of the population.

As in the field of equal rights for blacks, Spanish-Americans, the Indians, and other groups, laws will not change such deep-seated problems overnight. But they can be used to provide protection for those who are most abused, and to begin the process of evolutionary change by compelling the insensitive majority to reexamine its unconscious attitudes.

It is for this reason that I wish to introduce today a proposal that has been before every Congress for the last 40 years and that sooner or later must become part of the basic law of the land—the equal rights amendment.

Let me note and try to refute two of the commonest arguments that are offered against this amendment. One is that women are already protected under the law and do not need legislation. Existing laws are not adequate to secure equal rights for women. Sufficient proof of this is the concentration of women in lower paying, menial, unrewarding jobs and their incredible scarcity in the upper level jobs. If women are already equal, why is it such an event whenever one happens to be elected to Congress?

It is obvious that discrimination exists. Women do not have the opportunities that men do. And women that do not conform to the system, who try to break with the accepted patterns, are stigmatized as "odd" and "unfeminine." The fact is that a woman who aspires to be chairman of the board, or a Member of the House, does so for exactly the same reasons as any man. Basically, these are that she thinks she can do the job and she wants to try.

A second argument often heard against the equal rights amendment is that it would eliminate legislation that many States and the Federal Government have enacted giving special protection to women and that it would throw the marriage and divorce laws into chaos.

As for the marriage laws, they are due for a sweeping reform, and an excellent beginning would be to wipe the existing ones off the books. Regarding special protection for working women, I cannot understand why it should be needed. Women need no protection that men do not need. What we need are laws to protect working people, to guarantee them fair pay, safe working conditions, protection against sickness and layoffs, and provision for dignified, comfortable retirement. Men and women need these things equally. That one sex needs protection more than the other is a male supremacist myth as ridiculous and unworthy of respect as the white supremacist myths that society is trying to cure itself of at this time.

Questions:

- *How does the source present the intersection of ethnicity, class, and gender?*
- *What specifics does the source present on the serious problem of prejudice?*
- *What objections and obstacles to the amendment does the source indicate?*

Responses:

For more on this source, go to http://www.concisewesternciv.com/sources/sof14
.html.

TO THE BRINK, AGAIN AND AGAIN

The history of the Cold War involved a series of international crises and conventional wars around the world, where East and West confronted each other. Fortunately, there has not so far been a "hot" war between Russia and the West, which could be World War III and the end of civilization. Instead, the two sides faced a number of crises and proxy wars that regularly inflamed tensions and cost lives.

The first major crisis after the Berlin blockade centered on China. Further sealing the hostility between East and West was the "loss" of China to communism. As World War II ended, everyone expected Jiang's Nationalist Party to rebuild China from the devastation of the war. Because of this expectation, he gained a seat on the Security Council of the United Nations as a great power victor of World War II.

But westerners did not understand how divided China had become between Nationalists and Communists since the 1930s. Many Chinese reviled Jiang's government as incompetent and corrupt while admiring Mao's Communists as both dedicated guerrilla fighters against the Japanese and supporters of the common peasants. Despite American mediation, in 1947 civil war broke out in China. Most Western observers assumed the Nationalists would win since they controlled far more territory, weapons, and resources. The Communists, not having enough strength at first to engage in open battle, relied on guerrilla warfare. They expanded slowly their operations until they could field a national army. The Communists then drove Jiang and his allies off the mainland of China to the island of Taiwan (Formosa), where Jiang's followers proclaimed it as **Nationalist China**. Protected by the United States, Jiang ran the small island country as his own personal dictatorship until his death in 1975. Meanwhile on the Asian mainland, Mao proclaimed the state of the **People's Republic of China** (1 October 1949), a new rival to the West that drew on the Western ideas of Marxism and revolution.

Many Western intelligence analysts had long believed that Mao was merely Stalin's puppet. Instead, Mao began to forge his own unique totalitarian path. With the **Great Leap Forward** in 1958, Mao tried to modernize China, forcing it into the twentieth century and equality with the Western powers. Lacking capital or resources beyond the labor potential of an enormous population, Mao's crude methods turned into a disaster. Instead of investing in Western-style industrial and agricultural technology, he told his people to try to manufacture steel in their backyards and plant more seeds in the fields. Chinese peasants obeyed their leader's ignorant suggestions. In the resulting famine, tens of millions died of starvation. Even after moderates in the Communist Party ended these catastrophic policies, Mao went over their heads to proclaim the **Great Proletarian Cultural Revolution** (1965–1969). He encouraged young people to organize themselves as Red Guards who attacked their elders, teachers, and all figures of authority except for Mao. The Red Guards killed hundreds of thousands and shattered the lives of tens of millions by sending them to "reeducation" and prison camps. Although these policies were all aimed at making China's power competitive with the West, China took decades to recover from Mao's mistakes.

China's first major confrontation with the West took place over the division of Korea. The Allies had liberated the Korean Peninsula from Japan in 1945 but had not been able to agree on its political future. So they artificially divided the country: the Russian forces left behind a Soviet regime, the Democratic People's Republic of Korea (North Korea), and the Americans installed an authoritarian government, the Republic of Korea (South Korea). Unhappy with this arbitrary division of their nation, northern forces, with the permission of Stalin and Mao, invaded the South on 25 June 1950. The United States convinced the United Nations to defend South Korea, a member state, against aggression, beginning the **Korean Police Action** (1950–1953).[2] In the name of the UN, America provided the bulk of the money and sent the most arms and soldiers, although other Western nations also contributed. An American-led invasion drove back North Korean forces. But then, in turn, hundreds of thousands of Chinese "volunteers" (so named by the Chinese communist government that claimed no direct involvement) pushed back the UN forces to the original division along the thirty-eighth parallel. After several years of inconclusive fighting, a treaty reinstated the division of the peninsula between the communist-aligned North and the Western-aligned South.

Worried Americans saw the communists' actions in Berlin, Greece, Turkey, China, and Korea as part of an effort by the Soviet Union to gain world supremacy. A new Red scare tore through the West. This postwar reaction seemed credible at the time, given the power of Stalin's armies and their sway over eastern Europe. In reality, communist states were divided among themselves, and communist movements were weak outside of the Russian sphere. Communist Party successes in elections in the West were rare. Nevertheless, in America, the Red scare created *McCarthyism*, a movement named after a senator who used the fear of communism to destroy the careers of people he labeled as "commie pinko" sympathizers.

---

2. This armed conflict is, of course, more commonly known in America as the "Korean War." It was a war, involving large organized military forces causing much destruction and many casualties. But neither side ever officially declared war. Declaring war stopped being part of the procedure for making wars "legitimate." The military action is known in South Korea as the "6-25" after its starting date, in North Korea as the "Fatherland Liberation War," in China as the "War to Resist US Aggression and Aid Korea," and sometimes in America as "the Forgotten War."

But all the fear and hearings were wasted effort since communist organizations in the United States never seriously threatened America's security or its way of life.

In contrast, the military might of the Soviet Union unquestionably allowed it to remold eastern Europe. After Stalin's death, his successor, **Nikita Khrushchev** (r. 1953–1964), disavowed Stalin's cruelties and called for "peaceful coexistence" with capitalist countries (see Primary Source Project 14). That brief moment of optimism ended in 1956, however, when the Hungarians tested the limits of Khrushchev's destalinization by purging hard-line communists and asking Russian troops to leave the country. The Russian leadership interpreted these moves as a **Hungarian Revolt**. The tanks of the Warsaw Pact rolled in, and, since Hungary was clearly in the Soviet Union's sphere of influence, NATO could do nothing. Two hundred thousand people fled the country before the Iron Curtain fell again.

Berlin, for a second time, next focused Cold War tensions. The ongoing four-power occupation of Berlin had turned into a bleeding wound for communist East Germany. Many in the so-called workers' paradise in the eastern zone were envious of their brethren in the West. East Germans knew that if they moved to West Germany, they would be accepted as full citizens with special benefits. Thousands were soon leaving East Germany through Berlin. To stem the tide of emigration, the Russians gave permission for the East Germans to build the **Berlin Wall** (1961–1989) (see figure 14.3). The wall became a militarized barrier

Figure 14.3. In 1983, crosses by the Berlin Wall honor those who died trying to escape Soviet-occupied East Germany for West Germany.

to keep East Germans from West Germany. Since preventing the Berlin Wall from being built might have provoked World War III, there was little the West could do. The communists claimed that the Berlin Wall was a necessary bulwark to keep out Western imperialism and capitalism. Most people, however, recognized it as a symbol of the prison mentality of Soviet power. When American president John F. Kennedy (r. 1961–1963) visited in 1962, he proclaimed that all freedom-loving people should be proud to say, "Ich bin ein Berliner."[3]

Khrushchev's fall from power and replacement by Leonid Brezhnev again suggested to some that the enduring rivalry of the Cold War might calm down. Then Czechoslovakia experienced a virtual repeat of the Hungarian Revolt of 1956. In 1968 Czechoslovakia and its politicians tested Brezhnev's renewed proclamations of tolerance by initiating liberalizing reforms ("socialism with a human face"), a movement called the **Prague Spring**. When the Soviets decided the Czechs had gone too far, the tanks once again lumbered into the country, ending the experiment. Many Czechoslovakians were killed or imprisoned. And again, the West could do nothing without potentially triggering World War III. The new Russian leader proclaimed the Brezhnev Doctrine, clearly stating that any country's attempt at the "restoration of the capitalist system" would be stopped by its Warsaw Pact comrades, by force if necessary.

In this Cold War over different ideologies, even science became part of the ammunition. During the **Space Race** (1957–1969), both sides seized on efforts toward the legitimate scientific goals of space exploration to win advantage and prestige over each other. The Russians gained the first victory with their launch of the first functional satellite, **Sputnik** (4 October 1957). It surprised the Americans, who were usually technologically more advanced. The nearly two-hundred-pound device, the size of a beach ball, sent a simple radio signal as it circled the globe every ninety-five minutes. The Russians then proceeded to beat the Americans by sending the first animal, the first man, and the first woman into space. President Kennedy then decided to leap ahead of the Russians. He called on America to land a man on the moon by the end of the 1960s. Just as in a "hot" war, large forces were mobilized at high cost, great minds planned strategy, and people died (although in accidents, not by gunfire). In the end, the Americans won the race, as Neil Armstrong became the first person to walk in the lunar dust on 21 July 1969 (see figure 14.4). Hundreds of millions of people watched on live television. Western science proved its ability to move us beyond our earthly home. In the end, the moon turned out not to have much practical value. With the Space Race "won," lunar flights ended by 1972. But the Cold War continued, with other crises and costs on other foreign fronts.

---

3. Literally translated, the sentence could mean "I am a jelly doughnut." Some grammarians fuss that to precisely convey the meaning, "I am a person from Berlin," Kennedy should have said, "Ich bin Berliner." Regardless, the Berliners cheered.

Figure 14.4.   In July 1969 the American *Apollo 11* mission landed on the moon. Here the lunar module *Eagle* is seen returning from the moon's surface while the earth rises in the distance.

Review: How was the Cold War fought in the West and around the world?

Response:

LETTING GO AND HOLDING ON

The strains of World War II and the Cold War weakened the great powers of Europe so completely that they were forced to dissolve their colonial empires. The rise of the superpowers of America and the Soviet Union meant that the European ability to dominate the world was definitely finished after 1945. No longer could a European state send its gunboats, at will, to intimidate darker-skinned peoples. The colonies had failed to fuel the European states' economic growth. The costs of building the economic infrastructure and providing order and prosperity in both homeland and colony were finally deemed too expensive. The only motives slowing down the release of colonies were pride that the empires instilled and the sense of responsibility for all the peoples whose native societies had been replaced by European structures.

The colonial peoples of Africa and Asia began to increase their efforts toward independence. Some peoples fought for **decolonization**; others negotiated it; a few had it thrust on them before they were ready. All then faced the difficult challenge of finding prosperity in a world economy run according to the elites of Western civilization. Most colonial people were hastily freed with little preparation, suddenly becoming nations with imperialist-imposed borders that seemingly combined and separated ethnic groups arbitrarily. A few examples can illustrate the diverse ways such colonies became independent nations (see map 14.2).

Map 14.2. Decolonization of Africa. What factors have created instability or stability in African states?

The British let go of their colony of India immediately after World War II in, for them, a peaceful separation. As the war ended, the exhausted British caved to the demands for decolonization and negotiated a transition to Indian self-government by Gandhi and his ally Jawaharlal Nehru, leader of the Indian National Congress. The British decided to split the colony into two countries, recognizing the conflicting interests of Muslims and Hindus. The bulk of the subcontinent was to be **India**, run by Nehru as prime minister (r. 1950–1964), while the Muslim League was to control **Pakistan**, a new country with hastily drawn artificial borders. Pakistan took its name from the initials of several of its peoples (Punjabi, Afghans, Kashmiri, and Sindi, translating as "Land of the Pure"). Pakistan's peoples were united by Islam but geographically divided into two parts, West Pakistan and East Pakistan, separated by a thousand miles and very different languages and traditions.

A stroke of the pen led to Indian and Pakistani independence from Britain after midnight on 14 August 1948. Tragically, horrible violence broke out as millions of Muslims fled to Pakistan and Hindus escaped to India, each side killing hundreds of thousands along the way. Gandhi made some efforts to bring about peace and tolerance. These gestures were too much for one Hindu fanatic who assassinated Gandhi on his way to a prayer meeting (30 January 1949). Over the decades, both states have continued to quarrel over control of Kashmir province (where cashmere wool comes from). India became "the world's largest democracy," although electoral violence and assassinations of politicians intermittently continued. Meanwhile, Pakistan's prevailing political system has largely been a series of military dictatorships. In 1971, when East Pakistanis fought for independence from West Pakistan, starting a civil war, India helped them declare the independent state of Bangladesh, now notorious as one of the poorest countries on earth. By the 1990s, India and Pakistan remained mutually hostile and distrustful, each armed with nuclear weapons in a standoff reminiscent of the United States and the USSR during the Cold War.

A country that had to fight for its independence was **Algeria**. In 1954, the native-organized resistance movement, the National Liberation Front (FLN), began a campaign of terrorism against French colonists living there. The ruling French colonists struck back with their own use of terror: shootings by the military, torture of suspects, secret executions, mass arrests, and concentration camps. Even in Paris, police allegedly drowned Algerian demonstrators in the Seine River. Existentialist philosophers, such as Jean-Paul Sartre and Albert Camus (himself born in the colony), debated over the best path to take toward a resolution. The protracted violence in both Algeria and France put an end to the Fourth Republic in 1958. For the first time, a government's failure to handle a colonial conflict had brought down a European constitution. The World War II hero Charles de Gaulle subsequently helped France reorganize under the Fifth Republic.

As a newly empowered president, Charles de Gaulle (r. 1959–1969) dismantled France's empire. At first, he tried to organize colonies in a French Community, similar to the British Commonwealth, but only with moderate success. As deaths in Algeria piled up into the hundreds of thousands, de Gaulle finally allowed Algerians to vote for independence in 1962. Unfortunately for the Algerians, they could not develop a functional democracy. The FLN set up a one-party state that lasted for decades. After experimenting with democracy, a rival Islamic party finally won an election in 1990. Then a mysterious group of politicians and generals, called "the Power," seized control. The civil war that followed killed over 150,000 people, many of them hacked to death. Amnesties and reconciliation policies slowly ended the violence, at the price of the killers on both sides going unpunished. The FLN's authoritarian government allowed other parties to exist, but with little actual power. In 2019 and 2021, peaceful protests by hundreds of thousands of Algerians in the Hirak ("movement"), also called the "revolution of smiles," forced the ruling FLN party to concede some minor democratic and anticorruption reforms and formally abandon its association with the Socialist International. Nevertheless, the FLN regime still represses dissent with arrests and torture, just as the colonial French had done before independence.

The British colony of **Kenya** showed how a country could win independence by using both violence and negotiation. By 1952, the Kikuyu tribe resented colonial exploitation enough to begin the "Mau Mau" revolt against British rule. A few dozen deaths of Western colonists prompted the British to declare a state of emergency. The British then crushed the Mau Mau revolt by executing hundreds of suspected terrorists and rounding up hundreds of thousands more to live in either outright concentration camps or "reserves." There, many British and African guards humiliated, raped, and tortured their prisoners, often forcing them into hard labor and depriving them of food and medicine. Tens of thousands died.

By 1959, the British ended the campaign, and in 1963 they handed over rule to the new president, Jomo Kenyatta, a Kikuyu they had until recently held in prison for seven years. Kenyatta practiced a relatively enlightened rule, sharing involvement in government across ethnic lines. Since his death in 1978, the country has held together despite political rivals accusing each other of corruption and incompetence.

The Democratic Republic of the **Congo**, which had endured the worst of colonization under Belgium, then also suffered horribly with decolonization.[4] After decades of plundering, the Belgian colonial rulers simply abandoned the Congo in June 1960. The new nation lacked a single native Congolese college graduate, physician, lawyer, engineer, or military officer. The charismatic Patrice Lumumba became president but was tortured and assassinated with the connivance of the CIA and British MI6 in January 1961 because they thought he was a communist.[5] The country immediately dissolved into chaos. The mutinous army and rebel groups tried to seize different provinces that were rich in minerals, including cobalt. At first, the United Nations had some success in creating stability by sending in troops, but the effort waned the following year after UN secretary general Dag Hammarskjöld's death in a plane crash, perhaps because it was shot down.

---

4. The former Belgian Congo, now the Democratic Republic of the Congo with its capital of Léopoldville/Kinshasa, is not to be confused with the former French Congo, now the République du Congo/Congo Republic with its capital of Brazzaville.

5. His murderers destroyed Lumumba's bullet-riddled body with acid and fire. One Belgian officer, though, kept a tooth, which was returned and then buried with full honors on 30 June 2022, sixty-two years to the day after Congo's independence.

Colonel Joseph-Désiré Mobutu seized power in 1965. Weary of the conflict, Western powers accepted his claim to rulership and supplied him with technology, training, and cash. Mobutu developed a personal and corrupt dictatorship. He tried to discourage tribal identification and instead nourished a Congolese nationalism, *zairianization*. He rejected European names, renaming his country as Zaïre in 1971, the capital Léopoldville as Kinshasa, and himself as Mobutu Sese Seko kuku Ngbendu wa Za Banga. Mobuto's absolutism ended only in 1997 when international pressure after the end of the Cold War allowed a successful rebellion backed by the president of neighboring Rwanda. The country, soon named the Democratic Republic of the Congo again, suffered wars by armed groups who killed millions until about 2003. The Congo is still afflicted by too much illegal mining and deforestation, militia warfare (often using child soldiers), rape, disease, poverty, famine, and displaced people, as well as state-manipulated media and a corrupt authoritarian government that has nonetheless never fully controlled the entire country.

Even though almost all of Africa and Asia had been freed of official imperialism by 1965, the former imperialist powers continued to intervene in their former colonies' affairs. The Commonwealth of Nations (which dropped the adjective "British") supported democracy and human rights. Former French colonies failed to participate in the comparable French Community, which disbanded in 1995. Yet France kept many military arrangements with its former colonies, sometimes sending troops to protect the regimes from insurgencies (for instance against Tuareg rebels in Mali in 2013), other times toppling dictators (as in Chad in 1975 or the Central African Republic in 1979).

African states faced even more daunting economic challenges in a global trade system largely run by Western nations. Their model and competition were the nation-states of Europe, which they were ill equipped to imitate or compete with, especially because of their ethnic antagonisms. Economic growth was also hindered by minerals and agricultural products fetching low prices in the marketplace, poor decisions by corrupt strongman leaders, and economic aid that benefited industrialized countries more than African ones. Former colonies often grew cash crops for export to the West, such as bananas or cocoa, instead of staple foods to feed their own people. Farming only a single crop (monoculture) left the population deprived of a varied diet and the crops vulnerable to blight.

Further replacing the nineteenth-century colonization was the twentieth-century "Coca-colanization," a term combining the most famous American soft drink with the word *colonization*, implying a takeover through commerce rather than direct imperialism. Western products were marketed to meet the desires of the world's consumers. Natives abandoned regional and ethnic drinks, food, and clothing for American icons such as soda pop, hamburgers, fried chicken, T-shirts, and blue jeans. American blockbuster movies make more money in global sales than in the States.

From the 1970s on, **global debt** also hampered the worldwide economy, as many countries in Africa, Asia, and Latin America borrowed heavily from Western banks. The loans were supposed to be invested in industrialization but instead were too often wasted in corruption or on building from poor designs. As Third

World countries could not pay off their debts, Western banks threatened to fore-close. Increasing stress between rich nations and poor nations therefore burdened international relations. What little industry existed in former colonies was still owned and controlled by, and for, Western businesses, which kept the profits. The Third World countries also lacked support systems for sufficient education and medical care compared with industrialized nations. What little wellness and pros-perity existed, though, allowed populations to soar, often faster than jobs could be created. The population explosion fueled a cycle of urban poverty and criminality.

In addition, the new leaders of new nations too often seemed less interested in good governance than in *kleptocracy*, using political power to increase their own personal wealth. In this they practiced what their colonial masters had taught. Europeans had hardly ever bothered to teach democracy, but they had excelled at using authority for exploitation. The world economy was also skewed so that whenever things went wrong, the military was tempted to seize power. Many regimes repeatedly alternated between military dictatorship and civilian govern-ment. The few elected leaders who lasted in power often became dictators. Tran-sitioning to modern statehood so fast, the former colonies continued to prove that democracy was difficult.

The most problematic area for ending colonialism turned out to be in the Mid-dle East. Most colonies there had won independence either before or shortly after World War II or, like Saudi Arabia and Iran, had never been completely dominated by a Western power. By the third quarter of the twentieth century, the Middle East possessed the most accessible oil reserves. Since they were not industrialized, they required far less fuel for themselves than the energy-hungry West, which craved their petroleum exports. The desire to control the petroleum reserves in the Arab states kept Western powers intimately involved in Middle Eastern politics. But West-ern access to oil was complicated by Arab opposition to the new state of **Israel**.

Israel grew out of Zionism, the organized movement for Jewish nationalism begun in 1898. The Balfour Declaration during World War I had encouraged Jews to move to Palestine, then a British mandate and the site of the Jews' ancestral homeland of Judaea. The horror of the Holocaust, the Nazi attempt to extermi-nate the Jews during World War II, created much sympathy for creating a Jewish state. The British, caught between increasingly violent Jewish and Muslim terrorist attacks, handed over the problem to the United Nations in 1947. A UN commission proposed dividing up the territory into two new countries of roughly equal size: Israel (most of whose citizens would be Jews) and Palestine (most of whose citi-zens would be Arabs). The Jews eagerly accepted the proposal and declared their independence on 14 May 1948.

The Palestinian Arabs, however, refused the commission's proposal, which they considered to be giving away their homeland. On their behalf, the six mem-ber states of the newly formed Arab League launched the first Arab-Israeli War (1948–1949), intending to destroy the new Jewish state. They lost. Victorious Israel seized part of what the commission had apportioned to a Palestinian state, while Jordan and Egypt took control of the rest. The state of Palestine vanished from the map before it even had a chance to exist. Hundreds of thousands of Palestinians suddenly had no country, forced to live as refugees under the rule of Egypt and

Jordan (who refused to integrate them) or in exile in Lebanon and Syria in camps (without rights, seemingly without a future).

Meanwhile, Israel organized itself as a Western state, not surprisingly since so many of the immigrating Jews had lived in the West. Israel had a parliamentary government dominated by two parties (socialist and conservative), with several smaller ones (liberal and religious). Its economy was thoroughly Western, based on markets, investments, private property, and the welfare state. Some Israelis did experiment with socialist living in communes called kibbutzim, but these were more important for building a strong sense of community than for contributing to the overall economy and social structure. Most Israelis believed in Judaism, although the level of devotion varied widely. The government practiced religious toleration, a benefit for the 10 percent of its citizens who were Muslim Arabs and 2 percent who were Christians. Jews revived the virtually dead language of Hebrew as a living tongue, both for reading their scriptures and for daily interaction. Ongoing immigration by Jews from all over the world, including some from non-Western countries in North Africa, Russia, India, and even Ethiopia, caused tensions within the Israeli state, especially between the secularist and traditionalist religious factions.

Ongoing hostility from its Arab neighbors, however, meant that Israel had to fight for its existence, although it was supported by most states of the West. The next war between Israel and the Arabs, the **Suez Crisis** of October 1956, also marked the last time the Europeans acted as independent great powers. In that year, Egypt nationalized the Suez Canal and closed it to Israeli shipping, violating British property rights and international agreements. The British and French, in collusion with the Israelis, launched a surprise attack on Egypt. Overwhelmed by the successes of the enemy invaders, Egypt appealed for help from the Soviet Union. The United States feared that the Suez Crisis might escalate to involve the superpowers. America ordered its NATO allies to go home. They did. The former great powers of France and Great Britain could no longer intervene at will in world affairs.

The ongoing opposition to Israel by Arab states and Palestinians continued, however. By 1964, some Palestinians, who had by then remained homeless and without a state for almost twenty years, unified different political factions under the **Palestine Liberation Organization (PLO)**. The PLO began a more aggressive terrorist campaign, intending, ultimately, to destroy Israel. In turn, the Israelis carried out a preemptive strike against their Arab neighbors and won a significant victory in the Six-Day War of 1967. Israel conquered the Golan Heights from Syria, the West Bank from Jordan, and the Gaza Strip and the entire Sinai Peninsula from Egypt. These acquisitions, however, left millions of Muslim Arabs living without any civil rights under Israeli domination, as if under colonial power. Israel had no idea what to do about this situation, besides settling for a military occupation that deprived the stateless Palestinians of civil rights.

The brief Yom Kippur War in 1973 was the last war so far to attempt Israel's destruction. The Arab states attacked by surprise on the Jewish holy day and made some significant gains, especially in the Sinai. The Arab states also tried to weaken support for Israel among its Western allies by using their dominance in the petroleum trade group, the Organization of Petroleum Exporting Countries (OPEC). They imposed an oil embargo on Western states that supported Israel. While this embargo and the resulting fuel shortages did damage Western economies briefly, Israel survived. Subsequent peacemaking efforts, usually mediated by the United States, failed to fully remove hostility in the region. The 1978 Camp David Accords, which US president Carter used to bring peace between Egypt and Israel, did draw in other nations. Then an attack in 1983 by Hezbollah blowing up US Marines in their barracks in Lebanon frightened the United States into reducing its direct involvement.

Elsewhere, the legacy of occupation and ongoing economic and political interests (especially access to natural resources) kept Western states involved in Africa, Asia, and the Middle East, even if direct colonial imperialism had largely vanished by 1965. Only a century before, neo-imperialism had begun with noble aspirations and patriotic fervor, but it had obviously failed. The Europeans had used their power around the world to compete with one another, build up their own economies, and spread their culture. After letting their colonies go, the West still needed to cope with the ongoing political and economic ties of Europeans living in foreign parts and non-Western immigrants moving to Europe. Since the West controlled the bulk of the world's wealth and power, it could hardly avoid responsibility for the legacy of its century of colonialism.

Review: How did the decolonization of Africa and Asia succeed yet force choices between communist or Third World status?

Response:

AMERICAN HEGEMON

The unquestioned leadership of the West lay, of course, with the United States of America. In some ways, the United States fit the definition of an empire, as one nation that ruled over a variety of other peoples. It did let go of its colony of the Philippines in 1946 and turned Hawaii into its fiftieth state, but it held on to several other colonial possessions in the Pacific (Guam, the Northern Mariana Islands, and Samoa) and the Caribbean (Puerto Rico, the Virgin Islands) (see map 12.2). As the strongest shield against communism and the wealthiest warrior for capitalism, America's unique superpower status enabled it to dominate other nations without directly reducing them to colonies and protectorates. Within its immediate sphere of influence, though, the United States still intervened militarily and economically around the world. Closest to home, within the Western Hemisphere, the United States particularly intensified its involvement with Latin America (see map 14.3). In reaction, Latin Americans tended to blame the "Yankees" rather than themselves for their political, economic, and social problems.

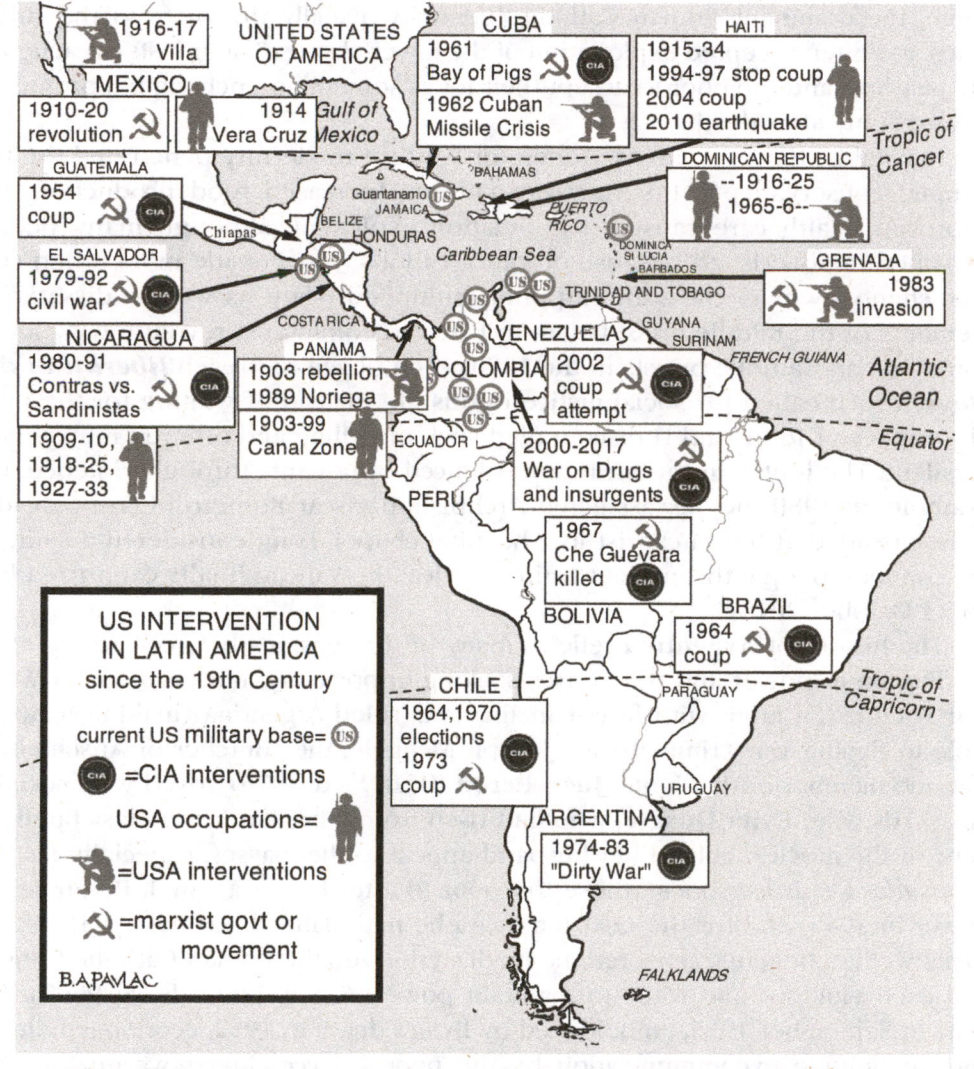

Map 14.3.   US Intervention in Latin America. American occupations meant troops marching in and policing for years. American interventions were armed forces fighting in Latin American countries for briefer time periods. The CIA involved itself through covertly providing information, training for local armed forces and police, money, weapons, and/or armed mercenaries and assassins. Marxist governments ranged from social democrats to communists to intervention by the Soviet Union, while movements included political activists and insurgents. Which countries are more vulnerable to US intervention than others?

Among these problems were great social inequities derived from class and ethnic divisions, dating back to Latin America's westernization as part of the Spanish and Portuguese Empires. Creoles, those of European descent, exploited those of Native American or African ancestry. Since the Creole elites feared the results of votes by the alienated poor majorities, they avoided expanding democratic participation beyond their own ranks. Many countries alternated between corrupt civilian leaders and juntas (cliques of military officers ruling as dictators). Meanwhile, the dominant Roman Catholic hierarchy, usually drawn from the ruling elites, too often accepted exploitation of the lower classes. The priests preached to the peasants and the poor to accept their lot as something unchanging, promising rewards only after death.

Inevitably, however, an awareness of Western modernity penetrated the traditional conservative Latin American culture. Increased food production and improved health care caused a population explosion, although many people remained impoverished because of a lack of jobs. Just outside most urban centers, shantytowns of the suffering poor multiplied. They, as well as dissatisfied members of the middle class, began to listen to communist revolutionary ideas. Some Roman Catholic priests in the 1970s even began to preach *liberation theology*, which called for social justice in this life instead of waiting for the next. The papacy of John Paul II discouraged such meddling and ordered ministers to be silent. The juntas in the meantime silenced opponents through violence. For example, in 1980 they assassinated Archbishop Oscar Romero of San Salvador as he presided at the Eucharist in a hospital chapel. Long considered a saint by the common people throughout Latin America, the Vatican finally canonized him on 13 October 2018.

The history of **Argentina** reflects many of the tensions between ruling elites holding on to power and the masses seeking opportunity and fairness. As World War II ended, a junta with fascist inclinations ruled Argentina (making it hospitable to fleeing war criminals like Joseph Mengele, the "Butcher of Auschwitz"). But one member of that junta, **Juan Perón** (b. 1895–d. 1975), toyed with socialist ideas. His wife, **Evita Duarte**, who had risen from a broken lower-class family to fame in the movies, helped her husband appeal to the masses, especially *los descamisados* ("shirtless ones," those too poor to afford even a shirt). Perón seized power in 1945, and for the next ten years he nationalized businesses, increased social welfare benefits, censored the media, criticized the Roman Catholic Church, and used violence and force to maintain power. A new junta drove Perón into exile in September 1955, emboldened by Evita's death in 1952, economic failures, and an oblique excommunication by the pope.[6] Succeeding governments that rejected socialism likewise failed to make Argentina prosper. Memories of Perón allowed him to return to power from exile in October 1974, but he died within

---

6. The government's forcible removal of a bishop and a deacon from office prompted the excommunication. The deposed clerics had protested the Peronist regime's legalization of prostitution, restriction of the Roman Catholic role in education, reduction of religious tax exemptions, and recognition of equal rights for illegitimate children. While the excommunication did not mention Perón by name, it provided one more excuse for a coup attempt in July that killed hundreds.

a year. His second wife tried to rule as his successor, but a coup replaced her in March 1976. The ensuing regime tried to adopt laissez-faire policies.

As the economy continued to fail, however, the government launched the so-called **Dirty War** against left-wing political opponents. The military secretly arrested suspected radicals, tortured them, and then murdered hundreds, often by tossing victims out of helicopters over the Atlantic Ocean. Refusing to accept a conspiracy of silence, hundreds of mothers and grandmothers began picketing before the presidential palace, asking for their lost children.

The government then tried to use a patriotic success to distract people's attention. Argentine forces invaded the nearby Falkland Islands, possessed by Great Britain but claimed by the Argentines (who called them Islas Malvinas). Fewer than three thousand British citizens inhabited the islands (along with almost half a million sheep). Surprisingly, the British decided to fight back. The **Falklands War** (April–June 1982) ended with almost a thousand dead but a British victory. Argentina's failure led to the collapse of the junta and the exposure of the secrets of its Dirty War. The new regime implemented unrestrained laissez-faire capitalism, following the advice of the "Chicago Boys," acolytes of economist Milton Friedman at the University of Chicago. By 2001, the policy had led to serious unemployment, massive debt to American banks, and riots. Neo-Peronist policies of state intervention and populism advocated by the husband and wife presidents Néstor Kirchner and Christina Fernández de Kirchner (r. 2003–2007–2015) stabilized and grew the economy again for a while.

While Argentina remained free of direct political intervention by the United States, the leaders of three other Latin American nations felt the power of their northern neighbor. First, President Jacobo Arbenz Guzman of **Guatemala** passed land reform policies that threatened the profits of US banana companies that controlled almost half the country's land. In 1954, the CIA organized covert subversion and even a military invasion to depose Guzman. By 1960, a virtual civil war had broken out between the government, usually run by juntas, and various guerrilla factions, often organized by communists. By the war's end in 1996, military, paramilitary, guerrilla, and terrorist forces had killed perhaps two hundred thousand Guatemalans.

In another case, the CIA likewise helped overthrow President Salvador Allende of **Chile** in 1973, as his socialist policies began nationalizing US businesses, especially copper mining. A military junta led by Augusto Pinochet bloodily seized power.[7] Then to maintain power, Pinochet's authoritarian regime suppressed opposition by torturing tens of thousands and killing (or "disappearing") several thousand more over the years. The recent president of Chile, the socialist Michelle Bachelet (r. 2006–2010, 2014–2018), was among those tortured. For a few years, Pinochet gave free rein to "neoliberal" economic policies, yet their lack of success led him to nationalize industries as Allende had previously done. Pinochet ruled until 1989, when the end of the Cold War made his dictatorship less useful to the

---

7. Many long claimed (and some still do) that Pinochet's troops murdered Allende. An official autopsy based on his body exhumed in 2011 declared his death a suicide. He had shot himself with an AK-47 given to him by Fidel Castro.

United States. In 1998, a Spanish court attempted to bring him to trial for crimes against humanity, albeit Pinochet argued for immunity first as a former head of state and then for reasons of health. Nevertheless, he was soon on trial or under investigation for many crimes. At his death in 2006, Pinochet remained not convicted in courts of law while judged guilty by his historical record.

In a third instance, the removal of the president of **Panama** came with the direct intervention of the US military. In 1978, America began a process to give the Panama Canal to Panama, completed at the end of 1999. In 1989–1990, however, twenty-five thousand American troops illegally invaded and literally kidnapped Panama's military dictator, Manuel Noriega (r. 1983–1989), who called himself "maximum leader of the national liberation." They brought him to trial in Miami for drug trafficking (an activity he claimed to have carried out on behalf of the CIA). Various international courts found him guilty of crimes such as tax evasion, drug money laundering, corruption, and murder. Ultimately, in 2011, a French court extradited Noriega back to Panama where he served out his sentences until his death in 2017.

The most notorious US intervention was with **Cuba**, which had been a US protectorate since the Spanish-American War. In the 1950s, Fulgencio Batistá, a semi-fascist dictator, offered Cuba as a haven for both legitimate US business interests and criminal organizations. Batistá faced a rebellion led by **Fidel Castro** (b. 1927–d. 2016), the illegitimate son of a Cuban sugar planter, who at first had wanted to play professional baseball. Castro converted to radical politics and began to promote revolution abroad and at home in Cuba. A failed attack on an army base led to his imprisonment and exile to Mexico. In 1956, he and a few revolutionaries invaded Cuba via a leaky yacht. His guerilla war finally achieved a surprising victory on New Year's Eve 1958. Once in control, Castro set up a one-party communist state that made him dictator. He arrested his enemies, nationalized most foreign property, tossed out crime syndicates, redistributed land, and provided free health care and education to all the people. Thousands of Cubans fled the island, most settling in the American state of Florida. Nevertheless, for many Latin Americans, Castro and the image of Castro's lieutenant Che Guevara symbolized a better, socialist future, free of Yankee capitalist exploitation.

The US reaction was to try to get rid of Castro. The CIA organized some 1,500 exiles in an attempted counterrevolution. These Cubans tried to reconquer Cuba with the **Bay of Pigs invasion** (17 April 1961), named after their landing site. Lacking both open support from the United States and popular backing from the Cuban people, the attack failed miserably and embarrassed the new administration of US president Kennedy. Castro became worried enough about future US intervention that he began to cooperate even more closely with the Soviet Union. He persuaded the Russians to build missile bases in Cuba.

In October 1962, American U-2 spy planes photographed the missile installations. The resulting **Cuban Missile Crisis** brought the superpowers closer to nuclear war than at any other time in history. Although Soviet ICBMs located in Russia and on Russian submarines could have easily targeted any place they wanted in the United States, the Cuban missile sites seemed a more direct threat because they were so close to American shores. From the Russian point of view, though, they were merely imitating American policy: US missiles based in NATO member Turkey were just as close and threatening to the Russian border as those in Cuba were to America. Not mentioned was that both sides had submarines armed with nuclear missiles off each other's shores.

Kennedy was determined to remove the missiles from Cuba. Nonetheless, he took the moderate step of declaring a "quarantine" of Cuba, meaning that while any military technology bound for Cuba would be stopped at sea by the US Navy, other ships could continue. This measure was not quite a blockade, which would have technically been an act of war. The Soviets declined to goad the United States into a shooting war. Instead of forcing the issue, both sides reached an agreement, because nobody wanted World War III. The Russian missiles left Cuba. Similarly, although less publicized, the American missiles left Turkey. Thus, while both sides gained something, the resolution of the crisis appeared to the public as an American victory. The United States also promised never to invade Cuba again (although the CIA later made some half-hearted and harebrained attempts at assassination with exploding cigars). Fidel Castro retired in 2008 because of declining health. His brother Raúl followed until he himself stepped aside in 2019, replaced by Miguel Mario Díaz-Canel Bermúdez. Cuba remains one of the few avowedly communist regimes.

Cold War rivalries continued in other countries throughout Latin America. The CIA-sponsored Operation Condor in the 1970s brutality repressed leftists and democrats throughout South America, while backing authoritarian regimes. Juntas tortured and killed their opponents in the name of fighting communism. Against them, communists organized revolts in the name of liberating the poor from capitalist oppression. US and European corporations dominated the economy to provide exports (and profits) for themselves. The lower classes benefited too little from that trade. These ideological differences guaranteed that Cold War tensions would continue to find their way into political and social divisions.

Review: *How was Latin America entangled in the Cold War?*

Response:

THE UNEASY UNDERSTANDING

Under the protection of NATO, the western European nations had managed to create stable parliamentarian, democratic governments that represented most people within each state through fair and competitive elections. Alternating coalitions of conservative, liberal, or social democratic parties, with occasional participation by regional, nationalist, or communist parties on the fringes, governed in most countries. Only tiny city-states such as Liechtenstein and Monaco remained ruled by princes with broad powers. The last fascist dictatorships, in Greece, Spain, and Portugal, ended in the 1970s with almost no violence during the transition to parliamentary democracies.

The only serious threat to stability broke out in the year 1968. Student riots and revolts flared up in cities from Warsaw to Madrid, Berlin to Paris, Chicago to Mexico City. The students protested against the Vietnam War (see below) or the proliferation of nuclear weapons; for improving university conditions; for civil rights of women, ethnic minorities, or indigenous peoples; or for more inclusive democracy. In France, after striking workers joined student riots, the government almost fell. By the end of the year, though, most governments remained firmly in control, enforced by police using clubs and tear gas, sometimes guns, and a few tanks. A radical "spirit" of 1968 nevertheless continued to inspire young people to question authority. In the next few years, sporadic attacks by terrorist groups, such as Red Brigades in Italy and Baader-Meinhof in West Germany, or by organized criminals, such as the Mafia, caused feelings of insecurity rather than any actual instability.

Although European economic prosperity recovered from World War II, Europe's standing as a center of military power did not. The western Europeans had grown used to being central to world affairs since the neo-imperialism of the nineteenth century. Western Europe found the Cold War duality of the United States versus the Soviet Union hard to deal with. These concerns led them to take a surprising step toward peace and cooperation with one another. For a thousand years, since the collapse of Charlemagne's empire, rival states had been fighting over which share of the European heartland each should reign supreme over. The horrors of the last such conflict, World War II, convinced western European leaders to take a new path.

In the early 1950s, the leaders of West Germany and France began to promote mutual cooperation. The movement started in Germany in 1950 with the nationalized coal and steel industries, creating an organization to regulate and supervise the joint Coal and Steel Authority of both France and West Germany. This arrangement succeeded so well that it expanded the next year into the European Coal and Steel Community, bringing in Italy and the Benelux countries (the Lowland nations of Belgium, the Netherlands, and Luxembourg).

Within a few years, these nations integrated their economic and political systems more intensively. They agreed to the Treaty of Rome on 25 March 1957, which founded the **Common Market** or the **European Economic Community**. Soon this international organization aimed at closer political as well as economic union, reflected in its name change to the European Community in 1967. Several neutral countries, such as Sweden, Switzerland, Finland, and Austria, formed themselves into a rival European Free Trade Association. At first the United Kingdom of Great Britain hesitated to join the Common Market, relying on its special friendship with the United States and the economic ties and trade with the Commonwealth. Still, Great Britain gained membership by 1973. Rivalries, political grudges, and inflation in the European Community took longer than hoped to overcome, but the improving prosperity of its members slowly made the European Community a serious competitor in the international economy. In addition, the European Community's unity changed the nature of international politics. Combined with NATO, the European Community has greatly reduced the chances of war among Europeans for the first time in history, at least for their member states.

Nevertheless, a possible outbreak of a global World War III remained a concern for Europeans. NATO troops based all over western Europe provided some reassurance of slowing down a possible Russian land invasion. Moreover, the nuclear weapons possessed by the United States, Britain, and France deterred possible Soviet aggression. Still, President de Gaulle of France remained resentful of American hegemony and vainly tried to assert French leadership by asking US forces to leave France in 1966. NATO headquarters shifted from Paris to Brussels, the capital of both Belgium and the European Community. Germany felt most painfully the divisions of the Cold War, separated into its East and West parts and aware that it was on the front line for any conventional war. To reduce the possibility of war, Social Democratic leaders of West Germany began a concentrated **Ostpolitik** (East politics) in the early 1970s. They began to talk with the leader of the Social Unity Party in East Germany, hoping to improve relations between communists and capitalists.

The real turning point in Cold War relations resulted from the United States' involvement in its **Vietnam War** (1964–1973), which the Vietnamese call the "Resistance War against America." In 1956, anticolonial and communist insurgencies forced the French out of their colonies of Laos, Cambodia, and Vietnam in Indochina, despite America's secret bankrolling of the French. A fragile Vietnam was left divided. In the North, the communists held power, led by Ho Chi Minh (meaning "Ho of Bright Spirit"; his birth name was Nguyen Ai Quoc). In the South, westernized (and Roman Catholic) elites ran the state. The Americans feared, rightly, that Ho Chi Minh would unite the country and make it part of the communist bloc. They believed, mistakenly, in the domino theory—which asserted that if one state fell to communism, so would its neighbor, followed by the next state, and so on, just like domino blocks knocking one another down. Thus, after Vietnam would go the rest of Indochina, followed by Thailand, the Philippines, and, perhaps, the rest of the world. Alleged attacks by the North Vietnamese in the Gulf of Tonkin that killed or injured not a single American provided the US president Lyndon Johnson with the "justification" to commit combat troops, beginning in 1964. Congress gave him a blank check to defend American interests as he saw fit, although without declaring war.

As more American troops poured in to protect South Vietnam, it seemed inconceivable that North Vietnam could defeat the strongest empire in world history.

Yet the Russians quickly claimed protection of North Vietnam under their nuclear umbrella. A troubling guerrilla war developed, one that the United States could not win as long as Russia and China supplied North Vietnam. By 1968, protesters in Europe and, more importantly, a majority of Americans called for US troops to pull out of Vietnam.

In 1968, **Richard Nixon** (r. 1969–1974) won the US presidential election partly because he claimed to have a secret plan to end the fighting in Vietnam. By that time the Cold War had been ongoing for twenty years. Again and again the superpowers had managed to annoy and provoke each other and frighten the globe with the risk of World War III. Nixon came to power mired in the unwinnable Vietnam conflict and looking for "peace with honor." The United States' heavy bombings of North Vietnam had failed. Indeed, over the course of the conflict, the US military dropped more bombs on Indochina (over 7.7 million tons) than American planes had on both Germany and Japan combined in all of World War II (under 2.2 million tons). Just as citizens of Germany and Japan supported their regimes despite horrible destruction, so did the North Vietnamese.

Suddenly and surprisingly, Nixon and his foreign policy advisors, especially the German immigrant Henry Kissinger, came to the realization that they had been mistaken about the Cold War. They finally figured out that China and Russia were not allies; the two communist states had not gotten along for years and were enemies and rivals themselves. Thus, the Americans began a new strategy to exploit Sino-Soviet tensions to preserve peace. Strangely enough, touring ping-pong or table-tennis teams paved the way for American and Chinese diplomats to begin talking. Soon the former anticommunist crusader Nixon was visiting China, toasting and treating the despot Mao as a respected equal. Next, Nixon visited Russia, toasting and treating Brezhnev, who had crushed Czechoslovakia, as a colleague. These leaders of the three most powerful nations on the planet then agreed to disagree on many ideological issues, while still working together to create order and stability. They called this policy **détente**, using a French term for an outwardly cordial yet distrusting relationship.

Securing the cooperation of China and Russia to manage their North Vietnamese ally, the United States was able to withdraw its armed forces from Vietnam in 1974. When the shooting stopped, more than fifty thousand US troops were dead, as were several million Vietnamese. Two years later, the communist North easily overran the South. When Laos and Cambodia also were seized by communists, some feared that the domino theory was about to succeed after all and that communism would roll through Southeast Asia and the Pacific. But the stability of Thailand and the quarrels among the communists halted any further toppling of regimes.

Unexpectedly, the Cold War afflicted Cambodia with the worst disaster of the Cold War. The communist group called **Khmer Rouge** (Red Cambodians) seized power, renaming their country Kampuchea. They then pushed certain Western ideas of anarchism and revolution further than any other prior political movement. In a drastic reaction against capitalism and industrialized society (and even

Marxist ideology), the Khmer Rouge agriculturalized the nation, driving urban populations into the countryside to become farmers, or die trying, in the notorious "killing fields." The Khmer Rouge burned and desecrated all evidence of past culture to create their version of modernity. Exalting equality, they rooted out all traditional or industrial social differences. They eliminated most scientists, teachers, artists, intellectuals, and priests. Even families were broken up. The Khmer Rouge slaughtered as much as a third of its own population in this self-inflicted genocide. By 1979, the communist government in Vietnam was so disgusted that it invaded Cambodia, drove the Khmer Rouge into the jungles, and installed a satellite regime. The United States, because of its dislike of communist Vietnam, then hypocritically found itself supporting the exiled communist Khmer Rouge in its attempts to throw out the Vietnamese. Once more, Western ideologies confronted and contradicted one another.

Still, détente continued as a policy among the major states of the world throughout the 1970s. The linkup of a Soviet Soyuz and an American Apollo spacecraft symbolized the high-flying spirit of cooperation. Détente peaked in August 1975 when representatives of most European states and the United States met in the capital of Finland to formulate a basis for future cooperation. These **Helsinki Accords** finally ended World War II, thirty years after the shooting had stopped. A new body, the Conference for Security and Cooperation in Europe (CSCE), provided a forum for representatives from all European states (along with the United States) to prevent any accidental outbreak of violence or war. The Helsinki Accords also asserted basic human rights of liberty and freedom for all the signatory states.

Détente provided a new way for the industrialized world to live with its ideological differences. Nonetheless, this uneasy truce probably could not have lasted for the long term. Sooner or later, fanatic ideologues probably would have provoked the Russians and Americans to shoot at or even annihilate each other. Instead, the West won a surprising nonviolent victory in the Cold War.

Review: How did the policies of détente ease Cold War tensions?

Response:

THE WALLS COME DOWN

The end of the Cold War followed directly from the collapse of the policy of détente. Support for coexistence weakened first when the Soviet Union sent troops to Afghanistan in December 1979 to prop up a recently installed communist regime. Afghanistan soon became the Soviet equivalent of Vietnam, as Muslim warriors (*mujahideen*) resisted the atheistic communists. Their guerrilla warriors fought in difficult terrain with supplies from the United States and kept the Russian occupying forces in turmoil.

Second, a number of labor strikes in Soviet-dominated Poland in late summer 1980 sparked a labor union movement called Solidarność (**Solidarity**). An ordinary worker, the mustachioed Lech Walesa, became the symbol of the conflict as he organized strikers from the barricades. The need for laborers in a socialist state to form a union for their own self-protection showed the failures of Soviet socialism. The Russians, though, made Polish authorities declare martial law in December 1981, which pushed the Solidarity movement underground and put Walesa under house arrest. These actions made the Soviet Union and its ideology of representing the worker class look both oppressive and incompetent.

Third, new leadership in the West became determined to take a harder line against Soviet domination and make a stronger push for "free market" capitalism. The West's economic success began to falter in the 1970s, ending years of unheard-of growth after World War II. The oil embargo by OPEC in 1974 marked a turning point. High fuel prices, international competition, inflation, the cost of good wages and benefits, and environmental regulations weakened the profits made in Western nations. Unemployment rates of between 5 and 10 percent burdened Western economies, even though such levels were well below the levels of the Great Depression.

Different Western governments tried following varying economic advice (see diagram 14.2). On the one hand, Sweden and Norway developed the welfare state to the highest possible degree outside communist regimes. On the other hand, many countries cut back on some state-managed benefits. By the 1980s, even the socialist leaders of France (Mitterand) and Austria (Vranitzky) trimmed social programs. To compensate for lower wages, western European regimes instead increased vacation time. The Americans encouraged hiring more women and immigrants, who were paid lower wages.

The welfare-state concept had come under attack by certain economists and politicians. Most famously, the "Chicago Boys," led by Milton Friedman, revitalized laissez-faire economic theory. They taught that the economy worked best when government avoided imposing regulations and spending on social programs. Instead, participants in markets should be as free as possible to make economic decisions. Their experiments in Latin America produced mixed results in the long term.

They found their strongest advocates, however, in Great Britain and America. In Great Britain, the Conservative Party's new prime minister, **Margaret Thatcher** (r. 1979–1990), disliked socialism in all its forms. She scaled back the British

MERCANTILISM

LAISSEZ-FAIRE / CLASSICAL
LIBERAL ECONOMICS

SOCIALISM

KEYNESIAN ECONOMICS

SUPPLY-SIDE / TRICKLE-DOWN / REAGANOMICS

Diagram 14.2. Economic Theories of Capitalism. To summarize
the various proposals dealing with the challenges of capitalism, these
cartoons highlight the alleged role of government (the man with the
crown) in dealing with capital (the bag of $) and contracts (the paper):
(1) In mercantilism (1600s), the government and businessmen work
together by establishing monopolies to benefit the state's balance of
trade. (2) In laissez-faire (early 1800s), the government takes a hands-
off approach, allowing the businessmen to make money according
to enlightened self-interest. (3) In socialism (late 1800s), the workers
demand a share of the wealth (an appeal usually resisted by government
and business). (4) In Keynesian economics (1930s), the government
steps in with regulations and capital investment to help the economy
recover from or to prevent a depression. (5) In supply-side or trickle-
down economics, or Reaganomics (1980s), a laissez-faire approach allows
businesses to make their own decisions, with the expectation that profits
will spread to government and workers.

welfare state, re-privatizing many businesses and industries and breaking unions. She also sharply criticized the totalitarian state of the Soviet Union. She found an ally in **Ronald Reagan** (r. 1981–1989), a former movie star who became president of the United States. He resolved to resist Soviet expansionism and even threatened the USSR, which he called an "evil empire," with the possibility of World War III. Some Americans were shocked that the Reagan administration could suggest that a nuclear war with the Soviet Union was winnable. Reagan proposed the Strategic Defense Initiative (SDI), a new high-tech antimissile system to shield the United States from ICBMs. Since the technology for such a program was decades away from being invented, much less activated, critics named this initiative "Star Wars" (after the popular science-fiction film). Even if successful, SDI would have left America's allies in Europe defenseless against Russian mid-range missiles. To counter this real threat, Reagan and NATO leaders installed mid-range nuclear weapons in western Europe. Many Western citizens protested, their resentment of American domination outweighing their fear of Russian invasion.

Reagan also continued the buildup of conventional armed forces of ships, planes, tanks, weapons, and soldiers in an effort to prevent possible Russian aggression anywhere. The vast US economy could still afford this expensive effort, although the country went deeply into debt to do so, borrowing money from abroad. President Reagan came into office promising to reduce government spending. While he did cut a few taxes, his Republican administration actually spent more on both social and military programs than the previous Democratic administration. The United States went from being the biggest creditor nation in the world to being the biggest debtor nation during Reagan's presidency. With all this new borrowing and debt, and with new competition from Germany and Japan, America's singular economic dominance of the West and the world was much reduced by the end of the 1980s.

Fourth, the new Reagan administration disliked the new Sandinista socialist regime in Nicaragua, which was backed by Cuba and the Soviet Union. After the US Congress refused to intervene, Reagan officials secretly and illegally financed a counterinsurgency by the "Contras" (right-wing paramilitary groups that were "against" the left-wing Sandinistas). The Reagan administration raised money for the Contras by selling weapons to Iran, a country the United States considered to be an international threat. In the civil war that followed, one side's "terrorists" were the other side's "freedom fighters" and vice versa. The Iran-Contra Affair exposed the secret deals, but the president's authority was left intact because his subordinates took the blame. The American military also defied international law by mining Nicaragua's harbors, technically an act of war. In the end, the leftist regime lost by the ballot box, not bullets. In 1990, the Sandinistas allowed free elections, which restored a tentative democracy. In 2021, the leader of the Sandinistas, Daniel Ortega (r. 1979–1990, 2007–), was elected to an unprecedented fourth consecutive term as president. Irregularities in the election and mistreatment of opponents, however, led US president Biden to put Ortega under sanctions.

The Cold War finally ended in the 1990s after **Mikhail Gorbachev** (r. 1985–1991) became secretary general of the Communist Party in the Soviet Union. He saw the flaws and corruption of the centralized communist system and attempted to reform Soviet society in order to save it. First, he promoted *perestroika* (restructuring) to allow more free-market competition within the economy. Second, he declared *glasnost* (openness). The regime reduced censorship, allowed more foreign travel, and imported more Western goods and entertainment. Third, Gorbachev allowed rival political parties to begin to organize, thus allowing a democratic process for the first time since the short-lived Russian Republic of 1917.

Despite Gorbachev's reform efforts, his communist state crumbled around him. The people resented their increasingly poor standard of living compared with that of western Europe. The transition to a market economy created shortages and unemployment. Political reform was clumsy because the Communist Party resisted giving up its privileged position. Finally, repression of protests in the Soviet Union's Baltic provinces of Latvia, Lithuania, and Estonia started to resemble the Hungarian Revolt of 1956 and the Prague Spring of 1968.

The Soviet satellite states in eastern Europe ultimately forced Gorbachev to prove his sincerity about openness by ending Soviet domination. Gorbachev finally decided against using force and violence to enforce the Brezhnev Doctrine. As a result, the satellite system collapsed swiftly, without much bloodshed. First, in 1988, workers' strikes in Poland pressured the military/communist government to launch reforms and organize free elections. Big changes came in the year 1989. In September, Solidarity came to power, and the next year Lech Walesa became president. Earlier in 1989, the Hungarians also held free elections. By the summer, they had torn down their portion of the Iron Curtain where it bordered Austria (which was just a barbed-wire fence with an electrified alarm system). In November, the totalitarian leader in Bulgaria, Zhivkov, resigned, beginning that country's transition to democracy. At the same time, protests in Czechoslovakia began to frighten the dictatorial regime. By December, Czechoslovakia had embraced its Velvet Revolution, so called because the separation from communism happened with comparatively little violence. The former political prisoner and playwright Václav Havel became president.[8] Finally, Romanians rejected the old system in a quick coup in which the long-reigning dictator Nicolae Ceauşescu and his wife were shot on Christmas Day, with video of their corpses then broadcast to the nation (see figure 14.5).

The most important sign of the Cold War's end was the reunification of Germany in 1990. The East German hard-liners began to lose control in August 1989 as East German citizens began fleeing across the new open border between Hungary and Austria. Through Austria they reached West Germany, where they were welcomed as free citizens. At home in East Germany, mass demonstrations organized by churches also began to seek openness. The communist dictator of many years was deposed, and moderates tried to find new directions. On the evening

---

8. Just four years after the Velvet Revolution, Czechoslovakia went through the "Velvet Divorce." Extremist politicians, with minimal popular support, arranged to divide the country into its two main parts, which became the Czech Republic (or Czechia) and the Slovak Republic (although usually called Slovakia). Havel resigned during the process rather than oversee the dissolution, but he then served as the first president of the Czech Republic.

Figure 14.5.   These statues of communist founders Marx and Engels were relegated to a museum outside Budapest, Hungary, after the Cold War.

of 9 November 1989, after a bureaucrat on television mentioned that some travel restrictions would be lifted, thousands of hopeful East Germans began to gather at crossing points at the Berlin Wall. They talked the guards into letting them through. By the next morning there was no sealing up the wall again. Indeed, the most potent symbol of the conflict, the Berlin Wall, was soon pounded into rubble as souvenirs for tourists. Within a year, the West German political leadership negotiated unification. On 3 October 1990, the communist East German state officially disappeared, absorbed into the Federal Republic of Germany.

In 1991, a failed coup by communist hard-liners in the Soviet Union led to the defeat of Gorbachev but not of the reforms. By 1992, the Soviet Union was in the "dustbin of history." The Russian Federation replaced the USSR. The new Russia remained linked with a few former Soviet republics, as part of a so-called Commonwealth of Independent States. This association included new nations in the Caucasus (Azerbaijan, Armenia, and Georgia), the Turkish states in Central Asia (Kazakhstan, Uzbekistan, Turkmenistan, Kyrgyzstan, and Tajikistan), and eastern Europe (Moldavia and Byelorussia or Belarus). Ukraine became only an associate member, while the Baltic states of Estonia, Latvia, and Lithuania left completely. The Warsaw Pact was soon gone as well. The Cold War was over.

The former Soviet satellite states in Europe quickly converted to Western-style capitalism. Indeed, in 2004 NATO expanded to include most former eastern European satellite states, right up to Russia's doorstep. The former Warsaw Pact members of Poland, Hungary, Romania, Bulgaria, the Czech Republic, Slovakia, and the three former Baltic "republics" of the Soviet Union (Estonia, Latvia, and Lithuania) officially entered the defensive military alliance with the West. Many of these states raised their standard of living to be comparable with those of their new Western allies, uniting their economies and destinies to the West's.

The Cold War's resolution even reached to the Union of South Africa and its repressive regime of apartheid. Over the years, the government had tortured, imprisoned, and killed members of the African National Congress. International pressure of boycotts, divestment, and sanctions; the absence of a communist threat; and worsening social strife all convinced the white racist regime to dismantle apartheid. In 1990, the regime released Nelson Mandela, leader of the African National Congress, who had been in prison since 1962. Mandela and his party won an overwhelming victory in free and fair elections in 1993. President Mandela (r. 1994–1999) passed a law that protected whites' property and advocated forgiveness rather than vengeance for decades of oppression. The Truth and Reconciliation Commission led by Anglican archbishop Desmond Tutu granted amnesty to the perpetrators of cruelty and violence in return for their honest accounts of their actions. South African citizens descended from the "white" British and Dutch as well as the "colored" Indians stayed to maintain the Western industrialized culture. Even so, poverty and violence continued to plague too many descendants of the "black" native South Africans.

Despite these successes, the collapse of communism did not result in the brilliant victory dreamed of by many in the West. A few communist dictatorships, namely China, North Korea, and Cuba, still held on to their ideology, despite losing subsidies from the Soviet Union. Although Russia no longer posed an invasion threat to Europe, it was armed with the nuclear weapons capable of destroying civilization. And Russia itself transitioned away from totalitarianism only with difficulty. During the switch from communism to capitalism, Russia saw much of its wealth fall into the hands of a few well-connected politicians and friends of the elites, since the rule of law and the checks and balances of good government had not been sufficiently established. Pollution, job loss, and military impotence lost the nation its superpower status. Meanwhile, other states that had broken away from the Soviet Empire, especially in Turkish Central Asia, established mini-dictatorships of their own. Their new authoritarian rulers merely substituted the language of Islam and nationalism for the communist rhetoric of Marx. Thus, ethnic and nationalist hatreds endured.

Review: *How did the Cold War come to an end?*

Response:

Make your own timeline.

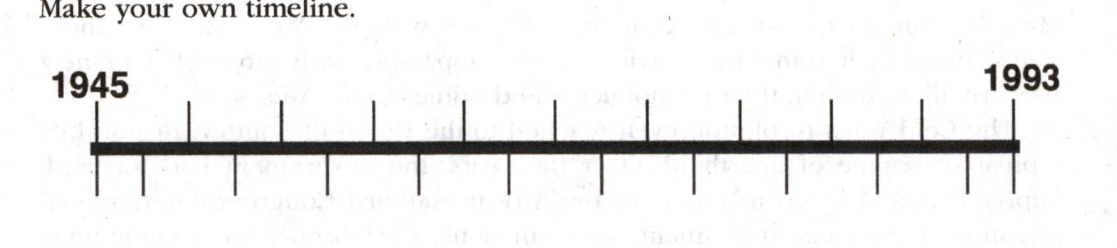

1945   **1993**

CHAPTER 15

Into the Future

The Contemporary Era, 1991 to the Present

The end of the Cold War startled most intelligence analysts, politicians, and pundits (a new kind of commentator in modern media who relies more on opinion than analysis). A conflict that had framed international actions and domestic policies for more than four decades came to a close with little warning. Nevertheless, the increasing interaction of the earth's peoples challenged the place of westerners and their wealth as never before. International commerce, science, industry, and politics still guaranteed that Western civilization would continue—and would also continue to change.

SEARCHING FOR STABILITY

As the Soviet Union was splitting apart, Europe was coming together. After a thousand years of warfare in Europe, war among Western states had become inconceivable instead of inevitable. Since the fall of Rome in the West in 476 and the failure of the Carolingians in the ninth century to replace it, rival states had quarreled with one another in one bloody conflict after another. The rivalries had contributed to making some European states great powers, but World War I, World War II, and the Cold War had then revealed how destructive war could be. NATO now mutually protected western European nations. The United States remained NATO's and the world's foremost military and economic nation, the sole superpower. But by the end of the century, US military installations wound down, no longer necessary for preventing a Soviet invasion. Thousands of American troops left Europe.

The political and economic unification of Europe that had begun with the Common Market accelerated after the Cold War's end. In 1991, the Maastricht Treaty turned the weak European Community into the stronger **European Union** (see map 15.1). Some politicians thought the various nations of Europe could even become a United States of Europe. In 2002, the union established its Common Security and Defense Policy (CSDP), which began missions to troubled countries

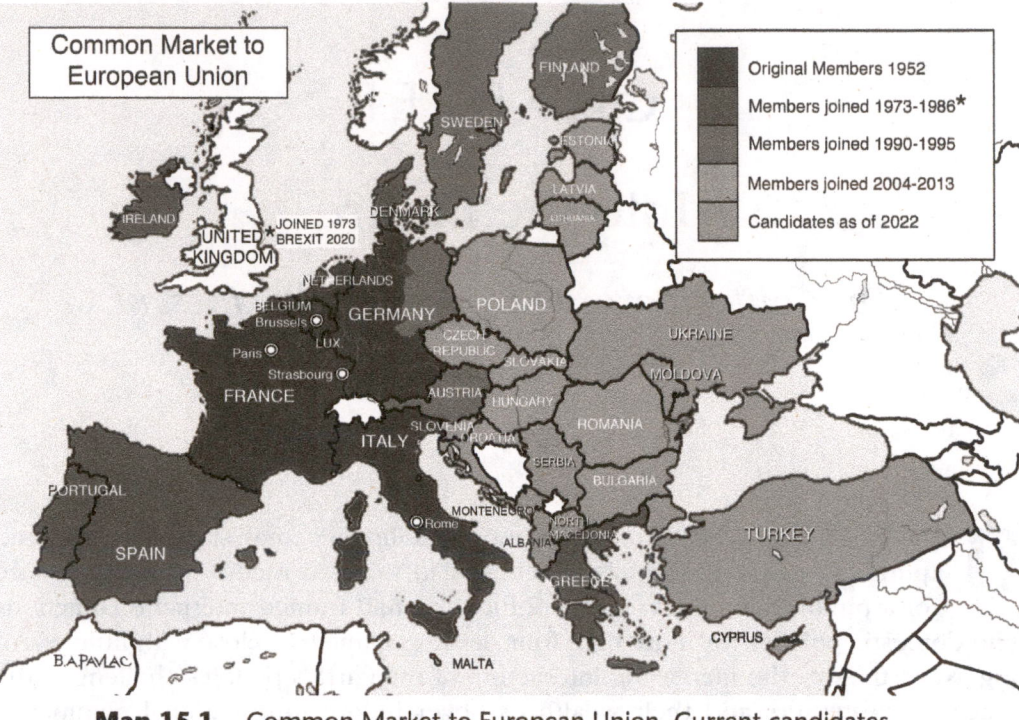

Map 15.1.   Common Market to European Union. Current candidates still have to improve market regulations, reduce corruption, and reform their justice systems before admission will be approved. In June 2022, Ukraine and Moldova were approved for candidate status due to the Russian attack on the former. (Note: The United Kingdom of Great Britain and Northern Ireland voted to leave in 2016, which they did on 31 January 2020. They are still negotiating the details of commerce.) How do the entrance dates or locations of various countries reflect their economic power and participation in the European Union?

around the world, such as the Congo, Indonesia, and Georgia. Today, its various operations support police and courts in maintaining law and order, monitor elections, try to prevent smuggling and piracy, and protect refugees and civilians in areas with violent conflict.

The European Union's greatest success remains in economics, although it values its culture as well. Its motto since 2000 has been "United in diversity." The EU removed trade and labor barriers among its members. Brussels's subsidies to the poorer member states, such as Ireland and Portugal, helped their economies to grow and to compare well with the more prosperous members, such as Germany. In 2002, a dozen competing monetary currencies within the EU countries, from the French franc to the Italian lira to the German mark, vanished into history and were replaced by a new common unit, the euro. By 2015, nineteen countries belonged to the "eurozone," with several other nonmember countries also using the euro as a currency. While many economists expected the euro to fail, it has usually remained strong against its international rival, the American dollar.

Ongoing economic success tempted still more countries to join the European Union. First, in 1995, the former neutral nations of Austria, Finland, and Sweden, with their advanced Western economies, were welcomed. The Schengen Agreement, put into action in 1995, created a "Europe without borders" that allowed free movement between the member states without going through customs and identity checks. Even non-EU countries like Norway, Switzerland, and Iceland joined in, although Ireland, Croatia, Romania, and Bulgaria opted out. Next, many of the newly freed Soviet satellites were eager to join the European Union. These nations, however, were required to develop their market economies and parliamentary democracies before they could be fully integrated. On 1 May 2004, the EU welcomed several new eastern European members, including the former Soviet republics of Estonia, Latvia, and Lithuania and the Soviet satellites of Hungary, Poland, the Czech Republic, Slovakia, and Slovenia, along with the island states of Malta and (non-Turkish-occupied) Cyprus. The most recent states to join were Romania and Bulgaria in 2007 and Croatia in 2013. Candidates as of 2022 include Montenegro, Serbia, the Republic of North Macedonia, and Albania, with potential candidates of Bosnia-Herzegovina and Kosovo. Turkey with its foothold in Europe applied for candidacy as far back as 1987. Still, several members of the European Union oppose Turkey's membership amid doubts that Turkey is, or ever will be, "Western" enough. Growing concerns about the authoritarian measures of President Recep Tayyip Erdoğan (r. 2014–) have only complicated the relations between Turkey and the EU.

Other obstacles slowed the path to true European unity. Some "Euroskeptics" saw the dangers of a vast bureaucracy in Brussels that demanded conformity and ignored local differences. The European Parliament in Strasbourg seemed to have little power or purpose. Many Europeans wanted to see more *subsidiarity*, in which decisions are made at the regional and local levels rather than by the European Commission in Brussels (see figure 15.1). While English grew more popular as a unified *lingua franca*, Europeans continued to speak more than fifty different regional and local languages and even more dialects. Some Europeans only reluctantly accepted new member states, afraid of the cost of supporting less-developed economies and opening up borders to more intra-European immigration, competition from cheap labor, redirection of agricultural subsidies, or lack of "proper" values. Even Germany had trouble integrating Germans from the former East Germany, especially as many businesses in the former socialist state failed to adapt to the new capitalist social-market economy.

Moreover, the prosperity of Europe made it a magnet for poor people and ethnic minorities from former colonies all over the world. "Economic" immigrants sought a better life through better employment in Europe's land of plenty. According to international treaties, "political" refugees (threatened by persecution, terrorism, or war) had the right to seek asylum. Yet Europeans saw a clash of civilizations as they feared being swamped by large numbers of people from foreign cultures. In point of fact, foreigners can integrate to Western culture over generations if they are given the right conditions (as seen with many immigrants to Western countries past and present, especially Canada and the United States). But

Figure 15.1. The Atomium built for the 1958 World's Fair in Brussels now dominates a park that celebrates the European Union with models of cultural icons from all over Europe. Replicas shown include buildings from Pisa and Venice.

since European governments and societies generally made few efforts to assimilate the newcomers, diverse immigrants often retained their own cultural customs. Modern communications also meant that immigrants easily received newspapers, radio, pamphlets, and television all in their own languages.

The fear of Islam in the West going back to the crusades continued to alarm many Europeans. The percentage of Muslims in the European Union had grown from less than 2 percent in 1950 to about 6 percent in 2020. That was about 26 million out of a total of almost 447 million. Not surprisingly, European countries that had once been part of the Ottoman Empire had much higher, even majority numbers. Some European Union member nations, like Portugal and Poland, had virtually no Muslims at all. The highest percentages in western Europe were almost 9 percent in France and Sweden. At any rate, some Europeans began to warn of "Eurabia": that Europe would convert into a Muslim territory. The call of the muezzin from minarets would drown out the church bells from steeples amid the traffic noise in the streets. And the European practice of tolerance allowed Muslim extremists to preach prejudice and resistance to assimilation. To use common metaphors about integration, would Christians and secular Europeans live together like metals becoming alloys in a melting pot, or would they blend as in a bowl of stew, or stay separated, as an assortment of fruits in a basket? Would these peoples from Asia and Africa become westernized, or would they change the West?

Immigration from without and within the European Union challenged how nation-states defined their populations according to unified ethnicity. The European Union bureaucracy called for better treatment and human rights for Sinti and Romany (formerly called Gypsy) people, while local governments discriminated and local mobs intimidated them. School officials in France, Germany, and Britain called for Muslim women and girls to stop wearing headscarves (hijabs). For many females who wore them, they were acts of religious obedience or symbols of their ethnic identity. For the opponents, the scarves, veils, and burkas subordinated women, undermined secularism (laïcité), or insulted Christianity (in ways that nuns' wimples supposedly did not).

Terrorist attacks by extremist Muslims recurred, especially in France. Coordinated shootings in Paris early in 2015 killed, among others, a number of cartoonists whose magazine Charlie Hebdo had published cartoons mocking the Prophet Muhammad. A larger onslaught at a wide variety of venues in November massacred dozens and injured hundreds more. Since then more isolated assaults by Muslims with knives and machetes have kept Islamist terrorism in French headlines.

Worried about the "traditional" populations of Europe, nativist or nationalistic parties campaigned to expel the growing number of non-Europeans. In the Netherlands, two killings changed politics: an environmentalist assassinated the politician Pim Fortuyn in 2002, and a Dutch Moroccan killed film director Theo van Gogh in 2004. These acts spurred the founding of the extreme nationalist Party for Freedom (PVV) under Geert Wilders. His open criticisms of Muslim culture eventually led to his being charged with (but not punished for) hate speech. Other populist politicians such as Marine Le Pen (daughter of the far-right-wing politician Jean-Marie Le Pen) in France and Jörg Haider in Austria sought both to limit the rights of foreigners and to resist the centralized control of the EU in Brussels. In the first decade of the twenty-first century, however, most politicians and voters still saw these nationalists as part of an extremist fringe, sure to fade away.

As fear of foreigners made some question the usefulness of Enlightened toleration, so also did some doubt the value of Enlightenment rationalism. In the 1980s, two French intellectuals proposed new techniques to interpret Western culture, called **postmodernism**. Jacques Derrida and Michel Foucault "deconstructed" texts to show how elites often camouflaged power and exploitation.

Their postmodern critique sought to undermine the accepted modern assertion that true knowledge can be obtained through human reason. Postmodernist criticism contributed to further uncertainty about truth and Western culture.

A concrete answer to the meaning of Western culture in Europe was supposed to be part of the Convention on the Future of the European Union in 2002. But as some politicians tried to enshrine the position of Christianity in the document, others successfully rejected the notion. Either way, the cumbersome and complicated constitution failed to win endorsement by 2005. Instead, European leaders reformed the EU through the Lisbon Treaty, which after delays went into effect in 2009. It clarified the competencies of institutions like the Council and Parliament and strengthened the rights and participation of citizens.

While the constitutional structures of Europe seemed stronger than ever, ethnic conflict and economic mistakes still troubled the EU's future. Some might say that Europeans had no one to blame but themselves for so many immigrants. Since the fifteenth century, they had bound the world's populace together in their practice of imperialism and capitalism. In a positive way, Europeans gladly consumed some foreign culture, especially regarding cuisine. Curry became a staple for British food like fish and chips, while Germans and Austrians ate *doner kebabs* as an alternative to bratwurst. Yet frustrations of enduring discrimination, poverty, and lack of adequate political representation among Muslims and other ethnic minorities flowing into Europe seems to predict future trouble.

Review: *How did the European Union attempt to provide a new economic and political basis separate from the United States?*

Response:

DIFFERENT FOLKS

The Cold War's end and the European Union's success at bringing diverse people together paradoxically encouraged some ethnic groups to seek separatist autonomy. The Cold War had bonded western Europeans together in fear of Soviet totalitarianism. With the Cold War over, some pundits now predicted that communism's collapse meant a victory for liberal democracy and for prosperity under capitalism. Many did not realize how separatist movements would actually increase.

Nationalism remained a potent political ideology, although in ever smaller units. While the Cold War's end drained wars of their communist versus capitalist dialectic, tensions within nation-states were still empowered by cultural and tribal rivalries.

Even during the Cold War, two areas of ongoing British imperialism illustrated how nationalist conflicts divided and killed. In **Cyprus**, the deep divisions between ethnic Greeks (about 80 percent of the population) and Turks (the other 20 percent) degenerated into terrorist attacks, especially by those who wanted unification with Greece. Britain pulled out in 1959, but the new Cyprus was forbidden to unify with Greece. Greeks and Turks never quite managed to live peaceably, relying on UN peacekeepers. In 1967, though, Greece's anti-communist military dictatorship decided to annex Cyprus as a distraction from its repression of domestic protests. In a preemptive strike, however, Turkish troops occupied the northern third of Cyprus. Tens of thousands of ethnic Greek Cypriots fled to the south. The two NATO allies, Greece and Turkey, just barely managed to avoid war (see figure 15.2). The whole island became a member of the European Union in 2004, but union authority does not quite apply to the northern third under Turkish rule.

In another example, Northern Ireland, which had remained part of the United Kingdom of Great Britain after independence for the rest of Ireland, experienced

Figure 15.2. A sign by peacekeepers of the United Nations marks the division of Cyprus.

renewed violence between Protestants and Roman Catholics. Roman Catholics in Northern Ireland saw themselves as oppressed. They often lived in ghettoes, had worse jobs, were paid less, and were allowed fewer political rights than Protestants in the same province. The "**Troubles**" began in 1968 when a splinter group of the long-dormant Irish Republican Army calling itself the **Provisional IRA**, or Provos, began terrorist attacks. The London government at first tried to be neutral but eventually sent in thousands of troops to maintain order. The British shooting of more than a dozen Roman Catholic demonstrators on "Bloody Sunday" (30 January 1972) convinced many Catholics to consider the English part of the enemy. In the following decades, violence among British troops, Ulster constabularies, and IRA fighters killed three thousand people and injured many more. Finally, the Good Friday Agreement of 1998 brought the Republic of Ireland, Great Britain, and parties in Northern Ireland toward a permanent, peaceful resolution.

During the Cold War, such ethnic fighting had been secondary to the larger possibility of World War III. To fight the Cold War on many fronts, both communist and capitalist industrialized states had spread modern military technology to many technologically primitive allies around the globe, whether they were ready for it or not. At first, the superpowers had supplied various dictators, tyrants, juntas, rebels, insurgents, and even terrorists with various kinds of advanced weapons: automatic rifles, grenades, land mines, plastic explosives, antitank rockets, and antiaircraft missiles. After the Cold War, when the superpower rivals reduced their gifts of arms, international drug trading provided money for weapons. As weapons became cheaper and more widespread, ordinary people acquired an easy ability to kill others. The result was increased violence for reasons of money, ideology, or power.

Ethnic groups seeking nationalist validity sparked much of this violence. Terrorists had already bombed, hijacked, kidnapped, and murdered to create ethnic states and enclaves during the Cold War. In western Europe, terrorists lashed out in defense of their minorities, including the Basques against Spain, the Corsicans against France, and even some South Tyroleans against Italy. In 1954, a few Puerto Ricans shot members of the US Congress in the Capitol to draw attention to freeing their island from the United States. In other parts of the world, civil wars and massacres broke out, giving the Western powers the choice of either standing by or intervening to stop the killing. After the Portuguese withdrew from their colony of East Timor in Indonesia, it was independent for only nine days (November–December 1975). Then Indonesians moved in and brutalized the native population, killing hundreds of thousands and sending more into exile. Only in 1999 did Australian troops backed by the United Nations begin to stabilize East Timor, creating a sovereign nation by 2002. In 1994, in the former Belgian colonies in Africa of Rwanda and Burundi, the legacy of ethnic rivalry stoked by colonial imperialism burst out in horrible slaughter. Mobs and military forces from the majority Hutus started butchering the minority lighter-skinned ethnic Tutsis with machetes, grenades, guns, and fire. In the course of one hundred days, Hutus had slain over eight hundred thousand Tutsi (and a few moderate Hutu) men, women, and children and had raped hundreds of thousands. They almost wiped out the former hunter-gathering Twa people. While the UN and France offered a minimal response, Uganda backed a Tutsi rebel invasion that momentarily stopped the slaughter, until Tutsis carried out some reprisals. An International Criminal Tribunal later convicted a few dozen Hutus of war crimes.

Europeans confronted their own massacres in the Balkans of the 1990s. During the Cold War, Soviet troops maintained stability in the nations of Hungary, Romania, and Bulgaria. Bulgarian communists in the 1980s were particularly extreme in enforcing ethnic conformity. They forced Turks to change their names and give up their customs or go into exile, which hundreds of thousands did. Although the postcommunist regime cut back on such discrimination against Turks, other politicians enflamed ethnic tensions as a way to win elections.

The unexpected breakup of Yugoslavia set in motion the worst violence in Europe since World War II. During that war, communist partisans led by Josep Broz, called **Tito** (r. 1945–1980), fought against both the Serbian fascist Chetnik insurgents and the Croatian fascist Ustaša regime installed by the Nazis. At war's end, Tito ruled the country.

Yet he avoided becoming a Soviet puppet and instead crafted his own brand of communist dictatorship. For his People's Republic of Yugoslavia, Tito maintained a beneficial balance in the Cold War rivalry. Officially a communist state, Tito's Yugoslavia broke quite early with Stalin and pursued friendship with capitalist western European states. At home, he mended the ethnic divisions that tormented the prewar Kingdom of Serbs, Croats, and Slovenes, culminating in the Serbian fascist dictatorship of Yugoslavia. Half Croat and half Slovene himself, Tito realized that he needed to deemphasize ethnic identity. He set up a federal system of six states: Slovenia, Croatia, Montenegro, Bosnia-Herzegovina, Serbia, and Macedonia. Each state remained somewhat autonomous from any potential Serbian bullying. Serbian nationalism was further weakened by carving out of Serbia the two autonomous provinces of Vojvodina and **Kosovo**, each with non-Serbian ethnic majorities (Hungarian and Albanian, respectively). Having dissolved ethnic tensions while situating itself between East and West, Yugoslavia became one of the more prosperous eastern European countries.

Tito's death in 1980 changed little at first. The presidents of the six republics rotated the central presidency. Already in 1981, however, disturbances began in Kosovo, where Albanians, who made up 90 percent of the population, wanted more use of their own languages and better living conditions. As the Cold War ended in 1989, the president of the Serbian federal state, Slobodan Milošević, decided to use ethnic tensions for his own political gain. A Serb himself, he fueled the ethnic resentment of the small Orthodox Christian Serbian minority in the province of Kosovo against the Muslim Albanian majority. He proclaimed that Serbians would not tolerate subservience in their own historic homeland.

With this revival of ethnic divisions, the leaders of the other federal states within Yugoslavia worried about a possible Serbian takeover that would repeat the fascist coup of 1929. In June 1991, **Slovenia** and **Croatia** preemptively proclaimed independence. When an invasion by the Serbian-dominated Yugoslav army failed, both countries were internationally recognized as sovereign states. Nonetheless,

Serbian-Croatian warfare was intense, and atrocities became the order of the day. The new term ***ethnic cleansing*** was coined, as both sides used destruction of homes and businesses, murder, and rape to drive away rival ethnic groups from villages and districts each wanted to claim as its own.

By early 1992, **Bosnia-Herzegovina** began its own attempt at independence. Unhappily for that state, Bosnia was the most ethnically divided of all. The dual province included Roman Catholic Croats, Orthodox Serbs, and large numbers of "Bosniaks," namely Serbo-Croatian Muslims. Croatia and the Serbian-dominated remnant of Yugoslavia both attacked. A siege from 1992 to 1996 shelled the provincial capital of Sarajevo. As recently as 1984, the historic town had hosted the Winter Olympics as a symbol of peaceful competition and excellence. After 1,425 days of bombardment, it smoldered in ruins.

Russia's sympathies lay with its old ally Serbia. Since Russia was a permanent member of the Security Council, it limited what the United Nations could achieve to stop the violence in the former Yugoslavia. UN peacekeepers stood by as Serb militias and military raped and murdered. Consequently, Western powers decided to realign the mission of NATO. The end of the Cold War and the breakup of the Warsaw Pact had removed the need to defend Europe against the extinct Soviet Union. Now the Western military alliance system took up peacekeeping in Europe. In August 1995, NATO planes began air strikes intended to reduce the warfare in Bosnia. After the Dayton Accords of November 1995, NATO sent in sixty thousand peacekeeper troops who successfully ended the fighting. Subsequently, Western armed forces slowly shrank in number until, by 2004, the European Union took over the mission with seven thousand soldiers. By the beginning of 2022, only a few hundred EU troops and bureaucrats remained stationed in Bosnia-Herzegovina to help with stabilization and state building. Some Bosnians even hoped for candidacy to the EU like the other Balkan states. Despite this success, many Bosnians remained frustrated with the ongoing slow implementation of legal reforms, quarreling politicians, high unemployment, official corruption, organized crime, genocide denial, and the continued craving of some ethnic Serbs and Croats to break up the state.

Another Balkan conflict exploded in the late 1990s over ethnic Albanians in Kosovo, where Milošević's nationalist rantings had sparked the breakup of Yugoslavia. The self-proclaimed Kosovo Liberation Army launched a rebellion in that province on behalf of the Albanian majority. Milošević's Yugoslav Federation retaliated for what it saw as Kosovar terrorism and began ethnic cleansing in January 1999. NATO then launched an aerial bombing campaign to stop the killings and expulsions. Soon NATO peacekeepers occupied the province, allowing the Kosovar Albanians to frame their own self-government and proclaim the Republic of Kosovo in 2008. A few thousand European Union bureaucrats in the "Rule of Law Mission in Kosovo" (EULEX) and several thousand NATO troops have kept the peace and continue to work toward building local political institutions. Nevertheless, the "Kosovo Question" remains open, since several EU members as well as Serbia still do not recognize its independence.

Meanwhile, the last two republics of former Yugoslavia, **Montenegro** and **Macedonia**, achieved independence without bloodshed. Macedonians had already voted for independence in 1991. They stayed out of the warfare raging among their northern neighbors, although a brief insurgency by ethnic Albanians in 2001 needed to be pacified by UN peacekeepers. The new country sought membership in both NATO and the EU but found its efforts obstructed on two sides. First, Greece objected to the use of the name "Macedonia," with its Hellenistic heritage from Philip II and Alexander. That attitude briefly forced that country to temporarily call itself the "Former Yugoslav Republic of Macedonia." Second, Bulgaria was reluctant to recognize Macedonians as a separate culture from Bulgarians. A compromise settled on the name "Republic of North Macedonia" in 2019. It became a member of NATO in 2020 but found its entry into the EU blocked by Bulgaria. Meanwhile, Montenegrins voted to abandon the Yugoslav Federation in 2006, leaving Serbia alone to its own destiny.

But even after hundreds of thousands had been displaced and over 130,000 people were dead because of the fragmentation of Yugoslavia, the consequences for some of those deaths continued long after the fighting stopped. Already in 1993, the United Nations Security Council was concerned about past atrocities and anxious to prevent future violence. It set up an International Criminal Tribunal for the former Yugoslavia in The Hague to hold leaders accountable for war crimes. Serbia's President Milošević was indicted while still in office. After he barely lost reelection in 2000, the new government handed Milošević over to be tried. He died unrepentant before a verdict could be rendered. The court considered 161 other accused war criminals, convicting and imprisoning ninety by 2017. Overall, these conflicts and policies have reduced ethnic differences in the Balkan states, but at the cost of much blood and destruction. The breakup of Yugoslavia demonstrated again how the passionate lures of ethnic separatism can thwart even honest efforts toward integration and unity.

Indeed, Western states continued to confront world problems made worse by nationalism and ethnic differences. Beginning in 1994, the ethnic minority of Mayan descent in the Mexican province of Chiapas organized a revolt under the Zapatistas. That conflict is still simmering today. Other countries suffered internal dissents, perhaps with less violence but still with important consequences. In Canada, beginning in the 1960s, the Québecois insisted on their own ethnic French identity. The Canadian government conceded to them the official use of the French language in Quebec, even if that preference drove millions of citizens of non-French heritage out of the province. Canadian governments further eased tensions by carefully promoting immigration to diversify national identity beyond Francophone versus Anglophone. Prime Minister Pierre Trudeau in 1971 fostered diversity rather than uniformity as the model for Canadian patriotism.

In Australia, tens of thousands of immigrants per year, especially from India and China, grew the population more than birth rates by citizens. But when hundreds of refugees from the Middle East and Afghanistan began to arrive by sea in 2001, they provoked anger and opposition. Refusing them entry, the

Australian government interned them offshore in costly concentration camps on remote islands until resettlement. Racial tensions against Lebanese and other ethnic immigrants from the Eastern Mediterranean sparked riots in the Sydney suburb of Cronulla in 2005. From the perspective of the Aboriginal and Torres Strait Islander peoples, all other persons in Australia were immigrants. But British colonizing regimes had long tried to westernize the descendants of the first inhabitants. Policies called Stolen Generations that took children from native families to be Europeanized only ended in the 1970s. And despite a court decision in 1996 that recognized native title to land that had been stolen from them, the government still sharply restricted those rights.[1] Efforts to have Aboriginal people recognized in the Australian constitution continue to limp along. The ongoing challenge of nationalism has been how to balance desires for ethnic diversity with ideals of nationalist conformity.

Review: *How did nationalism resurge after the Cold War?*

Response:

ELECTRIC DREAMS

Technological innovations transformed the economies of Western states and the world at the end of the twentieth and beginning of the twenty-first centuries. A "digital revolution" energized change based on new computers, affecting the use of information far more than the printing press had five centuries before. The Allies had invented programmable electronic calculating machines during World War II in order to break secret codes of the Axis powers. The computational ability of computers quickly increased as bureaucracies in business and government used them for collecting and analyzing data. New technologies such as transistors and microchips made computers cheaper and smaller. The electronics revolution accelerated with the invention of the **personal computer** as a consumer product in the 1980s. First used as advanced typewriters, they soon expanded into illustrations, spreadsheets, and databases, as well as games ranging from simple

---

1. The government was a coalition of the National Party, which represented miners' and farmers' rural interests, and the Liberal Party, which by most measures would be considered a conservative party.

solitaire to first-person shooter to multiplayer strategy and tactics simulations. At the same time, computer users began communicating via a new global network called the **internet**. Email allowed sending and receiving personal messages by the late 1980s. Then in 1991 the World Wide Web delivered graphic access through hyperlinks to information posted on the internet.

In modern industrialized societies, computers now control and regulate more lives than any human bureaucrat ever could. Also, for those who can afford to spend the time to learn to use them, computers help with the acquisition of new knowledge, which is power. With wireless and cellular technologies for phones and computers developed by the end of the twentieth century, people on the move easily connected both to each other and to a vast amount of data. Through search engines, most importantly Google since the turn of the century, users have more knowledge at their fingertips than anyone ever in history. Between 2004 and 2007, three new **social media** platforms, YouTube, Twitter, and Facebook, followed by the iPhone as the first "smartphone," connected users more intimately and empowered them to be more creative than almost any previous communications technology in history.

The ease with which words and images could be electronically distributed set an example for marketing goods and services. Beginning in the 1980s, *globalization* became the slogan of those who wanted to make more money by relying on the worldwide grasp of the modern corporation, cheap transportation and communication, and low or nonexistent trade barriers and regulations. Globalization's advocates suggested that worldwide marketing of material goods would be more influential in people's lives than the nation-state and its politics had ever been. Theoretically, a worldwide trade system could benefit rich and poor nations alike. Leaders of the most important economic powers began in 1975 to hold annual summit meetings about the global economy as the G7 (the United States, Japan, West Germany, Great Britain, France, Italy, and Canada).[2] These meetings coordinated select economic, social, and political policies to enable global trade.

Some economists, politicians, and citizens warned about the negative effects of globalization, especially where unchecked markets ignored social needs. Citizens concerned about issues of social justice and human rights began to organize NGOs (nongovernmental organizations), ranging from Amnesty International (to stop torture and cruelty) to Greenpeace (to protect the environment). They objected to Western corporations who paid low wages to impoverished natives for their country's natural resources while charging high prices to their comparatively wealthy Western customers. Broken pipelines and wrecked tankers spilled crude oil regularly, ruining vital watersheds and pristine coastlines while endangering wildlife and human health. Mountaintop removal and open-pit mining ravaged landscapes, too often with too little remediation afterward. Multinational or transnational enterprises seemed to show more loyalty to their managers and stockholders than patriotism or sympathy toward any one country or even toward

---

2. It became the G8 in the 1990s with the addition of Russia, although Russia's economy was the smallest of the members. It became the G7 again when the others excluded Russia after Putin's illegal seizure of the Crimea in 2014 (see below).

general human welfare. But consumers gained the mechanisms of middle-class life with microwaves, robot vacuums, washing appliances, cooking gadgets, battery-operated toys, and entertainment devices.

Meanwhile, industrial manufacturing expanded into Asia, which poured these products into the West. While low labor costs made them less expensive, Western corporations still earned good profits. Japan had led the way in the 1970s with exports of automobiles and electronics, subsidized by vigorous government policies and working with major manufacturing cartels. By the 1990s, the so-called Asian Tigers (Singapore, South Korea, Nationalist China/Taiwan, and the British colony of Hong Kong) likewise became competitive.

At the end of the twentieth century, China started its rise as a globally dominant power. By then, reforms by Chairman Deng Xiaoping (r. 1982–1987) had enabled communist China to recover from the mistakes of Mao. Deng had opened the path for China to become an economic powerhouse driven by a Western-style economy, while not allowing Western-style democracy. In 1989, protests in Tiananmen Square in Beijing demanded a more representative government, symbolized by their building a crude copy of the Statue of Liberty. The totalitarian, one-party regime dispersed the demonstrators, refusing to disclose how many it arrested or killed. For the Chinese, the history of this event remains heavily censored.

China's dynamism accelerated after 1997, when the British returned Hong Kong to China. The British had held Hong Kong as a colony by treaty since the Opium Wars in the 1840s. For Hong Kong and Macao (returned by the Portuguese in 1999), China promised to have "one country, two systems" for fifty years. That meant that democratic representation and free-market economics of private ownership of capital in Hong Kong and Macao would exist alongside the Chinese Communist Party's authoritarianism and socialist market economy of some private ownership and much nationalization. The design would not last even two decades.

Consequently, China began its own version of the Commercial and Industrial Revolutions. Western companies now found China to be an attractive business partner, and they invested huge amounts of Western capital to rapidly industrialize China. They even dismantled actual factories in their home countries and shipped them to China (firing, of course, the Western workers). This new Industrial Revolution likewise exploited Chinese workers as the West had a century before. The government ensured that workers would be diligent producers with long hours and high quotas. Many of the workers lived in spartan dormitories enclosed behind walls and barbed wire. The Chinese also have exploited child and prison laborers. As in the West in the nineteenth century, the government forbade workers to organize but did little itself to protect workers. Still, since factory workers' wages were superior to those offered by the collapsing rural economy, and as new modern cities rose from the dirt, many Chinese accepted this new revolution. And westerners willingly paid for cheap bedding, toothbrushes, clothing, toys, and, of course, electronics at their discount warehouse stores, so much of it "Made in China."

The ruling Chinese Communist Party had seemingly brought back the economic theory of mercantilism: capitalism as directed by the government. China has since used its new wealth to increase its international prestige and global intervention. In search of political influence to gain raw materials, Chinese economic imperialism invests its vast profits in developing nations around the world. The People's Republic of China offers a role model for how authoritarian one-party rule can transform a poor agrarian economy into an industrial giant. Indeed, once a second-rate nuclear power, China has the potential to become the world's most powerful state, militarily and economically, in the twenty-first century. The Chinese communists have adopted and adapted the ideas and methods of the West to become its most potent rival.

All this consumerism and industrialization increasingly had an impact on the environment. Chemical emissions seemed to have opened a hole over the Antarctic in the ozone layer that protects the earth's surface from destructive ultraviolet rays. Children of European descent in Australia and New Zealand were soon required to protect their light skin with sunscreen and floppy hats. Recent scientific studies have also added evidence that air pollution, carbon dioxide emissions, energy production, and deforestation have produced a greenhouse effect that is heating up the atmosphere. The largest forested area in the world, the Amazon, is laid waste as developers hack down trees and turn the land into cattle ranches (while dispossessing the native hunter-gathering peoples). Millions of acres of arable land in Africa, Asia, and even North America have been turned into desert, as rivers, lakes, and even the entire Aral Sea have dried up. The overwhelming number of scientific studies about **global climate change** have concluded that "anthropogenic global warming" is melting the glaciers and polar ice caps and then raising sea water levels to flood coastal areas.

The United Nations initiated meetings called Conference of Parties (COP) to deal with environmental issues in 1995, but saw little progress. Many politicians and economists have been reluctant to initiate reforms that would threaten standards of living. Yet at the COP21 in 2015, states began signing on to the Paris Agreement, supplementing the Kyoto Protocol of 2005, to cut carbon emissions (mostly from "fossil fuels" of coal, natural gas, and petroleum). By 2021, over 193 governments had ratified the agreement.[3]

Finding alternatives has been challenging. Nuclear power has faced continued opposition because of few alternatives to store spent fuel and worry about accidents. An earthquake and tsunami damaged a plant in Fukushima, Japan (2011), which continues to leak radioactivity from its dead zone into local groundwater and the ocean. Windmills and solar panels have become common, yet are still too few and too expensive to replace older power plants. Recent increases in heat waves, polar ice melting, permafrost warming, and wild fires, as well as more frequent hurricanes, floods, and droughts, show that the global climate is changing even faster than predicted. Conflicts over potable water and arable land seem certain to multiply.

Industrialization of our food supply has further shrunk rural populations and grown urban areas. Modern stock farms crowd thousands of caged pigs or

---

3. Although President Donald Trump withdrew American participation from the protocol, his successor President Biden rejoined the accord.

chickens into vast warehouses where they dwell in reeking darkness. They are fed hormones (to speed their growth), antibiotics (to prevent diseases that would normally destroy creatures living so closely together in filth), the recycled remnants of their fellow creatures (as cheap food), and laxatives (to make their excrement more manageable). The traditional family farm finds it hard to compete against aggressive agribusinesses.

And then there are advances in genetic science that promise to change the foundation of our being, from food supply to our physiology. The biggest leap in the study of life since Darwin was the discovery in 1953 of deoxyribonucleic acid, or DNA. This double helix of molecules is the basic building block of life. Among the uses of DNA science is fighting crime, having replaced fingerprints or dental impressions as the best means for identification of criminals or victims. Its real future, however, lies in scientists' tinkering with DNA's molecular structure. In 1988, the US Patent Office granted a patent on a genetically engineered mouse. Since then, synthetic organs, hormones, and compounds of all kinds for humans are being worked on. GMOs (genetically modified organisms) offer the potential to provide still cheaper and more nutritious food. Those opposed to their widespread use note corporate control of agriculture through patents (which prevents farmers from owning their own seeds) and the lack of long-term studies on their safety. Some consumer NGOs have campaigned to restrict the use of GMOs or at least have them clearly labeled when used in food products.

Aside from our food, the sex lives of our bodies have become increasingly commodified. The end of the Cold War brought the West's sexual revolution both to the newly liberated Soviet bloc and to the former colonial regions of the Third World. Business interests using the internet provided more access to pornography to more people than ever before in history. Westerners traveled to poor countries in Asia and eastern Europe for "sex tourism." The demands for the sex trade led organized criminals to virtually enslave women and children from poor countries to serve in brothels. Much of such commercial sex activity is still done behind closed doors and against the law, although a few countries have legalized sex work (Denmark, Germany, the Netherlands) or decriminalized it (New Zealand, Belgium).

Western societies have also led the way in challenging heteronormative expectations about sexual identities and activities. The term *homosexuality* (itself not much more than a century old) began to include a wide range of loving and sexual behaviors. What previously had legally been termed *sodomy* (usually meaning sexual acts between people of the same sex) began to be decriminalized. Same-sex relations had actually been legal in some Latin American countries (such as Brazil, Bolivia, and Paraguay) since the nineteenth century. The United States only legalized sexual activity by people of the same sex in 2003. In 1989, Denmark opened the door for homosexuals to enter civil unions, with rights similar to those of "traditional" heterosexual marriage. After the Netherlands allowed legal marriage for same-sex couples in 2001, more than two dozen other Western nations in Europe and the Americas, as well as New Zealand and South Africa, have done so, with others accepting civil unions and other forms of legally recognized partnerships (see the Sources on Families below).

More recently, issues about sex and gender identities have proliferated, as people sought labels for where they existed in a sexualized social order.[4] People identifying as transsexual or transgender resisted how society imposed the trappings of historically arbitrary manhood or womanhood. Medical surgery for sex reassignment began in the 1930s, becoming more common in the 1960s. While such operations could not change a person's genetics, successful surgeries helped individuals better align their inner sense of masculinity, femininity, or androgyny with their physical bodies. Who could have dreamed that attitudes toward sex could evolve so quickly?

Not everyone accepted these developments, of course. Opponents saw this change in sex and gender roles as a nightmare threat to "traditional" morality. Since many of the arguments are based on Christianity rather than science, the terms that describe divided Christians since the beginning of the twentieth century may be useful. On the one side, modernists have asserted that all people are inherently equal, regardless of sex or sexual orientation, and that differences in gender are socially insignificant. On the other side, fundamentalists have stated that God created only two sexes, male and female, each having a different defined role in society: men as leaders and women as mothers and caregivers. Permitting gender freedom or same-sex rights would contradict the divine order or offend decency. They conveniently forget or never learned about people born as intersex. Many African Christians have protested when Western churches have ordained women or homosexuals, although the South African Anglican archbishop Desmond Tutu notably called for toleration. Ironically, African leaders have claimed that Westerners are undermining "traditional" African identities regarding sex and sexuality, when actually imperialist laws first codified rigid heteronormative sex roles and punishment for deviation therefrom in the African colonies.

Review: How did Western economic practices dominate world trade?

Response:

---

4. The acronym LGBTQI+ is shorthand for a number of sex/gender perceptions: lesbian, gay, bisexual, trans (transvestite, transsexual, transgender), queer or questioning, intersex, etc.

SOURCES ON FAMILIES: SUPREME COURT OF THE UNITED STATES, *OBERGEFELL V. HODGES* (2015)

Any decision handed down by the Supreme Court is a combination effort among the main justice (in this case, Anthony Kennedy) who delivers the opinion, those who concur, those who dissent, and the law clerks who work for them. In the following decision, the court legalized same-sex marriages throughout the United States. This selection explains some of the rationale for doing so, providing context through the history of the institution.

From their beginning to their most recent page, the annals of human history reveal the transcendent importance of marriage. The lifelong union of a man and a woman always has promised nobility and dignity to all persons, without regard to their station in life. Marriage is sacred to those who live by their religions and offers unique fulfillment to those who find meaning in the secular realm. Its dynamic allows two people to find a life that could not be found alone, for a marriage becomes greater than just the two persons. Rising from the most basic human needs, marriage is essential to our most profound hopes and aspirations.

The centrality of marriage to the human condition makes it unsurprising that the institution has existed for millennia and across civilizations. Since the dawn of history, marriage has transformed strangers into relatives, binding families and societies together. . . . This wisdom was echoed . . . by Cicero, who wrote, "The first bond of society is marriage; next, children; and then the family." . . . It is fair and necessary to say these references were based on the understanding that marriage is a union between two persons of the opposite sex.

That history is the beginning of these cases. The respondents [those who oppose the petitioners or plaintiffs who brought the case] say it should be the end as well. To them, it would demean a timeless institution if the concept and lawful status of marriage were extended to two persons of the same sex. Marriage, in their view, is by its nature a gender-differentiated union of man and woman. This view long has been held—and continues to be held—in good faith by reasonable and sincere people here and throughout the world.

The petitioners acknowledge this history but contend that these cases cannot end there. Were their intent to demean the revered idea and reality of marriage, the petitioners' claims would be of a different order. But that is neither their purpose nor their submission. To the contrary, it is the enduring importance of marriage that underlies the petitioners' contentions. This, they say, is their whole point. . . .

Recounting the circumstances of three of these cases illustrates the urgency of the petitioners' cause from their perspective. Petitioner James Obergefell, a plaintiff in the Ohio case, met John Arthur over two decades ago. They fell in love and started a life together, establishing a lasting, committed relation. In 2011, however, Arthur was diagnosed with amyotrophic lateral sclerosis, or ALS. . . . Two years ago, Obergefell and Arthur decided . . . to marry before Arthur died. To fulfill their mutual promise, they traveled from Ohio to Maryland, where same-sex marriage was legal. It was difficult for Arthur to move, and so the couple were wed inside a medical transport plane as it remained on the tarmac in Baltimore. Three months later, Arthur died. . . . By statute, they must remain strangers even in death, a state-imposed separation Obergefell deems "hurtful for the rest of time." He brought suit to be shown as the surviving spouse on Arthur's death certificate.

April DeBoer and Jayne Rowse are co-plaintiffs in the case from Michigan. They celebrated a commitment ceremony to honor their permanent relation in 2007. They both work as nurses, DeBoer in a neonatal unit and Rowse in an emergency unit. In 2009, DeBoer and Rowse fostered and then adopted a baby boy. Later that same year, they welcomed another son into their family. The new baby, born prematurely and abandoned by his biological mother, required around-the-clock care. The next year, a baby girl with special needs joined their family. Michigan, however, permits only opposite-sex married couples or single individuals to adopt, so each child can have only one woman as his or her legal parent. If an emergency were to arise, schools and hospitals may treat the three children as if they had only one parent. And, were tragedy to befall either DeBoer or Rowse, the other would have no legal rights over the children she had not been permitted to adopt. This couple seeks relief from the continuing uncertainty their unmarried status creates in their lives.

Army Reserve Sergeant First Class Ijpe DeKoe and his partner Thomas Kostura, co-plaintiffs in the Tennessee case, fell in love. In 2011, DeKoe received orders to deploy to Afghanistan. Before leaving, he and Kostura married in New York. . . . Their lawful marriage is stripped from them whenever they reside in Tennessee, returning and disappearing as they travel across state lines. . . .

No union is more profound than marriage, for it embodies the highest ideals of love, fidelity, devotion, sacrifice, and family. In forming a marital union, two people become something greater than once they were. As some of the petitioners in these cases demonstrate, marriage embodies a love that may endure even past death. It would misunderstand these men and women to say they disrespect the idea of marriage. Their plea is that they do respect it, respect it so deeply that they seek to find its fulfillment for themselves. Their hope is not to be condemned to live in loneliness, excluded from one of civilization's oldest institutions. They ask for equal dignity in the eyes of the law. The Constitution grants them that right.

Questions:

- *How does the source place marriage in a historical context?*
- *How does the source use the personal experiences of the plaintiffs to make a case?*
- *How does the source argue against those who disagree with the decision?*

Responses:

For more on this source, go to http://www.concisewesternciv.com/sources/sof15.html.

VALUES OF VIOLENCE

The end of the Cold War seemed to bestow a dividend of peace and prosperity. Even nationalist terrorism interested in separatism seemed on the decline by the early 1990s in much of the West. The IRA in Northern Ireland and the ETA in Spain slowly stopped their bombings. In the United States, some homegrown terrorists struck against Planned Parenthood clinics, African Americans, and the government itself (such as the 1995 bombing of the Oklahoma City Federal Building that killed 168 people). But most Americans worried more about crime directly caused by gangs and the illegal drug trade. The collapse of the Soviet Union and its communist ideology validated what some saw as unique Western values of democracy, global capitalism, and the nation-state.

Unforeseen, tensions revolving around the place of hundreds of millions of Muslims provided global problems. The West's dependence on oil imports continued to force its attention toward the Middle East. Many Muslims there disliked both Western ideology, with its acceptance of changing social attitudes, and economic exploitation, with profits flowing out of Arab nations. Many also hated the existence of the state of Israel on land that they saw belonging to Palestinians. Certain fundamentalist Muslims, as individuals and as groups, began to oppose the West with force.[5]

The West could, of course, take much of the blame for the growing opposition of some Muslims. The Crusades, the *Reconquista*, and the rivalry with the Ottoman Empire built a legacy of suspicion, if not hostility. When westerners took over much of the Middle East in the nineteenth and early twentieth centuries, their arrogance further annoyed their imperialist subjects. It was merely unexpected good fortune for many Arab nations that geologists discovered petroleum beneath their desert sands just after the imperialists withdrew from the Middle East. Even then, Western leaders propped up local despots and dictators with whom they could conveniently make economic arrangements to control the flow of oil. Thus, many people in those new Middle Eastern countries resented such foreign intervention and the authoritarian governments it supported.

The tensions between diverse aspects of Islamic civilization and a modern world created by Western civilization were revealed with the **Iranian Revolution** (1978–1980). Through much of the Cold War, the shah of Iran, Mohammad Reza Pahlavi, had ruled as a near-absolute monarch. The CIA had put the shah in power in 1953 by overthrowing the democratically elected but socialist prime minister, Mohammad Mossadegh. The shah served as a loyal ally of the United States in the region, promoting secular modernization and westernization. He also oppressed those who disagreed with his secret police and absolutism. In

---

5. No one has yet come up with a satisfactory name for describing the wide range of different political agents who have recently combined Islam and terrorism. *Islamo-fascist* misapplies the nationalistic and state or corporate-based ideology of fascism, which is inherently based on "race," not religion. *Jihadist* validates those who believe *jihad* is compatible with slaughter and suicide, as opposed to every Muslim's duty to do good. This text will try *Islamist*, which differs some from the adjective *Islamic* for all Muslims, a great many of whom do not promote religious violence.

reaction, the Ayatollah Khomeini, a religious leader based in Paris, orchestrated a revolution in 1979 that forced the shah into exile. Khomeini then produced a new religious dictatorship, or theocracy, based on his interpretation of Islam.

The Iranian Revolution kept enough of the modern science needed to maintain oil wealth and military power, but it rejected much of the rest of Western culture. After American president Jimmy Carter (r. 1977–1981) allowed the ousted shah into the United States for medical treatment, Iranian students attacked the American embassy in Iran's capital of Tehran. They seized what they called a "spy den" and held its staff hostage for 444 days. Carter's failure to gain release or rescue of the hostages contributed to his defeat in his reelection campaign. The triumphant Iran championed anti-Western civilization and called on other Muslims to support its expansionist Shiite agenda.

Since the United States could not take direct action against Iran, it encouraged another friendly and more secular dictator, Saddam Hussein of Iraq (r. 1979–2004), to attack. The resulting Iran-Iraq War (1980–1988) killed hundreds of thousands, reviving trench warfare and even the use of poison gas. After the war ended as a draw, Saddam thought that exploiting his wealthy neighbor Kuwait could pay for the lost war. From Saddam Hussein's point of view, he just wanted to take back an Arab territory that the British had carved out of the Ottoman Empire in the nineteenth century. In August 1990 his armies invaded the tiny principality.

Kuwait was, however, a sovereign state and a member of the United Nations, whose purpose was to prevent wars against its members. Under the leadership of American president George H. W. Bush (r. 1989–1993), the United Nations intervened. During the **First Persian Gulf War** (1990–1991), half a million American and allied troops liberated Kuwait at the disproportionate cost of about eight hundred lives for the United States and its allies, versus probably one hundred thousand Iraqis. The UN forces left Saddam Hussein in power, though, since the United Nations Charter forbids intervention in the internal affairs of its members.

The First Gulf War only helped the new militant version of Islam to grow, supported by the Saudi royal family and their fundamentalist Wahhabi sect as a counterweight to Shiite Iran. Many Muslims in other Islamic countries had also become hostile against their own secular or Sunni regimes, and denounced Israel, the United States, and Western civilization as a whole. The dictator Muammar Gaddafi (r. 1969–2011) in Libya, for one early example, sponsored the bombing of a Pan Am flight to the United States that exploded over Lockerbie, Scotland, in 1988. In 1997, the so-called Islamic Group killed dozens of Western tourists at Luxor in Egypt.

The unending struggle between the Palestinians and Israelis fueled additional acts of terror. Israeli governments had failed to implement real Palestinian self-government as agreed in the Camp David Accords, while Western governments did little to force Israel to do so. Instead, Israel continued to dispossess Palestinians and encouraged Jewish settlers to create fortified enclaves within occupied areas. By the 1990s, Palestinians in the occupied territories carried out *intifadas* (uprisings), consisting of boycotts of Israeli businesses, strikes, demonstrations, and "wars of stones" (throwing rocks). The Israelis responded by restricting Palestinian movements (thus preventing them from going to their jobs), demolishing property (bulldozing wells, homes, and entire villages), and using force (such as rocket assassination attacks on Palestinian leaders). In a Second Intifada (2001–2005), Palestinian actions rose to having suicide bombers regularly blow up themselves and numerous Israelis on buses and in cafés. Divisions among Palestinians led to Fatah, a successor to the PLO, as the authority in the West Bank, while the rival Hamas (Islamic Resistance Group) in the Gaza Strip regularly launched chaotic missile attacks that killed dozens of Israelis. Israel usually responded disproportionately with its own missiles that demolished many buildings and killed hundreds. Neither Palestinian leaders nor Israeli politicians seemed able to end reciprocal exchanges of violence, while Western regimes too often failed to engage.

Another nest of hostility to the West developed in Afghanistan. When the Americans had armed the Muslim militant *mujahideen* in Afghanistan to fight the Soviets in the 1980s, they did not foresee how the Afghans would break down into near civil war. After the Cold War had ended, some religious students, or **Taliban**, became so disgusted with the ongoing violence that they organized their own attacks on everyone else, using the arms America had provided to defeat the Russians. The Taliban's religious devotion and militaristic discipline helped them to take over their country. They then imposed their own Islamist dictatorship, even harsher in cultural imperatives than Iran's. Their most notorious actions included both the forcible confinement of women and iconoclastically destroying priceless ancient sculptures.

The Taliban also provided a haven to yet another new kind of international Islamist terrorist group, **al-Qa'ida** (the Base). Osama bin Laden, a Saudi former oil and construction magnate, founded and financed al-Qa'ida to promote his militant version of Islam. Bin Laden was especially resentful of American intervention in the Middle East, whether in support of Israel or against Saddam Hussein. His Islamist organization launched the boldest terrorist attack in history on 11 September 2001 (**9/11**) by hijacking four passenger airliners to use as weapons. Two hit the twin towers of the World Trade Center in New York City, a symbol of Western commerce and capitalism. The resulting fires led to the skyscrapers' collapse. A third damaged the Pentagon (the US military's command center near Washington, DC), while a fourth crashed into a field in Pennsylvania after its passengers fought back against their hijackers. All told, about three thousand people (mostly Americans, but also dozens from other nations) died on that day from these attacks.

In response, President George W. Bush (r. 2001–2009) declared a "War on Terrorism." This declaration, unfortunately, was a confusing concept. For one, only Congress could constitutionally declare war. For another, terrorism has been a tactic, not an actual enemy against whom a state can easily fight. Terrorists have used small-scale violence to achieve their political goals since the end of the nineteenth century. Governments have found it nearly impossible to stop such terrorist attacks. As access to weapons became easier and grudges against specific state systems grew, terrorism offered an affordable substitute for sustained guerrilla war or conventional armies. Typical armed forces have been ill suited to combat terrorists, who blended so easily into the civilian population, both before and after they struck. Even in industrialized Western nations, such as Britain facing the IRA in Northern Ireland or Spain facing the ETA in the Basque regions, authorities could not completely crush terrorist cells. But by using the term *war*, the United States has become permanently, but vaguely, stuck "at war" ever since.

Since 9/11, some success against terrorism has come from either addressing the root political complaints of specific groups or using approaches similar to criminal investigations, such as expanding intelligence and police agencies. Some laws threatened to remove civil rights and legal due process from both citizens and aliens as they increased surveillance of public places, private computers and phone communications, and even persons' homes. Western states tended to favor security over civil liberty, invasive technology versus personal privacy, and ethnic intolerance against economic generosity.

Militarily, Article 5 of NATO's mutual self-defense agreement went into effect: an attack on one member state was an attack on all. The United States and allied troops retaliated for 9/11 by invading Afghanistan, where the Taliban had sheltered bases of al-Qa'ida. The United States and its allies won a quick victory. Yet most al-Qa'ida leaders, including Osama bin Laden, managed to escape. Unfortunately for peace, Afghanistan did not stabilize after the Taliban's defeat. Instead, warlords reasserted their divisive domination, even against tens of thousands of troops from NATO members and fifty partner states.

Then, despite being the world's lone superpower, the United States found itself unable to lead the West in dealing with terrorism, even with sympathy generated by the 9/11 attacks. Instead of finishing off al-Qa'ida, President Bush's attention turned to removing Saddam Hussein from power in Iraq. The Bush administration listened to "neoconservative" theorists who promoted a renewed American exceptionalism, believing that the United States could unilaterally intervene in troubled spots around the world to create Western-style capitalist democracies.

In this context, the American administration asserted that invading Iraq was part of that vague "War on Terrorism." Neocons suggested that Saddam had connections with al-Qa'ida and the attacks of 9/11 (which was not true). Specifically, the United States claimed that Iraq had defied UN resolutions about eliminating weapons of mass destruction (**WMDs**, a new name for the category "ABC" or atomic, biological, and chemical weapons). That also was not true, as UN inspectors (and later the US government) failed to find any evidence of such weapons. Neither the United Nations, nor NATO, nor indeed most of the world's nations supported invasion. Many westerners actively protested what they saw as the American rush into a distracting war. Nevertheless, the application of new bombing technology and rapid mobile forces, called "shock and awe," won the United States and its "Coalition of the Willing" (with Great Britain as the only serious participant) a quick initial military conquest in the **Iraq or Second Persian Gulf War** (2003–2011). Many countries in Asia and Africa, however, saw America's mission, called "Operation Iraqi Freedom," as a violation of international law, reinforcing the fear that America, or any strong power, could and would invade wherever it wanted, at will.

The quick declaration of "mission accomplished," however, did not end the conflict, as American and allied forces faced serious hostility to their occupation.

Iraqi insurgents regularly killed coalition troops with sniping and IEDs (improvised explosive devices) while terrorizing their own fragile government and weary population with kidnappings and beheadings. Human rights organizations and defenders sharply criticized the American government for its actions, including torture of "enemy combatants," which was against international law. Al-Qa'ida's terrorist bombings of commuter trains in Madrid in 2004 and subway bombings in London in 2005 proved that it could still operate despite the loss of bases in Afghanistan. Osama bin Laden himself remained at large until 2011, when American commandos under the orders of the next president, Barack Obama (r. 2009–2017), shot him in his secret refuge in Pakistan. By the end of that year, Obama carried out an agreement made by the previous Bush administration to pull out all American combat troops from Iraq, leaving it severely destabilized between Sunnis, Shiites, and Kurds.

The official end of America's Iraq War celebrated very little of a victory for "Western" values, much less American power. People of course feared terrorist kidnappings, shootings, hijackings, and suicide bombings. They resented the randomness, fatalities, and ultimate futility of most terrorist attacks. Yet many around the world also condemned the US course of preemptive war, torture, and bombing from the skies, especially since America had not created functional and prosperous democracies in its wake.

Review: How did Western and non-Western societies use violence to achieve political and cultural ends?

Response:

THE WALLS GO UP AGAIN

One of the sad ironies of history in the past few years has been the reappearance of political barriers. When the Berlin Wall and Iron Curtain fell at the end of the Cold War, many people hoped for a new age of toleration and prosperity (see figure 15.3). New and old fears, however, have brought back wall building with a vengeance. Desire for physical barriers had never quite disappeared. Militarized frontiers had continued between the Koreas and in parts of Asia and Africa. In Northern Ireland, the "Peace Lines" or "Peace Walls" that had gone up during the

Figure 15.3. Fragments of the Berlin Wall live on as art. This painting originated in 1979 when a photographer captured the moment when Soviet premier Leonid Brezhnev embraced East German president Erich Honecker in a "socialist fraternal kiss." After the wall's fall in 1989, Russian artist Dmitri Vrubel re-created the kiss on one section, with the title in Russian and German, "My God, help me to survive this deadly love." In 2009, twenty years after the fall, the wall remnant was cleaned, repaired, and repainted to be a more durable "gallery." The kiss painting survives today, covered with graffiti and blocked behind parked cars—somewhat symbolic of the messiness of the West.

Troubles remained standing, even if in 2007 a functional coalition government called for them to come down. At the turn of the twenty-first century, Israel began its roughly 25-foot-high and 440-mile-long "West Bank Barrier." Ostensibly it was to prevent suicide bombings, while Palestinians considered that its purpose was to reduce their economic and political freedoms and cement the theft of their territory. Some critics thought the wall more reminiscent of the ghettoes of the Renaissance or Third Reich, but this time it penned in Arabs.

A new barricade mentality began, however, after the globalized economy suffered a severe blow in 2008. In the years just before, many businesspeople and economists boasted from their towering skyscrapers that the constant capitalist cycle of boom and bust had been forever broken. Believing market bubbles and bursts were a relic of history, governments removed financial barriers that had prohibited banks from speculating with investments. Capitalists deregulated, increased debt, failed to require sufficient collateral, and encouraged rampant profit reaping. The superficial success of the unrestrained Reagan and Thatcher business practices drew in even Democrats under Bill Clinton (r. 1993–2001), Labour under Tony Blair (r. 1997–2007), and other social democratic parties. Many regimes agreed to loosen regulations for health and safety, lower taxes on the wealthy, encourage companies to merge and monopolize, allow exploitative interest rates on loans and credit cards, attack trade unionism, and transfer capital and manufacturing easily both between and outside Western nations (especially to communist China). Free trade agreements and cheaper transportation of goods in containers led to the dismantling of many factories in Western countries. Left behind were many unemployed workers unwilling or unable to follow jobs across country or overseas. Increasingly, capitalists invested in factories built in Third World nations, where they could pay a fraction of the wages expected by Western workers whether organized in unions or not. Many Western nations lost high-wage factory jobs, to be replaced by low-wage service jobs (cooking, cleaning, or clerking). Some economists considered this as mere "creative destruction," as described by the Austrian economist Joseph Schumpeter. Others worried that this postindustrial economy slowed the rise in the standard of living of the lower middle class, especially compared with the upper and upper middle classes.

Naive confidence in the wisdom of deregulated markets soon proved disastrously false, since many investments were not as safe as advertised. In America, stock markets and hedge funds had become overinflated with risky products called derivatives. In Europe, poor countries were showered with loans that would be difficult to repay, economic downturn or not. And a crash came in 2008, as the markets suddenly collapsed after investors finally realized how much bad debt had piled up. Trillions of euros and dollars and pounds completely disappeared over the following year in what some call the "Great Recession." The major banks of Iceland, for example, which had grown bigger than the rest of the national economy, completely crashed. That ruined that country's economy and stalled its admission to the European Union.

The eurozone itself added to its own financial crisis in 2009 after the Greek government admitted that it had ignored required limits on its national debt. The euro had been created with a significant flaw: the dominant Deutsche Bundesbank (German Central Bank) largely controlled its value, which meant that individual nations could not manipulate currency rates to help them recover from debt, as they had done before the currency union. As a result, Greece threatened to default. There was even talk of "Grexit," or Greece exiting from the European Union. To prevent widespread economic devastation, the EU poured billions of euros into bailouts in Greece while also imposing strict austerity measures (increasing taxes and cutting social welfare). The Greek economy still weakened and drove up unemployment numbers to over a quarter of the workforce. Soon Portugal, Ireland, Italy, and Spain sought similar relief because of their debts. Their failures earned those countries the insulting acronym of PIIGS.

How Europe, the West, and the global economic powers dealt with this crisis exposed the complex strengths and tensions that still lay within Western civilization. The responses to the collapse alternated between two economic theories. On one side, Keynesian policies recommended massive deficit spending, careful monitoring, and regulation. The other side pushed increasing privatization of public enterprises and imposing austerity by cutting social services, government pensions, and civil services. Each side claimed theirs was the right course.

In the United States, after the bankruptcy of the Lehman Brothers investment company shocked the markets, economists feared a complete crash. So the government threw taxpayer money at other "too big to fail" corporations and banks. That slowed the declining value of markets, but also allowed investors and owners to stay wealthy. Many executives paid themselves and major investors with the bailout money rather than funding pensions or raising wages for middle-class employees. Despite their reckless financial decisions, executives avoided jail (unlike in some previous financial mismanagement crises). Only in Iceland, whose banks had once driven vibrant economic growth, were executives sentenced to prison. When governments imposed fines for mismanagement, corporate leaders used shareholder money to pay them off. In the aftermath, the wealthy had accumulated a greater share of wealth than ever, while the middle class seemed threatened by the high costs of living on stagnant wages and by a rising revolution in robotics that replaced industrial workers. Which lessons governments and capitalists would learn from these failures, if any, remained unknown (see Primary Source Project 15).

Many common citizens seemed to lose confidence in the financial elites who led them into economic disaster. Populations reacted to rising unemployment and social welfare cutbacks by demonstrating, striking, and voting for extremist parties. Many became anti-globalization, anti–European Union, or anti–Wall Street. That somehow made sense, since such policies had largely caused the economic failure. Meanwhile, media outlets proliferated whose whole purpose was to agitate their audience into being upset with the "opposition" and rival media. They also deflected the blame for people's problems elsewhere: against minorities, the poor, "foreigners," and migrants.

Sudden increases in refugees from Muslim countries helped inflame those fears. The escalation originated in the so-called Arab Spring of 2011. As we have seen, many Arab states were ruled by authoritarian governments that rejected participation of the people around nationalist "traditions." During the Arab Spring, however, revolts broke out inspired by the hope for certain Western liberties, including free speech, open and fair elections with choice, checks and balances on authority, and honest and efficient bureaucracies. The conflicts began in Tunisia when in December 2010 police abuse on behalf of its dictator provoked riots. By the spring of 2011, people in various other North African and Middle Eastern countries began to protest and agitate for democratic change. Dictators toppled in Tunisia, Libya, Egypt, Syria, Bahrain, and Yemen. In many of the elections that followed, however, Islamist parties such as the Muslim Brotherhood tended to win and then tried to entrench themselves in power, while enforcing fundamentalist religious conformity. Rather than bringing freedom, therefore, the elections merely brought a different form of repression.

Revolutions went even more wrong in Libya and Syria. With the overt intervention of NATO through air support, Libyans overthrew and assassinated Colonel

Muammar Gaddafi after decades of dictatorship. Their inability to restore order left a failed state. Then, when a civil war broke out in Syria, Western powers declined at first to intervene. The dictator Bashar al-Assad (r. 2000–), who had inherited power from his father, had failed to address the crisis of a massive drought. Assad reacted to protests by having tens of thousands of Syrians arrested, tortured, and killed while reducing many neighborhoods to rubble. By 2015 he had invited the Russian military to help with the massacres.

These two failed regimes triggered a refugee crisis as thousands, then millions, of "economic" and "political" refugees headed toward Europe through Libya and from Syria. In 2013 and 2014, Italian border facilities became so overwhelmed with migrants crossing the Mediterranean in ramshackle boats that they could only be housed in conditions resembling concentration camps. At first, other European Union members offered little help for Italy's humanitarian crisis on its border. As migrant numbers climbed in 2015, however, leaders and citizens of some European countries, especially Chancellor Angela Merkel of Germany (r. 2005–2021), welcomed refugees. Eventually, the European Commission required all EU members to accept set quotas of refugees. Germany generously took in the most, a million refugees in 2015 alone (measured against a population of eighty-one million).

Then a reaction flared up. The seemingly never-ending flood of immigrants coupled with a few incidents of cultural conflict provoked a backlash of xenophobia, especially in the former East Germany. Its people still suffered from comparatively low income levels and high unemployment long after reunification. Then Hungary, Poland, Slovakia, and the Czech Republic banded together and refused to take any refugees, even while Spain, Greece, and Italy were overburdened. Several states, such as Hungary and Austria, began constructing physical barriers, mostly chain-link fences with barbed or razor wire, enforced by border guards, to control or prevent immigrants from entering their countries. Walls had returned.

These populist and nativist political movements worried about the loss of their various ethnic identities within and across Europe. Even though studies show that immigrants do not increase crime, many citizens continued to believe that newcomers did. And even though studies show that immigrants often enrich an economy, people resent their cost in social benefits. In France, *identitarianism* had been growing in reaction to Muslim immigrants. Identitarians promoted chauvinism and hostility to foreigners and rejected cosmopolitanism. Each country itself should be ethnically homogeneous, agreeing with nationalist ideas going back to the 1800s. It does seem paradoxical, though, that foreigners who were characterized as ignorant and inferior were simultaneously believed to be a threat capable of taking over the powerful, complex industrialized states of Europe.

The largest state in Europe, Russia, suffered the utter failure of democracy. The first president of the Russian Federation, Boris Yeltsin (r. 1991–1999), strengthened the presidency after an attempted coup by communist sympathizers. But then Yeltsin frittered away any serious rule by allowing "oligarchs" to dominate the economy and politics. Organized criminals allied with foreign investors to loot the assets of the Russian economy and create a new plutocracy (or kleptocracy) that financed their wealth by what they plundered. Coming out on top was Vladimir Putin, who had started as a KGB officer in East Germany when the Berlin Wall fell. Putin was nostalgic for the Soviet Union. He wanted a stronger Russia, unfairly (he believed) defeated and humiliated by its loss of the Cold War. As president, Putin (r. 2000–2008, 2012–) turned the Russian Federation even further away from democracy and established himself as a new, modern authoritarian leader. Putin used his intelligence agency connections to expand his power as head of state, and also to crush independent media, judiciary, and other oligarchs by threatening and sending some to prison. The ability of Russia to export gas and oil financed Putin's power grab. He solidified his authority by continuing to hand over major economic resources to loyal oligarchs (now defined as hugely wealthy beneficiaries of monopolies) and himself. They invested in Western markets, especially through London's financial institutions. Putin eliminated the free press and had reporters murdered, he rigged elections and arrested and even poisoned his adversaries, he had the constitution rewritten so he could be president until 2036, and he stacked the courts with supporters who legalized his autocracy.

More fatefully, Putin won support by boosting nationalistic Russian pride. Regretting the loss of the superpower status of the USSR, Russian imperialists still wanted a "Russian world" (*Russkiy mir*) to dominate peoples in former imperial and soviet neighboring states. As vice president, Putin crushed the efforts of Chechens to win independence from Russians. Russian bombs, missiles, and artillery flattened Grozny, the capital of Chechnya, first in 1994–1997 then in 1999–2000. Other nations paid little attention. Russian police used poison gas to resolve a hostage situation in a Moscow theater in 2002, killing over a hundred hostages along with several dozen Chechen gunmen. By 2009, Chechnya had been pacified. Farther south in the Caucasus, Georgia had succeeded in becoming independent. But in 2008 Russia invaded Georgia to support insurrections in its districts of Abkhazia and South Ossetia. Busy with the Beijing Olympics, few countries bothered about Russian military action. Russia continues its imperialist military occupations there, even if few nations recognize Abkhazia or South Ossetia as independent.

Inspired by Putin, other countries openly embraced autocracy, as they had between World Wars I and II. Like the "Democratic" and "Republican" and "People's" regimes during the Cold War (or still in North Korea, Cuba, and China), they exhibit the most superficial trappings of parliamentarianism, while allowing autocrats to wield arbitrary power almost without limits. In Hungary, Prime Minister Viktor Orbań since 2010 and in Poland Jaroslaw Kaczyński, leader of the PiS (Law and Justice Party) since 2015, have moved toward authoritarian regimes based on paranoid nationalism, called "illiberal democracy." Orbań and Kaczyński have followed Putin's success in Russia: restricting opposition parties, packing courts with subservient jurists, hiring cronies and partisans for the civil service, having the government take over businesses, funneling public contracts to family and friends, and limiting freedom of speech. In November 2017, tens of thousands of Poles gathered to chant, "White Europe, Europe must be white," while only a few thousand protested to "Stop fascism." In his reelections in 2018 and 2022, Hungary's

Orbán increased his popular support by campaigning against immigration, while united opposing parties were hamstrung by government-controlled media. His government then made it a crime to help migrants who lack proper documentation. Orbán had allies take over many of Hungary's universities and expelled the Central European University, founded after the fall of communism, claiming it promoted perverse and decadent values. The European Union did not know how to effectively respond to these new dictatorships. They declared his move illegal, but Orbán ignored them.

Right-wing conservatives in many countries and many Republicans in America actually hailed the intensifying autocracies of Putin, Orbán, and others as a win for the "traditional," "Christian," and "patriotic" values of Western civilization. They have attacked as "anti-Western" left-wing policies of economic justice, openness to sexual fluidity, and hostility to racism (see the Primary Source Project at http://www.concisewesternciv.com/sources/psc15.html). Extreme right-wing politicians openly questioned who belonged in any country or to Europe at all. The number of liberal democracies with functional multiparty systems and leaders with terms limited by voters has been shrinking.

In imitation of Putin, Venezuelan president Hugo Chávez (r. 1999–2013) did not so much create a fascist state, but an old-fashioned Soviet one. He came to power with a populist anti-American stance and blamed the United States for a failed coup in 2002. In 2007, he used the riches of nationalizing the prosperous oil industry to finance a Marxist revolution, imposing an authoritarian policy to control the economy called Chavezism or Bolivarianism (after one of the liberators of Latin America). His friendship with Putin once more escalated Russian involvement in Latin America. After Chavez's death, however, US efforts to isolate its southern neighbor and the incompetence of his successor both led to economic collapse and social chaos.

An actual anti-Western autocratic terrorist state, ISIS or ISIL, briefly alarmed the West in the wake of the US occupation of Iraq. It arose, in part, because the Western-backed regimes in Iraq and Afghanistan had difficulty sustaining democracies, despite having trillions of US dollars poured into the effort. In early 2014, the Sunni-inclined group ISIS or ISIL (standing for "Islamic State of Iraq and Greater Syria," or "the Levant") used the ongoing civil war in Syria to seize control of parts of that country and invade Iraq. ISIL proclaimed its hostility to Western values to a degree considered extreme even by the weakened al-Qa'ida. ISIL's anger reached back to the arbitrary borders drawn by the victorious Allies after the fall of the Ottoman Empire at the end of World War I. As its name implies, ISIL aspired to revive a new transnational caliphate that eliminated the modern borders. The group began its acts of terrorism by broadcasting videos of the beheadings of infidels. By seizing US weapons from retreating Iraqi troops and recruiting new members through social media on the internet, the terrorist group grew to become an army. Several victories won ISIL wide territory across Syria and Iraq, where group members blew up Christian, Yazidi, and Shiite homes and precious cultural artifacts and sacred places.

Figure 15.4. A predator drone armed with Hellfire missiles on patrol over Afghanistan. (US Air Force photo/Lt. Col. Leslie Pratt)

Determined US and Western joint military responses, in cooperation with Russia, broke up ISIL's army, especially through the use of **drones** (see figure 15.4). This latest advance in military technology at first enabled soldiers to pilot from a safe distance remote-controlled flying machines to spy on enemies. Then they could fire missiles or guide them to blow up specific targets. Drones are more precise than traditional strategic bombing used in previous wars, but nevertheless they have targeted and killed innocent victims as well. Such "collateral damage" has not slowed the use of these new killing machines. Meanwhile ISIS shrank to become just one more terrorist organization, reduced to using lone-wolf-driven trucks to plow into crowds on streets, on bridges, and in marketplaces in cities such as Nice, Columbus, Berlin, Jerusalem, London (twice in 2017), Stockholm, Barcelona, Edmonton, and New York.

Meanwhile, success was scarce in the Western alliance's war against the Taliban in Afghanistan. American-led NATO forces had briefly stabilized the country by deploying a record-high number of 130,000 troops by 2012. After that, the Obama administration started to wind down American involvement, handing over frontline combat to the Afghan military and leaving only about thirteen thousand NATO troops in advisory, training, and support roles. But a resurgence of Taliban forces (with links to Iran and Russia) complicated the withdrawal. The Obama administration tried to declare an end to the war in December 2014, but after November 2017, NATO troop numbers increased by a few thousand, with an additional fourteen thousand from the United States. Yet the Western alliance still lacked a clear path to end government corruption and bring peace or liberal democracy to the region, much less halt terrorism. President Trump abruptly signed an agreement to end the war in late 2020. Unfortunately, he neither consulted the Afghan puppet government nor made plans for an orderly withdrawal. Despite this lack of preparation, the newly inaugurated President Biden kept to the treaty, although he extended the withdrawal deadline by a few months. As American forces hastily pulled out in 2021, the Taliban rapidly took over the country as the national army threw down their weapons and the country's corrupt president fled. By then, Afghanistan had already become the longest war in American history. The Taliban largely returned to its old policies of Islamist dictatorship, anti-Western culture, and confining women. Afghanistan's economy collapsed into chaos, producing poverty and starvation. Both of the real wars, in Iraq and Afghanistan, fought in the "War on Terrorism" because of 9/11, provided little for which the West could claim victory.

Fears of foreign immigrants, whether suspected of terrorism, stealing jobs, or just being different, continued to rise in the West. In 2016 those afraid of outsiders began to make their opposition felt at the polls. Since many of those immigrants were pouring into the EU, politicians in Great Britain decided to hold a plebiscite on whether the United Kingdom should remain part of the European Union. The supporters of "**Brexit**" (an abbreviation for British Exit) compared the European Union with the Roman Empire, and not in a good way (see Primary Source Project 5). They airily boasted that the departure would be easy and would enable Britain to make its own decisions about immigration and the economy. Pro-EU voices pointed out that extricating the United Kingdom would be very complicated and unprofitable.

On the day of the referendum, 23 June 2016, many Britons went to bed expecting that the Brexit option would be defeated. Everyone woke to find that a slim majority led by English voters had prevailed for leaving the EU. The pro-EU prime minister David Cameron immediately announced his resignation. Elsewhere in the United Kingdom, many Scots, who had overwhelmingly voted against Brexit, even began to renew talk of independence from the United Kingdom in order to remain in the EU. Complicated negotiations between Britain and the EU (especially about what to do with the Irish–Northern Irish border) delayed an agreement on Britain's withdrawal until December 31, 2020. Discontent with the Northern Irish situation and among the Scots still troubles British politics.

Meanwhile, anti-immigration voices in the United States also gained political control. On 8 November 2016, the real estate magnate and former reality-show host Donald Trump won a surprise victory in the Electoral College (although not the popular vote) to become president of the United States. He had begun his campaign in 2015 by disparaging immigrants from Mexico as drug users, criminals, and rapists. His blustery rhetoric thrilled cheering crowds as he boasted that only he could make America great again. At his new golf course in Scotland the day after the Brexit vote, the presidential candidate cheered the results, saying people were angry at open borders and had taken back their country. His unique sensationalized tweets on social media won him more fans.

Figure 15.5. Prototypes of the new bigger, taller, see-through border wall for the US-Mexican border are shown to the public in the fall of 2017. Funding and progress on design and then building the new wall moved very slowly. And many immigrants were still able to get through, over, or around the sections that were built. (Mani Albrecht for US Customs and Border Protection)

President Trump tried a number of policies to keep foreigners out of America. During his election campaign, Trump repeatedly promised to build a wall on the Mexican border to stop illegal immigration. He boasted that his wall would cover at least half of the two-thousand-mile-long border, would be "big and beautiful," and would not cost Americans anything: Mexico would pay for it (see figure 15.5). Not surprisingly, Mexico did not pay for it. One of Trump's first executive acts was to ban citizens from seven Muslim countries from traveling to the United States, without any solid rationale for doing so. He also reduced the number of refugees that would be accepted from states like Syria that were torn by violence and civil war. To enforce a zero-tolerance policy of illegal entries, government agents at the Mexican border separated thousands of children from their parents and put some within pens or cages, also called "walls [made] out of chain-link fences." Very little planning was made about how family members could be reunited, and as of 2022, hundreds of detained children had not yet been restored to their parents.

After the 2016 votes in Great Britain and the United States, Western intelligence services began to reveal the extent of malicious interference from a new form of warfare: cyberattacks. Evidence made increasingly clear that Russian officials had worked to influence the voting in Britain and America through infiltration of politicians' email servers, probing of voting machines and databases, and made-up provocative memes posted on social media by "bots" (or software that simulates humans). President Trump's confused pronouncements on whether or not he accepted the findings of the Western intelligence agencies helped to erode the Western alliance system.

Trump also proclaimed policies of "America First" that echoed the position of isolationism before both World War I and World War II. He discontinued work on international trade agreements and instead initiated protectionist trade and tariff wars with other economies, including longtime American allies. He called the European Union a "foe" of the United States and regularly criticized his fellow NATO members. To many observers, Trump seemed to disrespect known allies and instead to defend Russia, in spite of its cyberattacks, its continued illegal occupation of Crimea, and its continuing intervention in Ukraine. Nevertheless, Trump often contradicted or denied his own recorded words and actions, leading to confusion both in the United States and abroad. His convenient practice for avoiding accountability was to accuse his opponents of "fake news" about any information or reports with which he disagreed, while his own people used "alternative facts." In all, the Republican administration's new troubled relationship with reality undermined the coherence of Western ideals.

Within the United States, Trump's policy of "America First" helped to launch a new cultural war that questioned what it was to be a citizen in the twenty-first century. Advocates of **multiculturalism** continued to call for the acceptance of more diversity and additional help for the disadvantaged. The **Black Lives Matter** movement challenged the system about how too many young Black men were shot by police. They partly blamed "white privilege," the idea that Americans whose ancestors came from Europe had certain inherent social advantages because of their race and identity.

The #MeToo movement drew attention to misogyny, sexual harassment, and "rape culture." Opponents, however, attacked these ideas as overextensions of "political correctness." Instead, the "alt-right" argued that "white" men themselves were being sidelined in their own country by those who failed to recognize the inherent differences either between men and women or among various "races." Neo-Nazis openly marched at the University of Virginia in Charlottesville in August 2017, bearing tiki torches and shouting about "Blood and Soil" and that "the Jews will not replace us." Increasing numbers both in the United States and in Europe voted against politicians who favored democracy's usual system of compromise reached through the use of civil discourse. Instead, they supported total victory solely for their own point of view by electing "their" strongmen (and occasional strongwomen), leading to further division and polarization rather than consensus.

Divided attitudes on race tore Americans apart on 25 May 2020 when a cell-phone video showed how a Minneapolis officer detained George Floyd on suspicion of passing a counterfeit twenty-dollar bill. The white policeman suffocated the Black suspect by kneeling on Floyd's neck for nine minutes and twenty-nine seconds on a public street. The murder lit protests about racism not only in America but around the world (see figure 15.6). While most protests were peaceful, in

Figure 15.6. The murder of George Floyd on 25 May 2020 by a police officer in Minneapolis outraged people around the world. For example, thousands marched in Paris by the Eiffel Tower soon afterward, showing solidarity with the "Black Lives Matter" movement (even as the French have their own racist issues with Muslim and African immigrants). The demonstrators wear masks because of COVID-19. (Thomas de Luze via Unsplash)

some cities violence by protestors, police forces, and outside agitators harmed some people, killed a few, damaged property, and heightened fear. Yet momentum increased for banning racist symbols, especially statues honoring the Confederacy, and, in Europe, slaveholders and imperialists.

Even while some Europeans attacked the racist legacy of imperialism, others worked to keep foreigners from such former colonies out of their countries. Nationalist parties in France, the Netherlands, Austria, Germany, Sweden, Denmark, and Finland surged in popularity and expanded their representation in parliaments. Nativist candidates were vocal in bashing European unity, as well as immigration, free trade, and deficit spending. They wanted instead more independent nations, closed borders, protectionism, and lower taxes. In France, the May 2017 presidential election required the cooperation of leftists, liberals, and moderates to unite around conservative Emmanuel Macron in order to defeat Marine Le Pen from the extreme-right National Front party. After his victory, however, instead of promoting policies to unite the left wing and moderates, Macron (r. 2017–) pushed hard-line economic austerity and anti-immigrant policies. The former provoked a populist movement called the *gilets jaunes* ("yellow vests," named after the reflective jackets that all drivers carried as safety equipment, then used by protestors as a sort of uniform). In April 2022, Macron and Le Pen faced off once more, although she had changed the name of her party to *Rassemblement National* (National Rally) to appear more moderate. Macron won again, but the extreme right gained strength, and parties on the left fell into disarray.

Nationalist parties made gains in several other EU member states. In October 2017, Catalonian nationalists tried to secede from Spain. The two nationalist parties in Germany, AfD (Alternative for Germany) and Pegida (Patriotic Europeans against the Islamization of the West), won seats in the German Reichstag in November 2017, weakening Merkel's ability to govern (see figure 15.7). A conservative-nationalist coalition government in Austria formed in late 2017, which proclaimed "Austria First!" In the Italian elections of 2018, and even more in 2022, far-right, some said neo-fascist, parties hostile to the European Union formed governments in Italy's parliament.

Figure 15.7. Almost every Monday, as shown here in July 2017, people marched in Dresden to protest the Merkel government and show their alignment with right-wing movements. The law forbids displaying actual Nazi symbols, but not criticizing politicians. So protestors carry flags of various nationalist associations and signs with political commentary. The sign with Chancellor Merkel's hands altered into a large circle reads, "Who still votes for me and my accomplices, has an asshole at least this wide open."

Thus, the post–Cold War consensus has been attacked from both sides of the political spectrum. From the left came complaints of freewheeling economic policies that enriched the few at the expense of the many. From the right, populism and nationalism resisted international cooperation and immigration. One international leader, Pope Francis I (r. 2013–), spoke with a soft voice of reconciliation. A Jesuit and former archbishop from Argentina, Francis was the first-ever head of the Roman Catholic Church to be chosen from outside Europe. Like his namesake, the medieval Francis of Assisi, the pope called on people to build bridges, not walls. His moral authority has been weakened, however, both by conservatives and ongoing sexual abuse scandals tied to Roman Catholic clergy.

Western civilization must decide how it is going to continue to manage its own, and the world's, affairs. Does it follow the lead of a unilateral United States of America? Try to promote international law and multilateral interventions? Is it united at all in the face of geopolitical dangers from varied terrorist groups and rogue nations? Does it turn back to its own religious roots? Are those roots fanatical or tolerant? Can the West spread prosperity with more fairness and less exploitation? Will the rest of the world accept any of this? How will the West continue to adapt to the rapid change created by science, capitalism, industry, transportation, and communication? How will the West adjust to the growing power of Asian nations? Of course, Western civilization is not one single entity but rather a collection of its individual citizens, who in turn are grouped into class, ethnicity, and citizenship. All of us, individually and together, must confront each of these questions.

Review: *What tensions and attitudes have weakened the unity of the Western alliances?*

Response:

PRIMARY SOURCE PROJECT 15: THE EUROPEAN CENTRAL BANK VERSUS THE NATIONAL FRONT ABOUT THE EU

The global economic crisis beginning in 2008 presented challenges for the European Union. A leading figure in the union, Yves Mersch, the former governor of the Banque Central du Luxembourg (BCL) and a current member of the executive board of the European Central Bank (ECB), offers his largely positive views on European integration. In opposition, a program paper supporting the 2012 presidential candidacy of Marine Le Pen, leader of the National Front, a nationalistic party in France, criticizes the EU's economic policies.

Source 1: Speech by Yves Mersch (15 May 2014)

[The first of] May this year, exactly two weeks ago, was more than just Labor Day. It was the tenth anniversary of the accession of no fewer than ten countries to the European Union. Three other countries—Bulgaria, Romania and, most recently, Croatia—have since joined. The European Union, despite its shortcomings, remains respected and influential. It also remains an aspiration for non-members and maybe even, in other ways, an inspiration. The Union has been and is a successful undertaking.

The EU has become a role model for regional cooperation. It has achieved its original objectives, namely to ensure peace and prosperity in a notoriously conflict-ridden part of the world. . . . Throughout its almost 60-year history, the EU has shown its ability to overcome important economic and political challenges. In fact, the euro area, the most integrated part of the Union, has grown since 1999 and the number of member states continues to increase—despite the challenges and setbacks of the recent crisis. Having started out with eleven countries, it has expanded over the years and now comprises eighteen. Most of them have experienced a slow but steady improvement in their economies. The number of countries having recently reset a target date for the adoption of the euro is a witness of unabated attraction of our common project subject to the agreed convergence path and criteria.

In many ways, EU membership and the prospect of euro adoption provided an impetus for reforms in these countries. . . . EU accession has also helped in the development of stronger institutions and a more business-friendly environment. Last but not least, EU funds, on a significant scale, have been invested in these countries, bringing noticeable improvements to the transport infrastructure and other domains. . . .

As the past few years of Economic and Monetary Union (EMU) have shown, temporary fulfillment of the convergence criteria does not, by itself, guarantee trouble-free membership of the euro area. Large and persistent macroeconomic imbalances accumulated in several euro area countries and were partly to blame for the economic and financial crisis which broke out in 2008.

In some countries, high public spending since the adoption of the euro has resulted in extremely high public deficits and an unsustainable accumulation of public debt. Other countries however have experienced excessive growth in private debt based on buoyant capital imports and low interest rates. This has resulted in surging imports and large current account deficits rather than strong trend potential growth. In some instances, excessive credit growth—closely associated with an unsustainable boom in real estate markets—has undermined the soundness of some financial institutions and given rise to an excessive accumulation of private debt. . . .

The EU has learnt its lessons. We now know what did not work properly. We have all realized that there needs to be a stronger set of institutions and rules to support the euro, that a monetary union needs to be accompanied by a banking union and a fiscal union, that, in the end, economic integration and political integration in Europe go hand in hand. . . .

In today's highly interconnected and competitive world, it means thinking beyond national economic interests and instead exploiting synergies and comparative advantages together. In short, it means working together to hold our own.

Source 2: "A Controlled End to Stimulate Growth" by the National Front (2014)

Ten years after its introduction into the daily life of the French, the euro as a single currency is proving to be a complete failure, despite the blindness of the proponents of Europe in Brussels and Frankfurt who refuse to admit the obvious. In fact, the euro is going to disappear, because the cost of maintaining it is every day becoming more unsupportable for the nations for which it is totally unsuitable. Since its inception, the euro has been an economic aberration, denounced by numerous economists. The tinkering and successive plans for bail-outs to save the euro will not solve the crisis. Therefore, an orderly plan for suspending the euro needs to be started now.

The single currency has become a symbol of a European federalist policy of an absurd brinksmanship by elite financiers ready to sacrifice the people on the altar of their own interests. Money should be put in its proper place, becoming once again an economic instrument in the service of growth and employment.

The euro was doomed from the start. At the time it was launched, the American Nobel Prize winner Milton Friedman, for example, predicted the failure of the euro, the crisis that would follow, and demonstrated the unsurpassable efficacy of monetary freedom. . . .

Today, the balance sheet of the euro is disastrous. The promises of prosperity, of growth, and of employment have not been kept. Since the creation of the single currency, the euro zone is the region of the world that has known the slowest growth. The exchange rate is much too high for France, accelerating outsourcing and de-industrialization of our country, which has also suffered for the last ten years from the non-union wage policy of Germany. . . . The euro did nothing to protect Europe from the first great crisis of 2008. . . .

It is advisable at present to refuse to engage in pointless policies of austerity in the name of preserving a currency that is stifling Europe. These successive plans for austerity always hit the same people: the working and middle classes, retirees, and civil servants. France should therefore veto useless and ruinous plans for bailing-out countries that are victims of the euro. French money should stay in France.

France must prepare, along with its European partners, for the end of the unhappy experience with the euro and for the beneficial return of national currencies that permit competitive devaluation, in order to breathe life into our economy and rediscover the path to prosperity.

The team of France and Germany should perform the driving role in this consultation and in the planned suspension of the euro experience. The team must rediscover the initiative and allow the euro zone to escape stagnation. A majority of Germans (54% in October 2011) favor a return to the mark. Abandoning the euro is a technical challenge, but in no way will it provoke the cataclysm described by ideologues and other fanatics of the single currency. Well prepared, coordinated with the other European nations, the orderly end of the euro is the requirement for the economic revival of France. To stay with the euro is to condemn ourselves "to die by inches," in the words of economist Alain Cotta.

Questions:

- *What details does each source use to prove its argument, positive or negative, for the euro?*
- *What specific changes does each source call for?*
- *On the basis of these two sources, without substantiating background, citations, or studies, how is one to decide which view is more credible?*

Responses:

For more on these sources, go to http://www.concisewesternciv.com/sources /psc15.html.

THE EQUIVALENT OF WAR

At the end of 2019 and in early 2022, two major events confounded Western civilization. First, the worst pandemic in a century broke out. Then, a vicious war on the edge of Europe burst forth. Both events continue on as of this writing. Both expose the contradictions inherent in Western civilization.

This history has covered contagious diseases that have been a hazardous part of civilization since its beginning. A hundred years ago, the murderous Spanish flu, caused by a virus named H1N1, killed more people after World War I than the war had. But that pandemic had been largely forgotten in the popular imagination. Vaccinations had their greatest success with eliminating smallpox by 1980 (except for samples stored in secret government labs). But as the twentieth century turned into the twenty-first, several outbreaks of plagues have alarmed those who studied and prepared for new epidemics.

In 1976 an outbreak of an H1N1 influenza (misnamed "swine flu") at a US army base frightened the government into a massive vaccination program for millions.

The disease, however, did not turn out to be as virulent as at first feared. And some flaws in vaccines led to illnesses that left people wary about the safety of public health mandates. Another outbreak of H1N1 in 2009 (again misnamed "swine flu") infected tens of millions of Americans, killing about twelve thousand, and another nine thousand worldwide. Public health agencies contained it with an aggressive vaccination campaign. In the first two decades of the twenty-first century, warnings about contagions of West Nile virus, SARS-CoV, mumps, whooping cough, MERS-CoV, Ebola, and Zika came and went as health officials managed their outbreaks.

In early 2020, health officials noticed a new virus, SARS-CoV-2, as it began to cause **COVID-19** (standing for *coronavirus disease* and 2019, the year it started). Although only a handful of Americans had died by March, the ease of transmission and the death rate of those who were infected alarmed epidemiologists. Some people called the effort to halt this new medical crisis "the equivalent of war." While governments supported the rapid development of safe and effective vaccines, supported by new mRNA technology, it would still take many months before they could be distributed. In the meantime, governments of many countries mandated an unprecedented quarantining, confining almost entire populations to their homes. Hospitals quickly found themselves overwhelmed with the sick and dying; mortuaries and funeral homes were inundated with the dead. For those who went out in public, governments also imposed mask mandates, at first made difficult by the shortage of effective protective coverings. People's encounters with one another shifted online "virtually" far more than in person physically. By the end of 2020, various vaccines became available. They improved resistance to catching COVID-19 and made symptoms milder and less deadly for those infected.

Just when it looked like the pandemic was in decline, increasingly virulent mutations of the virus surged the numbers of infected in waves. First, "Delta" peaked in 2021, then Omicron at the end of the year, followed by "B" subvariants in 2022. By June 2022, well over six million people worldwide had died from COVID-19, including over a million Americans.

Meanwhile, arguments about COVID-19 undermined the application of reason and science to these life-and-death medical issues. From the first, some people remained skeptical about the severity and risks of COVID-19, thinking it no worse than other previous influenza outbreaks. As time went on, more people became upset with quarantines because of their economic and personal costs. Many resented wearing masks, whether because of inconvenience or alleged infringement on personal freedoms. The unscientific anti-vaxx movement, which had been on the fringe for decades, attracted new believers. The American president, meanwhile, foolishly suggested dealing with the disease by ingesting bleach, filling the body with light, or using a veterinary antiparasitic drug. His administration actually had promoted the quick development of vaccines, but then did not effectively distribute them or advocate the idea that nearly everyone should take them once available. People who resented government controls disliked public health officials telling them what to do. British prime minister Boris Johnson found himself sharply criticized because he violated quarantine laws passed by his own administration by having parties in his offices at 10 Downing Street. At the same time, American politicians pandered to complaints by making it more difficult to implement public health recommendations.

While clashing views of rationality about the pandemic existed in many countries, discord over Donald Trump's loss of the 2020 presidential election to Obama's former vice president, Joe Biden, revealed how far partisan politics blinded reality. Trump became the first president not to accept the constitutionally mandated and valid decisions of election officials and Congress. He appropriated the term "the Big Lie," by which he meant that mainstream media, Democrats, and many Republican officials were lying that the election had been fair and square. The truth was, he claimed, that massive fraud had stolen the election from him. Like Hitler's "Big Lie," Trump was showing himself to be a teller of falsehoods. No consequential evidence has supported his claim, despite numerous lawsuits and recounts.

Trump's efforts to overturn the election culminated on 6 January 2021 when Congress was supposed to go through the formality of counting the Electoral College ballots from the states. After a rally where Trump called on the crowd to take back their country, a mob of Trump supporters stormed and broke into the Capitol building, chanting to hang Vice President Mike Pence, who presided over the count. The members of Congress barely escaped harm from this insurrection. As a result, the House impeached Trump a second time.[6] But most Republicans refused to convict the president. Republicans actually began to accuse the Democrats of their own "Big Lie": by which they meant Democrats were falsely accusing Republicans of passing laws to restrict voting and paving the way for future conservative minority rule. Many Americans refused to believe the reality that Biden had been legitimately elected.

Just as the war against COVID-19 seemed to be waning, a new crisis for the West appeared as Russia attacked Ukraine. What Russia's President Putin called merely a "special military operation" to help ethnic Russians was in reality a new modern war. The history of Ukrainians and Russians has long been intertwined, but Ukraine gained sovereign independence with the fall of the Soviet Union in 1991. At the time, Ukraine also gave up nuclear weapons that had been stationed in the country, and in return the new Russian Federation promised never to invade. The leadership of Ukraine since its new independence then walked a fine line between close relations to Russia or more integration into the "West," as embodied by NATO and the European Union.

Back in February 2014, the Maidan Revolution (named after a main square in Kyiv) broke out as massive protests resisted the Ukrainian president's efforts to align more with Russia. Those demonstrations intimidated their president into resigning and fleeing into exile in Russia. Right afterward, unmarked Russian troops blatantly seized the peninsula of Crimea by cutting it off from mainland Ukraine and declaring it Russian territory. In addition, Putin supported separatist movements by ethnic Russians living in the Ukraine in the eastern part of that country. The Russian Federation armed rebels and sent in Russian troops, but denied responsibility by claiming they were "volunteers."

Other nations now had to decide how to respond to this naked aggression. Most of the world had ignored Putin's earlier military interventions in the Caucasus.

---

6. For the first impeachment, see below.

The United Nations could do little, since Russia sat on the UN Security Council with its veto. Western nations imposed minor sanctions in 2014, but they did little to loosen Putin's grasp on Crimea. European states may have been reluctant to take more serious steps because they depended on natural gas imports from Russia. And, of course, no one wanted World War III.

Meanwhile, Putin increasingly accused the West of betraying Western civilization with its "political correctness" and "moral confusion," especially with its tolerance of homosexuality, gender fluidity, and same-sex marriages. In his defense of "moral (Christian) values," Putin had the vocal support of the patriarch of Moscow, leader of its Eastern Orthodox Church, especially since the ecumenical patriarch in Constantinople recognized a separate Orthodox Church of Ukraine in 2019. Many Western conservatives likewise actually admired Putin's image of strong leadership and his positions in the culture wars.

In 2019, the newly elected president of Ukraine, Volodymyr Zelenskyy (r. 2019–), again tried to find a safe path between Putin's increasingly anti-Western leadership and the advantages of possible admission into the European Union. He had run on the platform of fighting corruption and resolving tensions between ethnic Ukrainians and Russians, even if his only previous government experience was playing a president on a television comedy. As the real president of a country under threat, Zelenskyy asked for military aid from NATO to strengthen Ukrainian defense forces. In a phone call between Presidents Trump and Zelenskyy about such support, Trump asked first for a favor: to collect political dirt on the son of Joe Biden, Trump's political opponent in his reelection. That request led to President Trump's first impeachment.

Beginning in March 2021, Russian forces began a military buildup on Ukraine's border. Despite denials of any intentions to invade, on 24 February 2022, Russian forces crossed the border, allegedly to fight "Nazis." Instead of a swift victory, however, Russian forces bogged down because of poor planning, inadequate training, botched logistics, and fierce resistance by Ukrainian forces. President Zelenskyy became an international hero, building morale and obtaining more military aid for Ukraine's defense. Having failed to seize the capital of Kyiv, Russian efforts have concentrated on securing provinces in the east and bordering the Black Sea (see map 15.2).

And this time, unlike in the Caucasus, the West stepped in to confront Russian aggression. European Union and NATO nations imposed harsh economic sanctions on Putin himself, other prominent Russians, and the entire country. Corporations like McDonald's even shut down their operations in Russia. More crucial, the NATO alliance led by President Biden began sending desperately needed ammunition and supplies to Ukraine. NATO held back from sending troops or enforcing a no-fly zone, however, because that might provoke World War III. Supposedly nobody wants that, except Putin keeps hinting he might use nuclear weapons if he does not get his way. Instead of weakening NATO, the Russian attack on Ukraine strengthened its resolve, based on its original mission: preventing Russian advancement into Europe. Even historically neutral Sweden and Finland became so alarmed they both applied for membership in NATO.

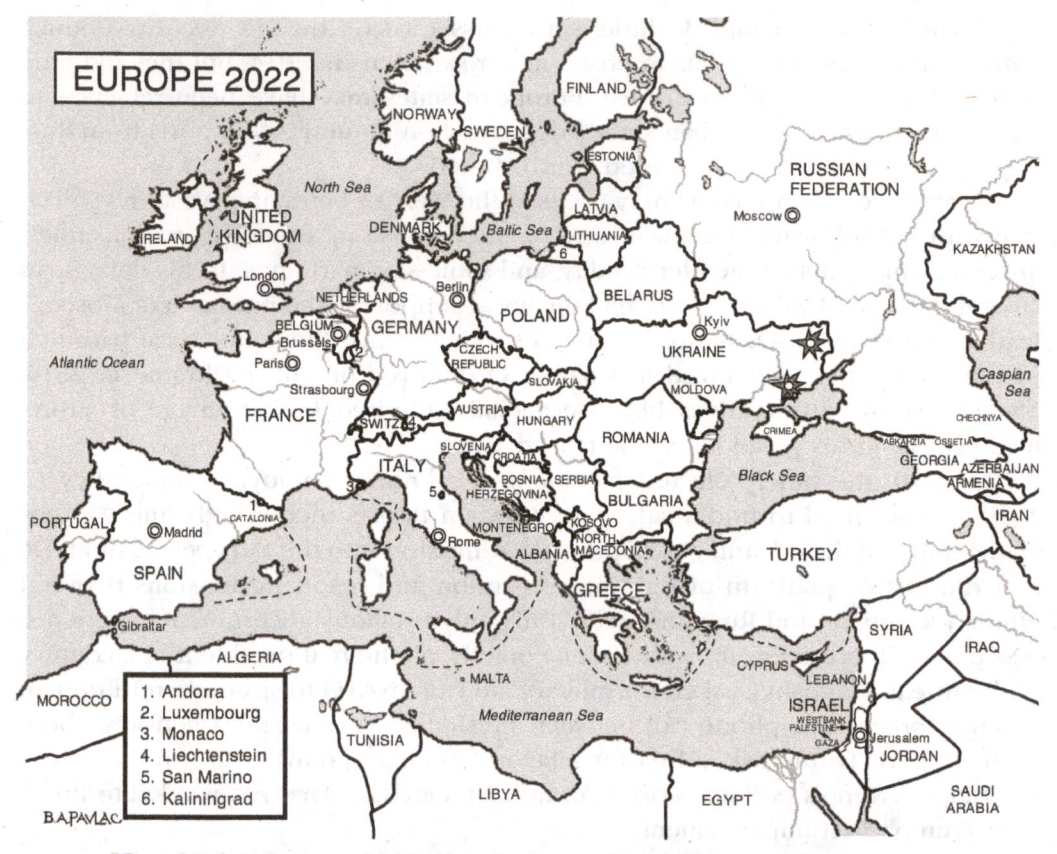

EUROPE 2022

1. Andorra
2. Luxembourg
3. Monaco
4. Liechtenstein
5. San Marino
6. Kaliningrad

B.A.PAVLAC

Map 15.2. Europe, 2022. How many countries belong to Europe and why? (Note that ongoing conflict in the Ukraine may change its borders, including the internationally unrecognized takeover of the Crimea by Russia.)

Just as the COVID-19 pandemic exposed diversity in opinions about scientific facts, trust in institutions like government, media, political parties, corporations, banks, stock markets, labor unions, think tanks, universities, and the courts has rapidly declined. Worse than distrust is the demonization of the opposition. Discourse has often degenerated into tribalism, where people consider those on the other side of ideological differences as the enemy, to be marginalized or even killed. Without compromise, though, democracies and even economies break down.

This so-called War on Truth has complicated our understanding of many recent events. With internet-connected computers in their pockets, people can look up anything instantly, often simply using the first links, which have been generated by manipulated algorithms. And new information created by anyone can spread like a pandemic. The gatekeepers of mainstream media are more easily bypassed or disputed. The problem clearly lies with the reliability of the information found and the ability to properly interpret it. Some websites have been established that try to help sort fact from falsehood.[7] One of the most-used information resources has been Wikipedia. Since its first edit in 2001, the online encyclopedia

---

7. See http://www.concisewesternciv.com/links/ferret.html.

has become more reliable (especially once it started to source articles with citations). Wikipedia rejected scholarly monopoly on expertise and offered everyone the opportunity to write an article that would be vetted by other volunteers to have a "neutral point of view." Perhaps we need one last basic principle:

> **To be worth discussing, opinions must be based on facts from reliable and well-researched sources.**

Nevertheless, conspiracy theories, hypocritical scandals, outrageous sound bites, and celebrity fads seem inherently more interesting than factual commentaries that carefully examine and explain important matters. Social media companies profit from fabrications peddled by advertisers and disinformation disseminated by populists. Moneyed interests contest facts and offer bogus studies to keep their profit margins. For example, the tobacco industry denied the medical proof that smoking causes lots of cancer, while oil and gas drillers refute their undeniable role in measurable pollution and climate change. Promoting reason seems not enough, since too many people refuse to be reasonable. Politicians and governments shamelessly deny basic facts about violence, discrimination, and corruption if they find them inconvenient or embarrassing to patriotic pride. How well democratic discourse can flourish under these conditions is the challenge of the future.

Review: *How did the COVID-19 pandemic and the Russian attack on Ukraine expose weaknesses in Western civilization?*

Response:

Make your own timeline.

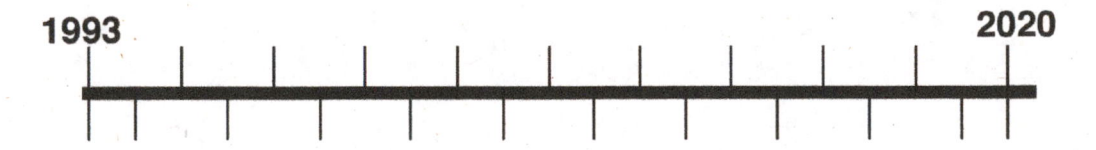

1993   **2020**

For more information online about history, go to **ConciseWesternCiv.com**.

Epilogue

Why Western Civilization?

Several hundred years ago, Western civilization took the worldwide lead in politics (often by success in war), economics (by accumulating wealth), and science and technology (by using machines to help with the first two). In each of these areas, states and social groups in the West gained more efficiency and effectiveness than organized societies elsewhere in the world. On the one hand, westerners used the power from these advantages to intimidate and oppress other human cultures and civilizations. On the other hand, westerners brought knowledge to those other societies that, in time, enabled some of them to become powerful in their own right by adopting parts of Western civilization. Cultures around the world are still deciding what to keep from the West and what to use against its dominance. Some would argue that Western values are uniquely essential to those who have inherited them. Others argue that anyone can adopt Western values, that they can be universal. And certainly what some consider to be values can be seen by others as vices. Regardless, the dynamism generated by the West guarantees that tomorrow will be different from today. Therein lie the difficulties of applying historical understanding. In a changing world, what should we ourselves choose to learn from the past of Western civilization?

A couple of decades ago, students at Stanford University chanted the phrase "Western Civ has got to go." They were saying that a Western civilization course requirement in their curriculum was more harmful than helpful. Although the incident was hardly significant, defenders of Western culture sometimes point to this specific episode as a signal of doom for the study of Western Civ. Ultimately, the West exists only as long as many of its members and opponents say it exists. It becomes real through self-identification or from labeling by others. Without being described, no civilization has inherent cohesion.

For many historians, the concept of "Western civilization" usefully frames for discussion the complicated history of Europe as it developed and then affected the rest of the world. Consequently, globally minded people have been arguing about "the West," now more than ever. Such is not unexpected, since every civilization has come under attack by someone at some time. The West has confronted external enemies, from Viking, Saracen, and Magyar hordes plundering the Carolingian Empire to al-Qa'ida blowing up commuters in New York, Madrid, and London. The West has also faced internal enemies who have caused peasant rebellions, civil wars over the role of government, the attempted genocide of Jews, criminal organizations taking the streets, and white supremacists committing mass shootings and blowing up buildings. All civilizations define themselves by the extent of their supremacy over their own subjects or against their neighbors, the "others." All cultures have, at one time or another, confronted new people and ideas and faced the necessity of either absorbing them or eliminating them. Since Western civilization is so widespread today, it cannot help but provoke opposition from those who do not accept the extent of its reach or agree with its values.

It is also important to remember that "the West" has never, at any time, been one single, monolithic entity. As described in this book, a long historical process of human choices about those values, many of them contradictory, has resulted in a divided West. In its belief systems, the West has experienced everything from myths to monotheisms, philosophical speculation to scientific secularism. In its culture, the West has expressed itself through epic poetry and prose history, theatricals and spectacles, novels and newspapers, all of which have been transmitted on stone and bone, clay and canvas, parchment and paper, celluloid film and streams of electrons. In its power over nature, the West is historically rooted together with all other worldwide cultures from the knife and knapsack of the hunter-gatherers to the plow and pottery of agriculturists. The West progressed further, with the steam engine and steel cruiser to today's computers and cars. But none of these inventions or attitudes necessarily made the West's culture better or superior. Nonetheless, through the power of its militaries, ideas, discoveries, and economies, the West indisputably came to reign supreme over world affairs by the nineteenth century.

Like any powerful civilization in world history, the West achieved its ascendancy most obviously by wielding weapons and wealth. Yet the West has never spoken with one unified voice. Both a strength and a weakness of Western civilization has been its division into many sovereign states. Their rivalries with one another spurred innovation and growth as well as destruction and death. This variety also enabled democratic and republican ideals to survive against prevailing absolutism and authoritarianism. The cooperation of individuals and groups in capitalism financed political growth and further fostered responsive government.

Some people believe that the West is based on freedom of the individual, but its own history shows an ambivalent interaction with that ideal. The nation-state as the primary way to organize people easily subsumes individuals, who only really matter when connected to larger social groups of family, class, and corporation. And when any state goes to war, few support the freedom of the individual to opt out from the collectivism of military service. Nation-states rose to great powers in Europe when, ironically, some individual states grew strong enough to create overseas empires. Around 1500, Western guns and galleons gave Europeans a lethal advantage over many other peoples in Asia, Africa, and the Americas. Imperialist Spain and Portugal were joined by France and England, then the Netherlands and Russia, next Germany and Italy, and finally, the United States and even Japan, which re-created itself in the West's own image. The official empires of the West largely collapsed in the twentieth century, partly because the West was drained by three global conflicts: World War I, World War II, and the Cold War.

At the end of these conflicts, the United States of America stood above all others as a superpower. The United States had achieved a unique global superiority through its money, media, and military. An economy and financial system allowed less than 5 percent of the world's population to consume more than 20 percent of its resources. Since World War II, the United States has wielded an influence without precedent. Its ideas have spread in television and movies, games, music, food, and fashion, while the power of its armed forces reflects a budget larger than roughly the next seven-most-powerful nations combined.

One of the most uncertain directions of Western civilization today is the extent to which the United States of America will continue to dominate it. Some American exceptionalists have suggested that its hegemony should allow the United States alone to define what the world should be in the future, acting unilaterally. To make the United States number one is to focus on its interests at the expense of other nations. Those who critique American exceptionalism believe that the United States should work in cooperation with the nations of Europe, and even the world. They would funnel war and power through the multilateral international institutions (such as NATO and the UN) created by the West in the second half of the twentieth century. President Obama proposed, "I believe in American exceptionalism, just as I suspect that the Brits believe in British exceptionalism and the Greeks believe in Greek exceptionalism." For true believers, his view was tantamount to contempt for the West. President Trump has said, "I declare today for the world to hear that the West will never ever be broken; our values will prevail; our people will thrive; and our civilization will triumph." Questions remain about what those values are, how Western people will dominate others, and what it means for those other cultures for Western civilization to triumph.

The study of the West has thus been undermined due to cultural warfare over which aspect of its past (and present) truly represents its traditional values and virtues. Some who argue for Western exceptionalism like to draw up little lists about what makes this civilization so special and worthy of emulation. This is history written by the victors. But if the losers have any history of their own at all, they often nurse their grudges until they can try to vanquish their oppressors. Should history remind us of our nobility or force us to acknowledge our crimes? People want their heroes and villains—although usually we want the heroes to resemble us and the villains to appear like some "other." It is hard to cope when the roles are reversed. Christianity had pacifists like Jesus, Saint Francis, and Martin Luther King Jr., as well as murderers like schismatics, crusaders, and inquisitors. Nations had their largely successful, yet flawed, rulers (King Henry II, King Louis XIV, or Chancellor Bismarck), as well as their failure-ridden, yet human, leaders (King John, King Louis XVI, or Kaiser Wilhelm II). Each has had, and will have, at least some proponents and some opponents. Good historians try to sort out the greatness and the failures that belong to each of us, recording all facets of events and people, both good and bad.

More important than the rulers and leaders of the past may have been the different ideologies that informed their choices. The Enlightenment consensus of reason and science has never completely overwhelmed religious and superstitious viewpoints. Ongoing resistance to Darwinian evolution by those who assert a literal interpretation of the Bible illustrates this lack of success. Yet Christianity has not been able to beget its "City of God." Neither has rationalism built its utopia, because people have never been able to agree on priorities. Some argue that capitalism should sanctify the pursuit of profit only by corporations, while others call for society to allow all persons active economic agency. Elites redefine democracy as the mere holding of elections, in which money makes some voices louder than votes. The masses often seek to be heard but speak in many different voices (quite literally, in the many languages from Basque and Breton to Welsh and Yiddish still spoken by citizens of the European Union). Most people want to win, which means usually that other people lose. Few people seem willing to agree, compromise, or forgive.

All these tensions among competing ideas interacted to create Western civilization. Fights over causation, civil rights, capitalism, class, high culture, and Christianity have all driven historical change. Influences from neighboring cultures and civilizations, small and large, from Mesopotamians, Egyptians, Assyrians, Persians, Muslims, North Africans, Byzantines, Slavs, Magyars, East Asians, South Asians, Central Asians, Native Americans, sub-Saharan Africans, Pacific Islanders, and others, helped to shape Western civilization over the centuries.

While advocates of multiculturalism have attacked Western expressions of power, history shows that the West has always been multicultural, in spite of efforts to enforce uniformity. In its earliest phases, Hebrews tried to Judaize their Canaanite neighbors in Palestine; the Greeks began to hellenize the peoples conquered by Alexander; the Romans romanized everyone from the Iberians to the Britains, Germans, Greeks, Mesopotamians, and Egyptians. They also subjugated the Etruscans, Carthaginians, Druids, and others. In the early Middle Ages, the church Christianized the ruling Germans and their neighbors. None of these "-izations" succeeded completely—elements of earlier cultures always survived. The alleged unity of medieval Christendom actually rested on the different "nations" of English, French, Germans, Italians, Spanish, and others. Then, from the Middle Ages into the nineteenth century, the diverse Germanic invaders who had toppled the western half of the Roman Empire melded into their conquered populations, in the process transforming and spreading new cultures. The Gothic Germans and old Romans (and Celts and a few others) diversified into the French, English, Italians, Spanish, Portuguese, Scandinavians, Norwegians, Danish, Swedes, Finns, Scots, Irish, Dutch, Swiss, Belgians, and others, including even Monegasques, Sammarinese, Luxembourgers, Liechtensteiners, Andorrans, and Maltese. The states of eastern Europe, with Albanians, Slavs, Balts, and Magyars, connected with the West after the fall of the Byzantines and the Ottomans (although complicated by the Russians and their ambivalent attitude toward "westernness"). As many of these westerners trekked out into the world, both colonizing and colonized peoples organized with indigenous peoples and enslaved Africans as Latin Americans,

"North" Americans, Australians, New Zealanders, South Africans, and others. All of them reflect multiculturalism; all of them share in Western civilization, insofar as they have appropriated large parts of it. Yet some people claim that Latin America is not "Western," even though the majority of the people believe in Christianity, speak European languages, are organized into industrial-age classes, apply economic theories, use modern science and technology, and live under modern nation-state political systems.

Does Western civilization have a future? At several moments in its past, Western civilization almost did not. Persia might have conquered Greece. The Romans might have self-destructed in their republican civil wars. The Germans might have resisted Christianity. Norse, Magyar, or Saracen invaders might have overwhelmed the Christendom of Charlemagne. The Mongols might have wiped out the West, as they did many societies that opposed them. Asian armies might have conquered Europe anytime up to the seventeenth century. Nuclear war might have ended it all during the Cold War (and still may).

Up to now, Western civilization has become a historical force by surviving numerous challenges and developing overwhelming power, partly because of the revolutions it has experienced and assimilated. It has been held together in the last few decades by a group of institutions such as NATO for a military alliance, and for economics, the International Monetary Fund, the World Bank, many trade agreements, the EU, and the G7. But nothing is stable. The Commercial Revolution, the intellectual revolutions of the Renaissance and Enlightenment, the religious revolution of the Reformation, the Scientific Revolution, the Industrial Revolution, and the political revolutions of England, America, and France all constantly continue to reshape our destiny. These revolutions encourage human creativity and the application of the "new" to improve people's lives.

The themes of supremacy and diversity reveal these ongoing changes. Some leaders and societies have sought domination, which bound allegiances into a unity that strengthened. Arguments over what justified supremacy recast societies: a divine mandate (decided upon by whose God?), tradition (choosing which part of the assorted past?), knowledge (as taught by whom?), or power (with what degree of violence?). Over time, though, supremacies have often stifled creativity. They demanded mere obedience and often oppressed. At the same time, humans obviously have sought diversity, fracturing into smaller unities while striving for what is new. Yet emphasis on too many differences, or focusing too much on them, has fragmented people into mutual hostilities, if not armed camps. Recent conflicts show clearly that there are no fundamental assumptions about which everyone agrees. The tendency toward diversity subverts supremacy.

Today, international and multiregional organizations continue to expand, while nationalistic groups persistently cling to their separate constructed identities. As the world economy binds peoples together, nationalists want to restrict immigration, and local patriotism resists international solidarity among human beings. Most people still fail to empathize with either the exploited or the enemy, although modern media zap their words, sounds, and images through screens mounted in public and commercial spaces, into our homes, and held in our hands every day. And with anyone able to put information on the internet, people who look can easily find both facts and falsehoods that confirm their convictions. Our collapsing world seems both smaller and more conflict ridden.

Where does that leave Western civilization? Globalization of all markets and cultures is taking place under pervasive Western methodologies of investment and profit. Superficially, Western culture is everywhere, in the commercial products of food, drink, and clothing; in the machines that make life easier and regulated; in the entertainment of music, games, and visual images. Those countries where Western civilization runs deepest are those whose populations largely descend from western Europe: in North America, both Canada and the United States, and in the South Pacific, Australia and New Zealand. The states of Latin America through the Caribbean, Central America, and South America are all Western, although with large doses of Native American and some African influences. Substantially westernized countries are also in eastern Europe, including Russia.

In the Middle East, Israel is largely Western, although increasingly at odds with Arab Palestinians inside and outside its borders. Oil riches have brought Western concepts to many other Muslim countries, provoking the hostility behind much of modern Islamist terrorism. On the African continent, South Africa with its British and Afrikaaner minority is most thoroughly westernized. Yet other African nations bear the scars and retain some of the benefits of Western colonialism while trying to adapt to a global economy run on Western principles. Japan has become largely a Western nation. Contemporary China has exploited Western capitalist policies, while it officially retains a communist authoritarian system (Western in its mechanisms). In the rest of the world, all former colonial areas of the West, the depth of Western penetration varies. Some nations have strong elements of rejection, while others are eagerly trying to assimilate.

What does it mean to be Western? Take your choice: science or supernaturalism, democracy or dictatorship, immigration or isolation, socialism or self-interest, class consciousness or ethnic identification, virtuosity or vulgarity, religiosity or rationality. All are rooted in our tradition, and all have flaws, at least according to those who choose one over the other. Perhaps the most significant Western value is a beautiful and dreadful changeableness (see figure E.1).

I once found a graffito written on a desk in a classroom where I taught history: "If history is so important, how come it is gone?" The writer obviously did not fully understand the point of studying history. The past isn't gone. History is all around us. And not just in dusty museums, crumbling monuments, or misty memories of old-timers. Could you understand your own self without remembering your childhood? The past is in the baggage of our minds, in the frameworks of our institutions, in the complexity of our problems. We cannot escape history. We may ignore it only at our peril, since it frames all events around us. Our common heritage has shaped the institutions and structures within which we live. Every significant event instantly becomes history the moment it is over.

Because of Western developments, more people have more choices to affect their politics, economics, and culture than ever before in history. The ability to choose is, of course, limited by one's position in society. The rich usually have more

Figure E.1. The city of Salzburg represents many of the varied aspects of Western civilization. It uses modern technology of electricity and automobiles, yet encourages pedestrians (with the footbridge across the river); its economy was once centered around its namesake salt, mined in the mountains in the distance, while today tourism dominates; also its river has been canalized to control flooding and increase property. Its politics have gone through many stages since the initial Stone Age settlement: a town under the Celts; a city under the Romans; a town rebuilt under the German Carolingians after being abandoned in late antiquity; a spiritual principality ruled by prince-bishops in the Holy Roman Empire, who built the powerful fortress; a province fought over by various powers; and finally a federal state today in Austria. Salzburg once had social structures of aristocrats, townspeople, and peasants, and now it has celebrities, professionals, laborers, and the poor. Some of its culture can be seen in the visible churches and their spires and heard in its music festivals. These churches indicate the traditional belief system of Christianity, but they seem increasingly to be tourist attractions rather than centers of faith.

options than the middle class, while the poor struggle with even fewer choices. Legitimate authorities (through law enforcement and war) as well as extralegal organized groups (through crime and terrorism) have the ability to restrict the choices of disconnected individuals. Nevertheless, many of us have some freedom to decide our own future because of the success of certain Western values.

Our future depends on the choices we make today. Those people who made decisions in the past changed the course of events to restrict our choices. All kinds of people have appeared in the past of the West, whether forward looking or backward leaning, tolerant or closed-minded, humanist or pragmatic, cruel or kind, tyrannical or populist. This diversity allows almost anyone to claim they are defending tradition, whether proposing a liberating innovation or clinging to oppressive preservation.

You should understand what you believe, whether inherited from family, imposed by society, or freely accepted as your own. You should then act according to your beliefs within our global society. This book offers one path to understanding the world's Western heritage. You can either learn more on your own, benefit from study of other scholars and teachers, be satisfied with what has been offered here, or forget it all. You can benefit, or not, from historical examples of wisdom, stupidity, greatness, and failure. It is ultimately up to you. Choose your story and how to live into it.

Review: *How should one shape one's own worldview by picking and choosing from the key legacies of Western civilization?*

Response:

For more about the idea of Western civilization, see http://www.concisewestern civ.com/sources/pse.html.

Timelines

Note: The timelines present key names, events, ideas, institutions, and inventions in chronological order, roughly according to their first appearance in history. Numbers along each side of the timelines indicate time segments and the name of the general historical period; older dates are at the top, more recent toward the bottom. Additionally, terms placed within the white and shaded boxes between the horizontal lines are in approximate chronological order. The six vertical columns spread across each timeline divide data according to categories explained in chapter 1. In the Politics column, information from similar geographic areas tends to be grouped together within the cells, aligned left, center, or right. For example, in timeline C, most of the Politics terms aligned at the left relate to Great Britain. Terms given in all capital letters are states or nations when they first appear, important wars, or regimes. Although some terms in the Culture column are not explained in the text, key works, genres, artists, and writers through history are listed to provide context. Book titles are italicized.

Timeline A. The Ancient Middle East and West before 500 BC

	SCIENCE & TECHNOLOGY	ECONOMY	POLITICS
Prehistory 30,000 Y.A.	Paleolithic Age clothing tools	hunter-gatherers	*Homo sapiens*
7000 B.C.	Neolithic Age	trade/commerce slavery	
	animal domestication agriculture copper Bronze Age	Neolithic Agricultural Revolution property	villages, towns, cities Mesopotamian city states war absolutism monarchy kings kingdoms MIDDLE-EASTERN CIVILIZATIONS Sumerians
2900 B.C.	writing		Egypt
	mathematics astronomy	taxes	pharaohs
2600 B.C.	calendar		dynasty
Ancient History 2300 B.C.			empires
2000 B.C.			Hebrews
			Middle Kingdom of Egypt Amorites/Babylonians
1700 B.C.			New Kingdom of Egypt
1400 B.C.			Hatshepsut Ahkenaton Exodus "Dark Age"
1100 B.C.	alphabet Iron Age		Phoenicians Israel & Judea colonialism
		money	
800 B.C.			*polis/poleis* Greek Archaic Age Rome
	hoplites-phalanx *thetes*-trireme		ASSYRIAN EMPIRE militarism Babylonian Captivity of the Hebrews PERSIAN EMPIRE
500 B.C.			

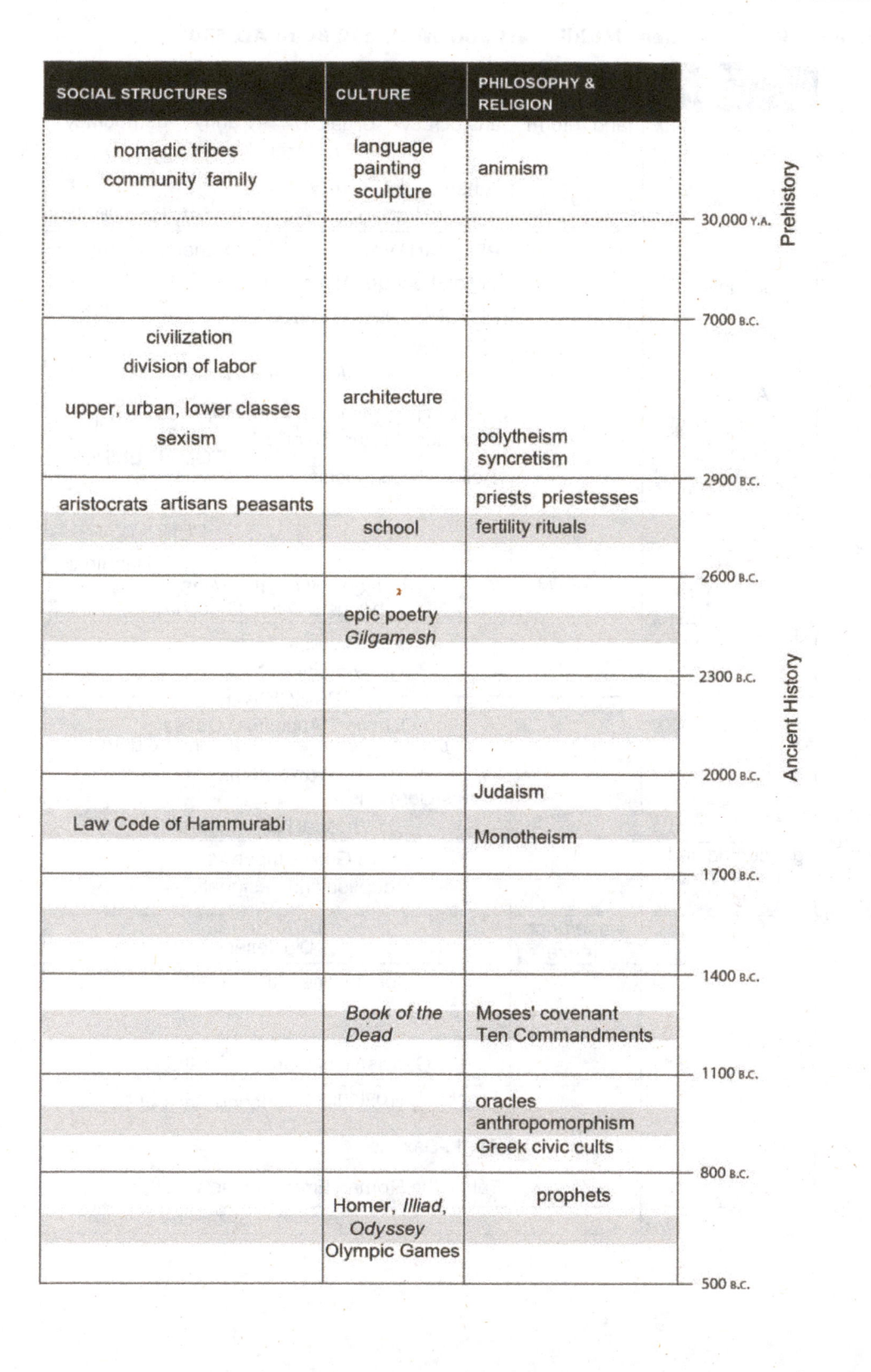

SOCIAL STRUCTURES	CULTURE	PHILOSOPHY & RELIGION	
nomadic tribes community family	language painting sculpture	animism	Prehistory
			30,000 Y.A.
			7000 B.C.
civilization division of labor upper, urban, lower classes sexism	architecture	polytheism syncretism	
			2900 B.C.
aristocrats artisans peasants	school	priests priestesses fertility rituals	
			2600 B.C.
	epic poetry *Gilgamesh*		
			2300 B.C.
			2000 B.C.
Law Code of Hammurabi		Judaism Monotheism	
			1700 B.C.
			1400 B.C.
	Book of the Dead	Moses' covenant Ten Commandments	
			1100 B.C.
		oracles anthropomorphism Greek civic cults	
			800 B.C.
	Homer, *Illiad*, *Odyssey* Olympic Games	prophets	
			500 B.C.

Ancient History

Timeline B. The Ancient Middle East and West, 550 BC to AD 530

	SCIENCE & TECHNOLOGY	ECONOMY	POLITICS
	hoplites-phalanx *thetes*-trireme	land reform	aristocracy- -oligarchy- -tyranny- -democracy *polis* citizenship
			Athenian democracy ostracism ROMAN REPUBLIC
500 B.C.			PERSIAN WARS Senate, consuls
	rationalism		Delian League, Athenian Empire
			PELOPONNESIAN WARS
	concrete		demagogues
400 B.C.			Gauls/Celts sack Rome
	Aristotle		tribunes
	dialectic logic		Philip II of Macedon proscription
	aqueduct		Alexander III "the Great" ROMAN EMPIRE
300 B.C.	Roman legion Roman roads		Hellenistic kingdoms
200 B.C.			PUNIC WARS
		latifundia	Hannibal
			ROMAN CIVIL WARS Tiberius & Gaius Gracchus
100 B.C.	Julian calendar		
			Julius Caesar
B.C.			Antony & Cleopatra
A.D.			PRINCIPATE
			Octavian "Augustus" Caesar *princeps, imperator*, Praetorian Guard
			Pax Romana
			Goths/Germans
			natural law, lawyers
A.D.100	geocentric and heliocentric theories		Five Good Emperors
			adoption and designation
A.D.200		wage/price freeze	DOMINATE
A.D.300			Diocletian
			Constantine I "the Great"
			Huns
			Germanic barbarian migrations
A.D.400			Franks, Merovingians Second Sack of Rome
			Anglo-Saxons
			Fall of the Roman Empire in the West
A.D.500			Justinian Byzantine Empire

(left axis label: Classical/Ancient History)

SOCIAL STRUCTURES	CULTURE	PHILOSOPHY & RELIGION	
	GREEK CLASSICAL AGE		
	lyric poetry		
patricians & plebians	Greek Golden Age theater history Parthenon	mystery religious cults philosophy Sophists	500 B.C.
		humanism	
	Lysistrata Oedipus	Socrates	
		Plato idealism Aristotle Jews	400 B.C.
	Hellenistic Age		
Alexandria		Diaspora anti-Semitism	
cosmopolitan		Epicureanism stoicism	300 B.C.
		rabbis	
proletariat			200 B.C.
optimates vs *populares*			
	Gallic War Vergil, *Aeneid*	Hebrew scriptures (Old Testament) deification	100 B.C.
		Yeshua of Nazareth Christianity martyrs	B.C. / A.D.
		Paul of Tarsus gospels councils apostolic succession	
		clergy mass saints apologists sacraments excommunication	A.D.100
			A.D.200
			A.D.300
Constantinople		Edict of Milan Council of Nicaea	
		Christian Bible (New Testament) orthodoxy heresy	A.D.400
		Augustine of Hippo *City of God*	
		monasticism regular clergy	
Justinian's Law Code			A.D.500

Classical/Ancient History

Timeline C. The Medieval West, 500–1640

	SCIENCE & TECHNOLOGY	ECONOMY	POLITICS
			Franks, Merovingians
			Clovis Justinian
			Justinian's Law Code
600			"Do-nothing kings"
		manorial economics	Anglo-Saxon kingdoms
700			
			CAROLINGIAN EMPIRE
	stirrups		mayors of the palace
			Pippin "the Short"
800		three-field planting	Charlemagne
			Vikings, Magyars, Moslems
	horse collars		Alfred "the Great"
			ENGLAND FRANCE GERMANY
			FEUDAL POLITICS
900	castles		SCOTLAND
			Otto I "the Great"
	knights		HOLY ROMAN EMPIRE
1000			HUNGARY DENMARK NORWAY SWEDEN
	reconquest of Toledo		
	Arab science in West	Domesday Book	William "the Conqueror"
		commune	Crusades Henry IV
1100		revival of towns & trade	Concordat of Worms
		industrialization	
	windmills	putting out/cottage guilds	Henry II PORTUGAL
		master, journeyman, apprentice	Philip II "Augustus"
1200			John Teutonic knights
	Scholasticism		Magna Carta
			Philip IV "the Fair"
1300			Parliament
	mini ice age begins		Estates-General
	pikes		OTTOMAN EMPIRE
	gunpowder, firearms	COMMERCIAL	SWITZERLAND
	cannons	REVOLUTION	Hundred Years War
1400		capitalism	Joan of Arc
		banks	Peace of Lodi
	printing press	public debt	AUSTRIA
			Habsburg dynasty Ferdinand & Isabella
	Columbus		SPAIN
	Vasco da Gama		Western European colonial imperialism
1500			Henry VIII Charles V
		Atlantic/African slave trade	DUTCH NETHERLANDS
		bourse, stock exchange	Elizabeth I St. Bart's Massacre Philip II
		mercantilism	Spanish Armada
1600			Wars of Religion
			Henry IV
			Thirty Years War
			English Civil War Peace of Westphalia

Left axis era labels:
Early Middle / Dark Ages — High Middle Ages — Later Middle Ages

SOCIAL STRUCTURES	CULTURE	PHILOSOPHY & RELIGION	
clan, kin, tribe, people, folk		monasticism Benedictine Rule	
free-unfree	Gregorian chant	caesaro-papism	— 600
personal justice vendetta/feud	Latin literature	Pope Gregory I Islam: Mohammed Qu'ran	
trial by ordeal customary law			— 700
	Carolingian Renaissance	Frankish-Papal Alliance Iconoclastic Controversy	— 800
	minuscule seven liberal arts		
seigneur & serf feudal society	Romanesque art		— 900
		Cluniac Reform	
	Gothic art	Peace & Truce of God	— 1000
nobility chivalry courtesy	tournaments rise of vernacular Chanson de Roland	"Great Schism" Eastern Orthodox Gregorian Reform Pope Gregory VII Investiture Struggle Crusades	— 1100
burghers, bourgeois patrician, artisan, common	universities Romance Goliards	Cistercian Reform canon law Peter Abelard Thomas Becket	— 1200
	colleges	Cathars, dualism Mendicants Francis of Assisi Inquisition Thomas Aquinas	— 1300
BLACK DEATH peasant revolts	Dante, Divine Comedy Chaucer Christine de Pizan	Pope Boniface VIII "Babylonian Captivity" "Great Western Schism"	— 1400
	RENAISSANCE textual criticism humanism Leonardo, Raphael	mysticism witch hunts Christian humanism Erasmus Spanish Inquisition	— 1500
	Machiavelli, The Prince Michelangelo Shakespeare	REFORMATION Martin Luther Jean Calvin Anabaptists English Reformation	— 1600
		Counter-Reformation Council of Trent	
		Loyola, Jesuits Inquisition, Index	

Early Middle / Dark Ages

High Middle Ages

Later Middle Ages

Timeline D. Early Modern West, 1540–1914

		SCIENCE & TECHNOLOGY	ECONOMY	POLITICS
		Copernicus		Wars of Religion
Renaissance & Reformation		heliocentric theory astronomy SCIENTIFIC REVOLUTION Gregorian calendar	COMMERCIAL REVOLUTION mercantilism	RUSSIA Elizabeth I DUTCH NETHERLANDS Philip II REPUBLICANISM divine right CONSTITUTIONALISM ABSOLUTISM
	1600	scientific method empiricism	joint-stock company	DUTCH REPUBLIC Henry IV "of Navarre" GREAT BRITAIN Thirty Years War Cardinal Richelieu
		Galileo physics		English Civil War Cromwell Peace of Westphalia sovereign nation-state balance of power
		scientific academies Newton	Scientific Agricultural Revolution	PRUSSIA Louis XIV "the Sun King" Glorious Revolution ancien régime Peter I "the Great"
Early Modern Europe	1700	mini ice age ends		cabinet, prime minister British Empire enlightened despotism
		spinning jenny		Frederick II "the Great" War of Austrian Succession Maria Theresa
		canals	INDUSTRIAL REVOLUTION mill/factory system laissez-faire	Seven Years War American Revolution partitions of POLAND USA federalism, president
		steam engine encyclopedia	Adam Smith classical liberal economics	Louis XVI FRENCH REVOLUTION National Assembly, Bastille, Reign of Terror, Thermidor Wars of the Coalitions
	1800			Napoleon Bonaparte guerrilla warfare Battle of Waterloo Metternich Congress of Vienna
			"iron law of wages" Luddites utopian socialism	liberalism nationalism conservatism Monroe Doctrine LATIN AMERICAN STATES
		railways		
Nineteenth Century		geology uniformitarianism evolution indoor plumbing	consumerism corporations	British reform bills GREECE Afrikaaners neo-imperialism Rev of 1830 US-Indian removals Mexico-US War BELGIUM Opium Wars Rev of 1848
		biology Darwin natural selection	Marxism trade/labor unions	Napoleon III Crimean War Sepoy Mutiny American Civil War Meiji Restoration ITALY Risorgimento Cavour Garibaldi Paris Commune Bismark 2nd GERMAN EMPIRE Third Republic
		oil chemicals electricity Pasteur, germ theory internal combustion engine	social democracy neo-mercantilism state socialism Christian socialism	SERBIA, BULGARIA, RUMANIA terrorism anarchism US-Plains Indian Wars Dollar Diplomacy pan-slavism yugo-slavism Hawaii partition of Africa Spanish American War Zionism
	1900	automobile airplane atomic theory Freud	cartels, trusts	Boer War SOUTH AFRICA Boxer Rebellion Balkan Wars Franz Ferdinand

SOCIAL STRUCTURES	CULTURE	PHILOSOPHY & RELIGION		
		Roman Catholicism		Renaissance & Reformation
estates clergy		Counter-Reformation Council of Trent		
nobility common-peasant	Shakespeare BAROQUE	Wars of Religion	— 1600	
	orchestra, opera Rembrandt Rubens			
westernization	Rococo art			
	ENLIGHTENMENT *philosophes*		— 1700	
	novels Bach	humanitarianism skepticism Pietism deism agnosticism atheism progress Great Awakening		Early Modern Europe
	Neoclassicism newspapers			
Wollstonecraft male suffrage *Declaration of the Rights of Man and the Citizen*	Rousseau Voltaire Mozart symphony ROMANTICISM		— 1800	
upper/middle/lower classes urbanization	Beethoven			
		materialism		
police public sanitation	Goethe, *Faust* Turner REALISM			Nineteenth Century
"family values"	Dickens professional sports	"higher criticism" Social Darwinism		
social sciences sociology anthropology	naturalism Richard Wagner impressionism Monet, Rodin, Van Gogh	Christian fundamentalism Christian modernism		
concentration camps		Pope Leo XIII	— 1900	

Timeline E. The Twentieth Century, 1900–present

	SCIENCE & TECHNOLOGY	ECONOMY	POLITICS
	telegraph, telephone	neo-mercantilism laissez-faire socialism	neo-imperialism conservative, liberal, socialist political parties
	Freud's subconscious auto	consumer economy trade unions	terrorism militarism Zionism
1900	airplane	"robber barons" trusts	"open door" policy, Boxer Rebellion Theodore Roosevelt
	atomic theory Einstein's relativity	cartels	alliance system
	plastic	department stores	progressivism
1910	gas warfare		Balkan crises ALBANIA
	U-boats tanks	"war socialism"	WORLD WAR I genocide Russian Revolution USSR Wafd
	bombers/fighters		CZECHO-SLOVAKIA ESTONIA LATVIA LITHUANIA HUNGARY AUSTRIA FINLAND
	influenza pandemic		KINGDOM OF SERBS, CROATS, and SLOVENES
1920	radio	era of big business USSR: NEP	IRELAND totalitarianism, authoritarianism League of Nations TURKEY
	air conditioning	USSR: 5-year plans	"Red scare" "Yellow Peril"
	Heisenberg's Principle	collectivization	Mussolini fascism Jiang, KMT
1930		Wall Street Crash	Stalinism YUGOSLAVIA Mao Zedong
	antibiotics	Great Depression	Hitler Naziism FDR
1940	radar	New Deal Keynesian Economics	Spanish Civil War Munich Conference WORLD WAR II Atlantic Charter
	jet computer		Blitzkrieg Pearl Harbor
	atomic bomb nuclear bomb	Great Leap Forward	United Nations Peron Israel Berlin Blockade apartheid Maoism Nehru
1950	television	baby boomers	NATO COLD WAR
	genetics Sputnik		CYPRUS McCarthyism Korean Police Action Warsaw Pact
	space flight Space Race		Treaty of Rome Suez Crisis EEC
1960	ICBMs	shopping malls	Castro decolonization
	laser transistor		Kennedy Berlin Wall Congo Crisis Cuban Missile Crisis Johnson race riots Vietnam War
1970	moon landing	German & Japanese economic "miracles"	Northern Ireland troubles Six-Day War PLO
	Earth Day pocket calculators	OPEC oil embargo G7	Nixon Allende détente Helsinki Accords Greens Sandinistas Solidarity Iranian Revolution
1980	Three Mile Island personal computer	Reaganomics	Reagan Thatcher Iran-Iraq War Falklands War
1990	Chernobyl	global debt	Gorbachev glasnost End of the COLD WAR
	Internet cell phones	globalization	SLOVENIA, CROATIA, BELARUS, UKRAINE, BOSNIA, MACEDONIA MOLDAVIA First Persian Gulf War
		G8	European Union Mandela Chinese Capitalist Revolution
2000	drones smartphones	global recession	9/11 invasion of Afghanistan and Iraq MONTENEGRO, SERBIA, KOSOVO

(left margin label: Twentieth Century)

SOCIAL STRUCTURES	CULTURE	PHILOSOPHY & RELIGION		
industrialization urbanization	advertising	Christian fundamentalism		
	fin de siècle	Christian modernism	— 1900	
suffragettes	ragtime			
	realism, naturalism			
	primitivism			
	cubism expressionism		— 1910	
	abstract art			
	movies			
Ku Klux Klan race riots	dada			
aristocracy depoliticized	Jazz Age	"Lost Generation"	— 1920	
	sports	"monkey" trial		
women's suffrage	Roaring Twenties			
Prohibition	surrealism			
Lindbergh		mass evangelists		
	International School		— 1930	
gulags	socialist realism	Gandhi		
	Picasso		— 1940	
	abstract expressionism	Holocaust		
welfare state	pop art	existentialism		
	television		— 1950	
suburbanization desegregation	"Coca-colanization"	Islamic fundamentalism		
civil rights movement	rock'n'roll			
sexual revolution 1968 student protests	The Beatles	Vatican II	— 1960	
	op art	Martin Luther King, Jr.		
women's liberation	rock concerts	drug culture cults		
abortion debate			— 1970	
NGOs	video games	televangelists		
			— 1980	
AIDS	music videos	The "Religious Right"		
		Pope John Paul II	— 1990	
ethnic cleansing	postmodernism			
homosexual rights				
			— 2000	
immigration debate	global climate change debate			

Twentieth Century

Common Abbreviations

AD   anno Domini, in the Year of the Lord (some historians instead use CE, Common Era)

AH   anno Hegirae, or Year of the Hegira (used as the starting date for Muslim calendars)

b.   born

BC   Before Christ (some historians instead use BCE, Before the Common Era)

ca.   circa, around or about

cent.   century

d.   died

fl.   flourished

r.   ruled

Glossary

The terms below cover many of the important ideas that Western civilization has either developed on its own, borrowed from others, or interacted with. The terms often end in *-ism* or *-ation* (and are ***boldface italicized*** in the text). Some of these ideas have been discredited by dominant attitudes of political institutions, social pressures, intellectual fashions, or religious organizations. Still, all of these diverse ideas, many of which contradict one another, are options that may be adopted and practiced.

absolutism: The idea and practice that one person should dominate in authority and decision making within a state. Historians and political theorists most often apply the term to European monarchs of the seventeenth and eighteenth centuries AD, although the concept does apply to all ages. *See also* **autocracy**; **dictatorship**; **fascism**; **Leninism**; **Stalinism**; **totalitarianism**; **tyranny**.

agnosticism: The belief that the existence of God or of any supernatural beings is impossible to prove.

Anabaptism: A religious belief that rejects infant baptism, an idea that united diverse groups of Christians during the Reformation. *See also* **Christianity**; **Protestantism**.

anarchism: A political idea that calls for the destruction of industrialized and bureaucratized societies so that a utopian agricultural society can appear. *See also* **terrorism**.

Anglicanism: A branch of Christians formed during the Reformation, first organized as the Church of England, which defines itself as a middle path between Protestantism and Roman Catholicism. British imperialism planted numerous Anglican churches around the world, now loosely connected to one another as the Anglican Communion. *See also* **Christianity**; **Protestantism**.

animism: The religious belief that nature is alive with spirits and ghosts that affect our natural world. Animism was probably the first religion, and many remaining hunter-gatherer societies still observe some form of it.

anthropomorphism: The idea that gods and deities look and act like human beings. Much of ancient Greek and Roman mythology was based on this concept.

anti-intellectualism: The criticism of the thoughts and opinions of educated elites as less useful than those of the "common" uneducated masses. *See also* **intellectualism**.

antisemitism: A euphemism for the hatred of Jews. *See also* **Judaism**; **racism**; **Zionism**.

apostolic poverty: The belief that it is virtuous for Christians to live like the poor, since Jesus and his followers did so. The height of its influence was in the Middle Ages with the Waldensians and Francis of Assisi's monasticism of the mendicants. *See also* **asceticism**.

apostolic succession: The belief in some parts of Christianity that the true church requires its leaders (bishops and priests) to be ordained in a direct line from Jesus and his apostles.

arabization: The process of making people conform to Arabic culture, especially Islam and its associated traditions. *See also* **islamization**.

Arianism: A religious belief in the third century AD that separated the human nature of Jesus from the divine. Most denominations of Christianity officially reject this division and see Jesus as fully human and fully divine at the same time. *See also* **heresy**.

aristocracy: The idea and practice that a few families are of a higher status than others (usually through bloodlines combined with wealth) and therefore as a class should rule society.

asceticism: The avoidance of worldly pleasures in living one's life.

assassination: The political practice of murdering leaders in order to force change.

atheism: The belief that denies the existence of the supernatural. *See also* **supernaturalism**.

atomic theory: The scientific idea that the smallest indivisible part of a unique substance is an atom (Greek for "not able to be cut"). Ancient Greek philosophers first suggested the idea, which was scientifically verified in the late nineteenth and early twentieth centuries.

authoritarianism: The modern political practice of a dictatorship, where a ruler and their party significantly control mass communication and bureaucracy while maintaining order through secret police, paramilitaries, and military forces. *See also* **absolutism**; **autocracy**; **dictatorship**; **fascism**; **Leninism**; **Stalinism**; **totalitarianism**; **tyranny**.

autocracy: A form of government dominated by one person. *See also* **absolutism**; **authoritarianism**; **dictatorship**; **fascism**; **Leninism**; **Stalinism**; **totalitarianism**; **tyranny**.

balance of power: A foreign policy idea most popular between 1648 and 1945 that the nations of Europe should league together against any one single state that tried to dominate the Continent.

balkanization: The practice of carving up larger empires into smaller states, as done after World War I in eastern Europe. Often it is used in a negative sense.

baptism: The religious idea in Christianity that a ritual with water binds one to that belief system.

barbarian: (1) A term used by civilized urban peoples to describe other peoples who are not civilized (that is, living in pastoral or hunter-gatherer economies); (2) a term used by one people to insult another as unjustifiably cruel, regardless of either's level of socioeconomic development.

Bolshevism: The name for the communist movement in early twentieth-century Russia led by Lenin. *See also* **communism**; **Leninism**.

bureaucracy: The practice of governing by means of written records and the offices that issue, administer, and store them.

caesaro-papism: The practice of the medieval Eastern Roman or Byzantine emperors of helping to organize and supervise the hierarchy and belief system of the Christian church in their empire. *See also* **Orthodox Christianity**.

Calvinism: The belief system held by churches formed during the Reformation that followed the theology of Jean Calvin. Predestination, the belief that God has already chosen who is saved or damned, is its most distinctive doctrine. *See also* **determinism**; **Protestantism**.

capitalism: In its simplest form, the practice of reinvesting profits. As part of our modern ideological conflicts, people apply the term to private ownership of the means of production with comparatively free markets, as opposed to communism, where the government carries out central planning of the economy. *See also* **communism**; **Marxism**; **mercantilism, economic theory of**; **socialism**.

catastrophism, theory of: A scientific idea that explains geology or the history and structures of the earth according to rare and unusual events of enormous power, resembling divine intervention. *See also* **uniformitarianism, theory of**.

Catharism: The medieval religion that mixed Christianity and dualism and was therefore identified by the Christian church as a heresy. *See also* **dualism**; **heresy**.

Christianity: The monotheistic religion that asserts that God became incarnate as his son, Jesus of Nazareth. The Romans executed Jesus, but as the Messiah, or Christ, he returned from the dead to offer salvation, or entrance into heaven for his followers. Since the first century, Christians have divided into many groups. *See also* **Anabaptism**; **Anglicanism**; **Arianism**; **caesaro-papism**; **Calvinism**; **heresy**; **Lutheranism**; **Orthodox Christianity**; **Pietism**; **Protestantism**; **Roman Catholicism**; **schism**.

Christian socialism: A socialist idea adopted by Christians, especially Roman Catholics, using religious ideology as a basis to improve conditions for workers while still respecting the private property rights of capitalists.

classical liberal economics, theory of: Also called laissez-faire (from the French for "allow to do"), the idea that the least interference by government provides the best opportunities for economic growth. It was developed in the eighteenth century in opposition to mercantilism. Some economists prefer to see this theory as identical to capitalism itself. *See also* **capitalism**; **mercantilism, economic theory of**; **socialism**.

collectivization: The practice of Stalin during the 1930s, where the state confiscated land from peasants and consolidated the large tracts into communal farms. Communists in other states, such as China and Cambodia/Kampuchea, later undertook similar policies. *See also* **communism**; **Leninism**; **Marxism**; **Stalinism**.

colonialism: The action of one state sending out some of its people to settle in another place. A colony may or may not retain close connections with the homeland. *See also* **imperialism**; **neo-imperialism**.

communism: The utopian idea proposed by Karl Marx in the nineteenth century of a perfect society where the means of production would be shared by all. *See also* **Leninism**; **Stalinism**.

conciliarism: The idea and practice that church councils should be the ultimate authority in resolving conflicts among Christians.

conservatism: A political inclination that developed into representative parties during the nineteenth century. It stands for resisting change in order to preserve political, social, and cultural advantages of the elites. Today conservatism often calls for reducing the role of government in the economy while increasing its role in preventing social and cultural change.

constitutionalism: The political idea that law limits a government's powers, whether formally written in an explicit document or by the precedent of tradition.

constitutional monarchy: The practice of having a democratically structured government while keeping a royal dynasty as a stabilizing force. *See also* **democracy**; **parliamentarianism**; **republicanism**.

cynicism: A philosophy originating among the ancient Greeks advocating the rejection of common social rules and human comforts. Today it often describes a pessimism that people's intentions are based on self-interest rather than the common good.

deification: The belief that a human being, usually a powerful leader, can be transformed into a god.

deism: The religious belief that God is the creator of the universe, although it deemphasizes the Christian dogma of Jesus's incarnation.

democracy: The political idea and practice that the best form of government involves the largest possible number of citizens making decisions. Democracies usually involve checks and balances upon authority. Also, various factions or parties discuss and compromise to resolve different political aims. Direct democracy in ancient Athens included all male citizens. Modern democracies usually use elected representatives. A democrat is not necessarily to be confused with a member of the modern American political party. *See also* **parliamentarianism**; **republicanism**.

democratic socialism: Also called social democracy, the effort of revisionists of Marxism to work through the political process instead of through a proletarian revolution. The various modern labor and social democratic political parties were the result. *See also* **Christian socialism**; **classical liberal economics**, theory of; **communism**; **Marxism**; **Naziism**; **socialism**; **state socialism**; **trade unionism**; **utopian socialism**; **war socialism**.

denazification: The policy after World War II to purge members of the Nazi party from leadership positions in occupied Germany. *See also* **Naziism**.

determinism: A philosophy that asserts humans have very little free will in deciding their fate. *See also* **Calvinism**.

dialectical materialism: The theoretical model of history suggested by Karl Marx, where a dominant class conflicts with an exploited class. *See also* **Marxism**.

dialectic logic: A method of gaining knowledge that uses two pieces of known data to produce or confirm other information. *See also* **Scholasticism**; **syllogism**.

dictatorship: The practice of one person seizing power in a government. While today the term is used in a negative way, the Romans originally used the method during political crises. *See also* **authoritarianism**; **autocracy**; **totalitarianism**; **tyranny**.

diversity: The term used in this text to describe the creative impulse as a force in history. New ideas and groupings of people create change. *See also* **particularism**; **toleration**; **universalism**.

divine right: The political idea that God has placed kings in power as part of his divine order.

dualism: A religious philosophy that sees the universe as divided between two powerful beings, one a good force inspired by spirit and ideas, the other an evil influence based on matter and flesh. *See also* **Catharism**; **Gnosticism**; **Zoroastrianism**.

ecumenism: The effort by religions, usually those of Christianity, to tolerate one another, work together, and perhaps unify. It was most influential in the mid-twentieth century. *See also* **toleration**.

egalitarianism: The idea that the best society tries to equalize the wealth, influence, and opportunities of all its citizens. It is exemplified by ancient Sparta, the radicals of the French Revolution, and much Marxist ideology.

empiricism: The idea that observations by our senses are both accurate and reasonable. It is the starting point of scientific knowledge. *See also* **rationalism**; **science**.

enlightened despotism: The political idea and practice that asserted that one person, usually a benevolent dynastic monarch, should rule, since unity encouraged simplicity and efficiency.

environmentalism: The idea and practice since the 1960s of reducing human interference with and damage to the natural world.

Epicureanism: A philosophy that suggests that the best way of life is to avoid pain. The good life lay in withdrawal into a pleasant garden to discuss the meaning of life with friends. Epicureanism originated among the Hellenistic Greeks and was popularized by the Romans. *See also* **hedonism**; **materialism**.

ethnicity: The idea of grouping humans into categories based on certain physical or behavioral differences. Ethnocentrism means that certain members of ethnic groups view members of other groups as inferior and dangerous. What separates ethnicity from the idea of race is the belief that race is unchangeable, while ethnicity is more fluid and open. *See also* **racism**.

evolution: The observed scientific phenomenon about the increasing diversity and complexity of life on earth from millions of years ago to the present. Darwin's theory of natural selection is the framework under which most scientists today understand the process of evolution. *See also* **natural selection, theory of**.

exceptionalism, American: A point of view that sees Americans as different from their fellow westerners or other peoples, usually as being more virtuous or free. The basis for this alleged virtue ranges from a special relationship with God to the unique genius of the Founding Fathers. *See also* **exceptionalism, Western**.

exceptionalism, Western: A point of view that sees Europeans as better than peoples in Asia, Africa, or the Americas. The basis for this alleged virtue ranges from the success of Western imperial colonialism, through superior moral upbringing, to divine favor. *See also* **exceptionalism, American**.

excommunication: The practice of various Christian churches of disciplining members by shunning them from society and cutting them off from the sacraments.

factionalism: The practice of refusing to cooperate with opposing political and social groups.

fascism: A political ideology, most popular in the 1920s and 1930s, where an extreme nationalist dictatorship seemed the best form of government. Fascist authoritarian and totalitarian regimes offered alternatives to socialism, communism, and parliamentary democracy. Many capitalists were able to accept fascist regimes, despite their violent tendencies toward outsiders, since fascism's concept of the corporate state still allowed some private property and profit. *See also* **authoritarianism**; **dictatorship**; **Naziism**; **totalitarianism**.

federalism: The political practice in republics of separating governmental power within a country, where a strong central administration both competes and shares power with provincial or state and local governments. It contrasts with a confederate system, where the central administration is weaker than the local governments.

feminism: The idea that women are not inferior to men, but rather should have equal access to education, political participation, and economic independence. Today it is often mischaracterized as hostility toward or sexism against men. *See also* **sexism**; **women's liberation**.

feudal politics: The system where knights bound one another together by oaths and rituals to rule society after AD 1000. The term *feudalism* should be avoided because of its many confusing meanings.

fundamentalism: A belief that values traditional, often preindustrial customs and attitudes, especially regarding religion. Fundamentalists reject modern ways of knowing based on the skepticism of literary criticism and the scientific and historical methods. In Christianity, it includes those who support an allegedly literal interpretation of the Bible rather than an interpretation through higher criticism. *See also* **higher criticism**; **textual criticism**.

germanization: The policy of making people conform to German culture. Used by some princes in the Holy Roman Empire, bureaucrats in the Second German Empire, and the Nazis of the Third Reich. *See also* **Naziism**; **pan-germanism**.

germ theory of disease: The scientific theory, argued by Pasteur in the nineteenth century, that microscopic organisms, such as bacteria and viruses, cause many sicknesses. While very successful as a means to understand illness, it does not, however, explain all disease.

globalization: The recent practice of the world's economies being tied more closely together, often bypassing the interests of nations, regions, and localities.

Gnosticism: The ancient philosophy or religion that drew on dualism and argued that its followers held secret knowledge about the meaning of life. Gnostics tried to influence early Christianity. *See also* **dualism**; **Zoroastrianism**.

heathenism: A synonym for the religion of polytheism. It was once a term of insult in late Rome applied to poor peasants (living in the countryside among the wild heath flowers) who were ignorant of Christianity; since the early Middle Ages, *heathen* has meant any non-Christian in or outside Christendom. *See also* **paganism**; **polytheism**.

hedonism: A philosophy originating among the ancient Greeks that suggested success came to those who pursued pleasure as the highest good. *See also* **Epicureanism**; **materialism**.

hellenization: The policy of making people under Greek authority conform to Greek institutions and culture. Practiced especially by the Greek rulers of the Hellenistic Age, after the death of Alexander "the Great." *See also* **pan-hellenism**.

heresy: Literally, a "choice" or a "sect," the term with which winners in a cultural or religious debate label the ideas of the losers. *See also* **orthodoxy**.

higher criticism: The practice of applying modern scholarly techniques to examining the Bible. *See also* **fundamentalism**; **textual criticism**.

history: The idea that the past is a product of human activity that needs to be interpreted. Since the eighteenth century, the historical method practiced by academics has been the most reliable way to produce objective and accurate descriptions and explanations of the past.

humanism: The philosophy begun by the ancient Greeks that the world is to be understood by and for humans. It gained a significant revival in the Renaissance, including a version called Christian humanism, inspired by the faith in Jesus. Recently some Christians attack what they call "secular humanism" which they believe undermines lives based on religion.

humanitarianism: The idea that humans ought to treat one another well. It is sometimes incorporated in Christianity and was promoted by many intellectuals of the Enlightenment.

idealism: Also known as the doctrine of ideas, idealism is a philosophical explanation of reality that proposed that particular things in the observable world are reflections of universal truths. It is famously formulated by Plato in his "Allegory of the Cave."

identitarianism: The racist belief that the "identity" or the socially constructed image of a group of people being an ethnicity or race is the most important form of community. *See also* **ethnicity**; **racism**.

imperialism: The practice of taking over different peoples in other countries and communities in order to build an empire. Empires usually surpass kingdoms or nations in the diversity of their subject peoples. *See also* **colonialism**; **neo-imperialism**.

individualism: The idea that political and social policies should favor opportunities for single human beings over those in collectives or groups. *See also* **collectivization**.

intellectualism: The attitude that educated elites and their production of knowledge should be respected. *See also* **anti-intellectualism**.

Islam: The religion begun by Muhammad in Arabia. Muslims believe that the one, true God has established a special relationship to those who submit to his will, as explained in the Qur'an.

islamization: The policy of making people conform to Islam and live as Muslims. *See also* **arabization**.

isolationism: The position that the best foreign policy is to remain as uninvolved as possible with neighboring nations.

Judaism: The religion begun by the ancient Hebrews. Jews believe that the one, true God has established a special relationship with them, as revealed in their sacred scriptures (called by Christians the Old Testament). *See also* **antisemitism**; **Zionism**.

just war theory: The argument, often made by Christians, that people should only participate in a war in order to defend others, limit hostile actions, and promote peace afterward.

Keynesian economic theory: An economic theory, part of which says that massive government spending can rescue a nation's economy from a depression. It is named after its creator, twentieth-century British economist John Maynard Keynes.

kleptocracy: The practice of government public officials using their authority to increase their personal wealth (from the Greek for "rule by those who steal").

Leninism: The ideological and political program put in place by Lenin during the Russian Revolution. He first established a dictatorship enforced by secret police, then had the state take over substantial portions of the economy (a policy called war communism), and carried out land reform. *See also* **Bolshevism**; **communism**; **Marxism**.

lesbianism: Sexual attraction or sexual activity between women. The term was coined in the nineteenth century, referring to the island Lesbos, where Sappho, the ancient Greek poet, had her school (although she herself was not strictly homosexual—another term invented at that time). *See also* **sapphism**.

liberalism: A political direction that developed into parties during the nineteenth century. It generally stands for changing laws in order to broaden political, social, and cultural opportunities for the middle classes. Today liberalism often calls for accepting a role of government to promote social change to help the poor and hold the wealthy accountable.

liberation theology: A religious idea in Latin America of the twentieth century that called for Christianity to look after the poor in this world and not merely preach about salvation for the next.

Lutheranism: The version of Christianity that originated with Martin Luther during the Reformation emphasizing justification through faith alone. *See also* **Christianity**; **Protestantism**.

manorial economics: The economic system in which serfs worked the lands of their seigneurial lords in exchange for the use of farmland for themselves; preferred instead of *manorialism*, a term to be avoided because of its confusing meanings.

Marxism: The particular socialist ideology developed by Karl Marx in the mid-nineteenth century that advocated a proletarian revolution to overthrow bourgeois capitalist society. Since then, Marxism has been used as a synonym for communism. *See also* **Bolshevism**; **communism**; **dialectical materialism**; **Leninism**; **socialism**; **Stalinism**.

materialism: The idea that the physical goods and pleasures in this observable world should take priority over any possible spiritual virtues or destinies. *See also* **Epicureanism**.

McCarthyism: A belief usually characterized as a paranoid and unfair attempt to persecute innocent people for their allegedly dangerous political views. It is named after a US senator who during the 1950s wanted to purge alleged communists from the government, politics, and the media.

mercantilism, economic theory of: The idea that government intervention provides the best opportunities for economic growth, especially in establishing monopolies and a favorable balance of trade. It was developed in the sixteenth century in order to manage early capitalism. *See also* **classical liberal economics, theory of**; **neo-mercantilism, theory of**.

militarism: The idea and practice that virtues such as discipline, obedience, courage, and willingness to kill for the state are the highest values a civilized society can hold. It is exemplified by the ancient Assyrians, the Spartans, and the modern Prussians.

Mithraism: An ancient religion, originating in Persia but most popular among the Roman military. Its cultic followers believed that Mithras was the son of the sun god, born on December 25, who killed the heavenly bull to bring fertility and whose own death helped human souls to an afterlife. *See also* **Zoroastrianism**.

modernism: A belief that accepts changes brought by the Enlightenment and the Commercial and Industrial Revolutions to bring about a more secular and materialistic society. In Christianity, it includes those who support rigorous scholarly examination of scripture. *See also* **higher criticism**.

monasticism: A religious way of life in which people live in a cloistered setting under strict rules, usually involving renunciation of property, physical pleasure, and freedom of choice.

monotheism: The religious belief that only one God exists and should be worshipped.

multiculturalism: The idea that knowledge of and appreciation for diverse ways of life are beneficial for society.

mysticism: The idea that humans can form a direct and meaningful connection to the supernatural, the divine, or God.

nationalism: The political idea that asserts that states should be organized exclusively around ethnic unities. The problem is, few states have only one ethnic group living within their borders. Nationalists often try to cultivate patriotism, or love of one's country, which can, but does not necessarily, lead to hostility between nations. An extreme form of nationalism is called chauvinism, named after an apocryphal French patriot. The word chauvinism is also applied to male sexism.

nativism: The political movement that promotes fears that foreigners and immigrants threaten the economic opportunities and social positions of the resident population. "Natives" in the West usually means those of European ancestry, not the oppressed native indigenous or aboriginal peoples.

naturalism: (1) The movement in classical sculpture and art since the Renaissance to portray objects exactly as they appear in nature rather than with an abstract interpretation; (2) the movement in literature since the late nineteenth century to focus on suffering caused by modern society. *See also* **realism**.

natural law, theory of: The belief that supernatural deities created the natural world so that humans could understand their proper place and create laws that would be more just and suitable to humankind.

natural selection, theory of: Also called "survival of the fittest," Darwin's theory explains how the fact of evolution took place. It proposes that the struggle of creatures for food and reproduction encouraged change as organisms adapted to their environment, competed with others, and then passed on useful characteristics to offspring. Thus some species went extinct while many living things became increasingly diverse and more complex. *See also* **evolution**.

Naziism or national socialism: The uniquely German version of fascism. Formulated by Adolf Hitler and brought into action during the Third Reich (1933–1945), it fulfilled many Germans' need for nationalistic pride. Its extreme germanization, however, aimed for the Nazi domination of Eurasia and the enslavement or extermination of "non-Aryan" peoples, especially Jews. *See also* **authoritarianism**; **fascism**; **germanization**; **pan-germanism**; **totalitarianism**.

neo-imperialism: The political practice used by Western industrialized states to build overseas colonial empires between 1830 and 1914. *See also* **colonialism**; **imperialism**.

neo-mercantilism, theory of: The economic idea in Western industrialized states between 1830 and 1914 that combined neo-imperialism abroad with laissez-faire practices at home. *See also* **classical liberal economics, theory of**; **mercantilism, economic theory of**; **neo-imperialism**.

nominalism: The medieval philosophy that proposed that only particular material things in the observable world exist, while collective ideas and categories are mere "names" created by the human mind. *See also* **idealism**.

objectivity: The attempt to remain neutral or interpret disagreements from an unbiased point of view. *See also* **subjectivity**.

oligarchy: The political idea that states are best run by the economic and social elites. *See also* **aristocracy**; **plutocracy**.

Orthodox Christianity: The version of Christianity originally centered in the Byzantine Empire. It became a separate branch after the Great Schism with Western Latin Christianity beginning in 1054. *See also* **Christianity**; **Protestantism**; **Roman Catholicism**; **schism**.

orthodoxy: Literally, the "right teaching," it is the label adopted by groups whose ideas win a cultural debate. *See also* **heresy**.

ostracism: The political practice in ancient Athens of exiling politicians who were considered too dangerous. Today it often means a social practice of shunning. *See also* **excommunication**.

pacifism: The political idea that wars are not a proper activity for states. Instead of warmongering, efforts to maintain peace should be prioritized. Some Christians and Christian groups promoted the idea in Western civilization.

paganism: A religion of polytheism. It was once a term of insult in late Rome leveled at poor peasants (from the Latin for those who lived in the countryside) who were ignorant of Christianity. Since the early Middle Ages it has meant any non-Christian in or outside Christendom. *See also* **heathenism**; **polytheism**.

pan-germanism: The ideology that all German peoples should be ruled together. As a policy of Adolf Hitler and his Third Reich, it had some success in the 1930s until Hitler showed his determination to rule non-Germans also. *See also* **Naziism**.

pan-hellenism: The idea that all Greeks should be united, at least culturally. *See also* **hellenization**.

pan-slavism: The political idea that called for all Slavs to live together in one nation-state. The Russians, as the dominant Slavic group, were most behind this movement. *See also* **yugo-slavism**.

pan-turkism: A version of Turkish nationalism that sought to promote unity among diverse Turkish peoples. "Young Turks" toward the end of the Ottoman Empire tried to encourage all subject peoples to become more like Turks.

parliamentarianism: The political idea and practice that elected representatives with limited terms are the best means of governing a state. Structurally, the person who leads the majority in the parliament, usually called a prime minister or a chancellor, is the most powerful political official in the government. *See also* **constitutionalism**; **democracy**; **republicanism**.

particularism: The political and social idea that specific local variations in institutions and beliefs are the best way to organize the state and society. *See also* **diversity**; **universalism**.

philosophy: Literally, "love of wisdom," any intellectual system that proposes explanations for the nature of the universe and the purpose of human beings. While a philosophy may or may not have a supernatural dimension, it should rely on rationalism.

Pietism: A form of Christianity that arose during the eighteenth century, especially among Lutherans, in which believers dedicated themselves to prayer and charity. *See also* **Lutheranism**; **Protestantism**.

plutocracy: A government run by and for the interests of the wealthy. *See also* **oligarchy**.

polytheism: The belief in many gods and goddesses. Divine beings usually reflected the values and needs of farming communities. *See also* **heathenism**; **paganism**.

populism: A political ideology that believes the masses of people (usually rural and middle and lower class) have more wisdom and virtue than elites (usually professionals, intellectuals, and capitalists), career politicians, and several social institutions (such as cities, the Roman Catholic Church, and secretive fraternal organizations). Its leaders often resort to demagoguery. *See also* **anti-intellectualism**; **fascism**; **nativism**; **tribalism**.

postmodernism: The academic practice of "deconstructing" texts and ideas to understand both how dominant elites perpetuate power and how "others" who resist subvert authority. Such poststructural relativism disputes the Enlightenment effort toward attaining objective truth. *See also* **objectivity**; **relativism**; **revisionism**; **subjectivity**.

progress: The idea that people should work to improve political, social, and living conditions in this world. It has been an important Western idea since the Enlightenment.

Protestantism: Any version of Christianity that appeared after Luther's Reformation and its break from Roman Catholicism and Orthodox Christianity; the name originates with those who protested the imperial attacks on Luther. *See also* **Anabaptism**; **Anglicanism**; **Calvinism**; **Christianity**; **Lutheranism**; **Pietism**.

racism: The social and political myth that genetically closely related people inherit immutable characteristics as if they were a species and that some "races" are superior to others. There is no good scientific proof of significant differences among these imaginatively constructed racial groups. Racism intensified as an influential Western political prejudice in the nineteenth century.

rationalism: The concept that the human mind can comprehend the natural world.

realism: (1) The movement in art since the Renaissance that strives to make paintings and sculptures portray objects as human eyes see them; (2) the movement in literature since the late nineteenth century that focuses on social problems. *See also* **naturalism**.

Realpolitik: The political practice of both pragmatically making compromise and using force to achieve desired ends, usually the strengthening of the state. Conservative nationalists promoted it in the nineteenth century.

regionalism: The political idea that people are best organized within smaller geographic areas rather than the typical large nation-state or centralized empire. *See also* **particularism**; **subsidiarity**.

relativism: An extreme attitude which holds that no objective, actual truth exists. Truth is constructed as determined by the point of view of each originator. *See also* **revisionism**.

religion: From the Latin word "to bind," a belief system that proposes a supernatural explanation for the nature of the universe and the purpose of human beings.

republicanism: The political idea and practice that elected representatives with limited terms are the best means of governing a state. Republicanism paired with the checks and balances of constitutionalism are the foundation of most modern democratic states. In its strict form, a republic elects all significant political figures, thus excluding constitutional monarchy. A republican is not necessarily to be confused with a member of the modern American political party. *See also* **constitutional monarchy**; **democracy**; **parliamentarianism**.

revisionism: The practice of historians to critically reexamine sources and arguments of established historians improves knowledge of the past. In contrast, some alleged experts declare themselves practicing "revisionism" when they attack established historical fact, such as the Holocaust. A third form of ideological revisionism applies to the social democratic rejection of strict Marxism. *See also* **democratic socialism**; **Marxism**; **relativism**.

Roman Catholicism: The version of Christianity that developed in the Middle Ages in what had been the western portion of the ancient Roman Empire. It is characterized by being under the authority of the bishop of Rome, eventually called the pope. It defined itself as uniquely Roman first after the schism from Orthodox Christianity in 1054 and finally with the rise of Protestantism in the sixteenth century. *See also* **Christianity**; **Orthodox Christianity**; **Protestantism**; **schism**.

romanization: The process carried out by ancient Romans of conforming their subject peoples, institutions, and attitudes to those of the Roman Empire.

Romantic movement: The intellectual movement begun in the nineteenth century that appreciated nature, admired the Middle Ages, and emphasized emotion as a reaction against the rationalism of the Enlightenment.

sapphism: Sexual attraction to and sexual activity between women. The term (as was *homosexuality*) was coined in the nineteenth century, referring to Sappho, the ancient Greek poet who had a school on the island of Lesbos (although she herself was not strictly homosexual—another term invented at that time). *See also* **lesbianism**.

schism: Literally, a "rip," usually used to describe one religious group splitting away from another. *See also* **heresy**; **Orthodox Christianity**; **orthodoxy**; **Protestantism**; **Roman Catholicism**.

Scholasticism: The medieval philosophy "of the schools," which applied Aristotle's dialectic logic to better explain Christianity. *See also* **dialectic logic**; **syllogism**.

science: The idea that knowledge of nature can best be gained through rigorous experimentation and observation according to the scientific method. Scientific theories provide coherent explanations for the facts of natural phenomena. Science's many verifiable successes have made it the dominant modern methodology of acquiring reliable knowledge. *See also* **empiricism**; **rationalism**.

sexism: The belief that one sex (usually the male and its expected gender expression of masculinity) is better than the other (usually the female and its imposed gender expression of femininity). *See also* **feminism**; **women's liberation**.

skepticism: The intellectual idea of doubting everything and trusting only what can be tested through reason.

Social Darwinism: The idea of understanding human society through perspectives influenced by the debate over evolution. Social Darwinists usually rationalized the supremacy of rich European elites over the impoverished masses both in the West (through laissez-faire policies) and around the world (through colonialism). *See also* **colonialism**; **classical liberal economics, theory of**; **evolution**; **imperialism**; **natural selection, theory of**; **neo-imperialism**; **racism**.

socialism: Several ideas and practices that have developed since the Industrial Revolution to address the political, social, and economic inequalities between capitalists and workers. In principle, socialism stands for helping the workers. Over time, socialist theories and systems have developed in many directions. *See also* **Christian socialism**; **classical liberal economics, theory of**; **communism**; **democratic socialism**; **Marxism**; **Naziism**; **state socialism**; **trade unionism**; **utopian socialism**; **war socialism**.

sovietization: The practice of the Soviet Union during the Cold War of transforming states under their influence to conform to Stalinism. *See also* **Stalinism**.

Stalinism: The developments in the early Soviet Union that both modernized state and society and created a totalitarian dictatorship based on Stalin's cult of personality. *See also* **Leninism**; **Marxism**; **sovietization**.

state socialism: The practice of conservative governments legislating practices to improve the condition of workers. *See also* **socialism**.

stoicism: A philosophy that calls for people to do their duty in difficult circumstances. It originated among the Hellenistic Greeks and was popularized by the Romans.

subjectivity: The inclination to take sides or interpret disagreements from a biased point of view. *See also* **objectivity**; **postmodernism**; **relativism**; **revisionism**.

subsidiarity: The political idea and practice where decisions should be made at the regional and local levels rather than by a distant national, imperial, or global authority. *See also* **particularism**; **regionalism**.

suburbanization: The process of moving people to live in areas around cities that mixed traditional urban dwellings with rural landscapes. It became common in the late twentieth century with the increasing use of automobiles.

supernaturalism: The belief that another realm exists apart from the reality that can be empirically observed and sensed. Forces or beings in the supernatural realm are often believed to have influence or power within the natural world.

supremacy: A term used in this text to indicate historical change through the enforced domination of ideas or by those with power.

syllogism: An element of dialectic logic as developed by the ancient Greek philosopher Aristotle, where two pieces of known information are compared in order to reach new knowledge. *See also* **dialectic logic**; **Scholasticism**.

syncretism: The process in which elements of an idea, philosophy, or religion are blended with those of another.

terrorism: The political idea and practice of using small-scale violence, usually against civilians, to achieve specific political ends. Large-scale violence becomes guerrilla war, rebellion, or actual war. *See also* **anarchism**.

textual criticism: The intellectual tool developed during the Renaissance of comparing different manuscript versions of an author in order to find the best, most accurate text. *See also* **higher criticism**.

theocracy: The political idea and practice that religious leaders should rule the state.

toleration: The idea that people and society should accept others who believe in different worldviews, philosophies, or religions, and live in different cultures. *See also* **diversity**; **ecumenism**.

totalitarianism: The modern political practice of a strong dictatorship, where a ruler and his party substantially control mass communication, bureaucracy, and the economy and maintain order through secret police and a strong military. *See also* **authoritarianism**; **dictatorship**; **fascism**; **Leninism**; **Naziism**; **Stalinism**.

trade unionism: The practice of organizing labor unions (trade unions in Britain, *syndicats* in France) to help workers. At first illegal, unions often successfully improved conditions for workers to the point that much of the working class blended into the middle class during the twentieth century. *See also* **socialism**.

tribalism: The tendency of humans to form groups with whom they strongly identify, while recognizing other groups as hostile enemies. *See also* **ethnicity**; **racism**.

tyranny: The practice of one person seizing power in a government. While today the term is used in a negative way, tyrants among the ancient Greeks often opened politics to become more egalitarian and democratic. *See also* **dictatorship**.

uniformitarianism, theory of: A scientific theory to explain the history of the earth. It states that the same (uniform) processes that are shaping the earth today have always acted to mold the planet. *See also* **catastrophism, theory of**; **science**.

universalism: The attitude that the same beliefs and practices should be applied or open to everyone. *See also* **diversity**; **particularism**; **supremacy**.

urbanization: The process of moving rural people to live in ever-larger cities, carried out after the Industrial Revolution. Today most people live in urban areas.

utopian socialism: The first version of socialism, which called on capitalists to improve conditions for workers. *See also* **socialism**.

vandalism: The practice of writing on or damaging property, either out of spite or to make a statement. It is named after the Vandals, a Germanic tribe, which sacked Rome in AD 455. The name is perhaps unfair, since later sacks were worse.

war socialism: A common policy during World War I and World War II when governments took control of large sectors of the economy, creating a new military-industrial complex. In doing so, they often had to appease workers to prevent strikes. *See also* **socialism**.

westernization: The process of conforming non-European institutions and attitudes to those of Western civilization.

women's liberation: A movement in the 1960s and 1970s that promoted the rights of women to education, political participation, and economic independence. It was largely successful in Western industrialized states. *See also* **feminism; sexism**.

yugo-slavism: The political idea that called for all southern (*yugo*) Slavs to live together in one nation-state. The Serbs, as the dominant group of southern Slavs, were most behind this movement. *See also* **pan-slavism**.

zairianization: A political idea of Congolese nationalism, where the authoritarian kleptocrat Mobuto in the 1960s rejected European culture and tried to re-adapt his country to more native African ways. *See also* **kleptocracy**.

Zionism: Originally the idea of Jewish nationalism, namely that Jews, like any other nationality, should have their own nation-state. Zionism culminated in the modern state of Israel in 1948. Ever since, the term has sometimes been used to describe the alleged racist and imperialist policies of Israel against Arab Palestinians. *See also* **antisemitism; Judaism**.

Zoroastrianism: A dualistic religion in ancient Persia founded by the legendary Zoroaster or Zarathustra. *See also* **dualism**.

Index

Letters after page numbers indicate the following: d = diagram; f = figure; n = note; ps = primary source; sf = sources on families; t = timeline; tb = table. Terms in **boldface** designate a person.

About the Author

Brian A. Pavlac is a professor emeritus of history from King's College in Wilkes-Barre, Pennsylvania, where he served as chair of the department, director of the Center for Excellence in Learning and Teaching, and a Herve A. LeBlanc Distinguished Service Professor. He is the author of *Witch Hunts in the Western World: Persecution and Punishment from the Inquisition through the Salem Trials* and articles on Nicholas of Cusa and excommunication, editor of and contributor to *Game of Thrones versus History: Written in Blood*, coauthor of *The Holy Roman Empire: A Historical Encyclopedia*, and translator of Balderich's *A Warrior Bishop of the 12th Century: The Deeds of Albero of Trier*.